OWYA

a first time for everything

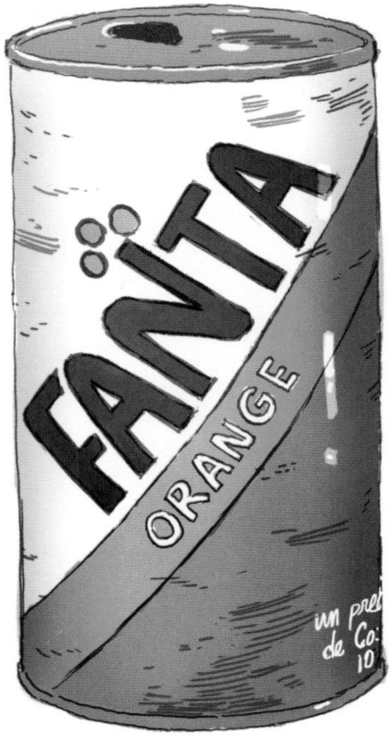
FANTA
ORANGE

a true story by DAN SANTAT

:01
First Second
new york

First Second

Published by First Second
First Second is an imprint of Roaring Brook Press,
a division of Holtzbrinck Publishing Holdings Limited Partnership
120 Broadway, New York, NY 10271
firstsecondbooks.com
mackids.com

Library of Congress Control Number: 2022908849

Our books may be purchased in bulk for promotional, educational, or business use.
Please contact your local bookseller or the Macmillan Corporate and Premium Sales Department
at (800) 221-7945 ext. 5442 or by email at MacmillanSpecialMarkets@macmillan.com.

The names and identifying characteristics of some persons
described in this book have been changed.

First edition, 2023
Edited by Connie Hsu
Cover design by Kirk Benshoff
Interior book design by Sunny Lee and Yan L. Moy
Production editing by Helen Seachrist
Coloring assistance by Abe Erskine

This book was illustrated digitally in Adobe Photoshop.

Printed in China by 1010 Printing International Limited, Kwun Tong, Hong Kong
ISBN 978-1-250-85104-8 (paperback)
1 3 5 7 9 10 8 6 4 2

ISBN 978-1-62672-415-0 (hardcover)
1 3 5 7 9 10 8 6 4 2

Don't miss your next favorite book from First Second!
For the latest updates go to firstsecondnewsletter.com and sign up for our enewsletter.

"We didn't know
we were making
memories, we were
just having fun."
—A. A. MILNE

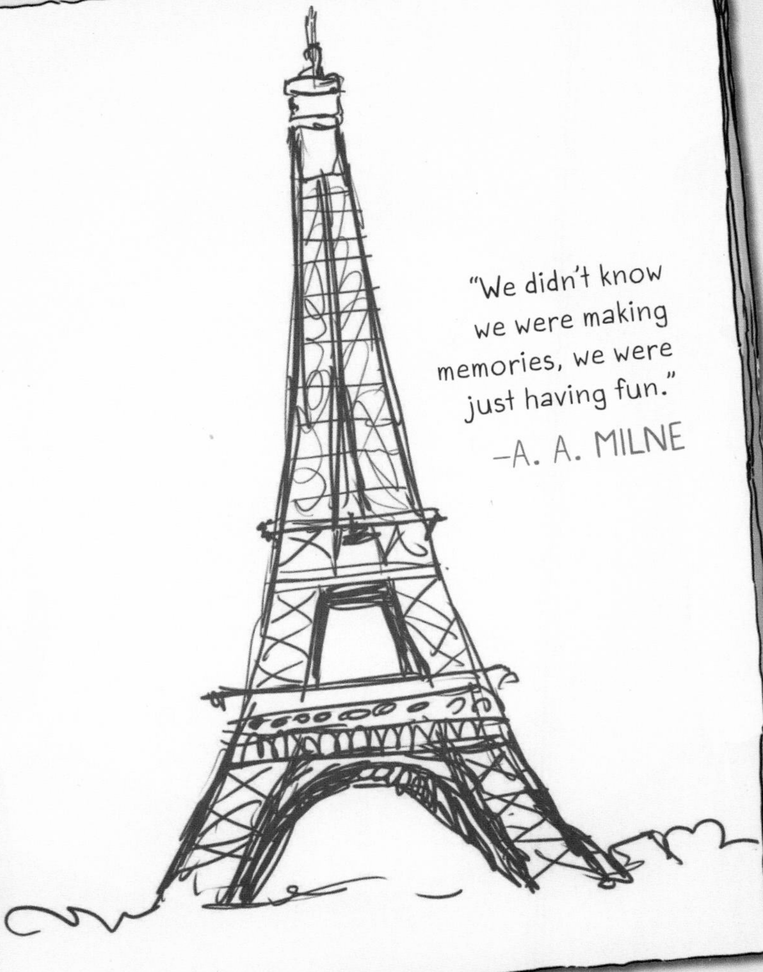

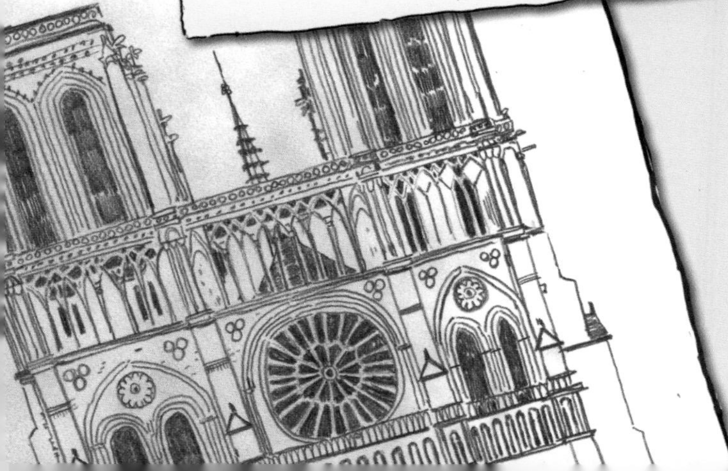

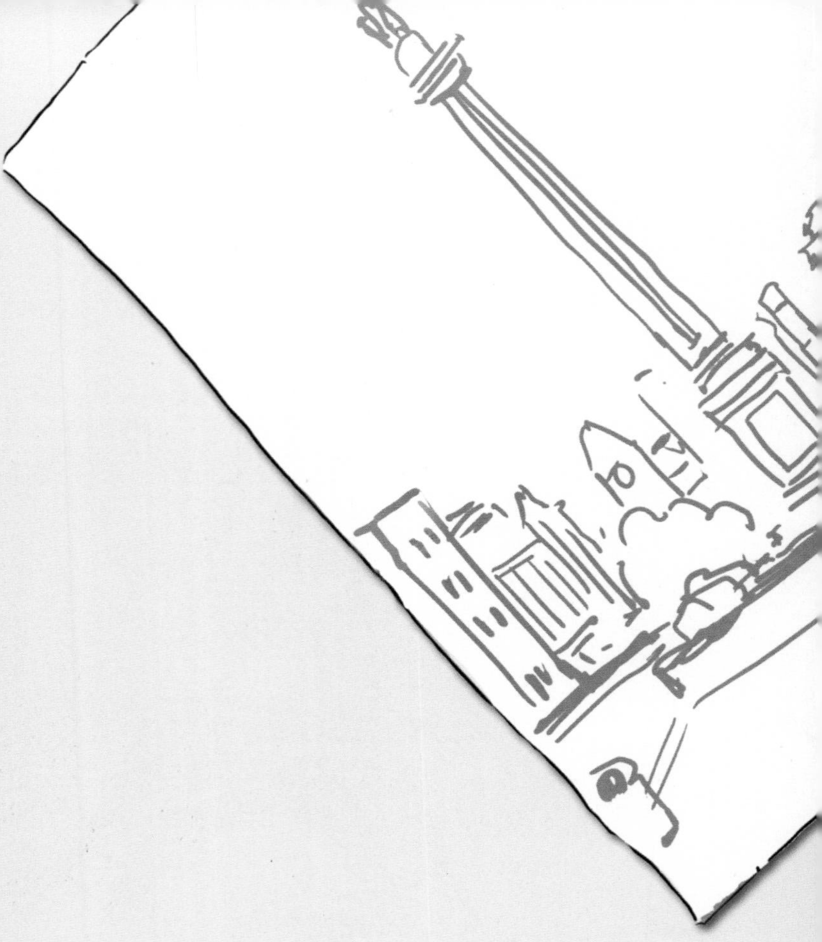

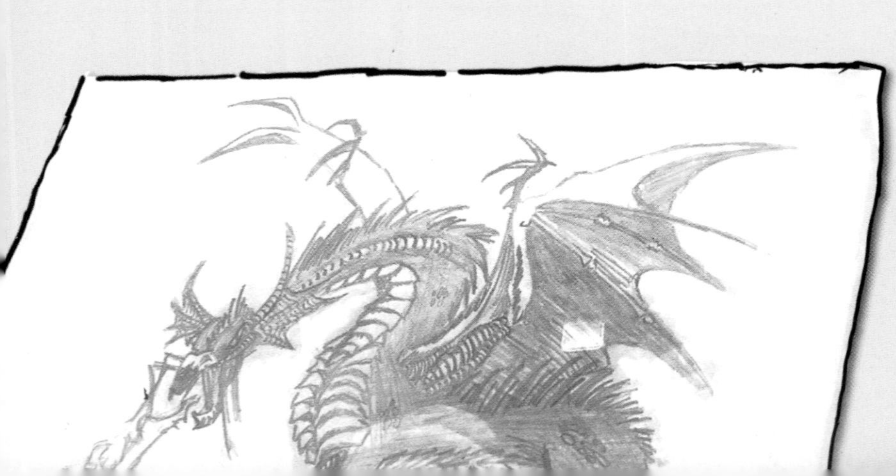

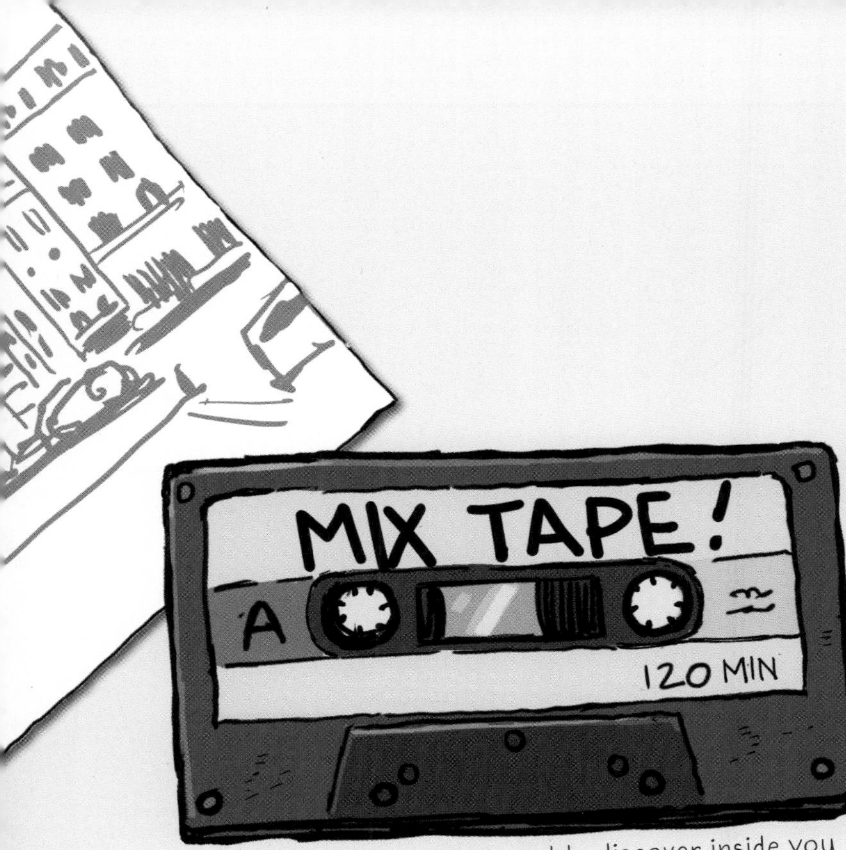
MIX TAPE!
A
120 MIN

for the person you have yet to discover inside you

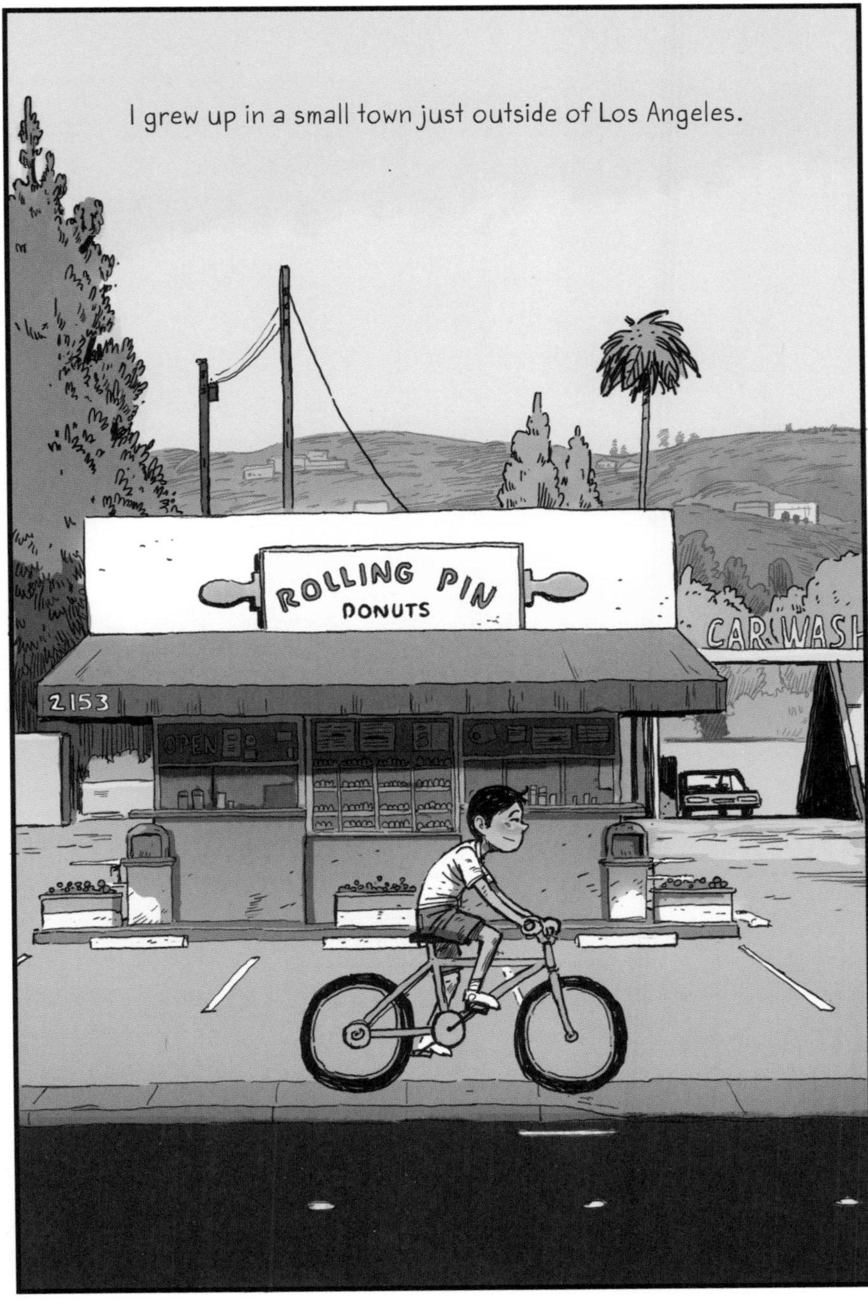
I grew up in a small town just outside of Los Angeles.
ROLLING PIN
DONUTS
CAR WASH
2153
OPEN

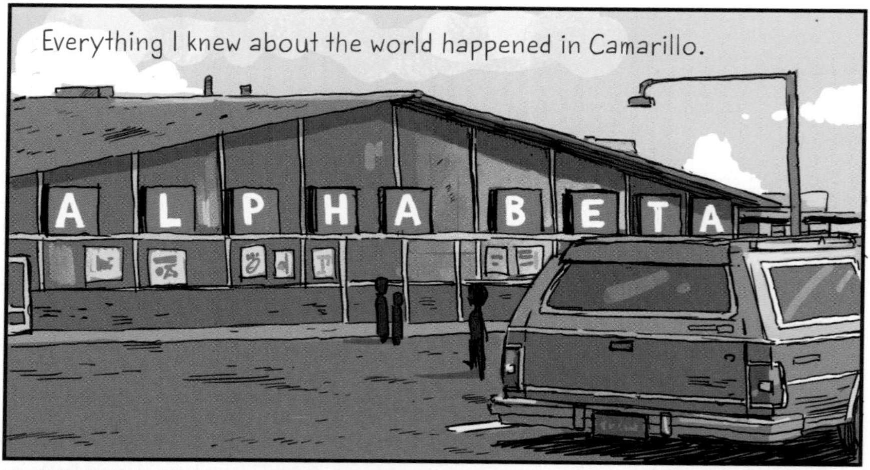
Everything I knew about the world happened in Camarillo.
ALPHABETA

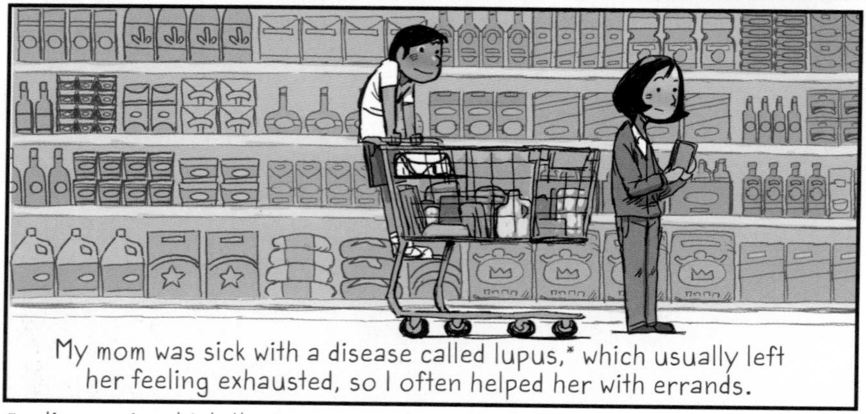
My mom was sick with a disease called lupus,* which usually left her feeling exhausted, so I often helped her with errands.

*a disease in which the immune system attacks its own tissues

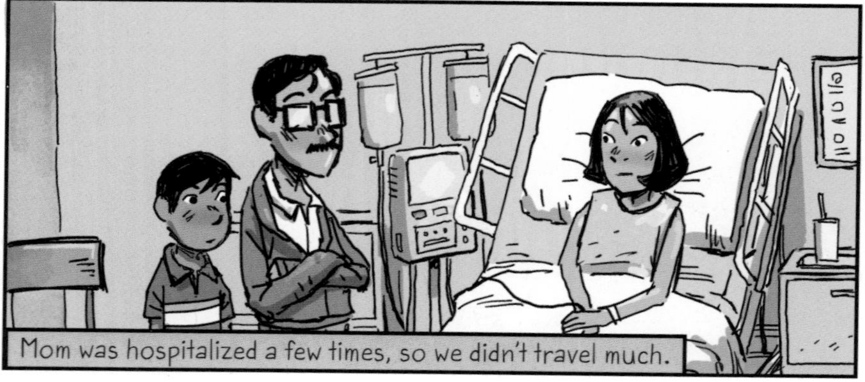
Mom was hospitalized a few times, so we didn't travel much.

I was an only child, so I kept myself busy at home.

I stayed out of trouble.

I tried my best in school.

I did normal kid stuff.

I played with friends on playgrounds and Little League sports.

Life was good.

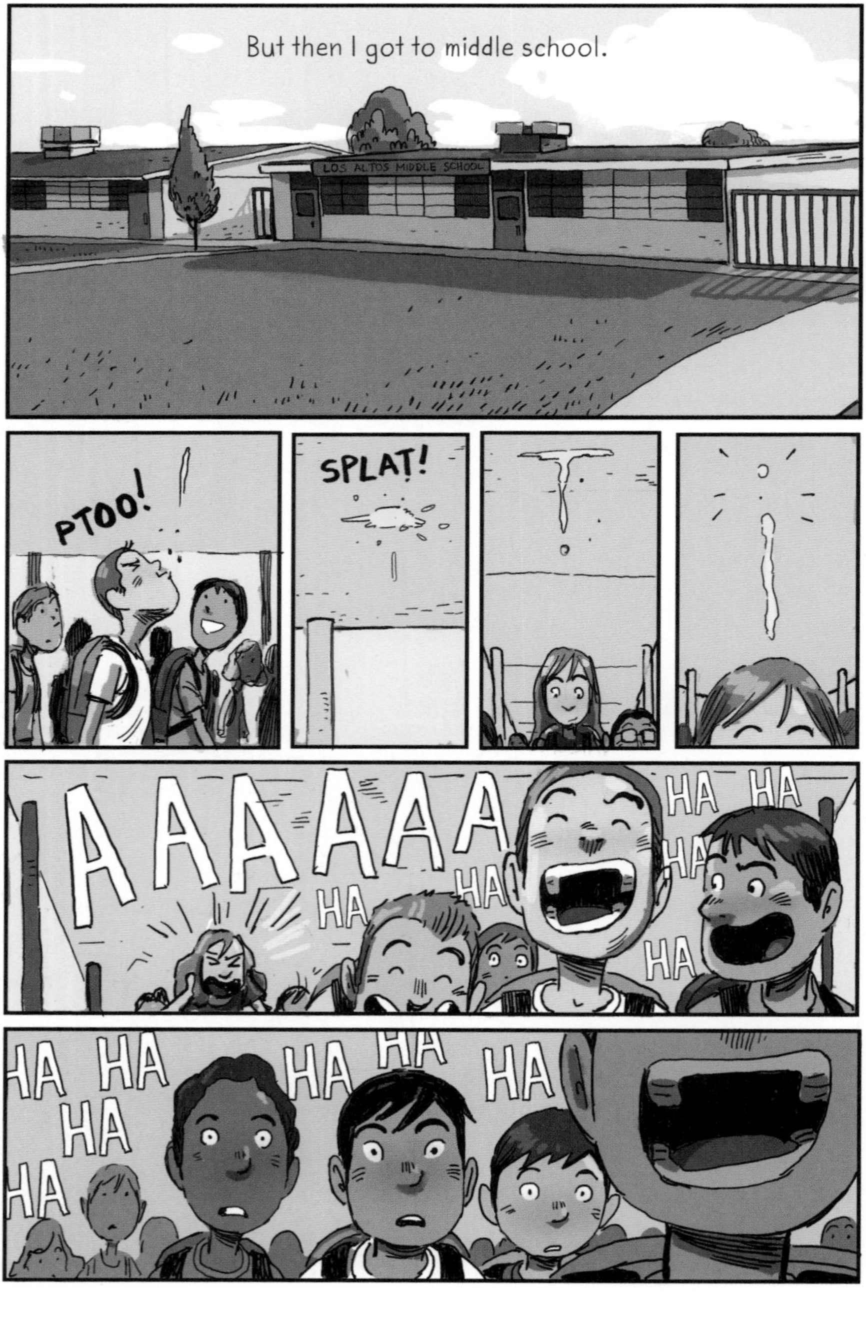

But then I got to middle school.
LOS ALTOS MIDDLE SCHOOL
PTOO!
SPLAT!
AAAAAAA
HA HA
HA
HA
HA
HA
HA HA
HA HA HA
HA
HA

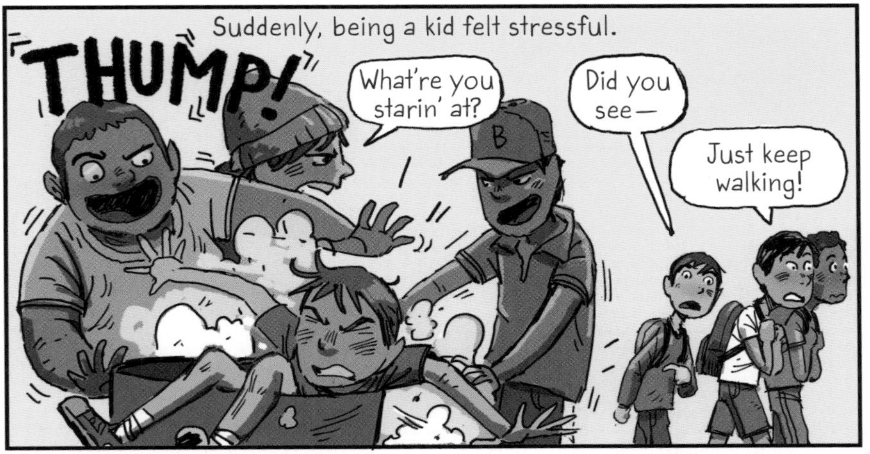
Suddenly, being a kid felt stressful.
THUMP!
What're you starin' at?
Did you see—
Just keep walking!

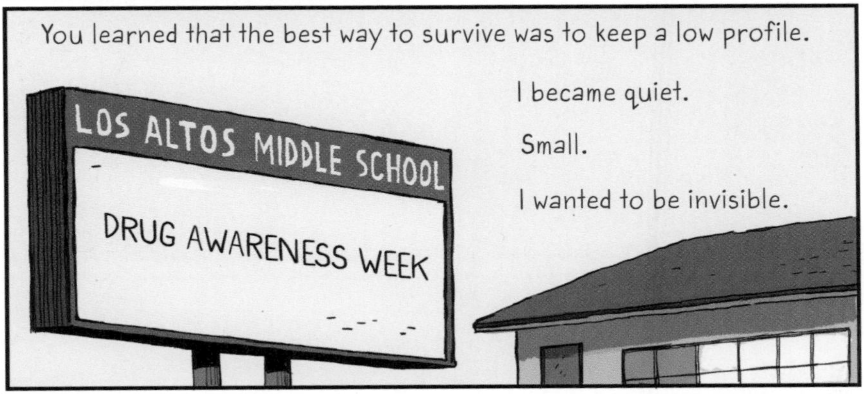
You learned that the best way to survive was to keep a low profile.
LOS ALTOS MIDDLE SCHOOL
DRUG AWARENESS WEEK
I became quiet.
Small.
I wanted to be invisible.

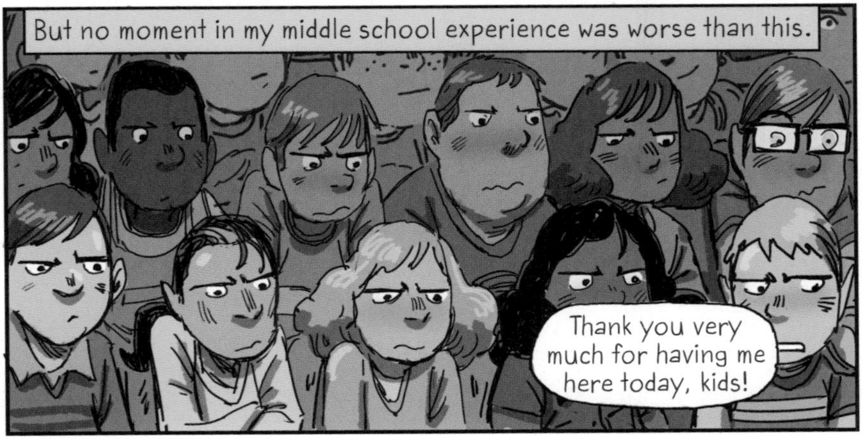
But no moment in my middle school experience was worse than this.
Thank you very much for having me here today, kids!

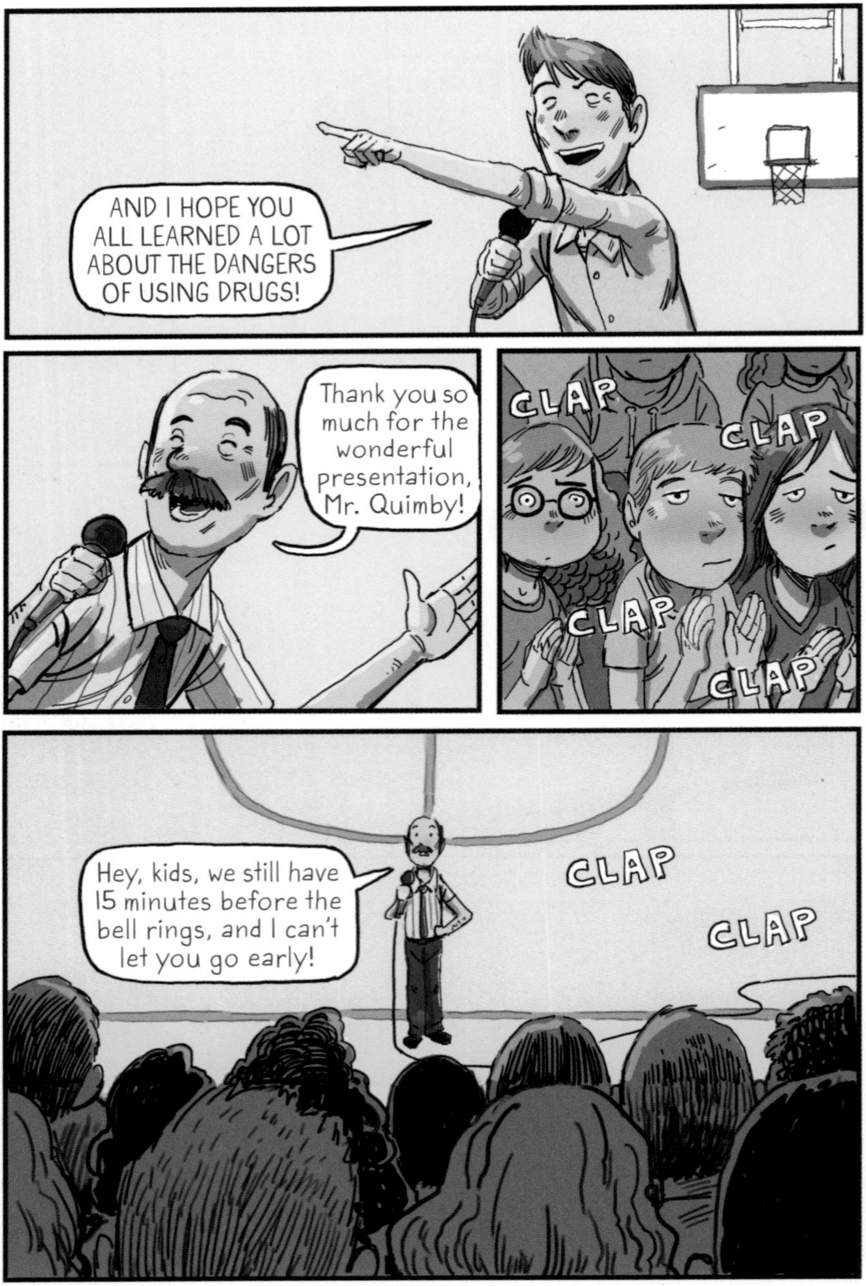
AND I HOPE YOU ALL LEARNED A LOT ABOUT THE DANGERS OF USING DRUGS!
Thank you so much for the wonderful presentation, Mr. Quimby!
CLAP
CLAP
CLAP
CLAP
Hey, kids, we still have 15 minutes before the bell rings, and I can't let you go early!
CLAP
CLAP

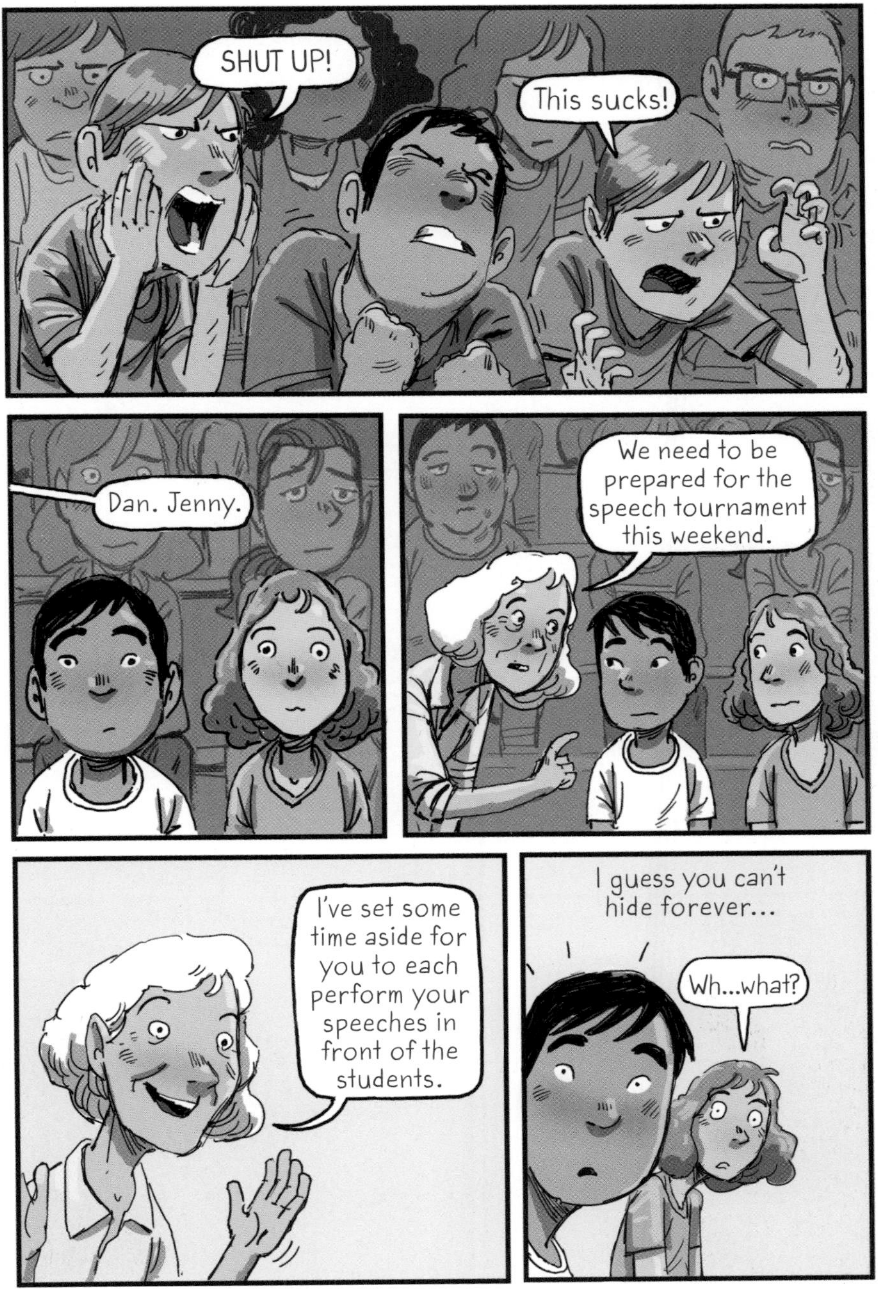
SHUT UP!
This sucks!
Dan. Jenny.
We need to be prepared for the speech tournament this weekend.
I've set some time aside for you to each perform your speeches in front of the students.
I guess you can't hide forever...
Wh...what?

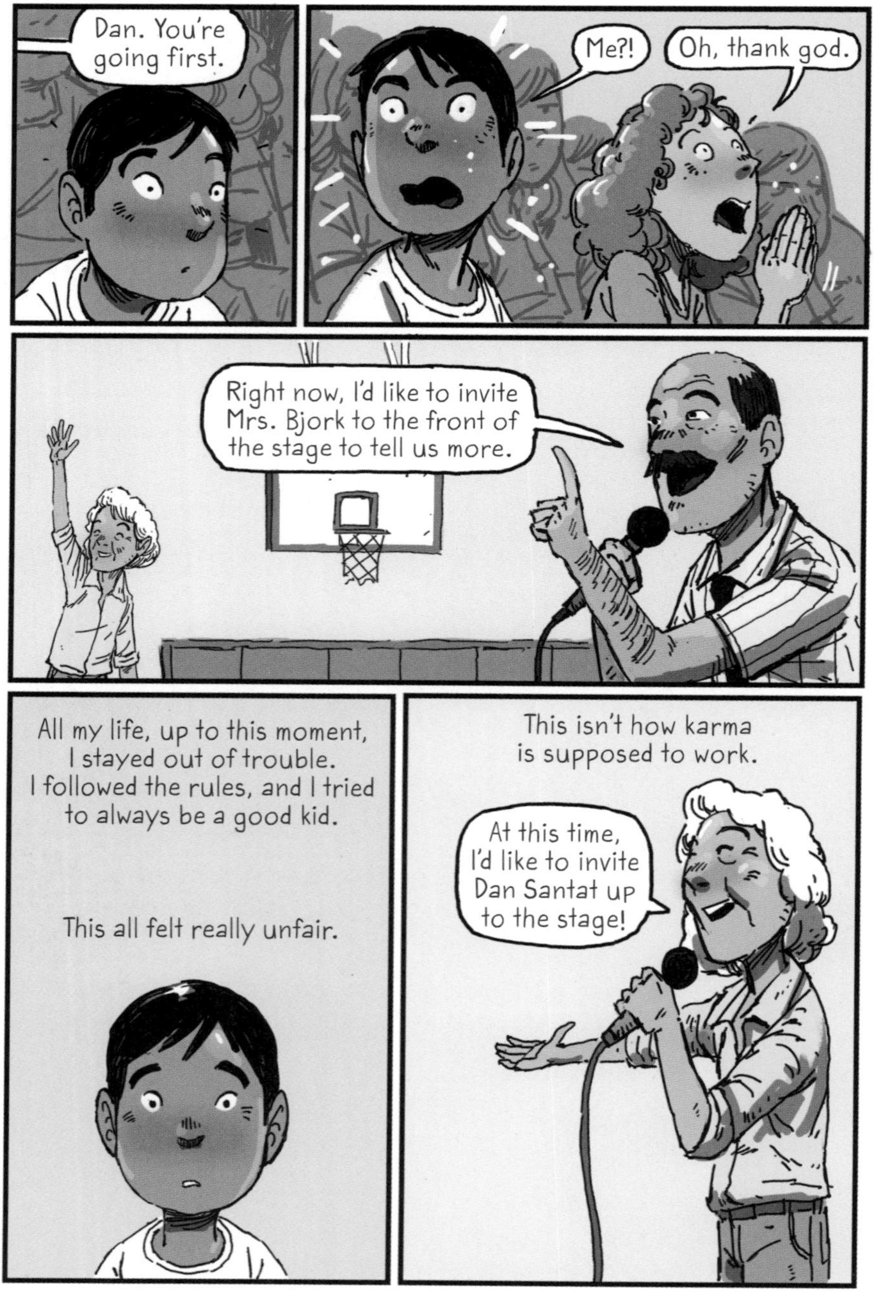

Dan. You're going first.
Me?!
Oh, thank god.
Right now, I'd like to invite Mrs. Bjork to the front of the stage to tell us more.
All my life, up to this moment, I stayed out of trouble. I followed the rules, and I tried to always be a good kid.
This all felt really unfair.
This isn't how karma is supposed to work.
At this time, I'd like to invite Dan Santat up to the stage!

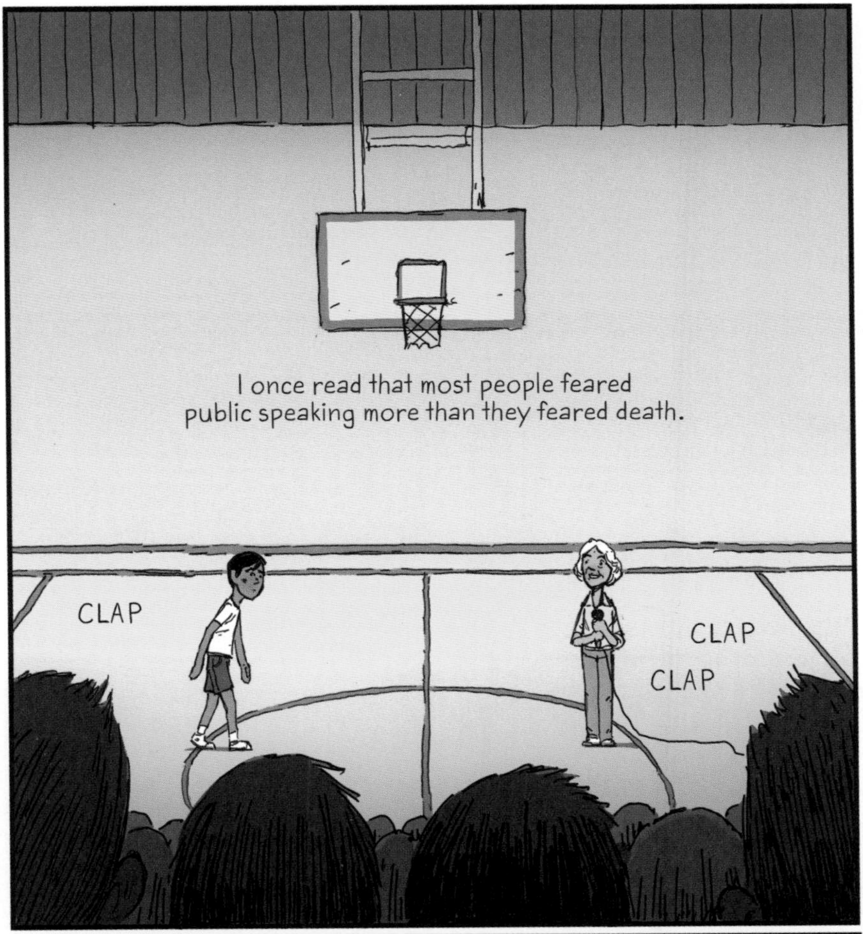
I once read that most people feared public speaking more than they feared death.
CLAP
CLAP
CLAP

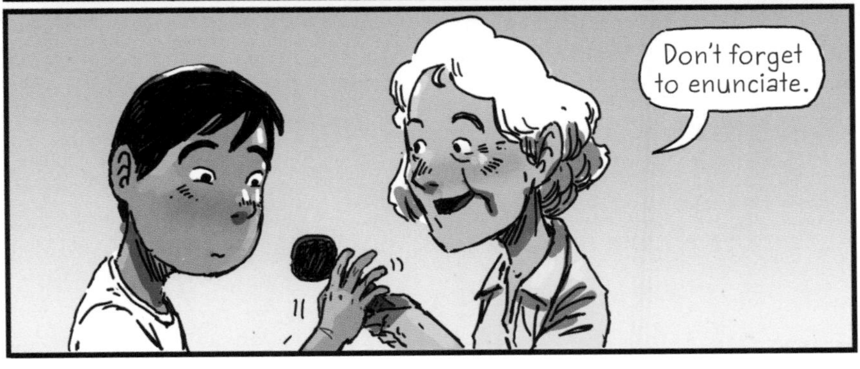
Don't forget to enunciate.

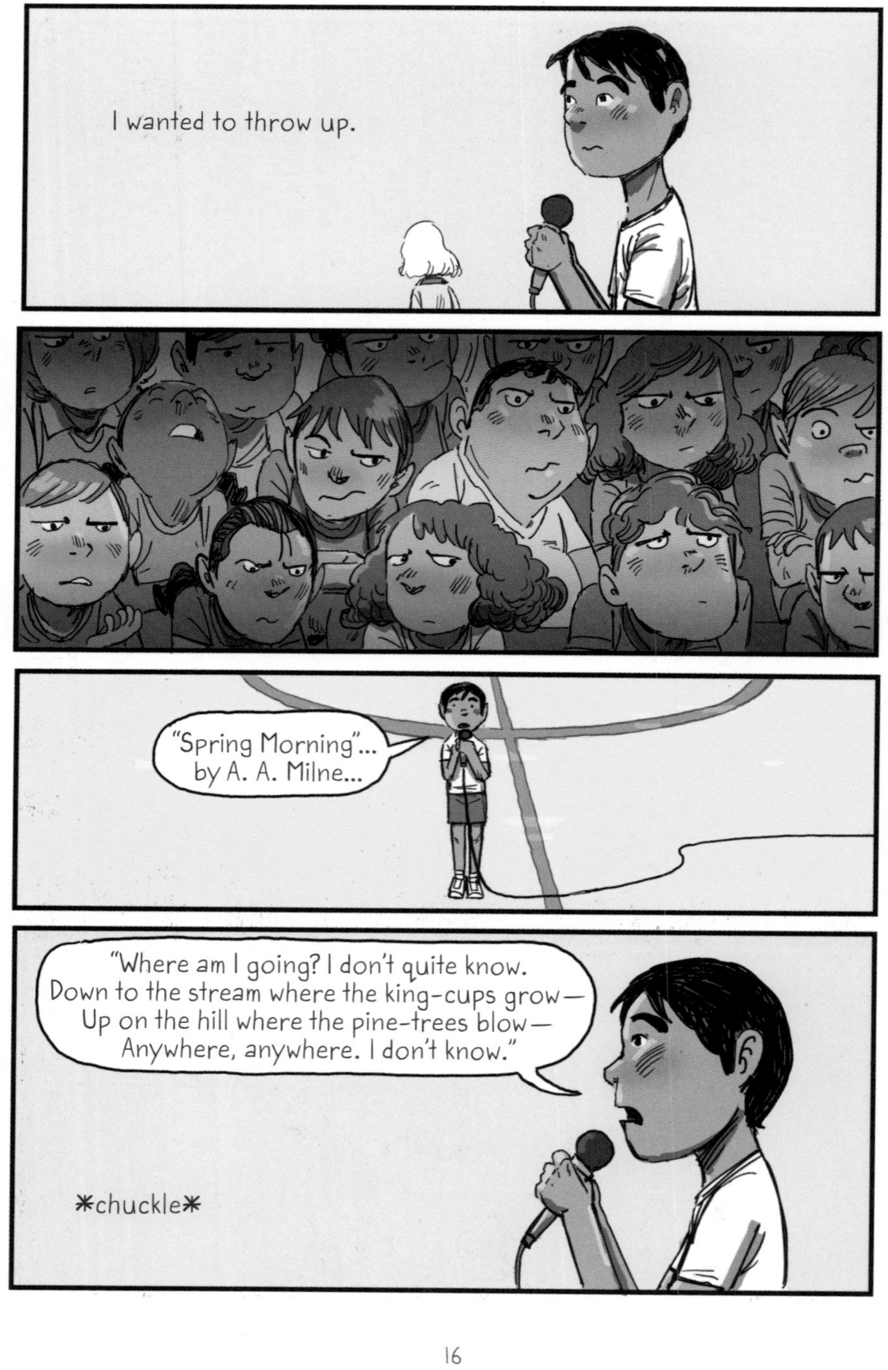
I wanted to throw up.
"Spring Morning"... by A. A. Milne...
"Where am I going? I don't quite know. Down to the stream where the king-cups grow— Up on the hill where the pine-trees blow— Anywhere, anywhere. I don't know."
chuckle

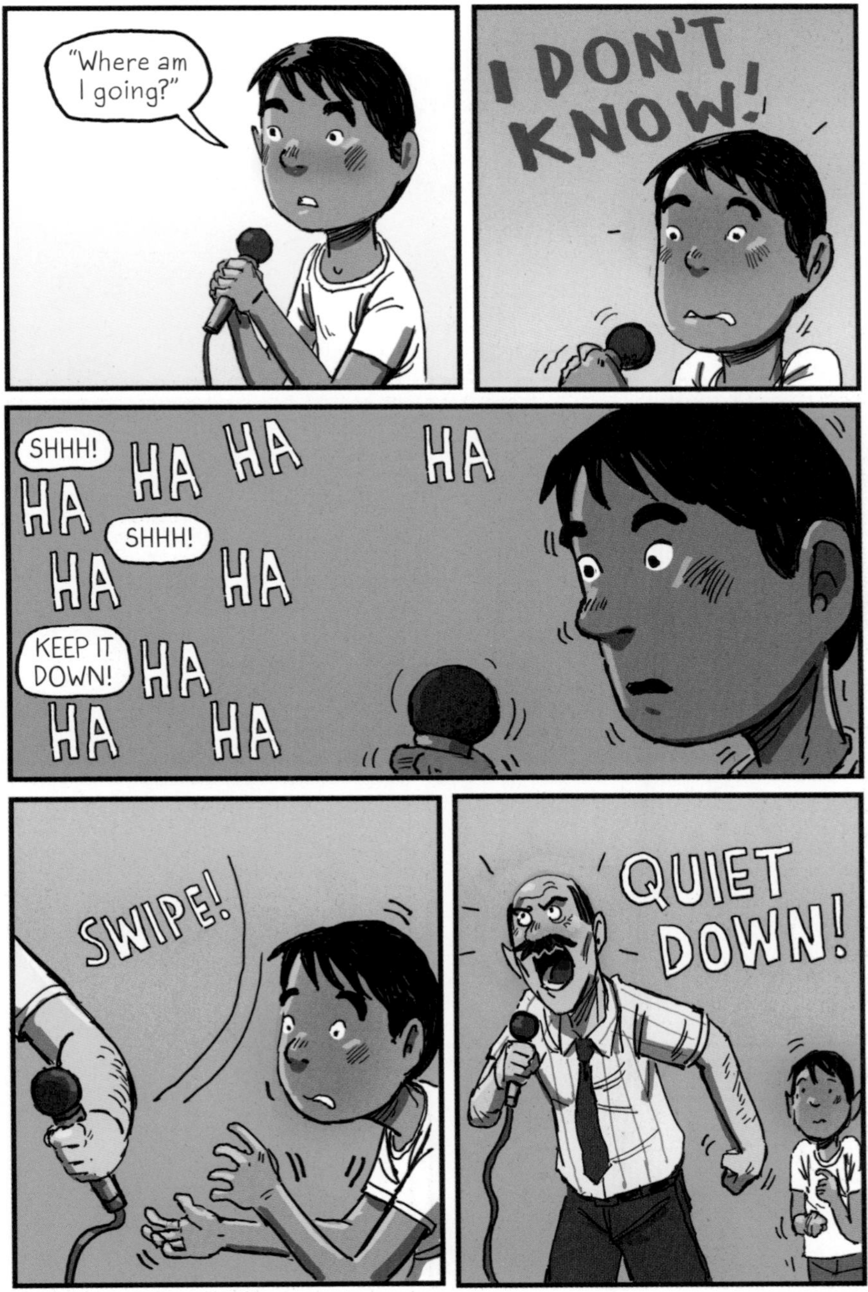
"Where am I going?"
I DON'T KNOW!
SHHH!
HA HA HA HA
HA
SHHH!
HA HA
KEEP IT DOWN!
HA
HA HA
SWIPE!
QUIET DOWN!

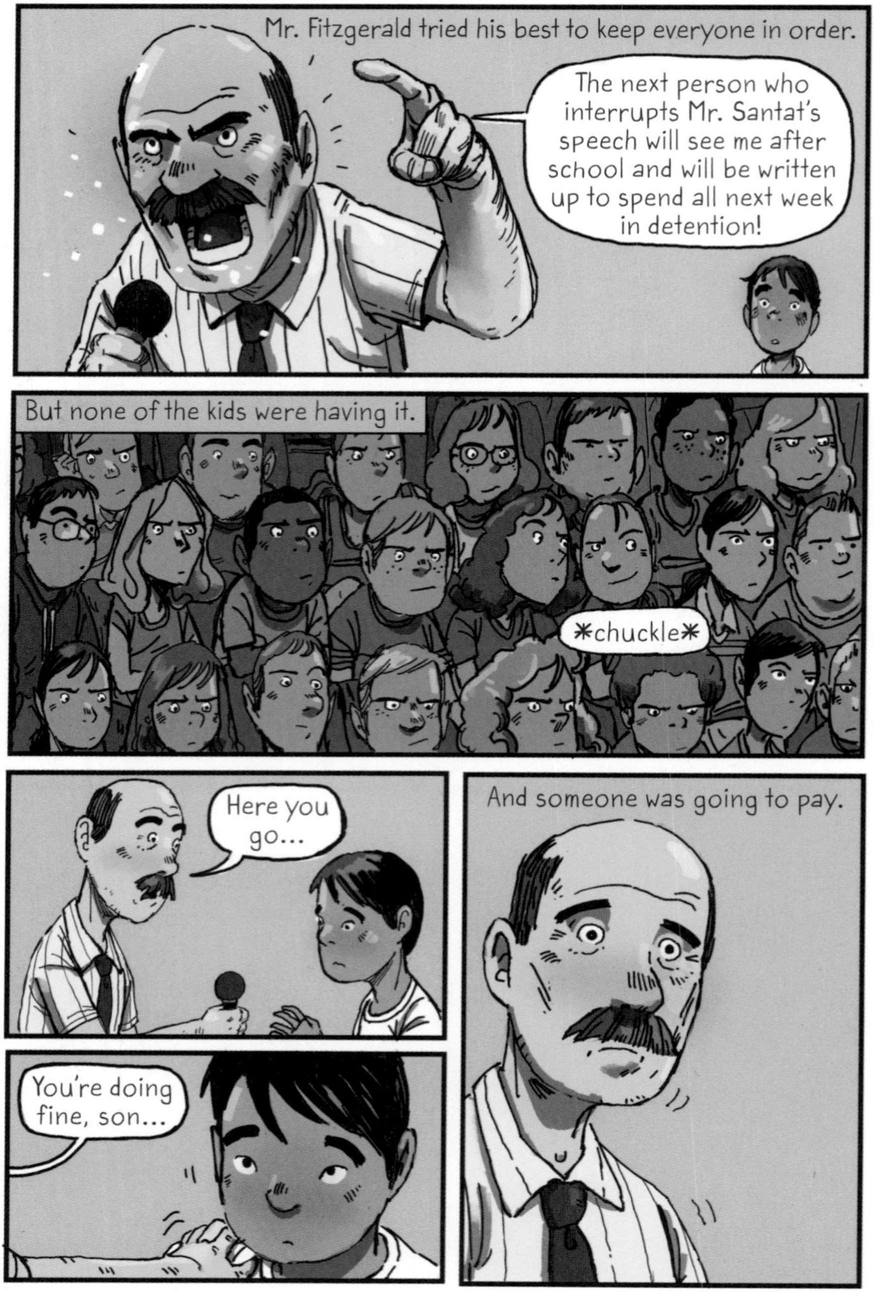

Mr. Fitzgerald tried his best to keep everyone in order.
The next person who interrupts Mr. Santat's speech will see me after school and will be written up to spend all next week in detention!
But none of the kids were having it.
chuckle
Here you go...
You're doing fine, son...
And someone was going to pay.

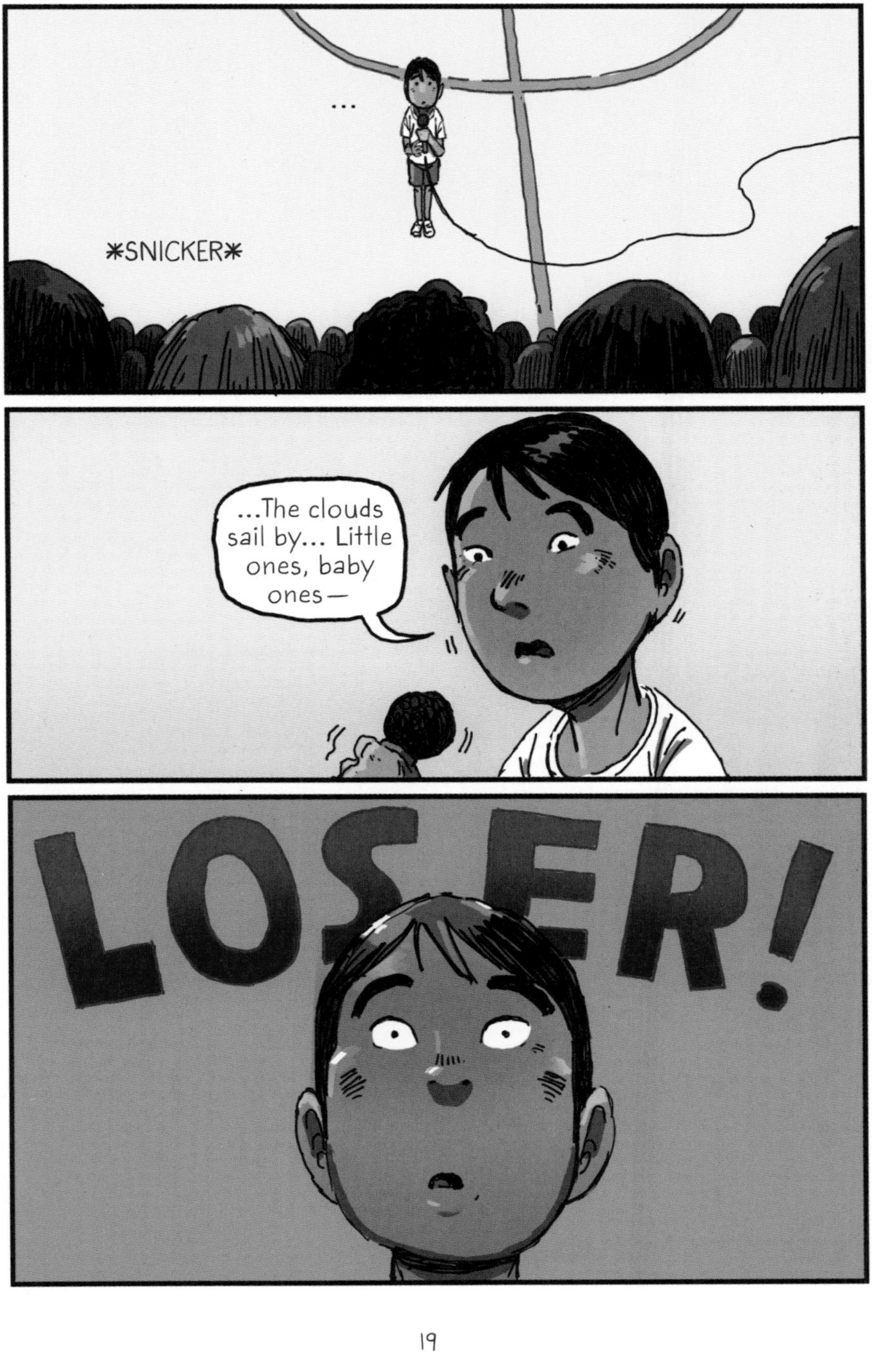
...
SNICKER
...The clouds sail by... Little ones, baby ones—
LOSER!

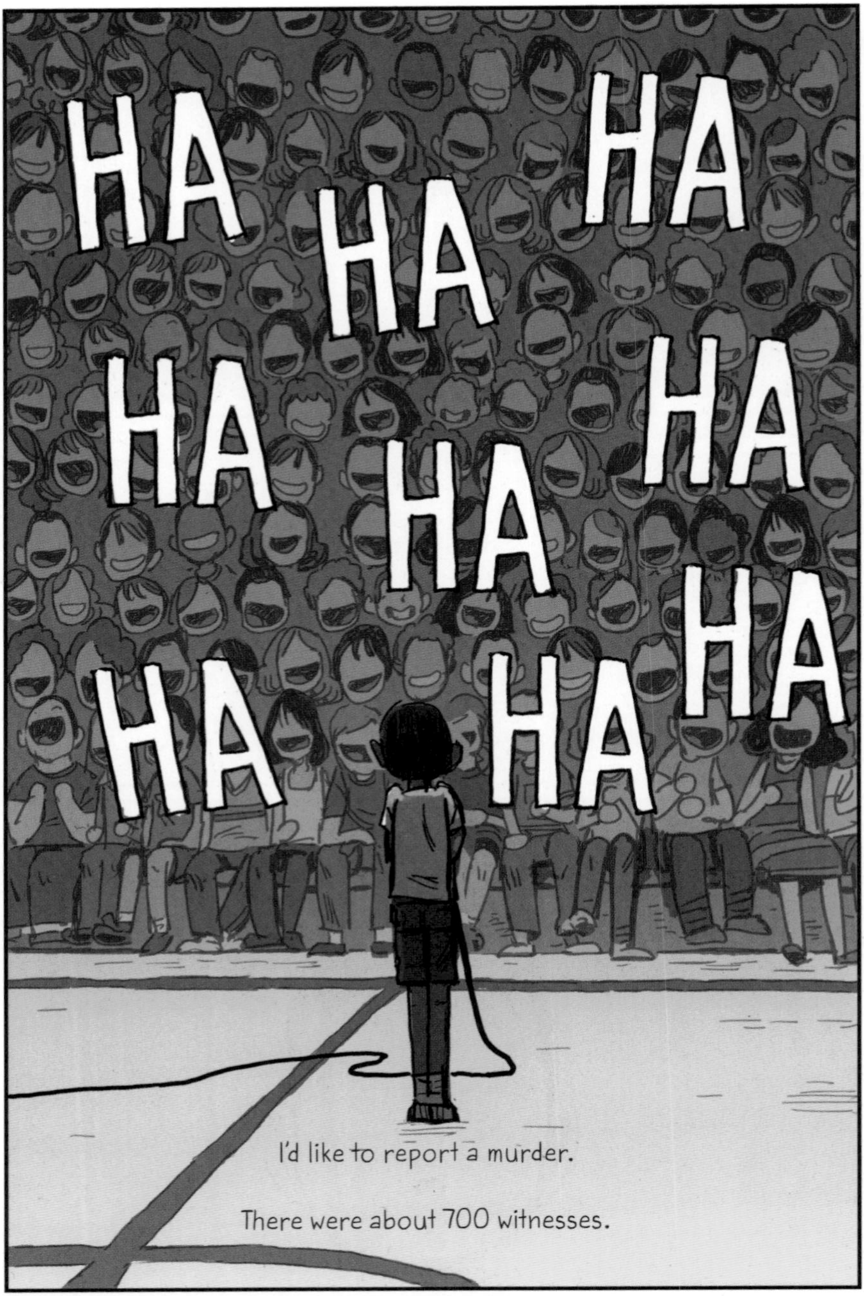
HA HA HA HA HA HA HA HA HA
I'd like to report a murder.
There were about 700 witnesses.

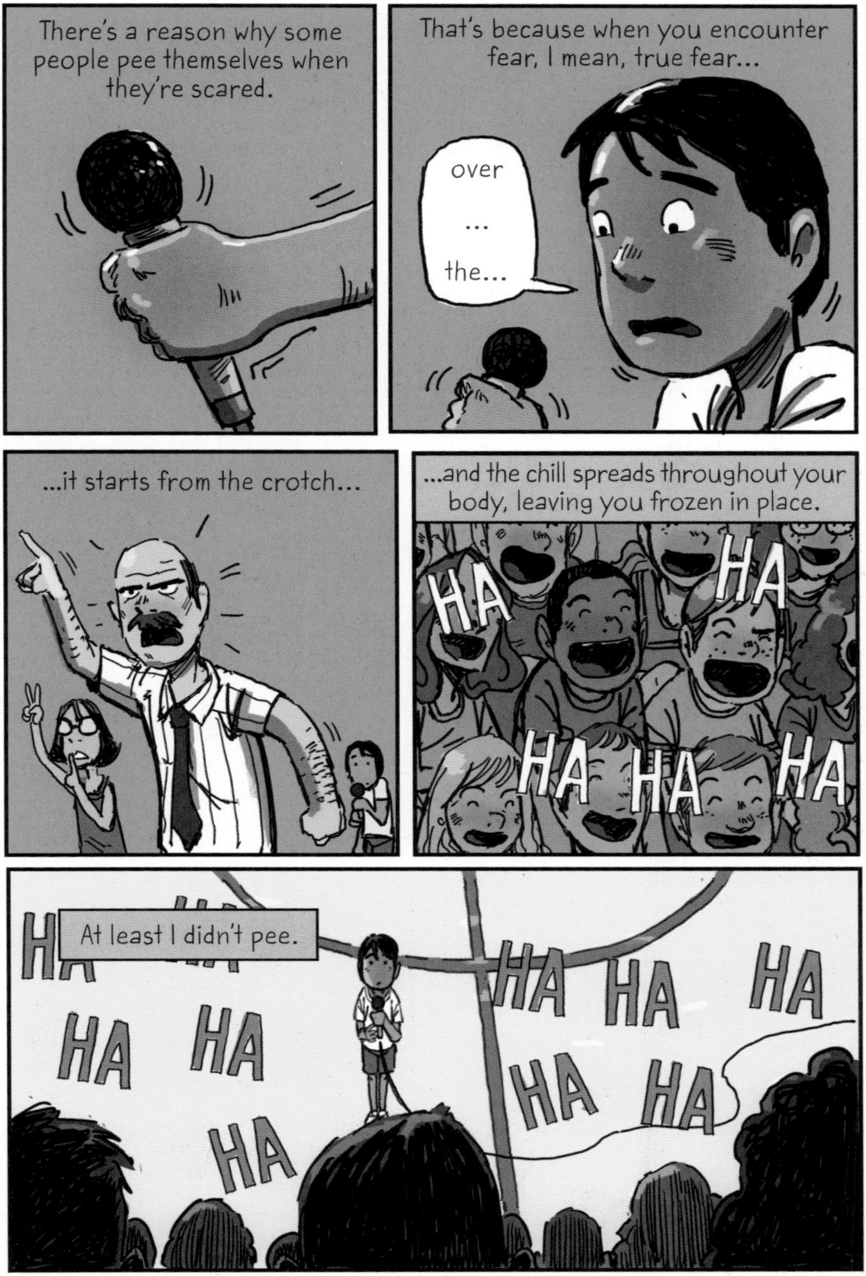
There's a reason why some people pee themselves when they're scared.
That's because when you encounter fear, I mean, true fear...
over ... the...
...it starts from the crotch...
...and the chill spreads throughout your body, leaving you frozen in place.
HA
HA
HA HA HA
At least I didn't pee.
HA HA HA HA HA HA HA HA HA HA

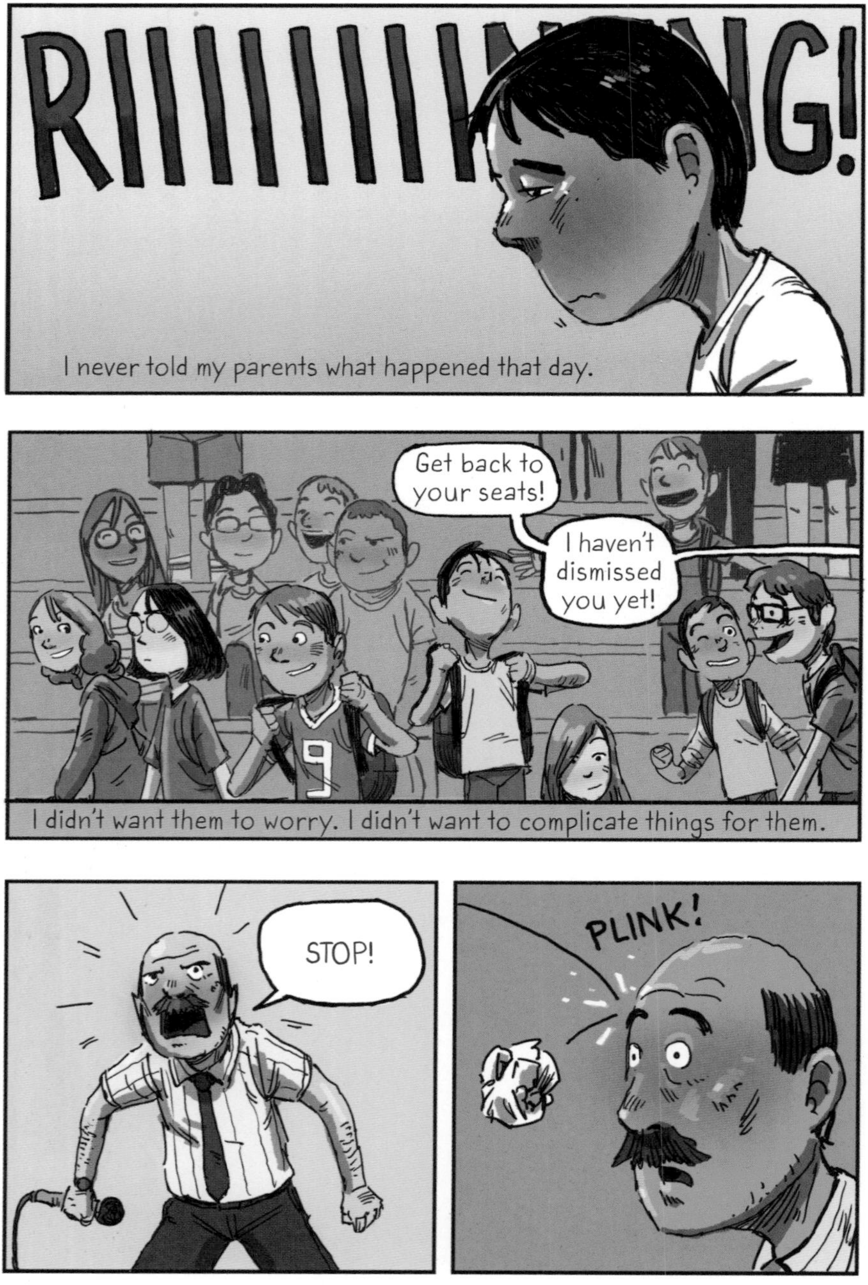
RIIIIIIIING!
I never told my parents what happened that day.
Get back to your seats!
I haven't dismissed you yet!
I didn't want them to worry. I didn't want to complicate things for them.
STOP!
PLINK!

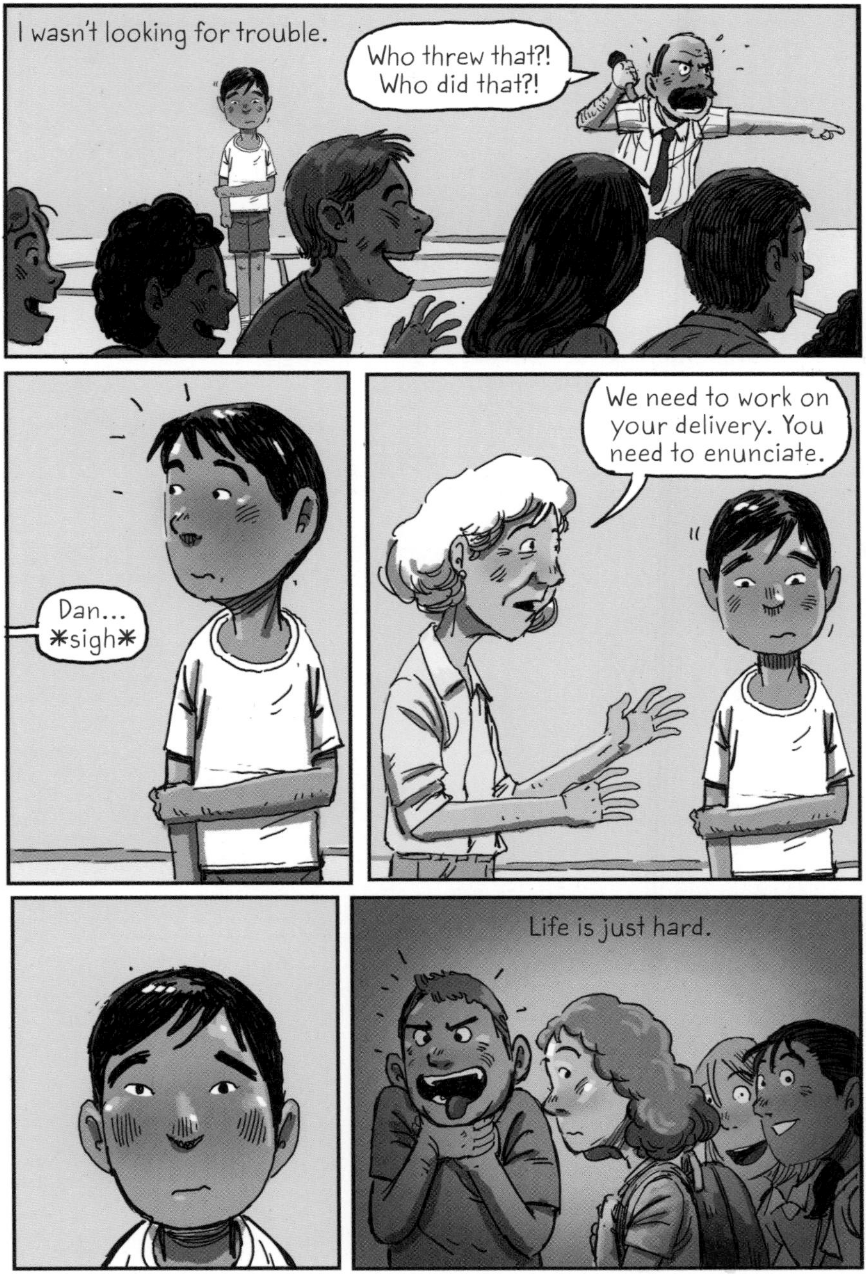
I wasn't looking for trouble.
Who threw that?! Who did that?!
Dan... *sigh*
We need to work on your delivery. You need to enunciate.
Life is just hard.

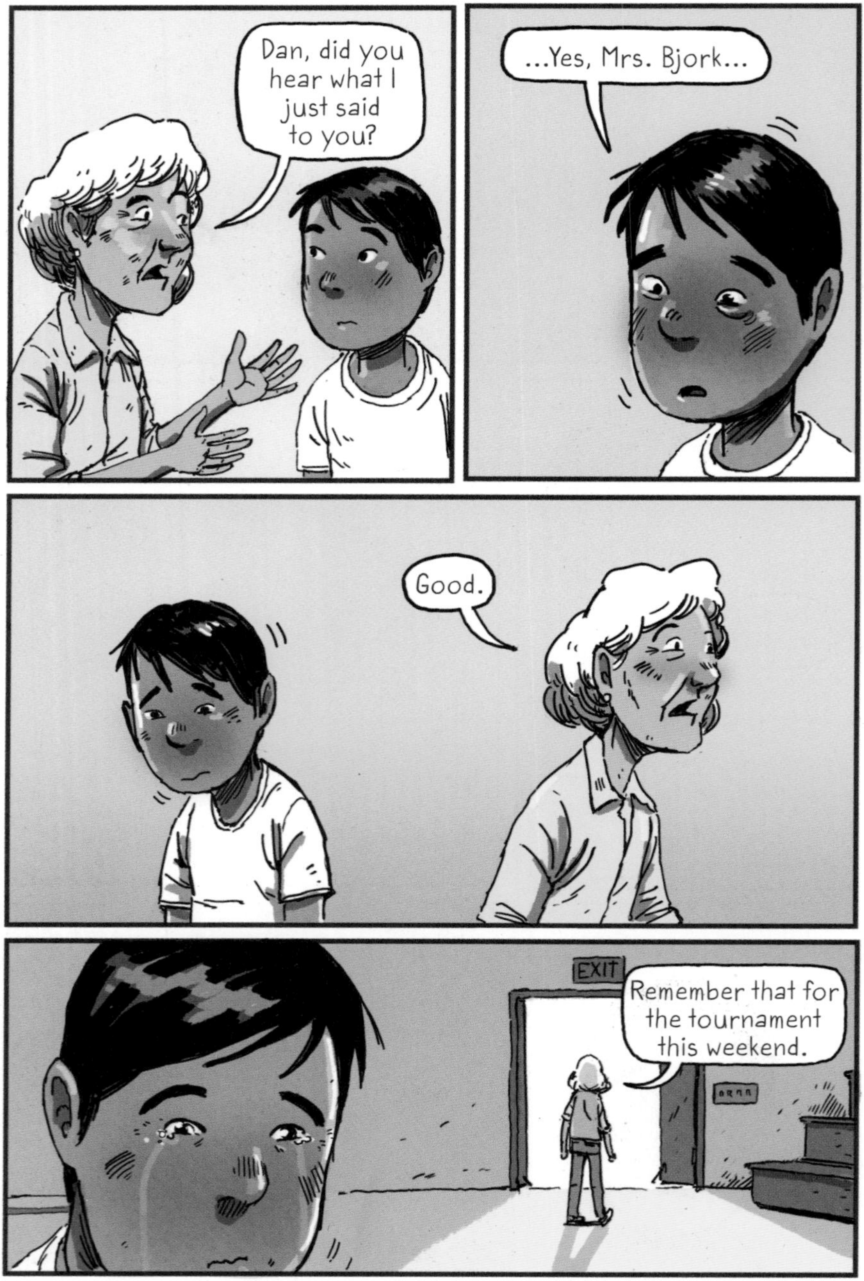
Dan, did you hear what I just said to you?
...Yes, Mrs. Bjork...
Good.
EXIT
Remember that for the tournament this weekend.

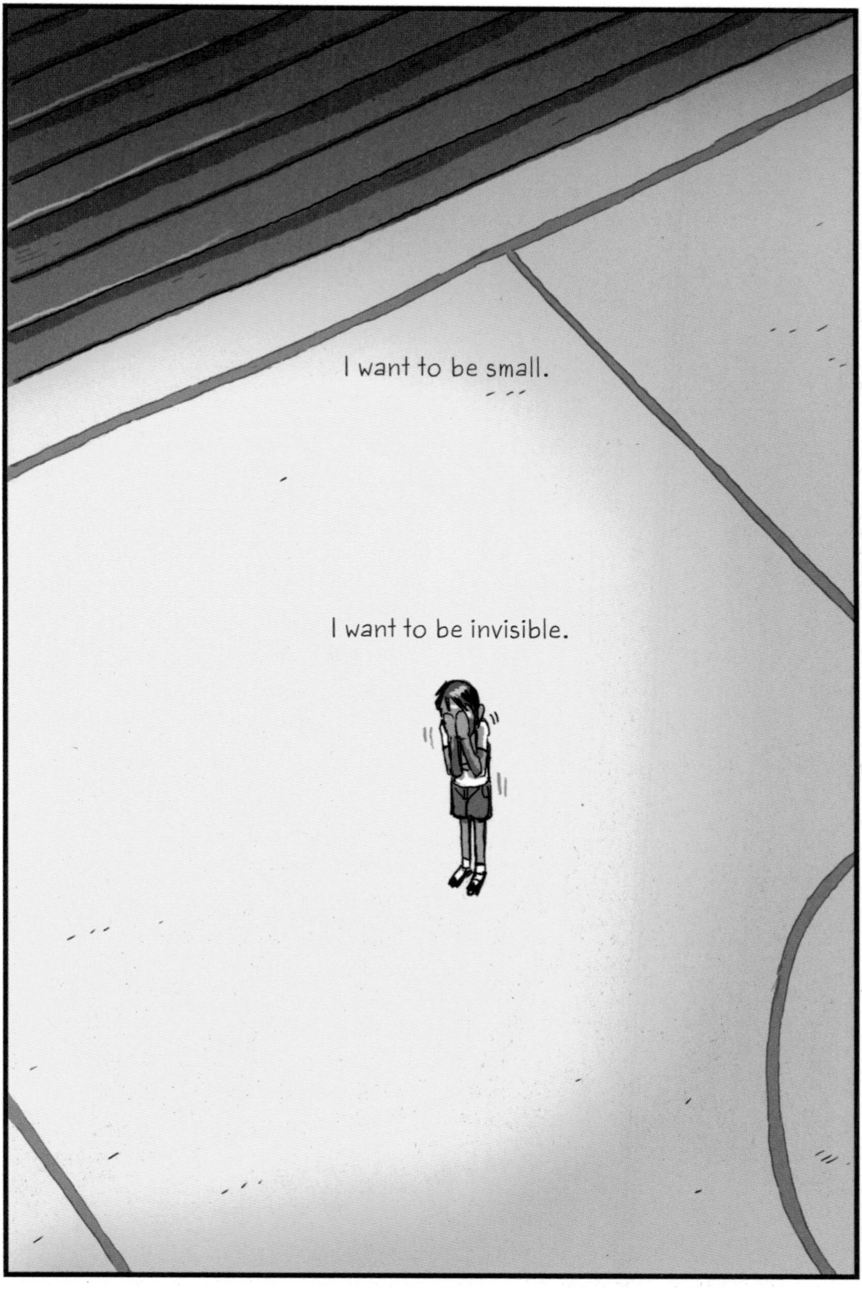
I want to be small.
I want to be invisible.

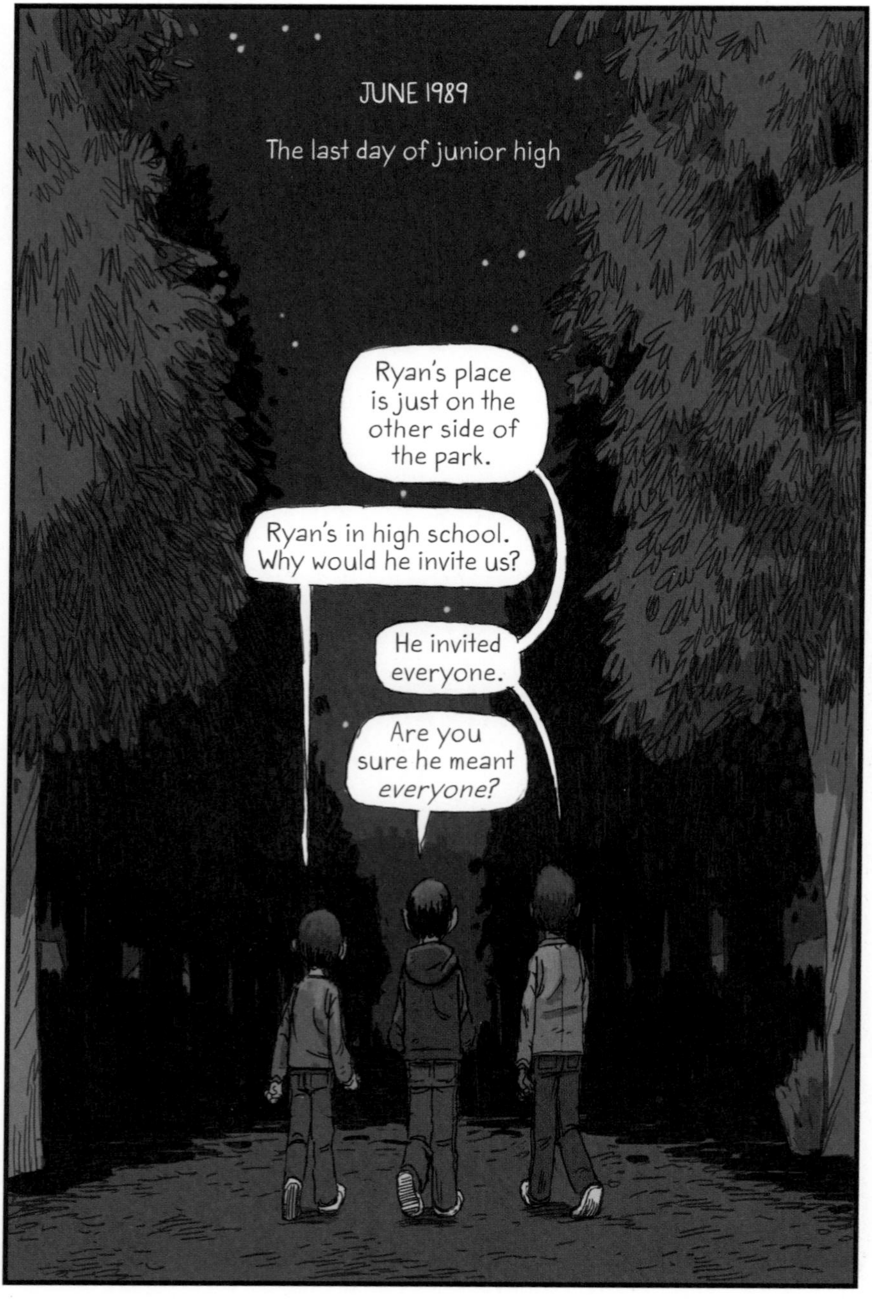
JUNE 1989
The last day of junior high
Ryan's place is just on the other side of the park.
Ryan's in high school. Why would he invite us?
He invited everyone.
Are you sure he meant *everyone?*

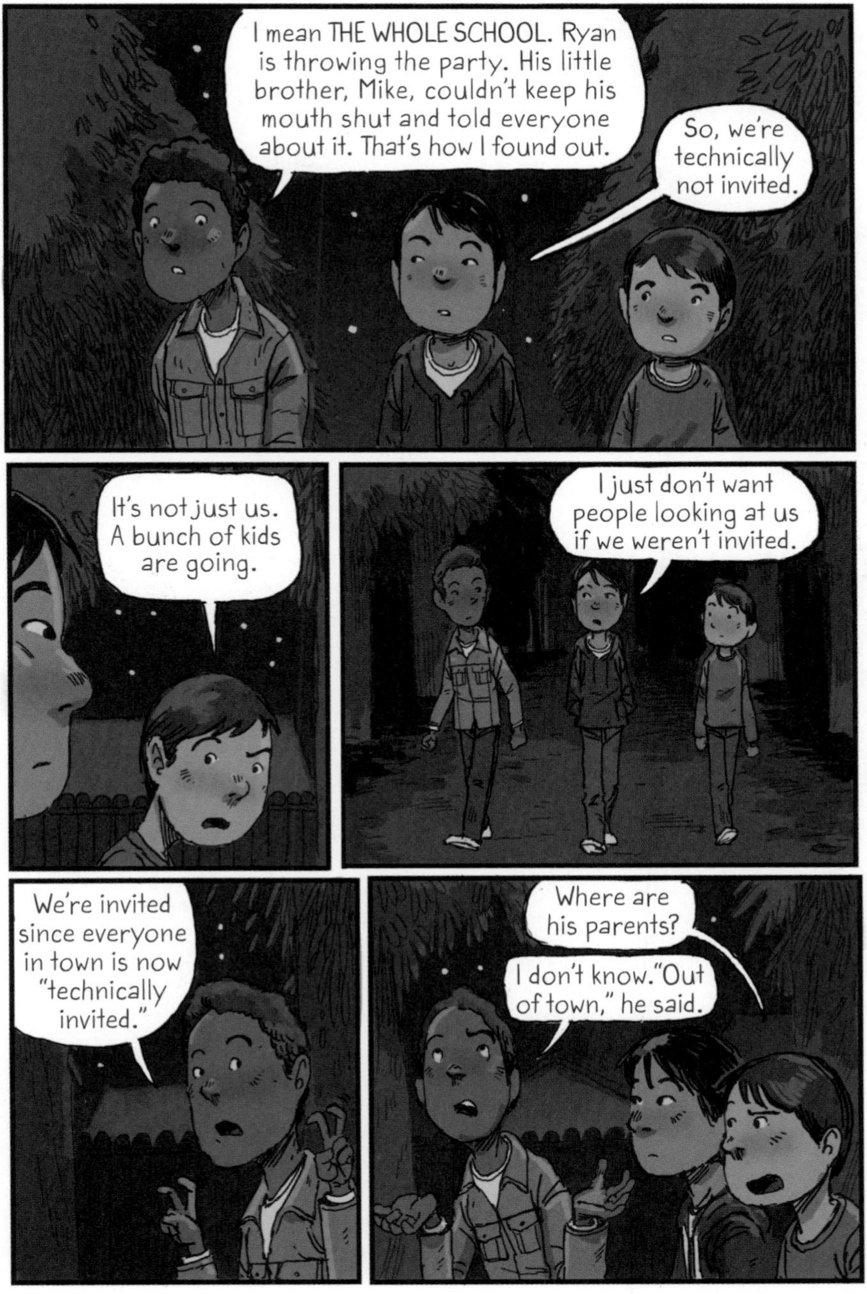
I mean THE WHOLE SCHOOL. Ryan is throwing the party. His little brother, Mike, couldn't keep his mouth shut and told everyone about it. That's how I found out.
So, we're technically not invited.
It's not just us. A bunch of kids are going.
I just don't want people looking at us if we weren't invited.
We're invited since everyone in town is now "technically invited."
Where are his parents?
I don't know. "Out of town," he said.

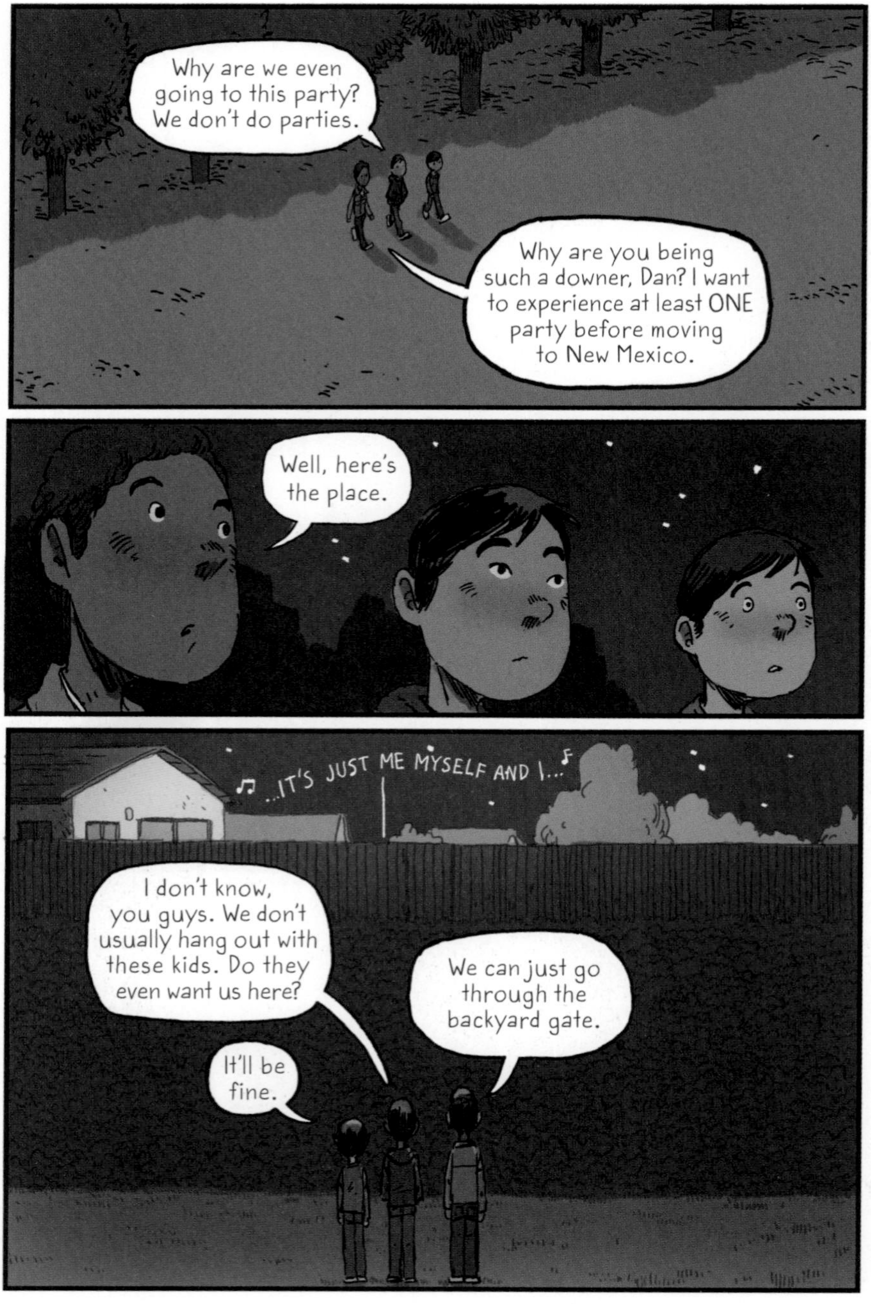
Why are we even going to this party? We don't do parties.
Why are you being such a downer, Dan? I want to experience at least ONE party before moving to New Mexico.
Well, here's the place.
♫ ...IT'S JUST ME MYSELF AND I... ♪
I don't know, you guys. We don't usually hang out with these kids. Do they even want us here?
We can just go through the backyard gate.
It'll be fine.

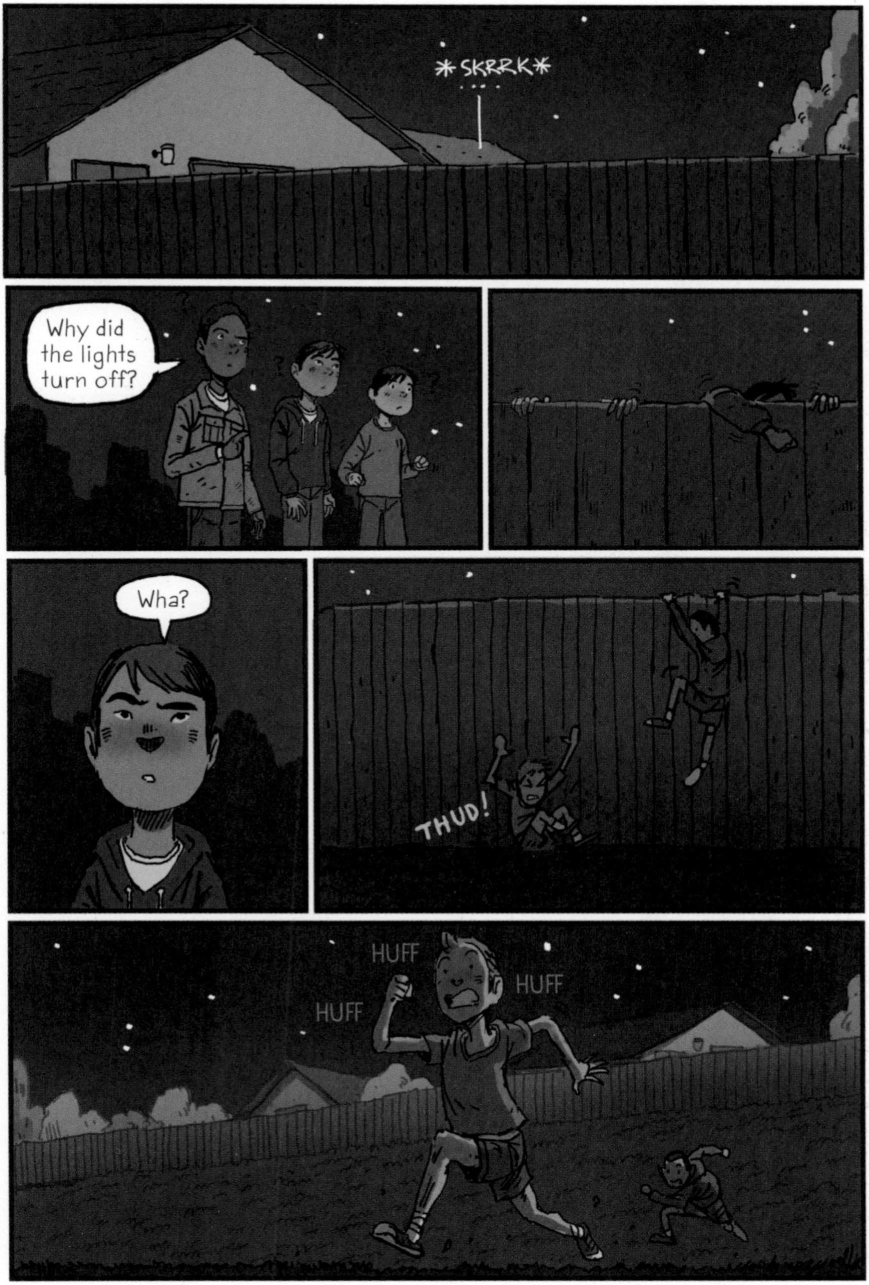
SKRRK
Why did the lights turn off?
Wha?
THUD!
HUFF
HUFF
HUFF

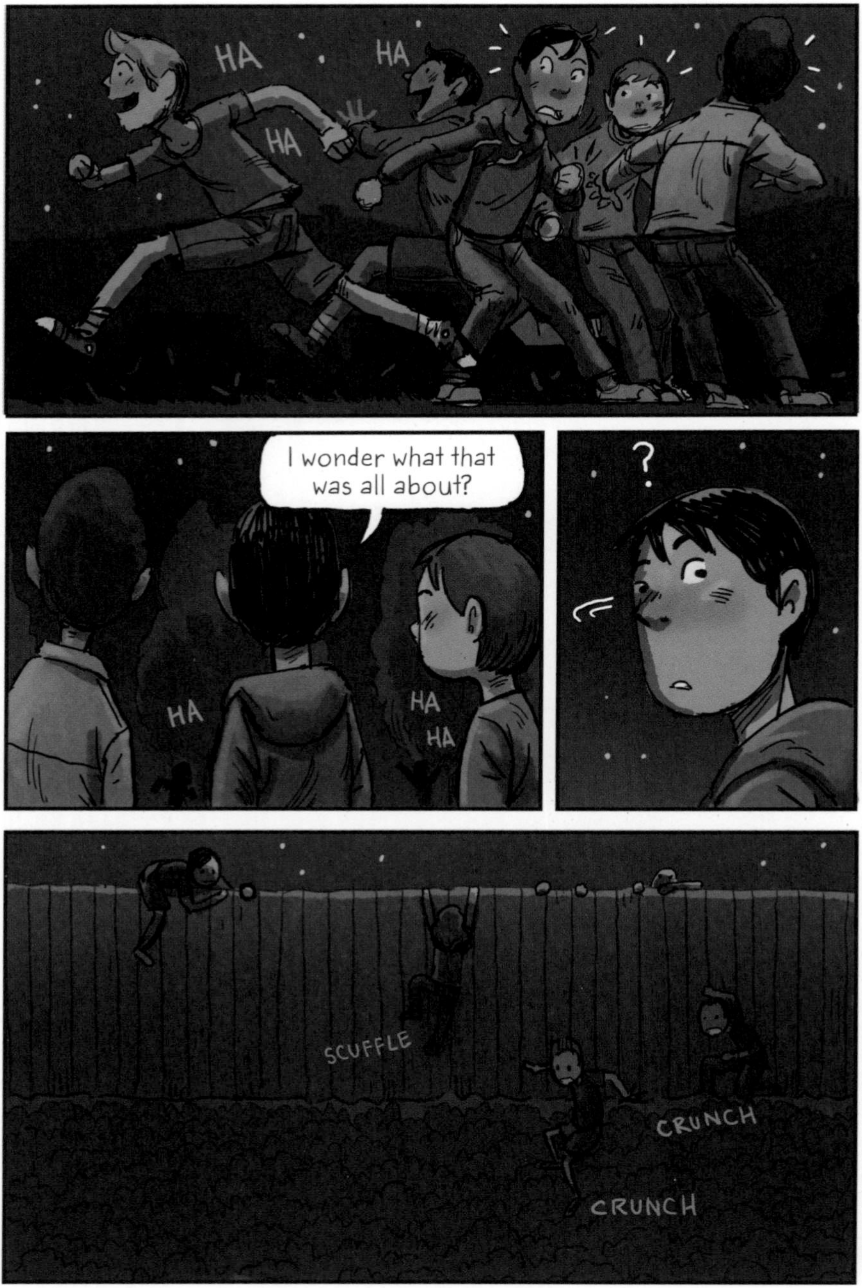
HA
HA
HA
I wonder what that was all about?
HA
HA
HA
?
SCUFFLE
CRUNCH
CRUNCH

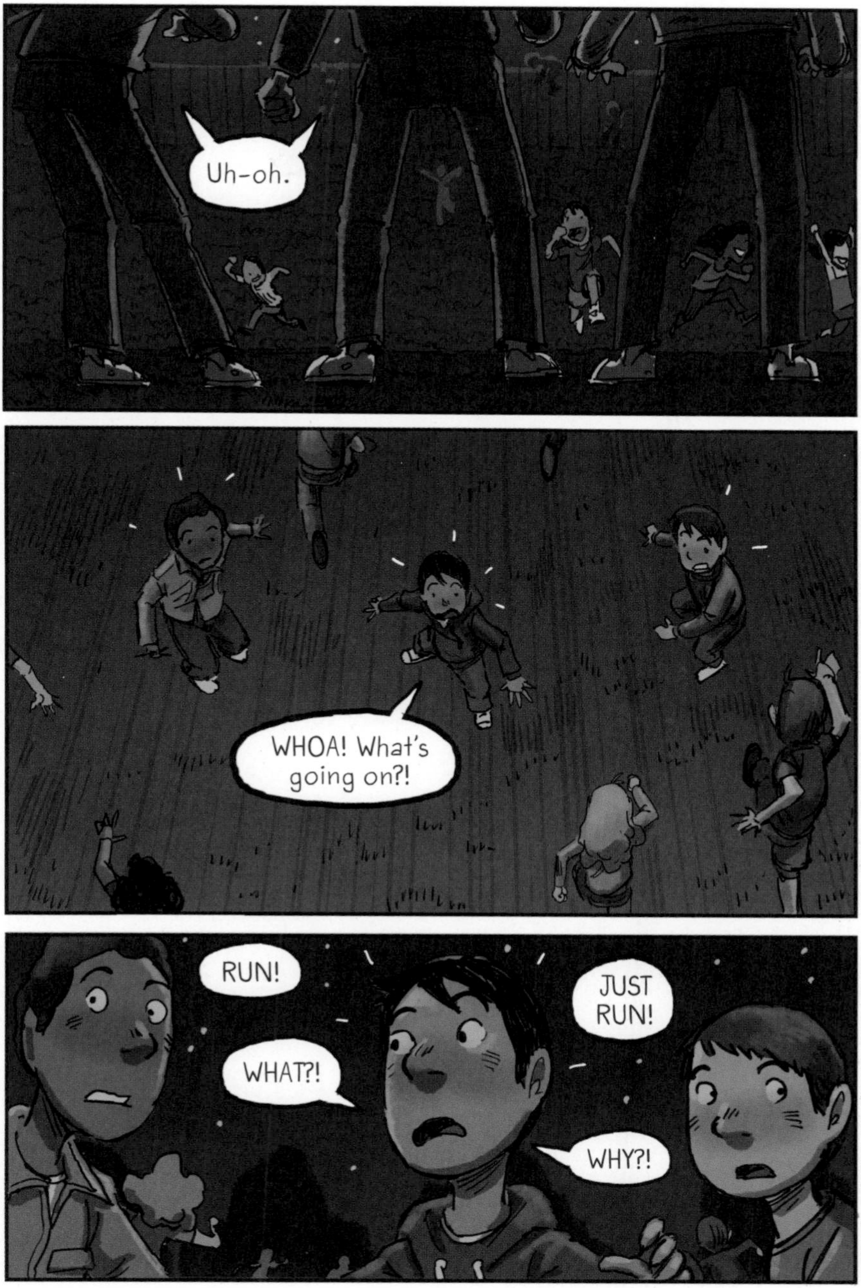
Uh-oh.
WHOA! What's going on?!
RUN!
WHAT?!
JUST RUN!
WHY?!

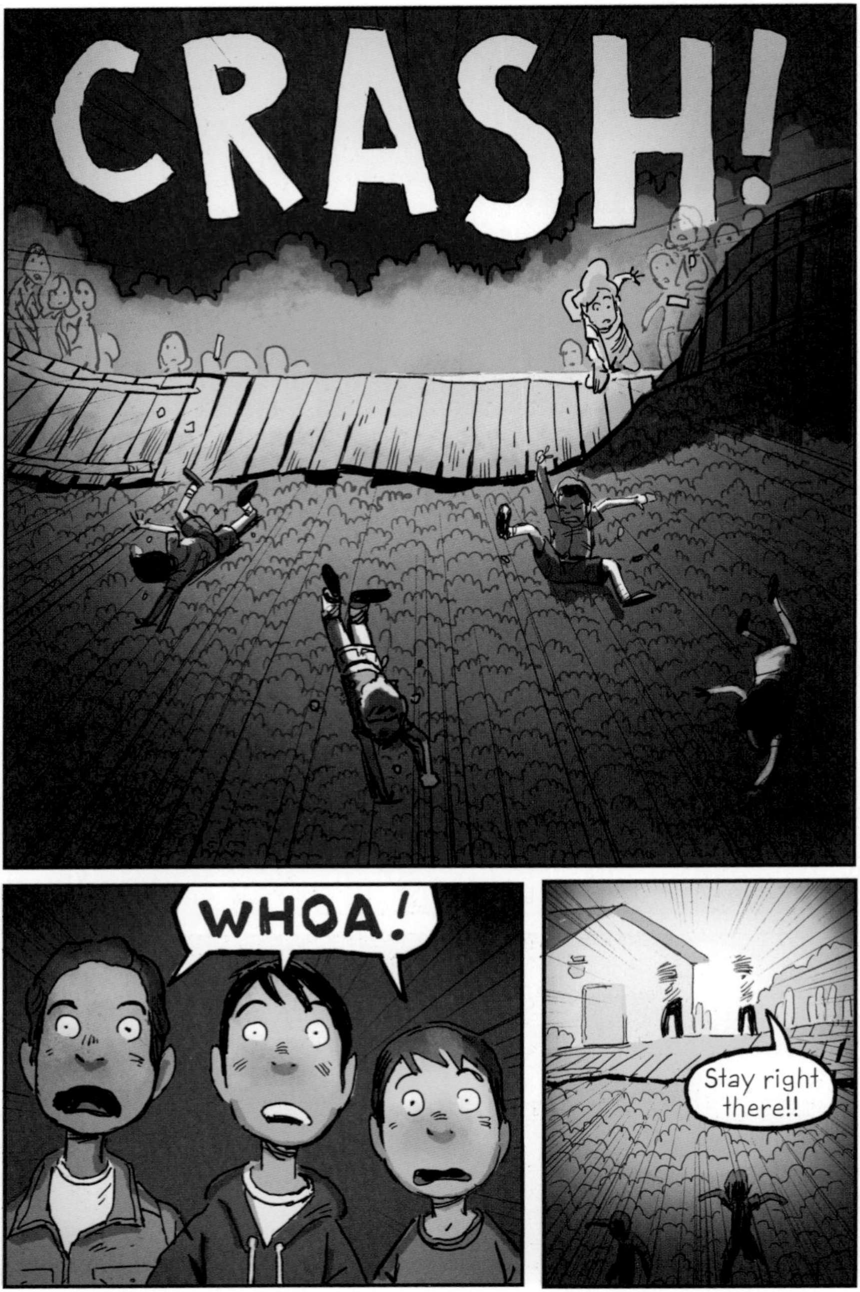
CRASH!
WHOA!
Stay right there!!

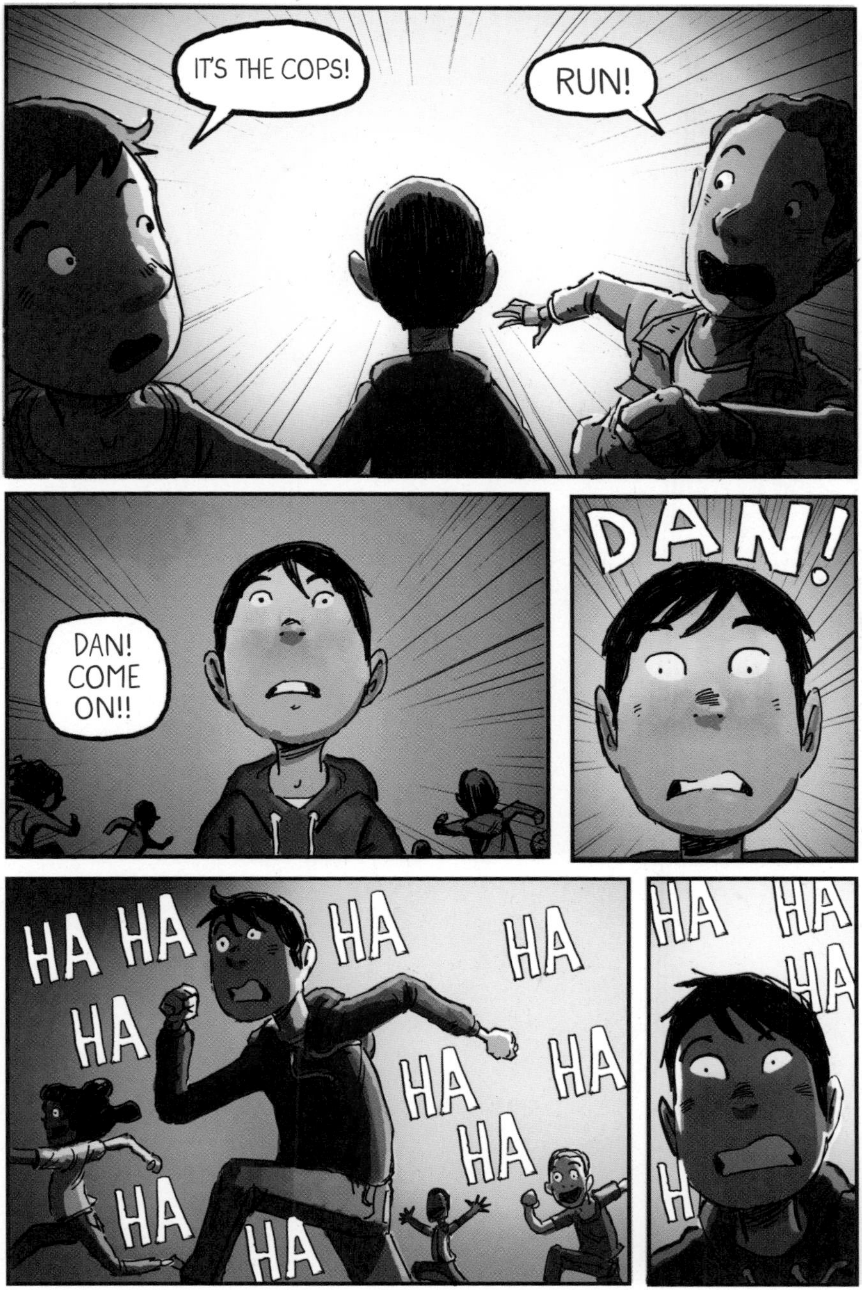
IT'S THE COPS!
RUN!
DAN! COME ON!!
DAN!
HA HA
HA
HA
HA
HA
HA
HA
HA
HA
HA
HA
HA
HA

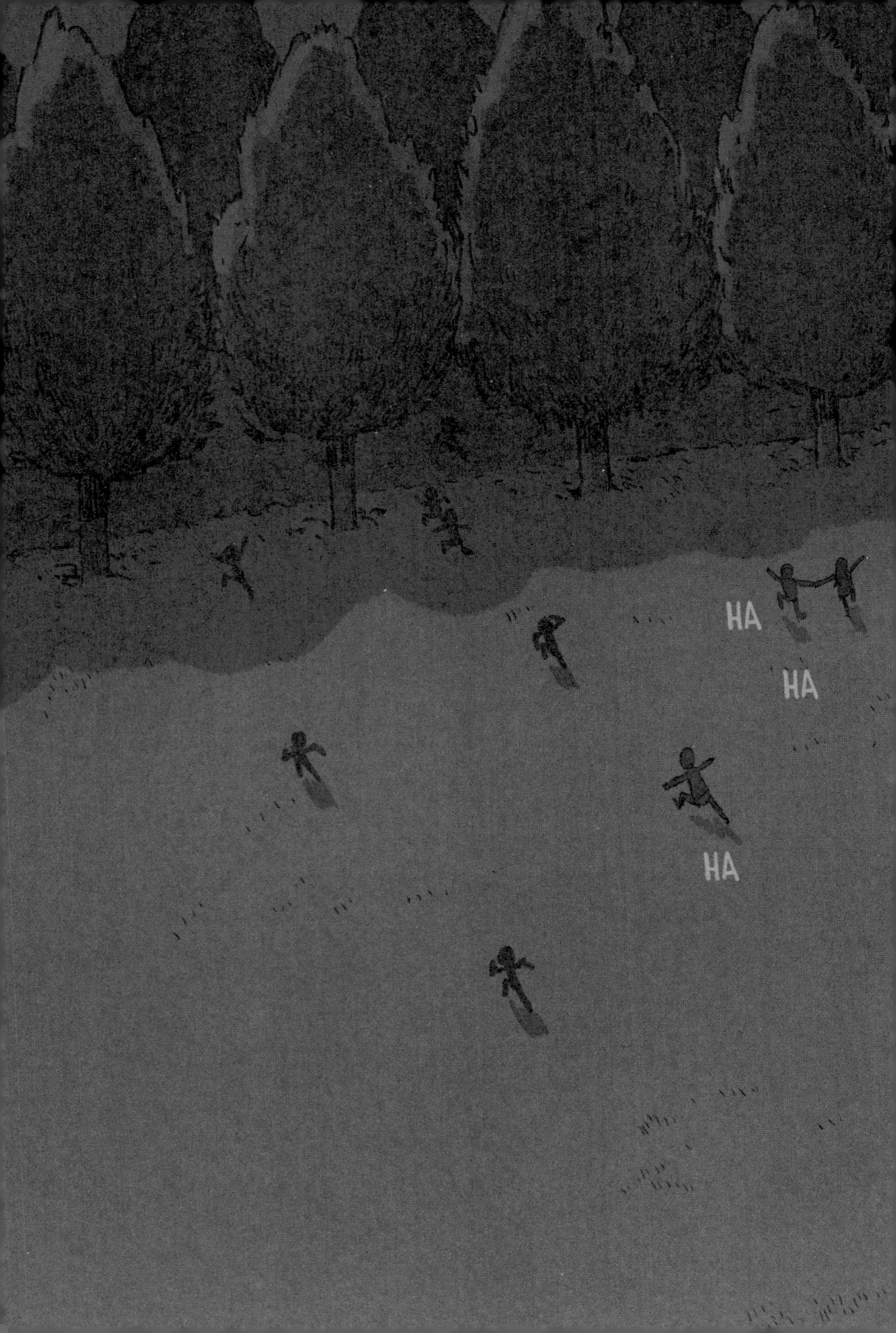
HA
HA
HA

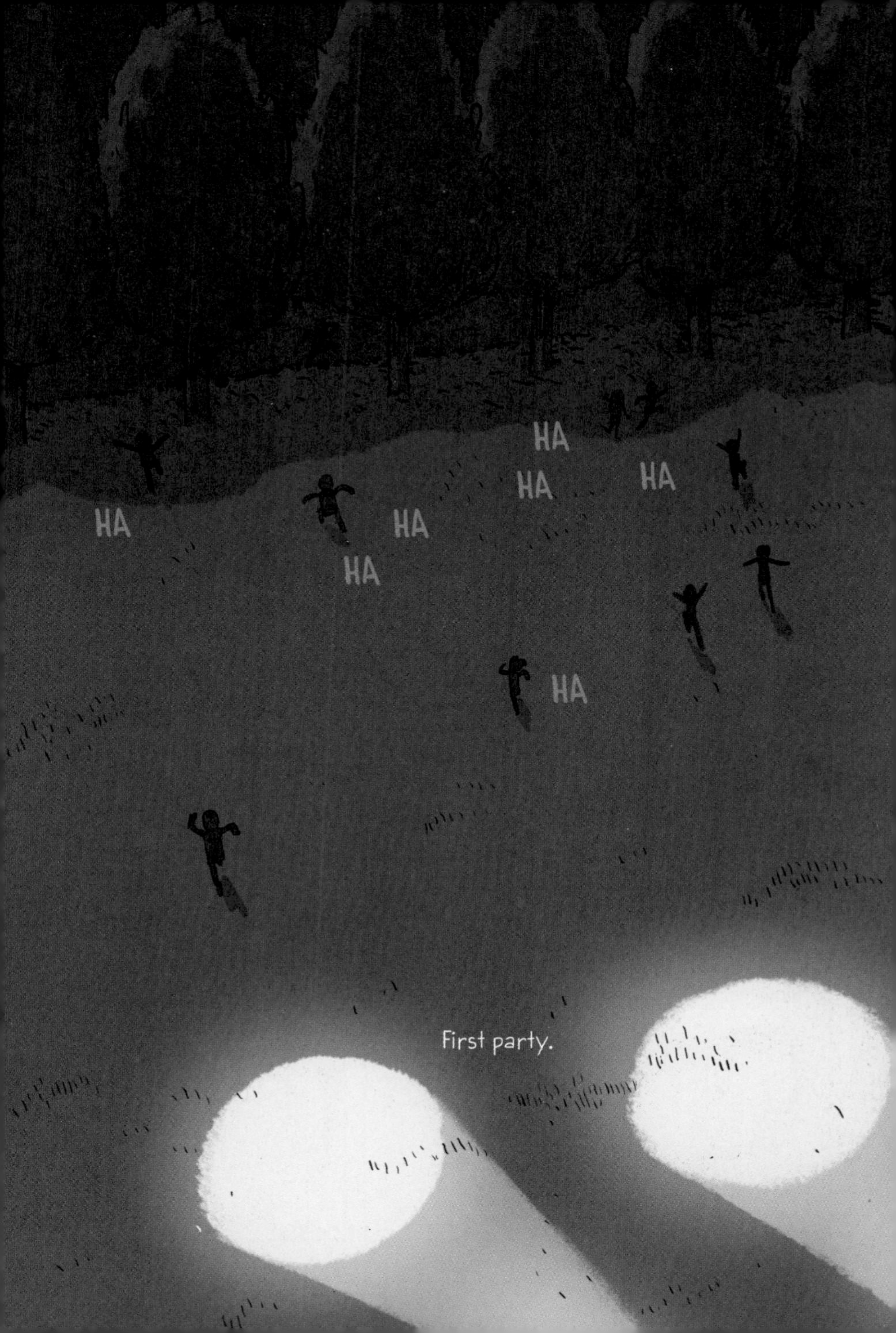
HA
HA
HA
HA
HA
HA
HA
First party.

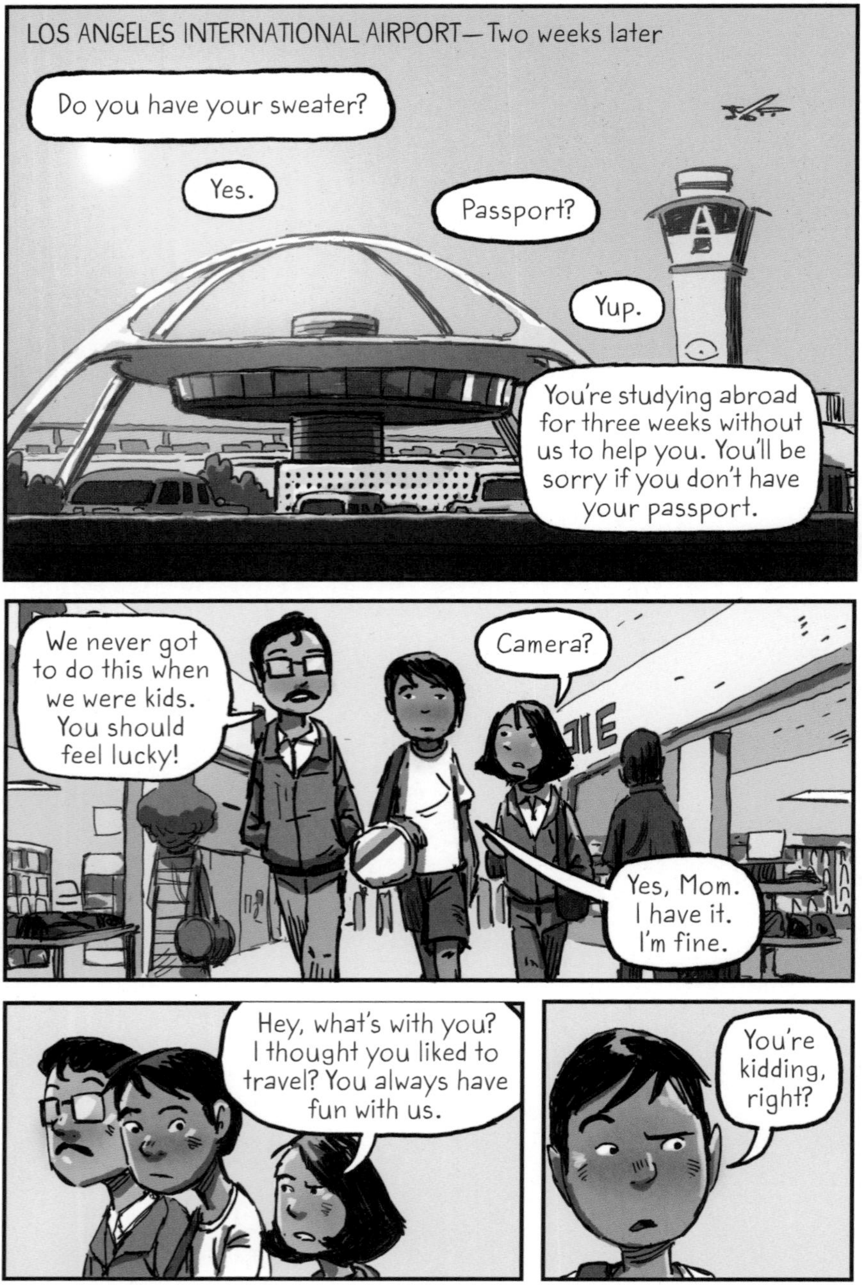
LOS ANGELES INTERNATIONAL AIRPORT—Two weeks later
Do you have your sweater?
Yes.
Passport?
Yup.
You're studying abroad for three weeks without us to help you. You'll be sorry if you don't have your passport.
We never got to do this when we were kids. You should feel lucky!
Camera?
Yes, Mom. I have it. I'm fine.
Hey, what's with you? I thought you liked to travel? You always have fun with us.
You're kidding, right?

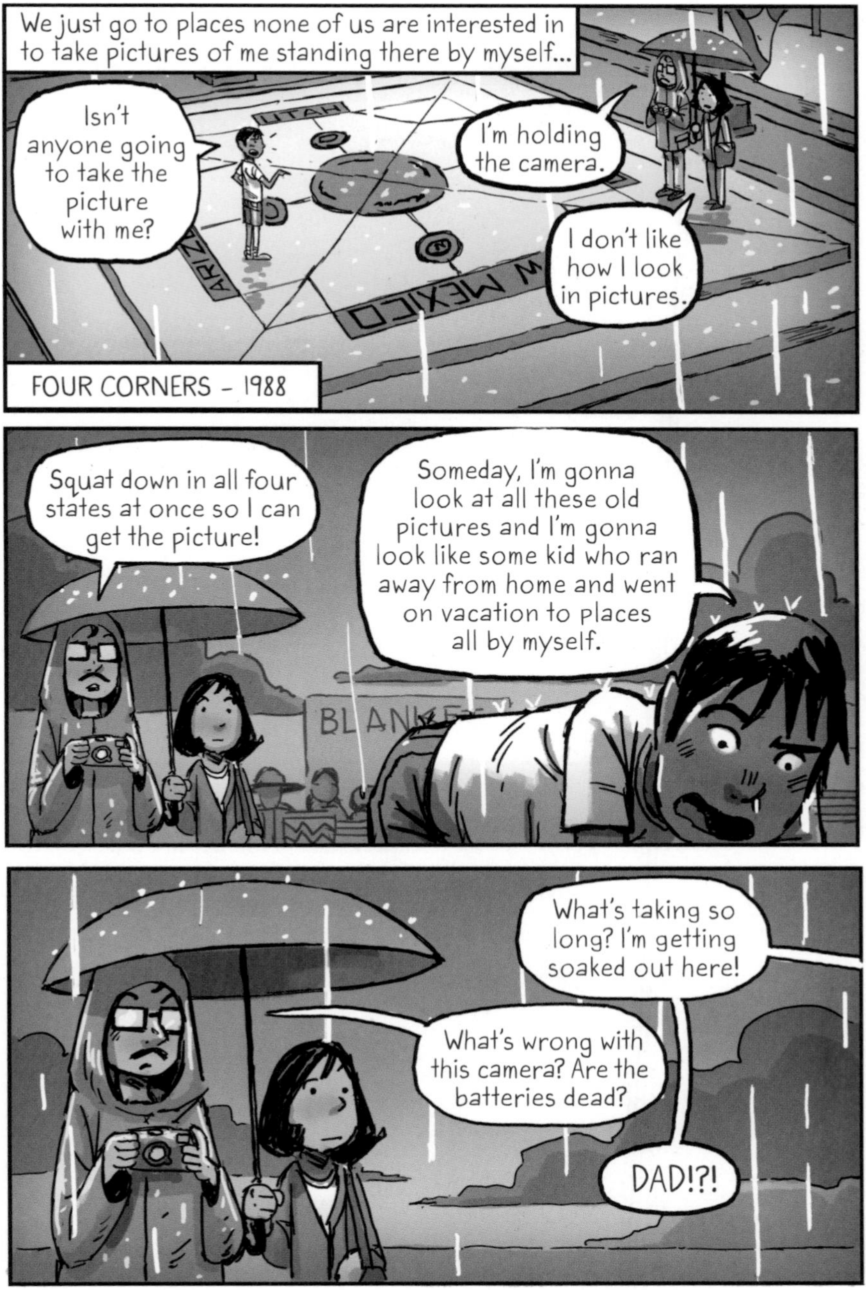
We just go to places none of us are interested in to take pictures of me standing there by myself...
Isn't anyone going to take the picture with me?
I'm holding the camera.
I don't like how I look in pictures.
UTAH
ARIZ
W MEXICO
FOUR CORNERS - 1988
Squat down in all four states at once so I can get the picture!
Someday, I'm gonna look at all these old pictures and I'm gonna look like some kid who ran away from home and went on vacation to places all by myself.
What's taking so long? I'm getting soaked out here!
What's wrong with this camera? Are the batteries dead?
DAD!?!

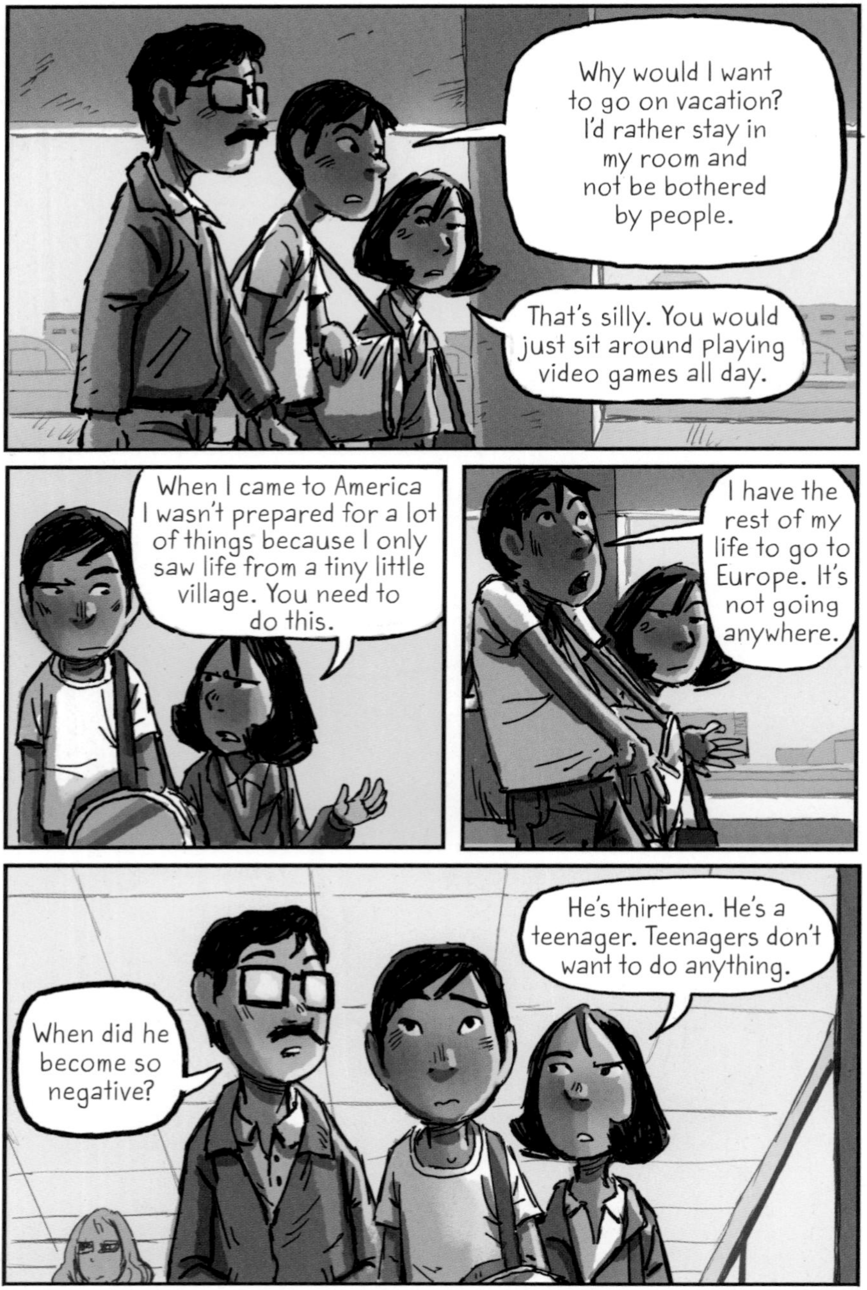
Why would I want to go on vacation? I'd rather stay in my room and not be bothered by people.
That's silly. You would just sit around playing video games all day.
When I came to America I wasn't prepared for a lot of things because I only saw life from a tiny little village. You need to do this.
I have the rest of my life to go to Europe. It's not going anywhere.
He's thirteen. He's a teenager. Teenagers don't want to do anything.
When did he become so negative?

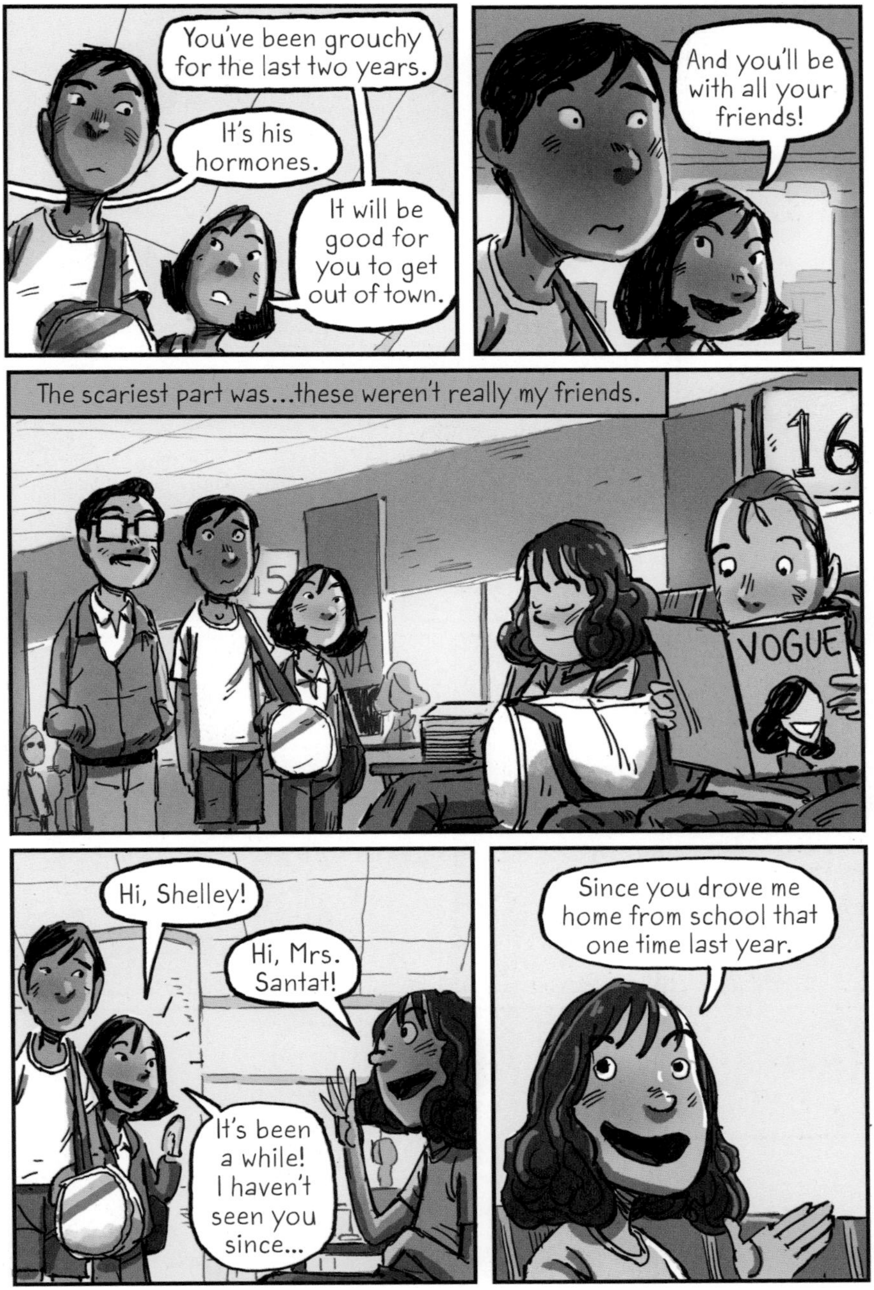
You've been grouchy for the last two years.
It's his hormones.
It will be good for you to get out of town.
And you'll be with all your friends!
The scariest part was...these weren't really my friends.
16
15
VOGUE
Hi, Shelley!
Hi, Mrs. Santat!
It's been a while! I haven't seen you since...
Since you drove me home from school that one time last year.

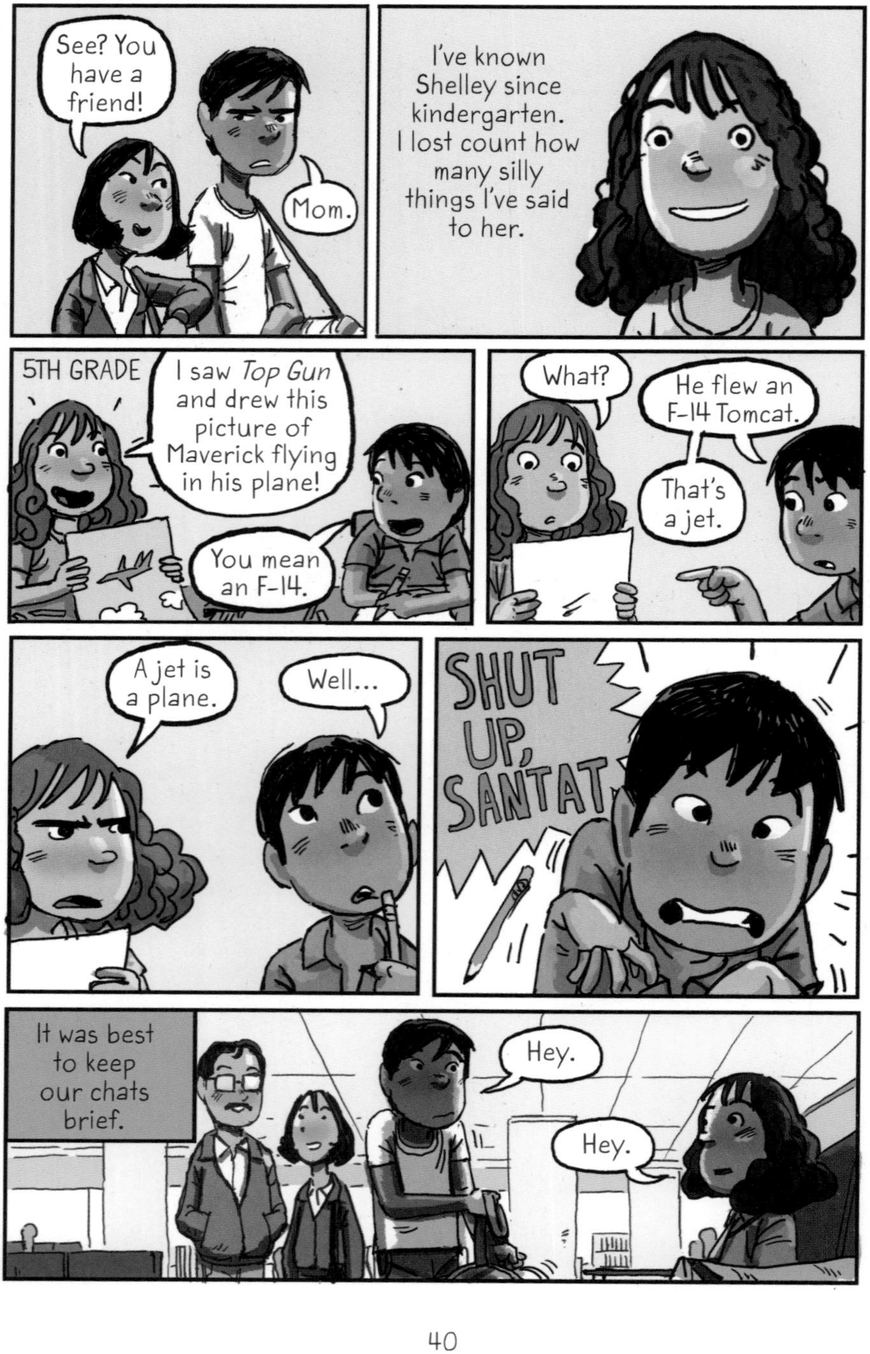
See? You have a friend!
Mom.
I've known Shelley since kindergarten. I lost count how many silly things I've said to her.
5TH GRADE
I saw *Top Gun* and drew this picture of Maverick flying in his plane!
You mean an F-14.
What?
He flew an F-14 Tomcat.
That's a jet.
A jet is a plane.
Well...
SHUT UP, SANTAT
It was best to keep our chats brief.
Hey.
Hey.

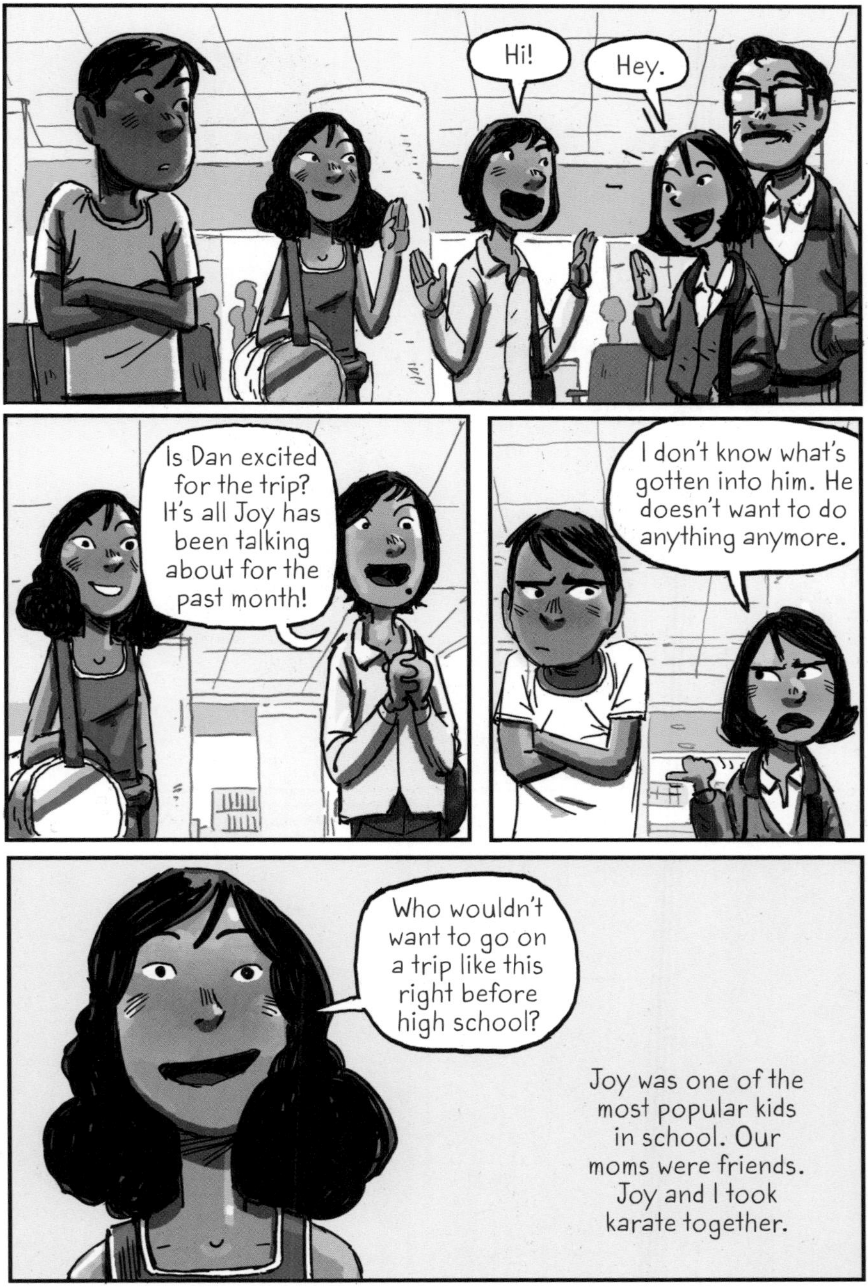
Hi!
Hey.
Is Dan excited for the trip? It's all Joy has been talking about for the past month!
I don't know what's gotten into him. He doesn't want to do anything anymore.
Who wouldn't want to go on a trip like this right before high school?
Joy was one of the most popular kids in school. Our moms were friends. Joy and I took karate together.

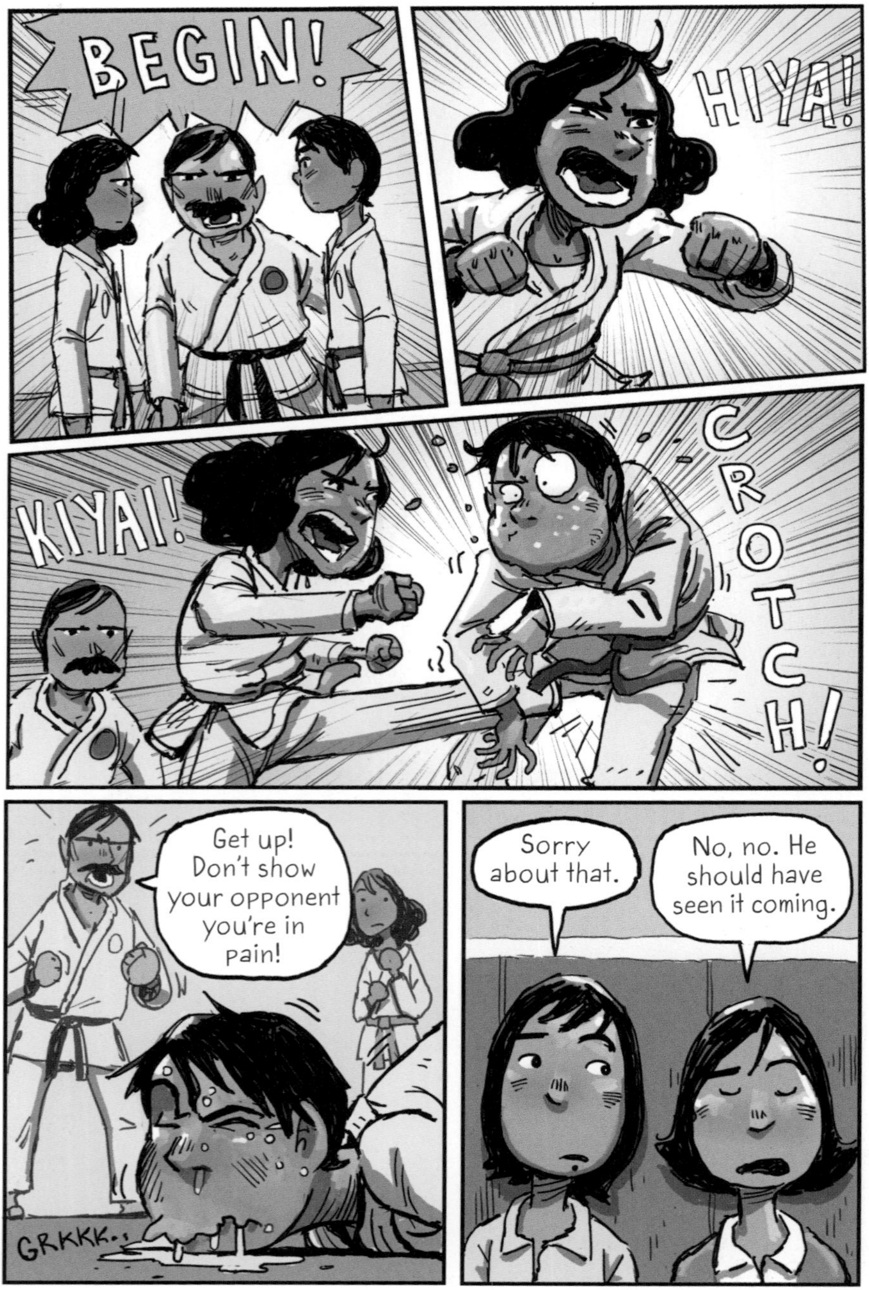
BEGIN!
HIYA!
KIYAI!
CROTCH!
Get up! Don't show your opponent you're in pain!
GRKKK..
Sorry about that.
No, no. He should have seen it coming.

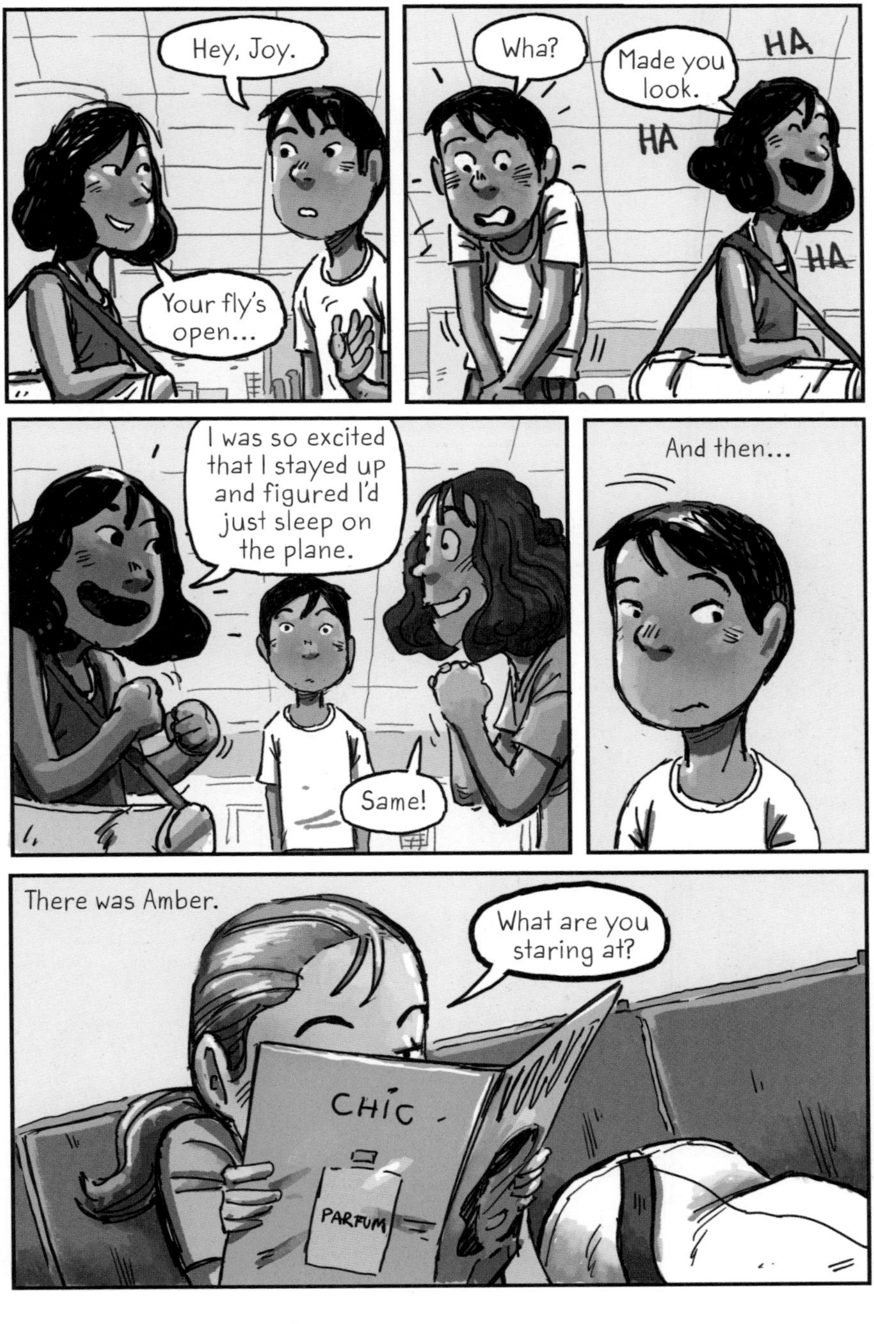
Hey, Joy.
Your fly's open...
Wha?
Made you look.
HA
HA
HA
I was so excited that I stayed up and figured I'd just sleep on the plane.
Same!
And then...
There was Amber.
What are you staring at?
CHIC
PARFUM

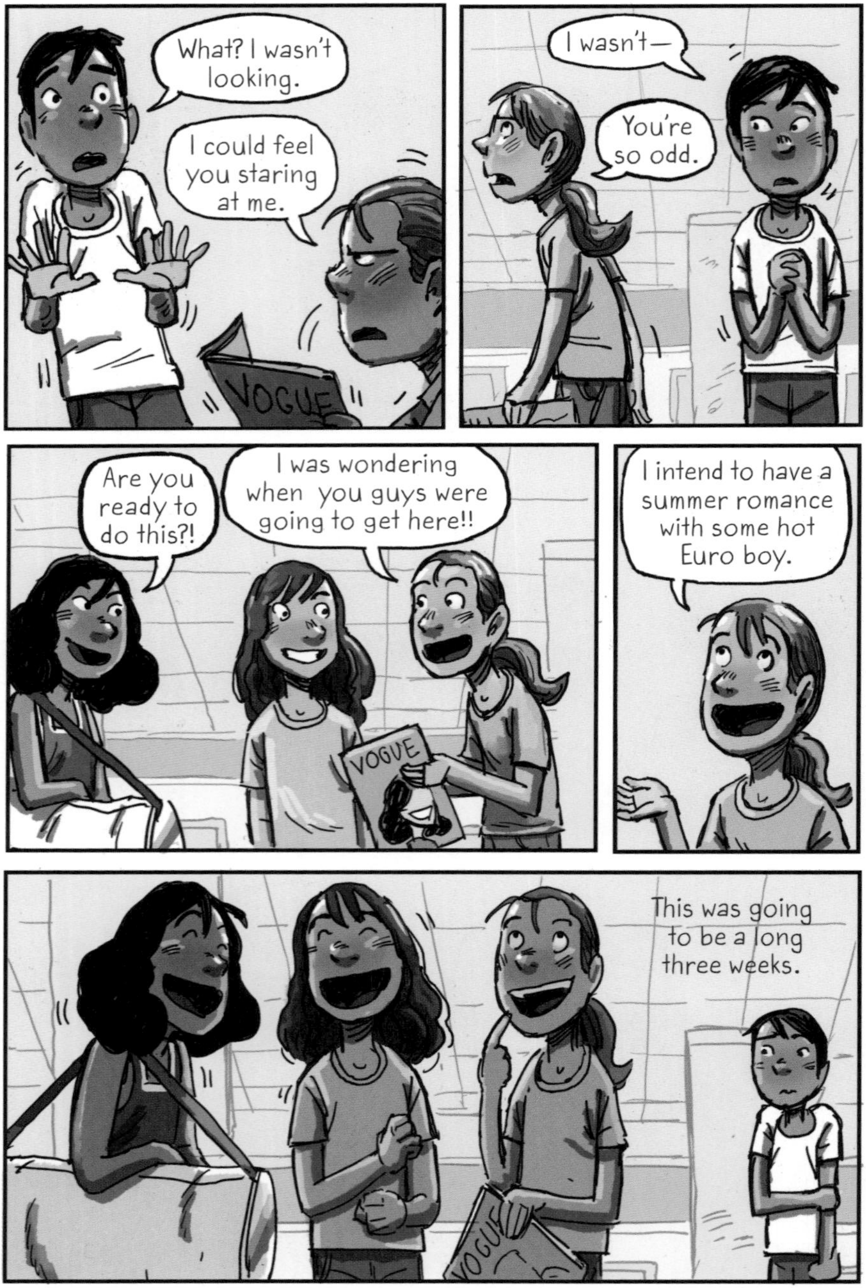
What? I wasn't looking.
I could feel you staring at me.
VOGUE
I wasn't—
You're so odd.
Are you ready to do this?!
I was wondering when you guys were going to get here!!
VOGUE
I intend to have a summer romance with some hot Euro boy.
This was going to be a long three weeks.
VOGUE

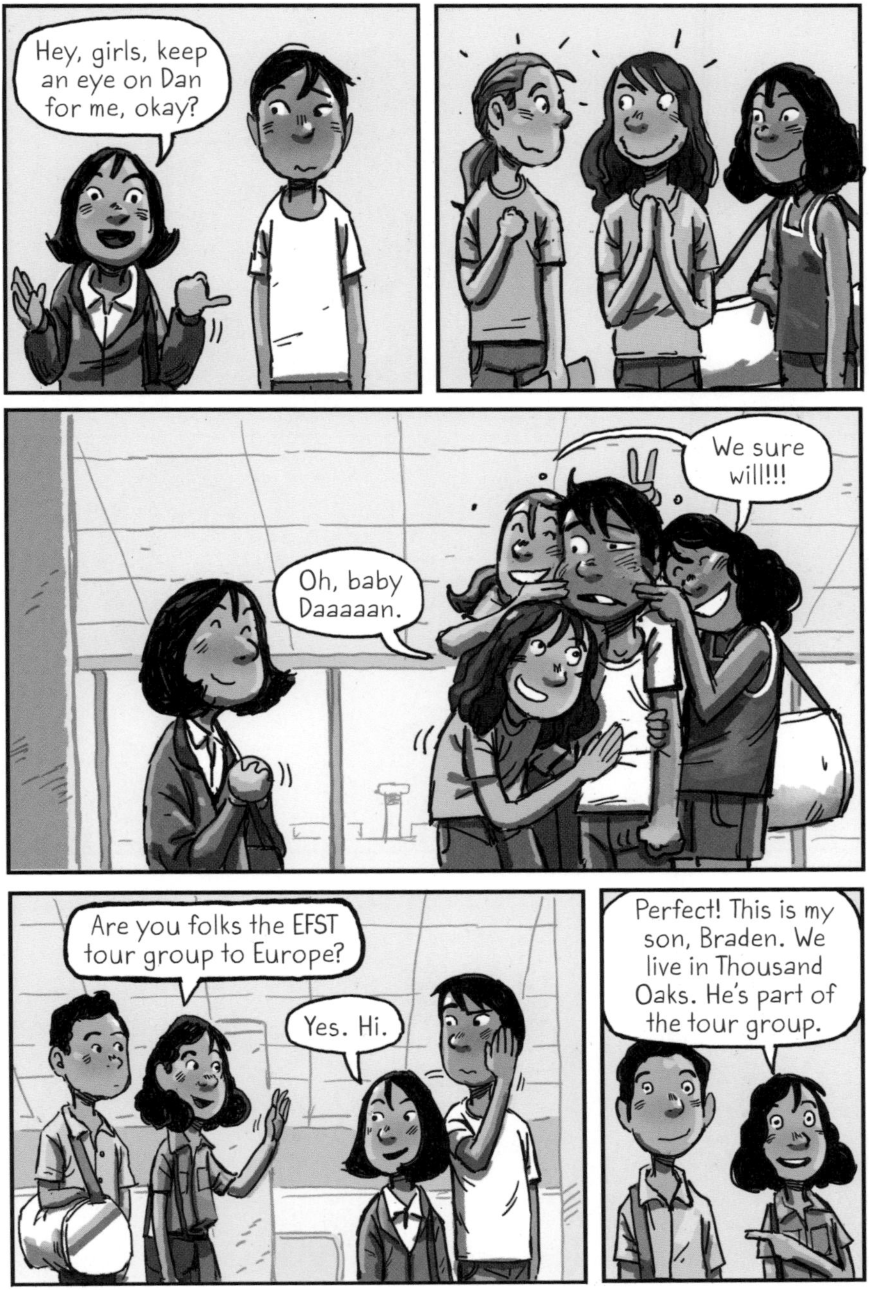
Hey, girls, keep an eye on Dan for me, okay?
We sure will!!!
Oh, baby Daaaaan.
Are you folks the EFST tour group to Europe?
Yes. Hi.
Perfect! This is my son, Braden. We live in Thousand Oaks. He's part of the tour group.

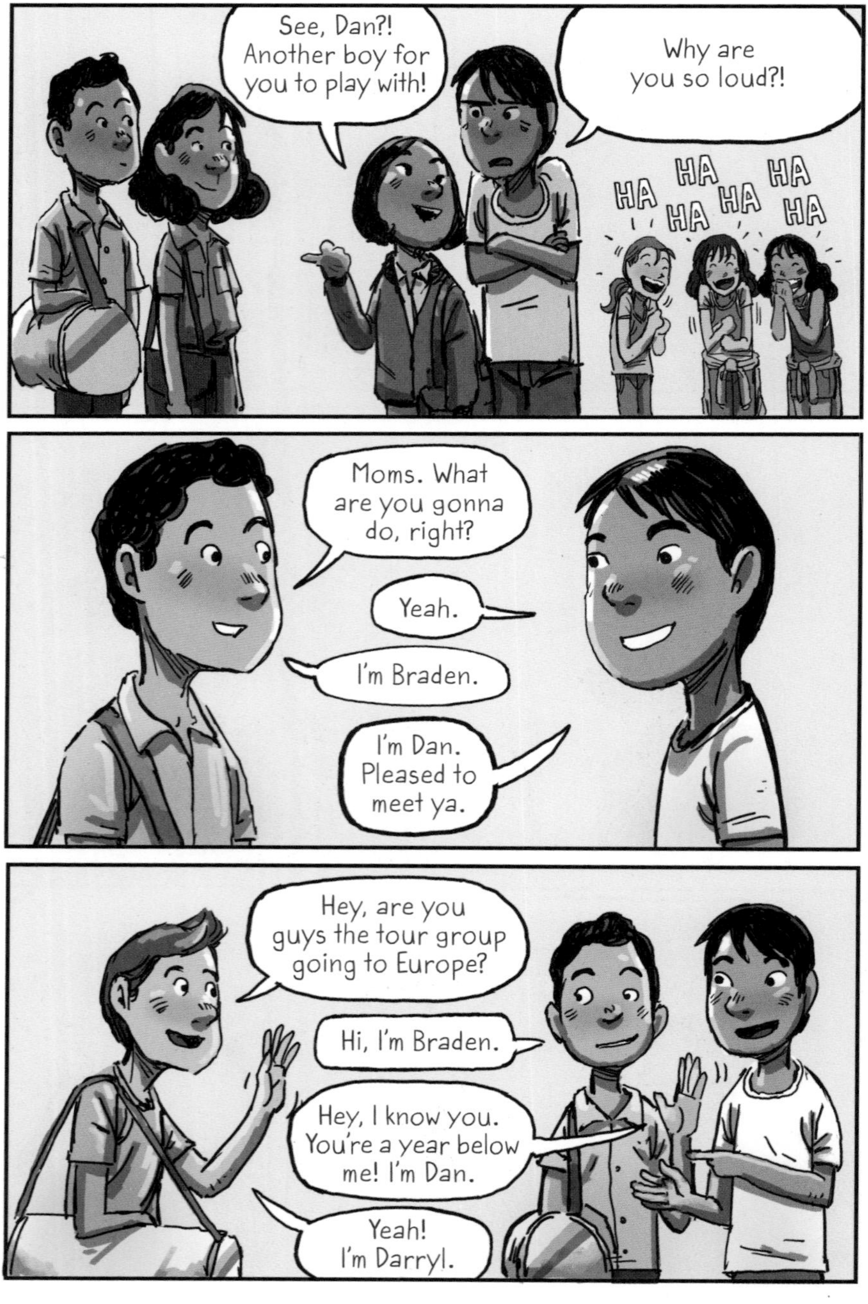
See, Dan?! Another boy for you to play with!
Why are you so loud?!
HA HA HA HA HA HA HA
Moms. What are you gonna do, right?
Yeah.
I'm Braden.
I'm Dan. Pleased to meet ya.
Hey, are you guys the tour group going to Europe?
Hi, I'm Braden.
Hey, I know you. You're a year below me! I'm Dan.
Yeah! I'm Darryl.

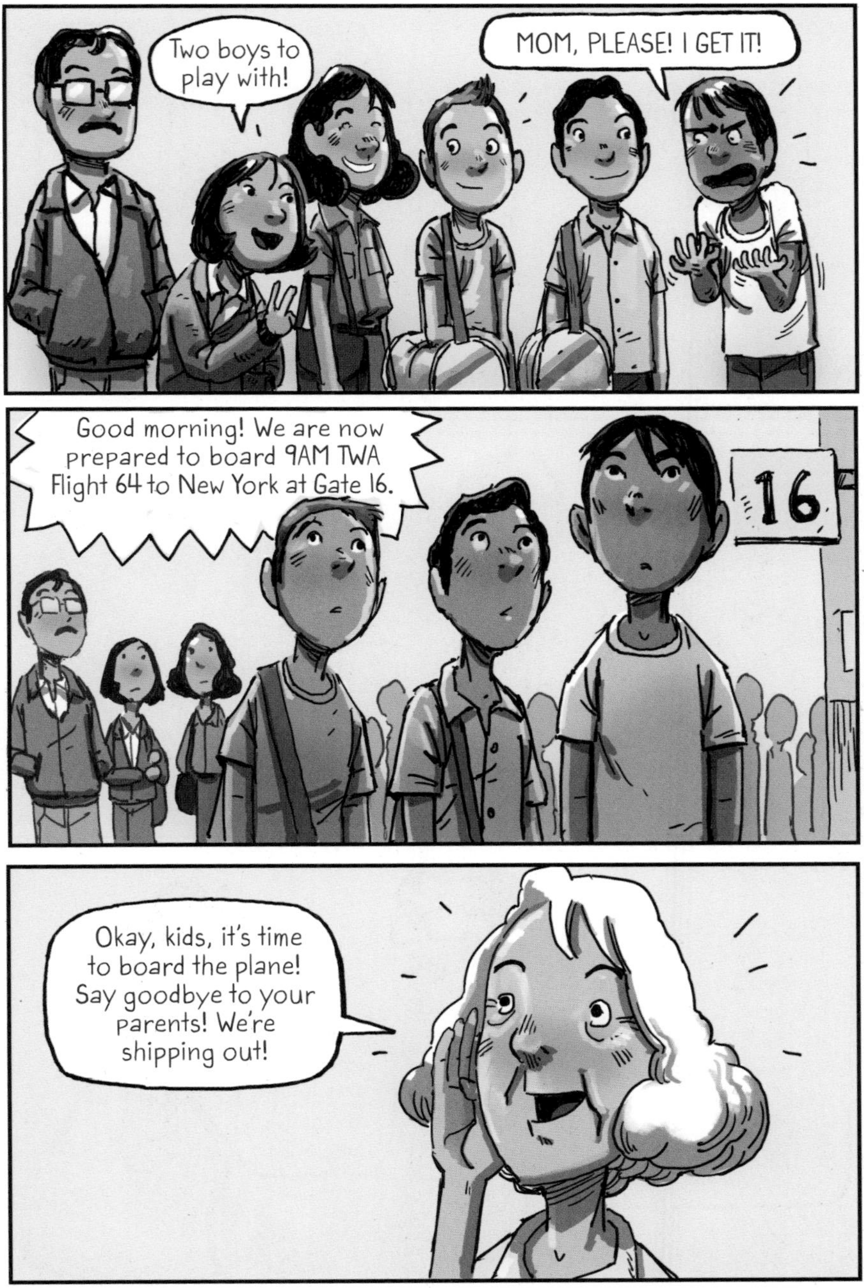
Two boys to play with!
MOM, PLEASE! I GET IT!
Good morning! We are now prepared to board 9AM TWA Flight 64 to New York at Gate 16.
16
Okay, kids, it's time to board the plane! Say goodbye to your parents! We're shipping out!

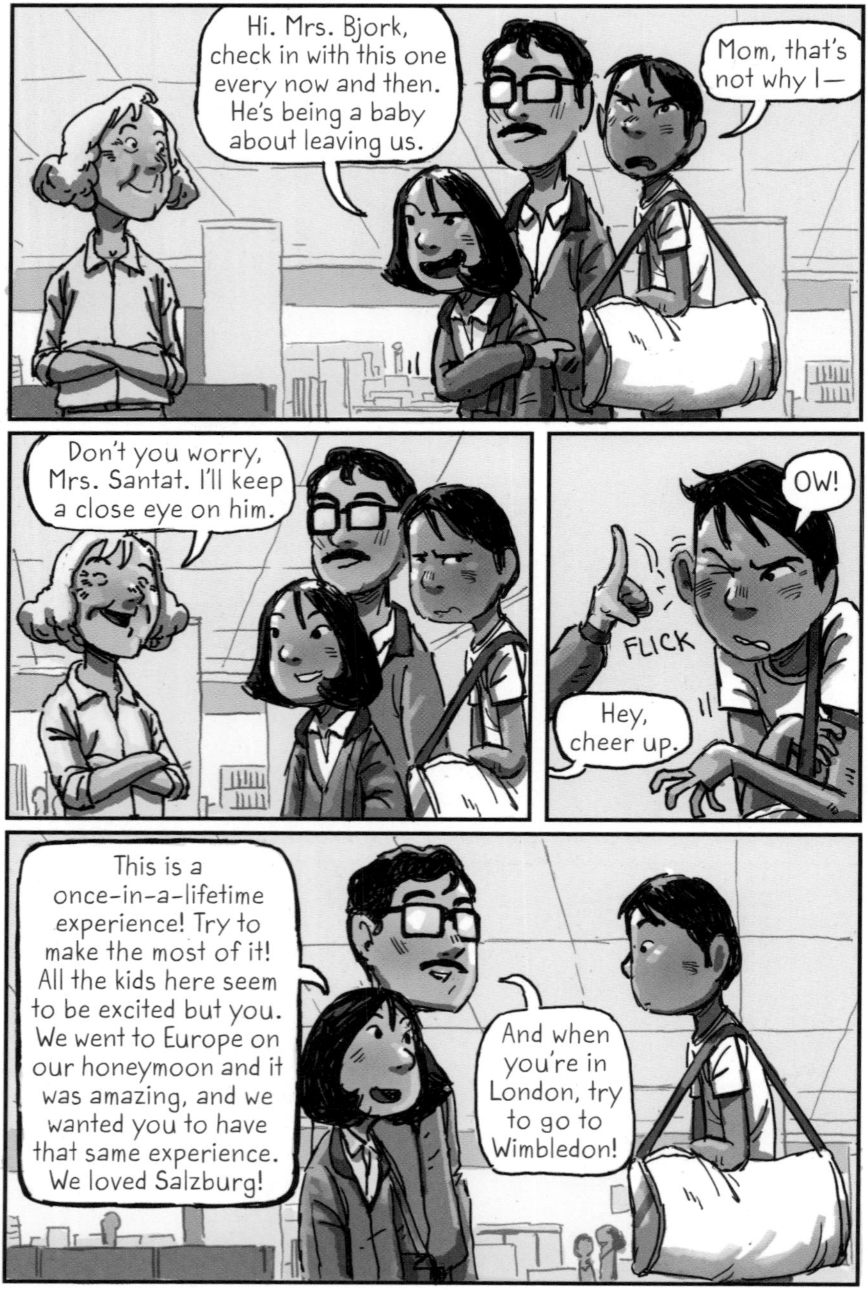
Hi. Mrs. Bjork, check in with this one every now and then. He's being a baby about leaving us.
Mom, that's not why I—
Don't you worry, Mrs. Santat. I'll keep a close eye on him.
OW!
FLICK
Hey, cheer up.
This is a once-in-a-lifetime experience! Try to make the most of it! All the kids here seem to be excited but you. We went to Europe on our honeymoon and it was amazing, and we wanted you to have that same experience. We loved Salzburg!
And when you're in London, try to go to Wimbledon!

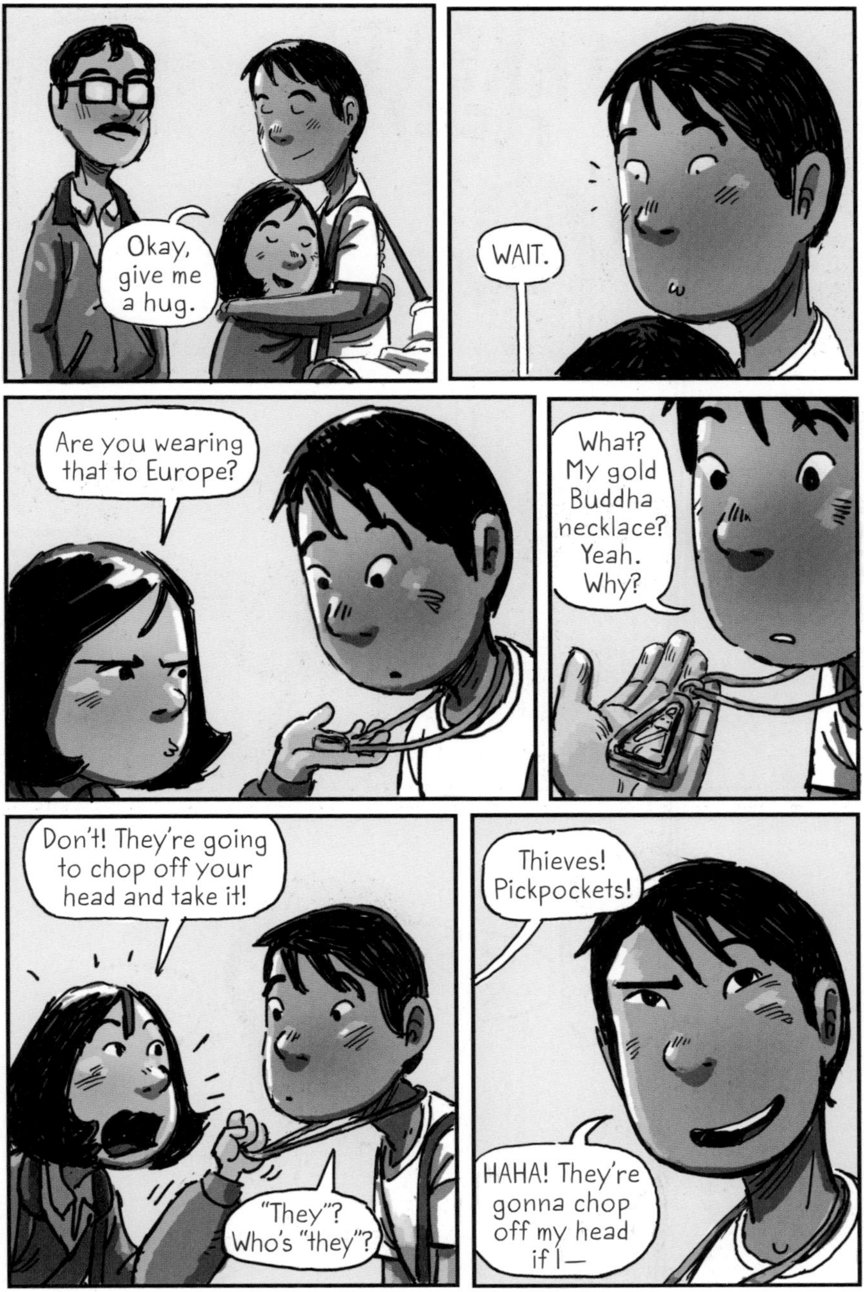
Okay, give me a hug.
WAIT.
Are you wearing that to Europe?
What? My gold Buddha necklace? Yeah. Why?
Don't! They're going to chop off your head and take it!
"They"? Who's "they"?
Thieves! Pickpockets!
HAHA! They're gonna chop off my head if I—

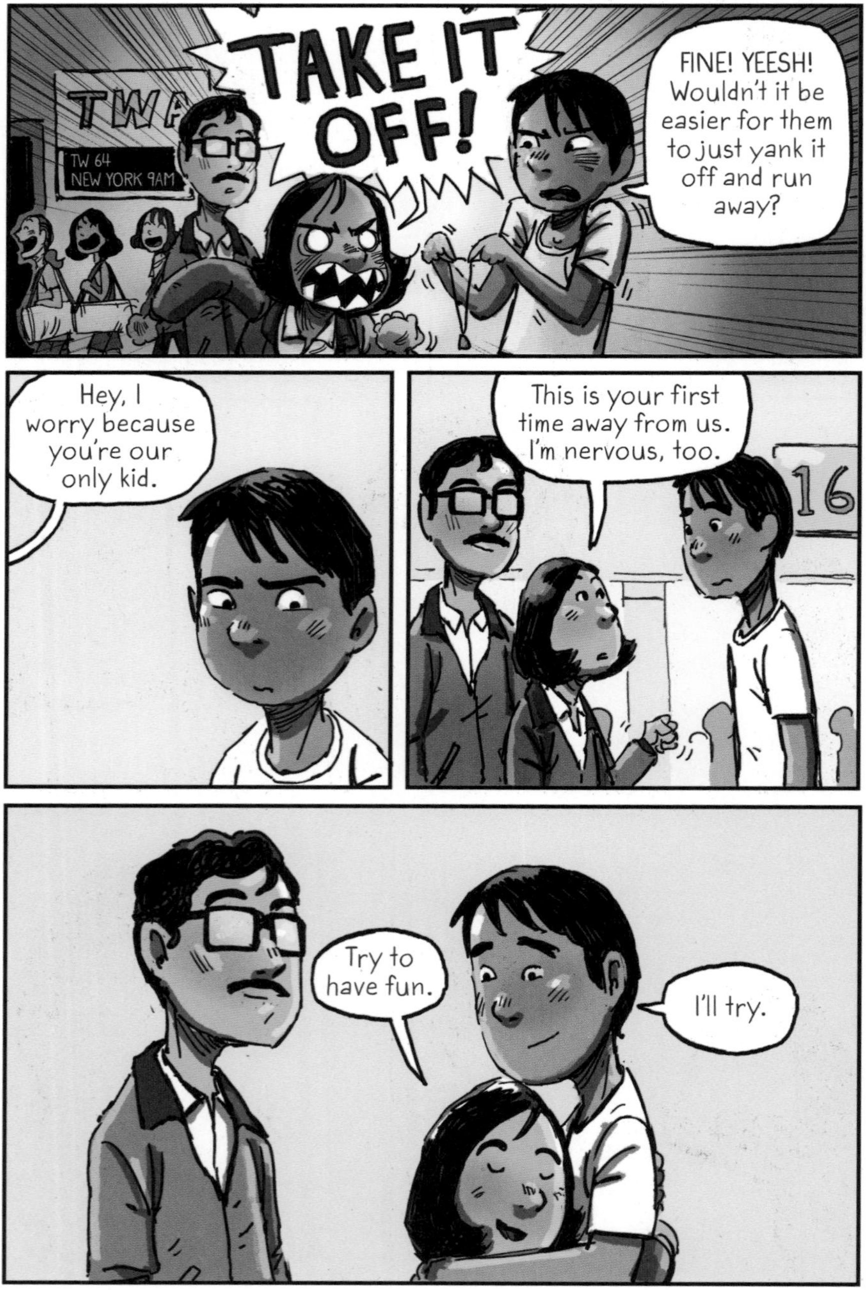
TWA
TW 64
NEW YORK 9AM
TAKE IT OFF!
FINE! YEESH! Wouldn't it be easier for them to just yank it off and run away?
Hey, I worry because you're our only kid.
This is your first time away from us. I'm nervous, too.
16
Try to have fun.
I'll try.

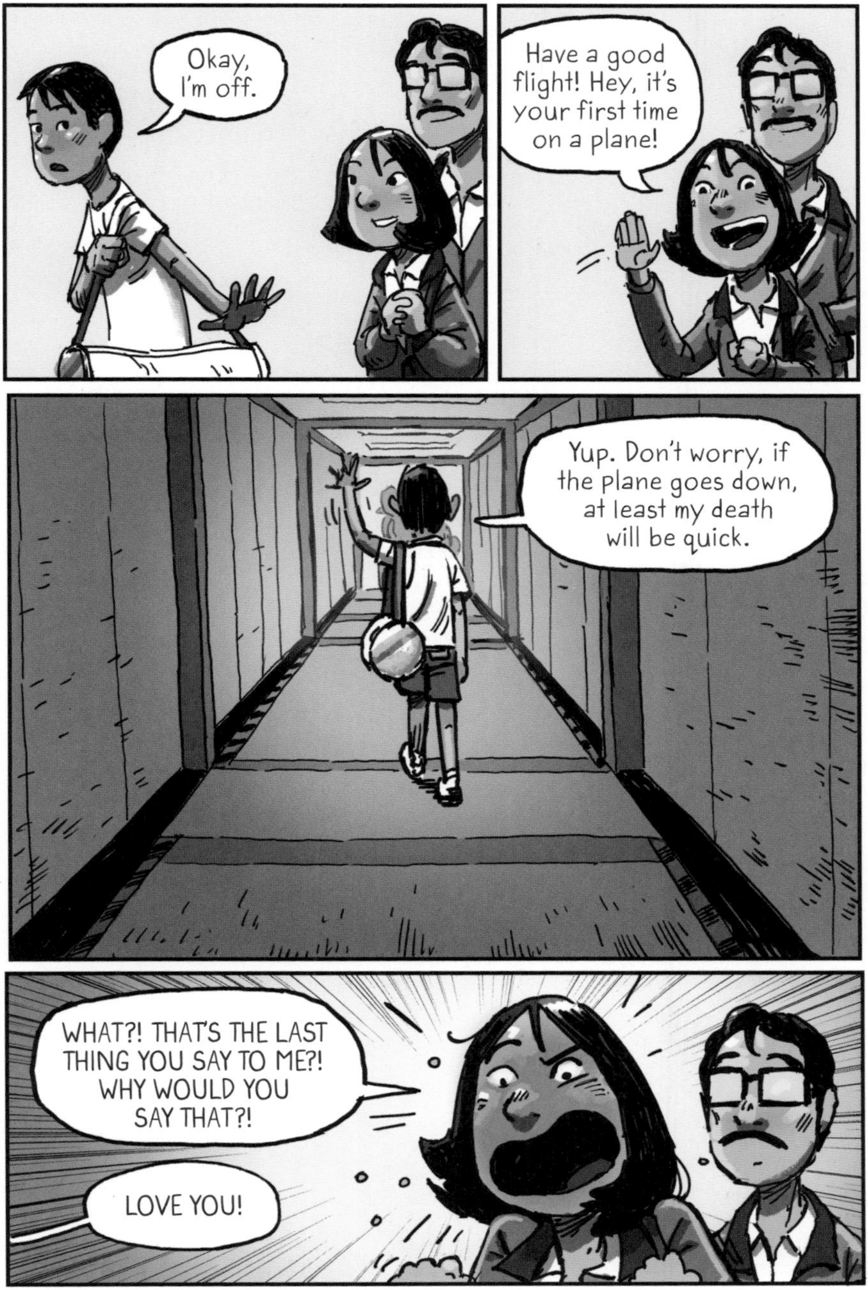

Okay, I'm off.
Have a good flight! Hey, it's your first time on a plane!
Yup. Don't worry, if the plane goes down, at least my death will be quick.
WHAT?! THAT'S THE LAST THING YOU SAY TO ME?! WHY WOULD YOU SAY THAT?!
LOVE YOU!

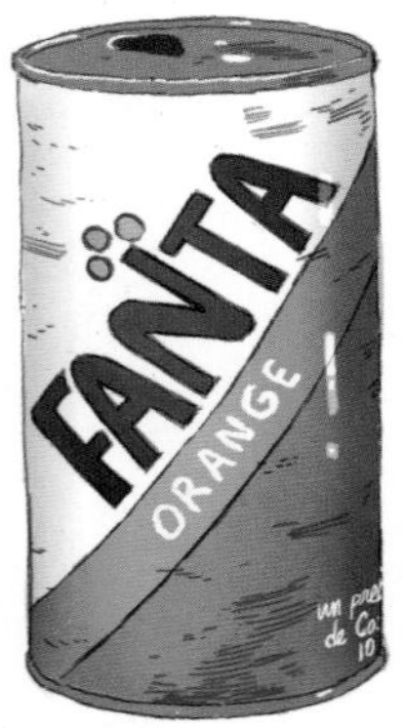
FANTA
ORANGE

PARIS

(21 DAYS LEFT IN THE TRIP)

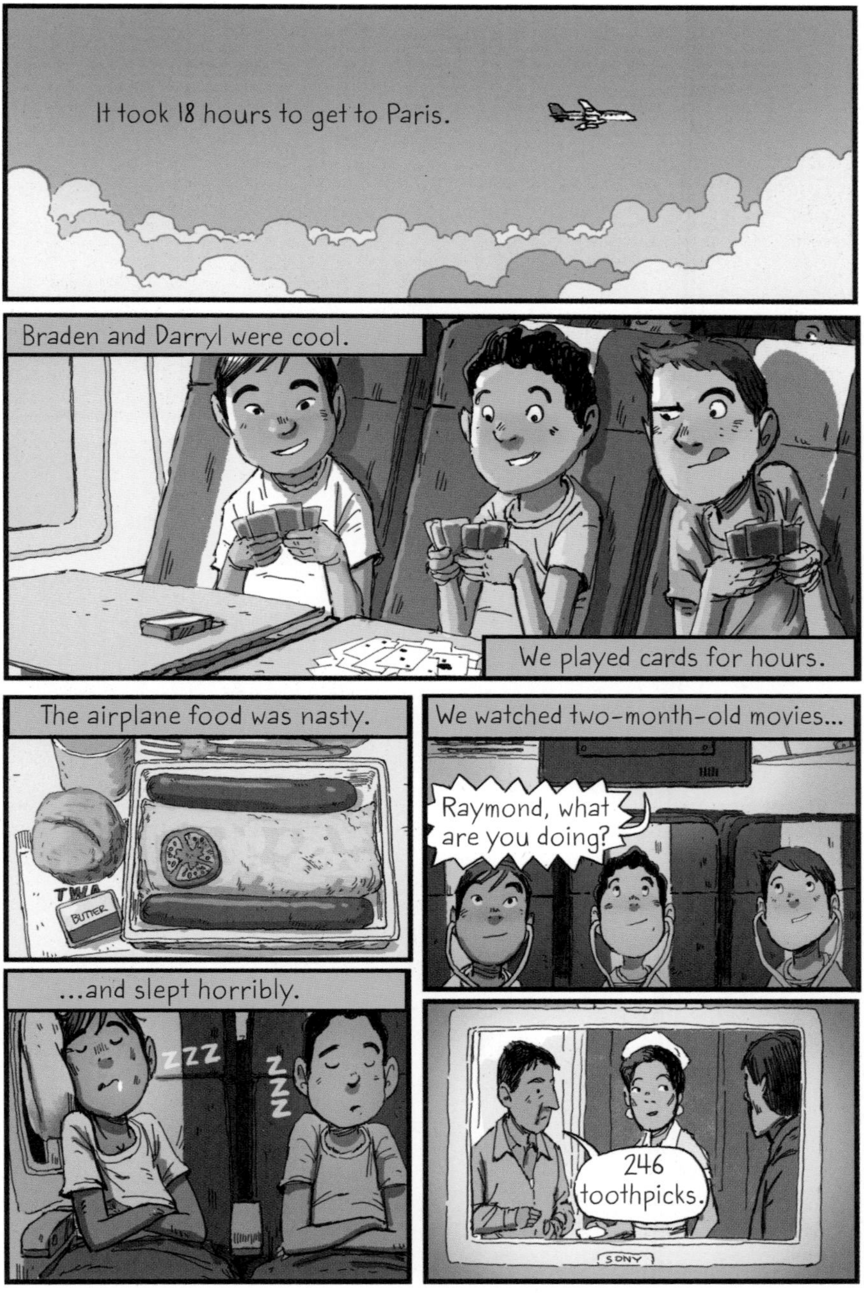
It took 18 hours to get to Paris.
Braden and Darryl were cool.
We played cards for hours.
The airplane food was nasty.
TWA
BUTTER
We watched two-month-old movies...
Raymond, what are you doing?
...and slept horribly.
ZZZ
ZZZ
246 toothpicks.
SONY

Maybe this trip won't be so bad?

VACANT

But I was still way out of my element.

sigh

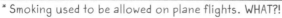

* Smoking used to be allowed on plane flights. WHAT?!

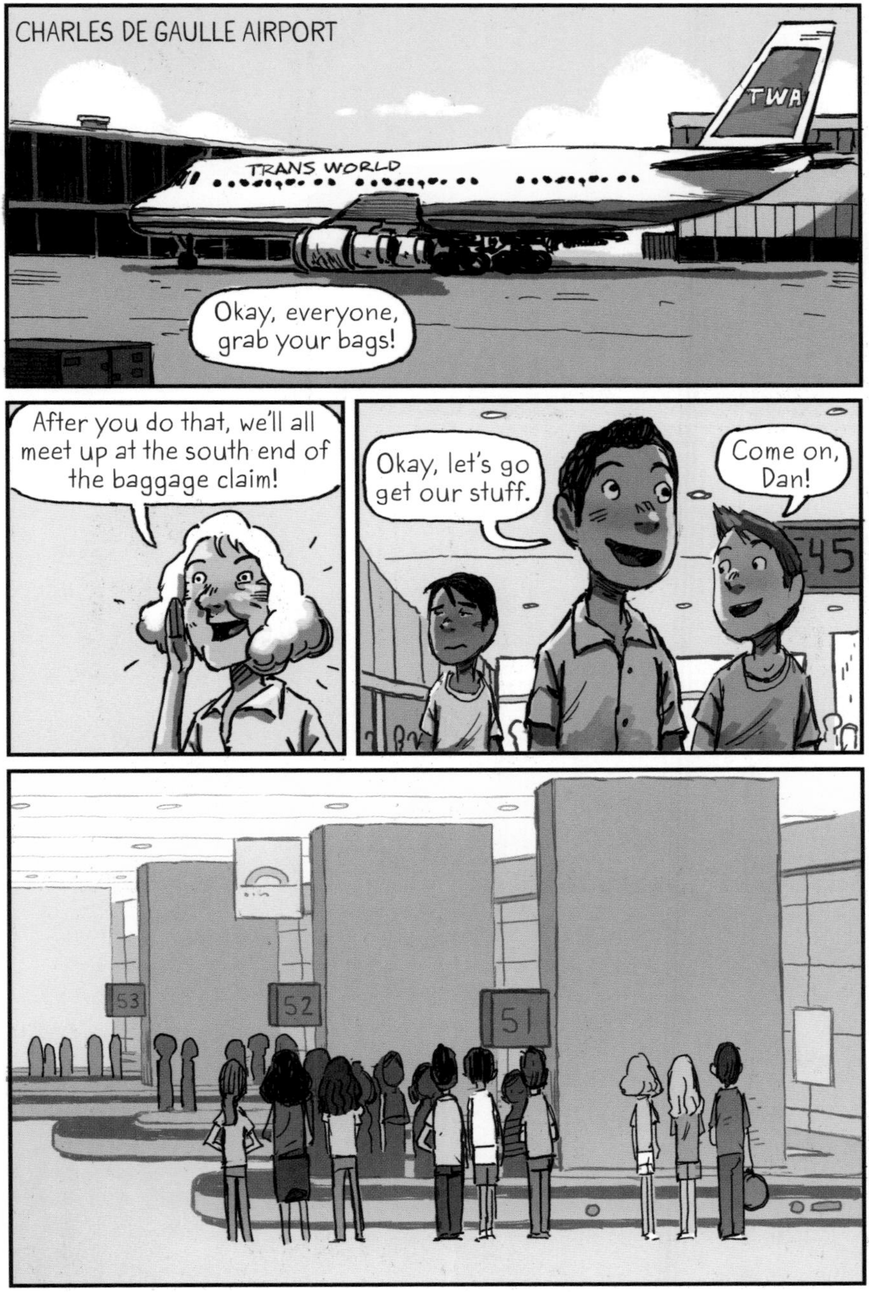
CHARLES DE GAULLE AIRPORT
TWA
TRANS WORLD
Okay, everyone, grab your bags!
After you do that, we'll all meet up at the south end of the baggage claim!
Okay, let's go get our stuff.
Come on, Dan!
45
53
52
51

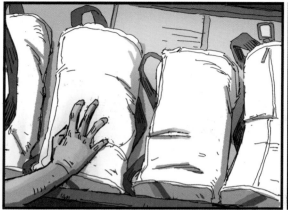

S'il vous plaît, prenez vos sacs et mettez-vous de côté pour que les autres puissent récupérer leurs valises.

Huh?

Par ici s'il-vous-plait. Avancez !

What...?

Avancez !!!

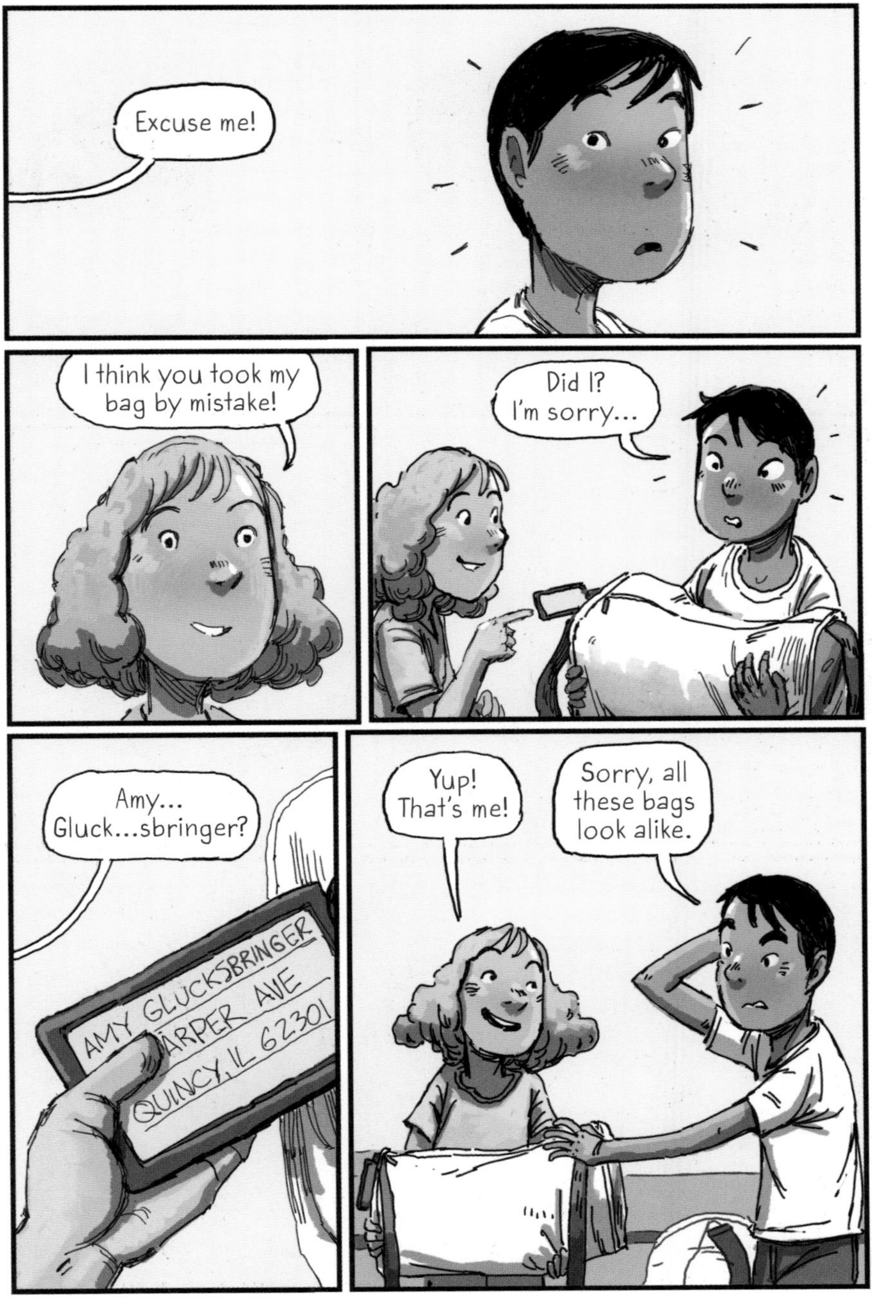
Excuse me!
I think you took my bag by mistake!
Did I? I'm sorry...
Amy... Gluck...sbringer?
AMY GLUCKSBRINGER
ARPER AVE
QUINCY, IL 62301
Yup! That's me!
Sorry, all these bags look alike.

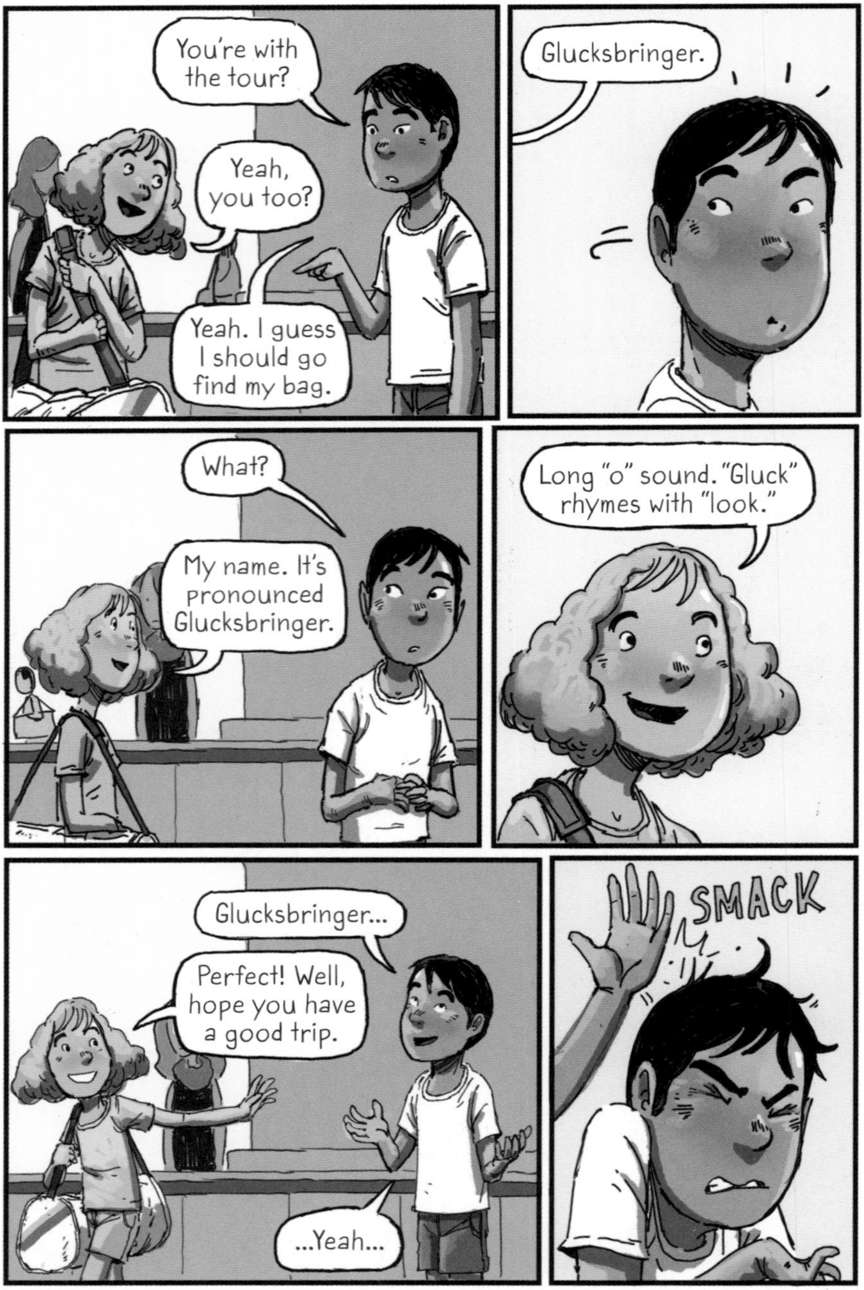
You're with the tour?
Yeah, you too?
Yeah. I guess I should go find my bag.
Glucksbringer.
What?
My name. It's pronounced Glucksbringer.
Long "o" sound. "Gluck" rhymes with "look."
Glucksbringer...
Perfect! Well, hope you have a good trip.
...Yeah...
SMACK

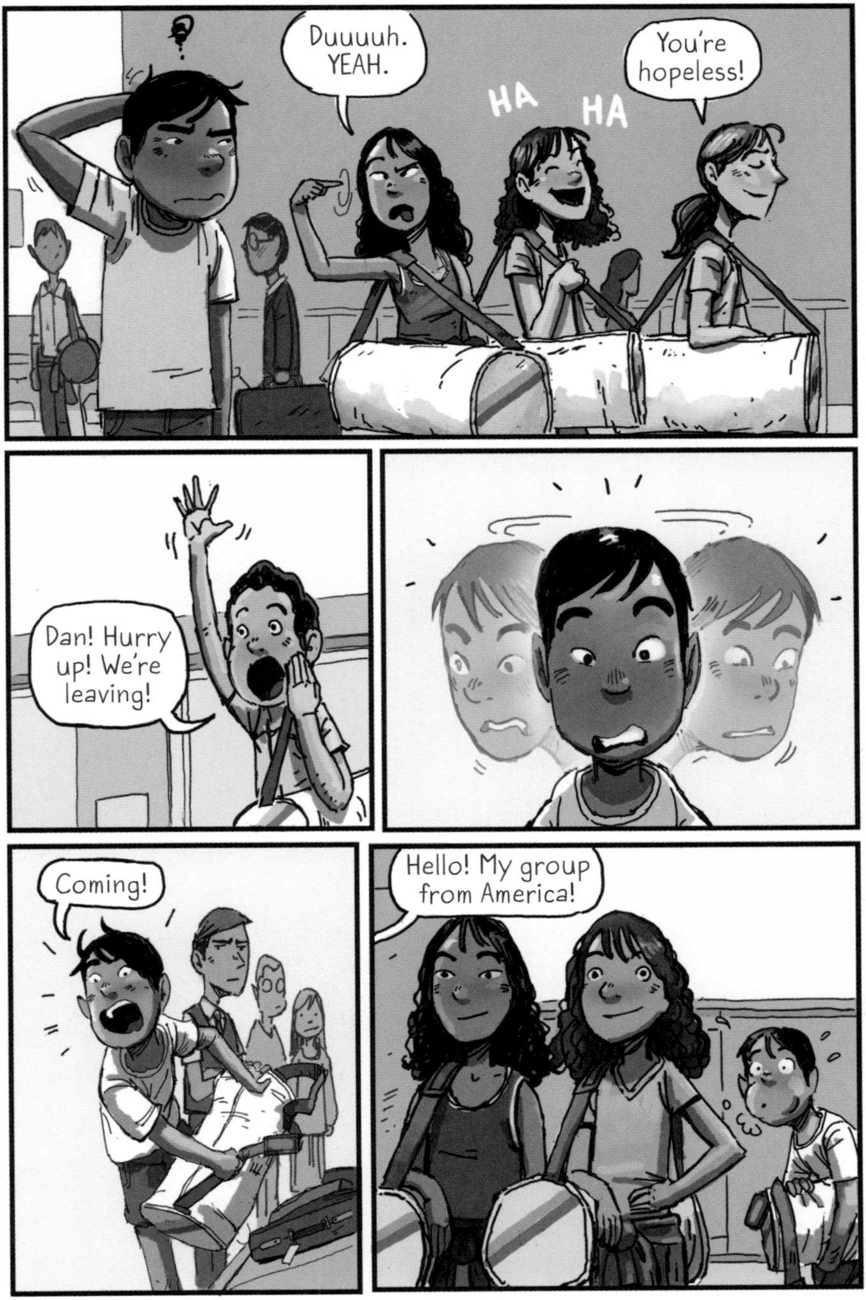
Duuuuh. YEAH.
HA
HA
You're hopeless!
Dan! Hurry up! We're leaving!
Coming!
Hello! My group from America!

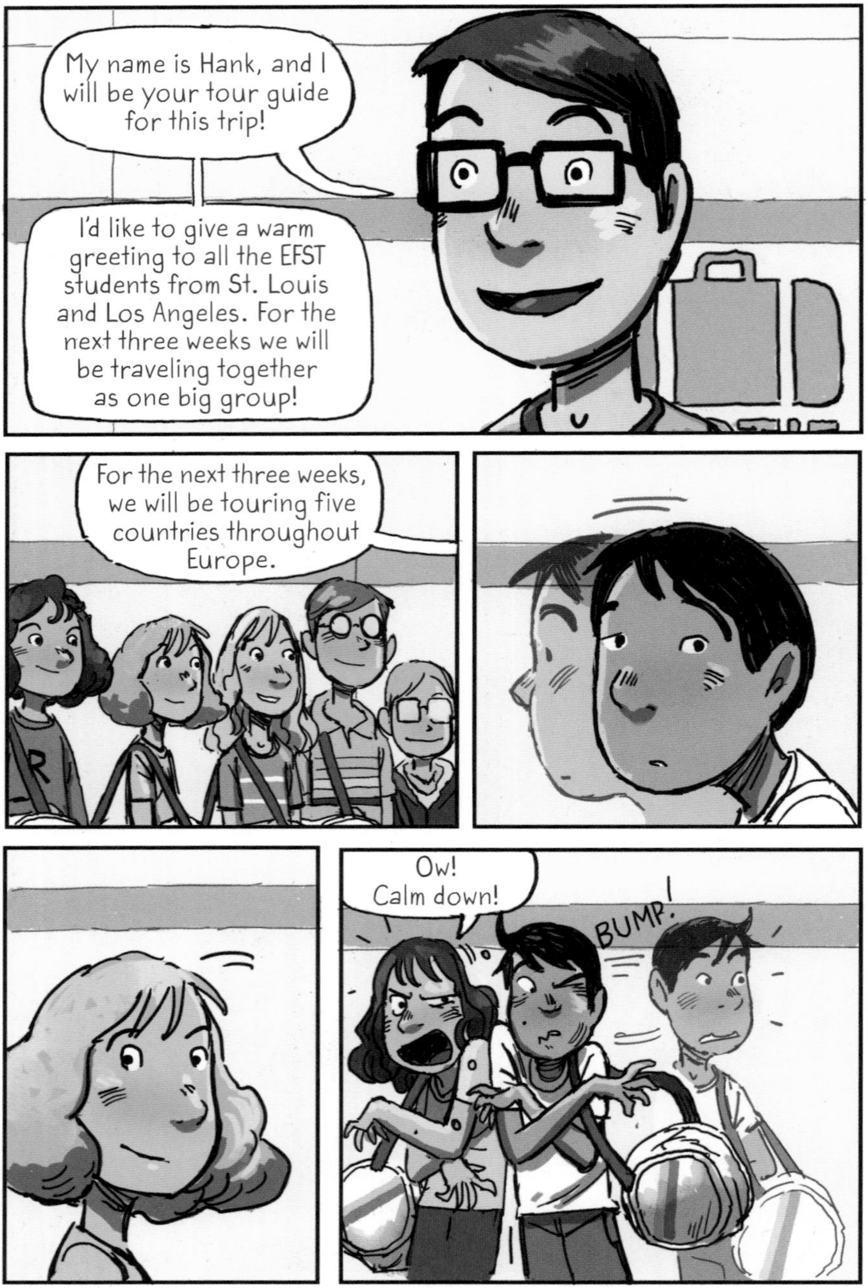
My name is Hank, and I will be your tour guide for this trip!
I'd like to give a warm greeting to all the EFST students from St. Louis and Los Angeles. For the next three weeks we will be traveling together as one big group!
For the next three weeks, we will be touring five countries throughout Europe.
Ow! Calm down!
BUMP!

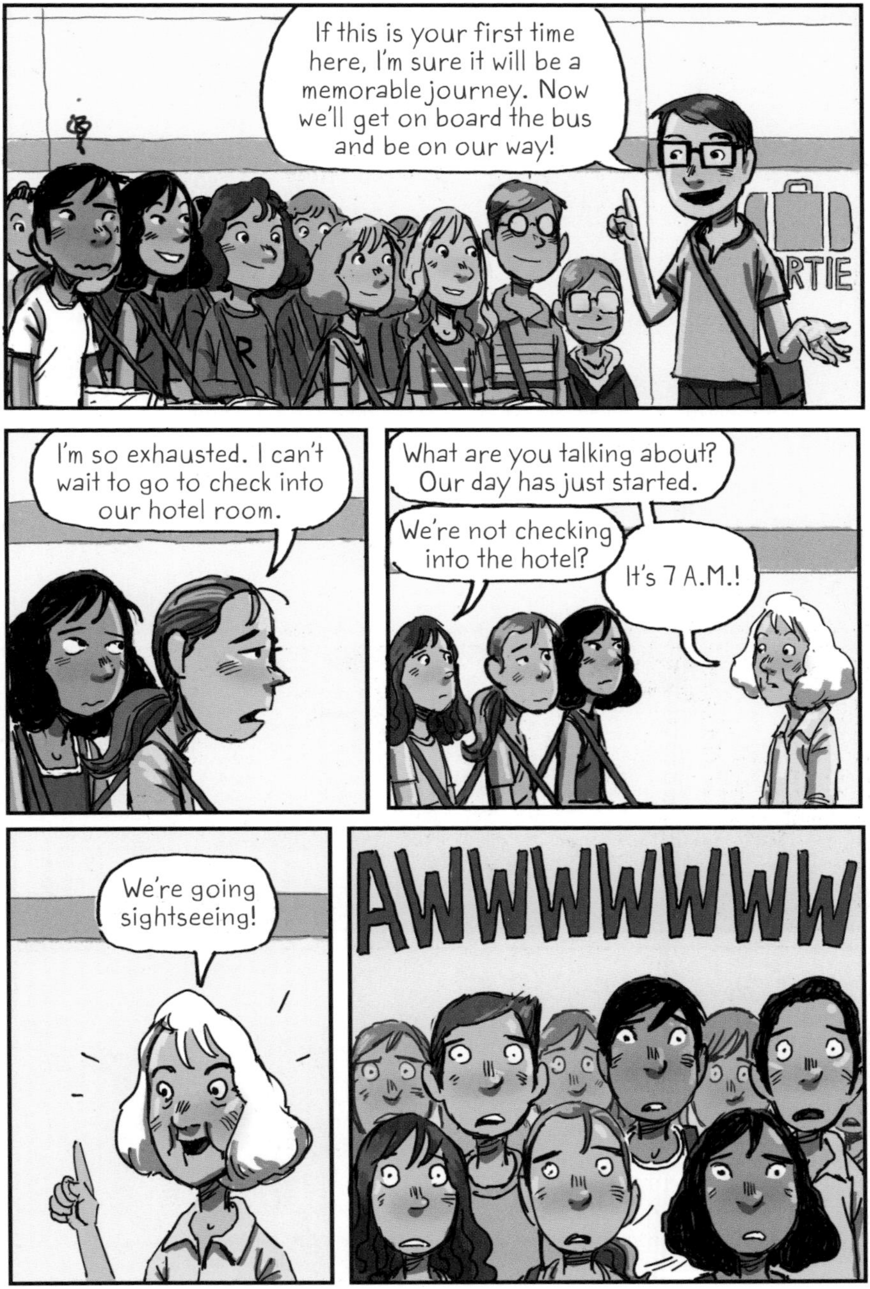

If this is your first time here, I'm sure it will be a memorable journey. Now we'll get on board the bus and be on our way!
RTIE
I'm so exhausted. I can't wait to go to check into our hotel room.
What are you talking about? Our day has just started.
We're not checking into the hotel?
It's 7 A.M.!
We're going sightseeing!
AWWWWWWW

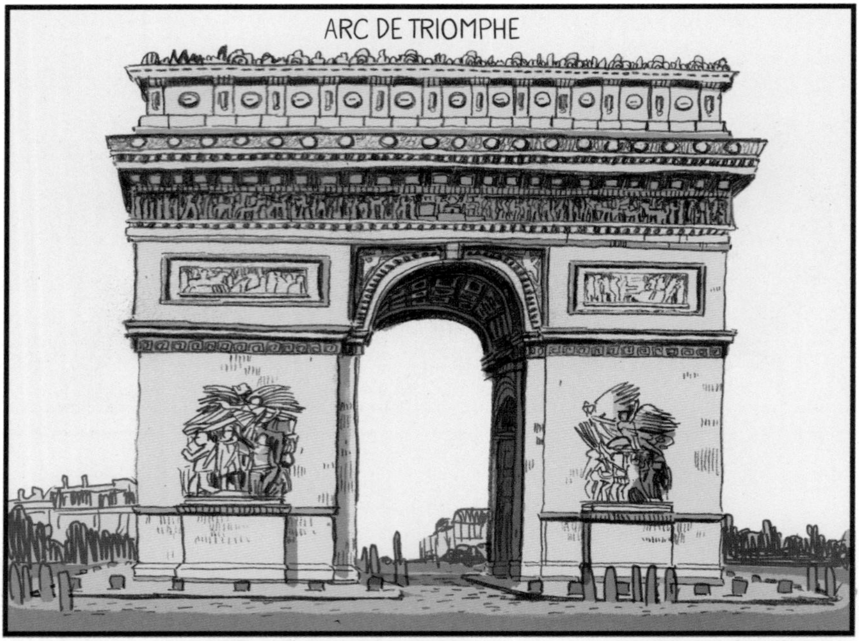
ARC DE TRIOMPHE

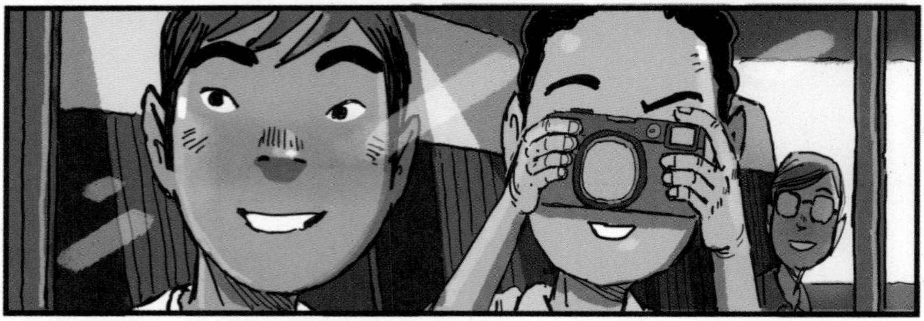

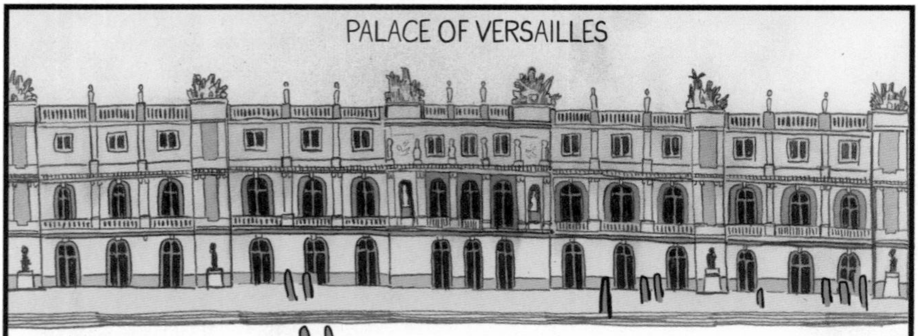
PALACE OF VERSAILLES

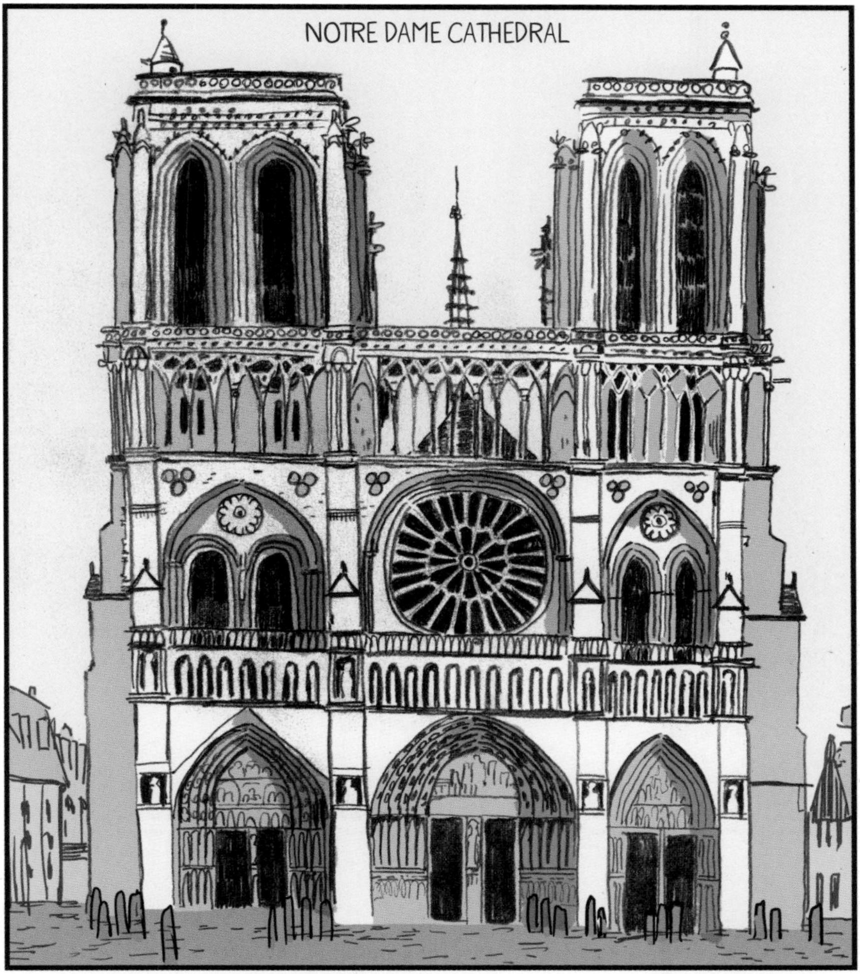
NOTRE DAME CATHEDRAL

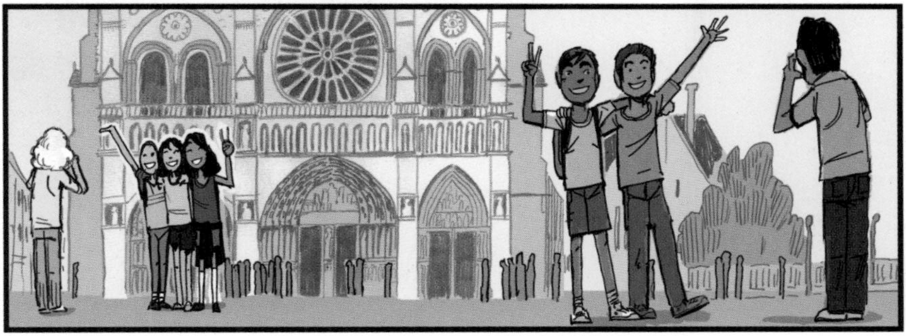

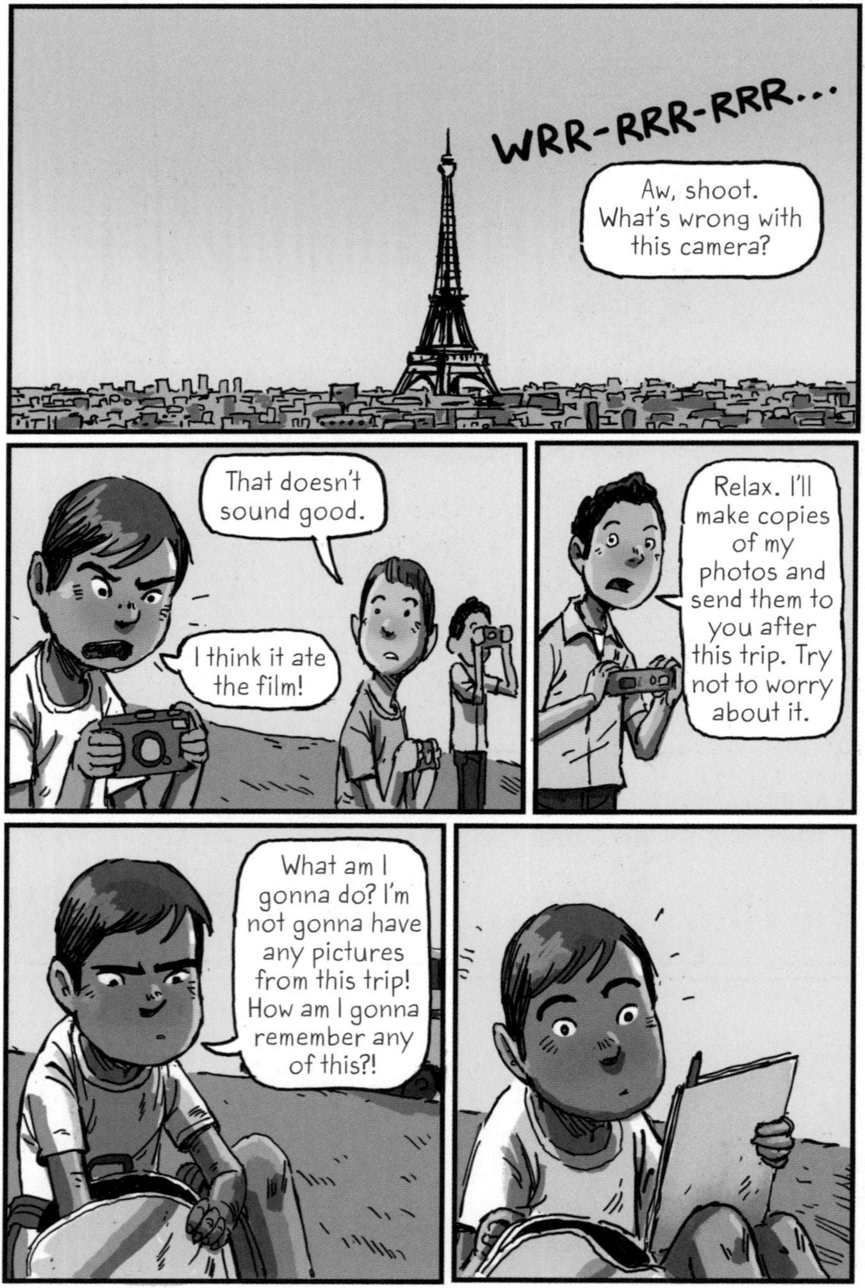
WRR-RRR-RRR...
Aw, shoot. What's wrong with this camera?
That doesn't sound good.
I think it ate the film!
Relax. I'll make copies of my photos and send them to you after this trip. Try not to worry about it.
What am I gonna do? I'm not gonna have any pictures from this trip! How am I gonna remember any of this?!

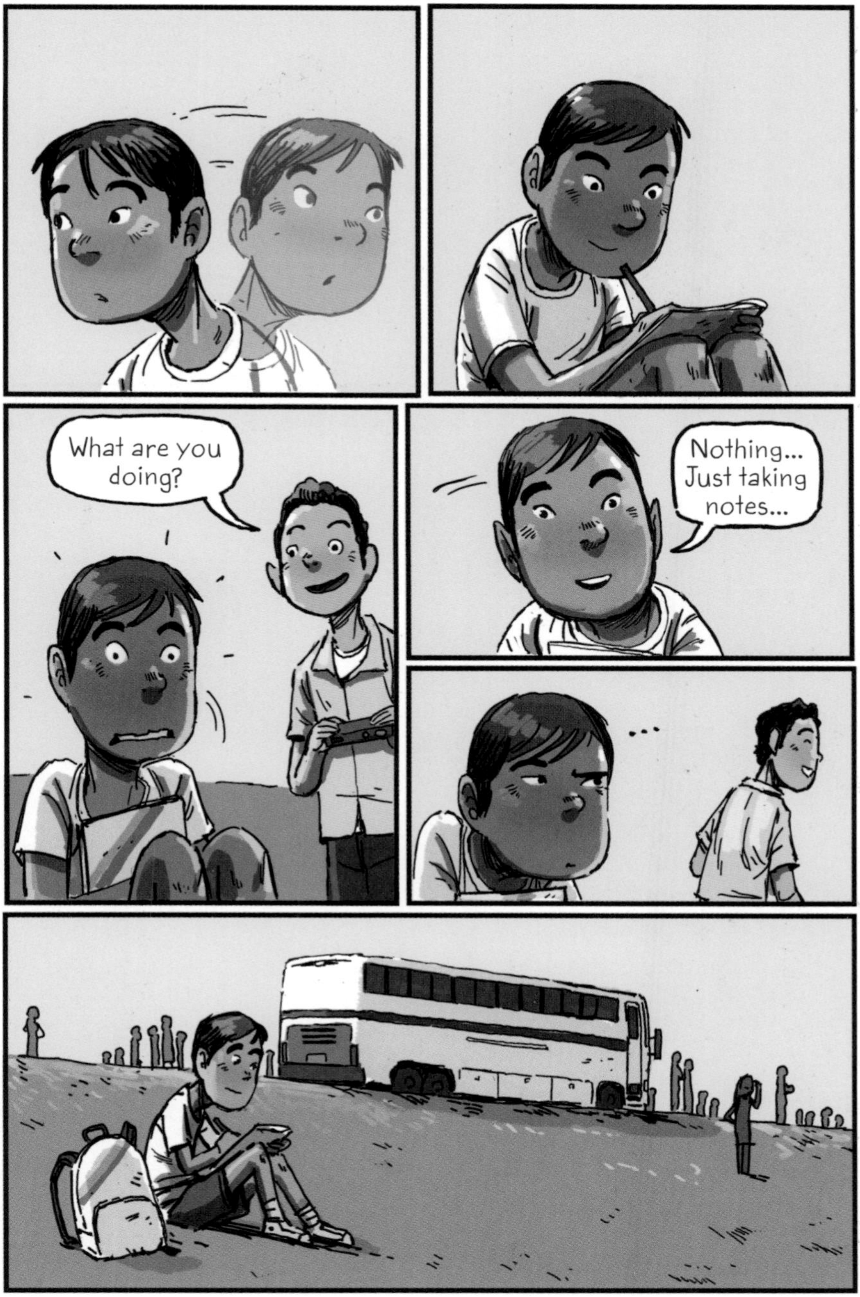
What are you doing?
Nothing... Just taking notes...
...

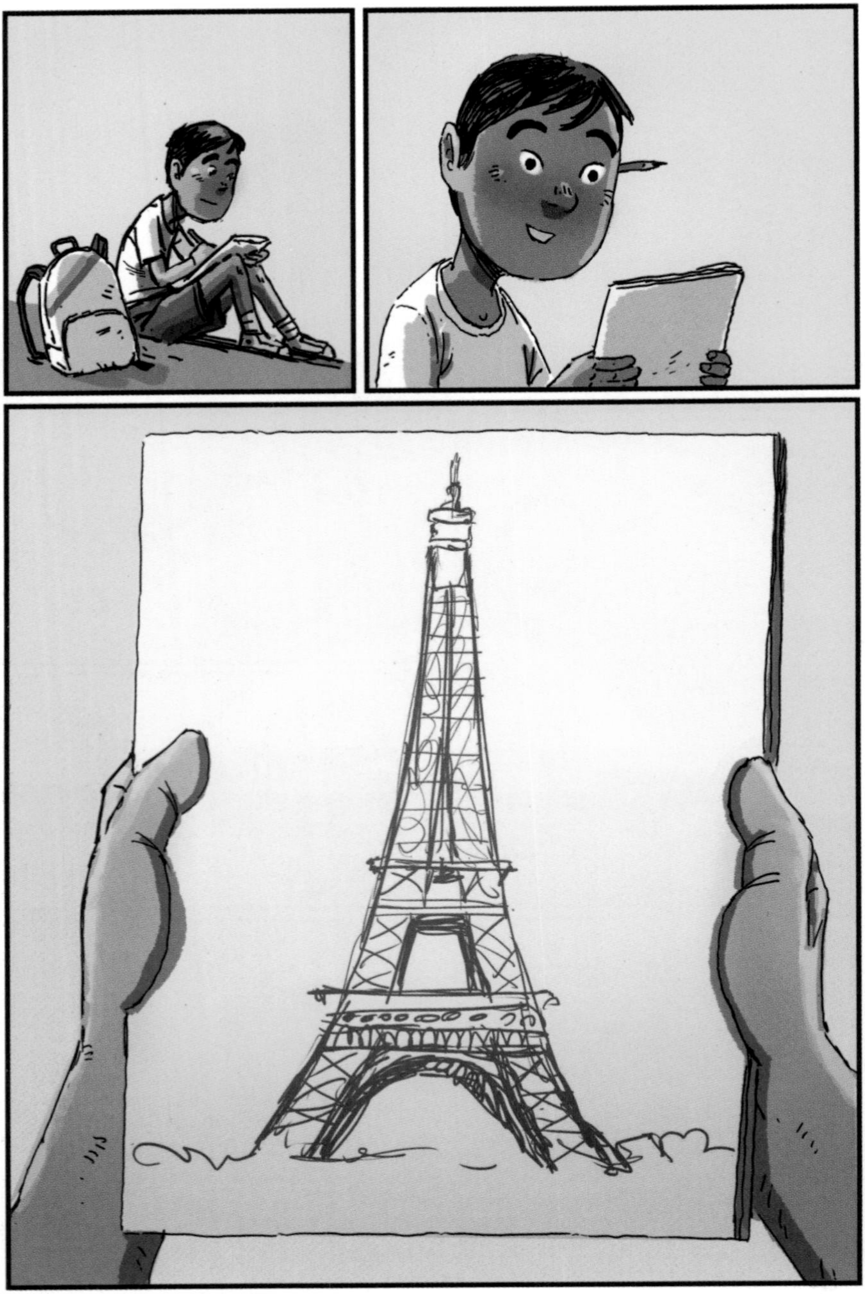

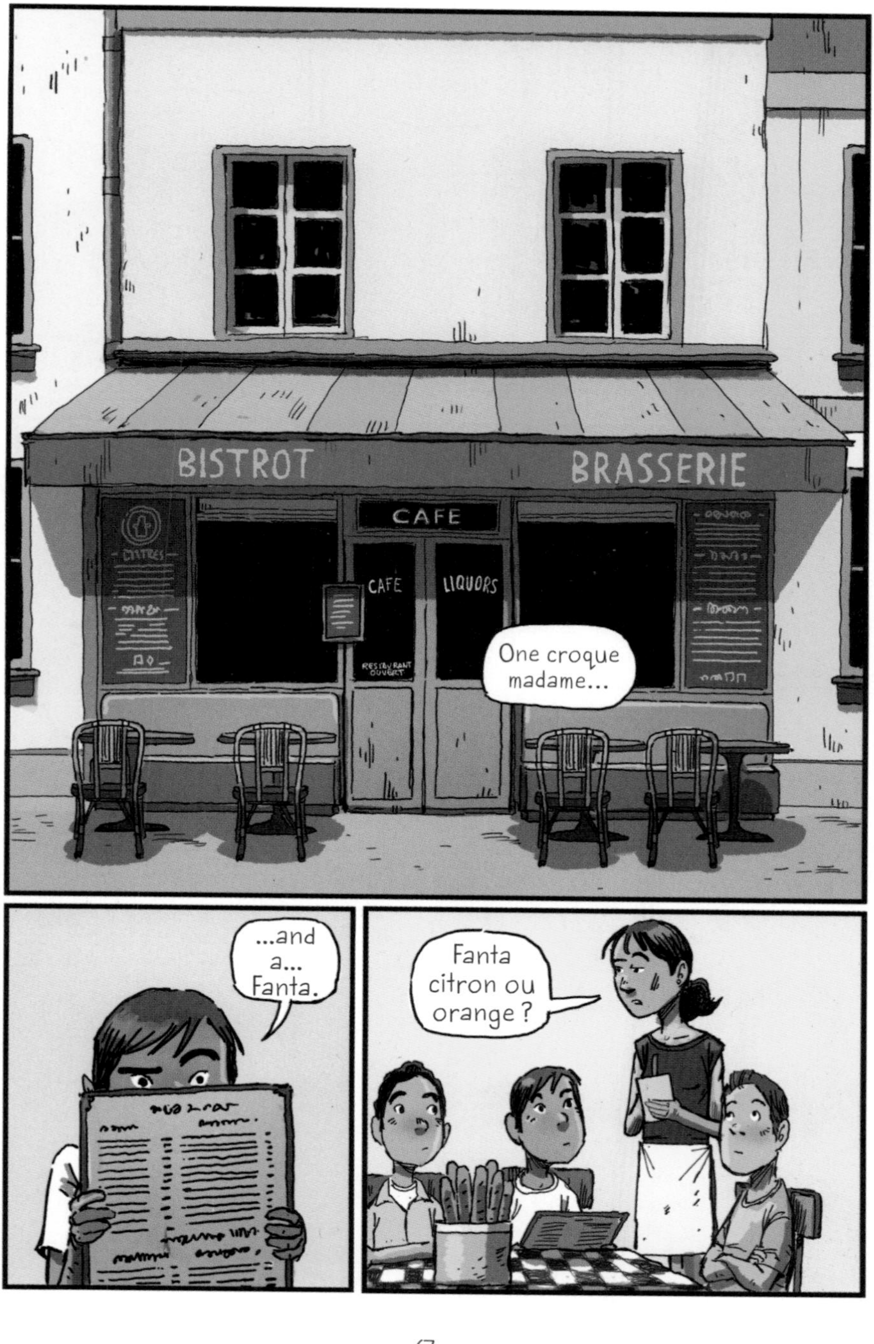
BISTROT
BRASSERIE
CAFE
CAFE
LIQUORS
RESTAURANT OUVERT
One croque madame...
...and a... Fanta.
Fanta citron ou orange ?

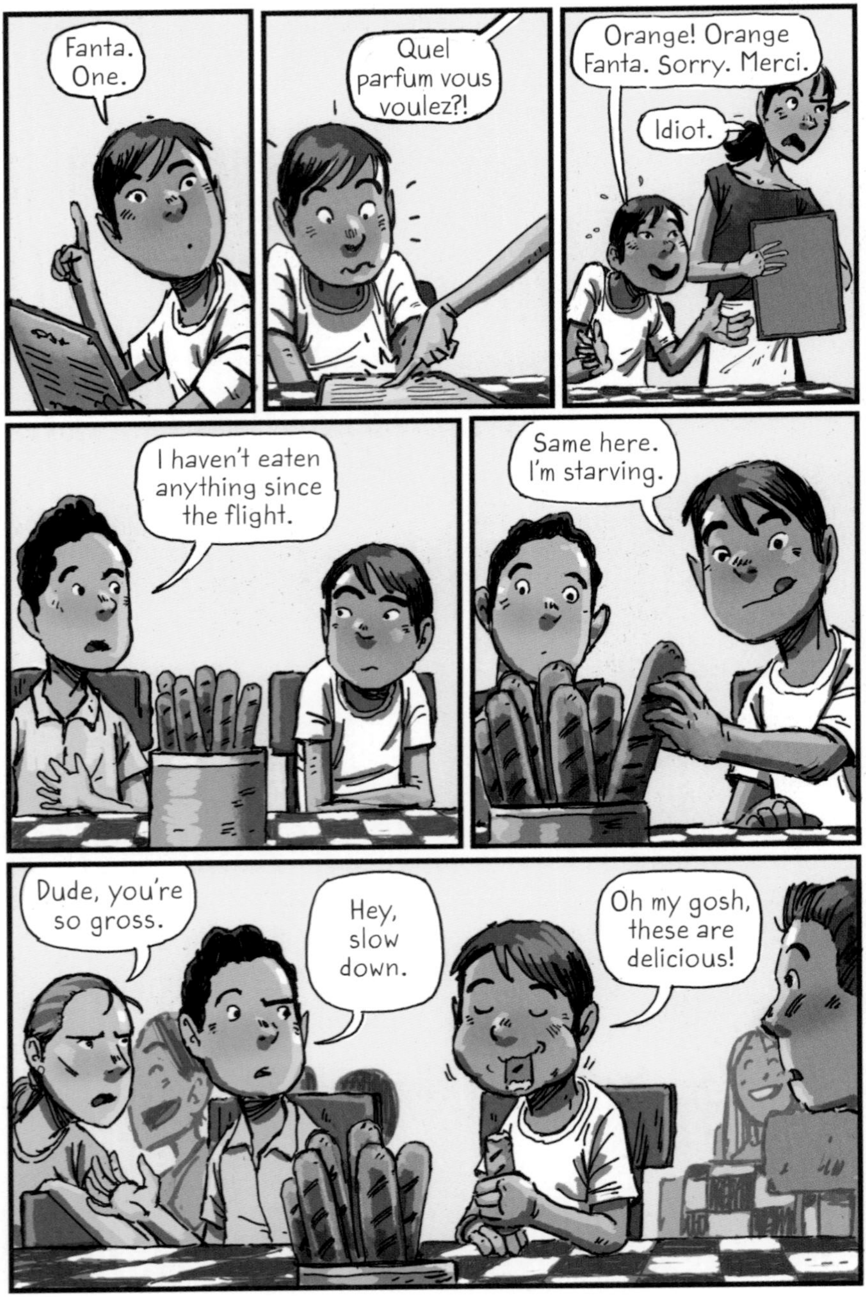
Fanta. One.
Quel parfum vous voulez?!
Orange! Orange Fanta. Sorry. Merci.
Idiot.
I haven't eaten anything since the flight.
Same here. I'm starving.
Dude, you're so gross.
Hey, slow down.
Oh my gosh, these are delicious!

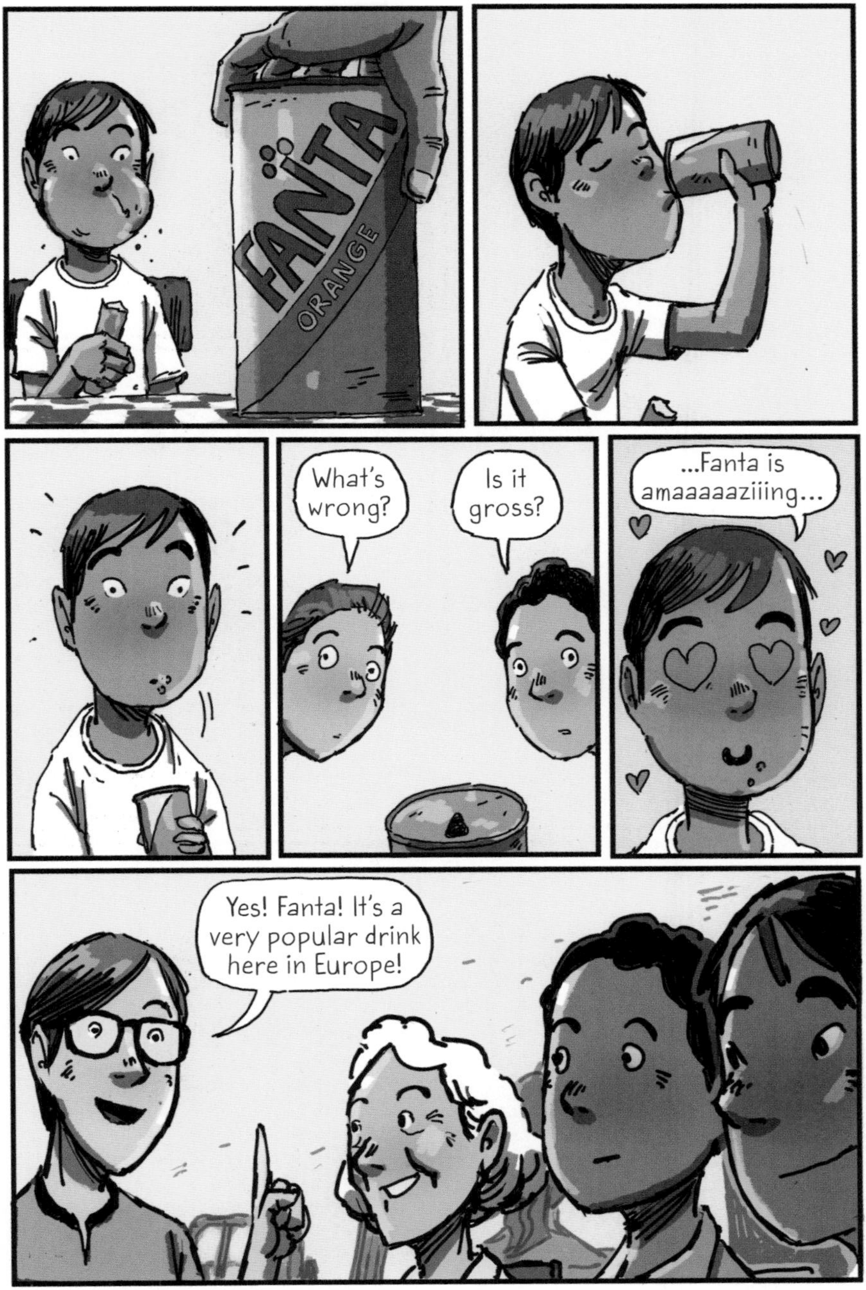
FANTA
ORANGE
What's wrong?
Is it gross?
...Fanta is amaaaaaziiing...
Yes! Fanta! It's a very popular drink here in Europe!

That was a product of World War II. After the US declared a trade embargo against the Nazis, they couldn't import syrup from the States and decided to make their own soda with only natural ingredients from Germany. You can find various flavors all over Europe like grape, strawberry, lime, mango...

...I must have them all...

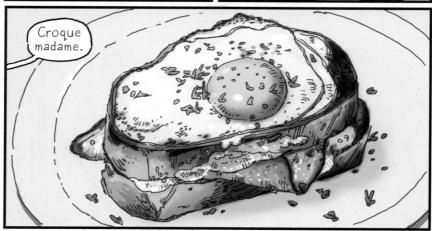

Croque madame.

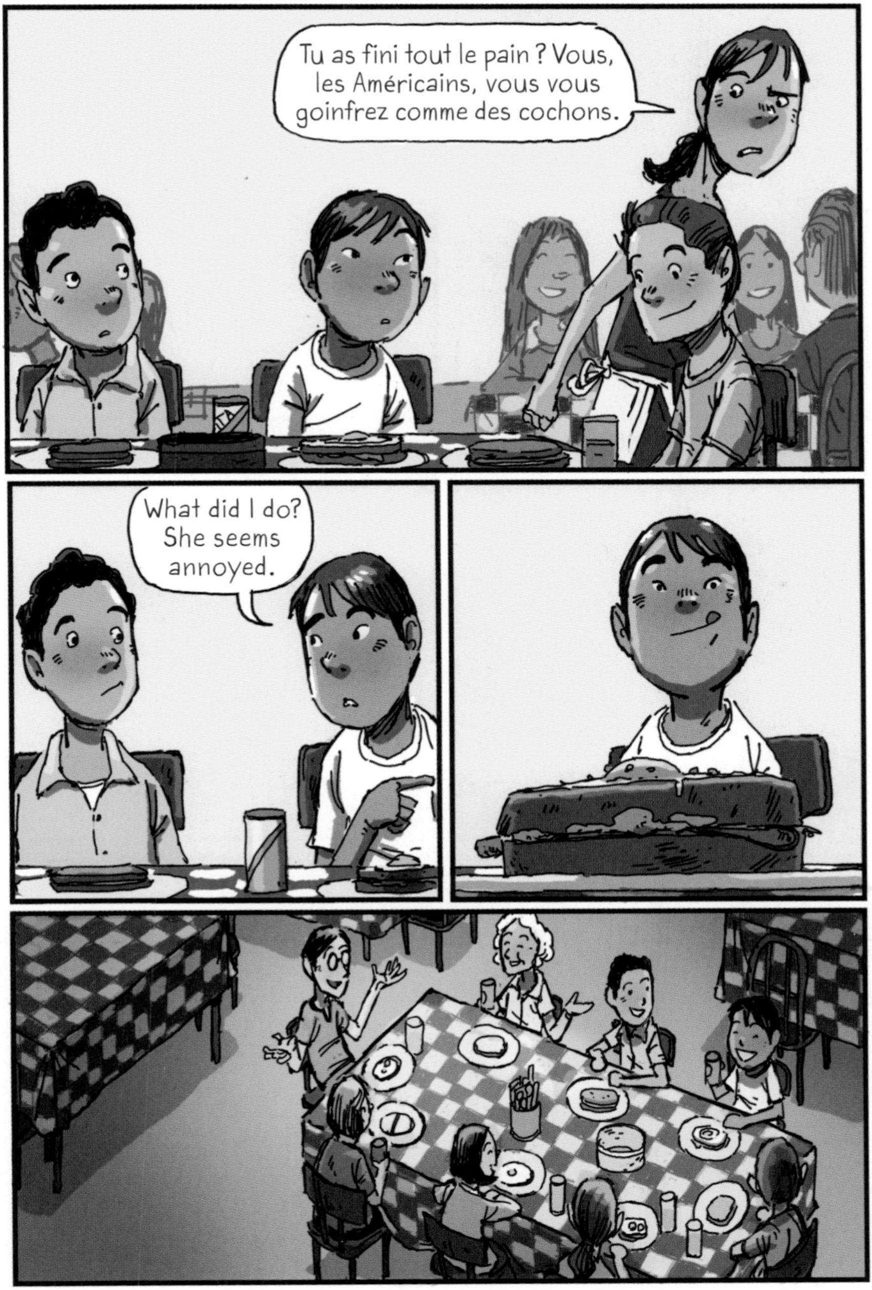
Tu as fini tout le pain ? Vous, les Américains, vous vous goinfrez comme des cochons.
What did I do? She seems annoyed.

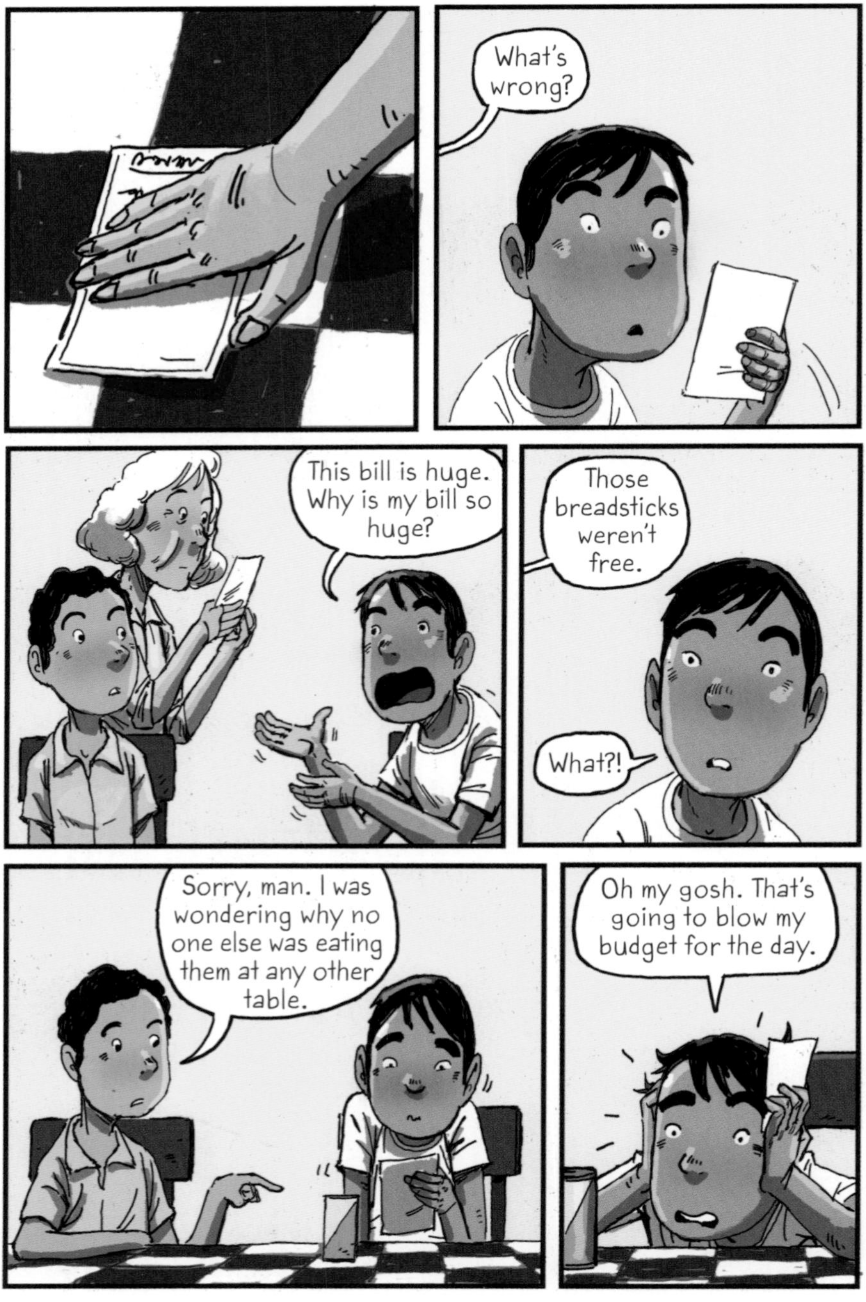
What's wrong?
This bill is huge. Why is my bill so huge?
Those breadsticks weren't free.
What?!
Sorry, man. I was wondering why no one else was eating them at any other table.
Oh my gosh. That's going to blow my budget for the day.

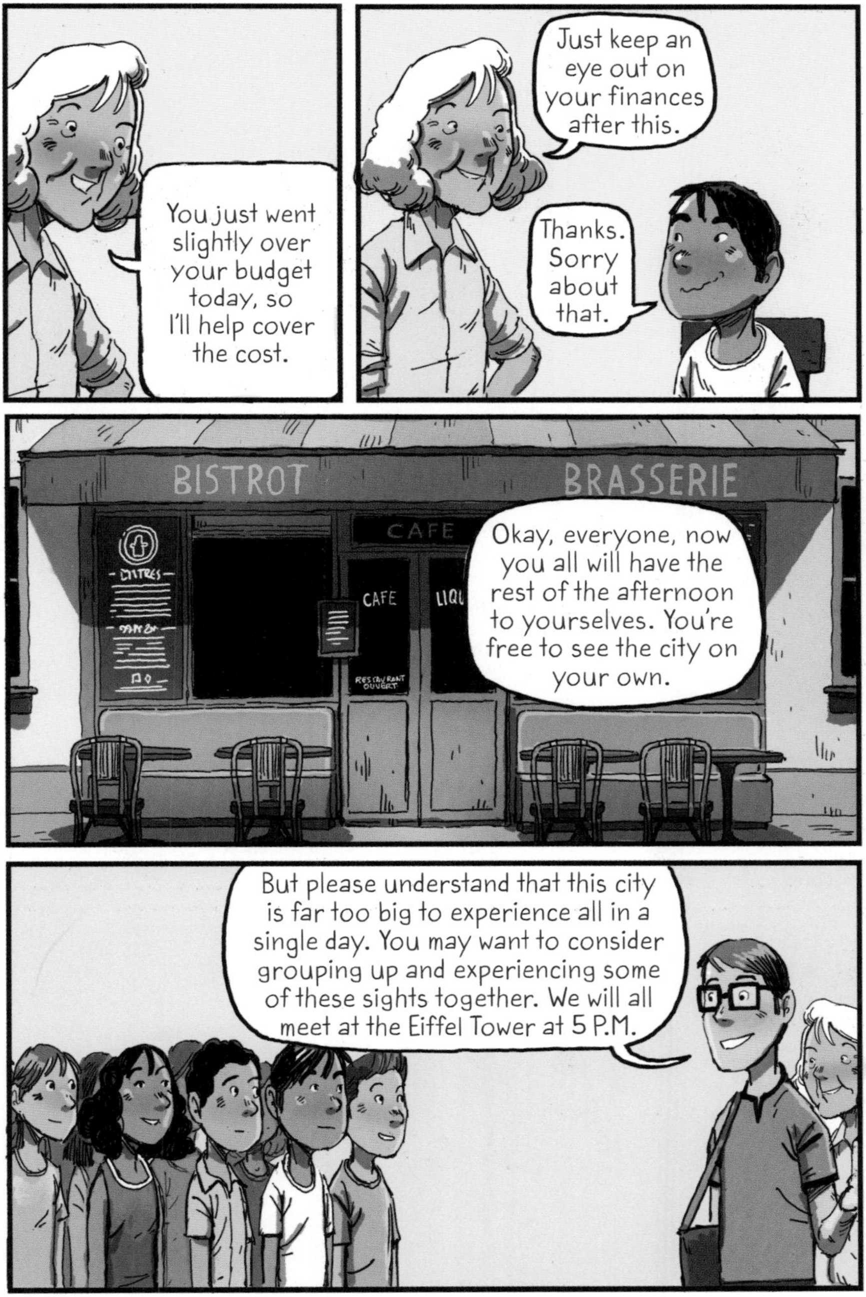
You just went slightly over your budget today, so I'll help cover the cost.
Just keep an eye out on your finances after this.
Thanks. Sorry about that.
BISTROT
BRASSERIE
CAFE
CAFE
RESTAURANT OUVERT
Okay, everyone, now you all will have the rest of the afternoon to yourselves. You're free to see the city on your own.
But please understand that this city is far too big to experience all in a single day. You may want to consider grouping up and experiencing some of these sights together. We will all meet at the Eiffel Tower at 5 P.M.

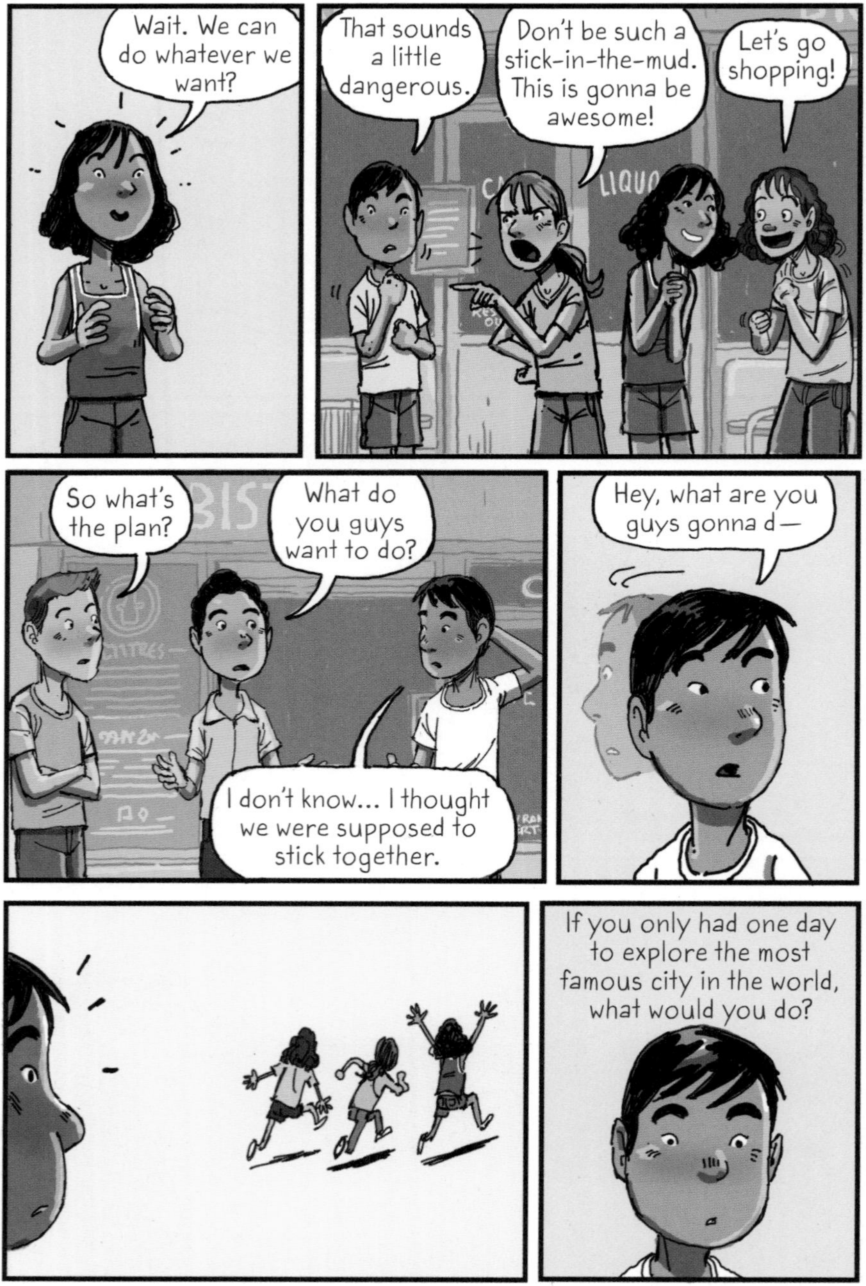
Wait. We can do whatever we want?
That sounds a little dangerous.
Don't be such a stick-in-the-mud. This is gonna be awesome!
Let's go shopping!
So what's the plan?
What do you guys want to do?
I don't know... I thought we were supposed to stick together.
Hey, what are you guys gonna d—
If you only had one day to explore the most famous city in the world, what would you do?

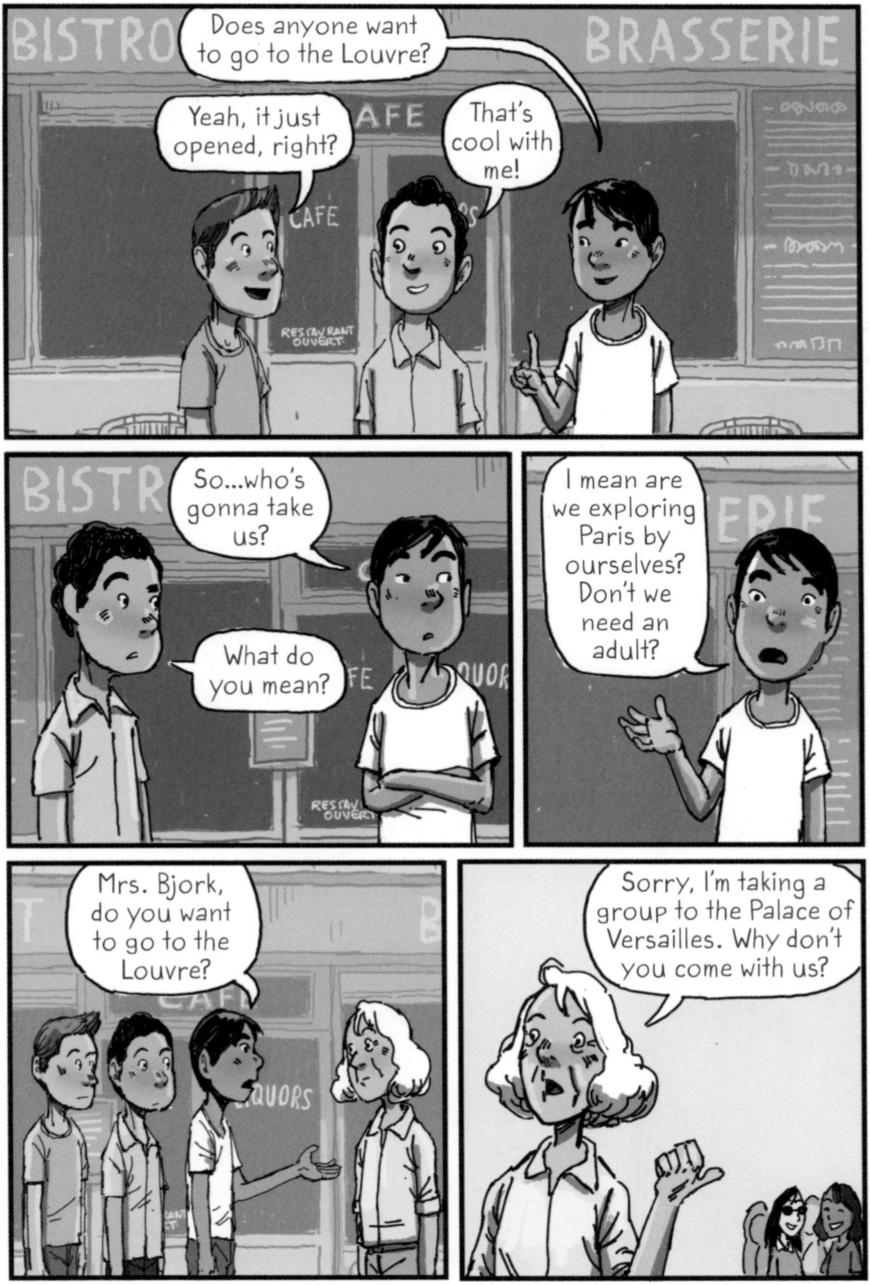
BISTRO
BRASSERIE
Does anyone want to go to the Louvre?
CAFE
Yeah, it just opened, right?
That's cool with me!
CAFE
RESTAURANT OUVERT
BISTR
So...who's gonna take us?
What do you mean?
I mean are we exploring Paris by ourselves? Don't we need an adult?
Mrs. Bjork, do you want to go to the Louvre?
Sorry, I'm taking a group to the Palace of Versailles. Why don't you come with us?

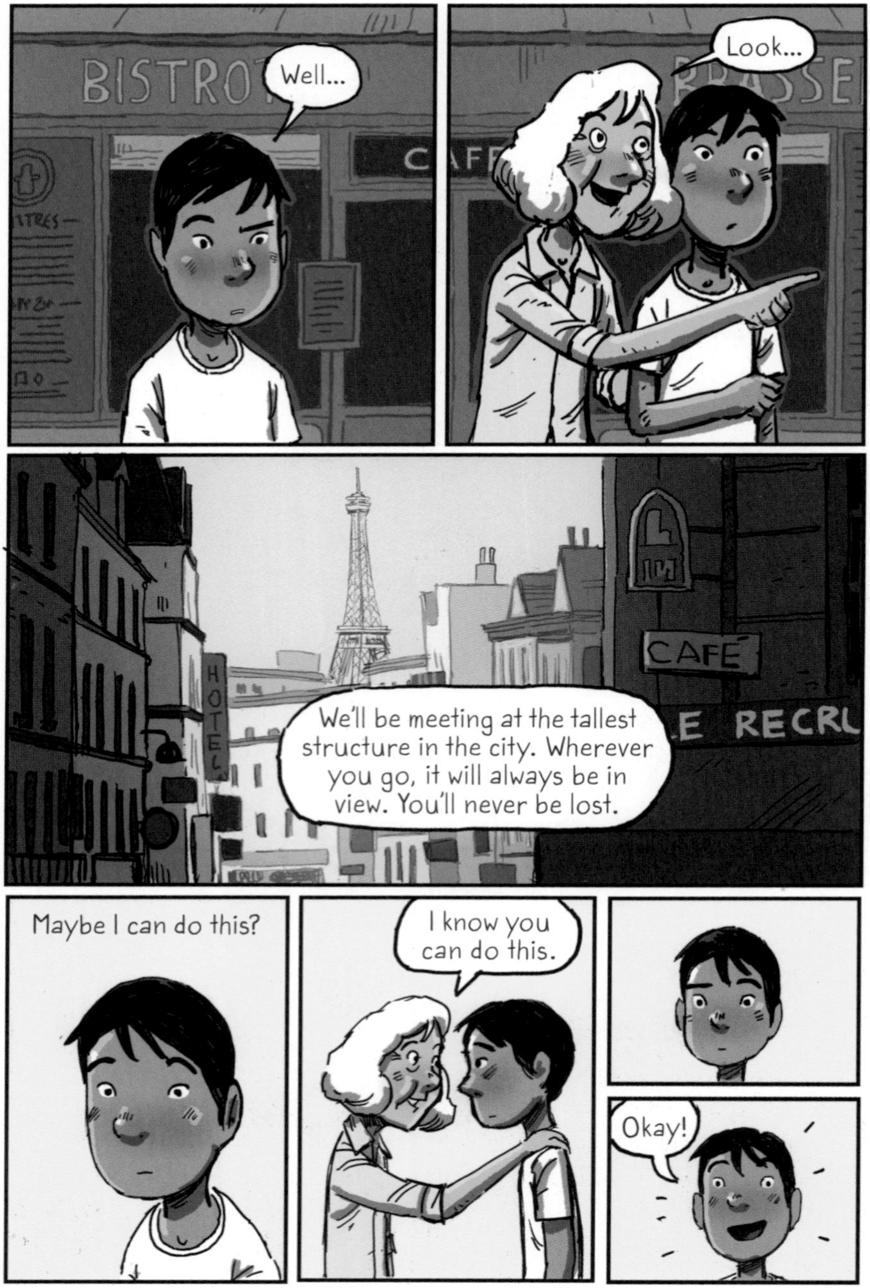
BISTRO
Well...
CAFE
Look...
BRASSE
HOTEL
CAFE
E RECRL
We'll be meeting at the tallest structure in the city. Wherever you go, it will always be in view. You'll never be lost.
Maybe I can do this?
I know you can do this.
Okay!

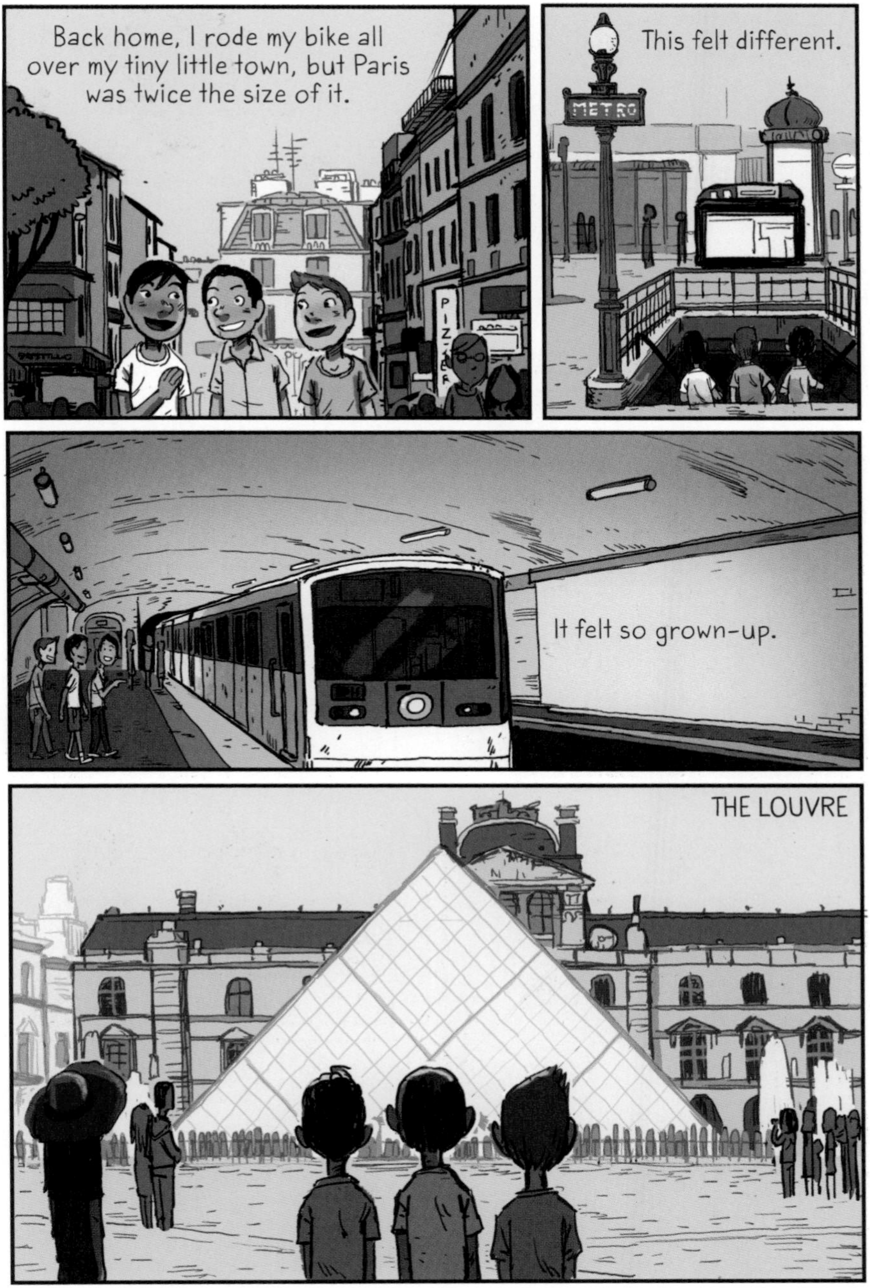
Back home, I rode my bike all over my tiny little town, but Paris was twice the size of it.
This felt different.
METRO
It felt so grown-up.
THE LOUVRE

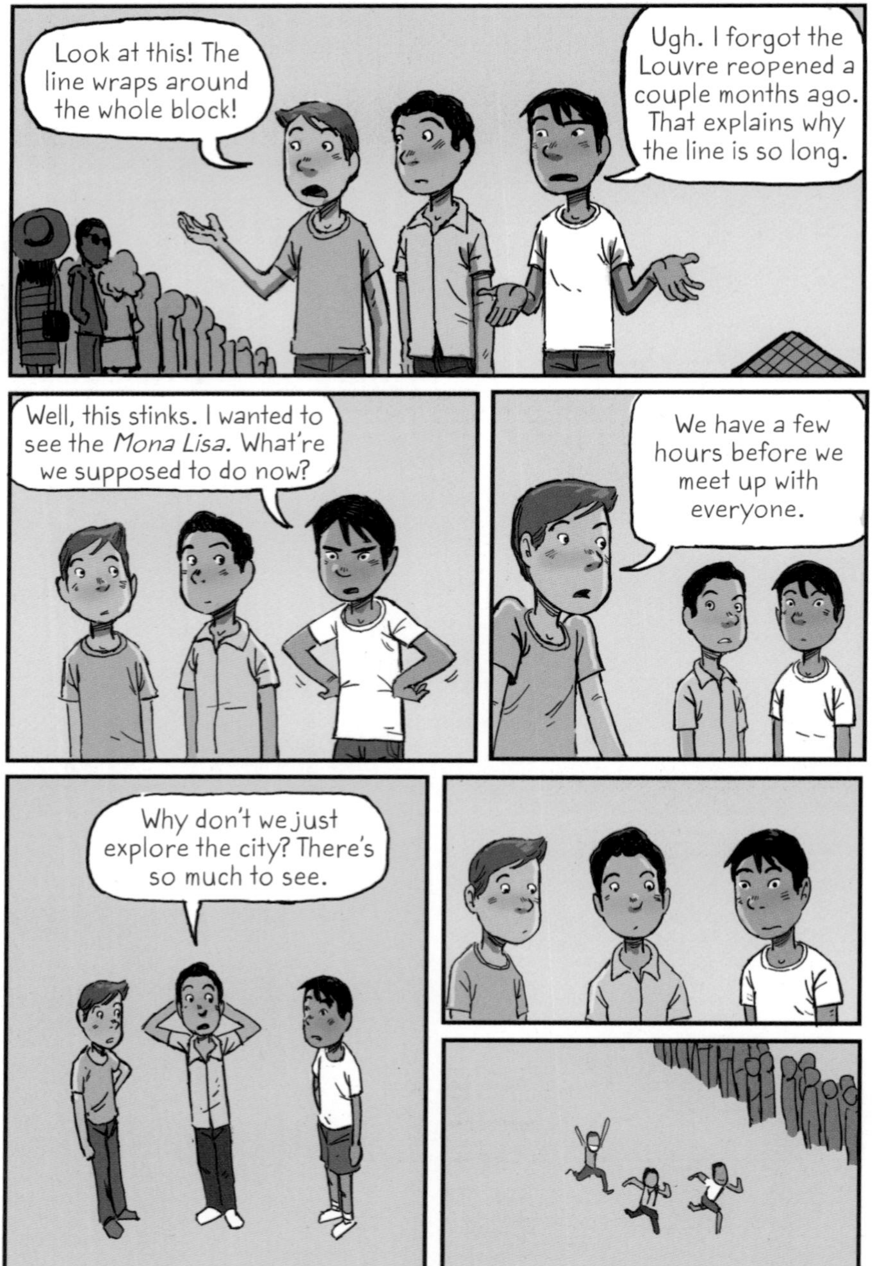
Look at this! The line wraps around the whole block!
Ugh. I forgot the Louvre reopened a couple months ago. That explains why the line is so long.
Well, this stinks. I wanted to see the *Mona Lisa.* What're we supposed to do now?
We have a few hours before we meet up with everyone.
Why don't we just explore the city? There's so much to see.

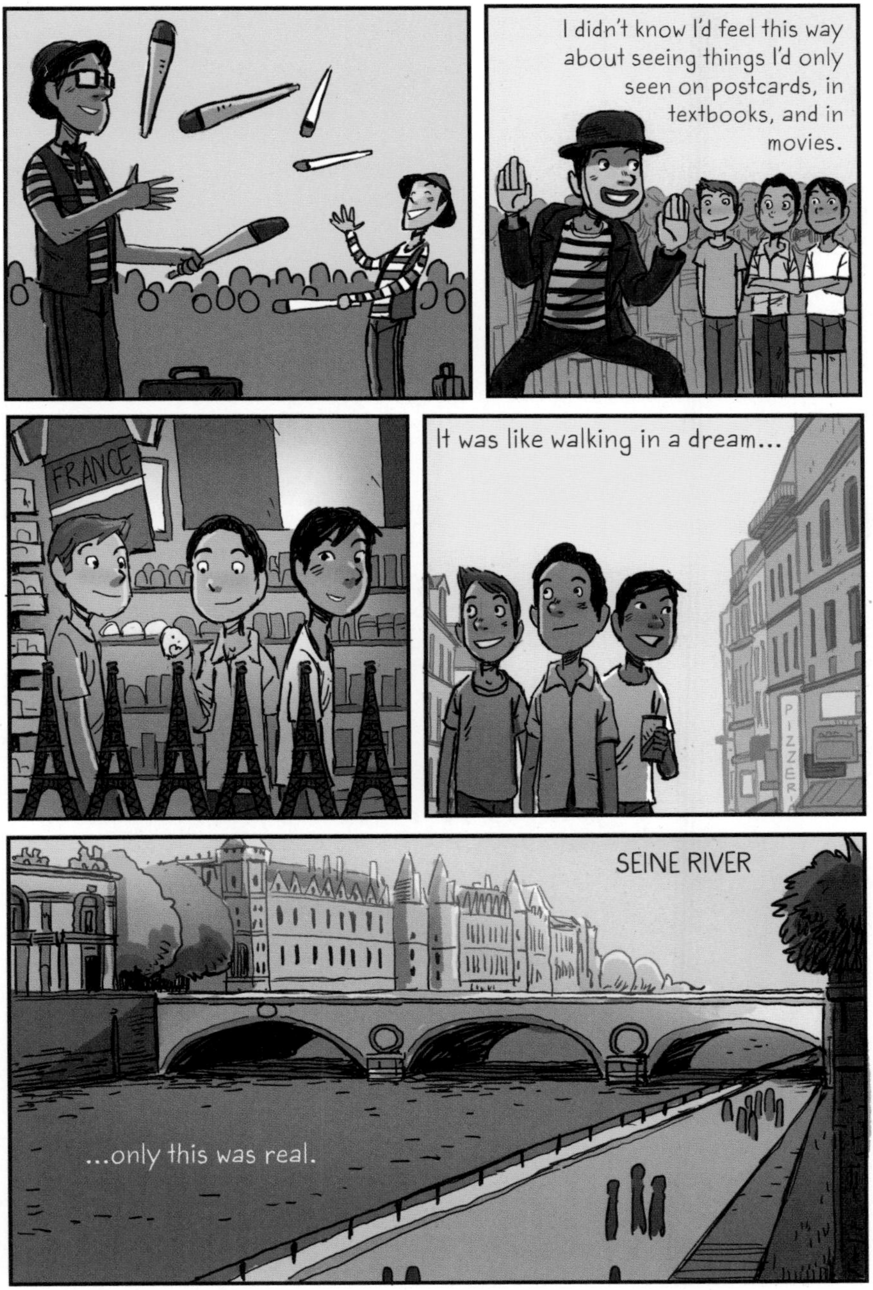
I didn't know I'd feel this way about seeing things I'd only seen on postcards, in textbooks, and in movies.
FRANCE
It was like walking in a dream...
PIZZERI
SEINE RIVER
...only this was real.

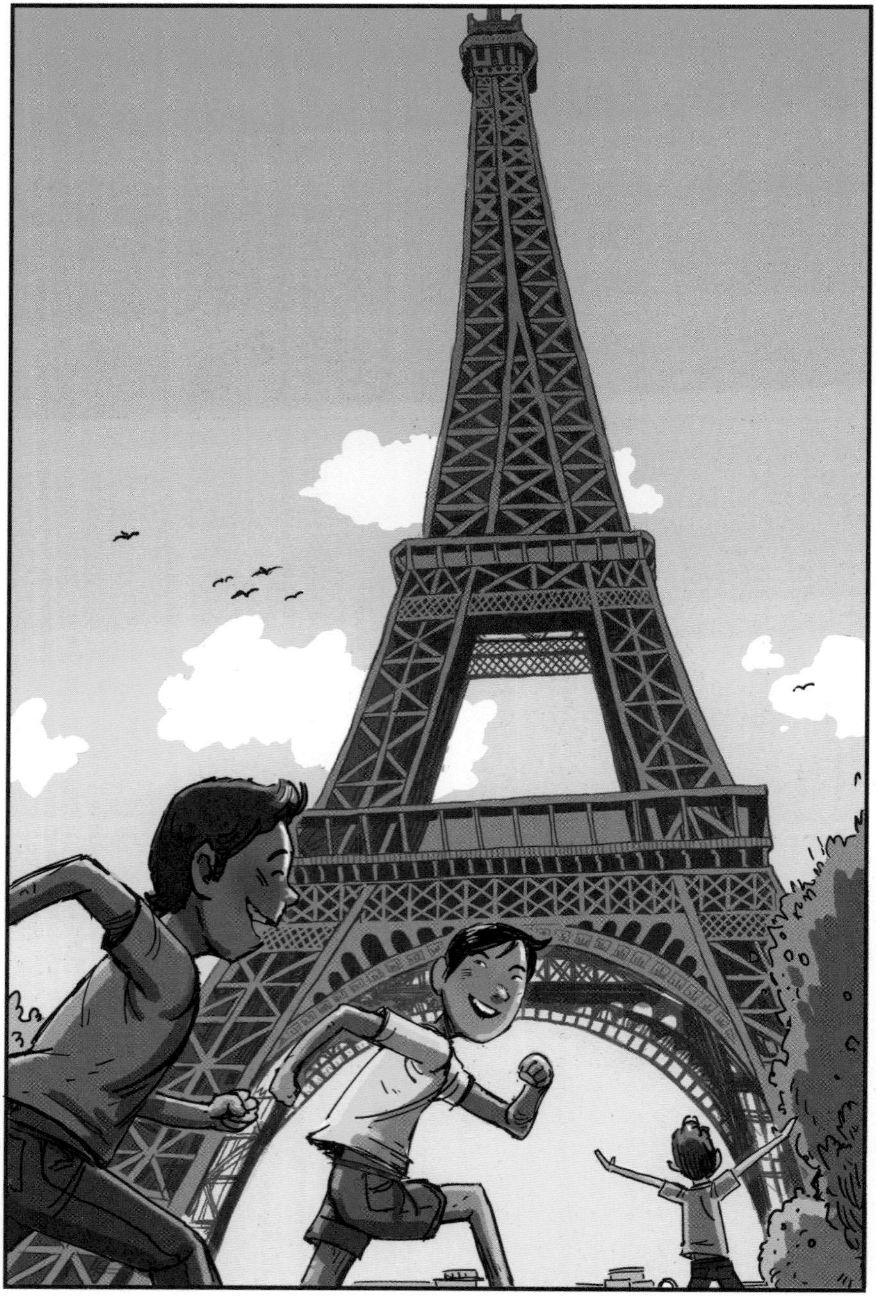

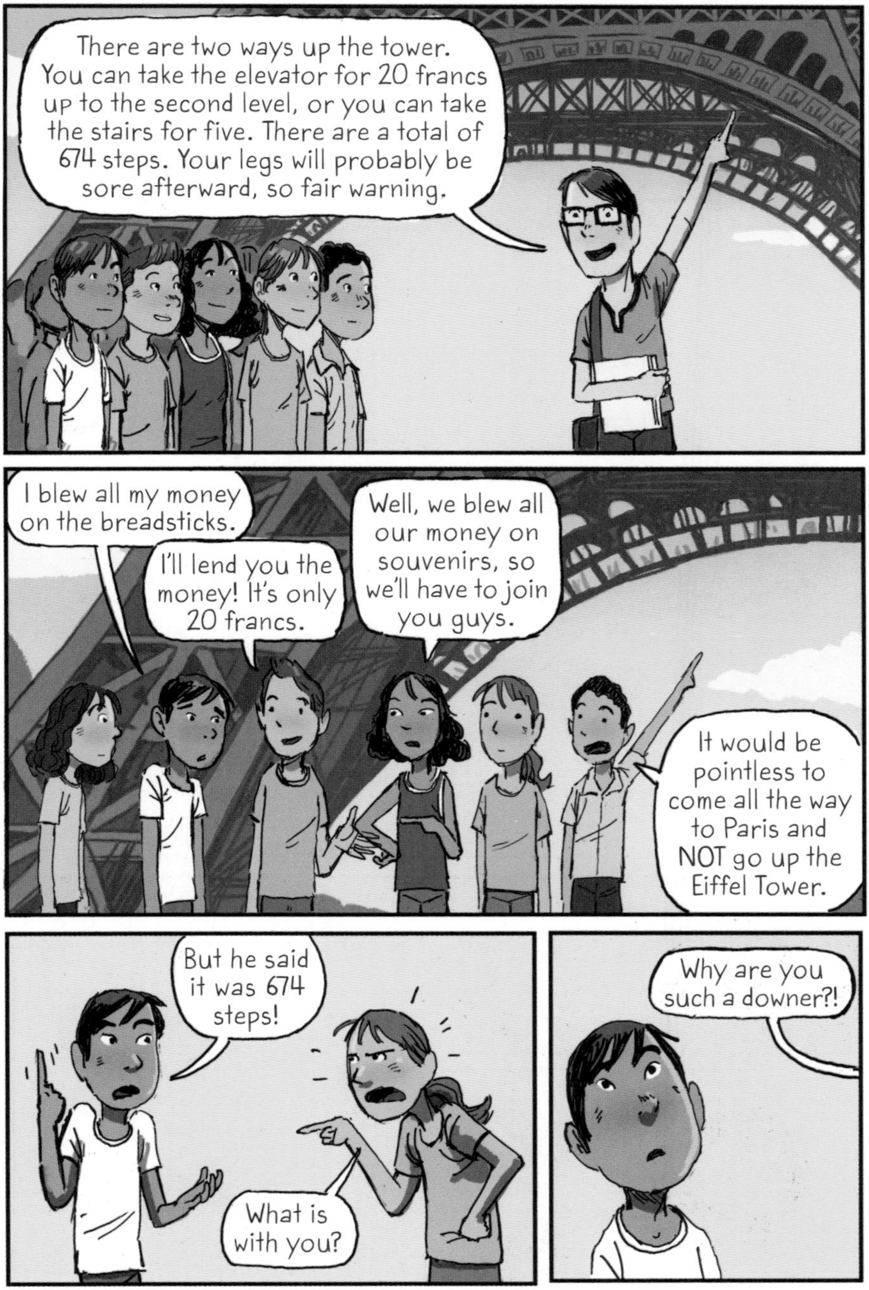
There are two ways up the tower. You can take the elevator for 20 francs up to the second level, or you can take the stairs for five. There are a total of 674 steps. Your legs will probably be sore afterward, so fair warning.
I blew all my money on the breadsticks.
I'll lend you the money! It's only 20 francs.
Well, we blew all our money on souvenirs, so we'll have to join you guys.
It would be pointless to come all the way to Paris and NOT go up the Eiffel Tower.
But he said it was 674 steps!
What is with you?
Why are you such a downer?!

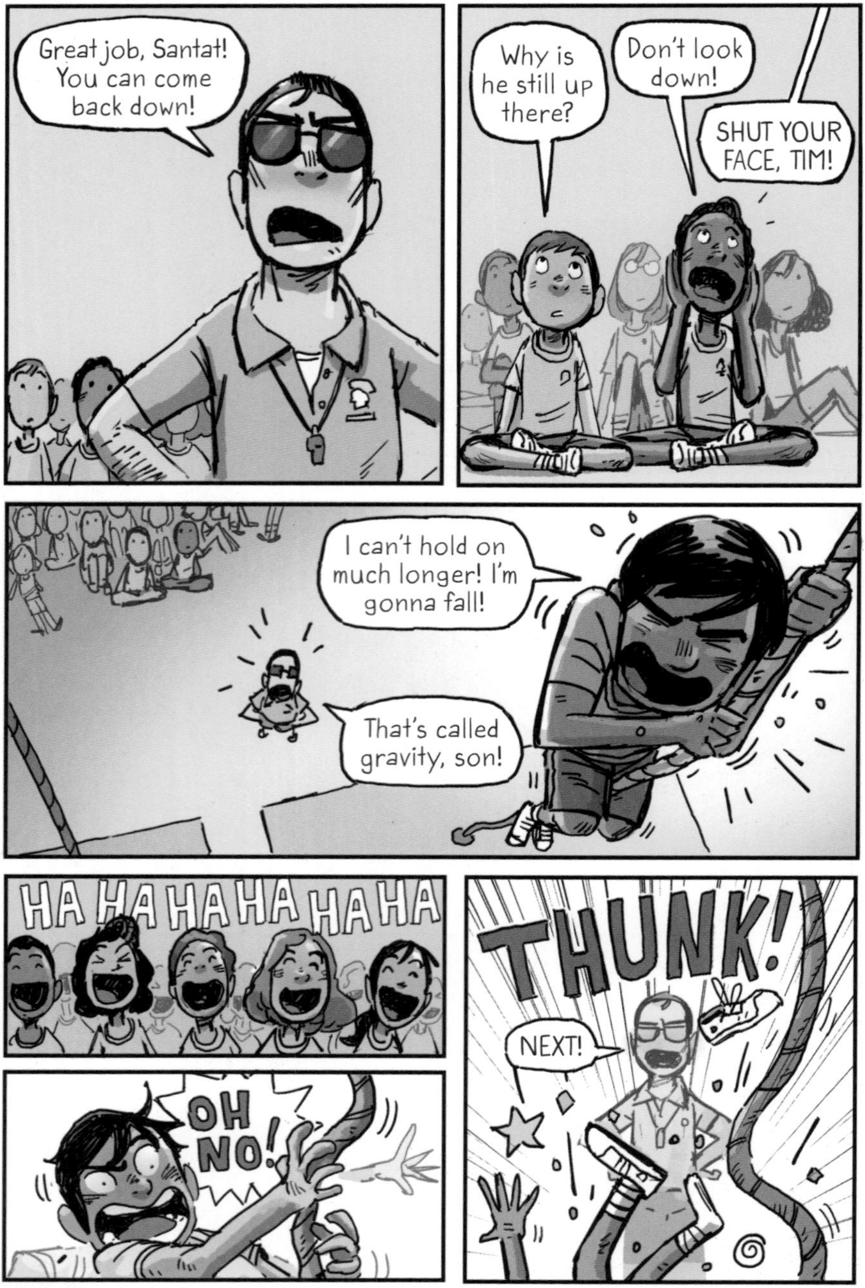
Great job, Santat! You can come back down!
Why is he still up there?
Don't look down!
SHUT YOUR FACE, TIM!
I can't hold on much longer! I'm gonna fall!
That's called gravity, son!
HA HA HA HA HA HA HA HA
OH NO!
THUNK!
NEXT!

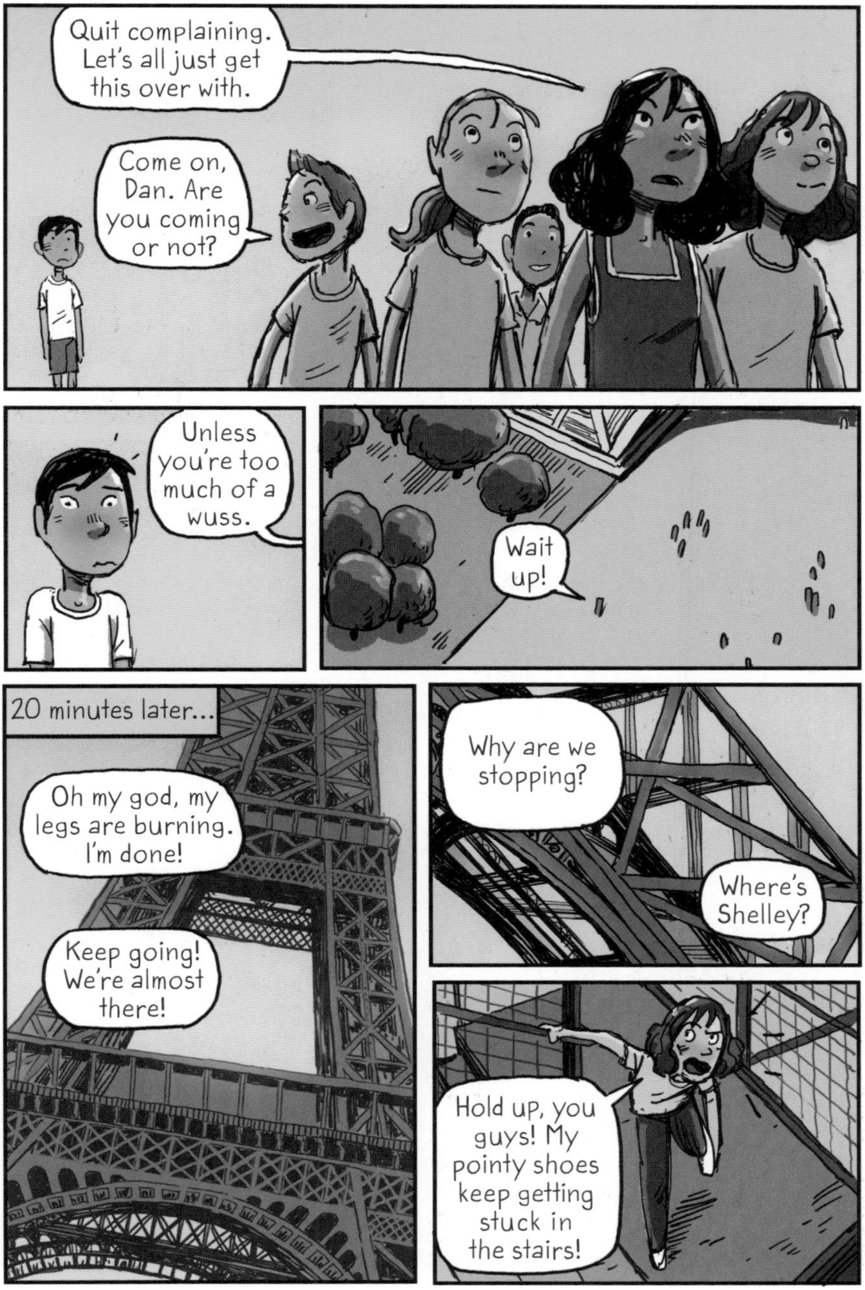
Quit complaining. Let's all just get this over with.
Come on, Dan. Are you coming or not?
Unless you're too much of a wuss.
Wait up!
20 minutes later...
Oh my god, my legs are burning. I'm done!
Keep going! We're almost there!
Why are we stopping?
Where's Shelley?
Hold up, you guys! My pointy shoes keep getting stuck in the stairs!

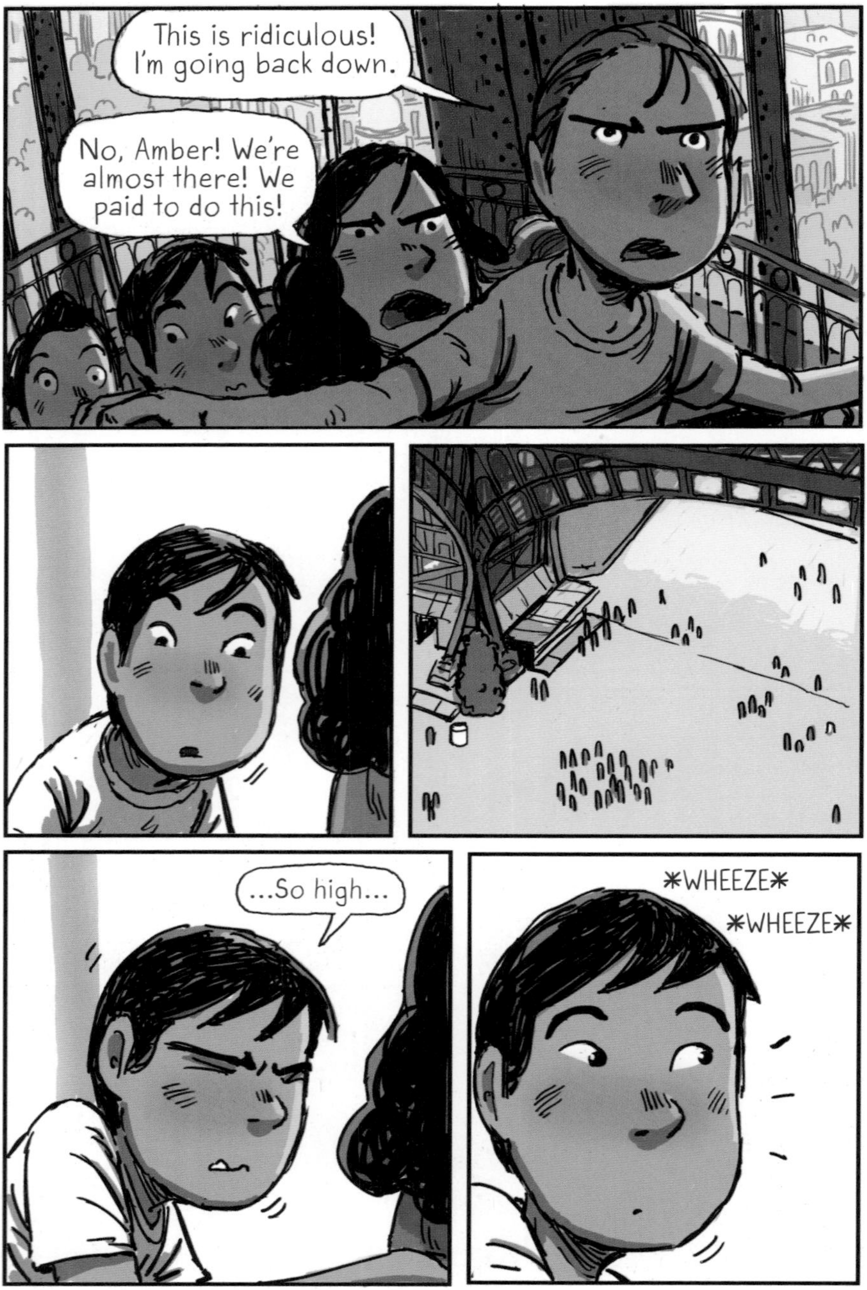
This is ridiculous! I'm going back down.
No, Amber! We're almost there! We paid to do this!
...So high...
WHEEZE
WHEEZE

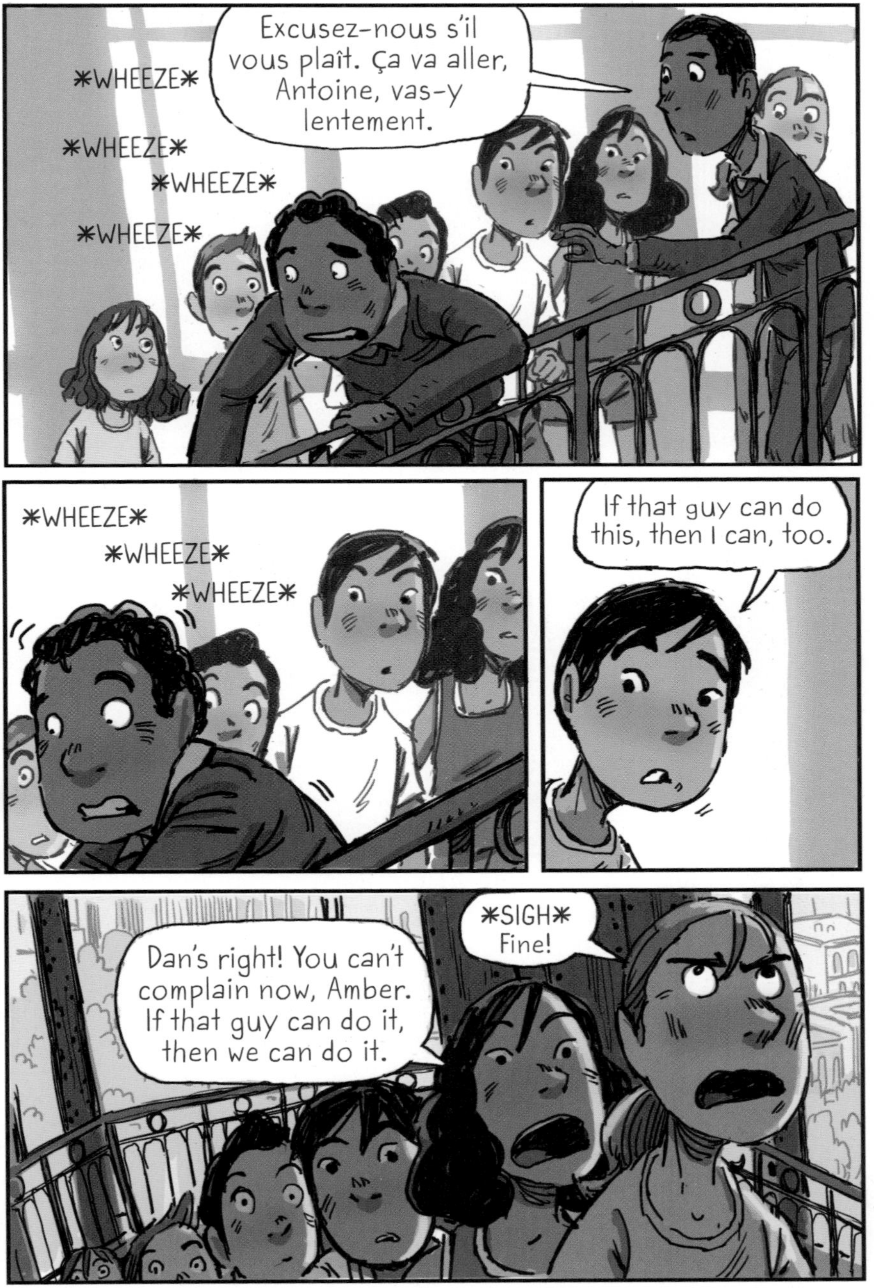
WHEEZE
WHEEZE
WHEEZE
WHEEZE
Excusez-nous s'il vous plaît. Ça va aller, Antoine, vas-y lentement.
WHEEZE
WHEEZE
WHEEZE
If that guy can do this, then I can, too.
Dan's right! You can't complain now, Amber. If that guy can do it, then we can do it.
SIGH Fine!

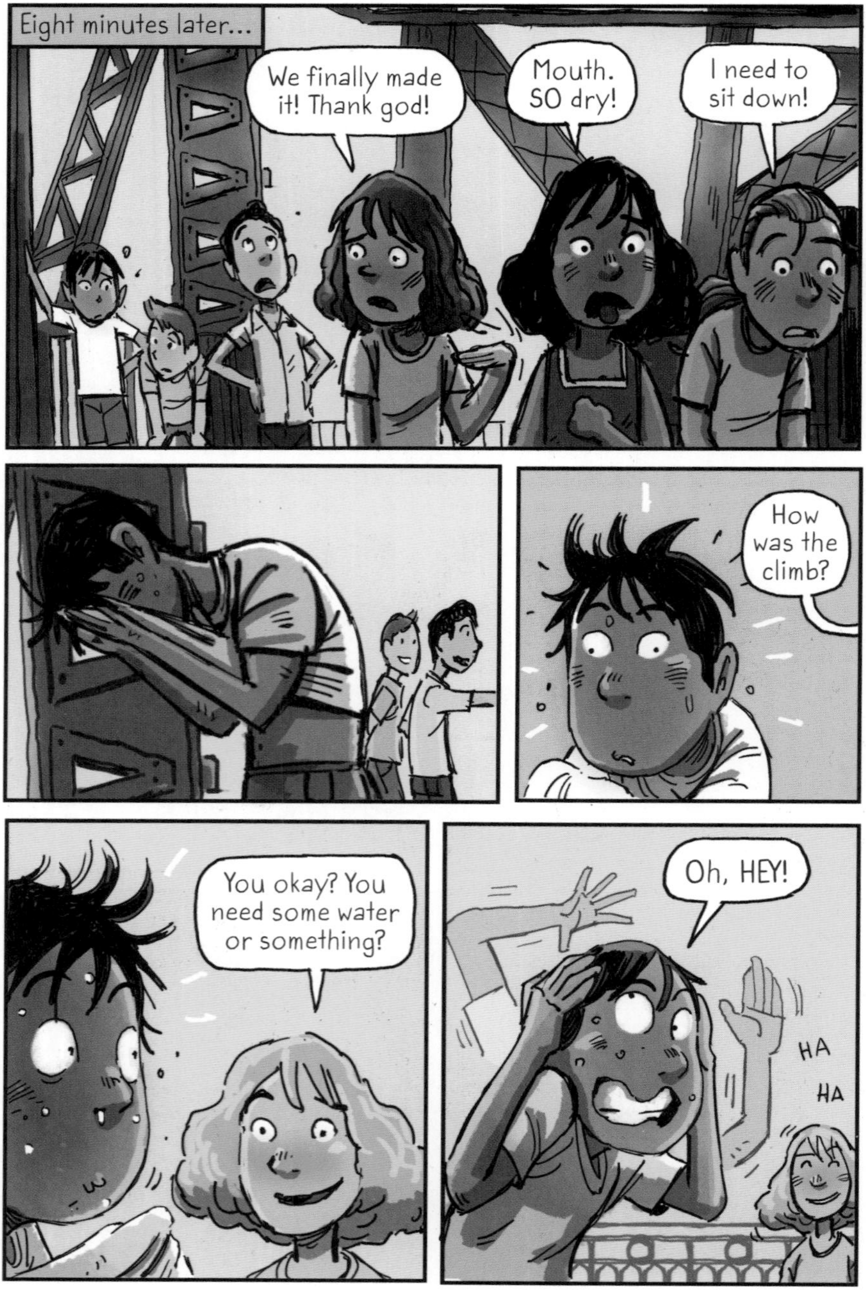
Eight minutes later...
We finally made it! Thank god!
Mouth. SO dry!
I need to sit down!
How was the climb?
You okay? You need some water or something?
Oh, HEY!
HA
HA

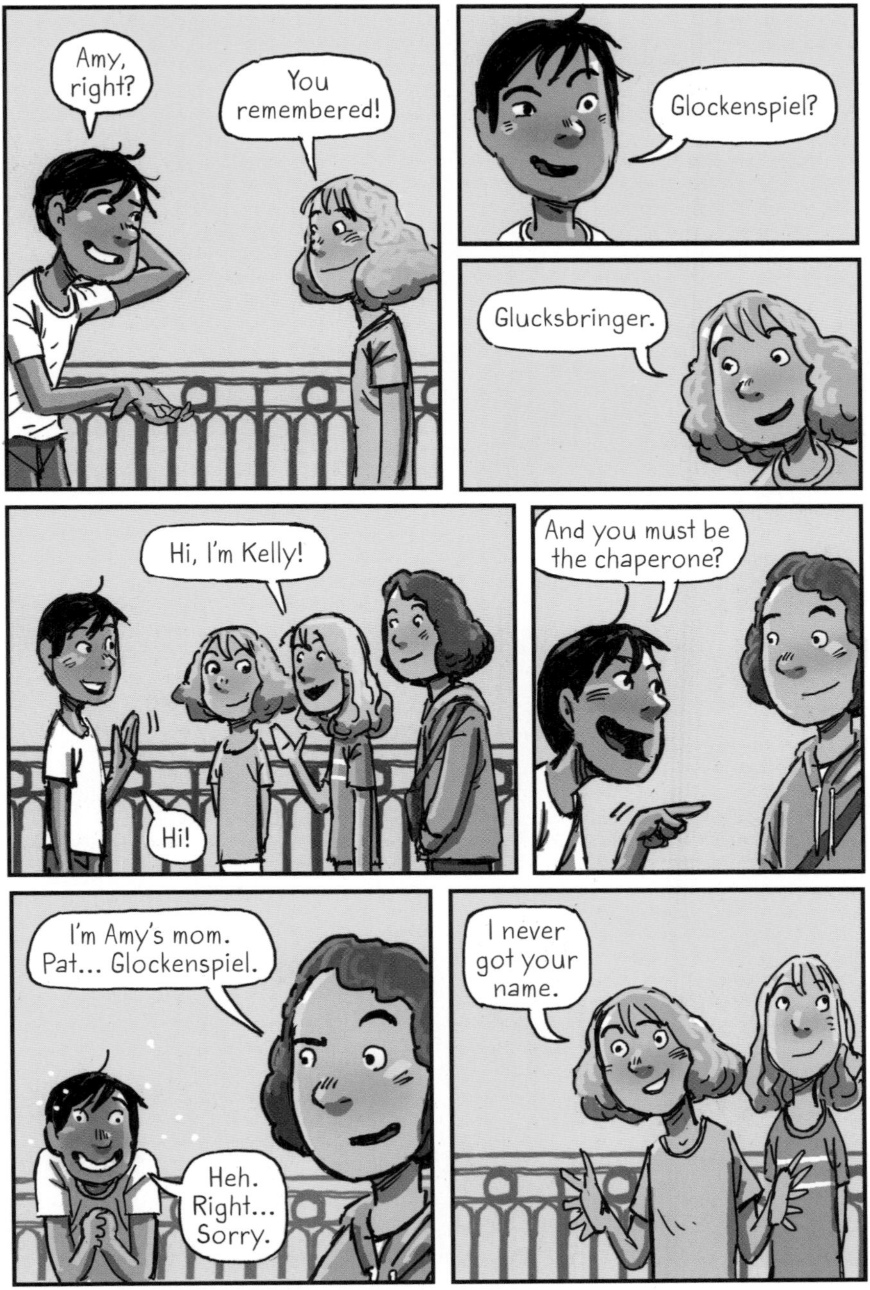

Amy, right?
You remembered!
Glockenspiel?
Glucksbringer.
Hi, I'm Kelly!
Hi!
And you must be the chaperone?
I'm Amy's mom. Pat... Glockenspiel.
Heh. Right... Sorry.
I never got your name.

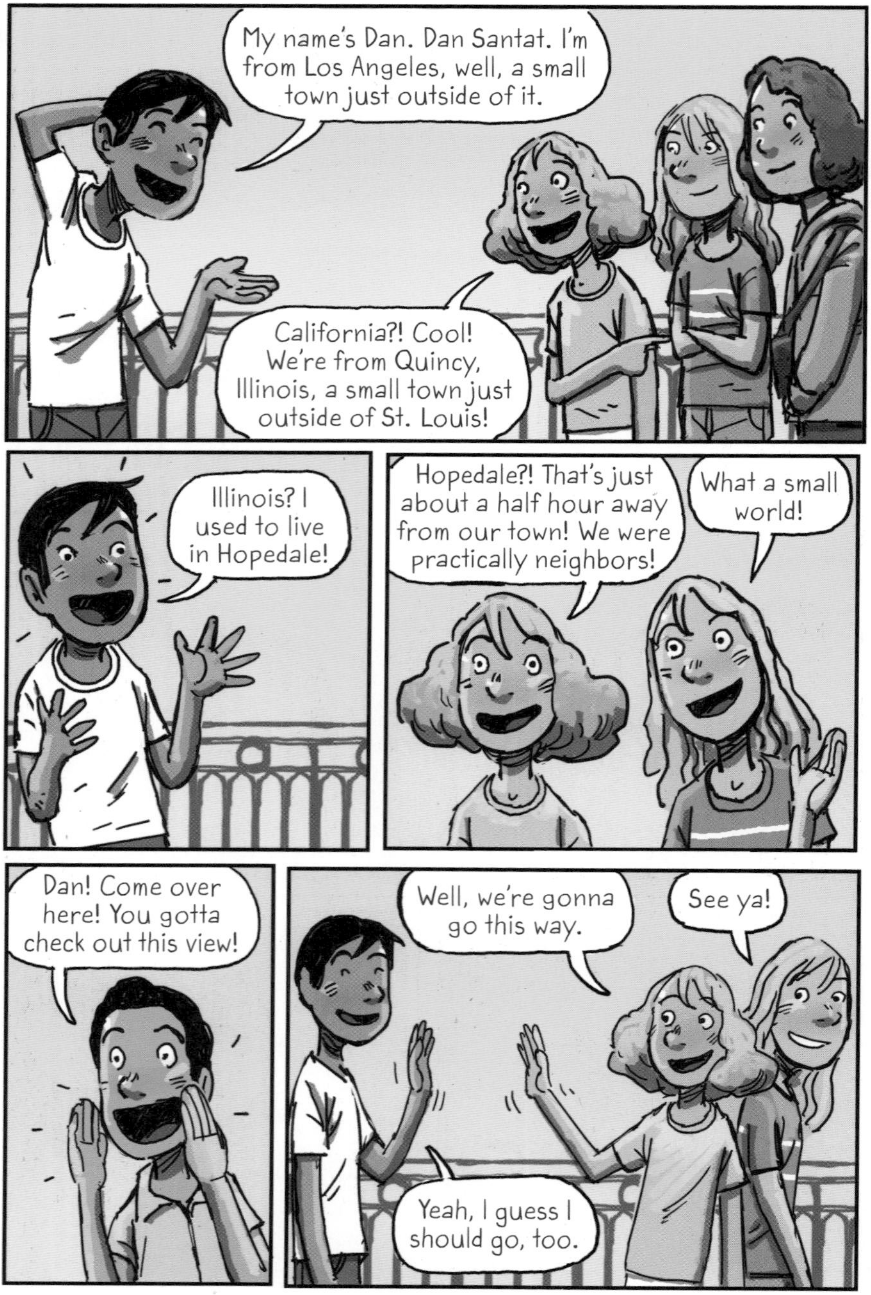
My name's Dan. Dan Santat. I'm from Los Angeles, well, a small town just outside of it.
California?! Cool! We're from Quincy, Illinois, a small town just outside of St. Louis!
Illinois? I used to live in Hopedale!
Hopedale?! That's just about a half hour away from our town! We were practically neighbors!
What a small world!
Dan! Come over here! You gotta check out this view!
Well, we're gonna go this way.
See ya!
Yeah, I guess I should go, too.

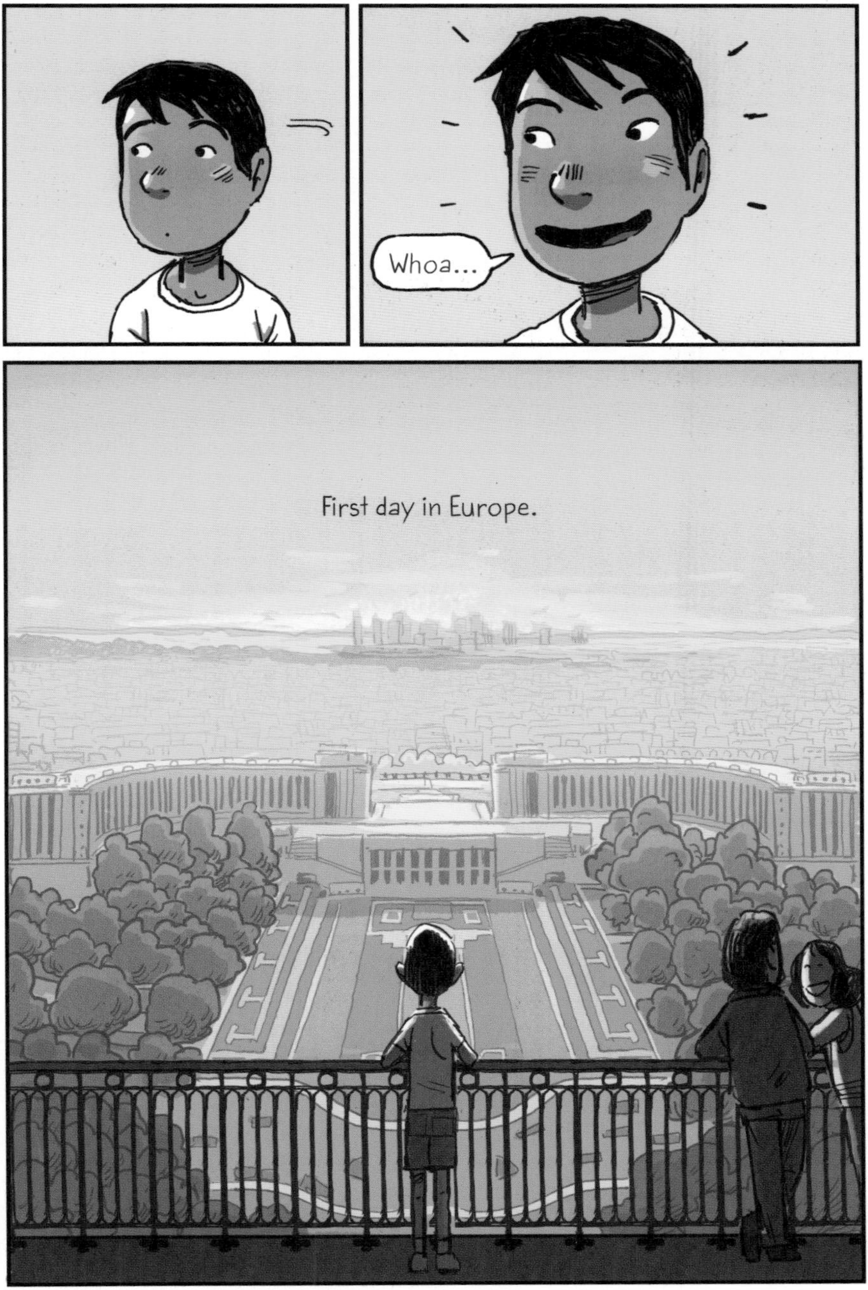
Whoa...
First day in Europe.

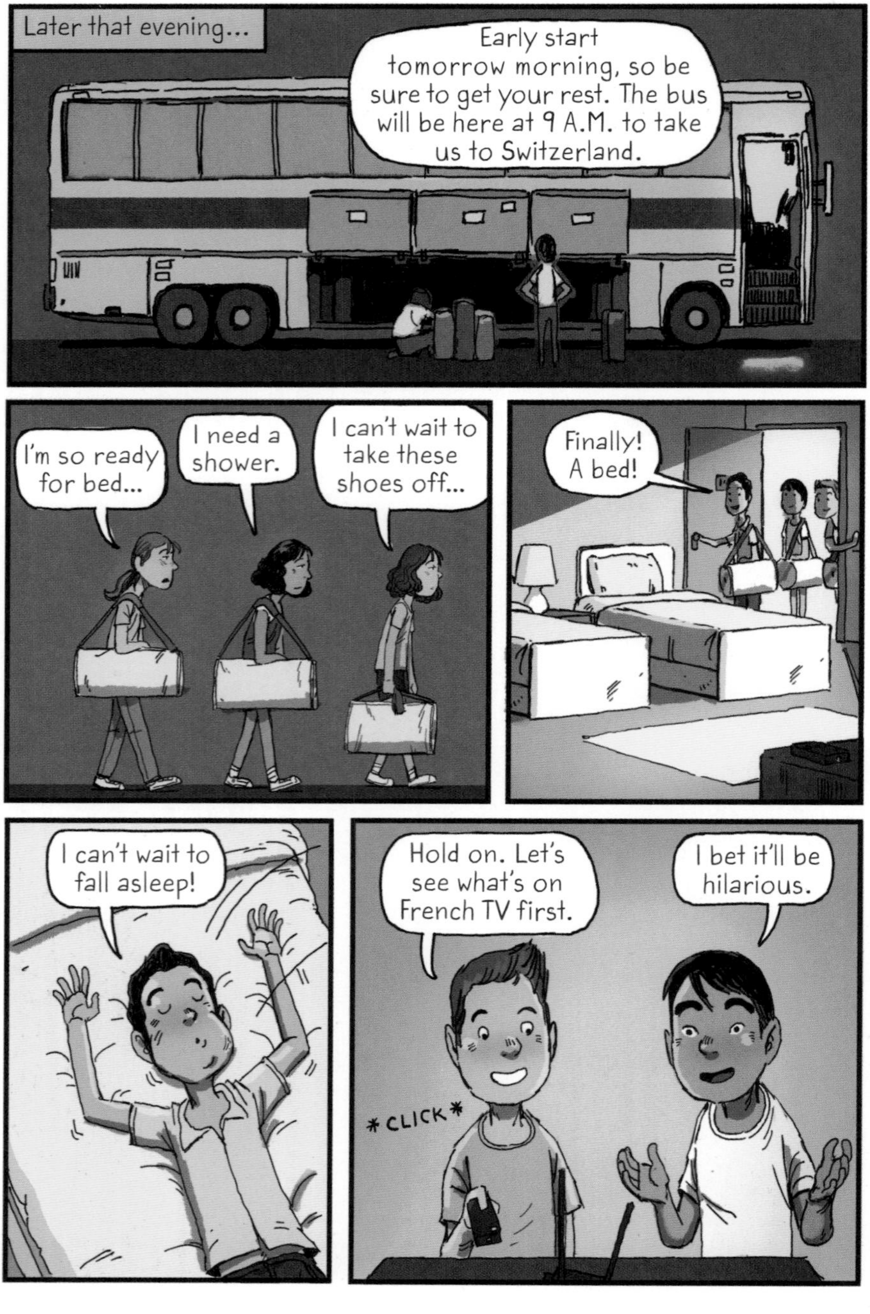
Later that evening...
Early start tomorrow morning, so be sure to get your rest. The bus will be here at 9 A.M. to take us to Switzerland.
I'm so ready for bed...
I need a shower.
I can't wait to take these shoes off...
Finally! A bed!
I can't wait to fall asleep!
Hold on. Let's see what's on French TV first.
I bet it'll be hilarious.
CLICK

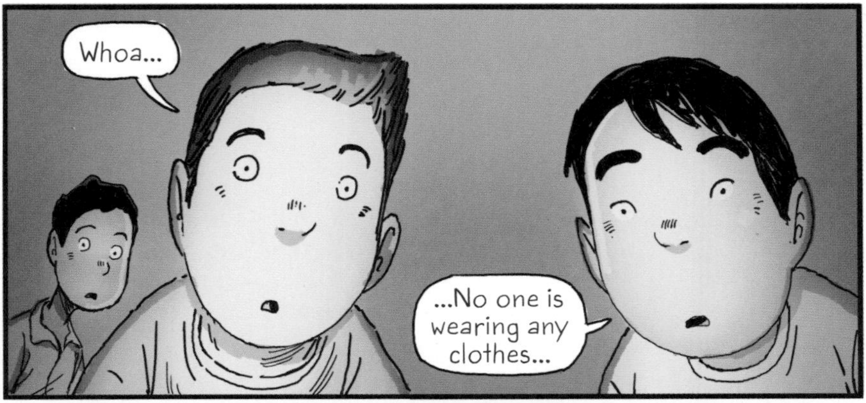
Whoa...
...No one is wearing any clothes...

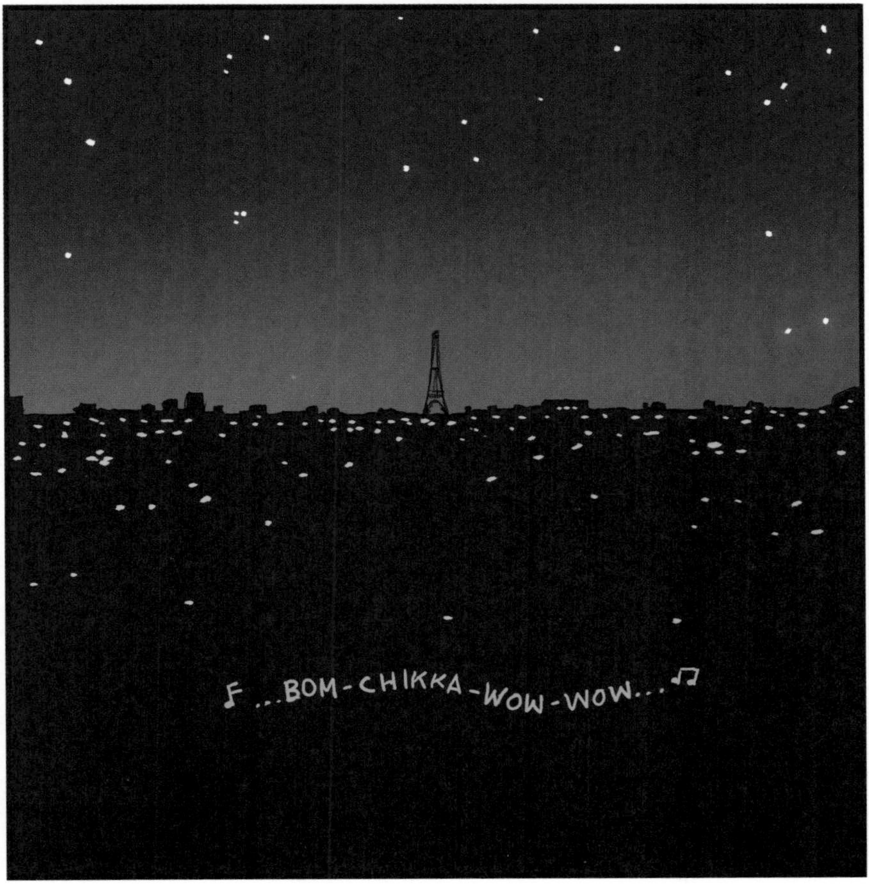
...BOM-CHIKKA-WOW-WOW...

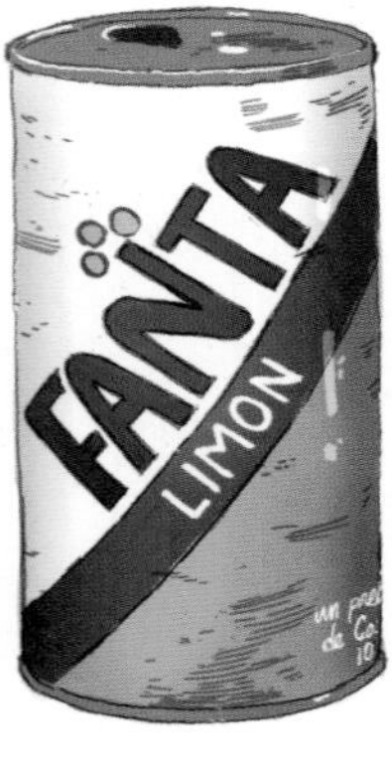
FANTA
LIMON

SWITZERLAND

(19 DAYS LEFT IN THE TRIP)

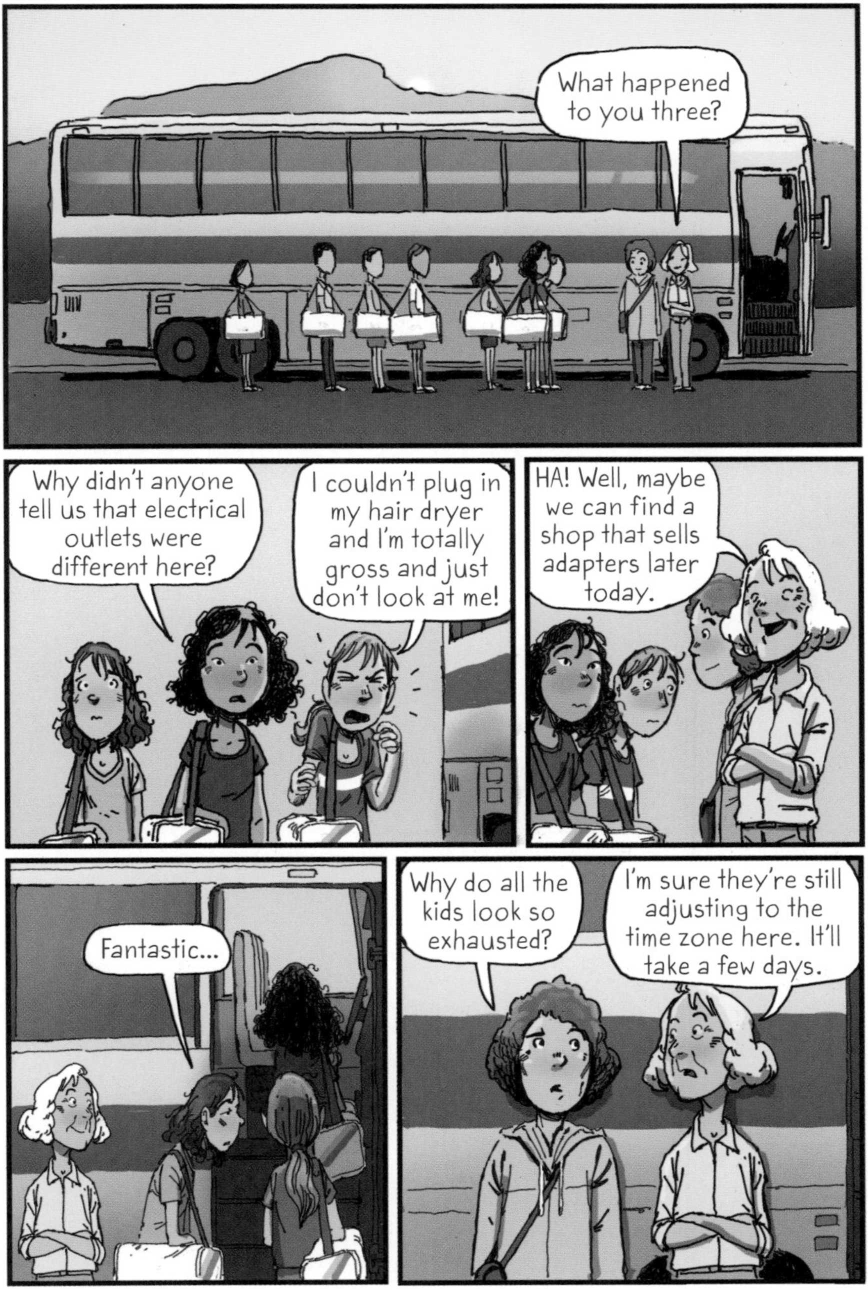
What happened to you three?
Why didn't anyone tell us that electrical outlets were different here?
I couldn't plug in my hair dryer and I'm totally gross and just don't look at me!
HA! Well, maybe we can find a shop that sells adapters later today.
Fantastic...
Why do all the kids look so exhausted?
I'm sure they're still adjusting to the time zone here. It'll take a few days.

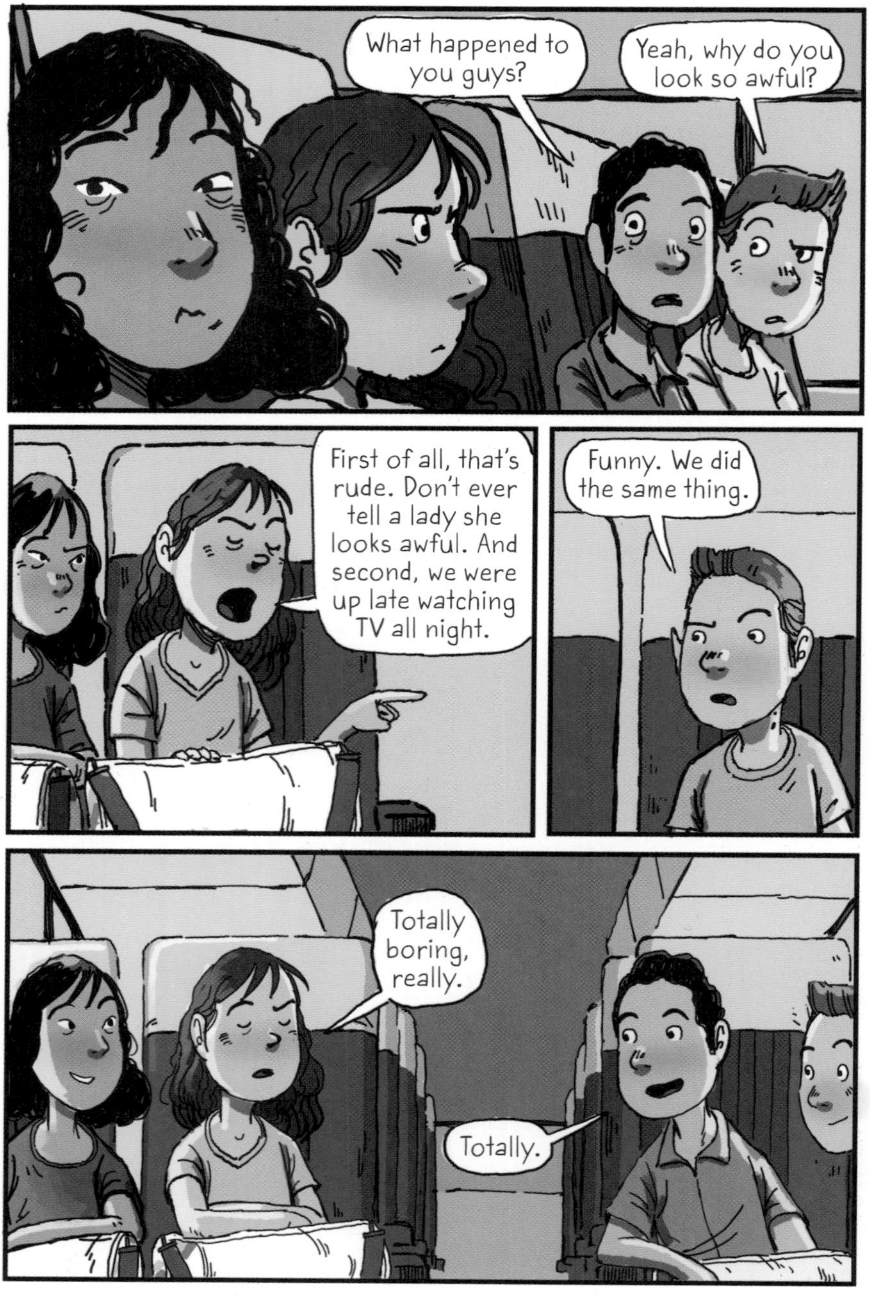
What happened to you guys?
Yeah, why do you look so awful?
First of all, that's rude. Don't ever tell a lady she looks awful. And second, we were up late watching TV all night.
Funny. We did the same thing.
Totally boring, really.
Totally.

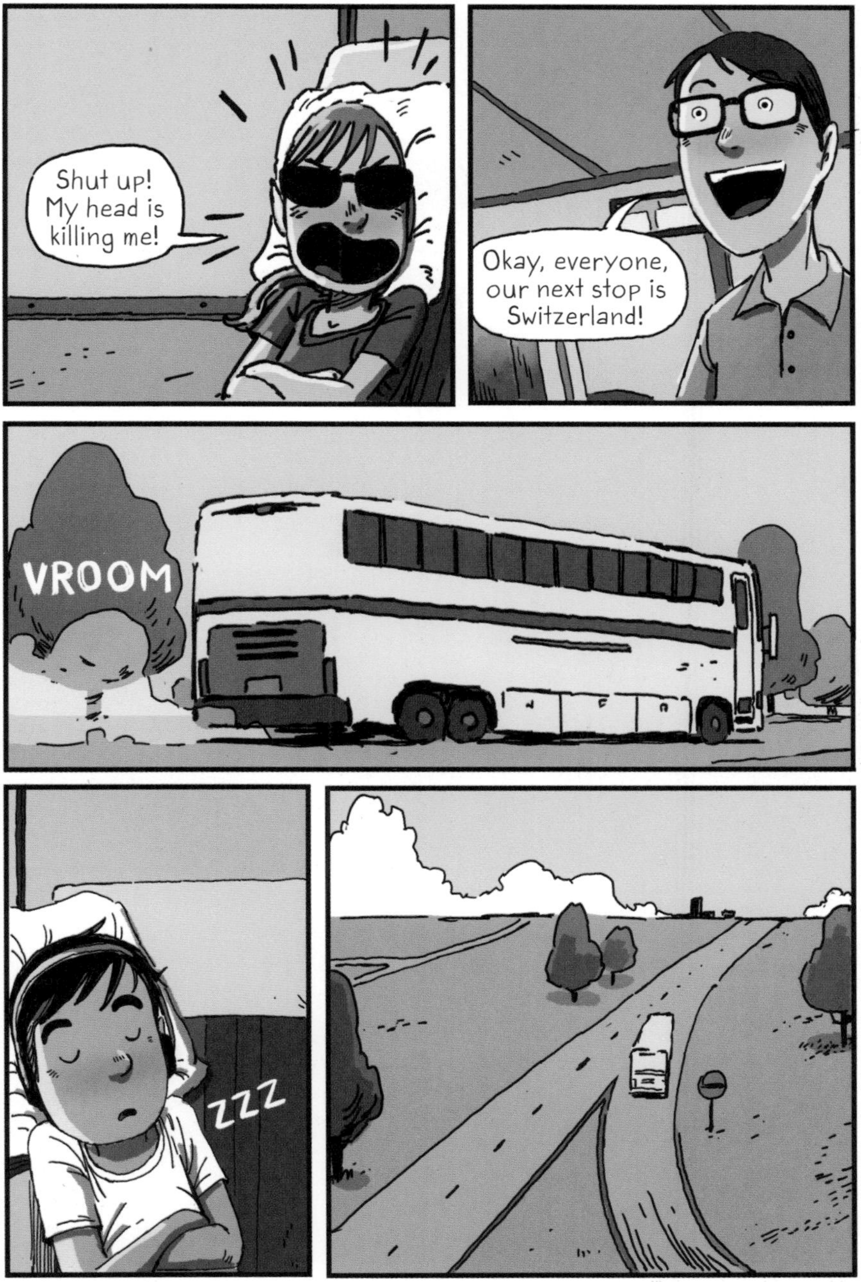
Shut up! My head is killing me!
Okay, everyone, our next stop is Switzerland!
VROOM
ZZZ

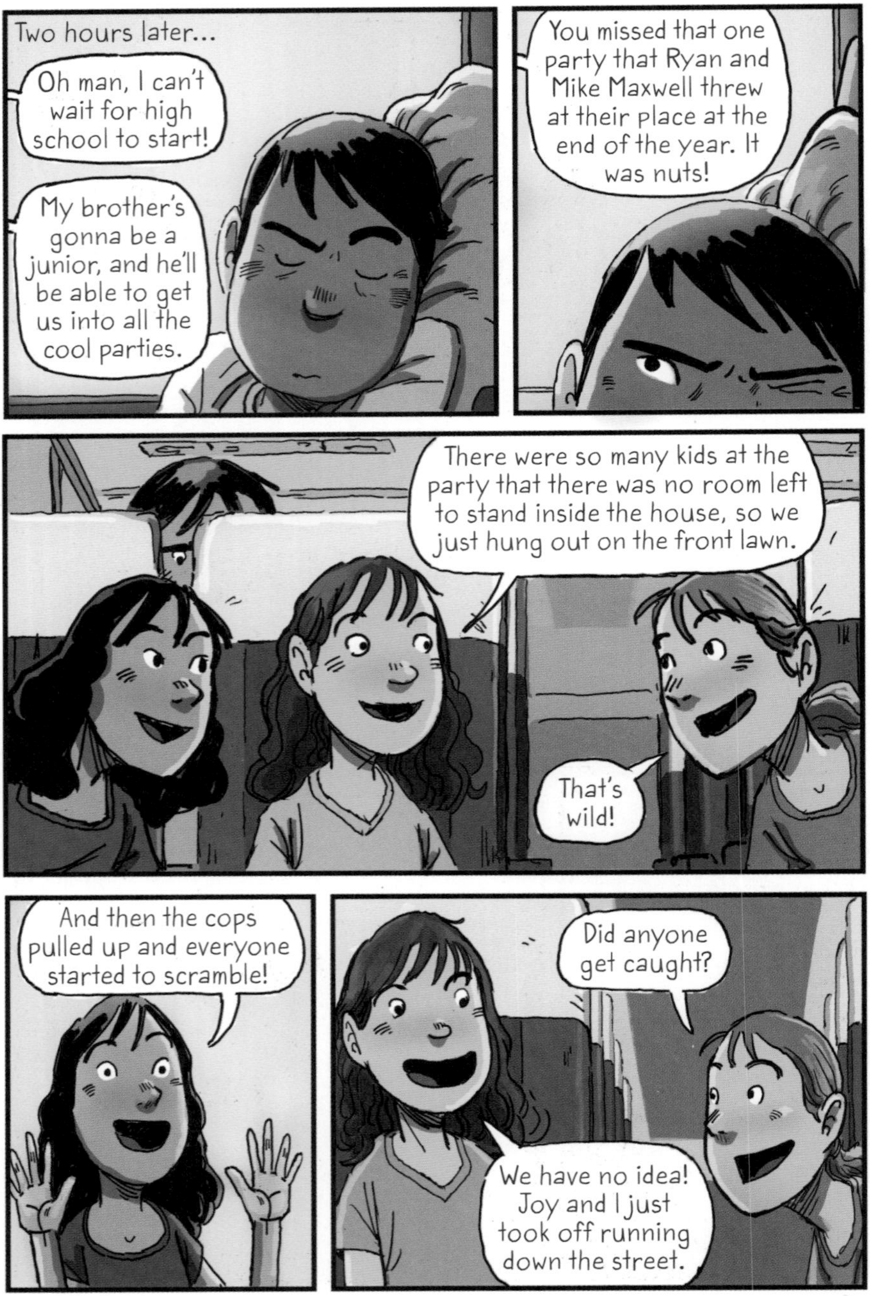
Two hours later...
Oh man, I can't wait for high school to start!
My brother's gonna be a junior, and he'll be able to get us into all the cool parties.
You missed that one party that Ryan and Mike Maxwell threw at their place at the end of the year. It was nuts!
There were so many kids at the party that there was no room left to stand inside the house, so we just hung out on the front lawn.
That's wild!
And then the cops pulled up and everyone started to scramble!
Did anyone get caught?
We have no idea! Joy and I just took off running down the street.

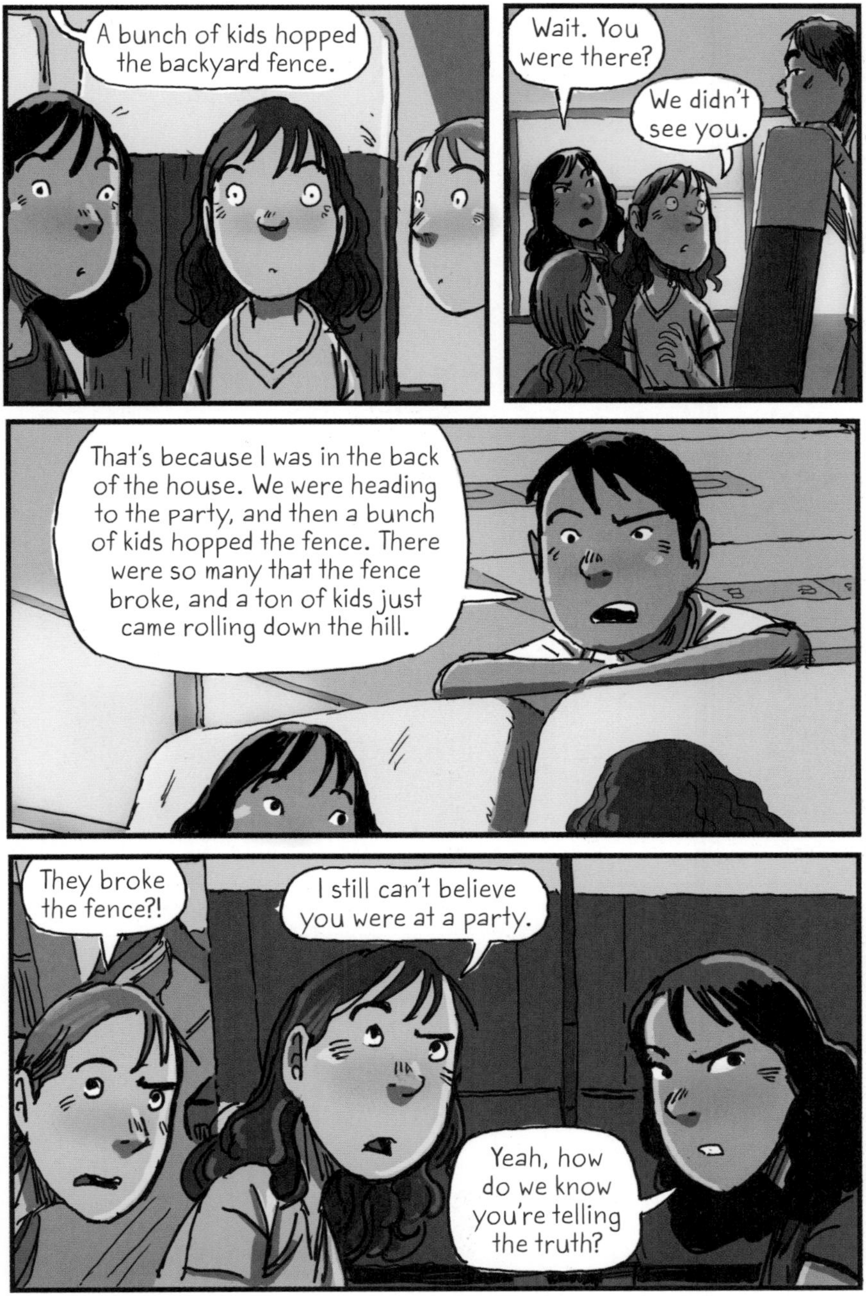
A bunch of kids hopped the backyard fence.
Wait. You were there?
We didn't see you.
That's because I was in the back of the house. We were heading to the party, and then a bunch of kids hopped the fence. There were so many that the fence broke, and a ton of kids just came rolling down the hill.
They broke the fence?!
I still can't believe you were at a party.
Yeah, how do we know you're telling the truth?

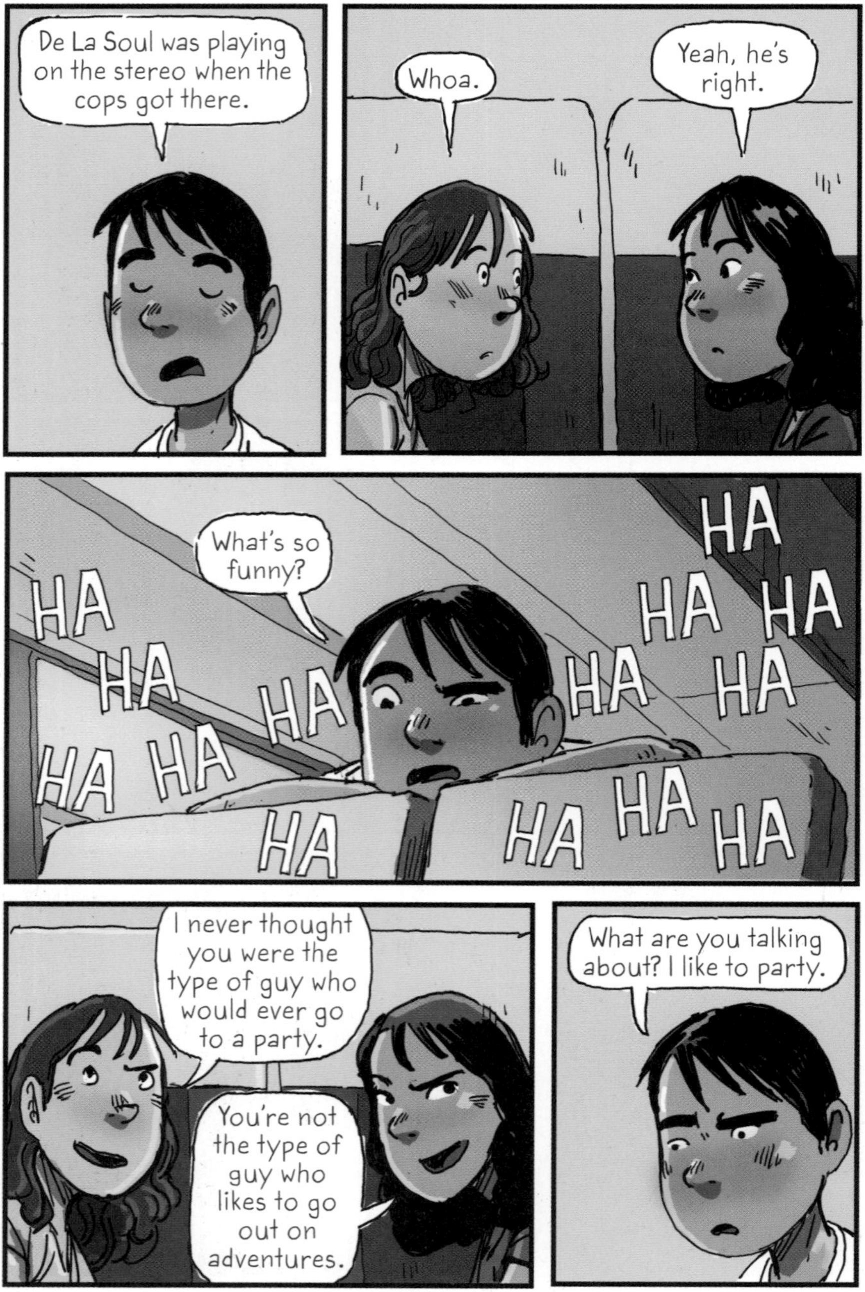
De La Soul was playing on the stereo when the cops got there.
Whoa.
Yeah, he's right.
What's so funny?
HA HA HA HA HA HA HA HA HA HA HA HA HA HA HA
I never thought you were the type of guy who would ever go to a party.
You're not the type of guy who likes to go out on adventures.
What are you talking about? I like to party.

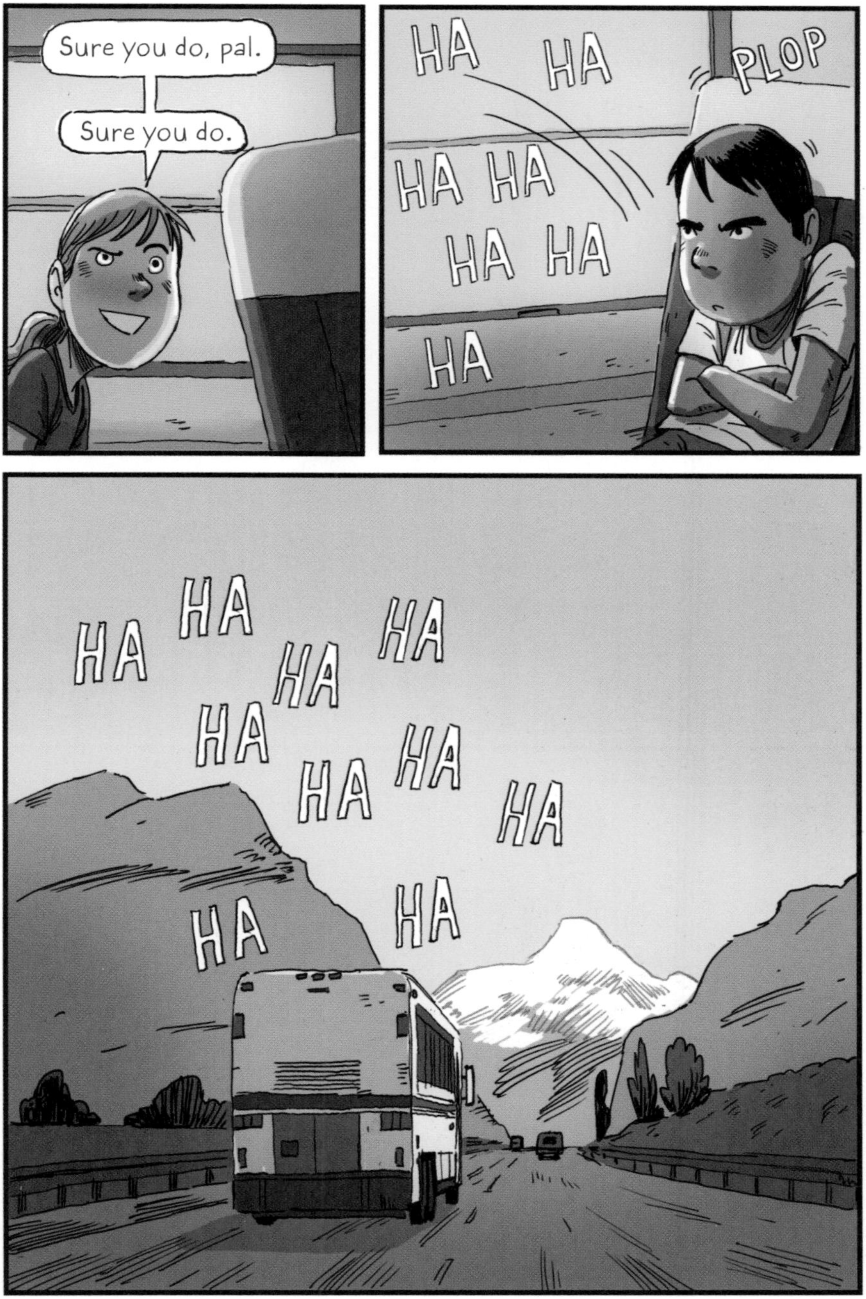
Sure you do, pal.
Sure you do.
HA HA
PLOP
HA HA
HA HA
HA
HA HA HA
HA
HA
HA HA
HA
HA HA

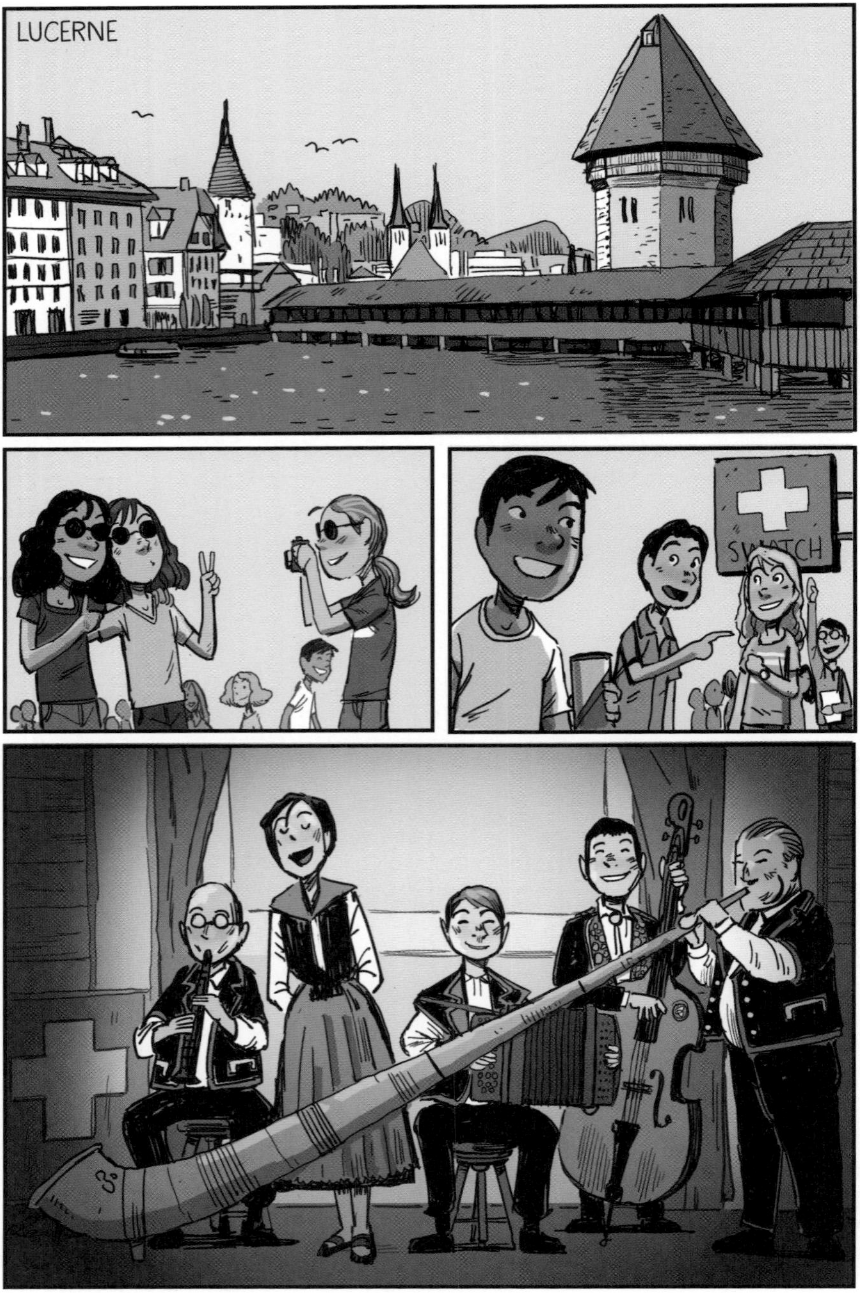
LUCERNE
SWATCH

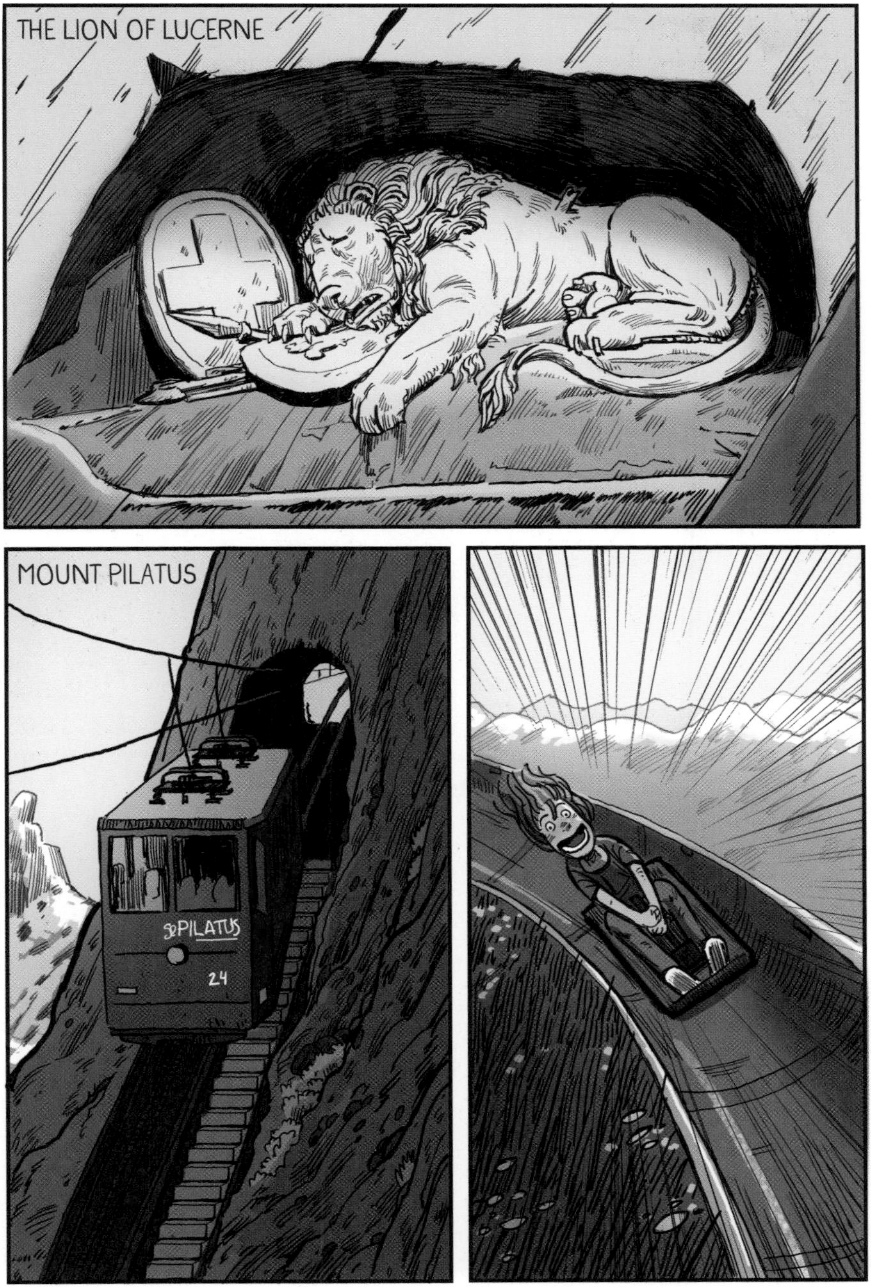
THE LION OF LUCERNE
MOUNT PILATUS
PILATUS
24

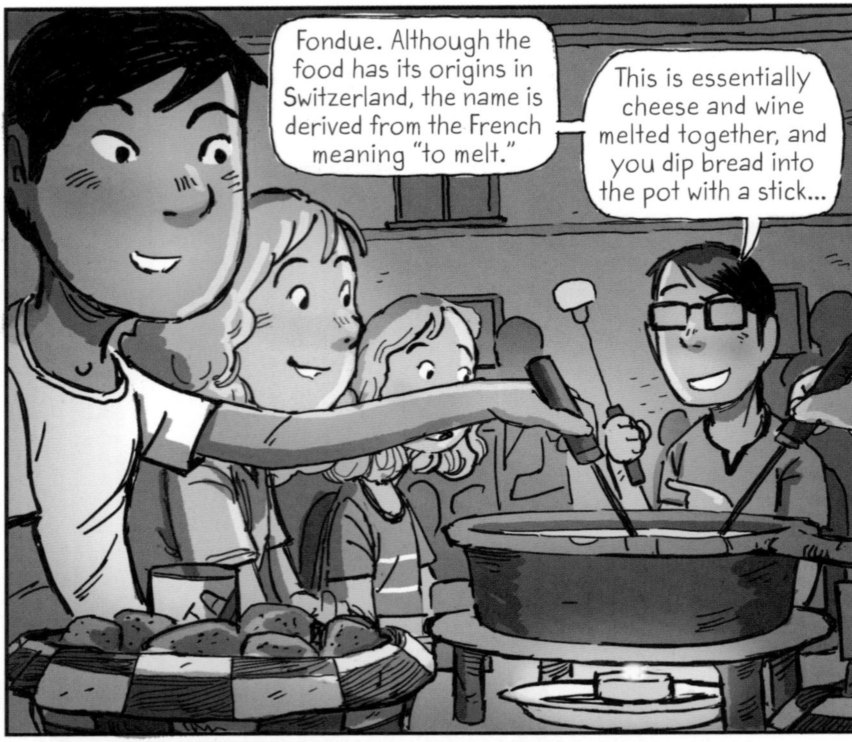
Fondue. Although the food has its origins in Switzerland, the name is derived from the French meaning "to melt."
This is essentially cheese and wine melted together, and you dip bread into the pot with a stick...

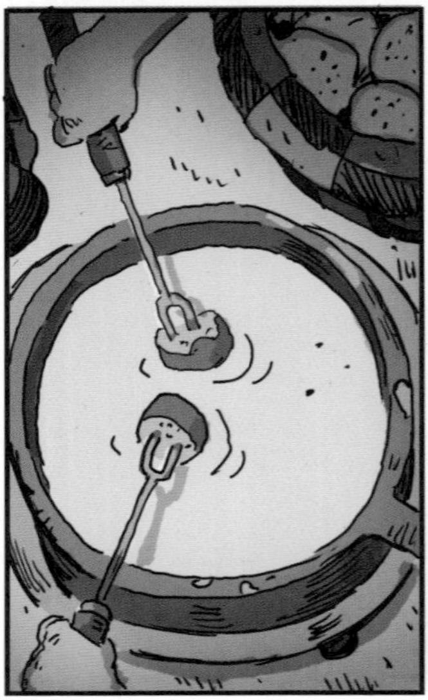

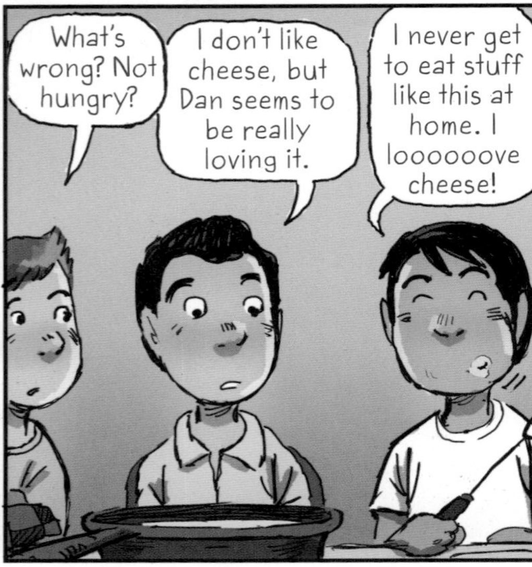
What's wrong? Not hungry?
I don't like cheese, but Dan seems to be really loving it.
I never get to eat stuff like this at home. I loooooove cheese!

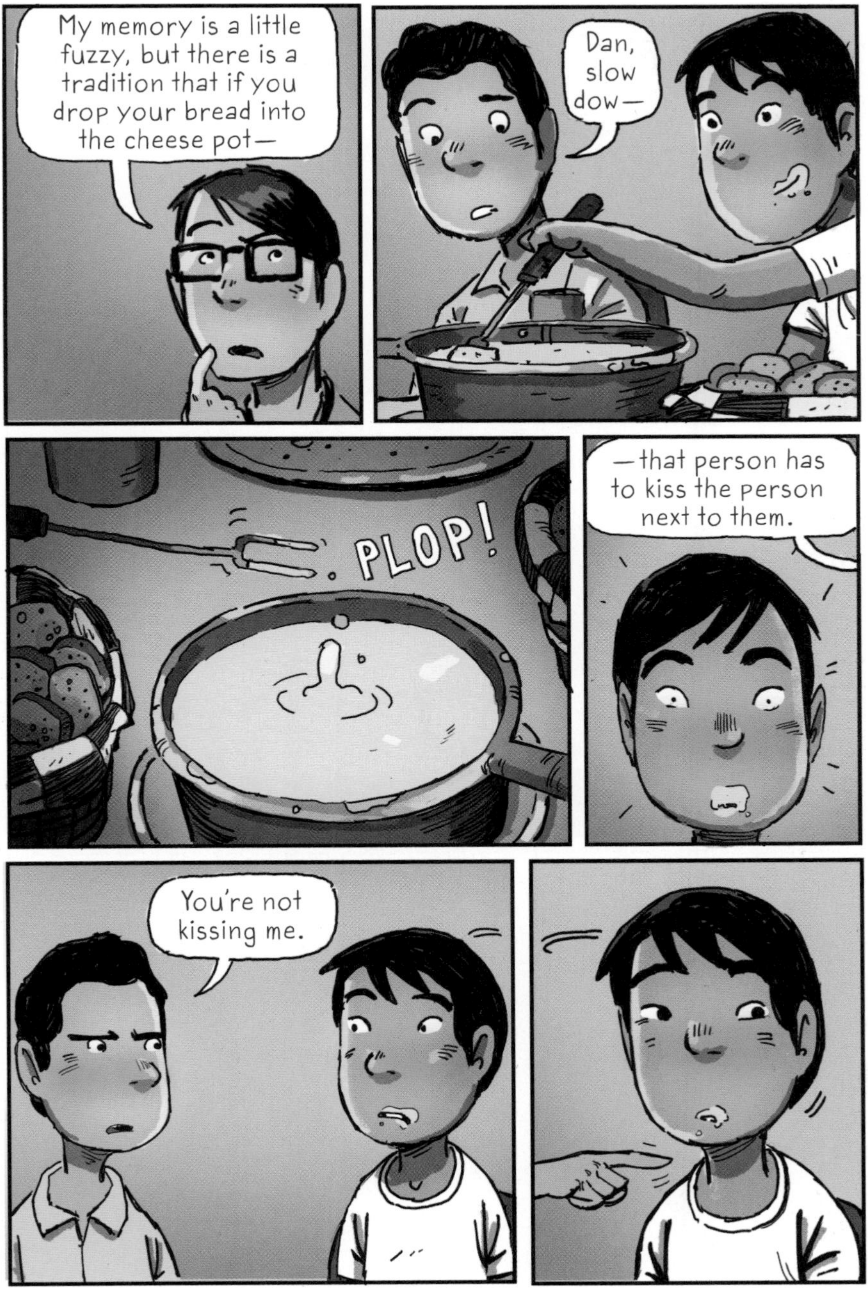
My memory is a little fuzzy, but there is a tradition that if you drop your bread into the cheese pot—
Dan, slow dow—
PLOP!
—that person has to kiss the person next to them.
You're not kissing me.

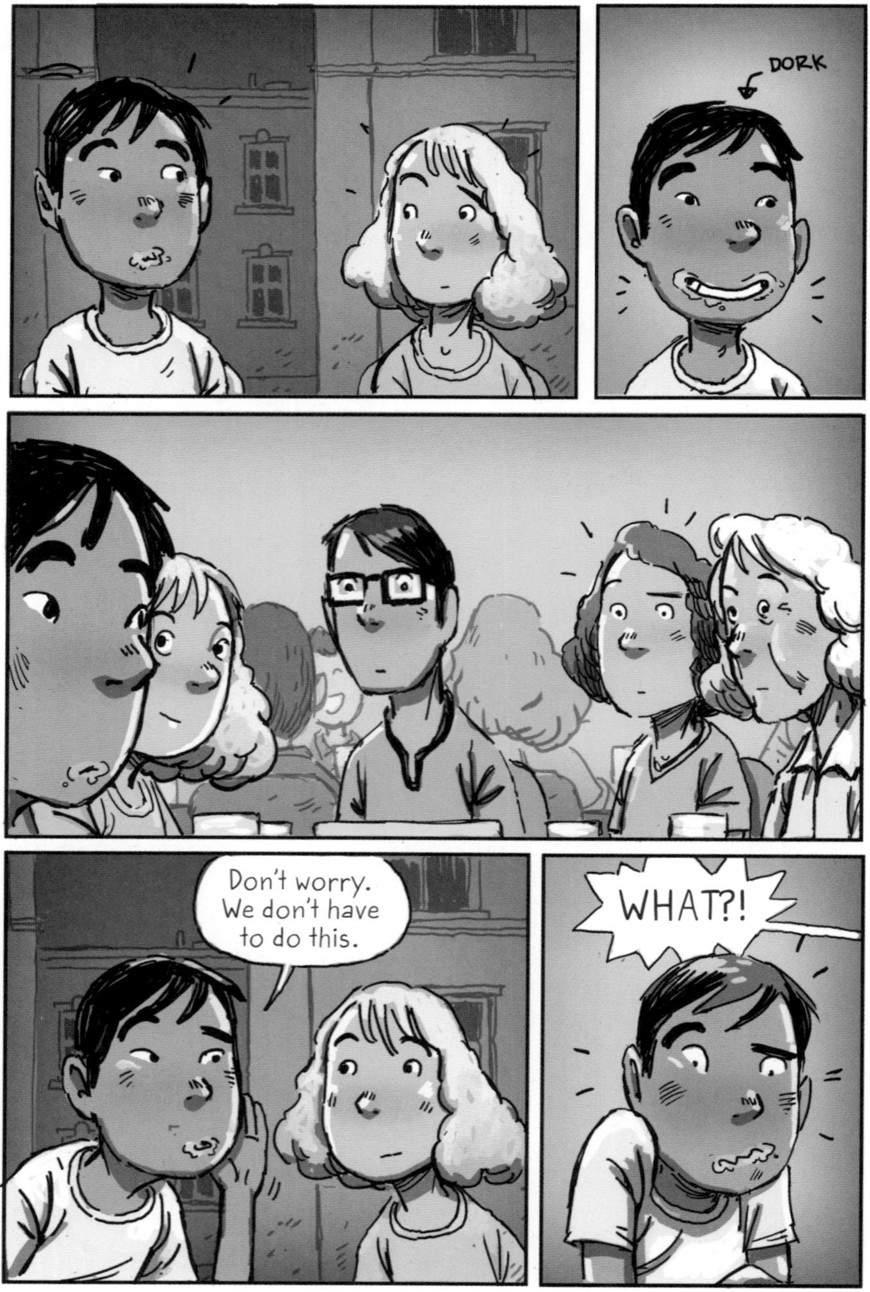
DORK
Don't worry. We don't have to do this.
WHAT?!

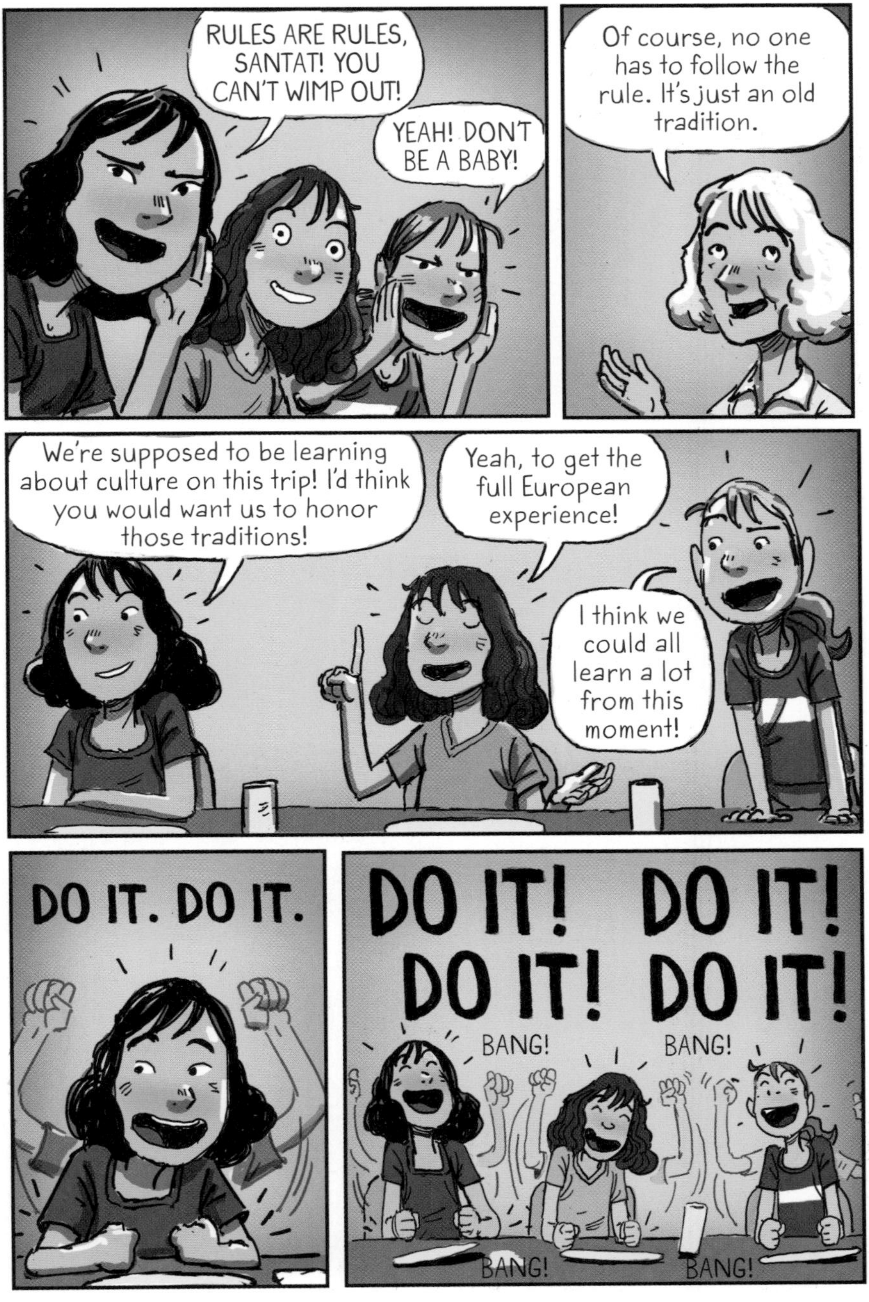
RULES ARE RULES, SANTAT! YOU CAN'T WIMP OUT!
YEAH! DON'T BE A BABY!
Of course, no one has to follow the rule. It's just an old tradition.
We're supposed to be learning about culture on this trip! I'd think you would want us to honor those traditions!
Yeah, to get the full European experience!
I think we could all learn a lot from this moment!
DO IT. DO IT.
DO IT! DO IT! DO IT! DO IT!
BANG!
BANG!
BANG!
BANG!

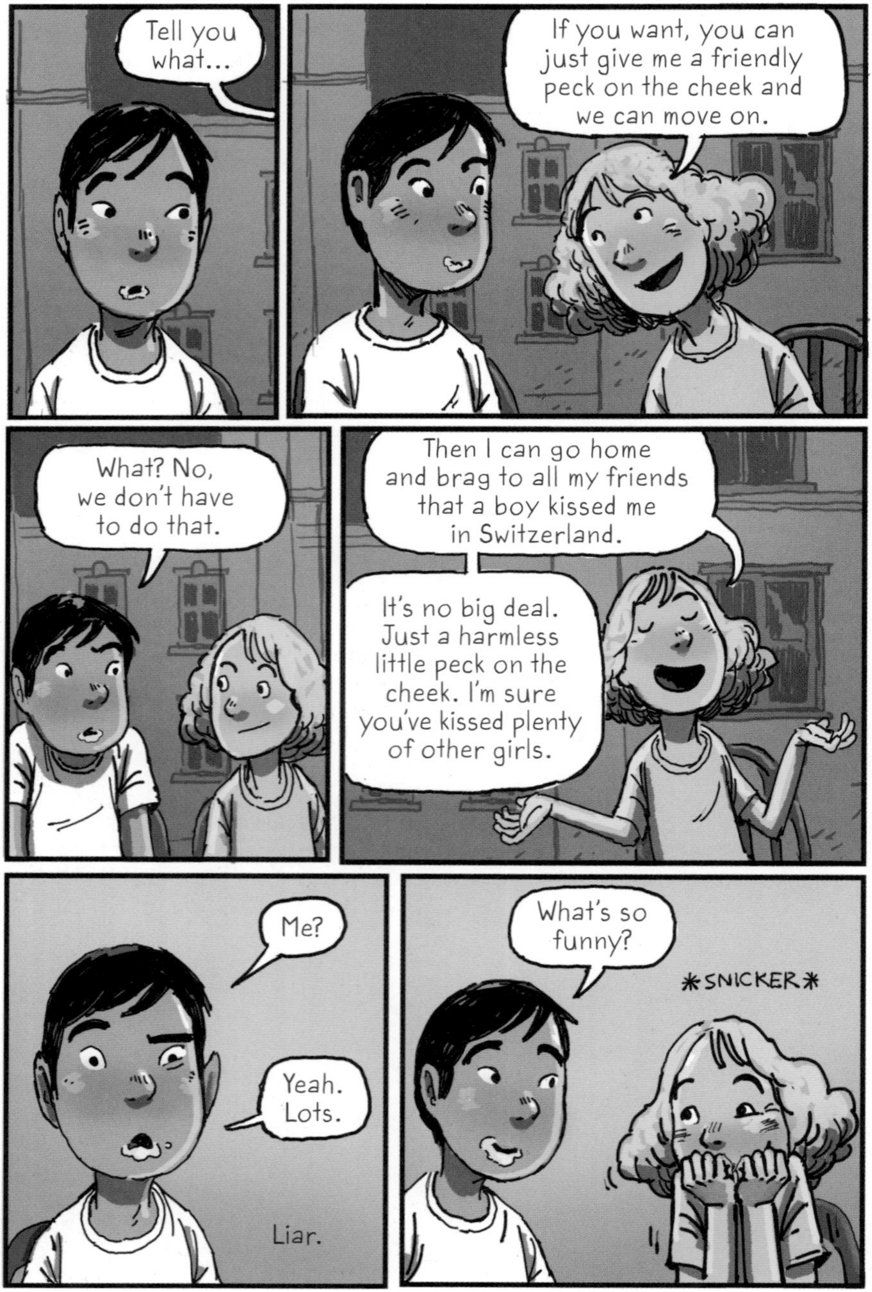
Tell you what...
If you want, you can just give me a friendly peck on the cheek and we can move on.
What? No, we don't have to do that.
Then I can go home and brag to all my friends that a boy kissed me in Switzerland.
It's no big deal. Just a harmless little peck on the cheek. I'm sure you've kissed plenty of other girls.
Me?
Yeah. Lots.
Liar.
What's so funny?
SNICKER

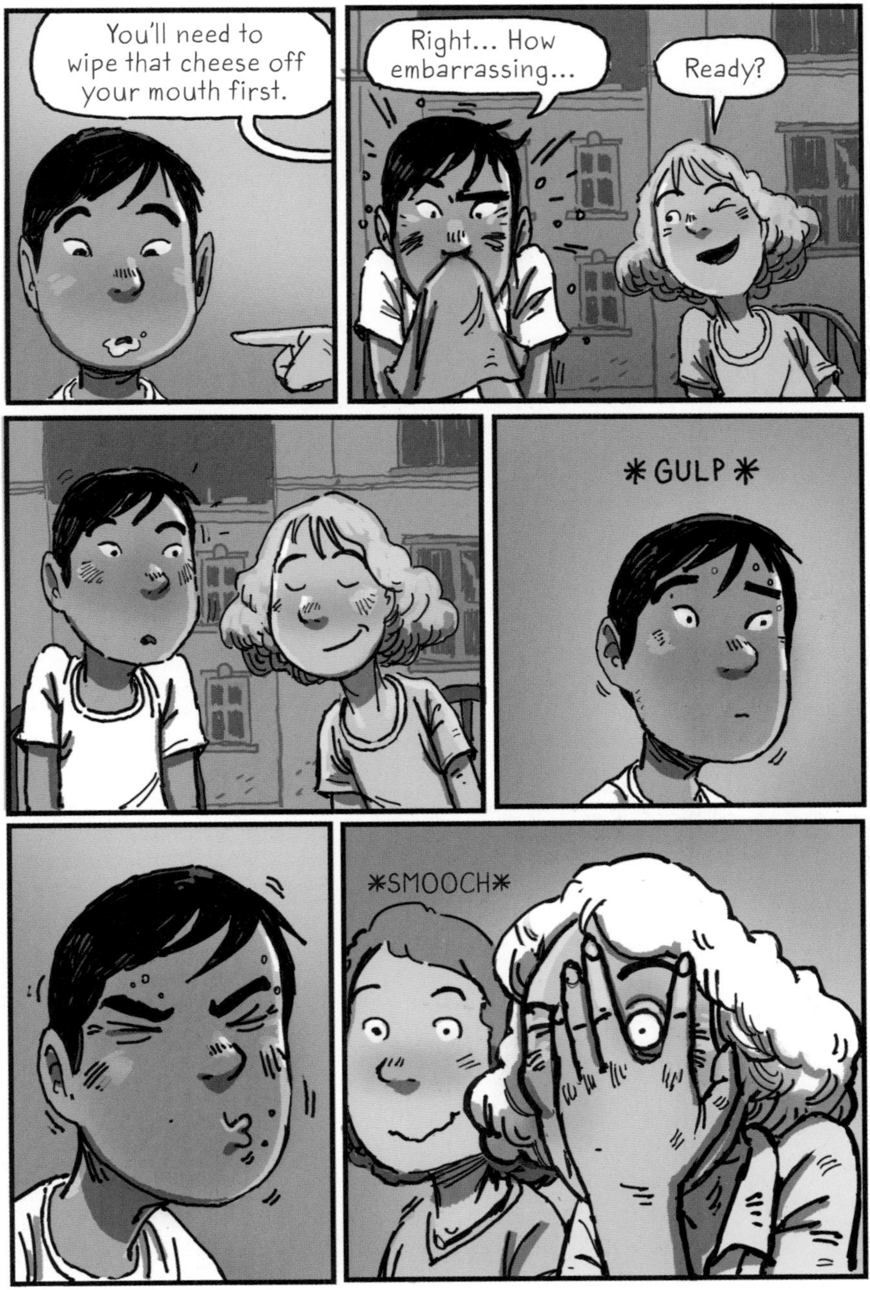
You'll need to wipe that cheese off your mouth first.
Right... How embarrassing...
Ready?
GULP
SMOOCH

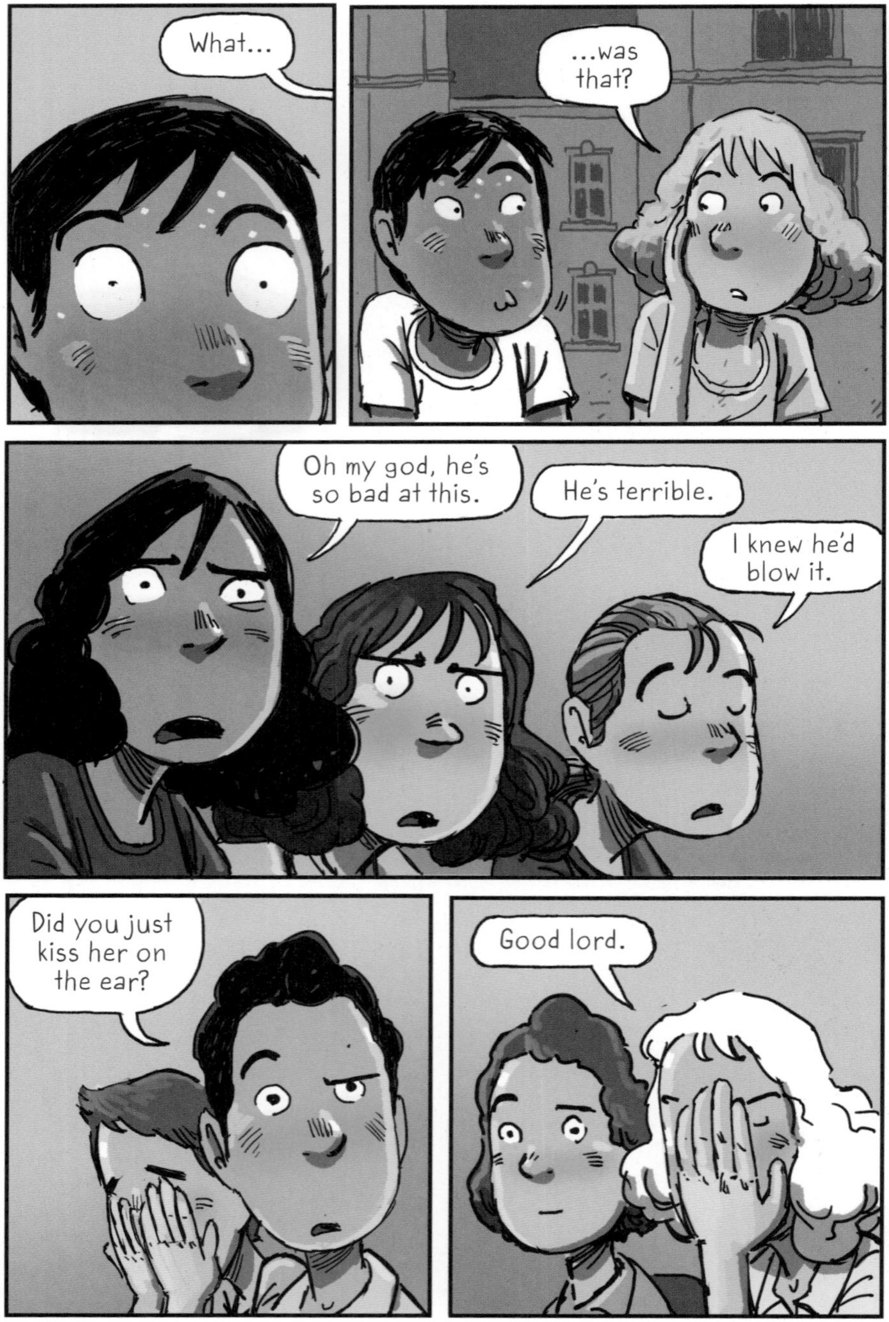
What...
...was that?
Oh my god, he's so bad at this.
He's terrible.
I knew he'd blow it.
Did you just kiss her on the ear?
Good lord.

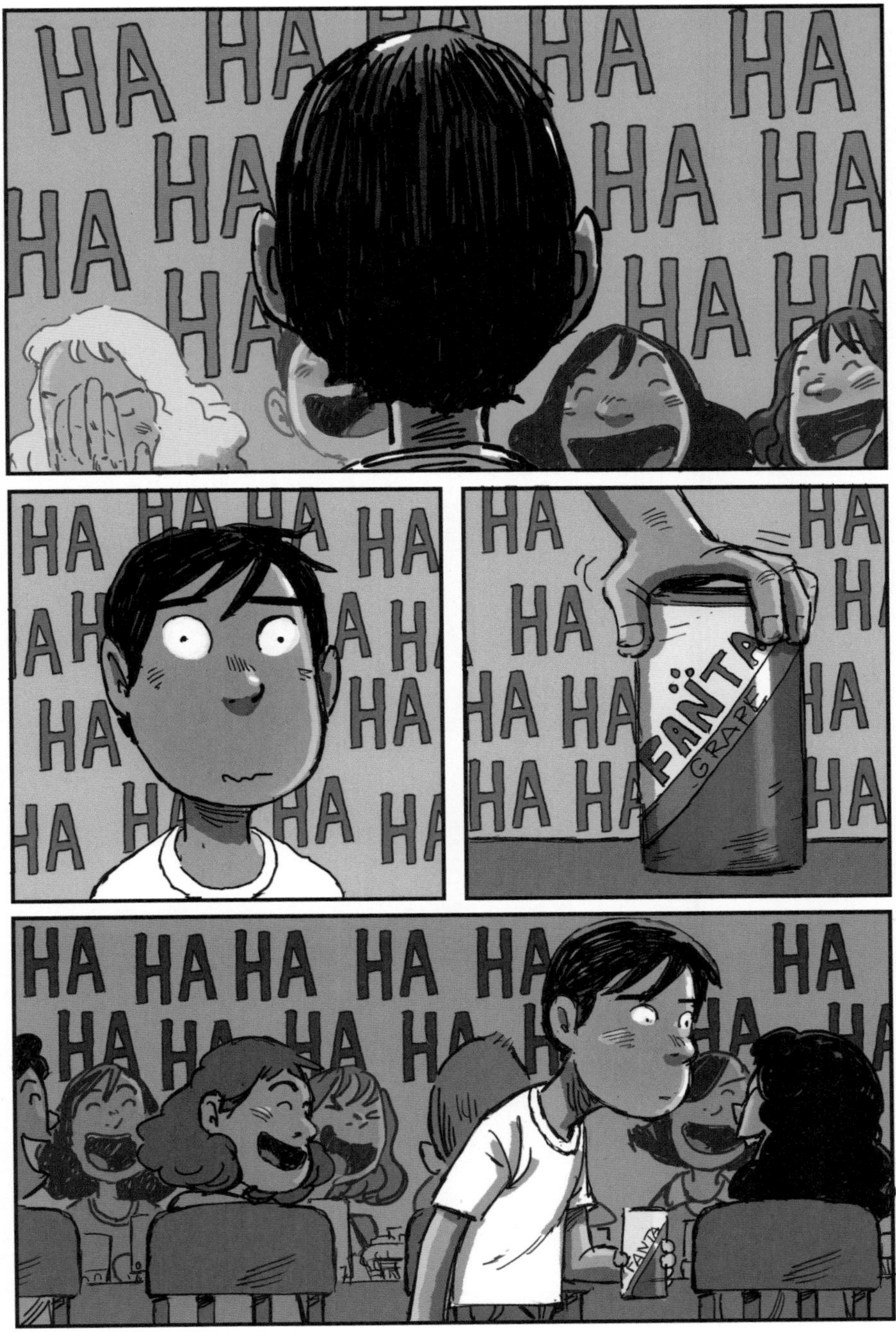
HA HA HA HA HA
HA HA HA HA
HA HA HA HA HA HA HA HA
HA HA HA HA HA HA HA HA
FANTA
GRAPE
HA HA HA HA HA HA HA HA HA HA
HA HA HA HA HA HA HA HA HA

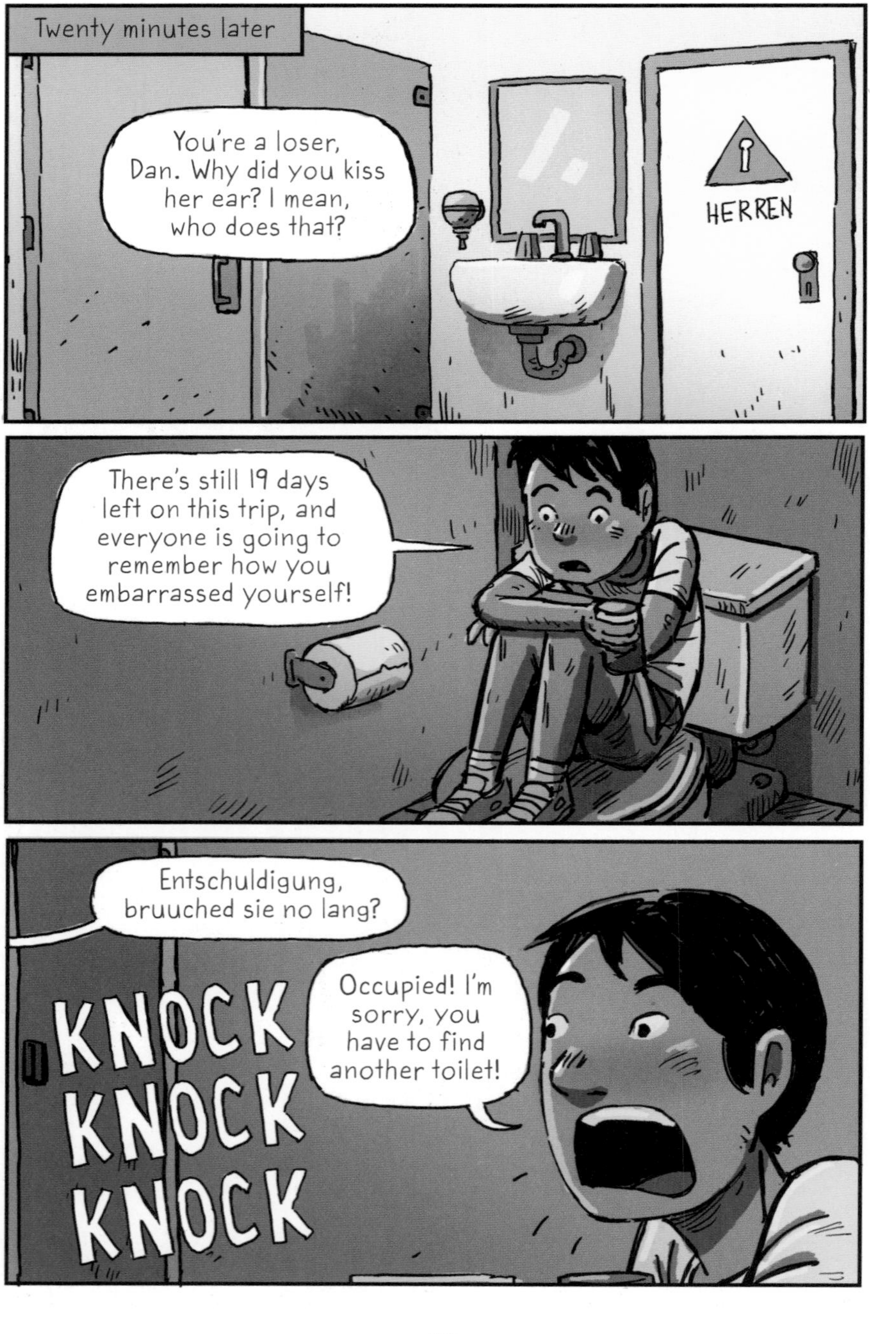
Twenty minutes later
You're a loser, Dan. Why did you kiss her ear? I mean, who does that?
HERREN
There's still 19 days left on this trip, and everyone is going to remember how you embarrassed yourself!
Entschuldigung, bruuched sie no lang?
KNOCK KNOCK KNOCK
Occupied! I'm sorry, you have to find another toilet!

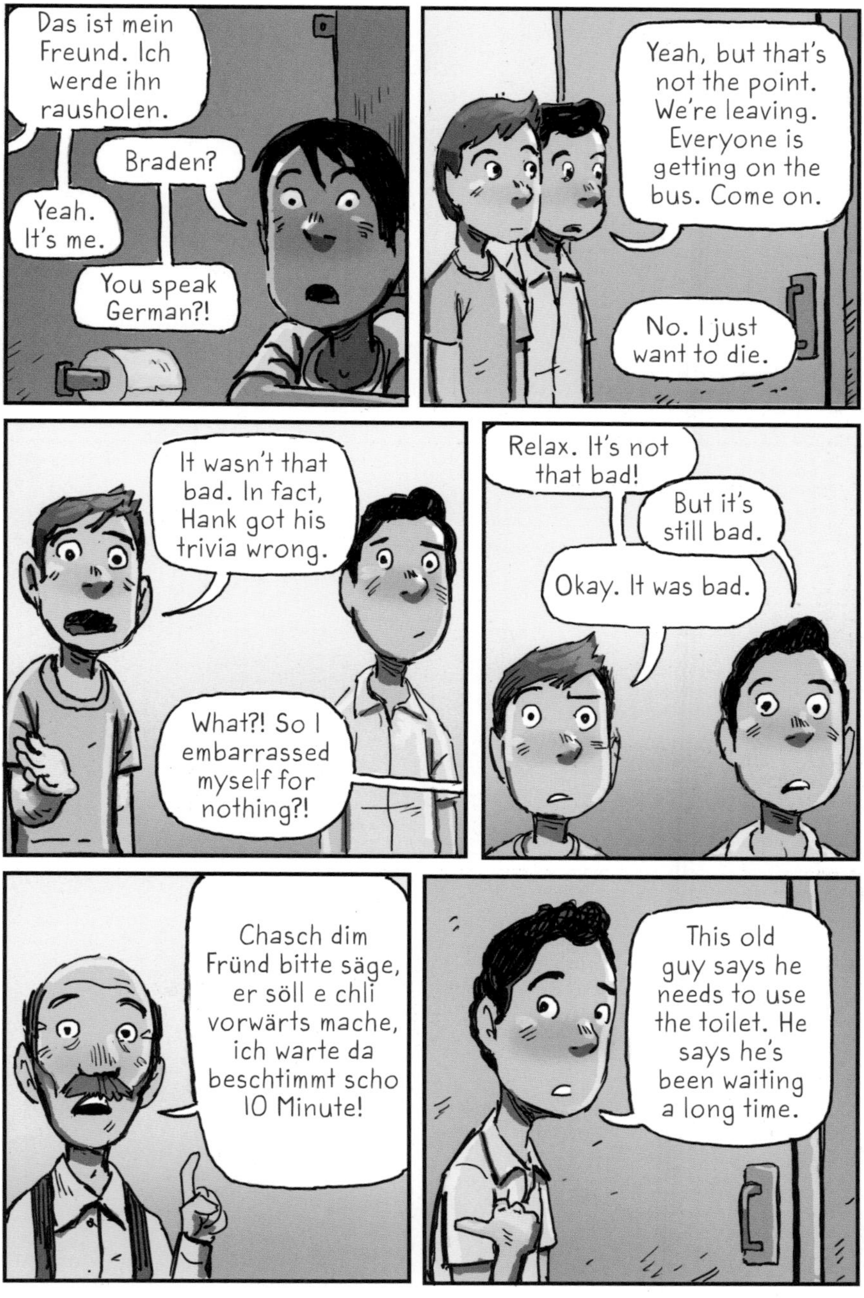
Das ist mein Freund. Ich werde ihn rausholen.
Braden?
Yeah. It's me.
You speak German?!
Yeah, but that's not the point. We're leaving. Everyone is getting on the bus. Come on.
No. I just want to die.
It wasn't that bad. In fact, Hank got his trivia wrong.
What?! So I embarrassed myself for nothing?!
Relax. It's not that bad!
But it's still bad.
Okay. It was bad.
Chasch dim Fründ bitte säge, er söll e chli vorwärts mache, ich warte da beschtimmt scho 10 Minute!
This old guy says he needs to use the toilet. He says he's been waiting a long time.

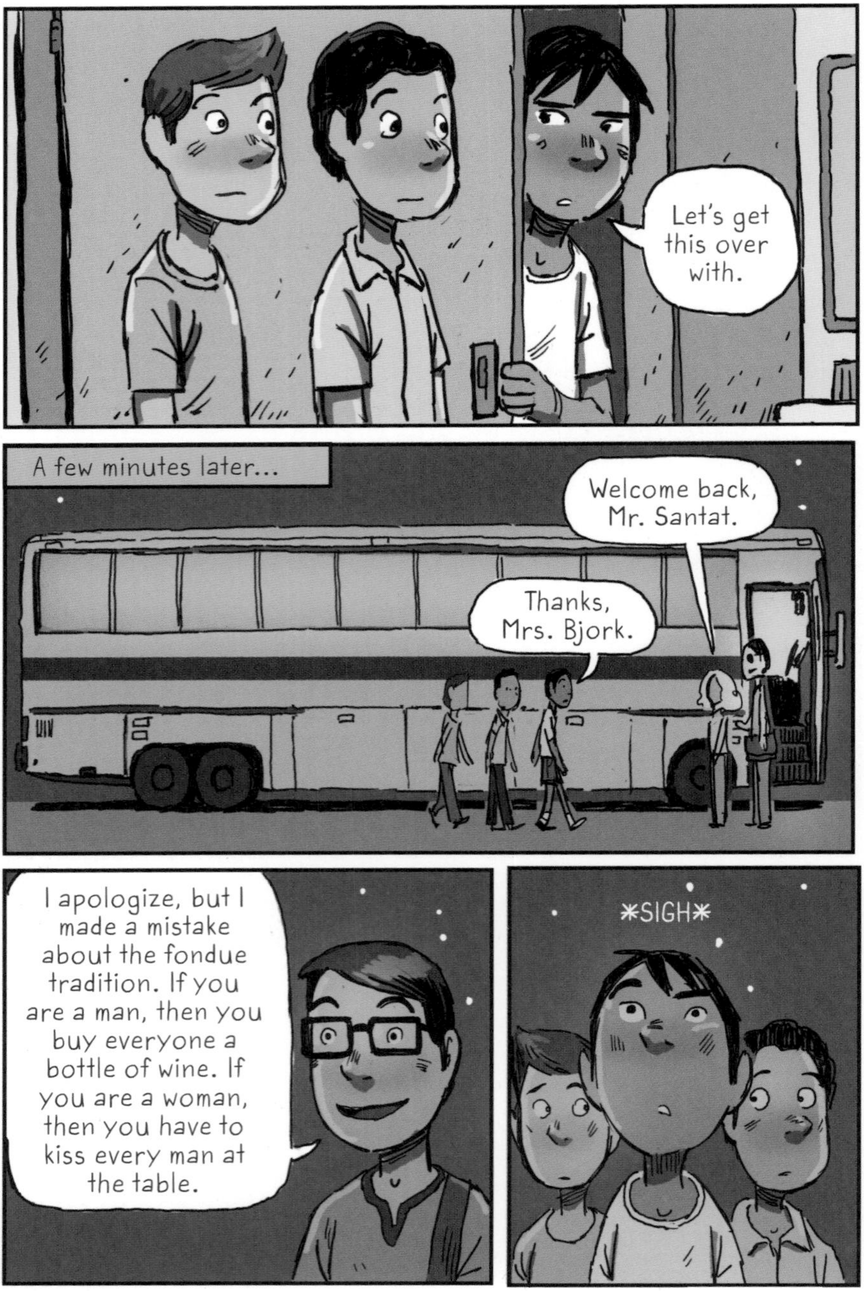
Let's get this over with.
A few minutes later...
Welcome back, Mr. Santat.
Thanks, Mrs. Bjork.
I apologize, but I made a mistake about the fondue tradition. If you are a man, then you buy everyone a bottle of wine. If you are a woman, then you have to kiss every man at the table.
SIGH

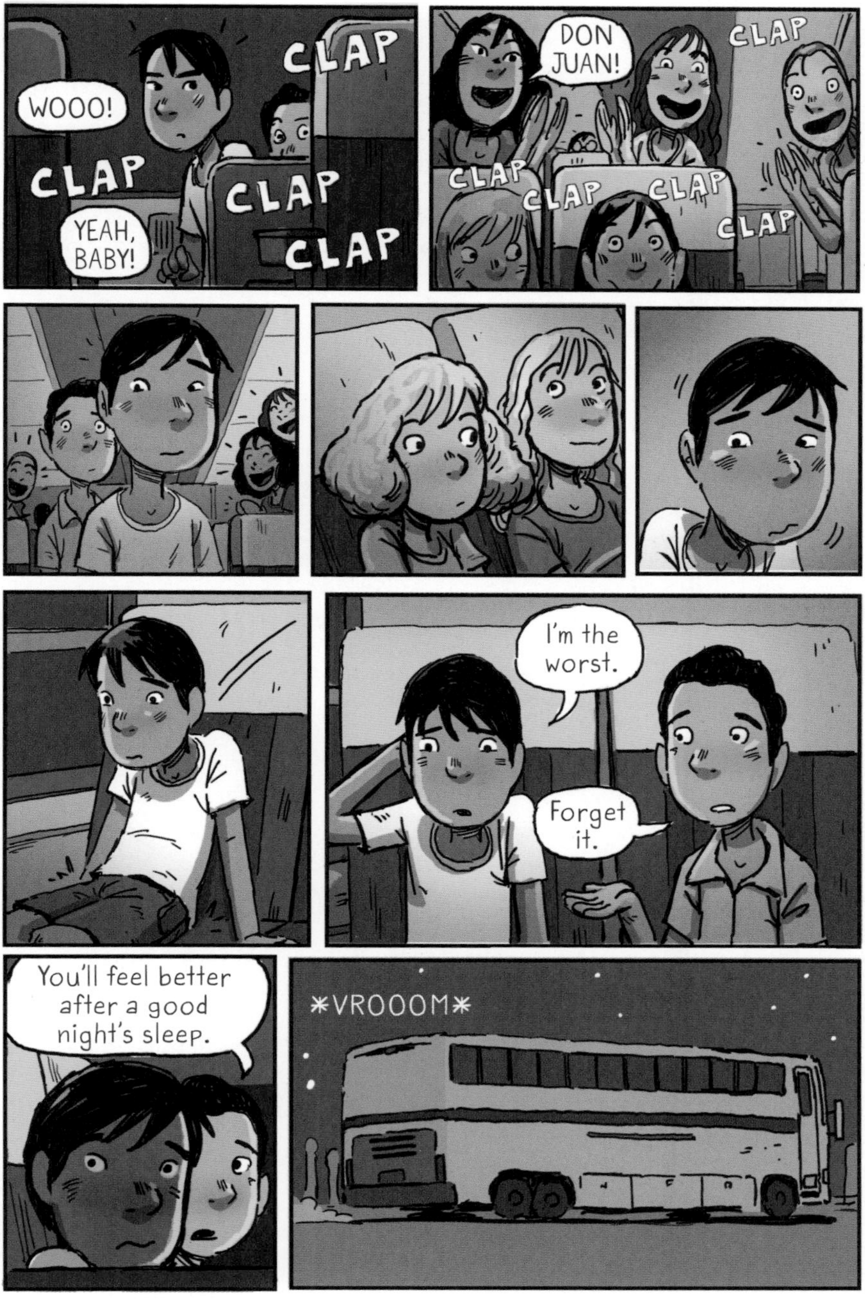
WOOO!
CLAP
CLAP
CLAP
CLAP
YEAH, BABY!
DON JUAN!
CLAP
CLAP
CLAP
CLAP
CLAP
I'm the worst.
Forget it.
You'll feel better after a good night's sleep.
VROOOM

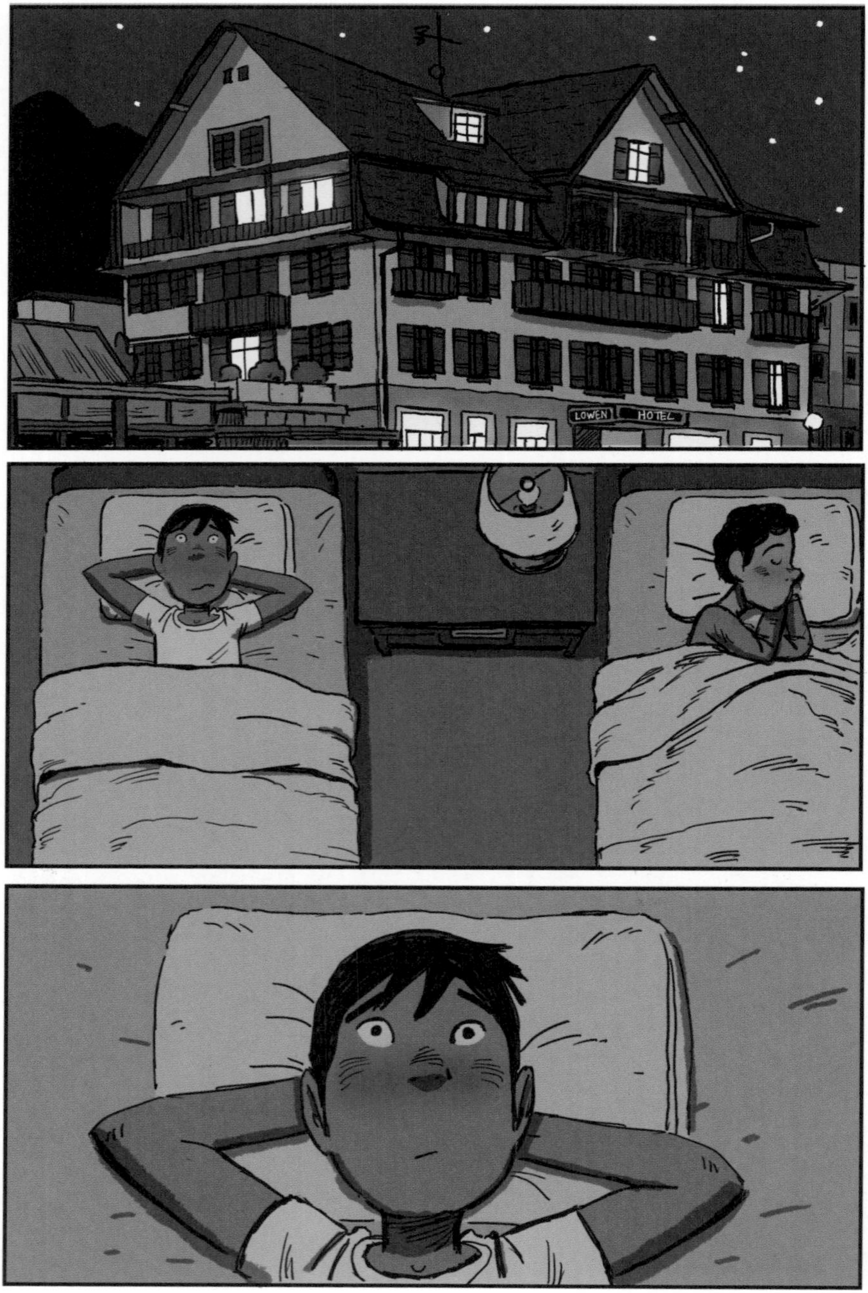
LOWEN
HOTEL

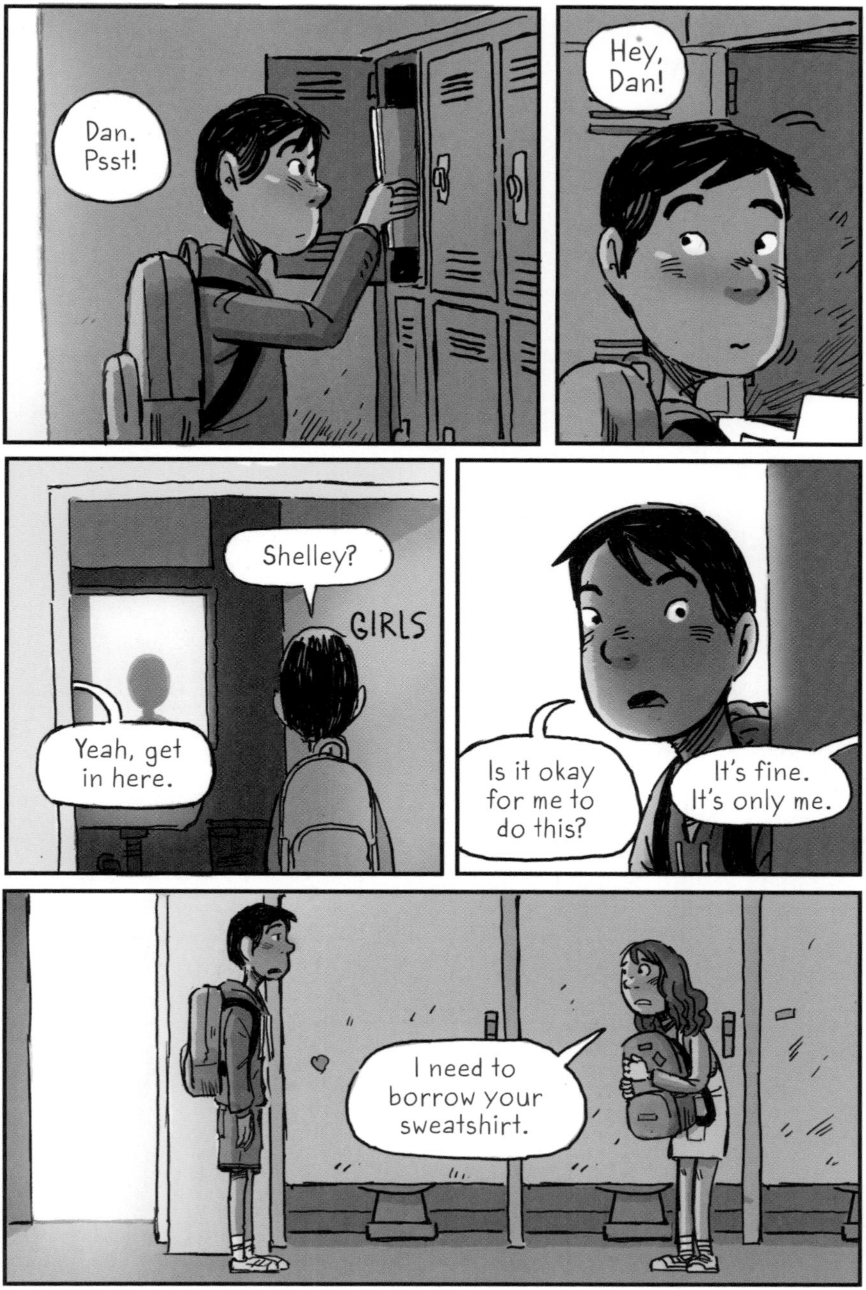
Dan. Psst!
Hey, Dan!
Shelley?
GIRLS
Yeah, get in here.
Is it okay for me to do this?
It's fine. It's only me.
I need to borrow your sweatshirt.

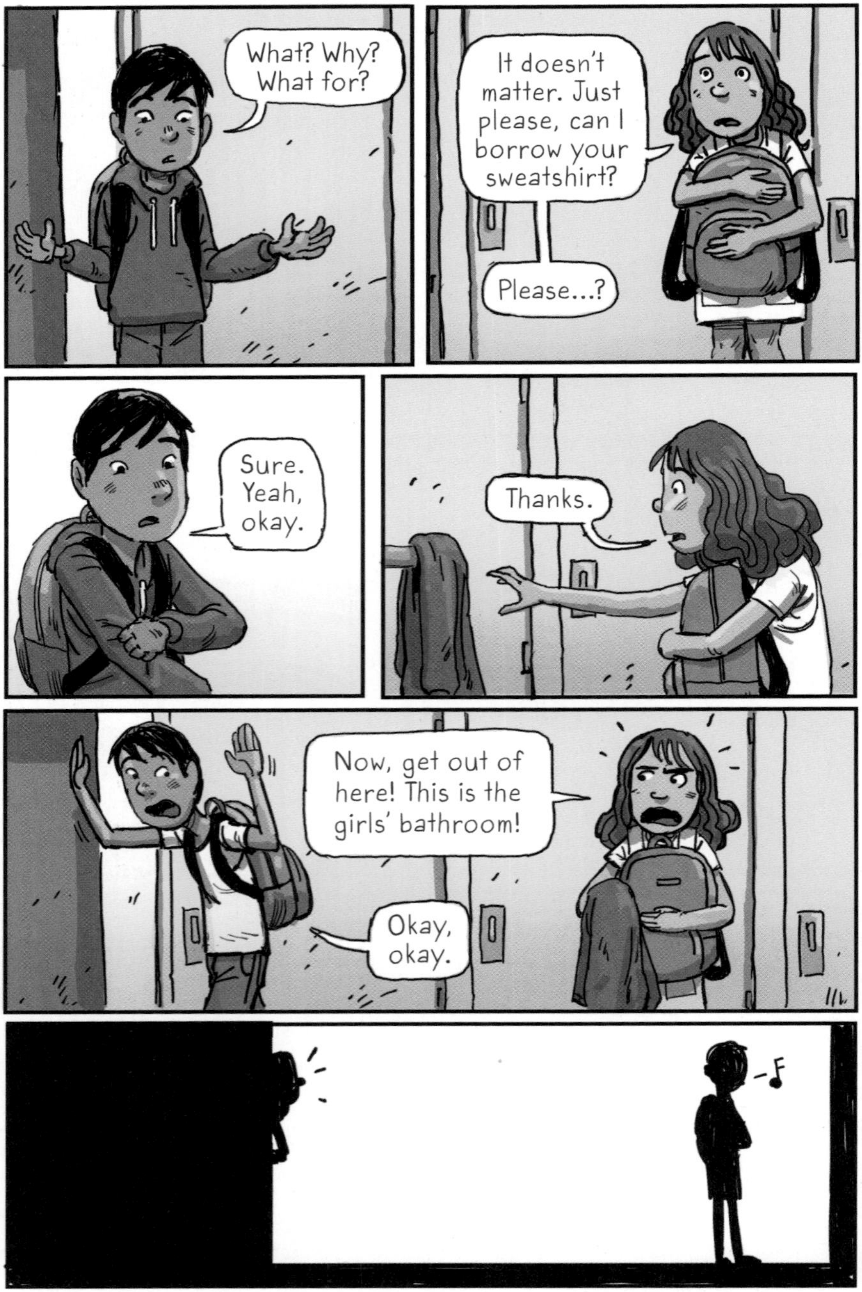
What? Why? What for?
It doesn't matter. Just please, can I borrow your sweatshirt?
Please...?
Sure. Yeah, okay.
Thanks.
Now, get out of here! This is the girls' bathroom!
Okay, okay.

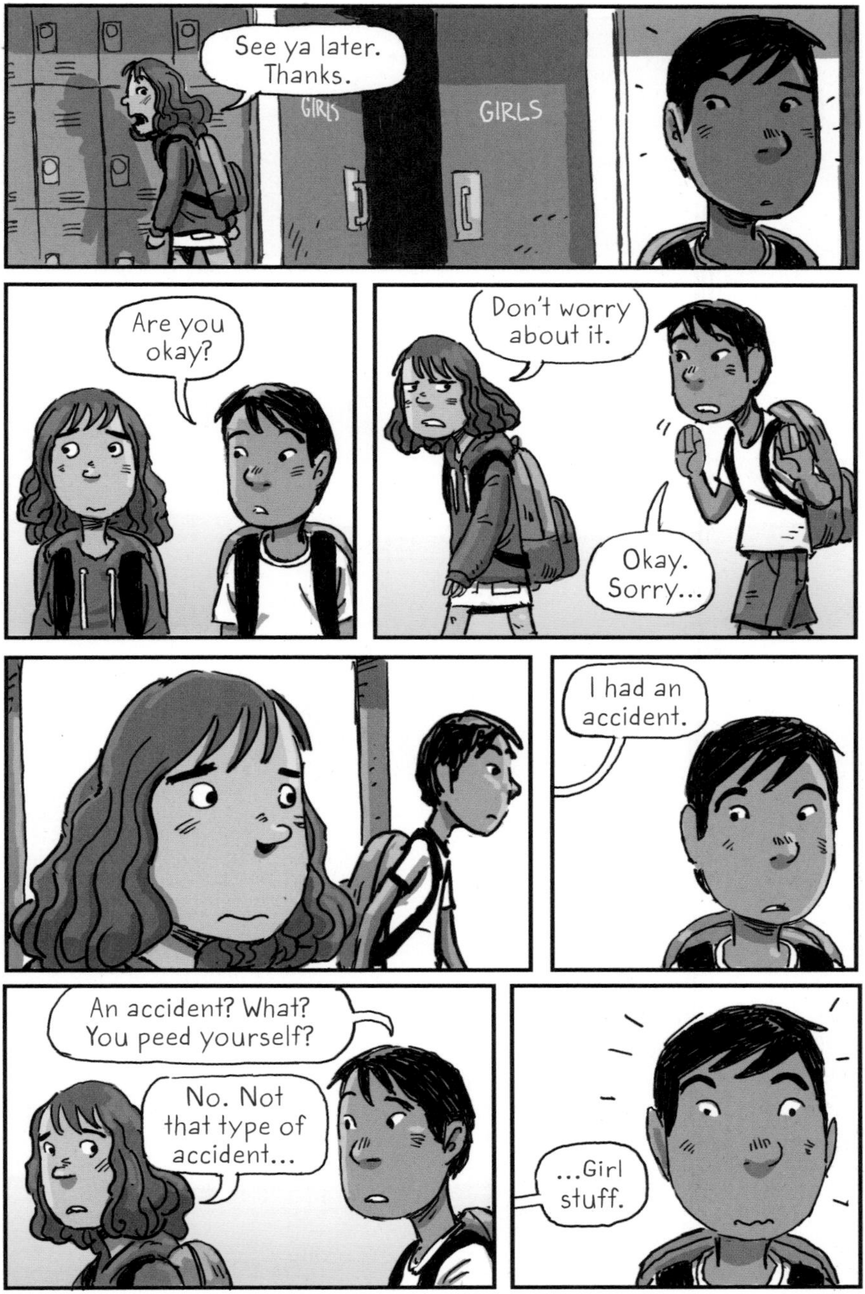
See ya later. Thanks.
GIRLS
GIRLS
Are you okay?
Don't worry about it.
Okay. Sorry...
I had an accident.
An accident? What? You peed yourself?
No. Not that type of accident...
...Girl stuff.

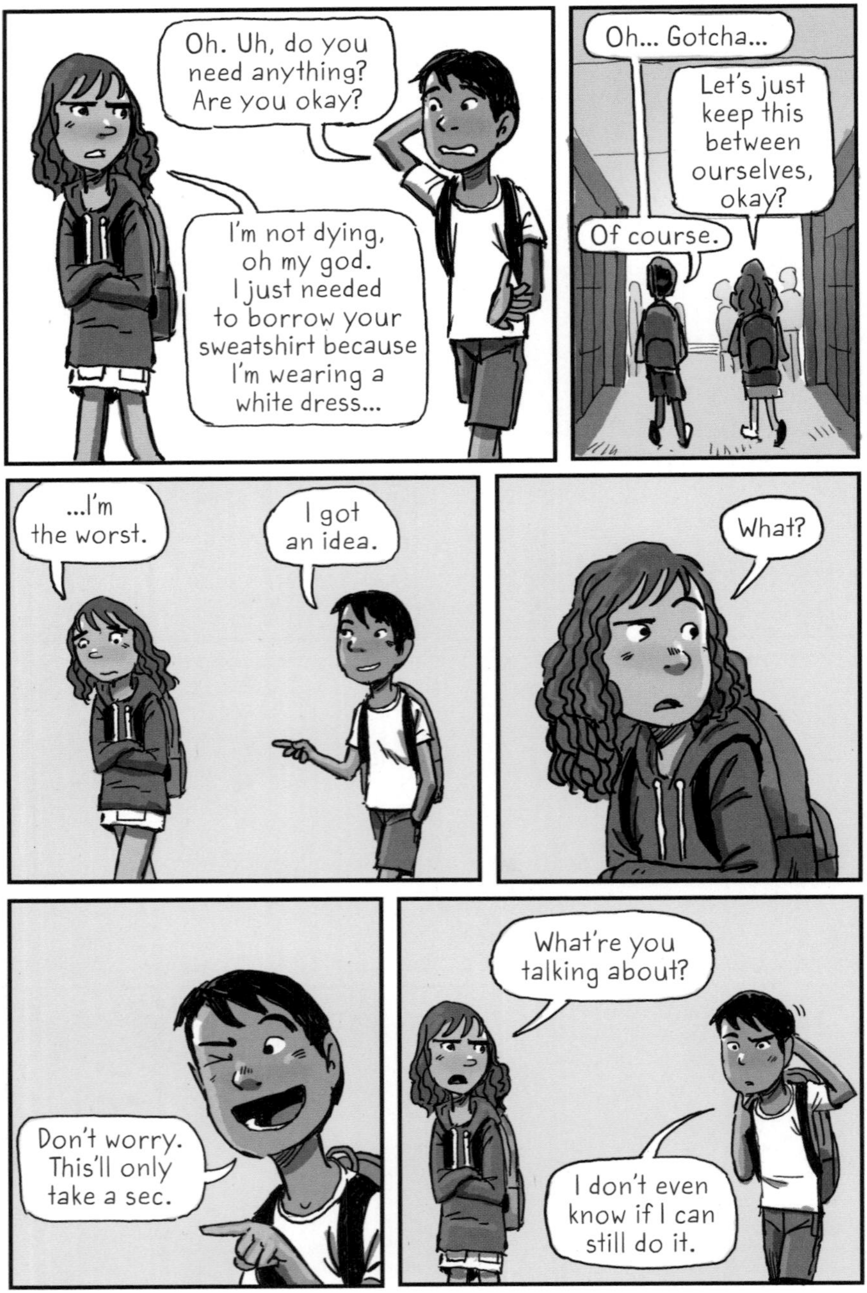
Oh. Uh, do you need anything? Are you okay?
I'm not dying, oh my god. I just needed to borrow your sweatshirt because I'm wearing a white dress...
Oh... Gotcha...
Let's just keep this between ourselves, okay?
Of course.
...I'm the worst.
I got an idea.
What?
Don't worry. This'll only take a sec.
What're you talking about?
I don't even know if I can still do it.

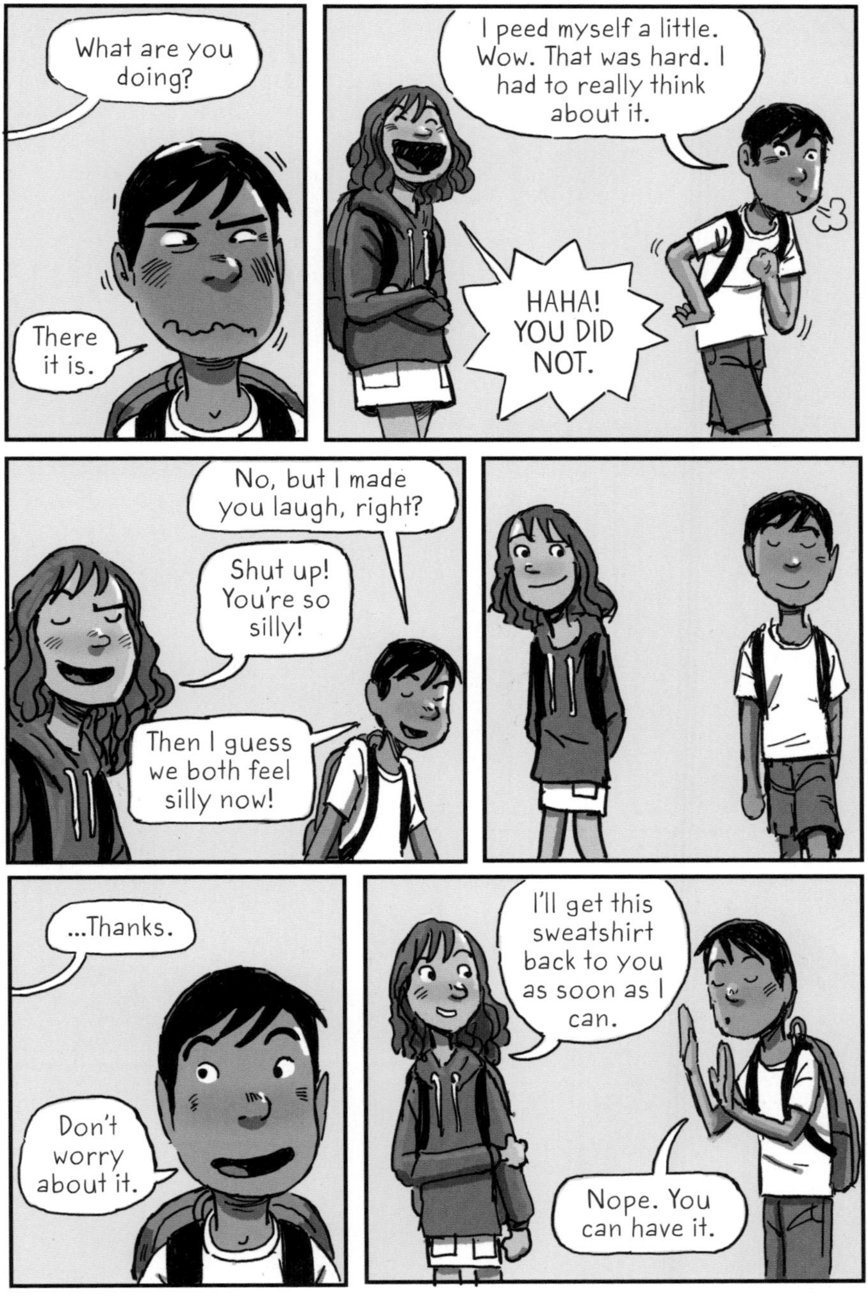
What are you doing?
There it is.
I peed myself a little. Wow. That was hard. I had to really think about it.
HAHA! YOU DID NOT.
No, but I made you laugh, right?
Shut up! You're so silly!
Then I guess we both feel silly now!
...Thanks.
Don't worry about it.
I'll get this sweatshirt back to you as soon as I can.
Nope. You can have it.

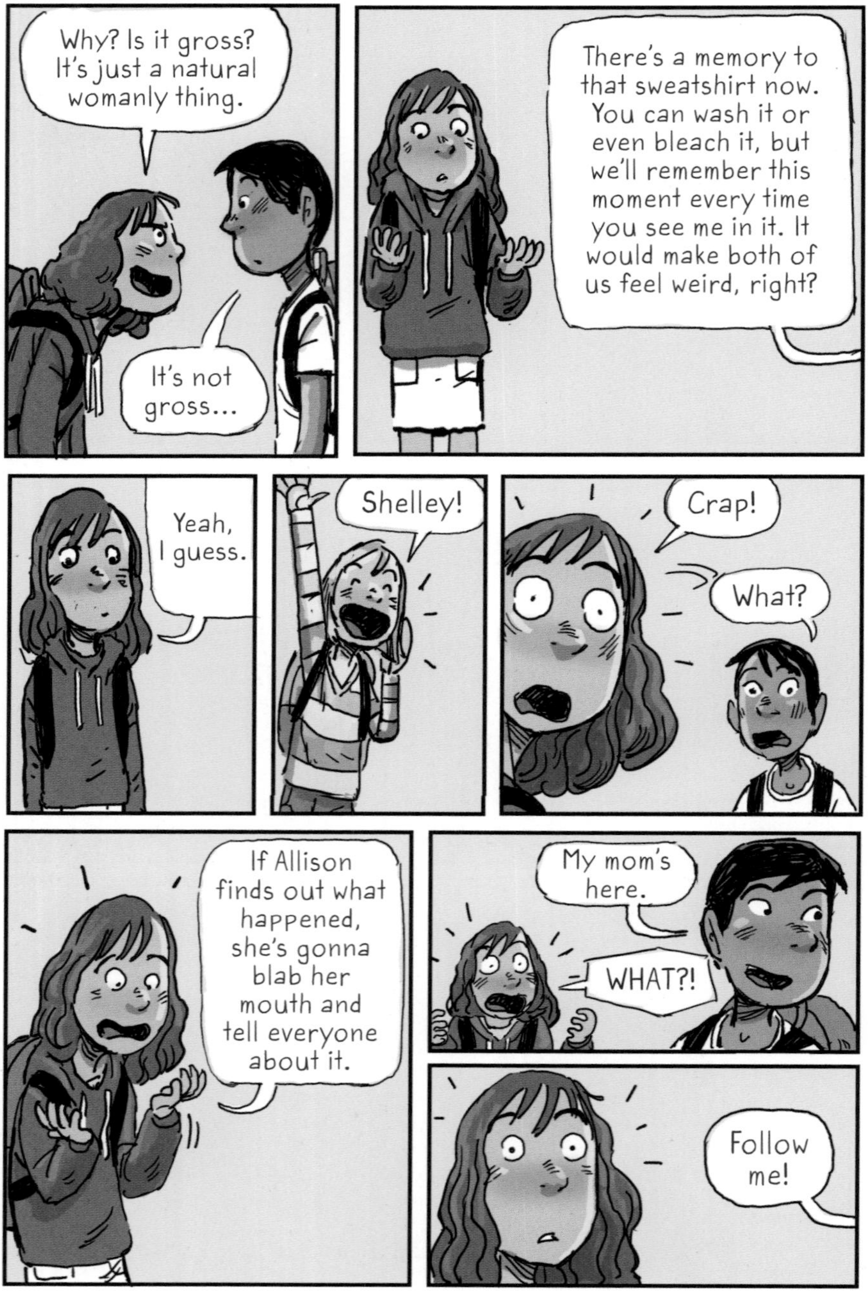
Why? Is it gross? It's just a natural womanly thing.
It's not gross...
There's a memory to that sweatshirt now. You can wash it or even bleach it, but we'll remember this moment every time you see me in it. It would make both of us feel weird, right?
Yeah, I guess.
Shelley!
Crap!
What?
If Allison finds out what happened, she's gonna blab her mouth and tell everyone about it.
My mom's here.
WHAT?!
Follow me!

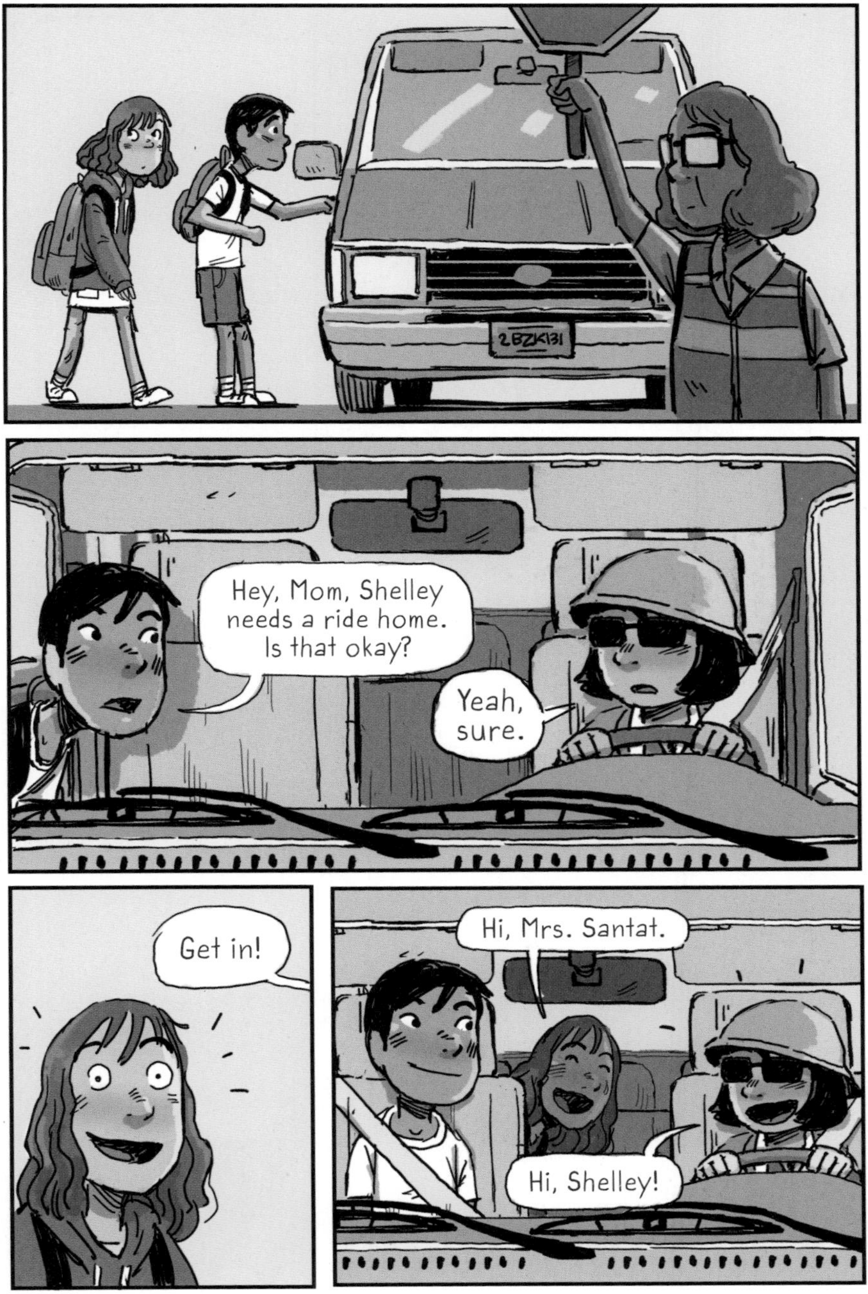
2BZK131
Hey, Mom, Shelley needs a ride home. Is that okay?
Yeah, sure.
Get in!
Hi, Mrs. Santat.
Hi, Shelley!

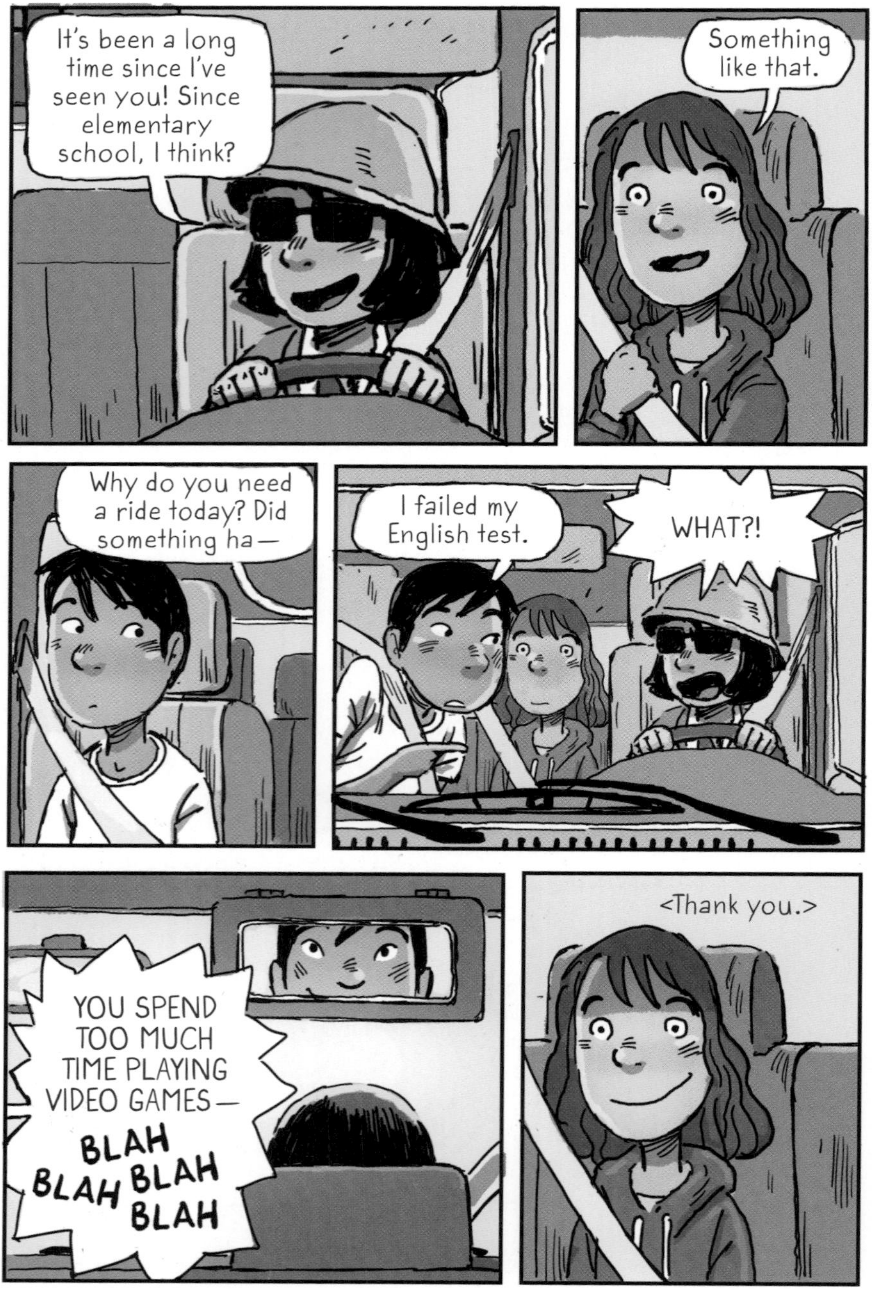

It's been a long time since I've seen you! Since elementary school, I think?
Something like that.
Why do you need a ride today? Did something ha—
I failed my English test.
WHAT?!
YOU SPEND TOO MUCH TIME PLAYING VIDEO GAMES—
BLAH BLAH BLAH BLAH
<Thank you.>

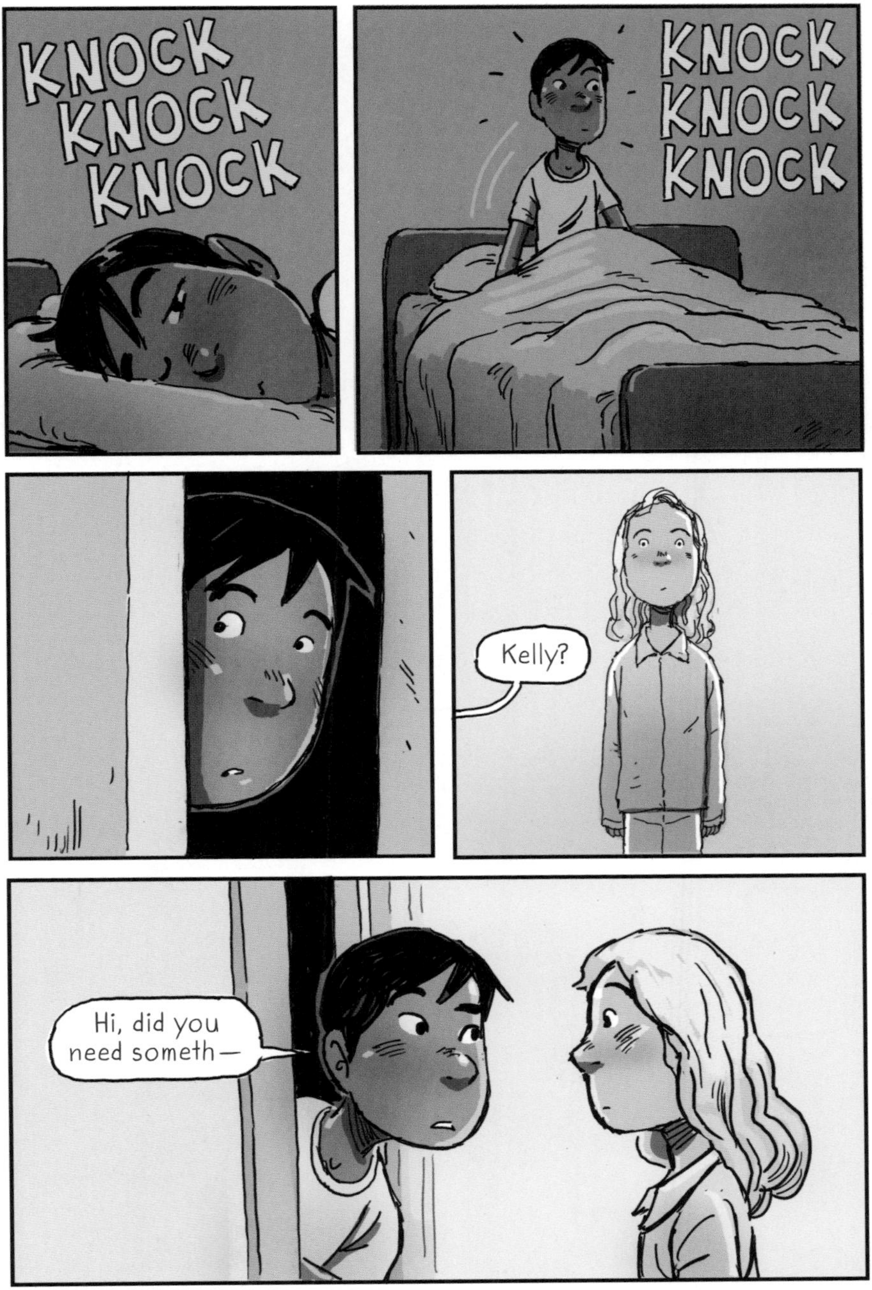
KNOCK KNOCK KNOCK
KNOCK KNOCK KNOCK
Kelly?
Hi, did you need someth—

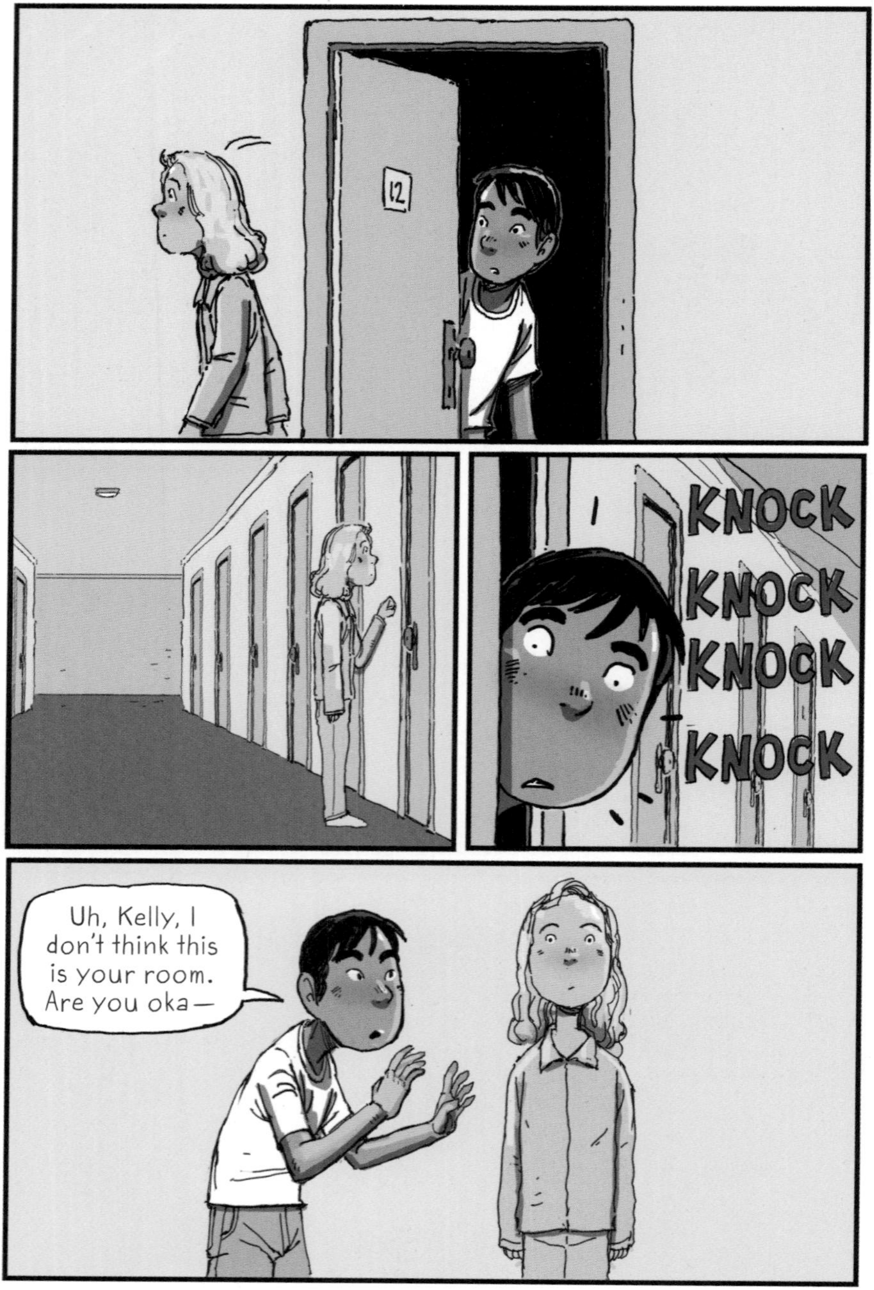
12
KNOCK
KNOCK
KNOCK
KNOCK
Uh, Kelly, I don't think this is your room. Are you oka—

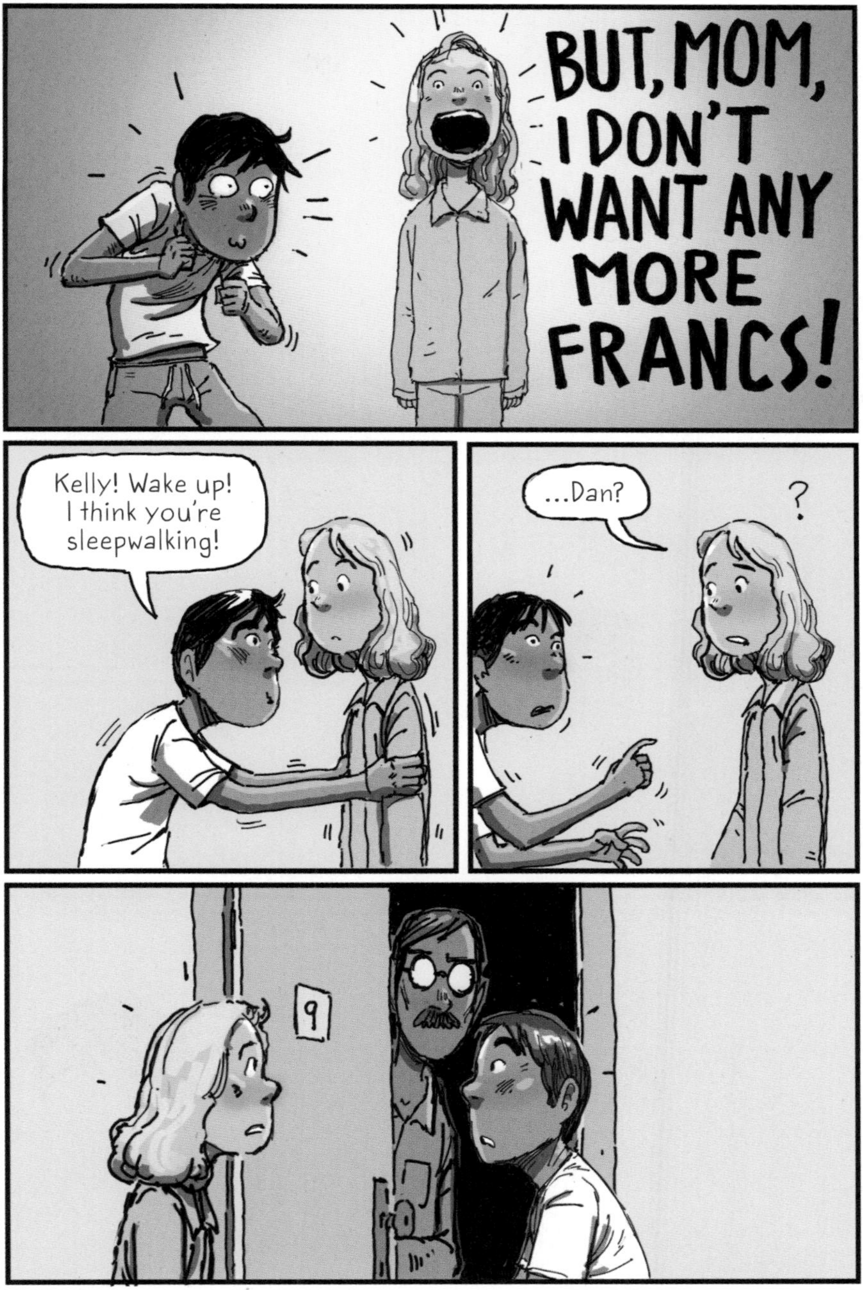
BUT, MOM, I DON'T WANT ANY MORE FRANCS!
Kelly! Wake up! I think you're sleepwalking!
...Dan?
?
9

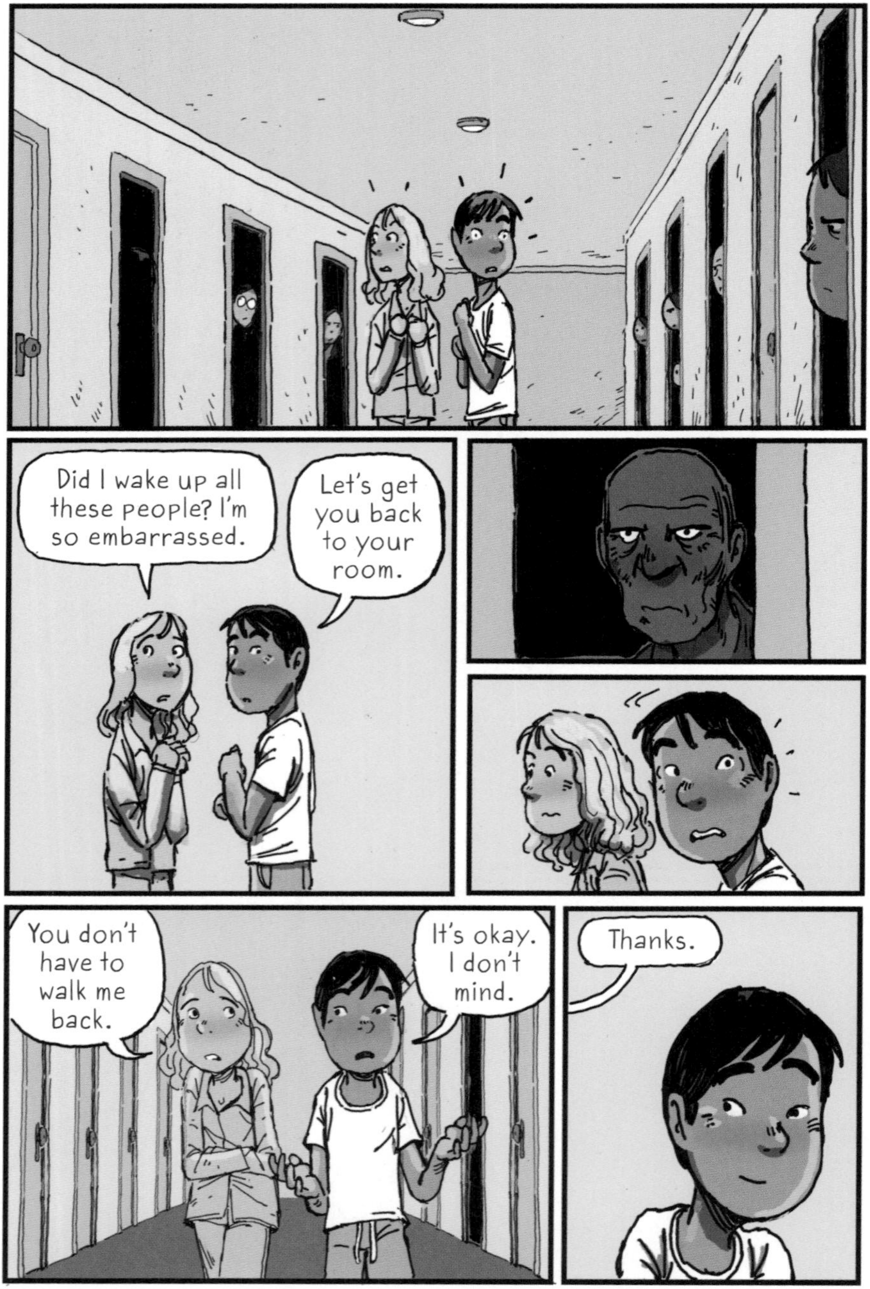
Did I wake up all these people? I'm so embarrassed.
Let's get you back to your room.
You don't have to walk me back.
It's okay. I don't mind.
Thanks.

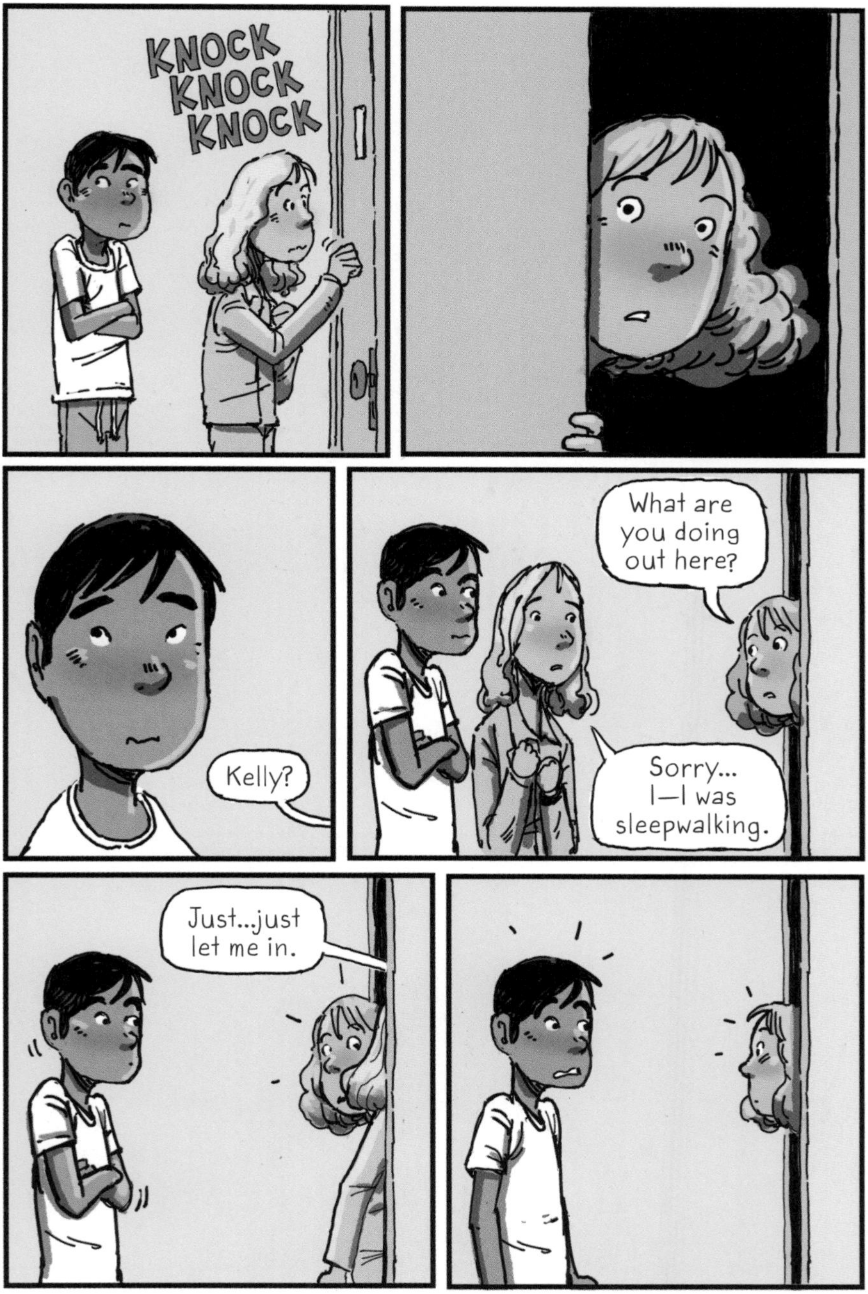
KNOCK
KNOCK
KNOCK
Kelly?
What are you doing out here?
Sorry... I—I was sleepwalking.
Just...just let me in.

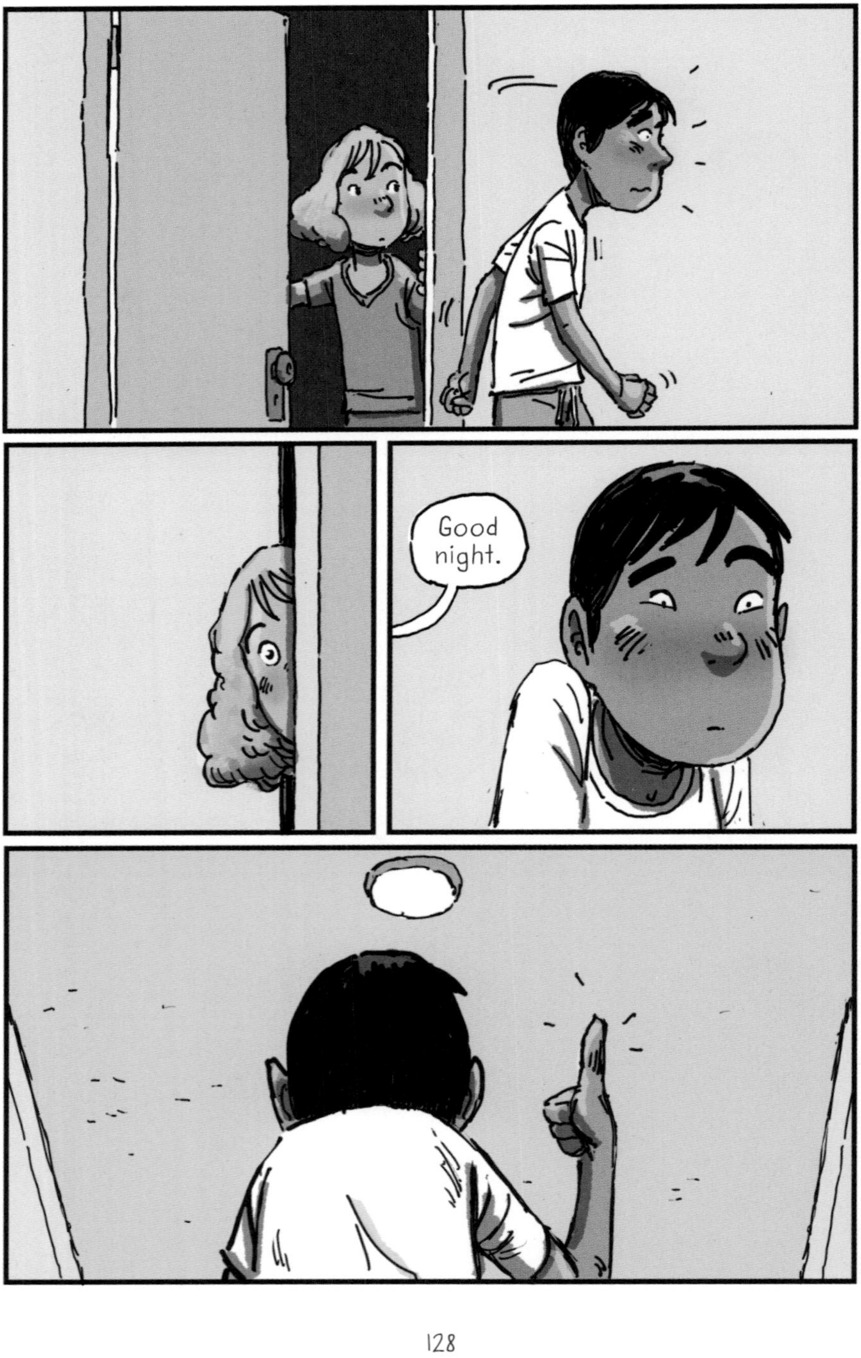
Good night.

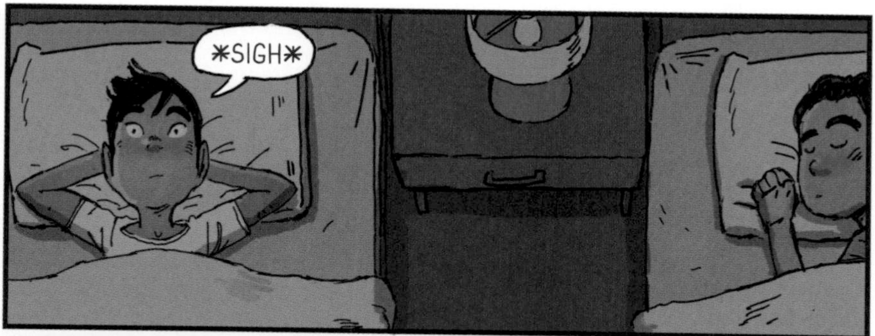
SIGH

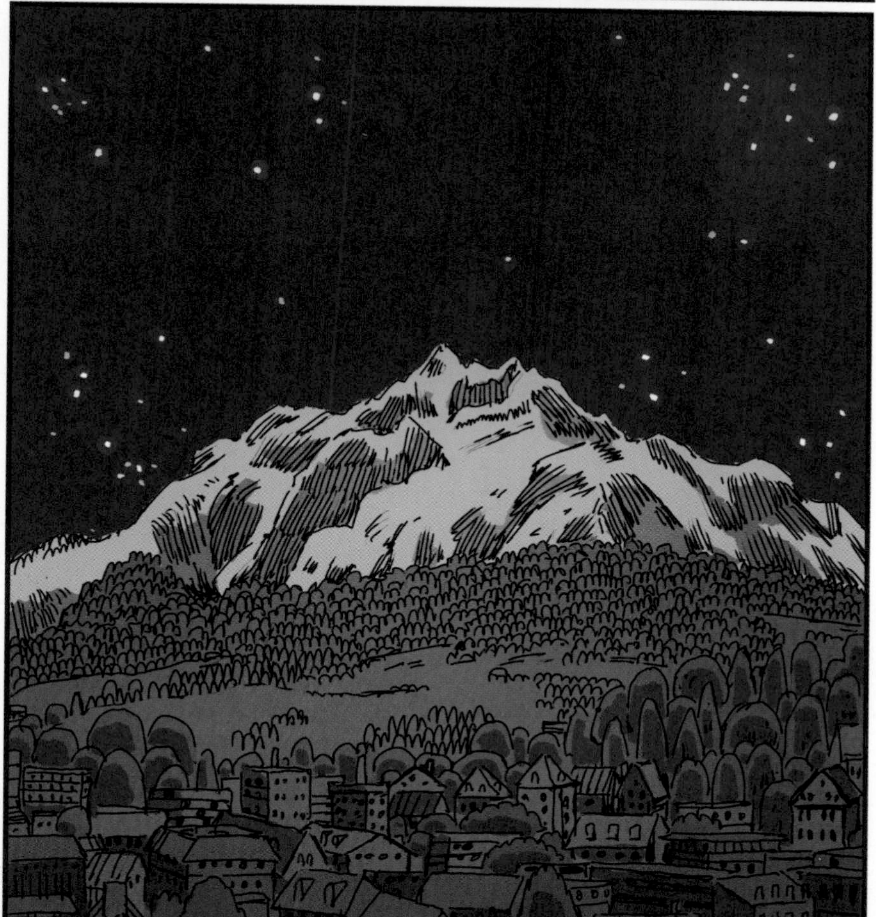

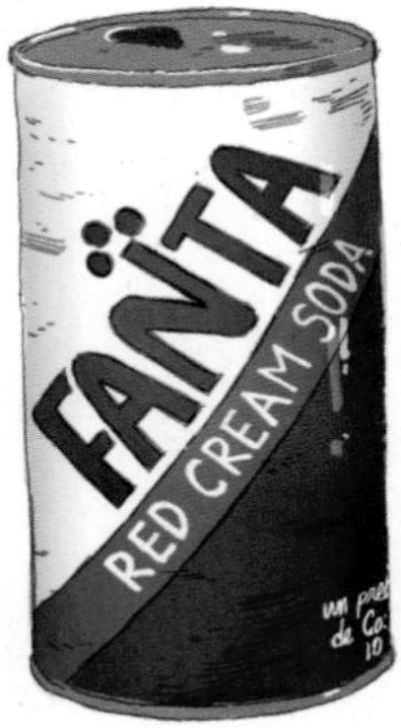
FANTA
RED CREAM SODA

MUNICH

(17 DAYS LEFT IN THE TRIP)

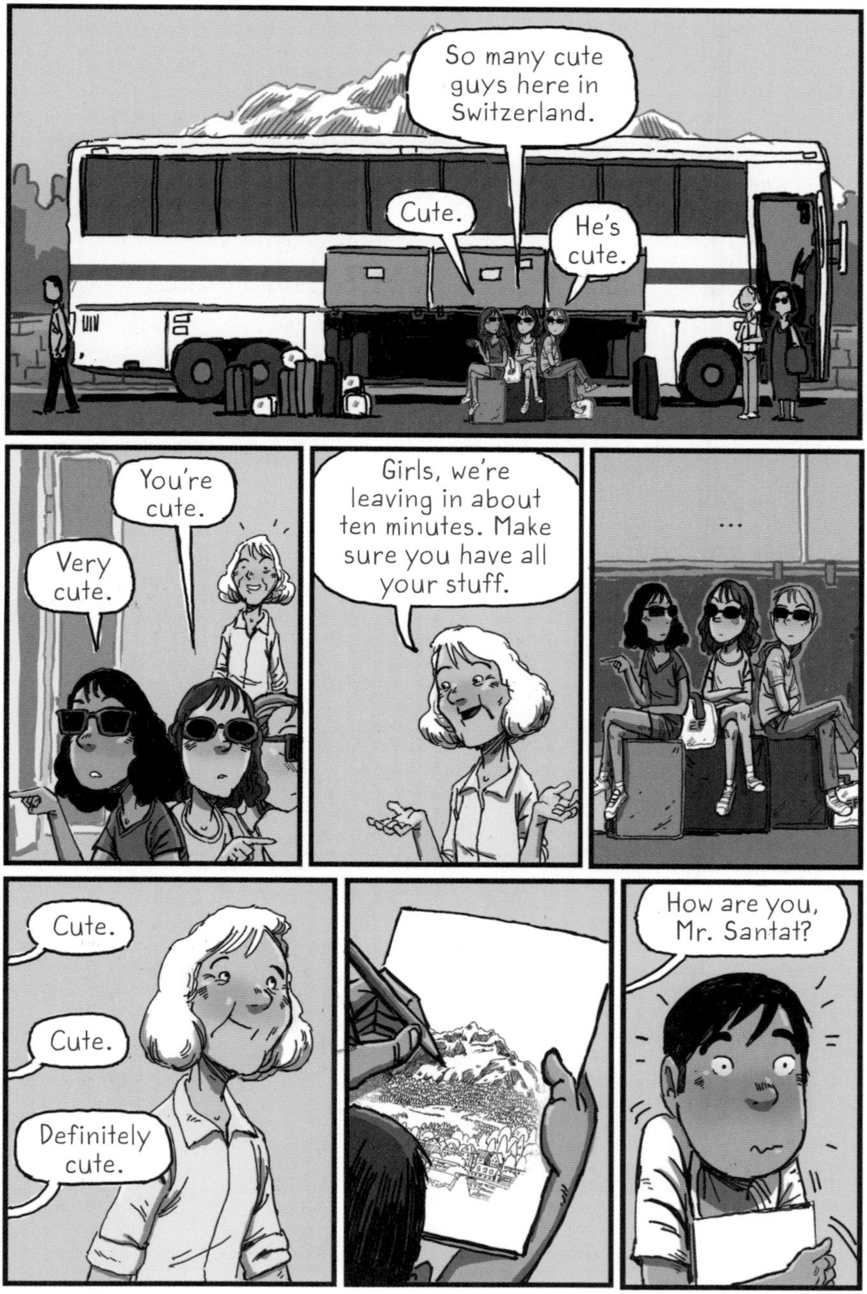
So many cute guys here in Switzerland.
Cute.
He's cute.
You're cute.
Very cute.
Girls, we're leaving in about ten minutes. Make sure you have all your stuff.
...
Cute.
Cute.
Definitely cute.
How are you, Mr. Santat?

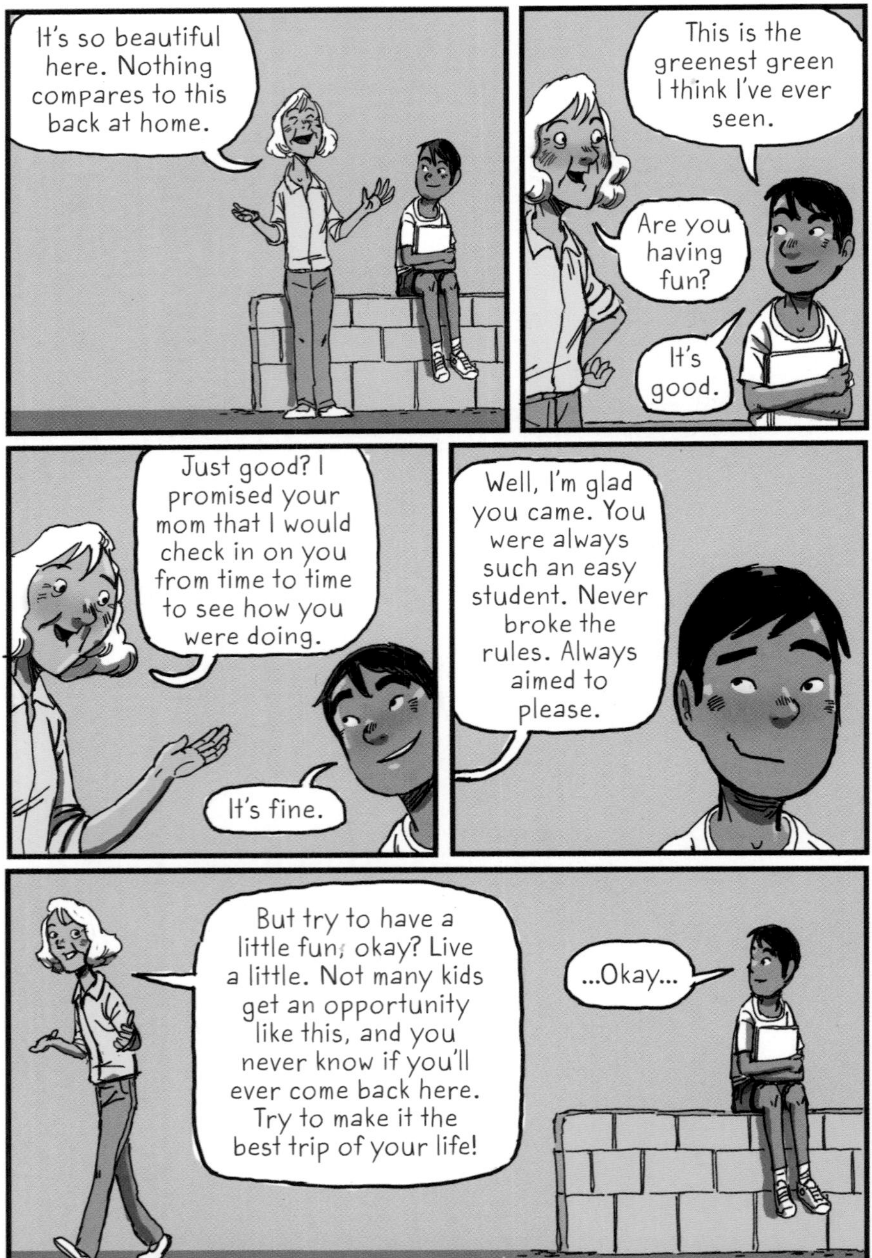
It's so beautiful here. Nothing compares to this back at home.
This is the greenest green I think I've ever seen.
Are you having fun?
It's good.
Just good? I promised your mom that I would check in on you from time to time to see how you were doing.
It's fine.
Well, I'm glad you came. You were always such an easy student. Never broke the rules. Always aimed to please.
But try to have a little fun, okay? Live a little. Not many kids get an opportunity like this, and you never know if you'll ever come back here. Try to make it the best trip of your life!
...Okay...

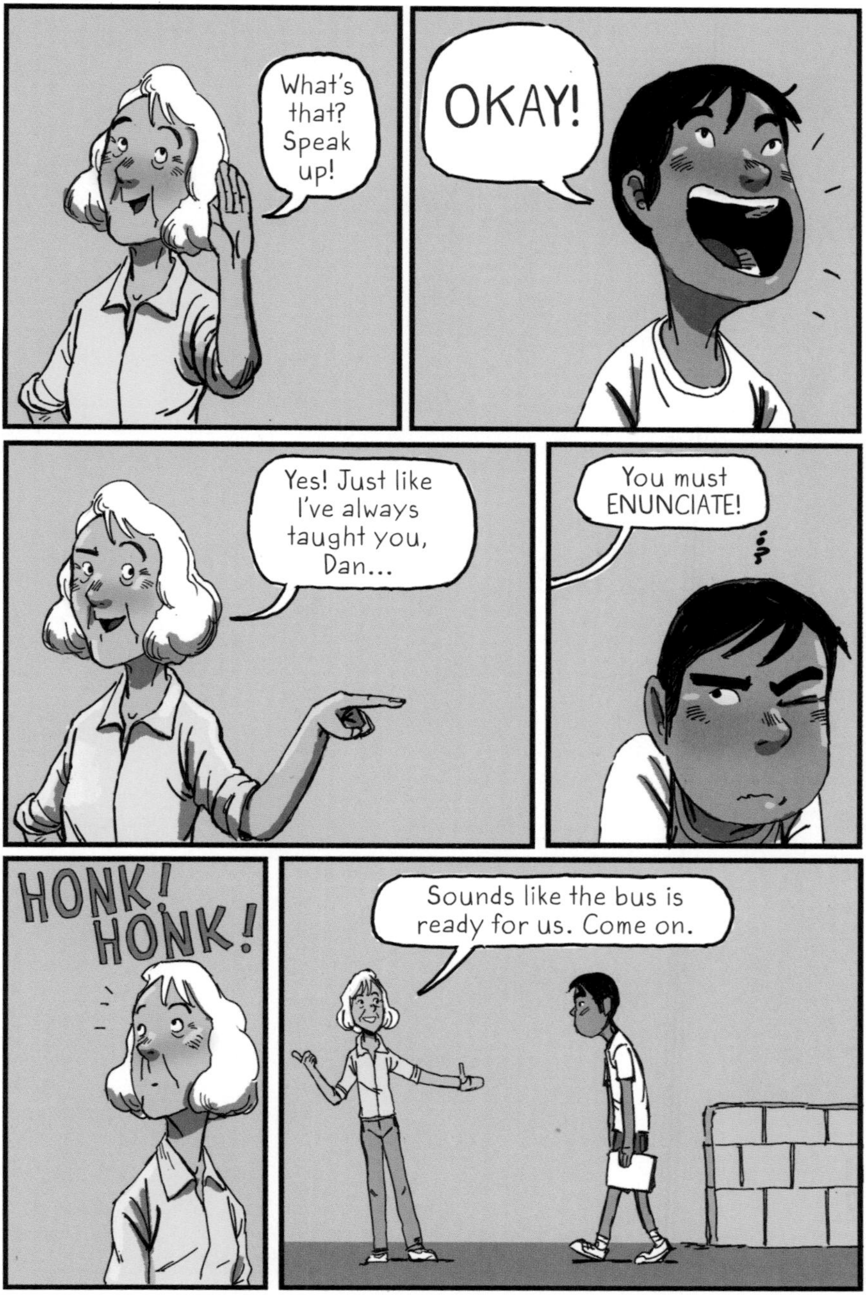
What's that? Speak up!
OKAY!
Yes! Just like I've always taught you, Dan...
You must ENUNCIATE!
HONK! HONK!
Sounds like the bus is ready for us. Come on.

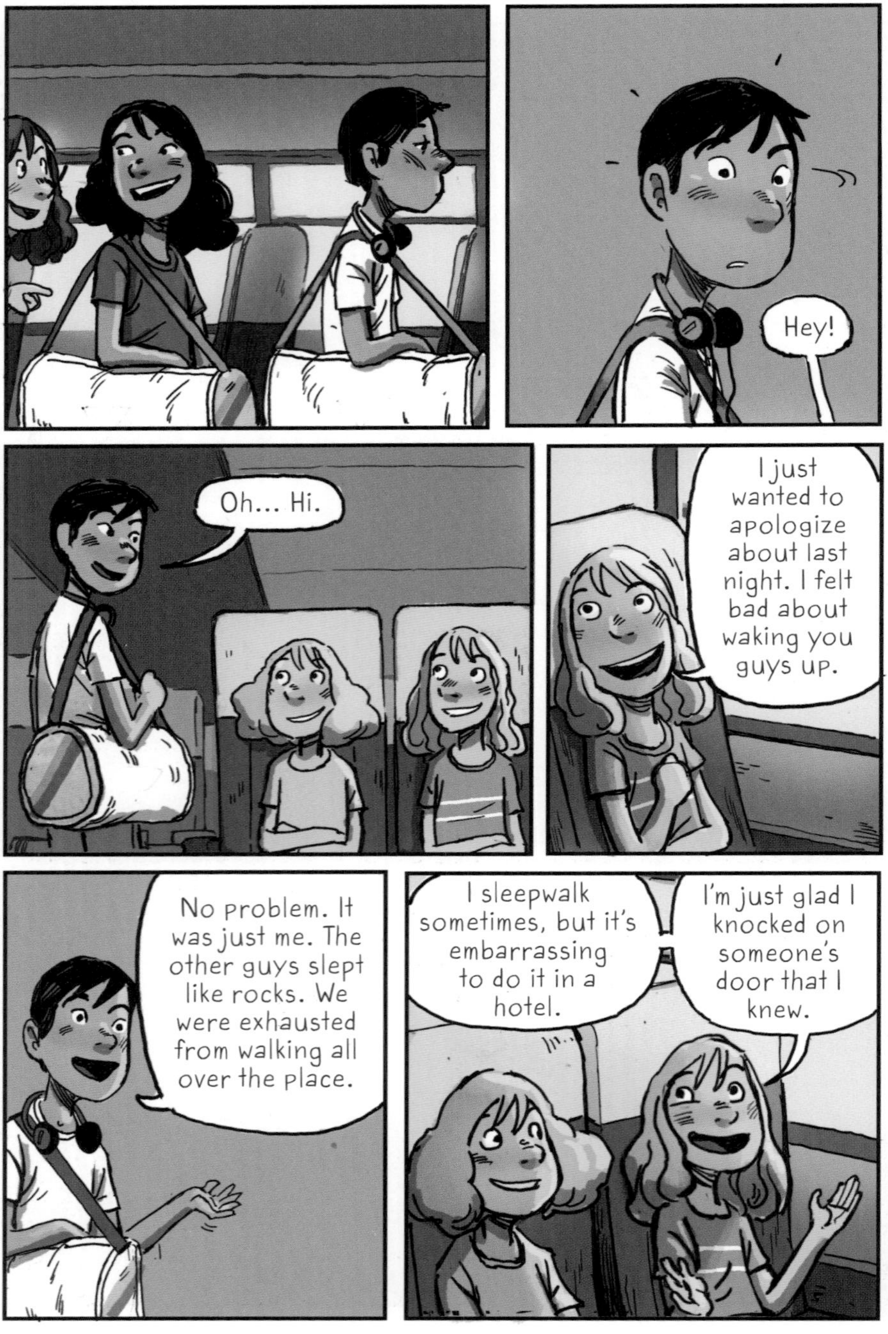

Hey!
Oh... Hi.
I just wanted to apologize about last night. I felt bad about waking you guys up.
No problem. It was just me. The other guys slept like rocks. We were exhausted from walking all over the place.
I sleepwalk sometimes, but it's embarrassing to do it in a hotel.
I'm just glad I knocked on someone's door that I knew.

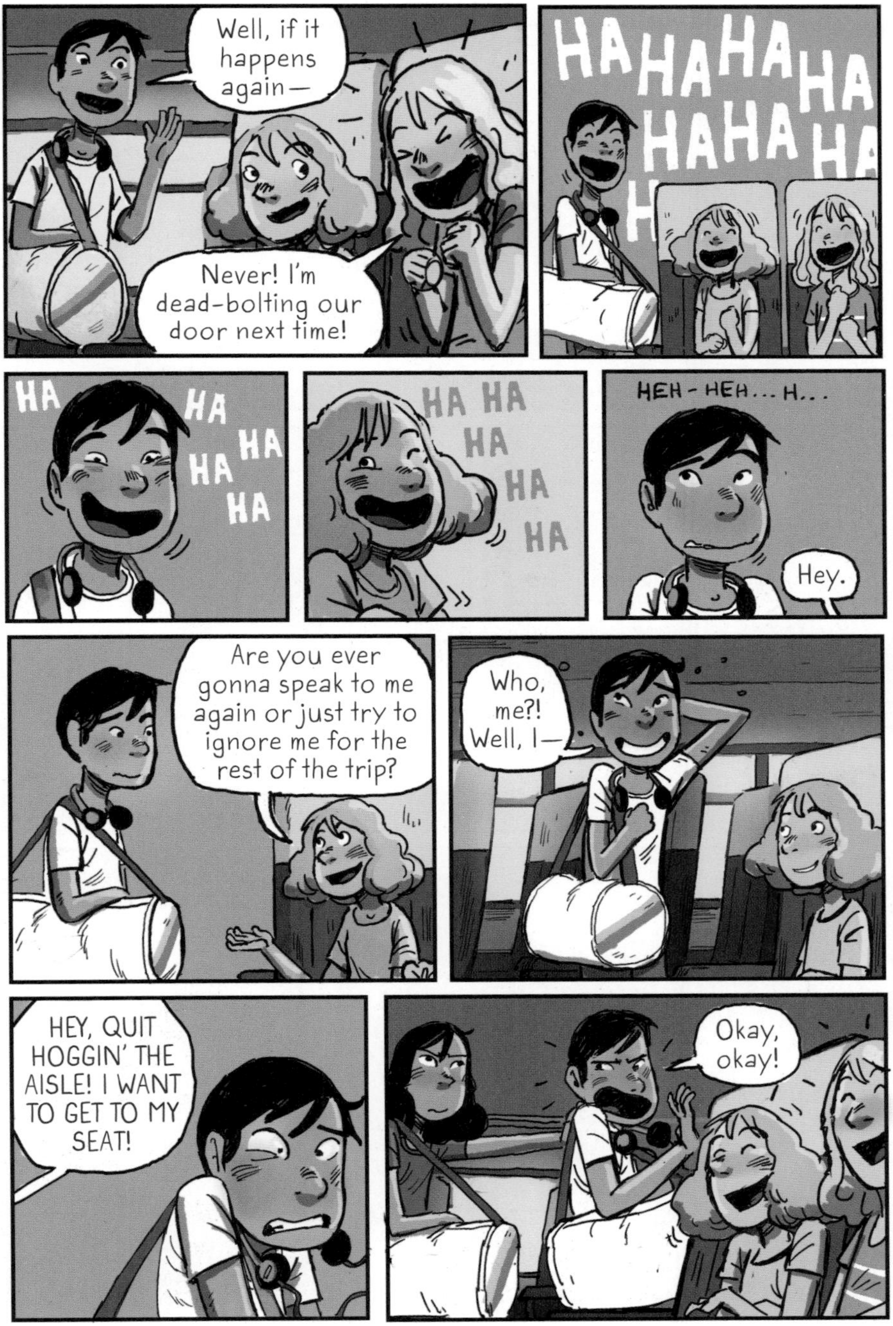
Well, if it happens again—
Never! I'm dead-bolting our door next time!
HAHAHAHAHA HAHAHA HA H
HA HA HA HA HA HA
HA HA HA HA HA
HEH-HEH... H...
Hey.
Are you ever gonna speak to me again or just try to ignore me for the rest of the trip?
Who, me?! Well, I—
HEY, QUIT HOGGIN' THE AISLE! I WANT TO GET TO MY SEAT!
Okay, okay!

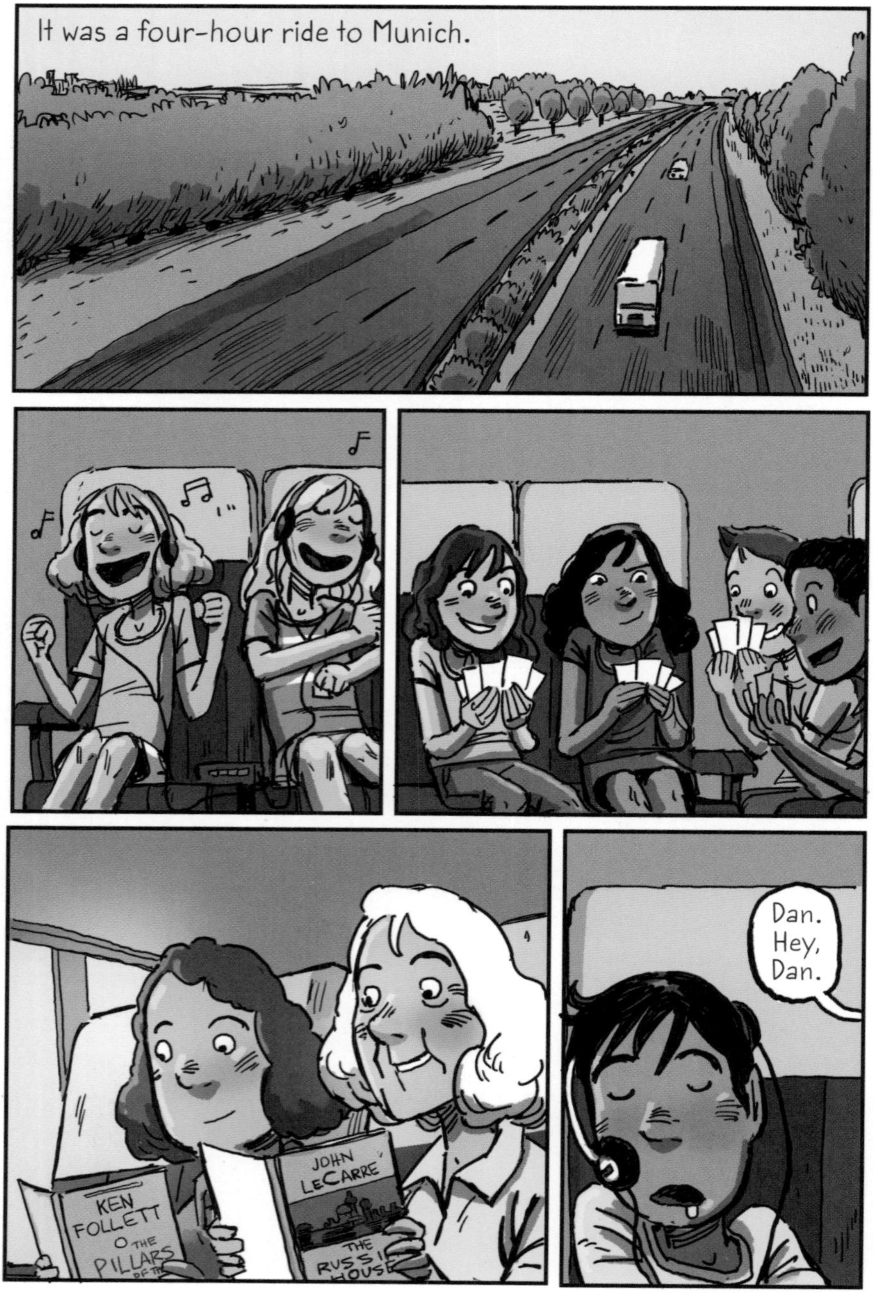
It was a four-hour ride to Munich.
KEN FOLLETT
THE PILLARS
JOHN LeCARRE
Dan. Hey, Dan.

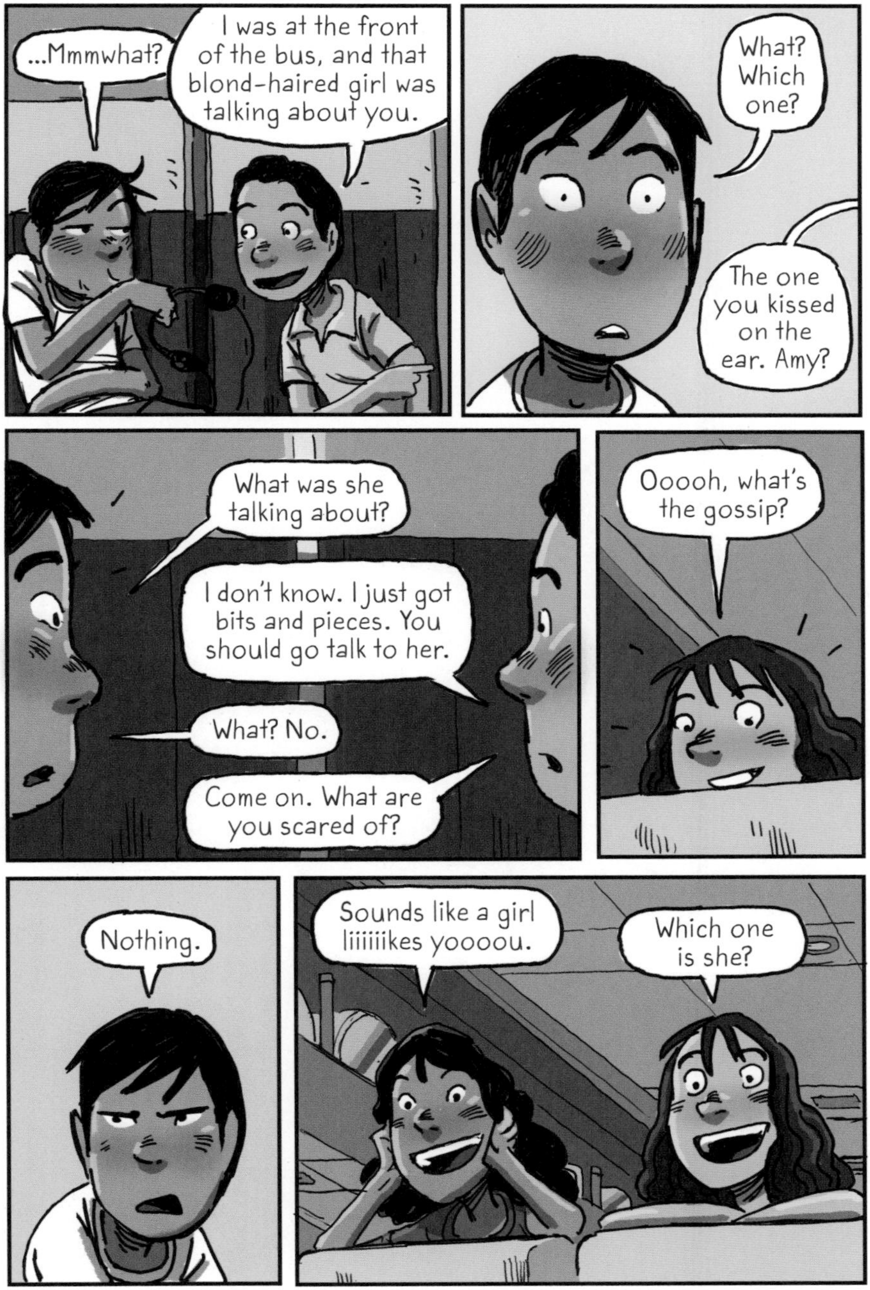
...Mmmwhat?
I was at the front of the bus, and that blond-haired girl was talking about you.
What? Which one?
The one you kissed on the ear. Amy?
What was she talking about?
I don't know. I just got bits and pieces. You should go talk to her.
What? No.
Come on. What are you scared of?
Ooooh, what's the gossip?
Nothing.
Sounds like a girl liiiiiikes yoooou.
Which one is she?

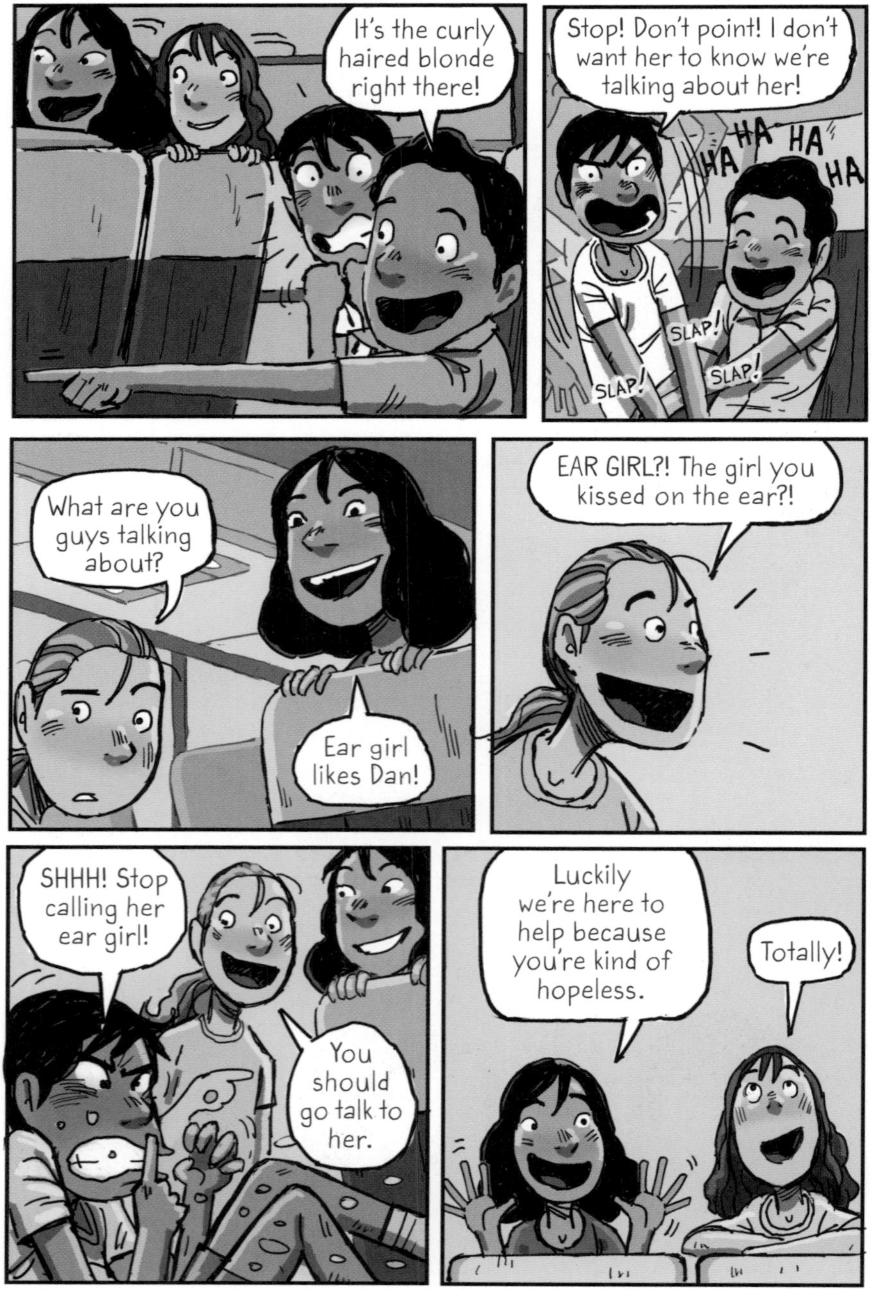
It's the curly haired blonde right there!
Stop! Don't point! I don't want her to know we're talking about her!
HA HA HA HA HA
SLAP!
SLAP!
SLAP!
What are you guys talking about?
Ear girl likes Dan!
EAR GIRL?! The girl you kissed on the ear?!
SHHH! Stop calling her ear girl!
You should go talk to her.
Luckily we're here to help because you're kind of hopeless.
Totally!

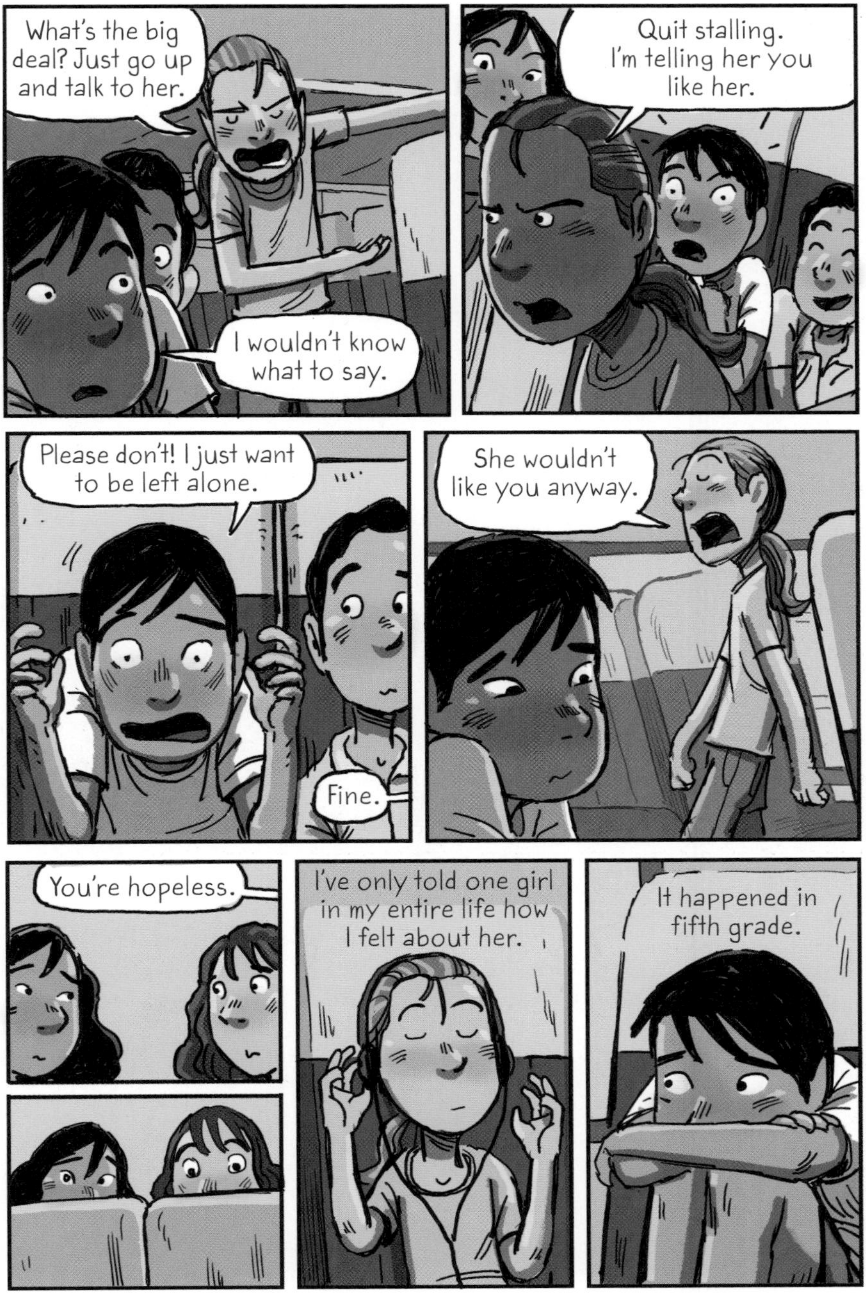
What's the big deal? Just go up and talk to her.
I wouldn't know what to say.
Quit stalling. I'm telling her you like her.
Please don't! I just want to be left alone.
Fine.
She wouldn't like you anyway.
You're hopeless.
I've only told one girl in my entire life how I felt about her.
It happened in fifth grade.

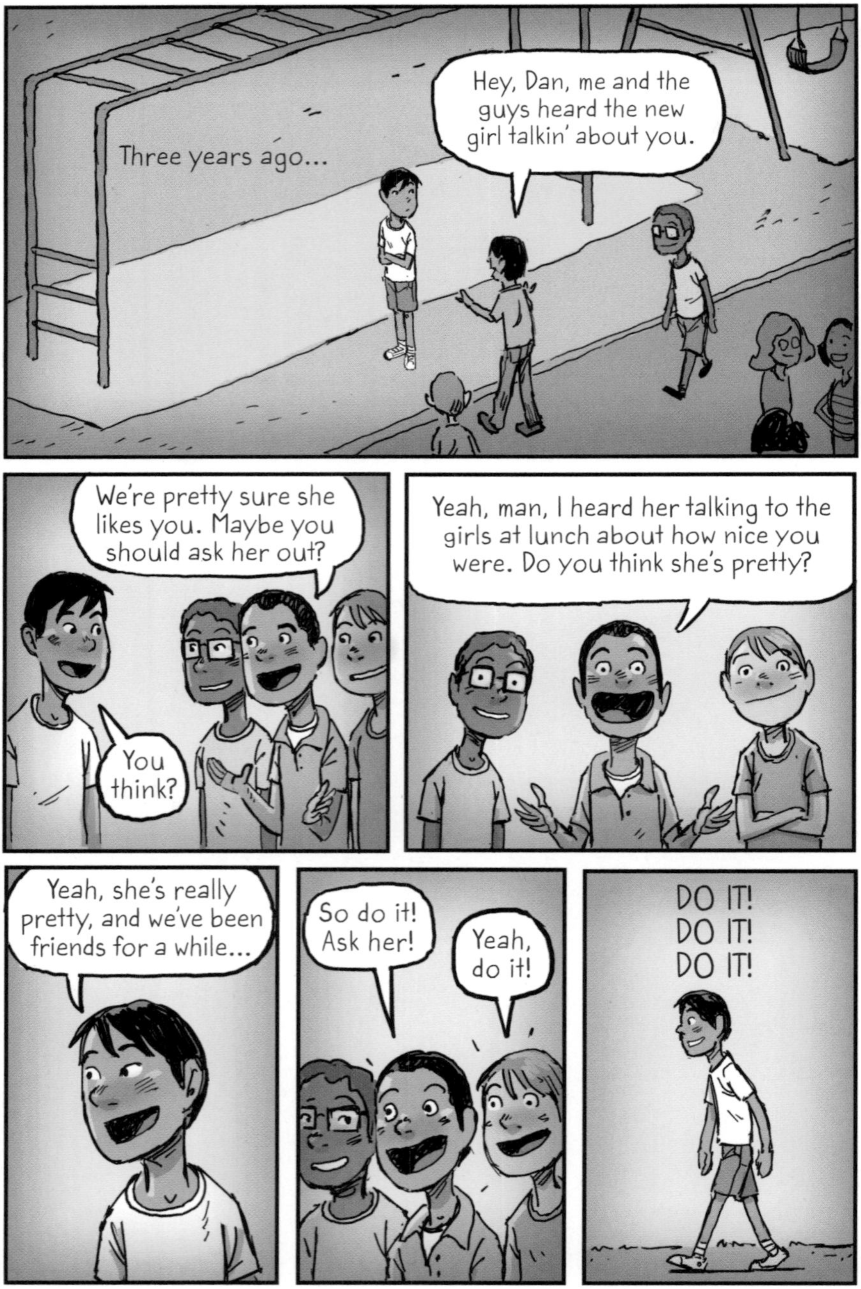
Three years ago...
Hey, Dan, me and the guys heard the new girl talkin' about you.
We're pretty sure she likes you. Maybe you should ask her out?
You think?
Yeah, man, I heard her talking to the girls at lunch about how nice you were. Do you think she's pretty?
Yeah, she's really pretty, and we've been friends for a while...
So do it! Ask her!
Yeah, do it!
DO IT!
DO IT!
DO IT!

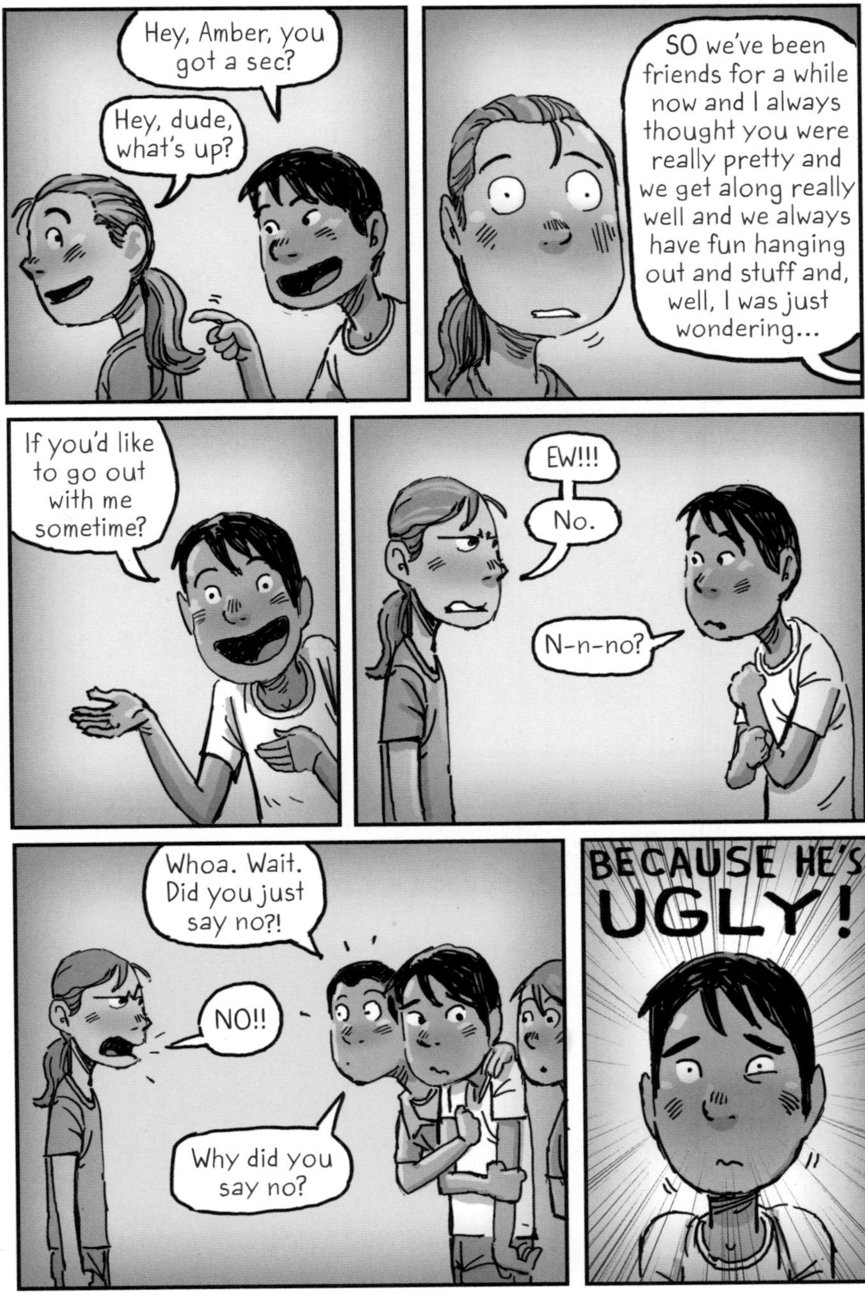
Hey, Amber, you got a sec?
Hey, dude, what's up?
SO we've been friends for a while now and I always thought you were really pretty and we get along really well and we always have fun hanging out and stuff and, well, I was just wondering...
If you'd like to go out with me sometime?
EW!!!
No.
N-n-no?
Whoa. Wait. Did you just say no?!
NO!!
Why did you say no?
BECAUSE HE'S UGLY!

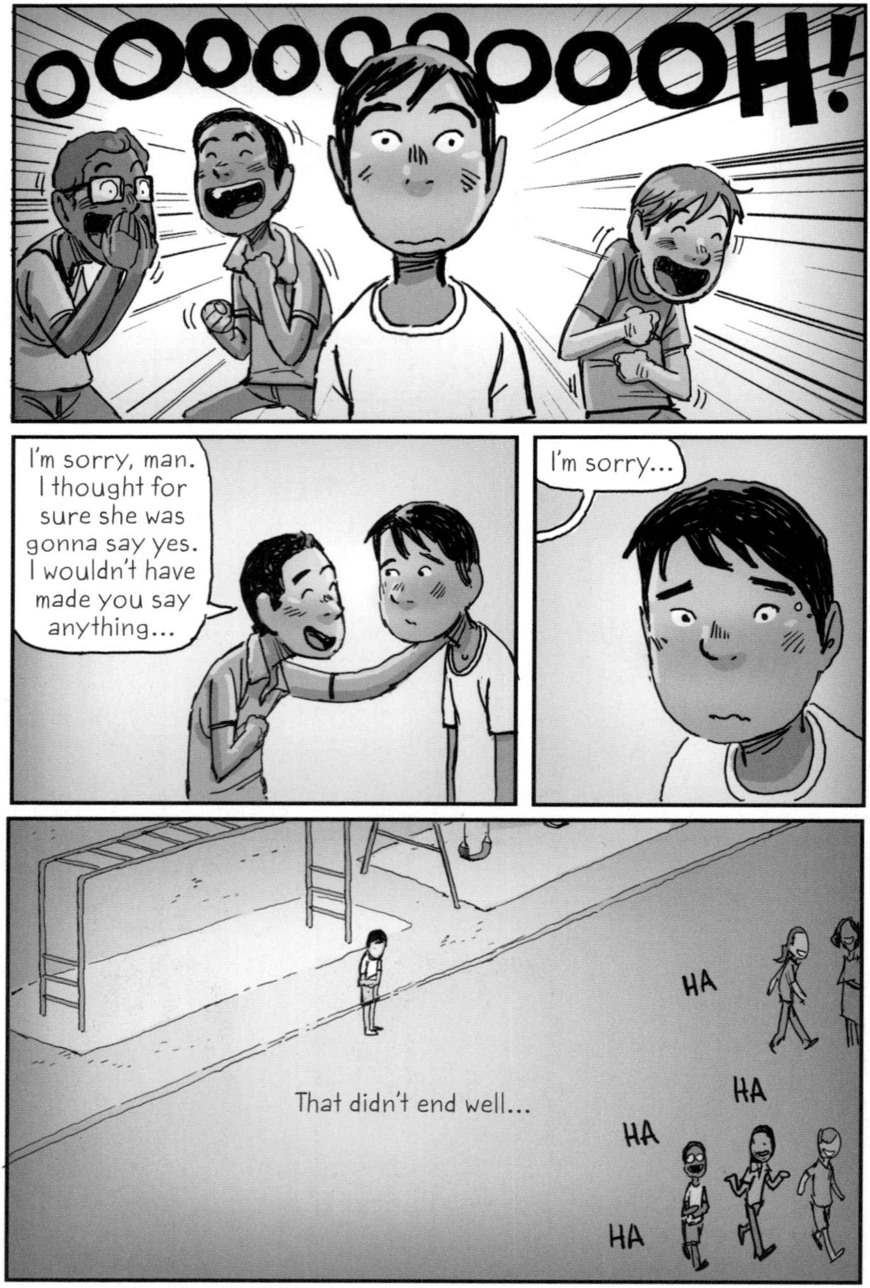
OOOOOOOOOOOH!
I'm sorry, man. I thought for sure she was gonna say yes. I wouldn't have made you say anything...
I'm sorry...
HA
That didn't end well...
HA
HA
HA

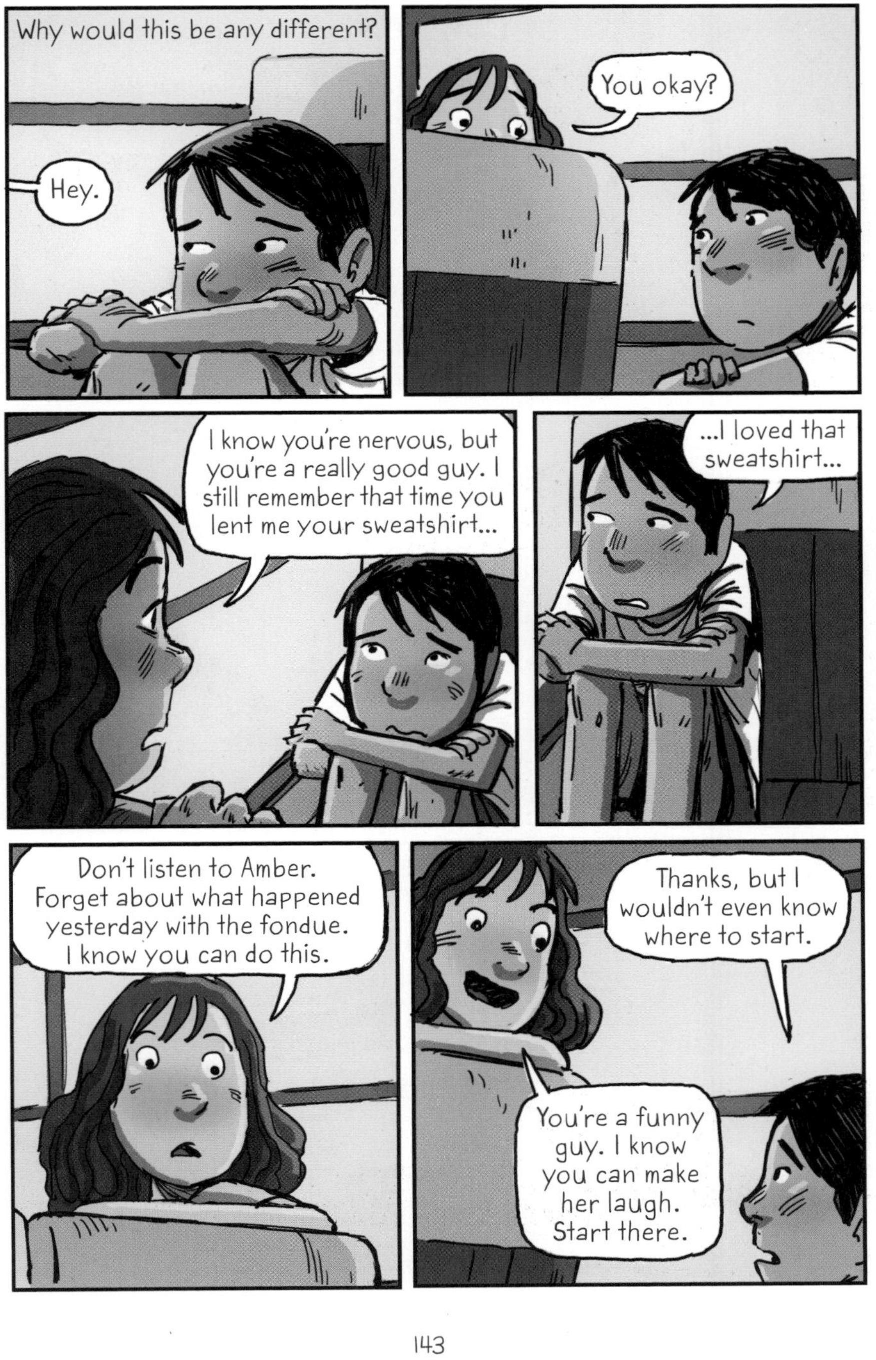
Why would this be any different?
Hey.
You okay?
I know you're nervous, but you're a really good guy. I still remember that time you lent me your sweatshirt...
...I loved that sweatshirt...
Don't listen to Amber. Forget about what happened yesterday with the fondue. I know you can do this.
Thanks, but I wouldn't even know where to start.
You're a funny guy. I know you can make her laugh. Start there.

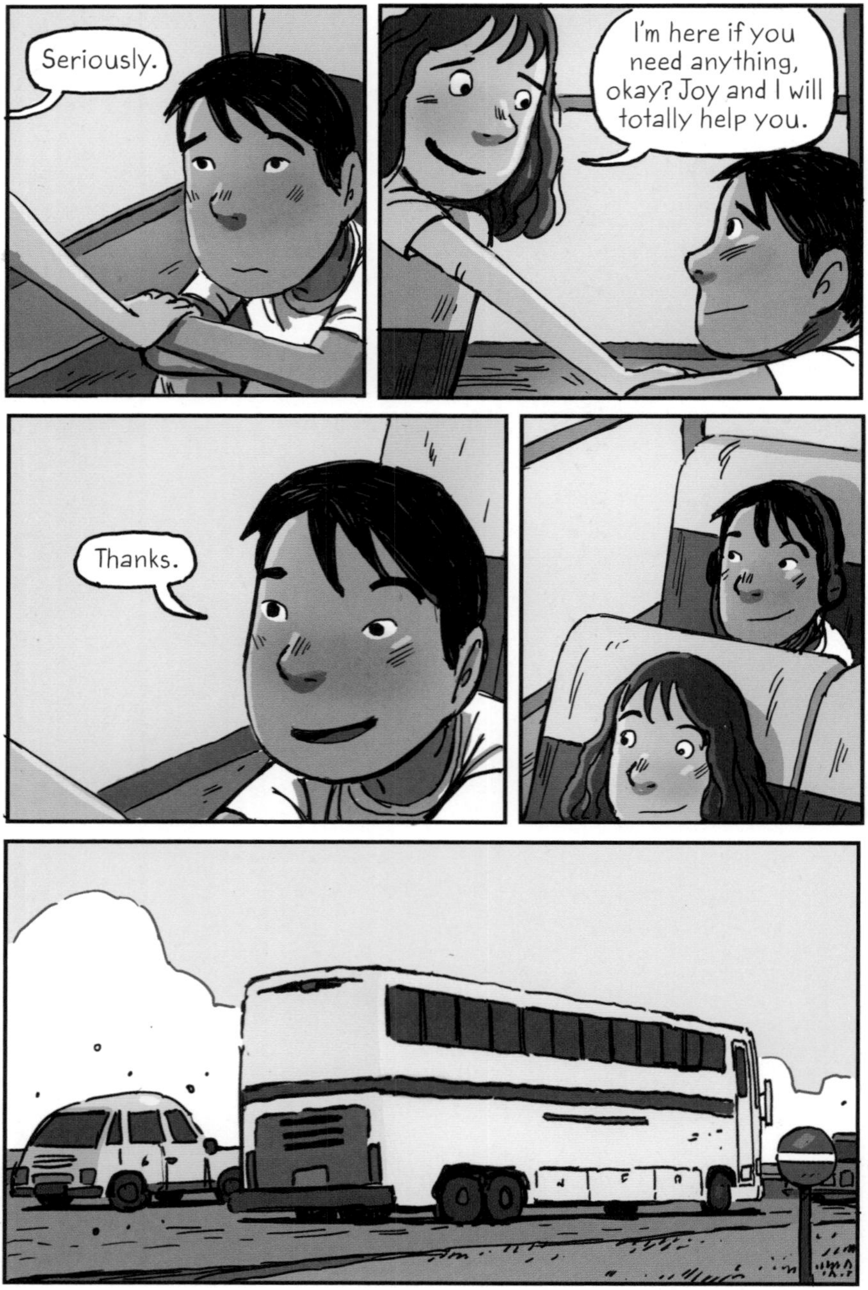
Seriously.
I'm here if you need anything, okay? Joy and I will totally help you.
Thanks.

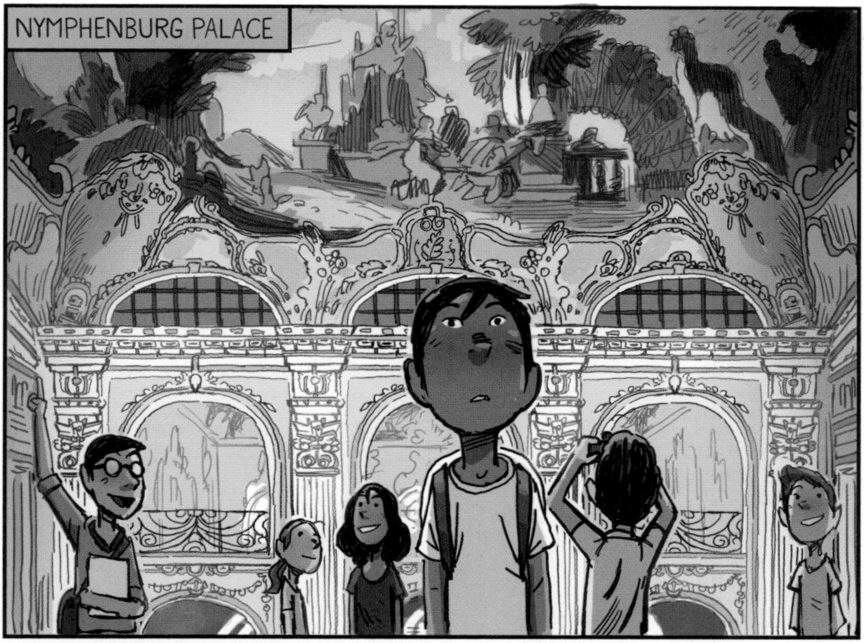
NYMPHENBURG PALACE

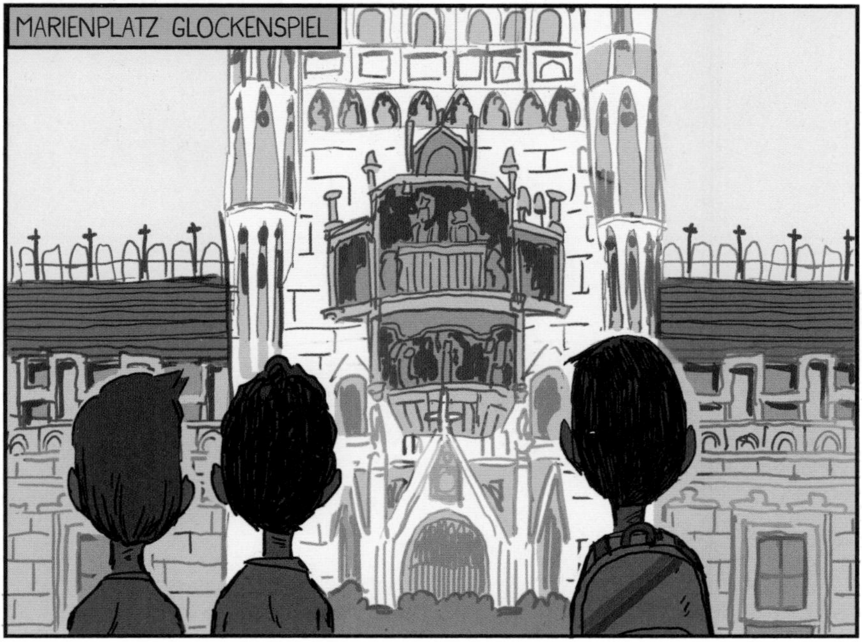
MARIENPLATZ GLOCKENSPIEL

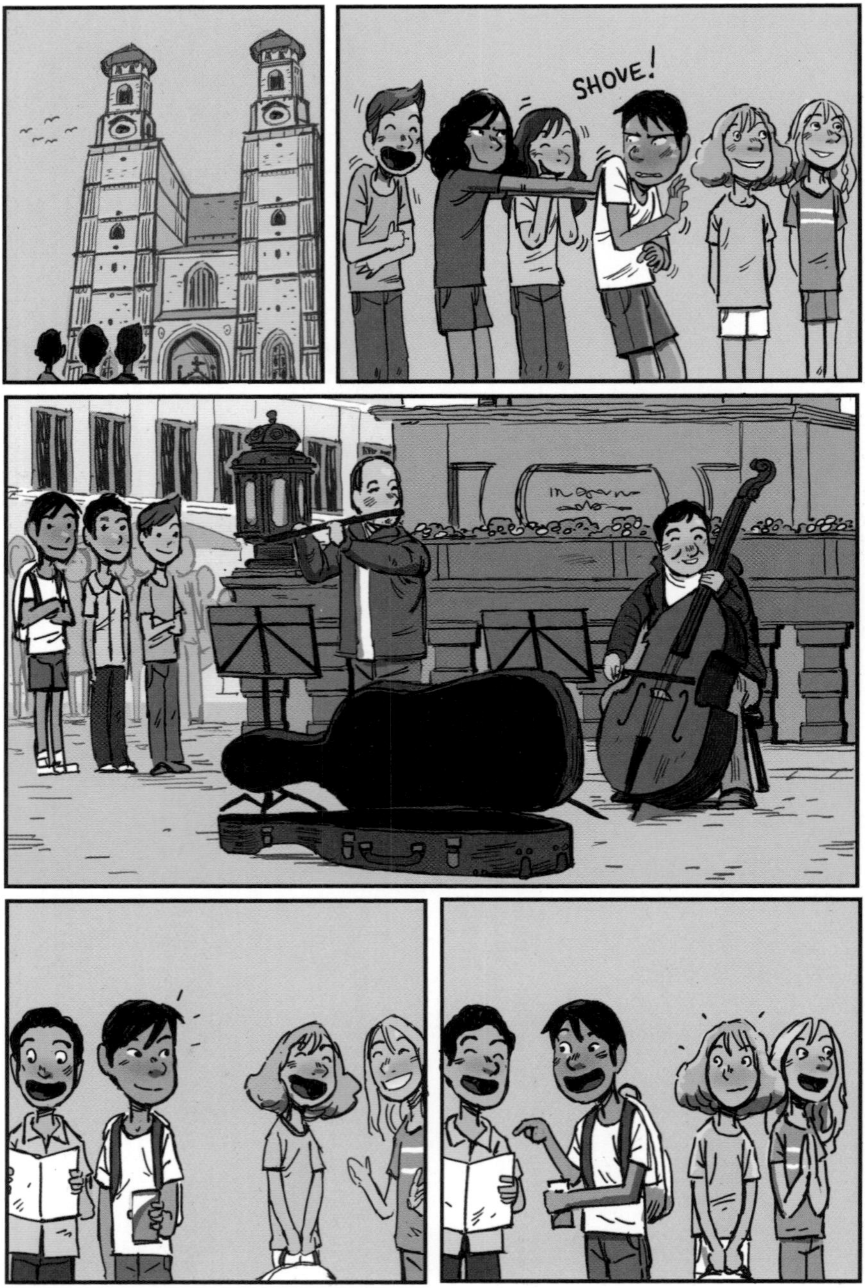
SHOVE!

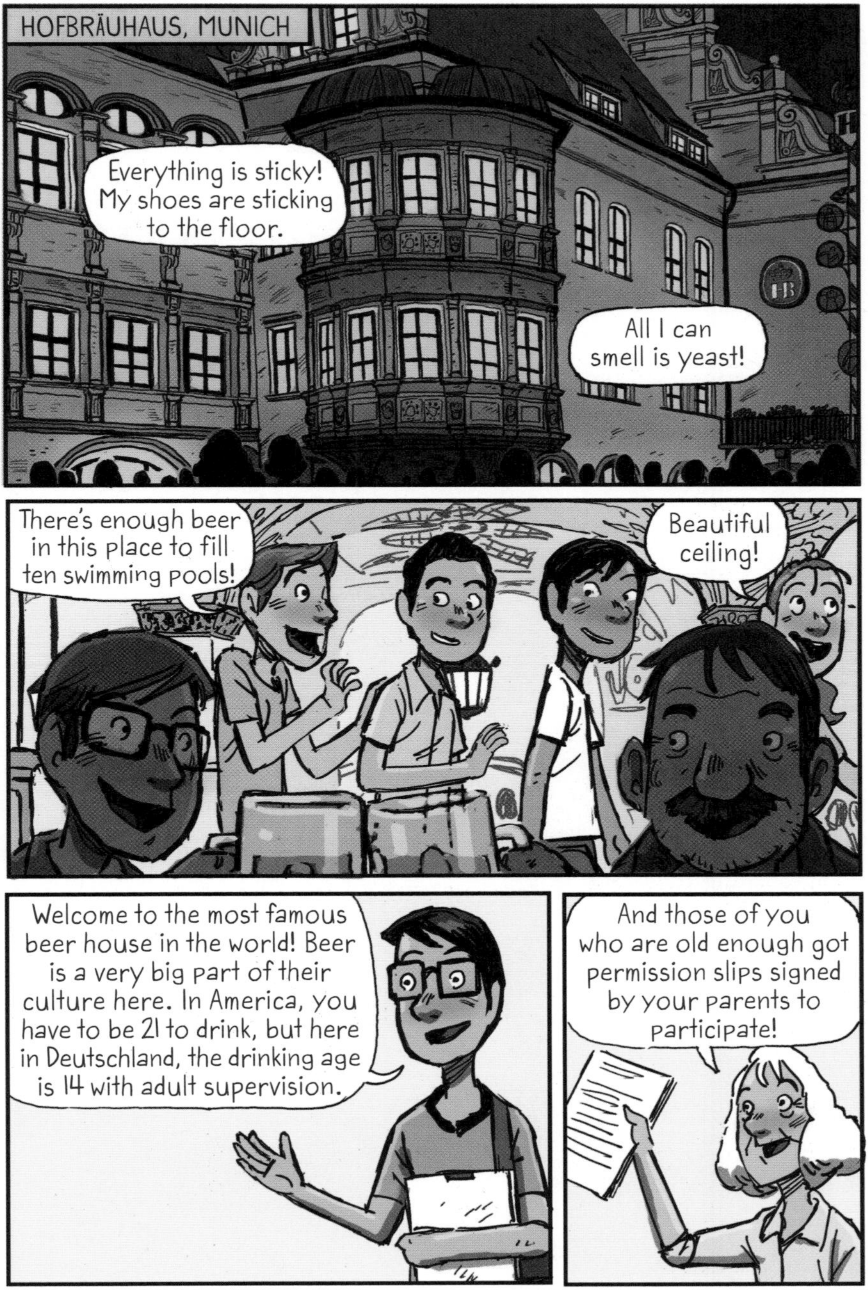
HOFBRÄUHAUS, MUNICH
Everything is sticky! My shoes are sticking to the floor.
All I can smell is yeast!
There's enough beer in this place to fill ten swimming pools!
Beautiful ceiling!
Welcome to the most famous beer house in the world! Beer is a very big part of their culture here. In America, you have to be 21 to drink, but here in Deutschland, the drinking age is 14 with adult supervision.
And those of you who are old enough got permission slips signed by your parents to participate!

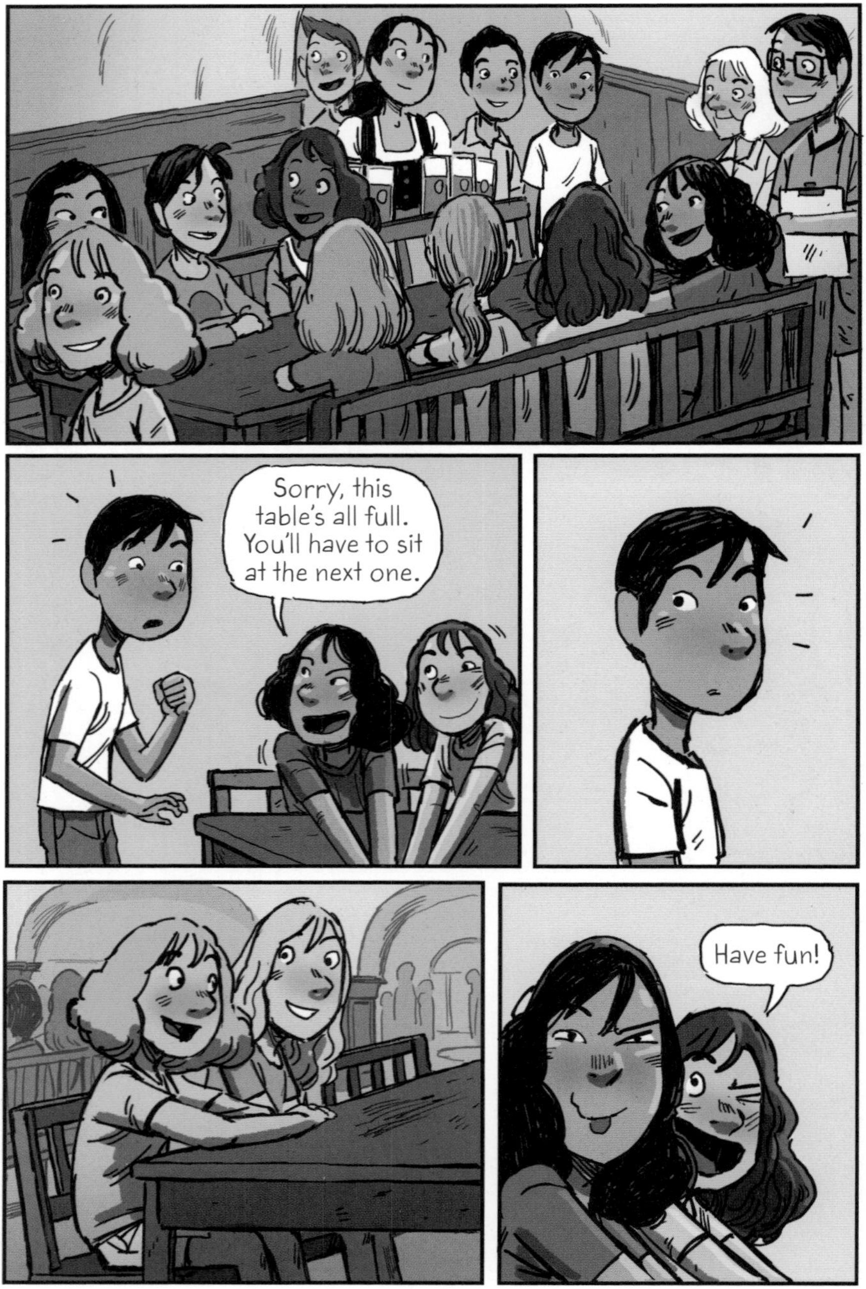
Sorry, this table's all full. You'll have to sit at the next one.
Have fun!

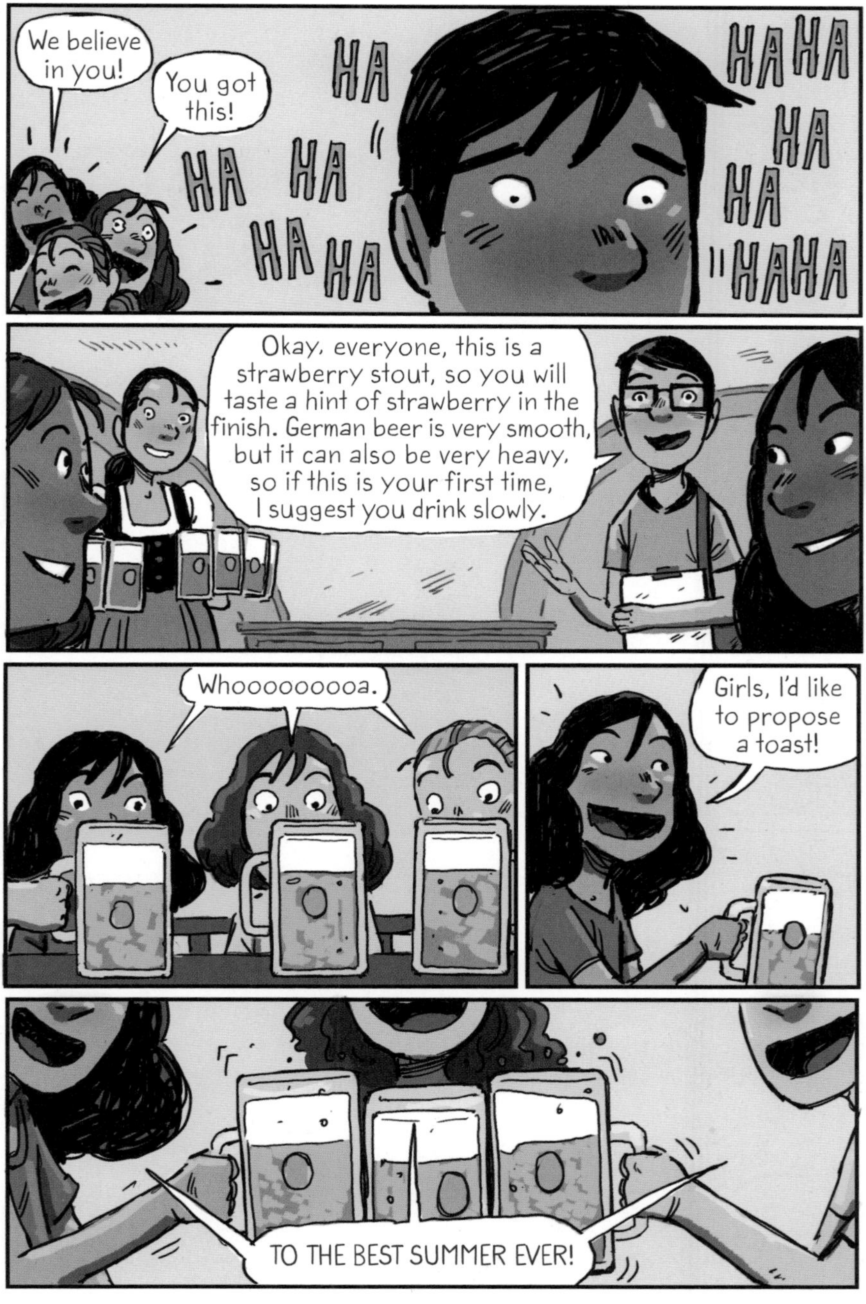
We believe in you!
You got this!
HA
HA HA
HA HA
HAHA
HA
HA
HAHA
Okay, everyone, this is a strawberry stout, so you will taste a hint of strawberry in the finish. German beer is very smooth, but it can also be very heavy, so if this is your first time, I suggest you drink slowly.
Whoooooooooa.
Girls, I'd like to propose a toast!
TO THE BEST SUMMER EVER!

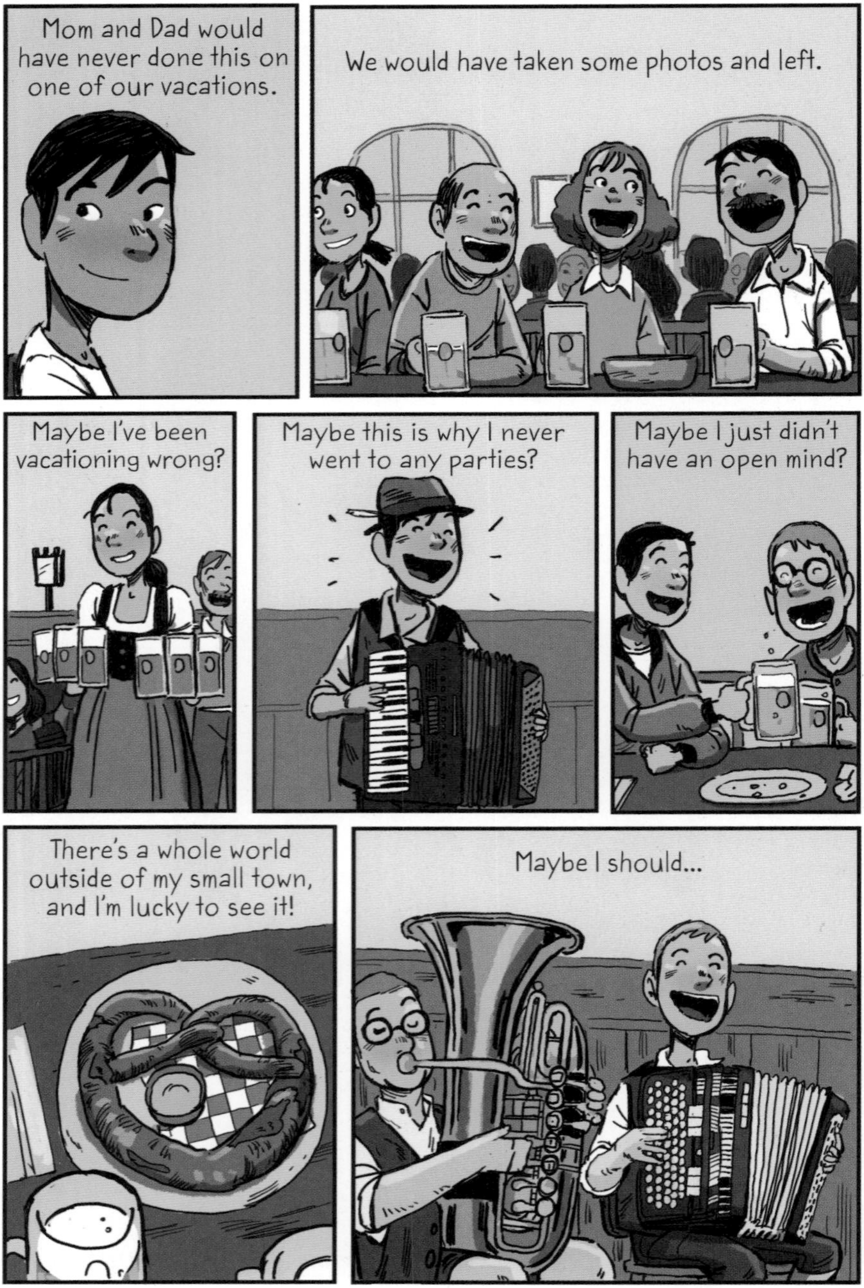
Mom and Dad would have never done this on one of our vacations.
We would have taken some photos and left.
Maybe I've been vacationing wrong?
Maybe this is why I never went to any parties?
Maybe I just didn't have an open mind?
There's a whole world outside of my small town, and I'm lucky to see it!
Maybe I should...

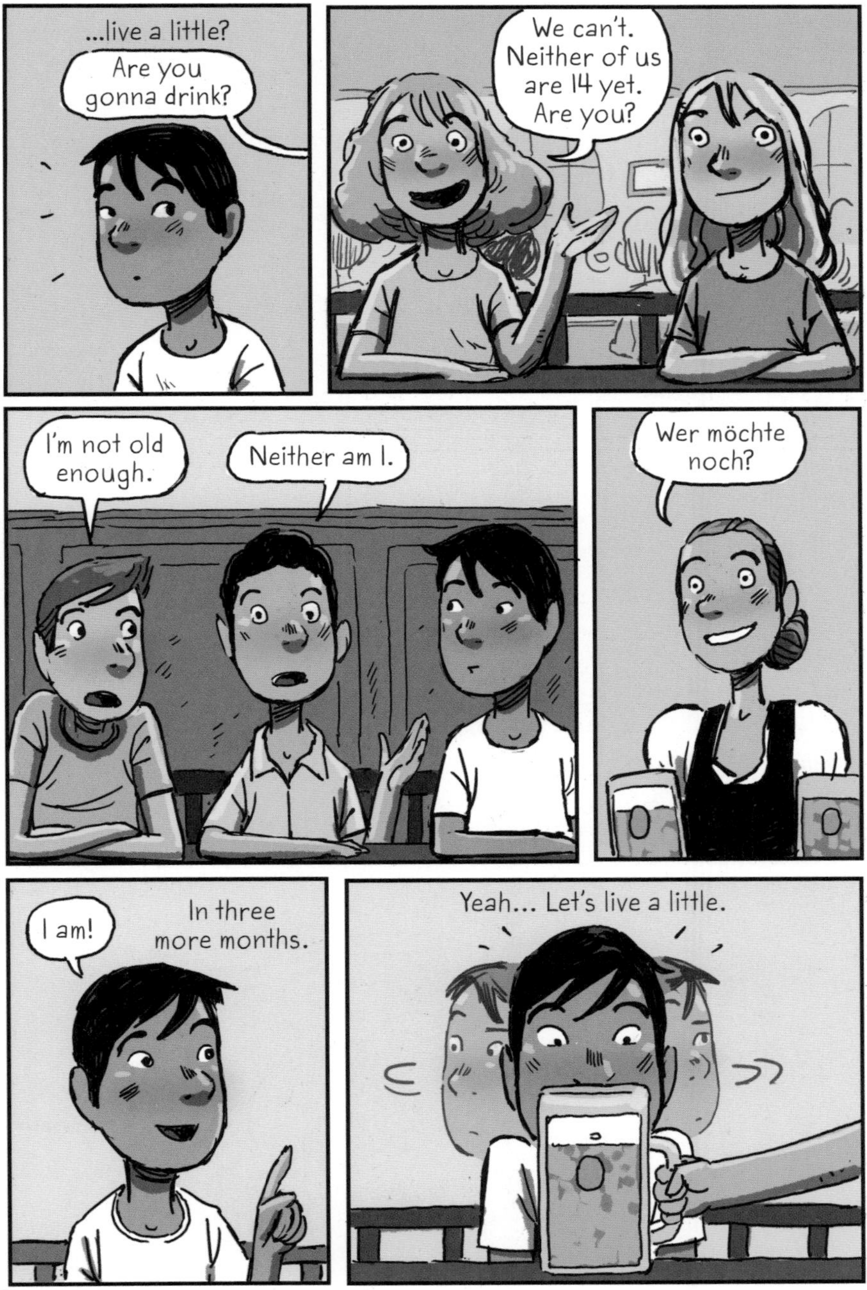
...live a little?
Are you gonna drink?
We can't. Neither of us are 14 yet. Are you?
I'm not old enough.
Neither am I.
Wer möchte noch?
I am!
In three more months.
Yeah... Let's live a little.

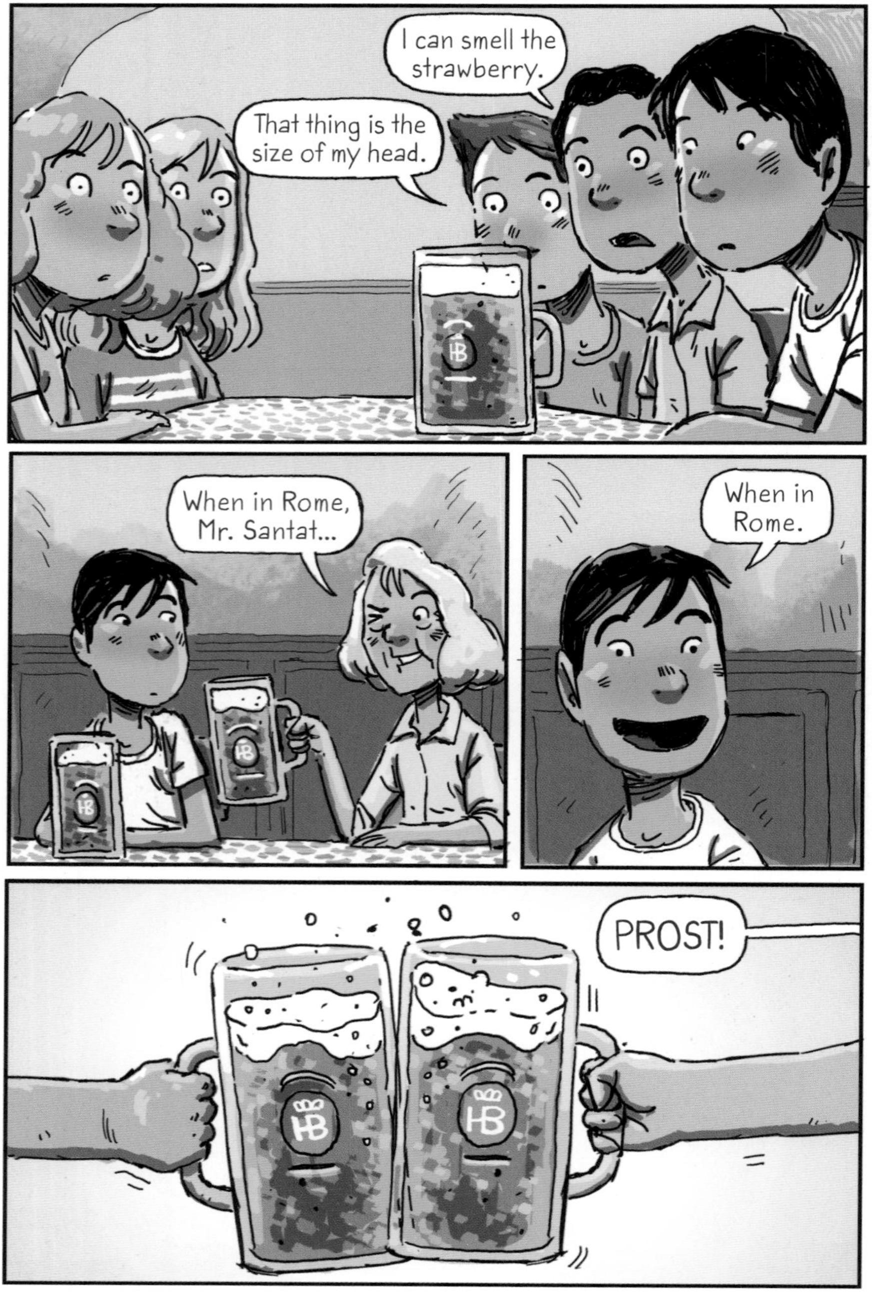
I can smell the strawberry.
That thing is the size of my head.
When in Rome, Mr. Santat...
When in Rome.
PROST!

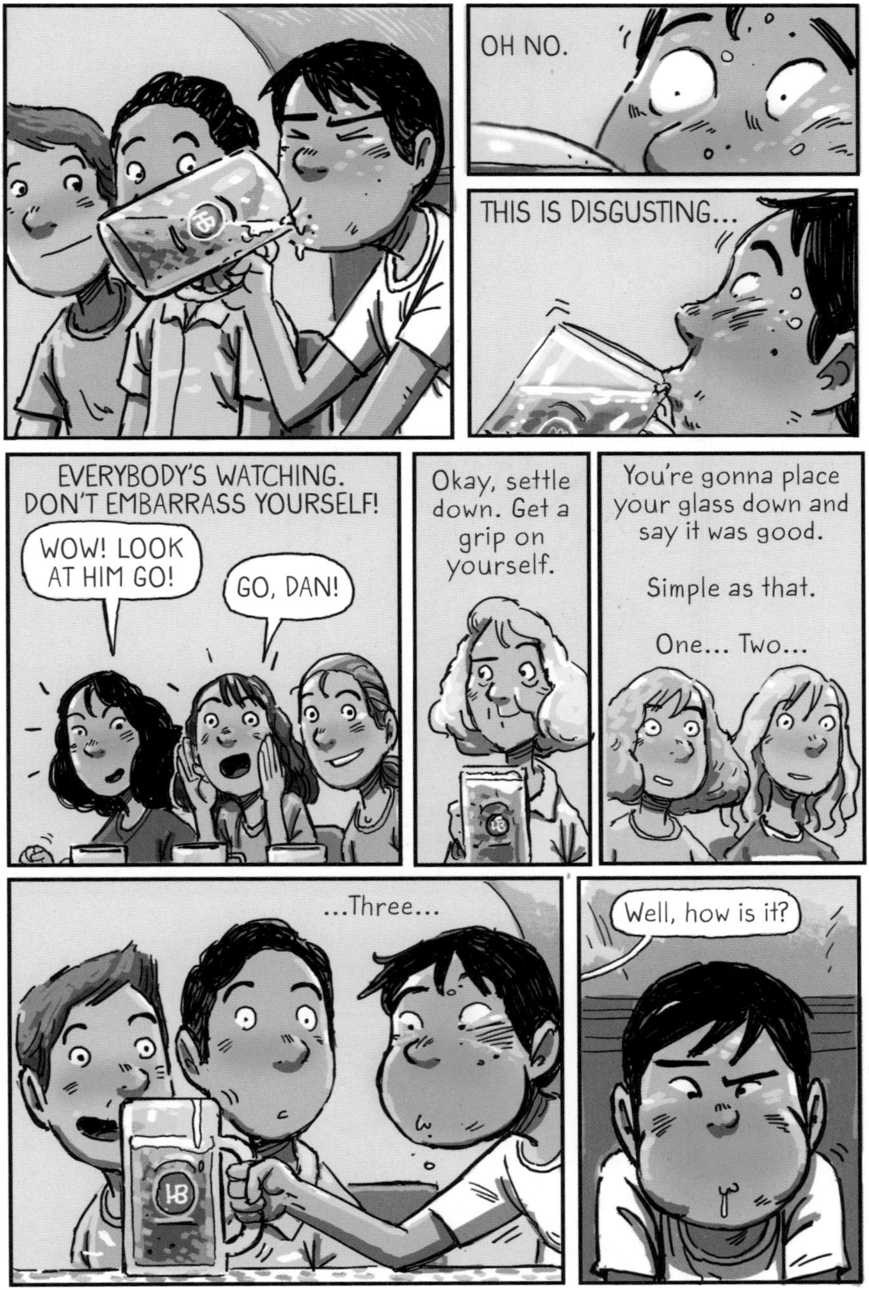

OH NO.
THIS IS DISGUSTING...
EVERYBODY'S WATCHING. DON'T EMBARRASS YOURSELF!
WOW! LOOK AT HIM GO!
GO, DAN!
Okay, settle down. Get a grip on yourself.
You're gonna place your glass down and say it was good.
Simple as that.
One... Two...
...Three...
Well, how is it?

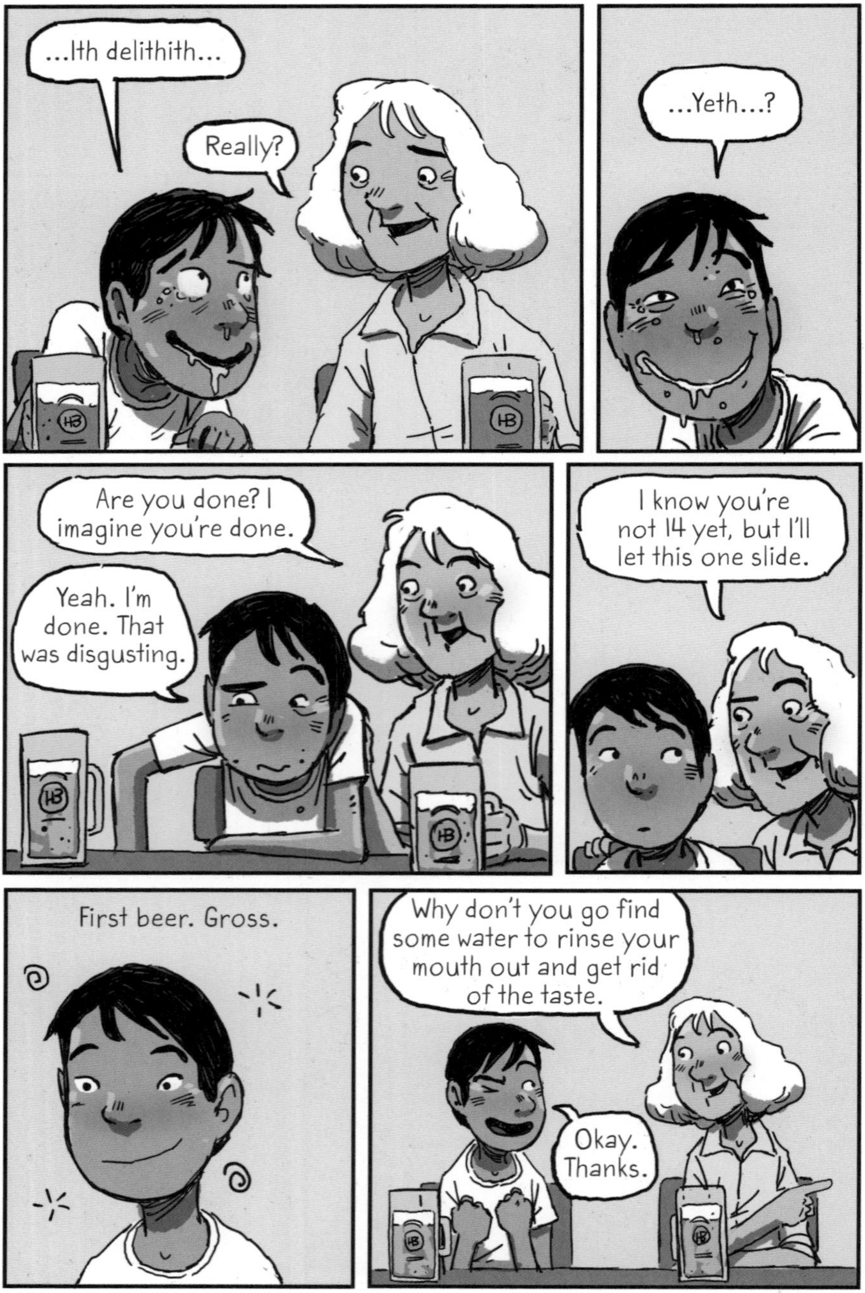
...Ith delithith...
Really?
...Yeth...?
Are you done? I imagine you're done.
Yeah. I'm done. That was disgusting.
I know you're not 14 yet, but I'll let this one slide.
First beer. Gross.
Why don't you go find some water to rinse your mouth out and get rid of the taste.
Okay. Thanks.

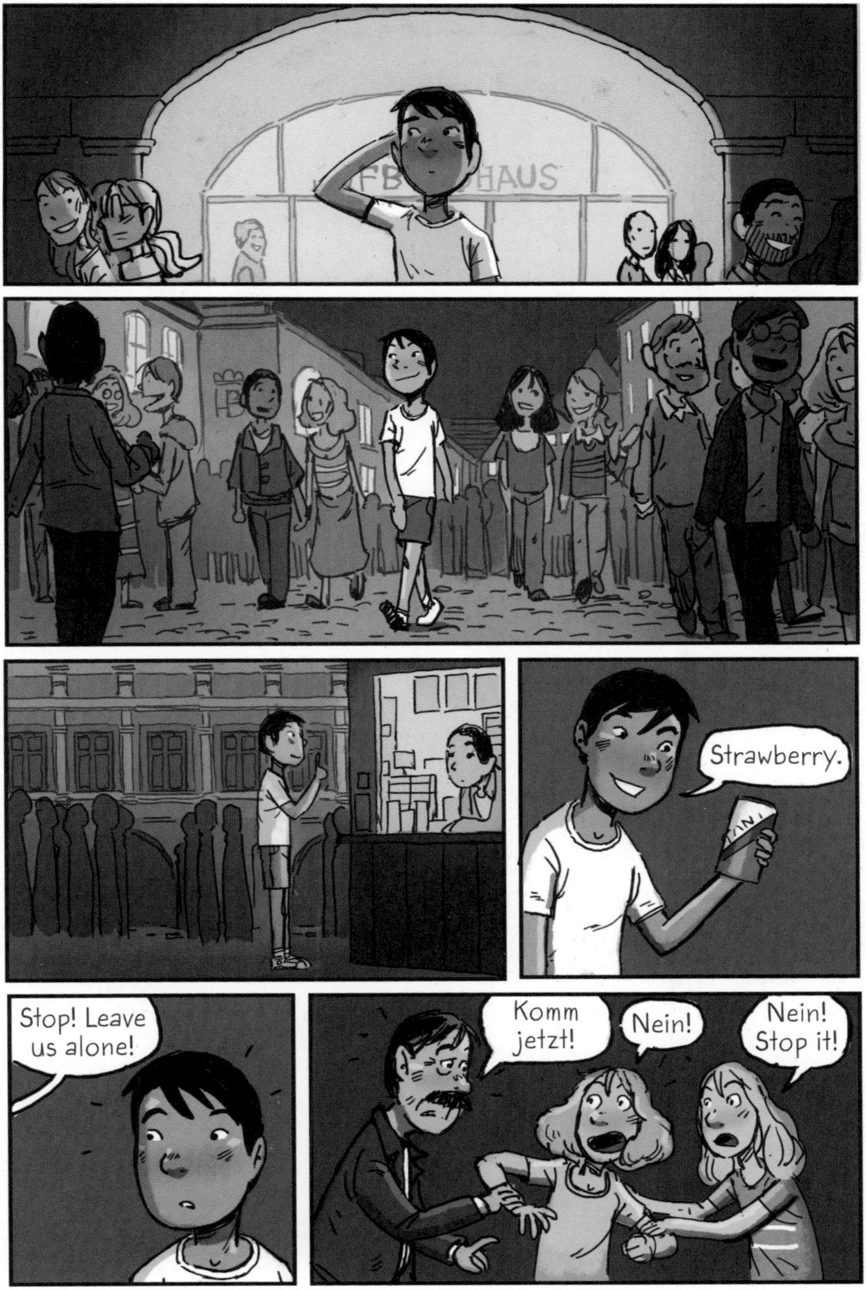
FB HAUS
Strawberry.
Stop! Leave us alone!
Komm jetzt!
Nein!
Nein! Stop it!

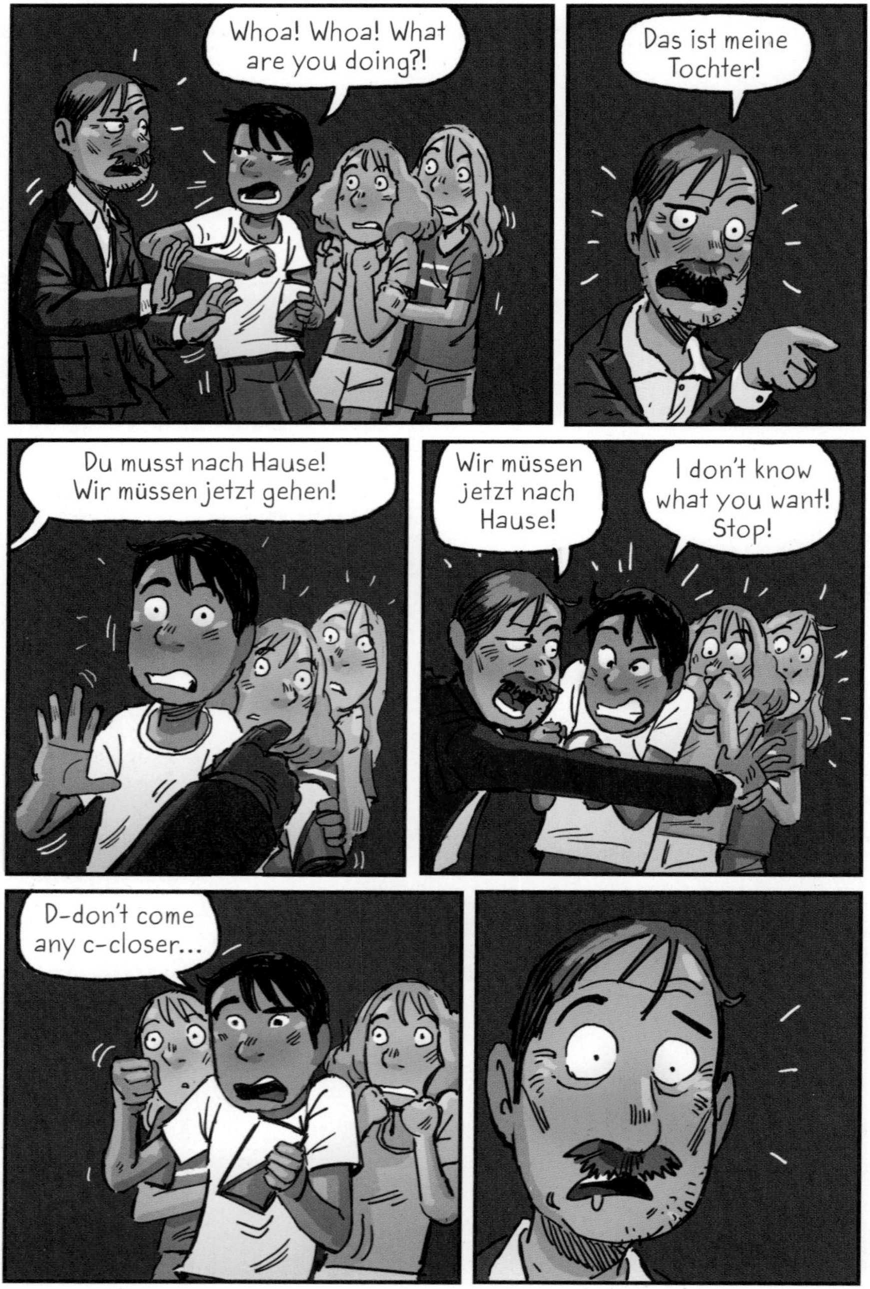
Whoa! Whoa! What are you doing?!
Das ist meine Tochter!
Du musst nach Hause! Wir müssen jetzt gehen!
Wir müssen jetzt nach Hause!
I don't know what you want! Stop!
D-don't come any c-closer...

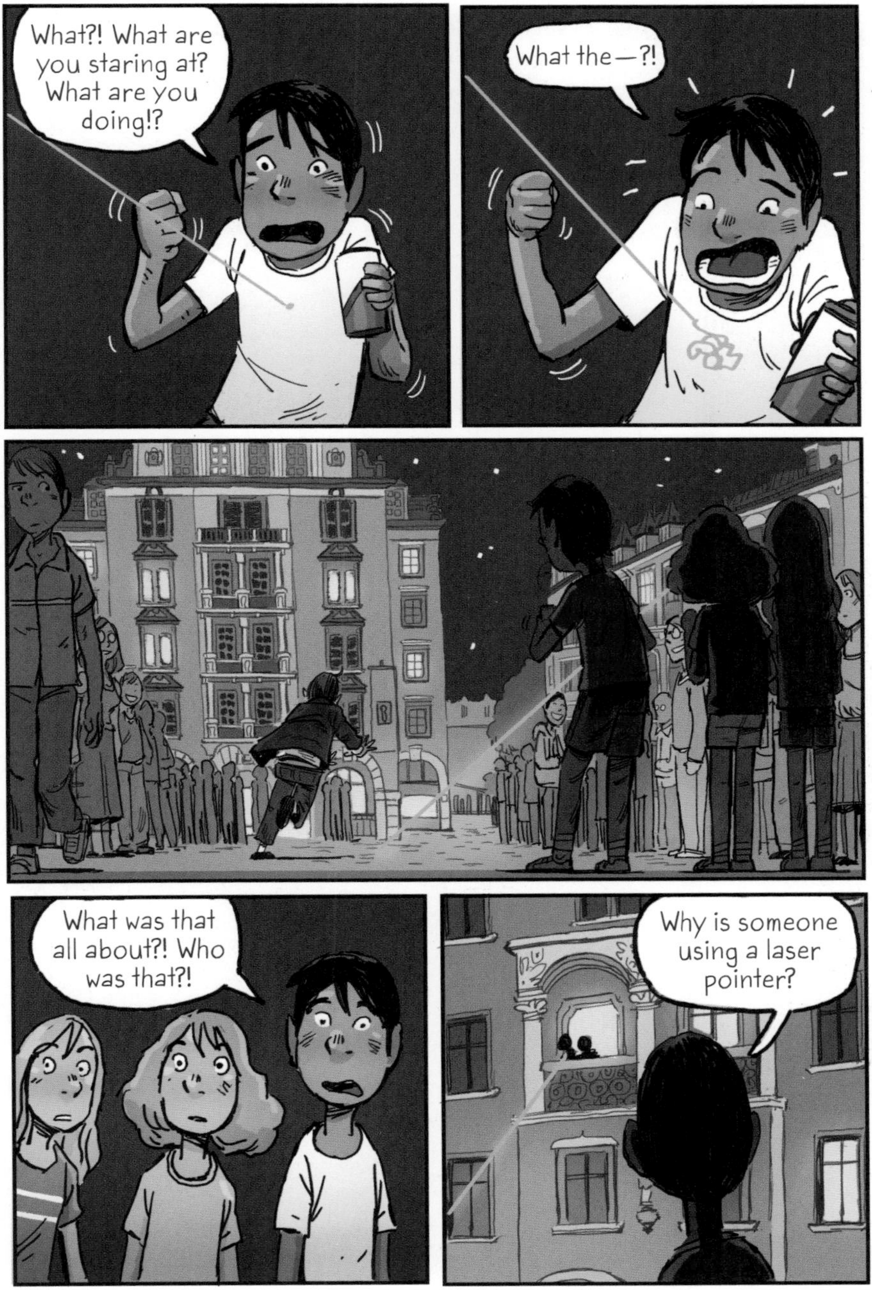
What?! What are you staring at? What are you doing!?
What the—?!
What was that all about?! Who was that?!
Why is someone using a laser pointer?

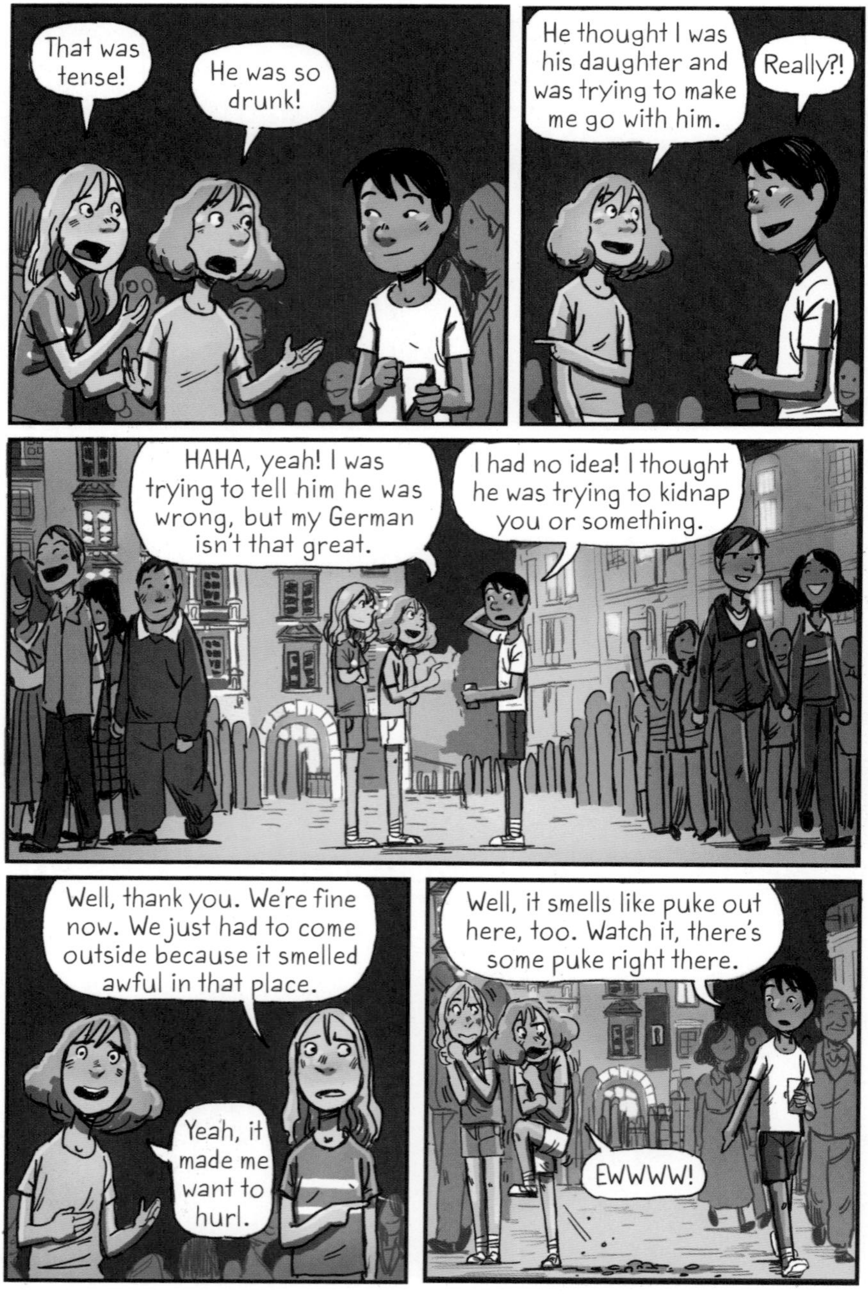
That was tense!
He was so drunk!
He thought I was his daughter and was trying to make me go with him.
Really?!
HAHA, yeah! I was trying to tell him he was wrong, but my German isn't that great.
I had no idea! I thought he was trying to kidnap you or something.
Well, thank you. We're fine now. We just had to come outside because it smelled awful in that place.
Yeah, it made me want to hurl.
Well, it smells like puke out here, too. Watch it, there's some puke right there.
EWWWW!

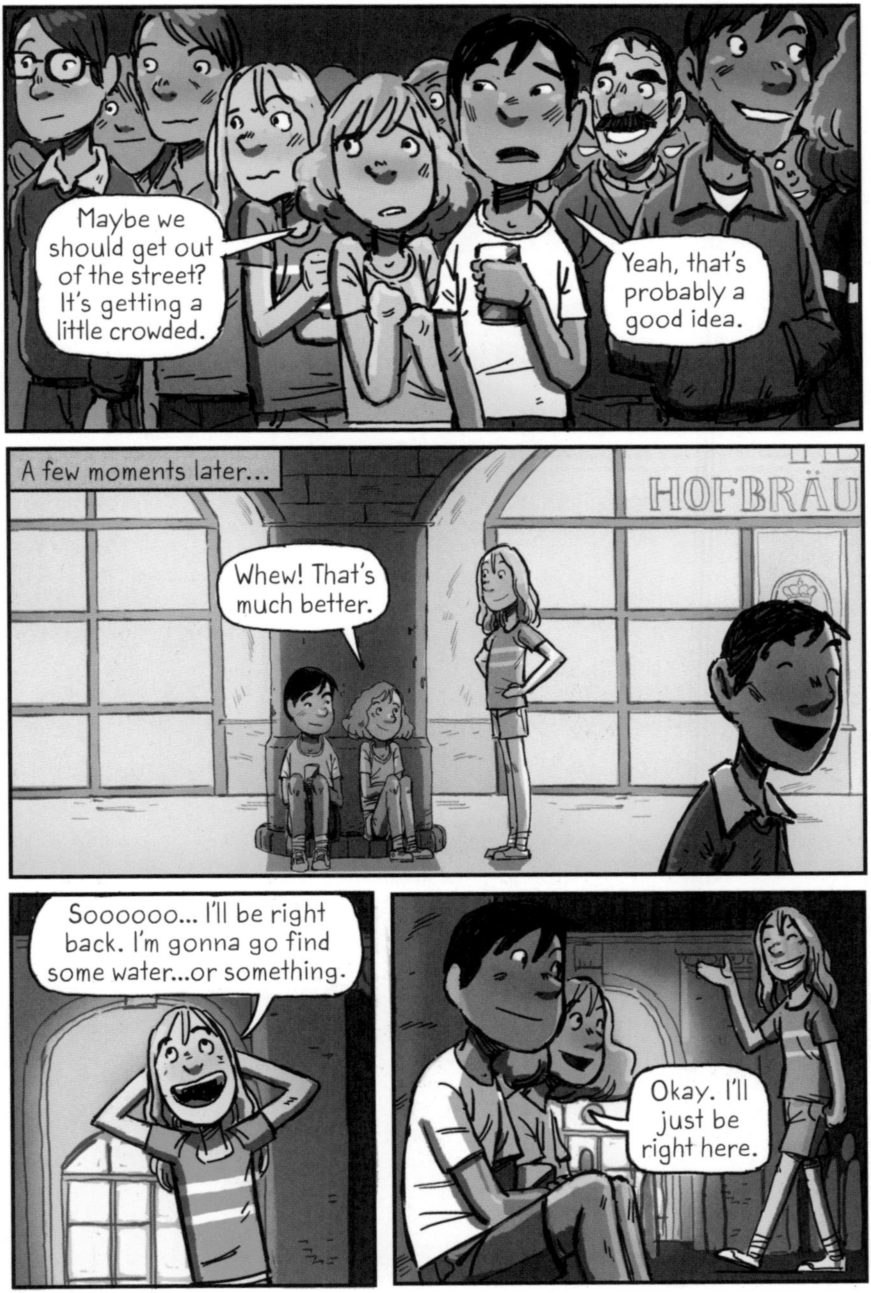

Maybe we should get out of the street? It's getting a little crowded.
Yeah, that's probably a good idea.
A few moments later...
HOFBRÄU
Whew! That's much better.
Sooooooo... I'll be right back. I'm gonna go find some water...or something.
Okay. I'll just be right here.

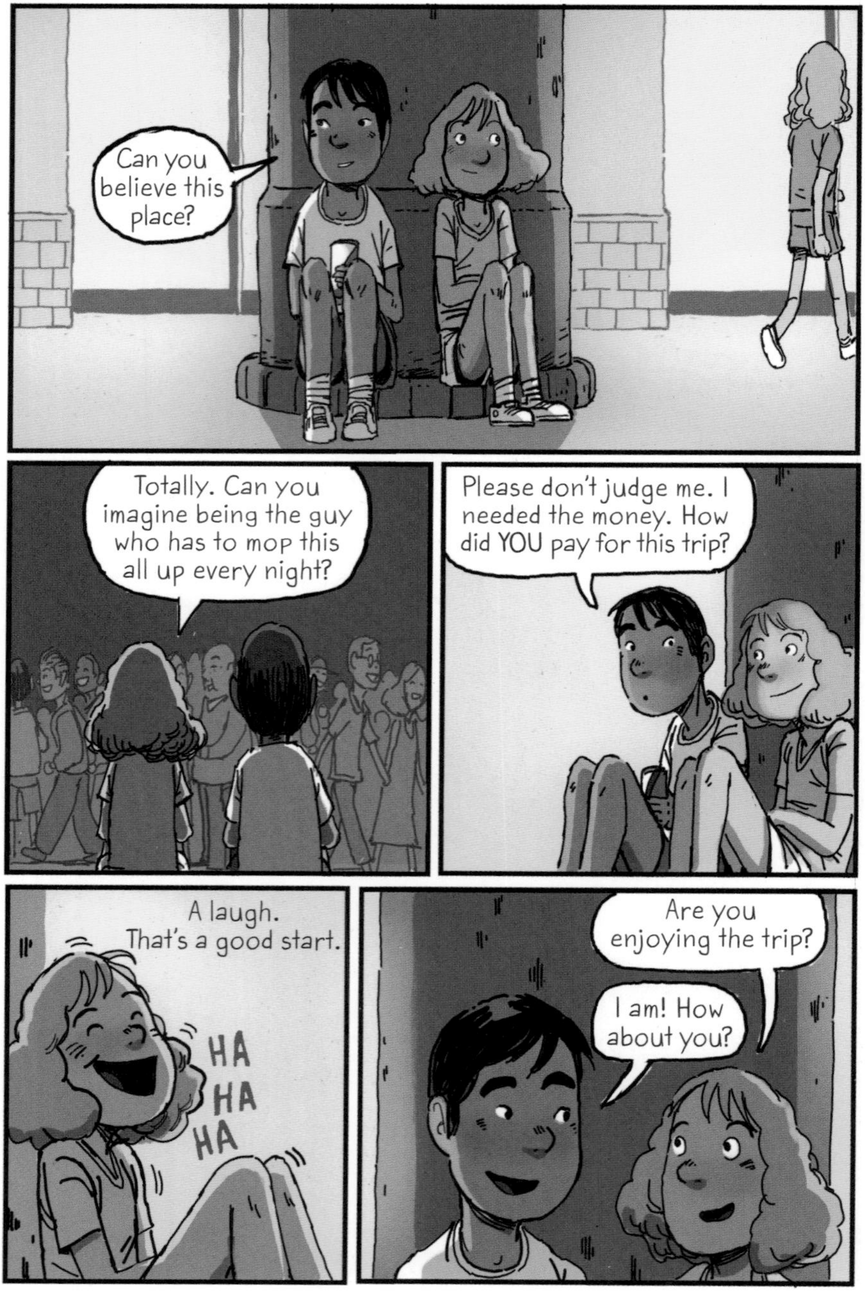
Can you believe this place?
Totally. Can you imagine being the guy who has to mop this all up every night?
Please don't judge me. I needed the money. How did YOU pay for this trip?
A laugh. That's a good start.
HA HA HA
Are you enjoying the trip?
I am! How about you?

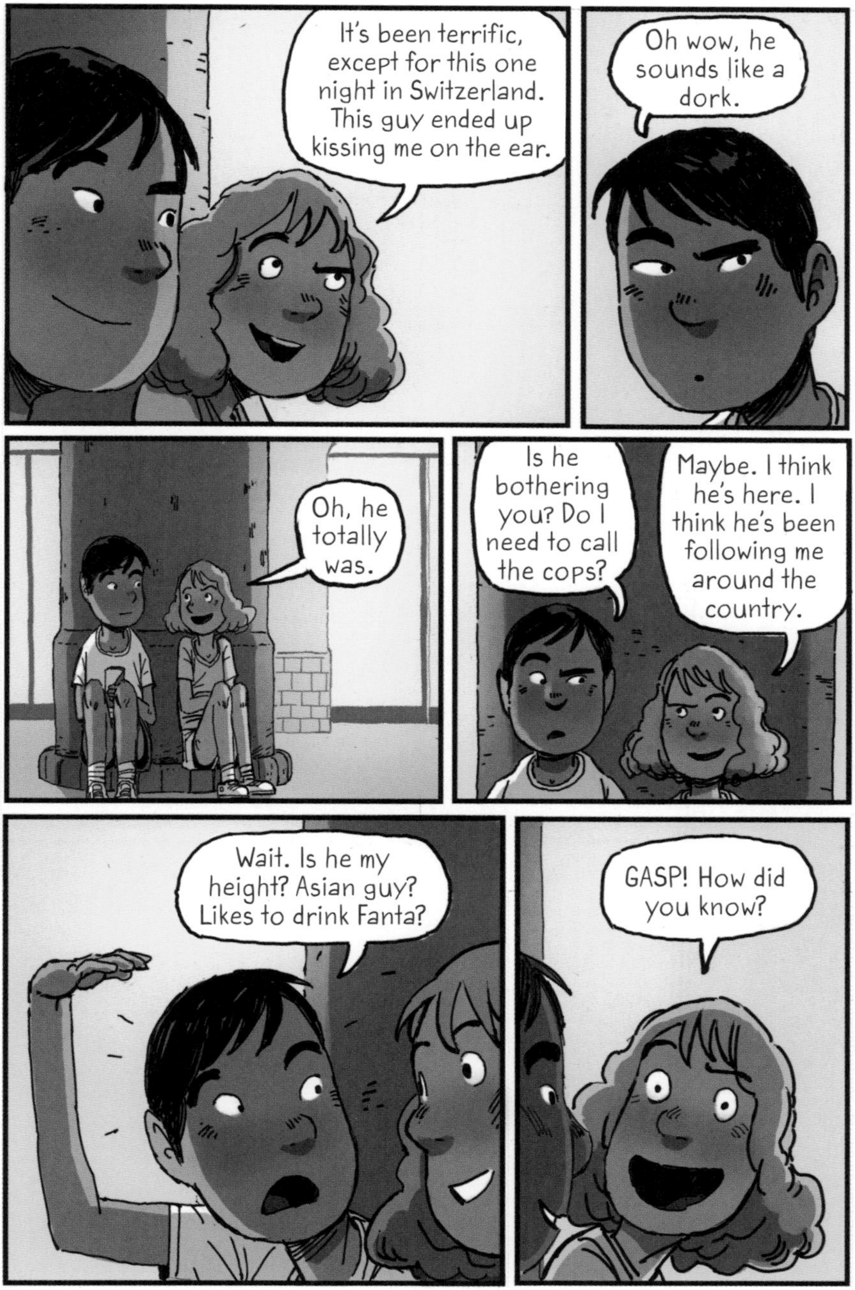
It's been terrific, except for this one night in Switzerland. This guy ended up kissing me on the ear.
Oh wow, he sounds like a dork.
Oh, he totally was.
Is he bothering you? Do I need to call the cops?
Maybe. I think he's here. I think he's been following me around the country.
Wait. Is he my height? Asian guy? Likes to drink Fanta?
GASP! How did you know?

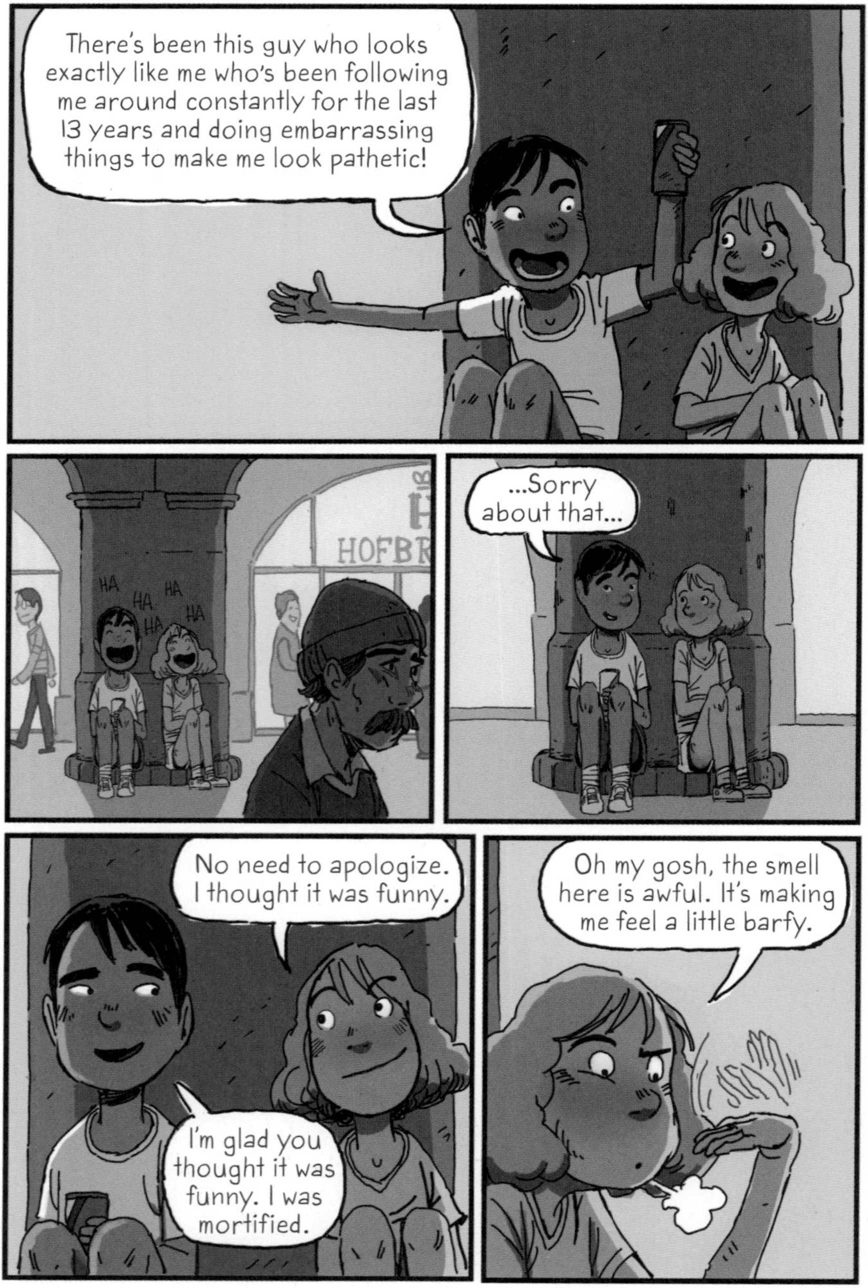
There's been this guy who looks exactly like me who's been following me around constantly for the last 13 years and doing embarrassing things to make me look pathetic!
HOFBR
HA HA HA HA HA
...Sorry about that...
No need to apologize. I thought it was funny.
I'm glad you thought it was funny. I was mortified.
Oh my gosh, the smell here is awful. It's making me feel a little barfy.

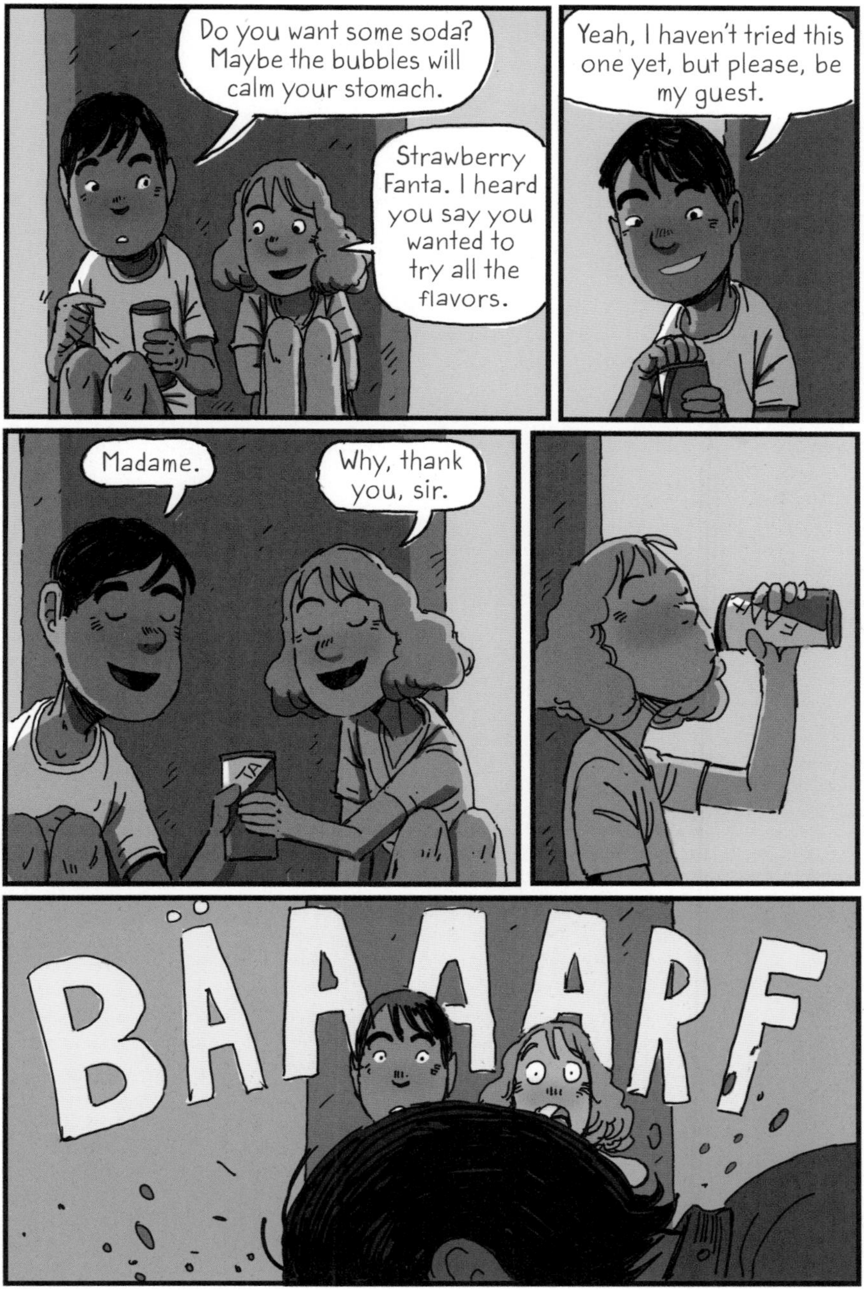
Do you want some soda? Maybe the bubbles will calm your stomach.
Strawberry Fanta. I heard you say you wanted to try all the flavors.
Yeah, I haven't tried this one yet, but please, be my guest.
Madame.
Why, thank you, sir.
BAAARF

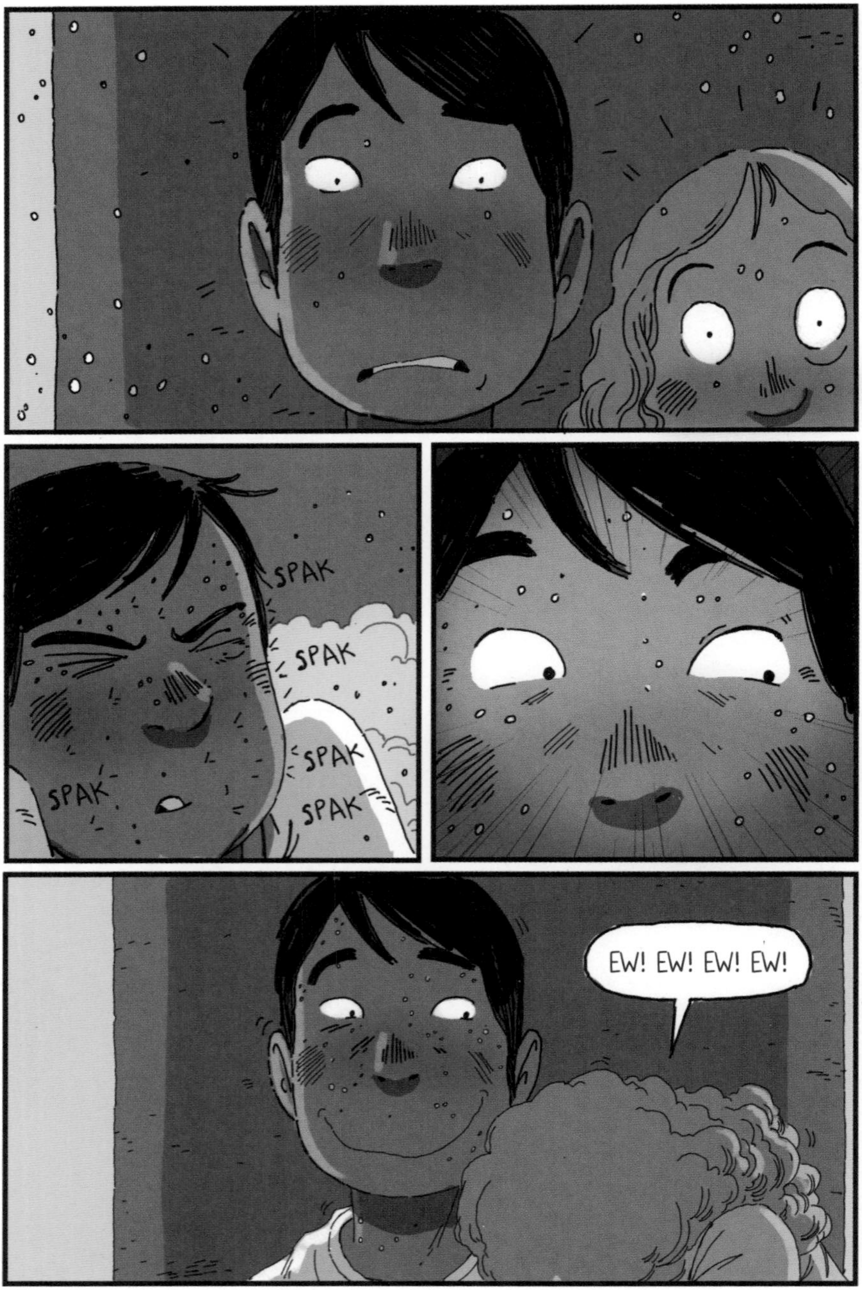
SPAK
SPAK
SPAK
SPAK
SPAK
EW! EW! EW! EW!

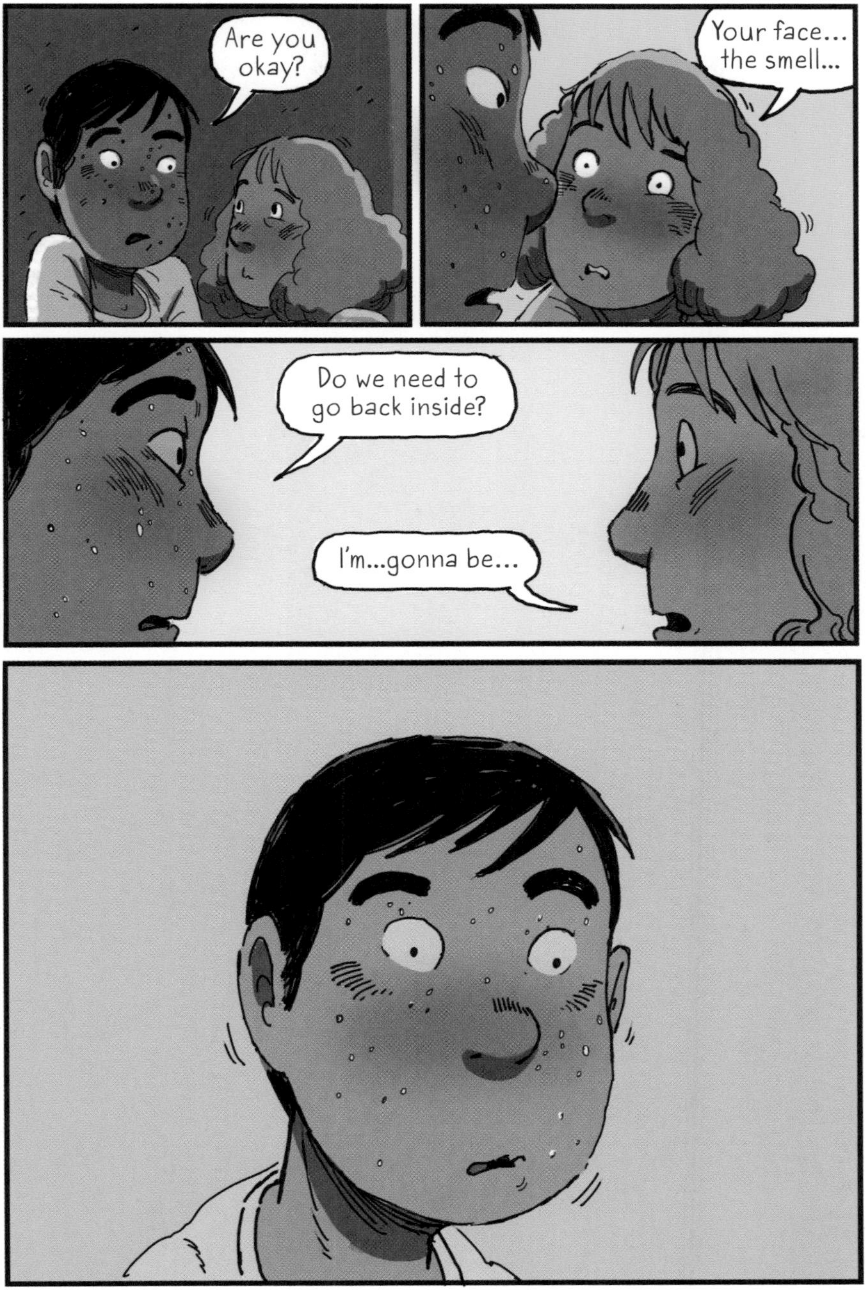
Are you okay?
Your face... the smell...
Do we need to go back inside?
I'm...gonna be...

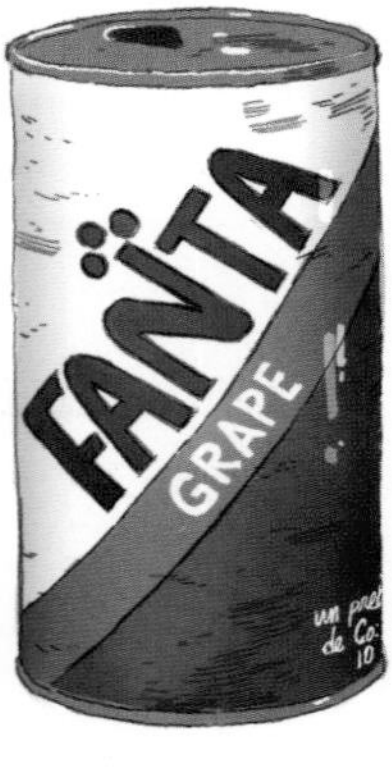
FANTA
GRAPE

SALZBURG

(13 DAYS LEFT IN THE TRIP)

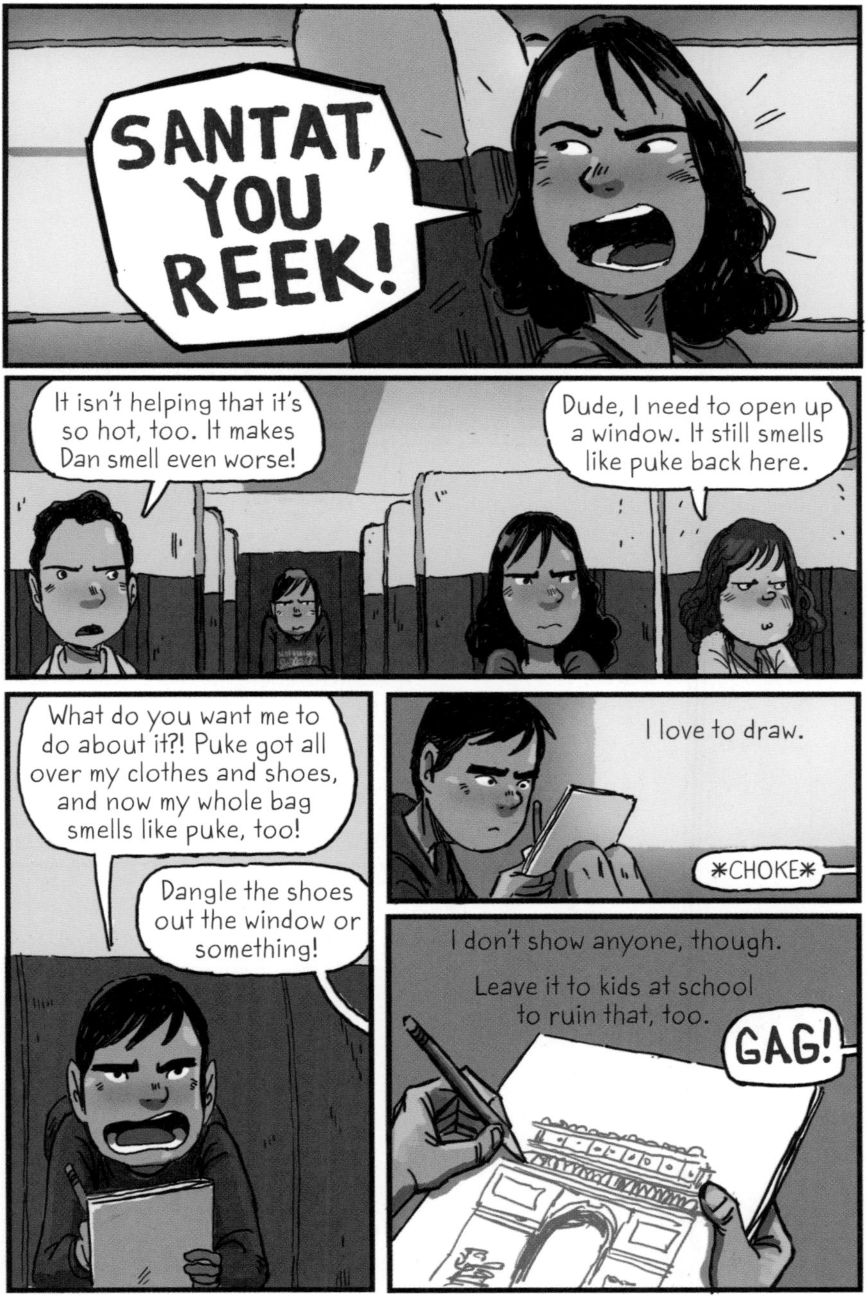
SANTAT, YOU REEK!
It isn't helping that it's so hot, too. It makes Dan smell even worse!
Dude, I need to open up a window. It still smells like puke back here.
What do you want me to do about it?! Puke got all over my clothes and shoes, and now my whole bag smells like puke, too!
Dangle the shoes out the window or something!
I love to draw.
CHOKE
I don't show anyone, though.
Leave it to kids at school to ruin that, too.
GAG!

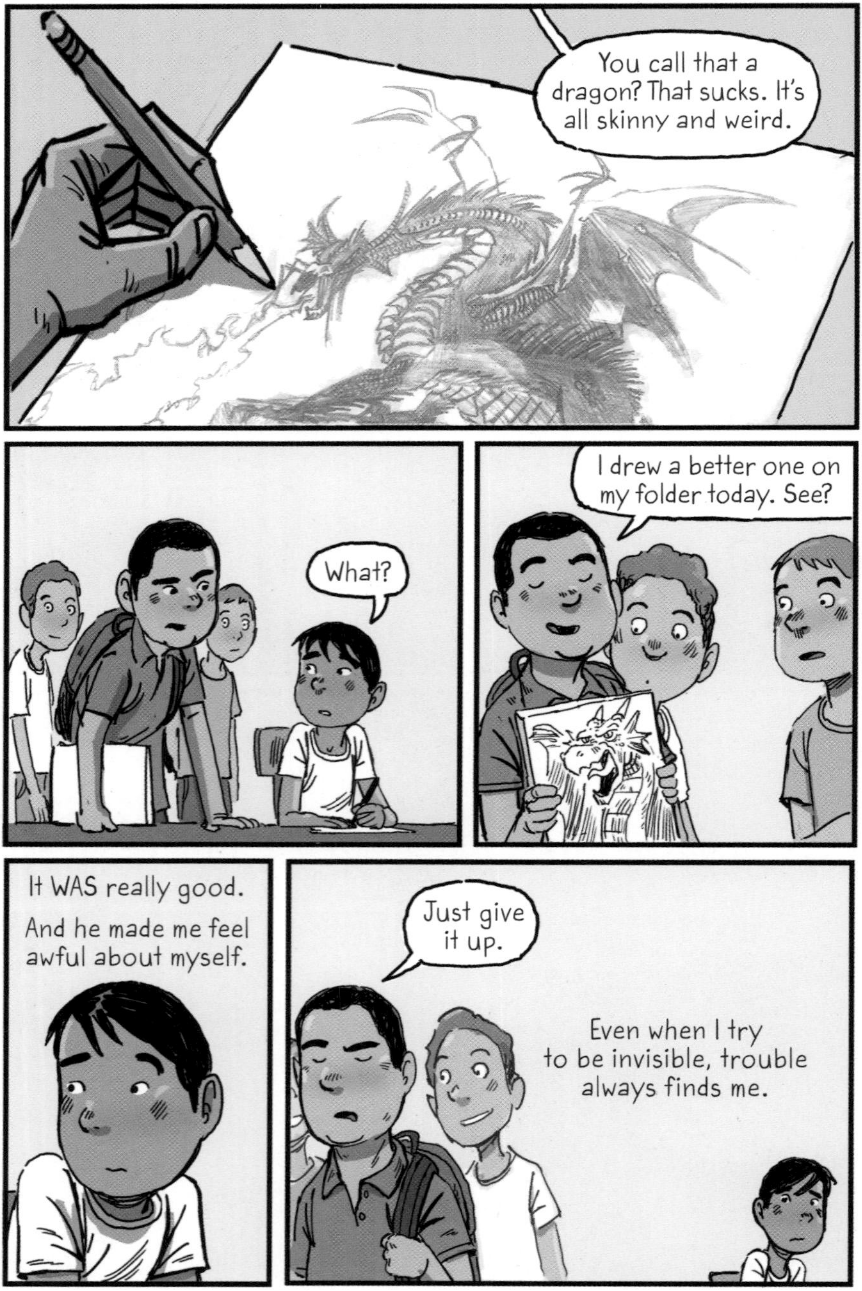
You call that a dragon? That sucks. It's all skinny and weird.
What?
I drew a better one on my folder today. See?
It WAS really good.
And he made me feel awful about myself.
Just give it up.
Even when I try to be invisible, trouble always finds me.

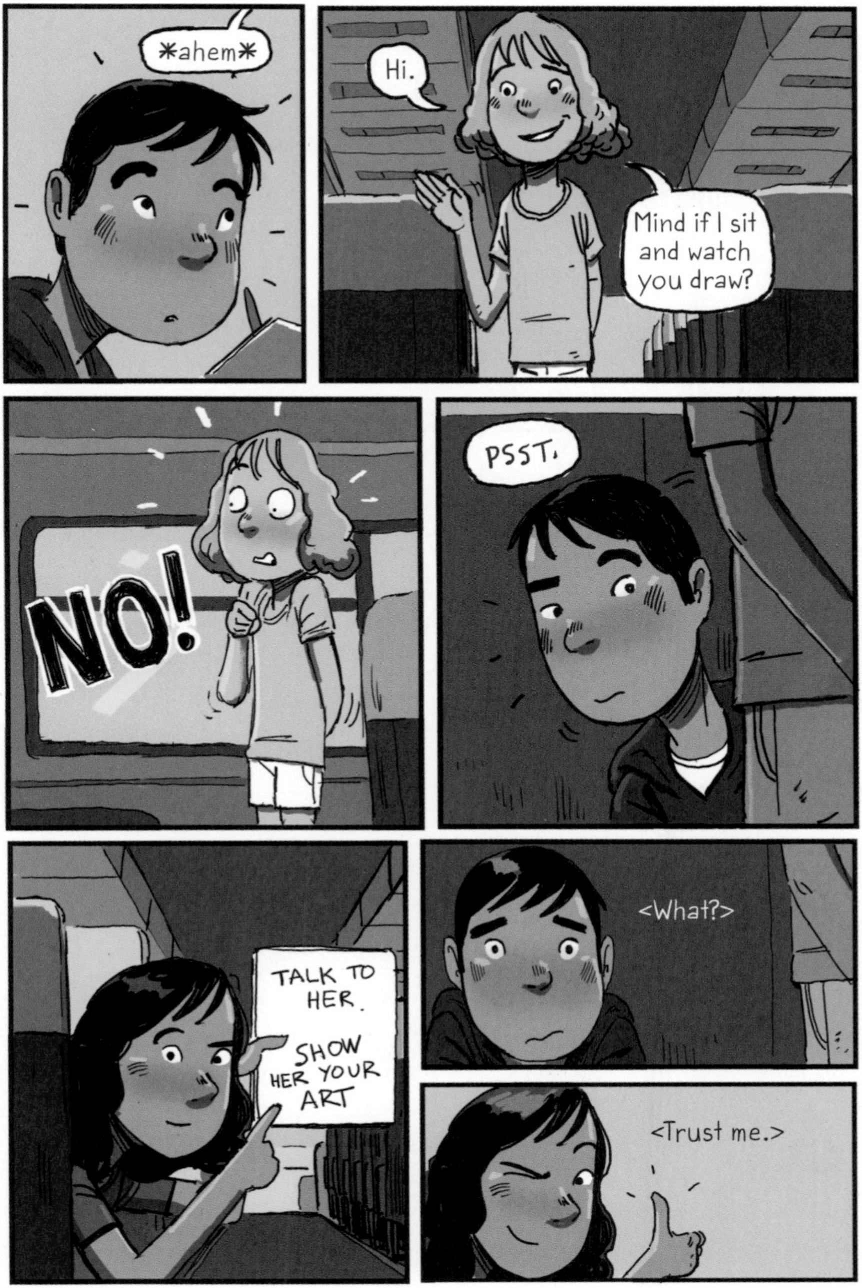
ahem
Hi.
Mind if I sit and watch you draw?
NO!
PSST.
TALK TO HER.
SHOW HER YOUR ART
<What?>
<Trust me.>

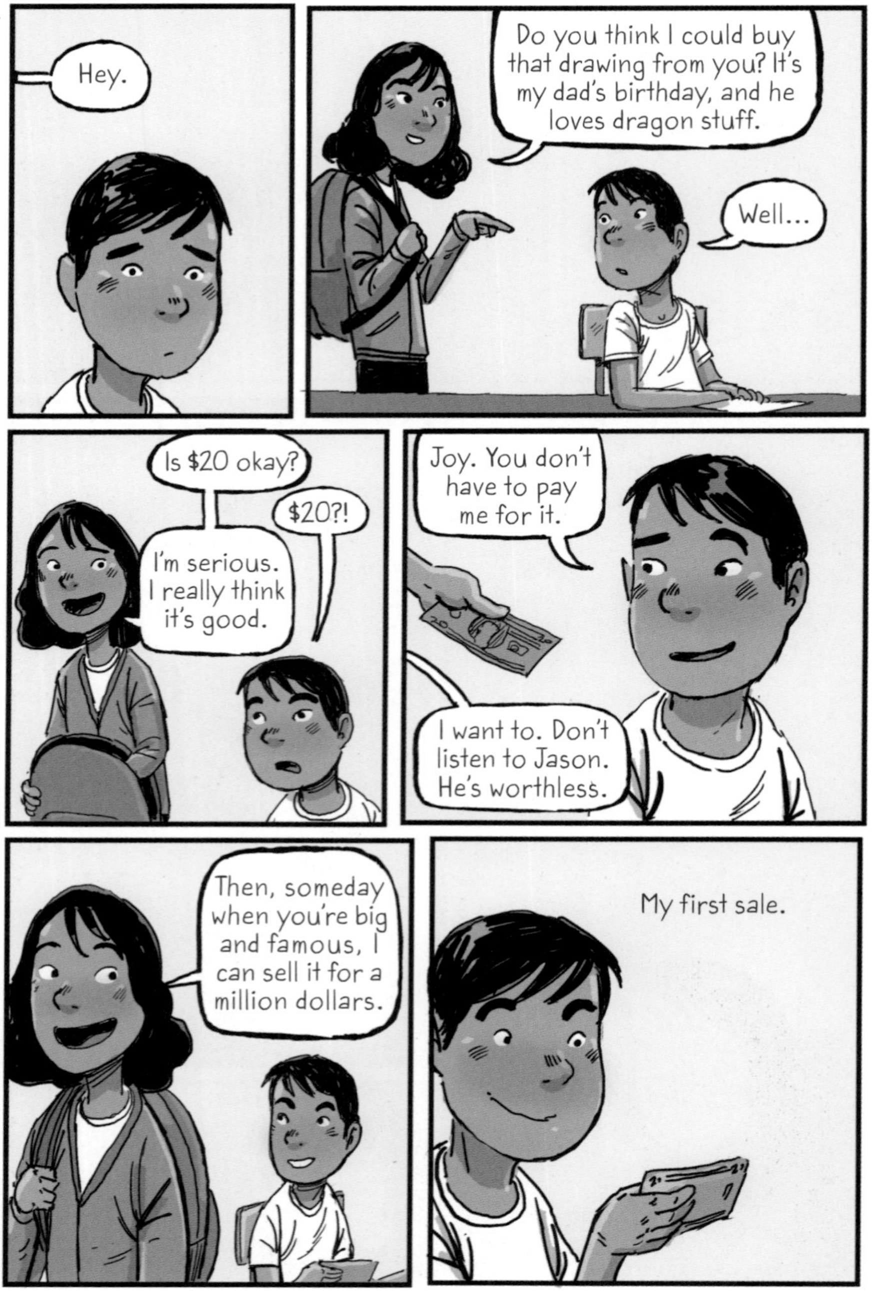
Hey.
Do you think I could buy that drawing from you? It's my dad's birthday, and he loves dragon stuff.
Well...
Is $20 okay?
$20?!
I'm serious. I really think it's good.
Joy. You don't have to pay me for it.
I want to. Don't listen to Jason. He's worthless.
Then, someday when you're big and famous, I can sell it for a million dollars.
My first sale.

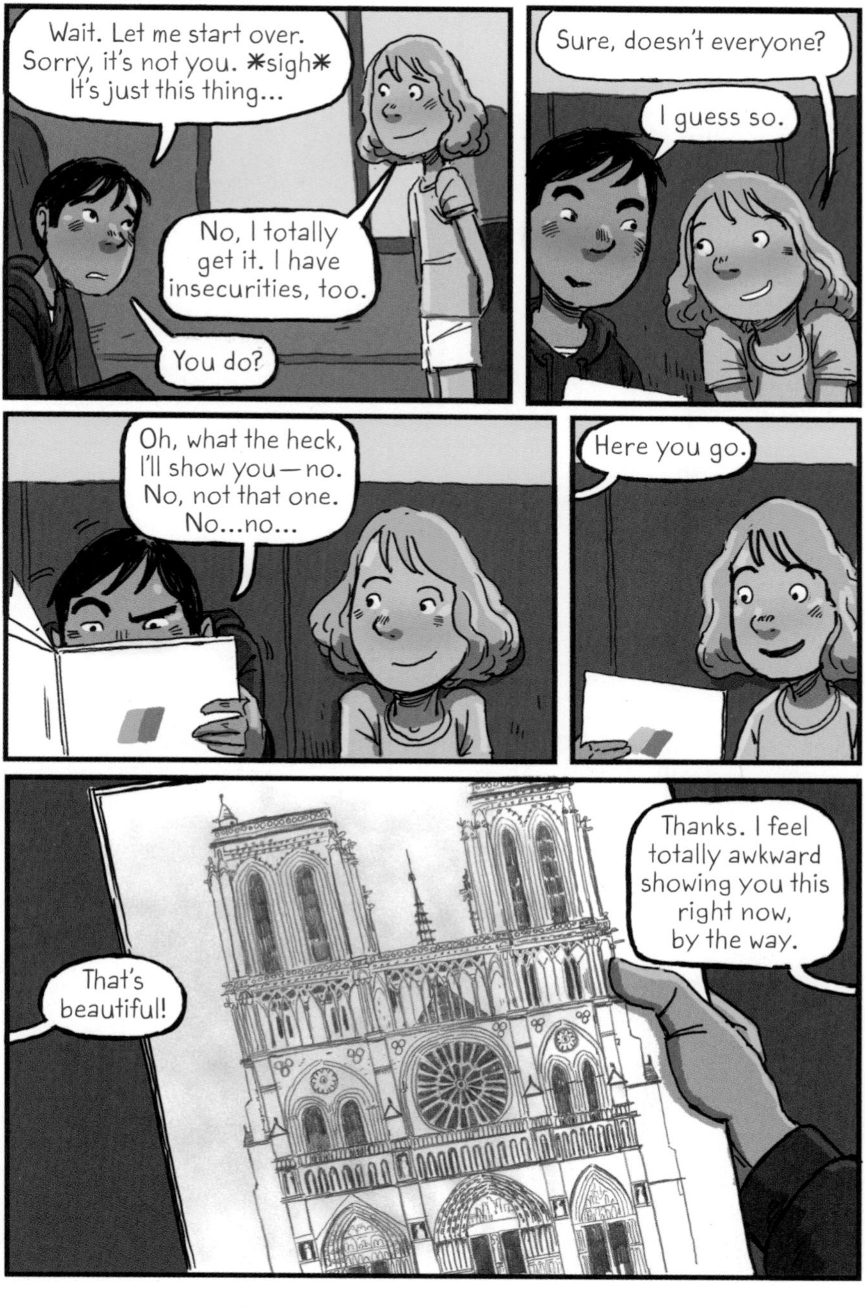
Wait. Let me start over. Sorry, it's not you. *sigh* It's just this thing...
No, I totally get it. I have insecurities, too.
You do?
Sure, doesn't everyone?
I guess so.
Oh, what the heck, I'll show you—no. No, not that one. No...no...
Here you go.
Thanks. I feel totally awkward showing you this right now, by the way.
That's beautiful!

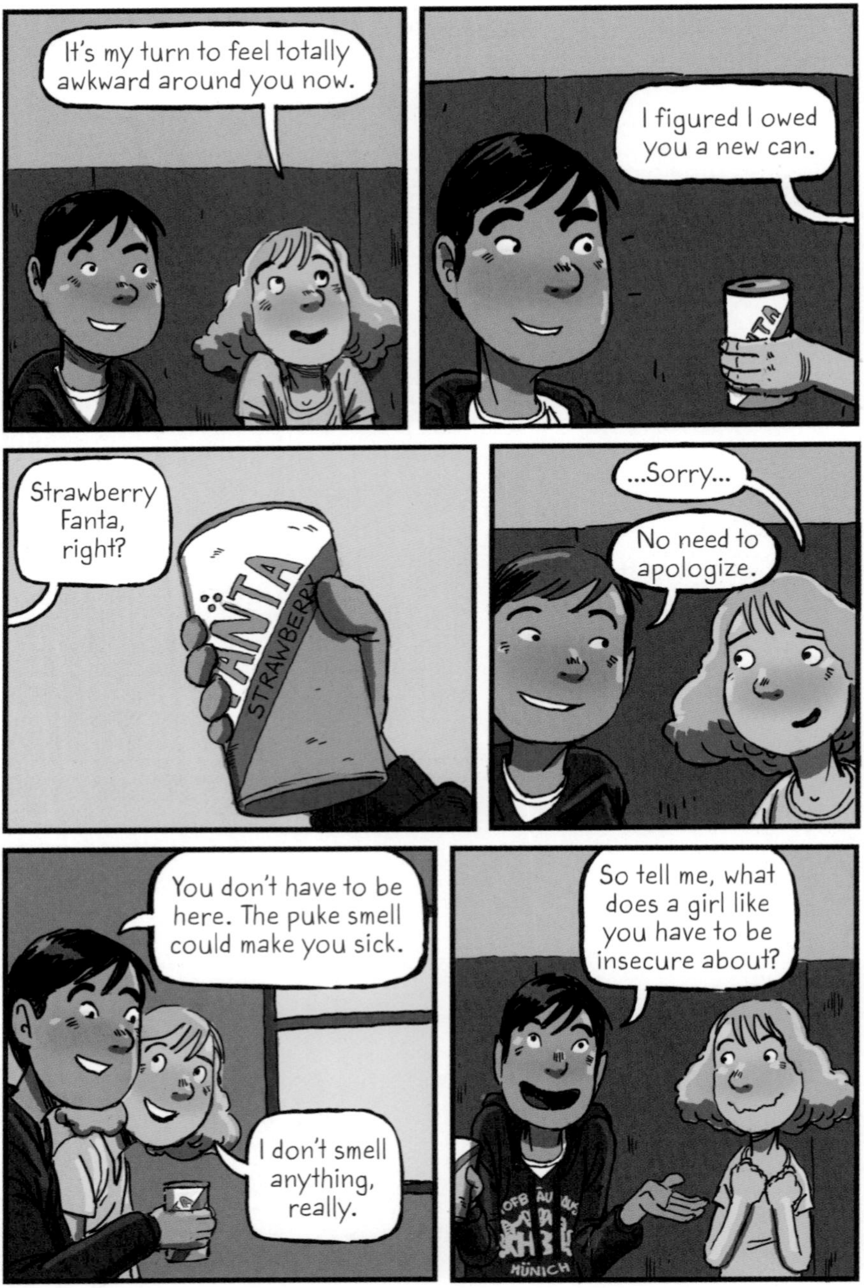
It's my turn to feel totally awkward around you now.
I figured I owed you a new can.
FANTA
Strawberry Fanta, right?
FANTA
STRAWBERRY
...Sorry...
No need to apologize.
You don't have to be here. The puke smell could make you sick.
I don't smell anything, really.
So tell me, what does a girl like you have to be insecure about?
MÜNICH

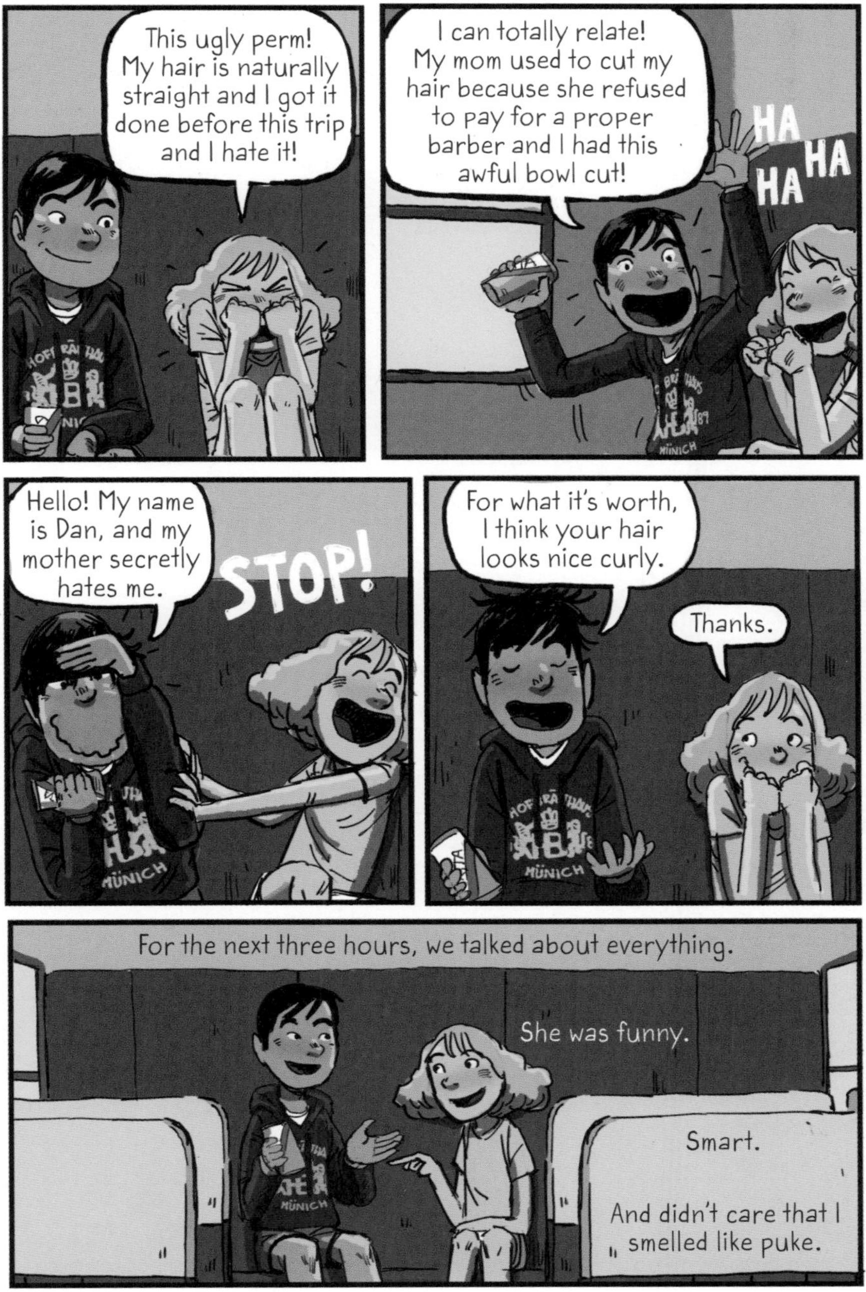
This ugly perm! My hair is naturally straight and I got it done before this trip and I hate it!
I can totally relate! My mom used to cut my hair because she refused to pay for a proper barber and I had this awful bowl cut!
HA HA HA
Hello! My name is Dan, and my mother secretly hates me.
STOP!
For what it's worth, I think your hair looks nice curly.
Thanks.
For the next three hours, we talked about everything.
She was funny.
Smart.
And didn't care that I smelled like puke.

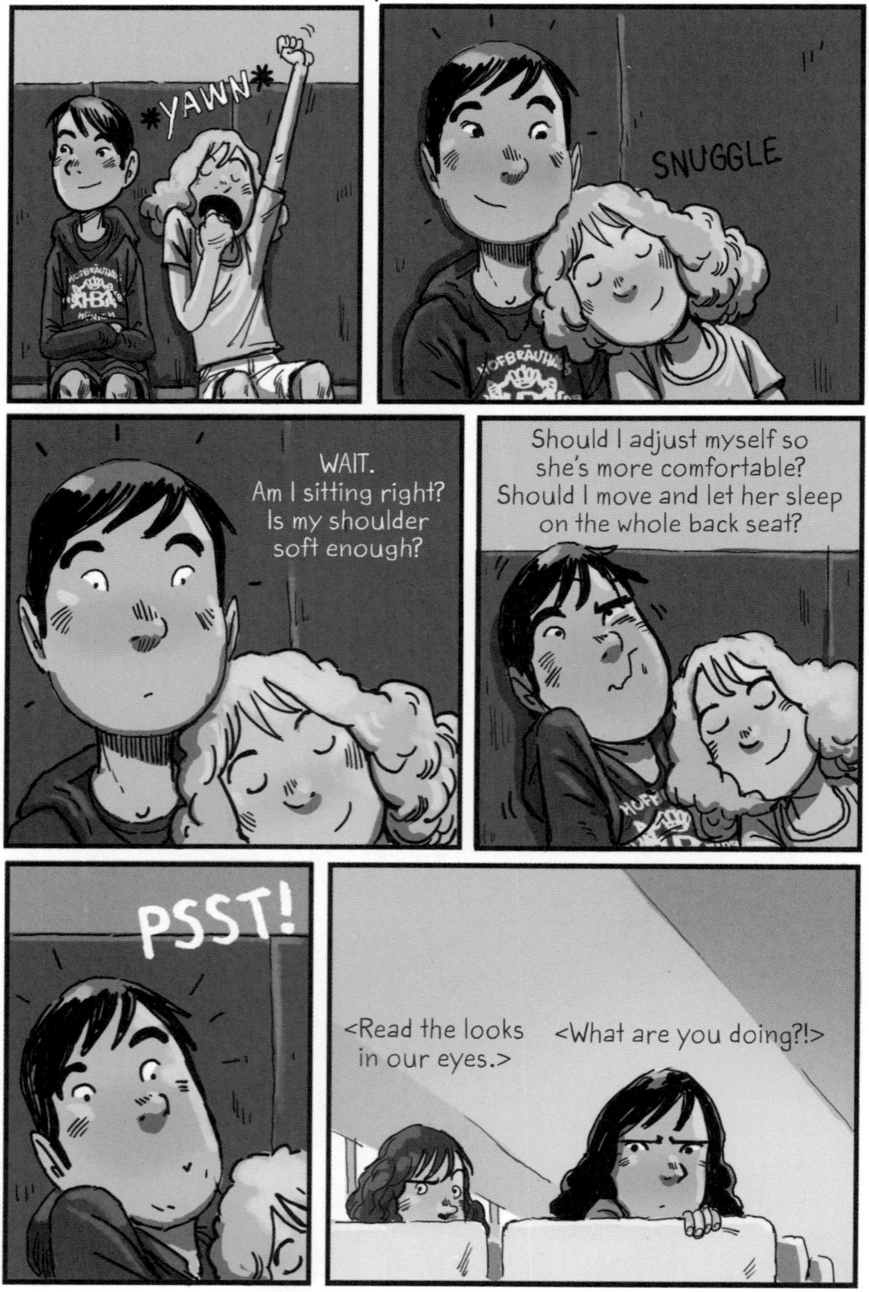
YAWN
SNUGGLE
WAIT.
Am I sitting right?
Is my shoulder
soft enough?
Should I adjust myself so
she's more comfortable?
Should I move and let her sleep
on the whole back seat?
PSST!
<Read the looks
in our eyes.>
<What are you doing?!>

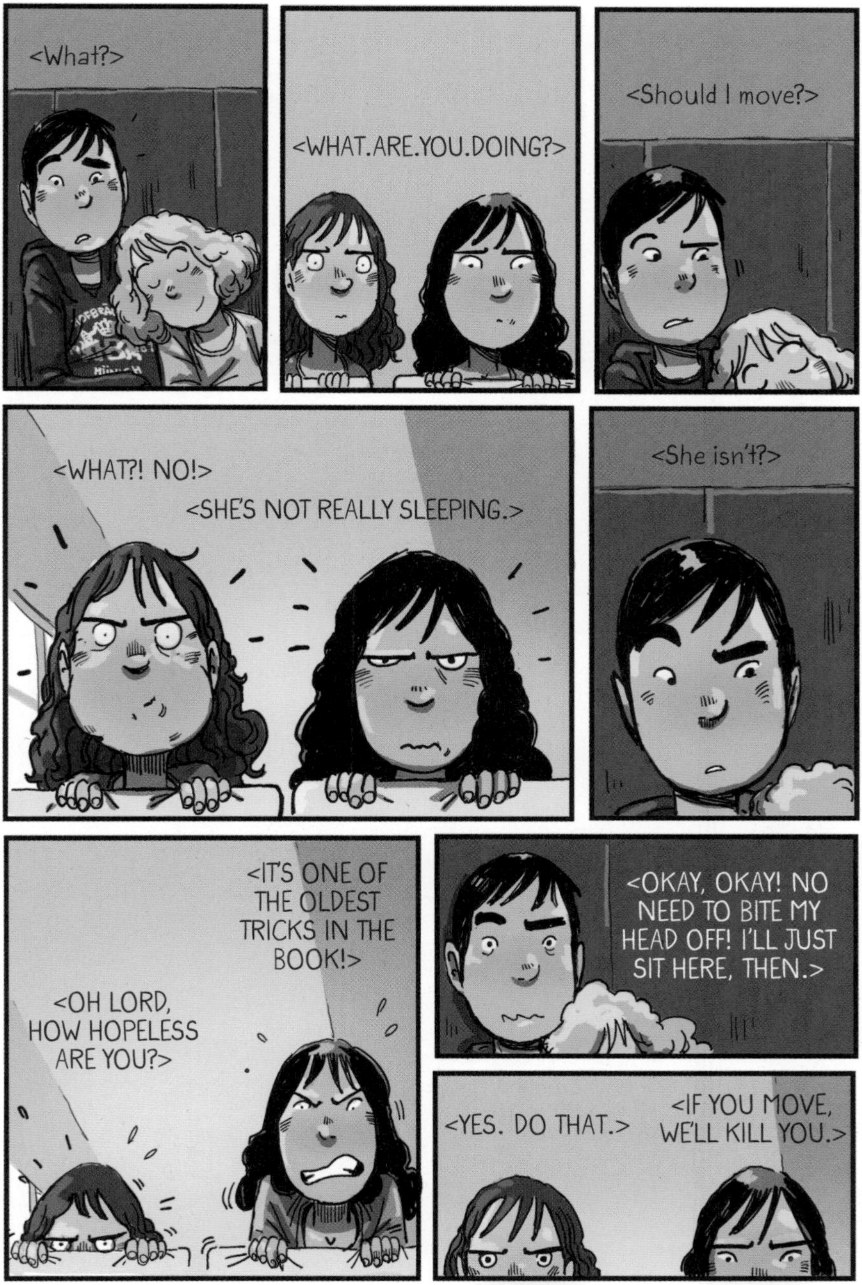

<What?>
<WHAT.ARE.YOU.DOING?>
<Should I move?>
<WHAT?! NO!>
<SHE'S NOT REALLY SLEEPING.>
<She isn't?>
<IT'S ONE OF THE OLDEST TRICKS IN THE BOOK!>
<OH LORD, HOW HOPELESS ARE YOU?>
<OKAY, OKAY! NO NEED TO BITE MY HEAD OFF! I'LL JUST SIT HERE, THEN.>
<YES. DO THAT.>
<IF YOU MOVE, WE'LL KILL YOU.>

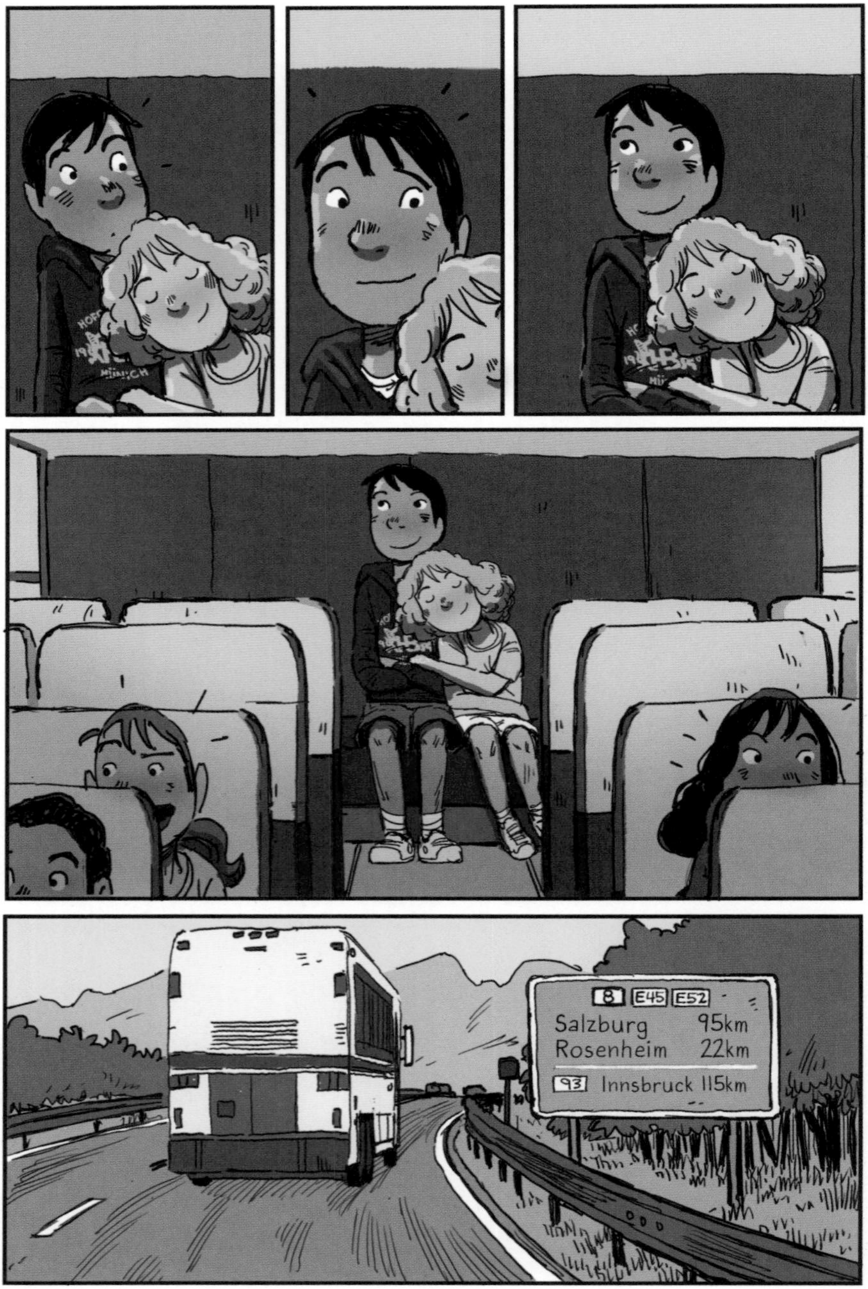
HOF 19 MÜNCH
8 E45 E52
Salzburg 95km
Rosenheim 22km
93 Innsbruck 115km

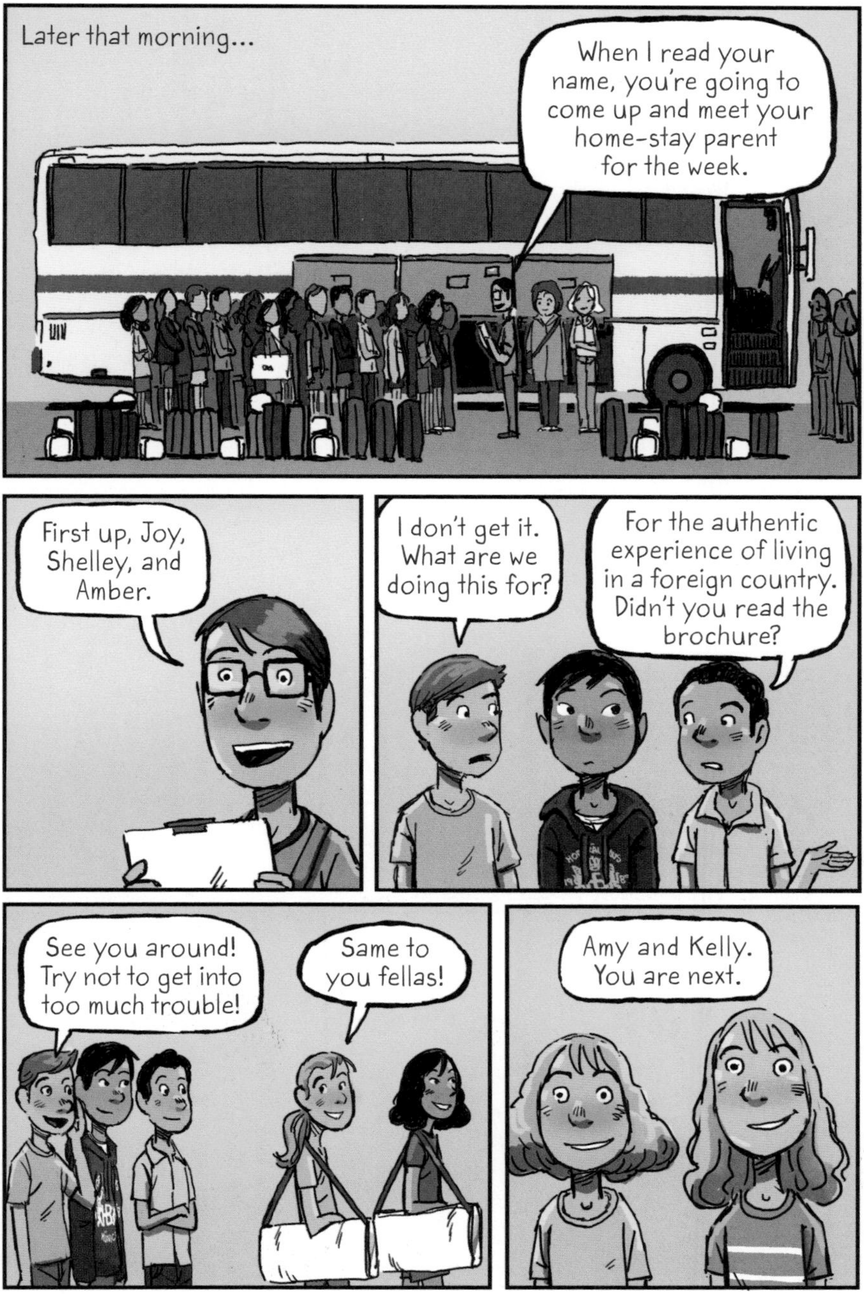

Later that morning...
When I read your name, you're going to come up and meet your home-stay parent for the week.
First up, Joy, Shelley, and Amber.
I don't get it. What are we doing this for?
For the authentic experience of living in a foreign country. Didn't you read the brochure?
See you around! Try not to get into too much trouble!
Same to you fellas!
Amy and Kelly. You are next.

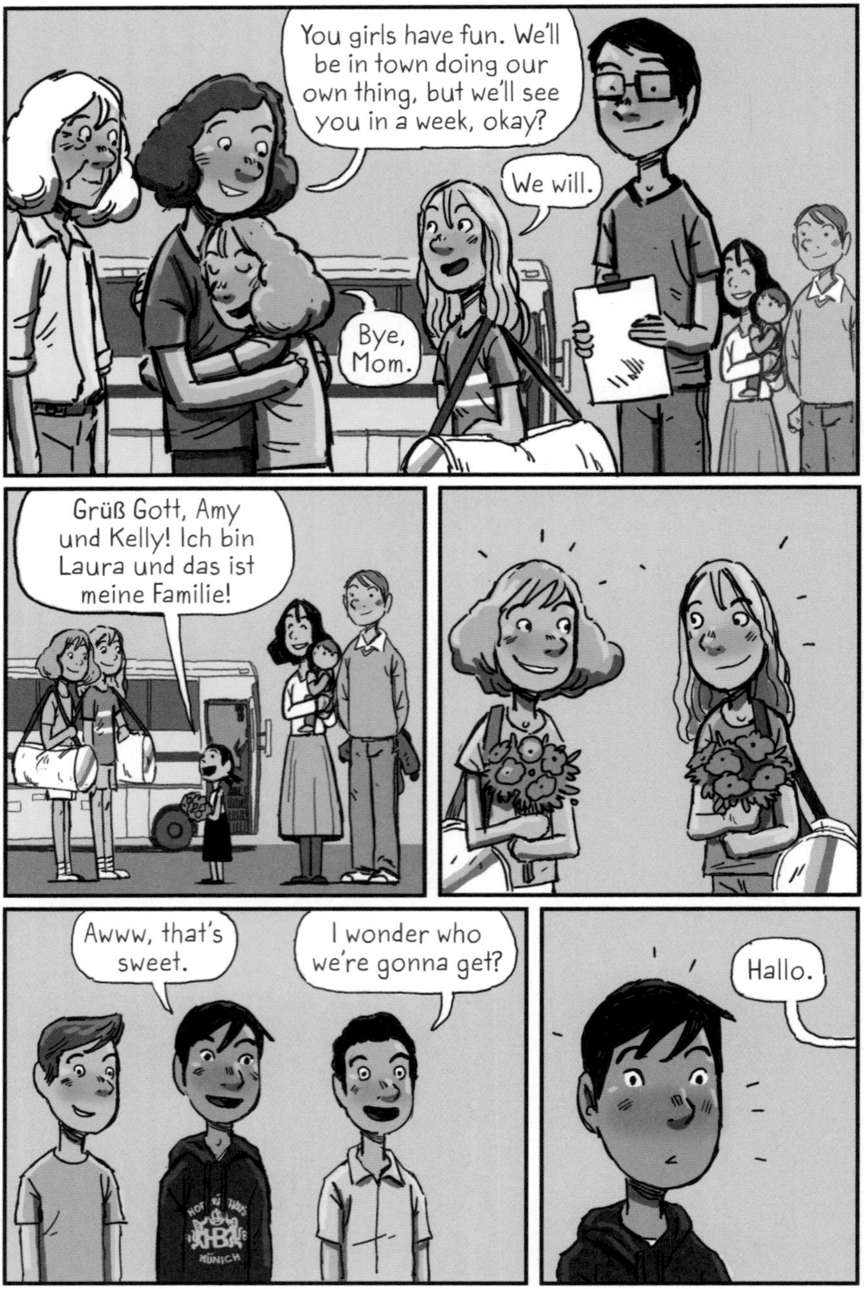
You girls have fun. We'll be in town doing our own thing, but we'll see you in a week, okay?
We will.
Bye, Mom.
Grüß Gott, Amy und Kelly! Ich bin Laura und das ist meine Familie!
Awww, that's sweet.
I wonder who we're gonna get?
Hallo.

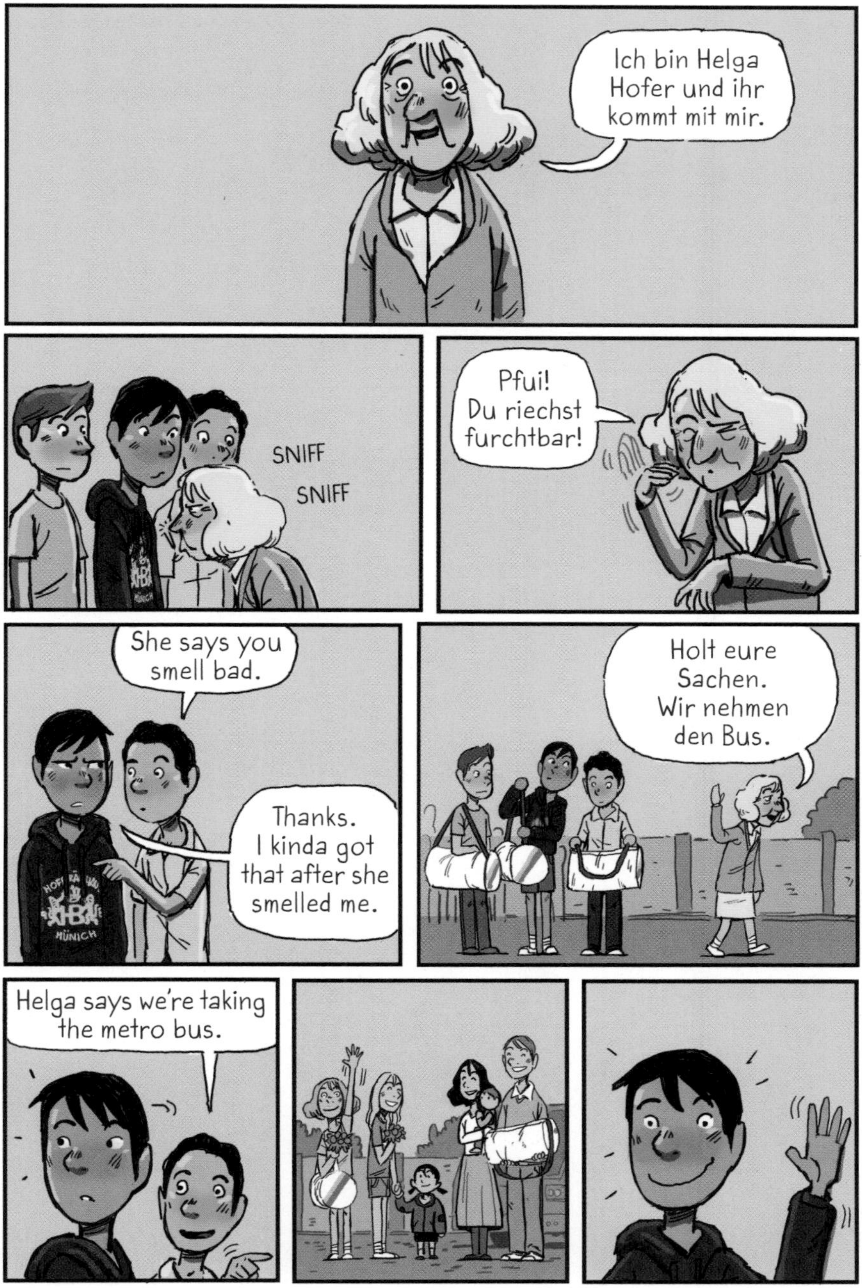
Ich bin Helga Hofer und ihr kommt mit mir.
SNIFF
SNIFF
Pfui! Du riechst furchtbar!
She says you smell bad.
Thanks. I kinda got that after she smelled me.
Holt eure Sachen. Wir nehmen den Bus.
Helga says we're taking the metro bus.

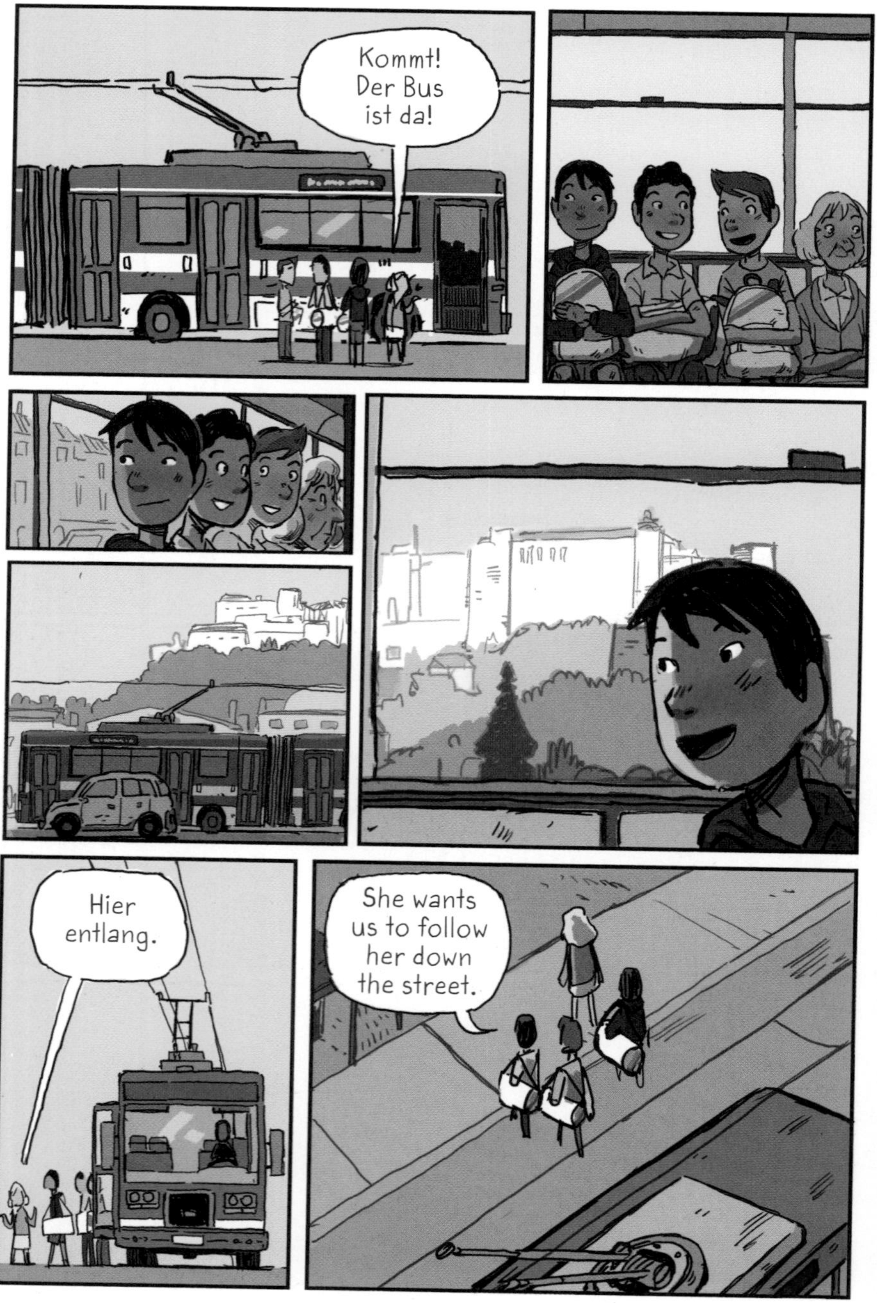
Kommt! Der Bus ist da!
Hier entlang.
She wants us to follow her down the street.

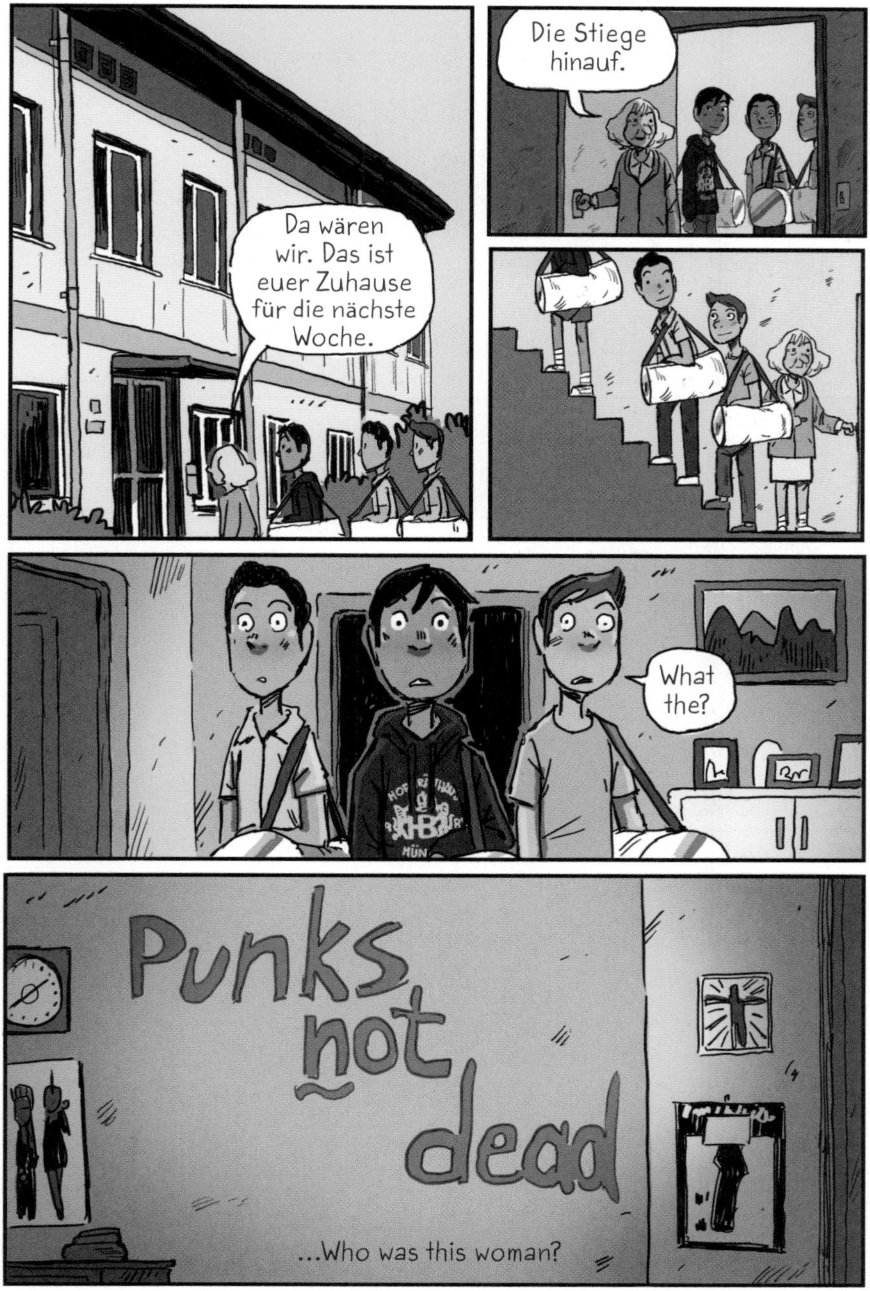

Da wären wir. Das ist euer Zuhause für die nächste Woche.
Die Stiege hinauf.
What the?
Punks not dead
...Who was this woman?

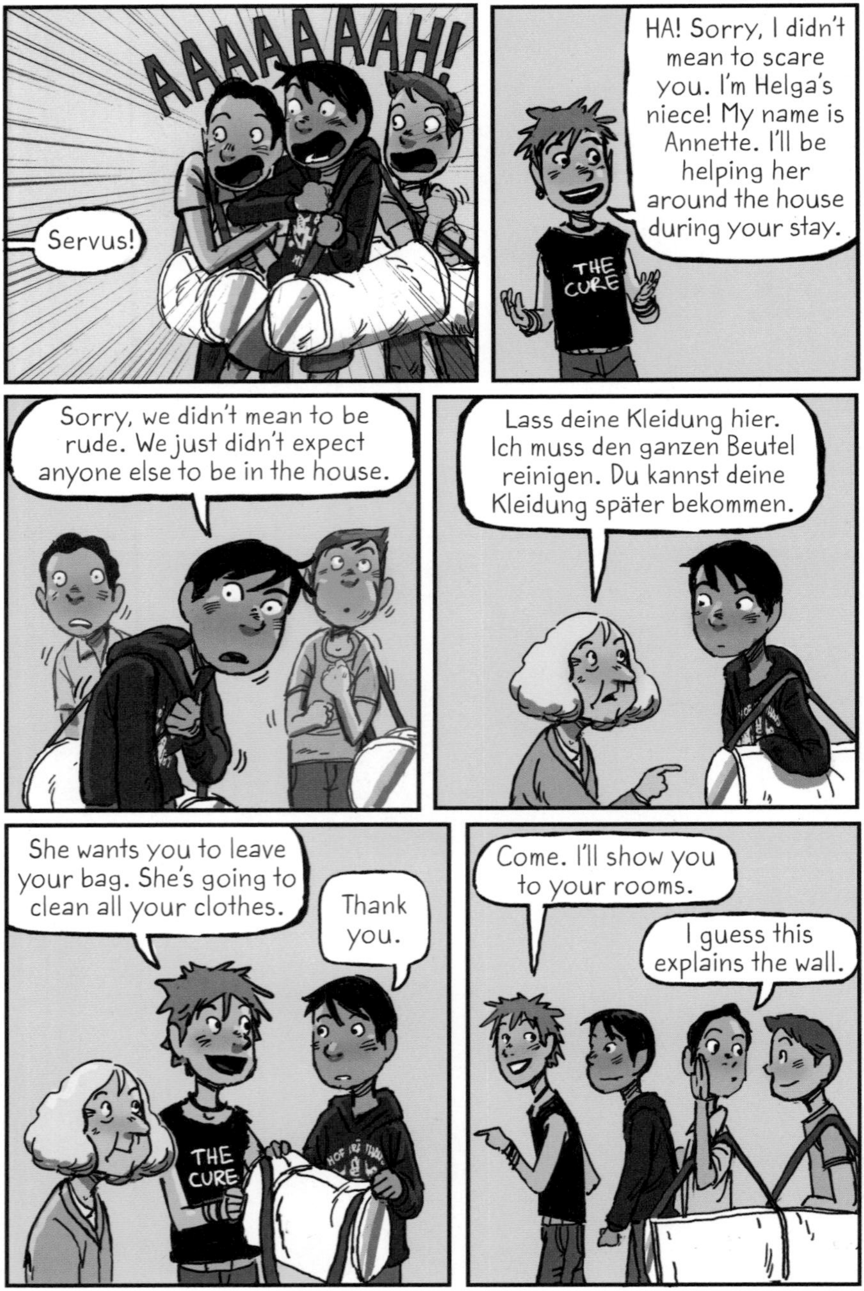
AAAAAAAH!
Servus!
HA! Sorry, I didn't mean to scare you. I'm Helga's niece! My name is Annette. I'll be helping her around the house during your stay.
THE CURE
Sorry, we didn't mean to be rude. We just didn't expect anyone else to be in the house.
Lass deine Kleidung hier. Ich muss den ganzen Beutel reinigen. Du kannst deine Kleidung später bekommen.
She wants you to leave your bag. She's going to clean all your clothes.
Thank you.
THE CURE
Come. I'll show you to your rooms.
I guess this explains the wall.

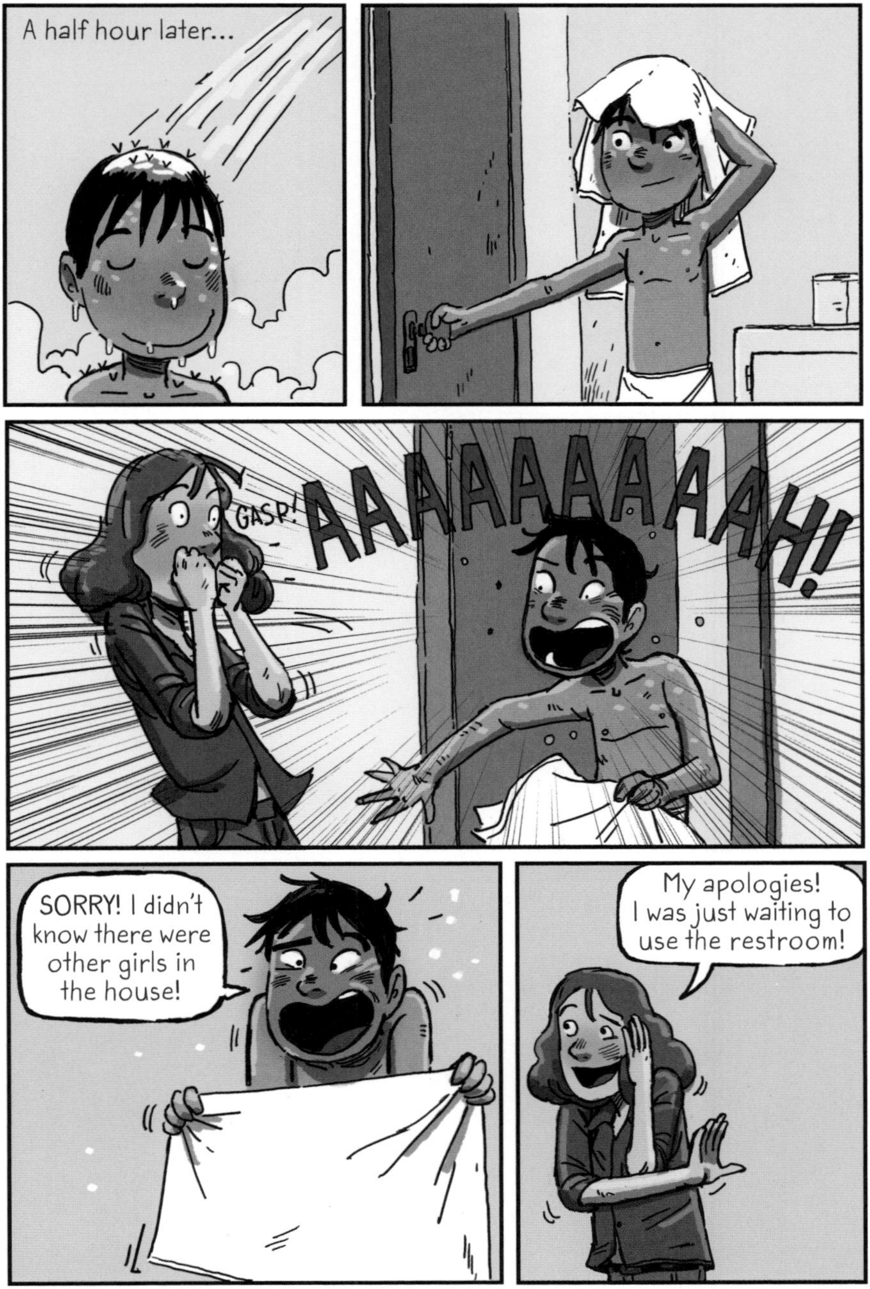

A half hour later...
GASP!
AAAAAAAAAH!
SORRY! I didn't know there were other girls in the house!
My apologies! I was just waiting to use the restroom!

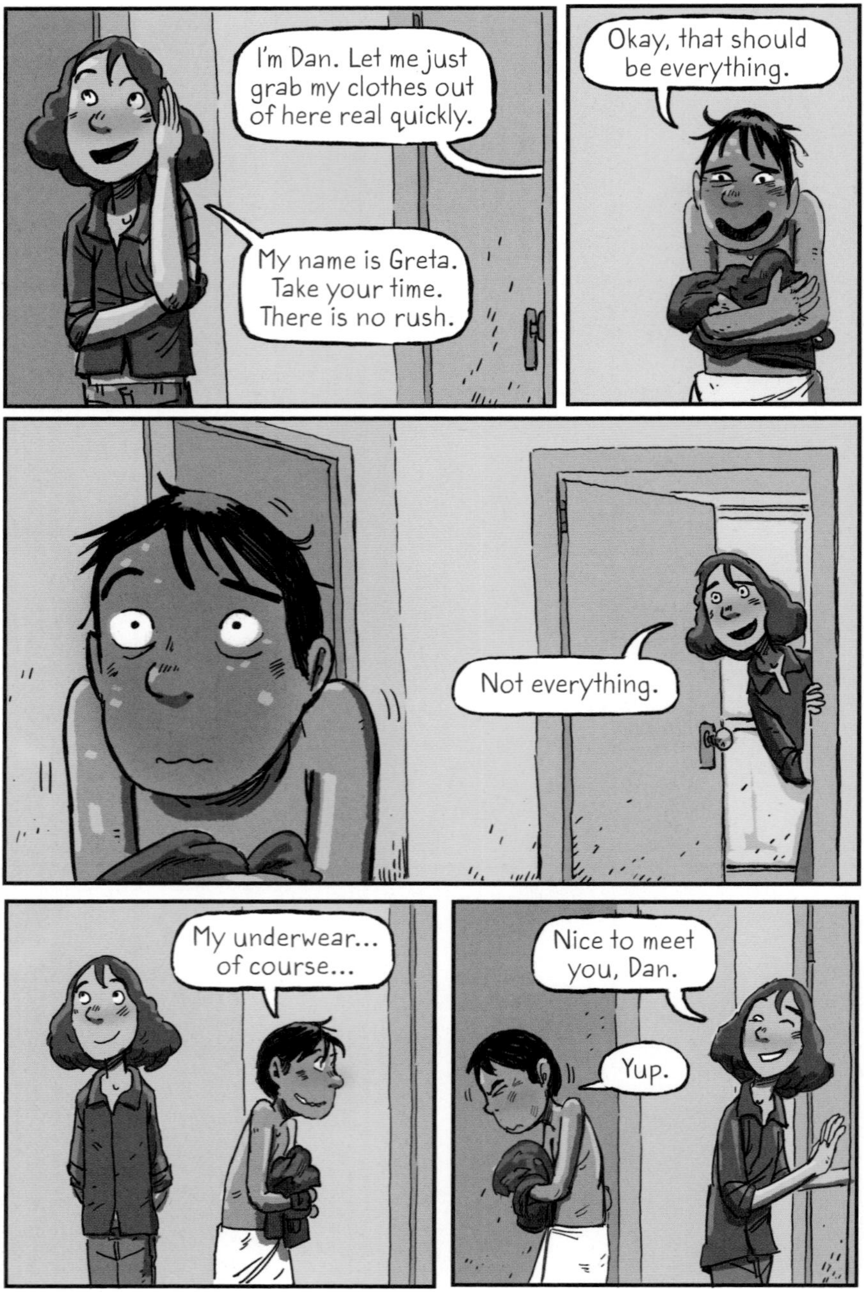
I'm Dan. Let me just grab my clothes out of here real quickly.
My name is Greta. Take your time. There is no rush.
Okay, that should be everything.
Not everything.
My underwear... of course...
Nice to meet you, Dan.
Yup.

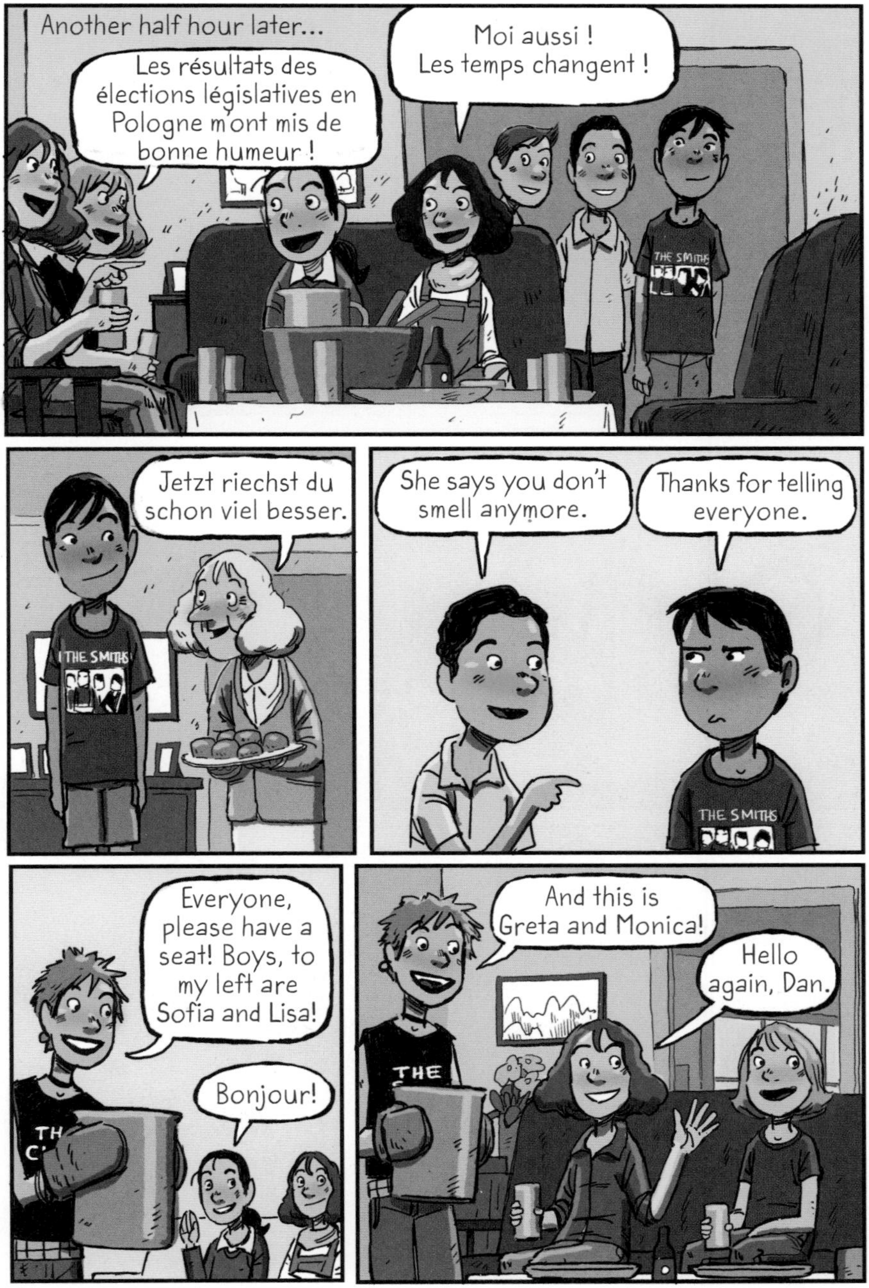
Another half hour later...
Les résultats des élections législatives en Pologne m'ont mis de bonne humeur !
Moi aussi ! Les temps changent !
THE SMITHS
Jetzt riechst du schon viel besser.
THE SMITHS
She says you don't smell anymore.
Thanks for telling everyone.
THE SMITHS
Everyone, please have a seat! Boys, to my left are Sofia and Lisa!
Bonjour!
And this is Greta and Monica!
Hello again, Dan.

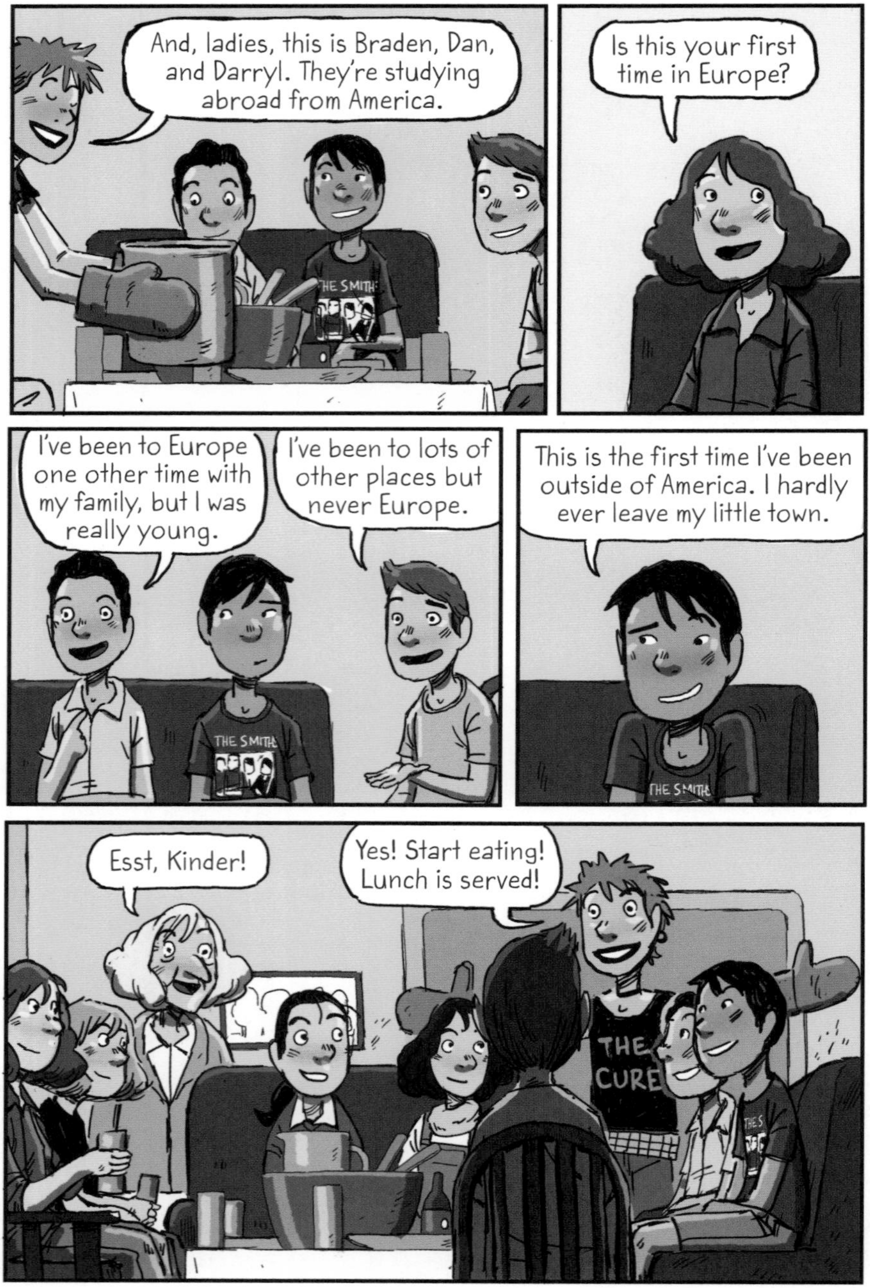
And, ladies, this is Braden, Dan, and Darryl. They're studying abroad from America.
Is this your first time in Europe?
I've been to Europe one other time with my family, but I was really young.
I've been to lots of other places but never Europe.
This is the first time I've been outside of America. I hardly ever leave my little town.
Esst, Kinder!
Yes! Start eating! Lunch is served!

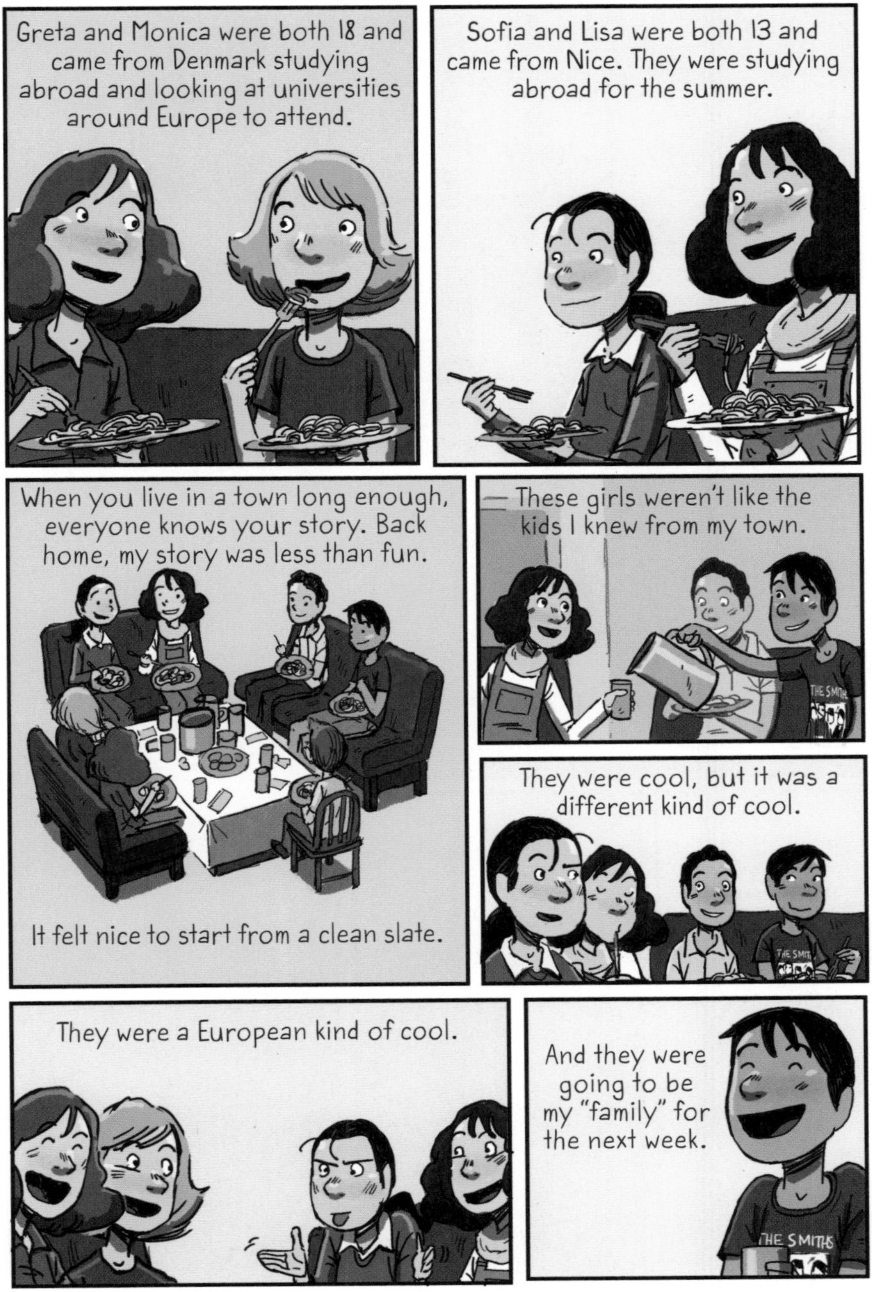
Greta and Monica were both 18 and came from Denmark studying abroad and looking at universities around Europe to attend.
Sofia and Lisa were both 13 and came from Nice. They were studying abroad for the summer.
When you live in a town long enough, everyone knows your story. Back home, my story was less than fun.
It felt nice to start from a clean slate.
These girls weren't like the kids I knew from my town.
THE SMITHS
They were cool, but it was a different kind of cool.
THE SMITHS
They were a European kind of cool.
And they were going to be my "family" for the next week.
THE SMITHS

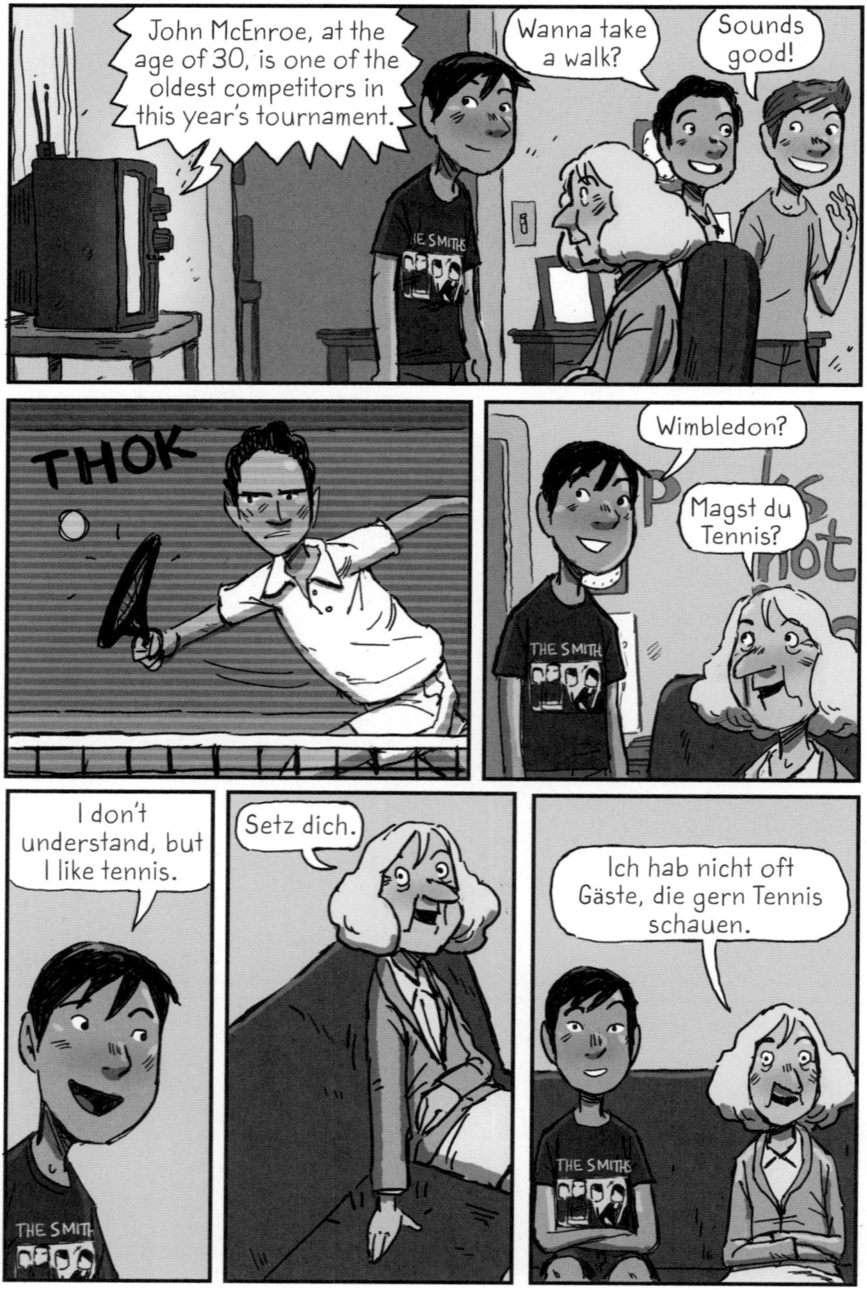
John McEnroe, at the age of 30, is one of the oldest competitors in this year's tournament.
Wanna take a walk?
Sounds good!
THE SMITHS
THOK
Wimbledon?
Magst du Tennis?
THE SMITH
I don't understand, but I like tennis.
THE SMITH
Setz dich.
Ich hab nicht oft Gäste, die gern Tennis schauen.
THE SMITHS

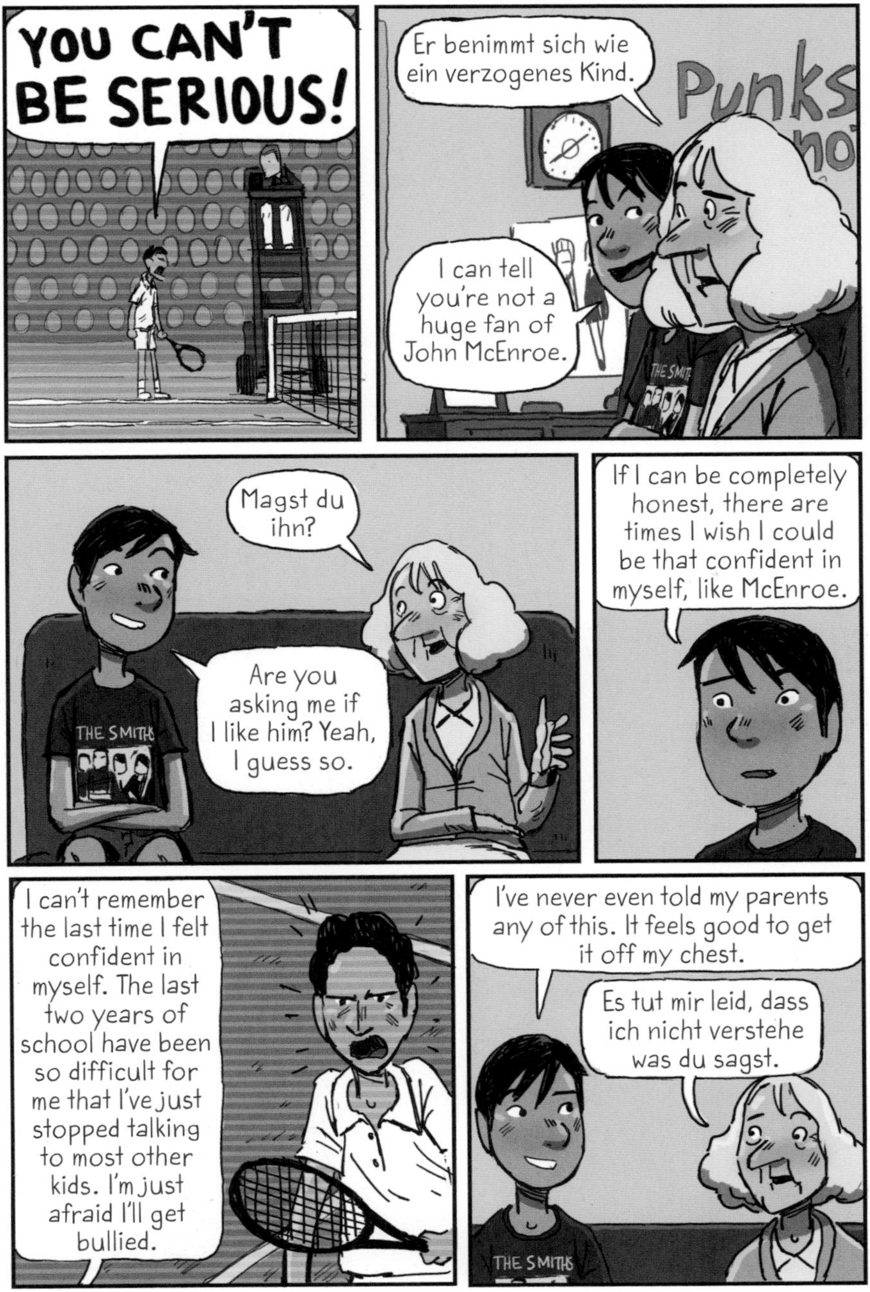
YOU CAN'T BE SERIOUS!
Er benimmt sich wie ein verzogenes Kind.
Punks
I can tell you're not a huge fan of John McEnroe.
THE SMITHS
Magst du ihn?
Are you asking me if I like him? Yeah, I guess so.
THE SMITHS
If I can be completely honest, there are times I wish I could be that confident in myself, like McEnroe.
I can't remember the last time I felt confident in myself. The last two years of school have been so difficult for me that I've just stopped talking to most other kids. I'm just afraid I'll get bullied.
I've never even told my parents any of this. It feels good to get it off my chest.
Es tut mir leid, dass ich nicht verstehe was du sagst.
THE SMITHS

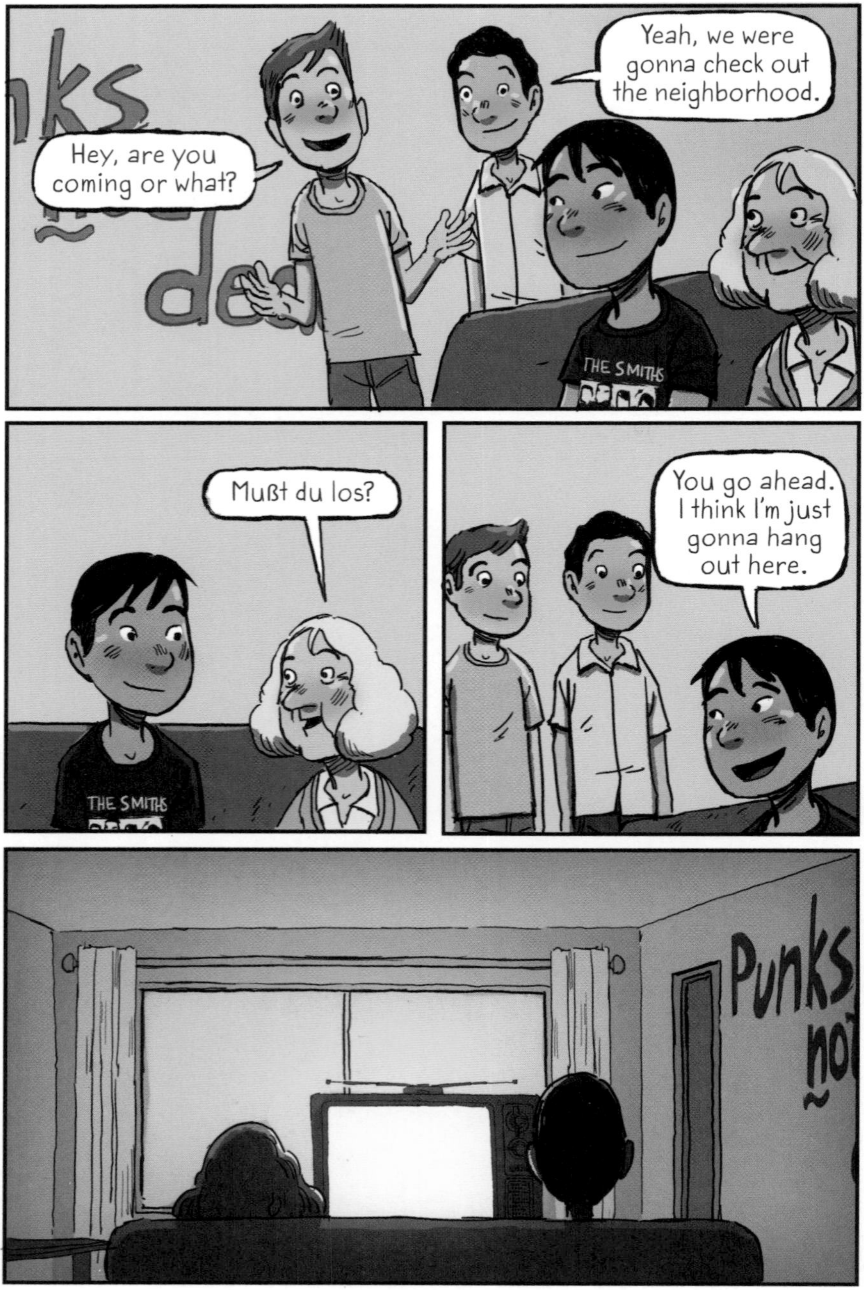
Hey, are you coming or what?
Yeah, we were gonna check out the neighborhood.
THE SMITHS
Mußt du los?
THE SMITHS
You go ahead. I think I'm just gonna hang out here.
Punks

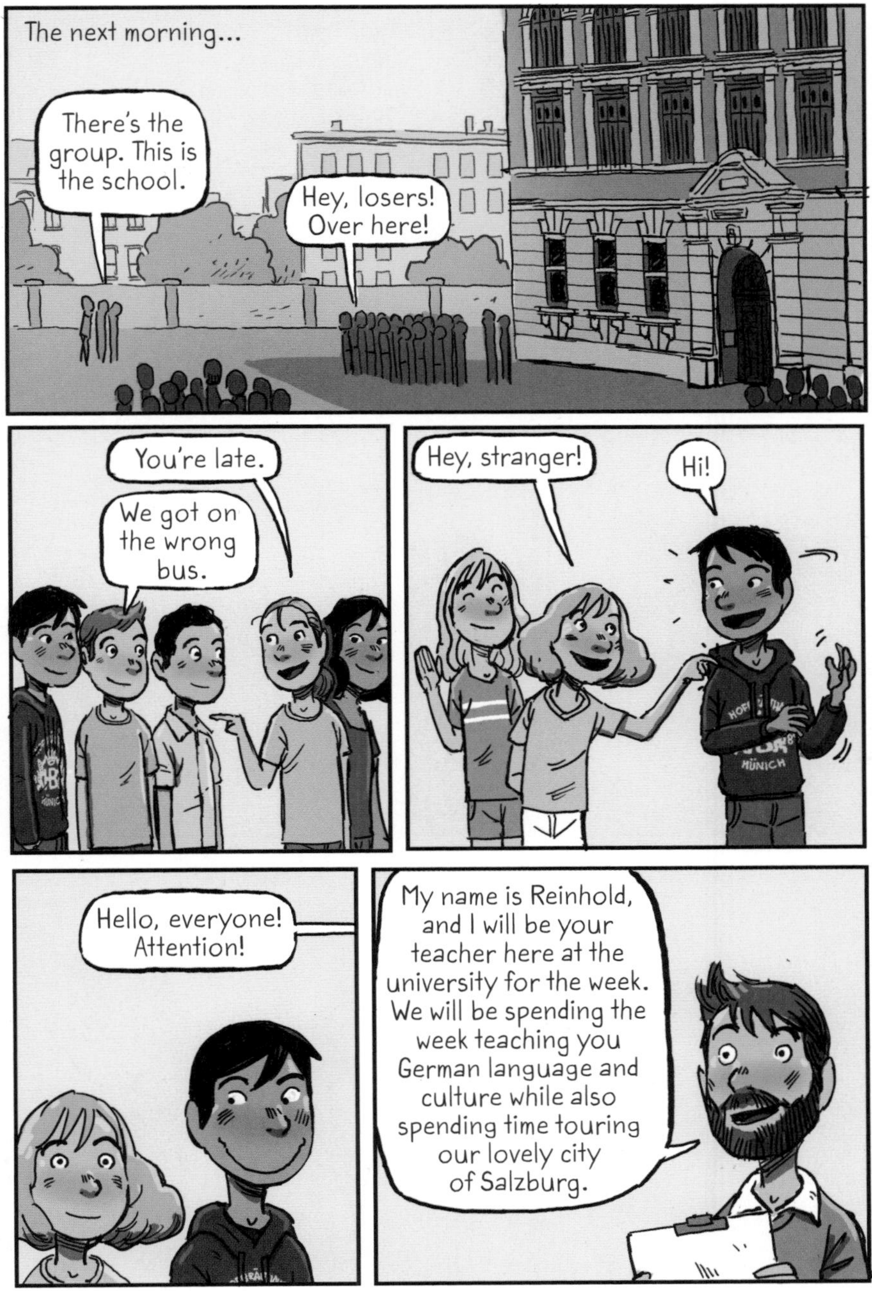
The next morning...
There's the group. This is the school.
Hey, losers! Over here!
You're late.
We got on the wrong bus.
Hey, stranger!
Hi!
Hello, everyone! Attention!
My name is Reinhold, and I will be your teacher here at the university for the week. We will be spending the week teaching you German language and culture while also spending time touring our lovely city of Salzburg.

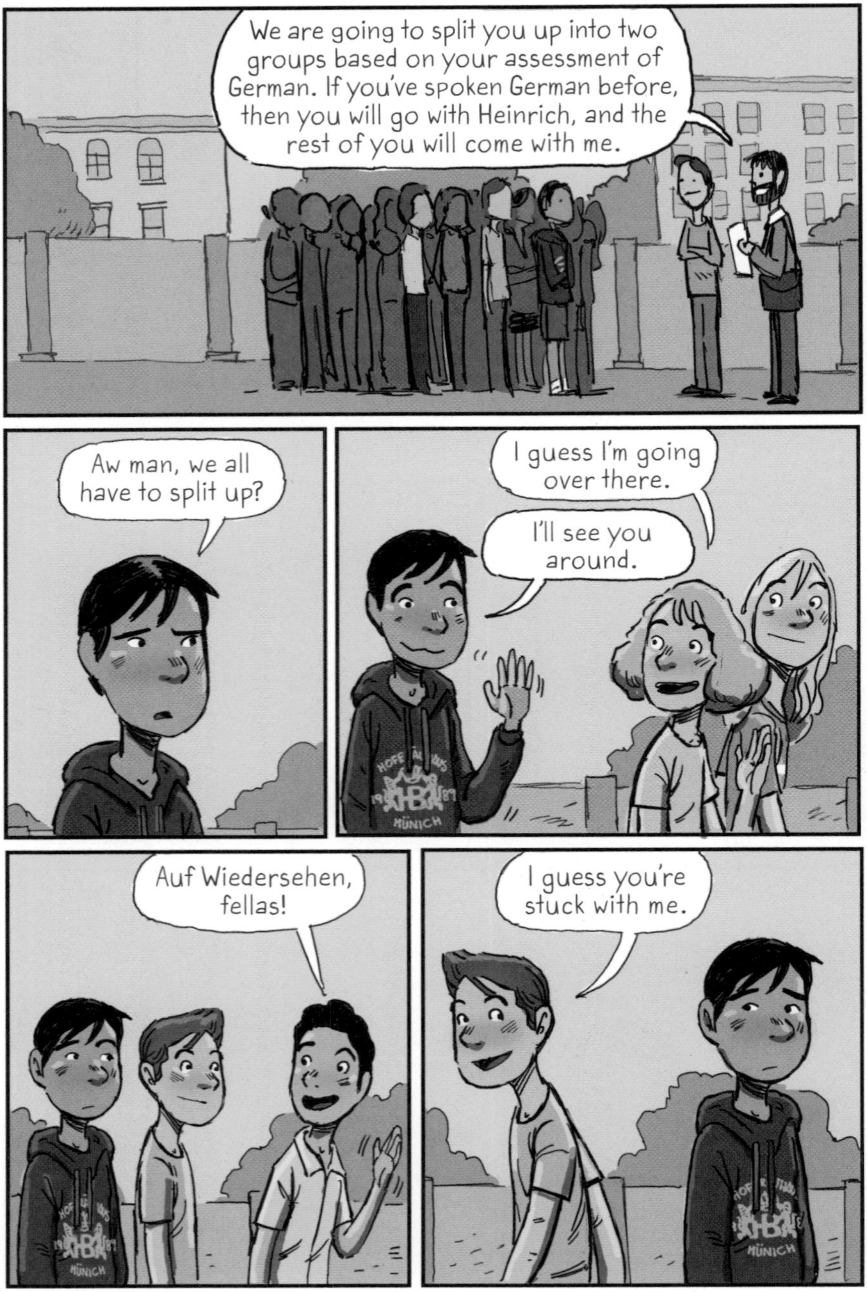
We are going to split you up into two groups based on your assessment of German. If you've spoken German before, then you will go with Heinrich, and the rest of you will come with me.
Aw man, we all have to split up?
I guess I'm going over there.
I'll see you around.
HOFBRÄUHAUS
1987
MÜNICH
Auf Wiedersehen, fellas!
I guess you're stuck with me.

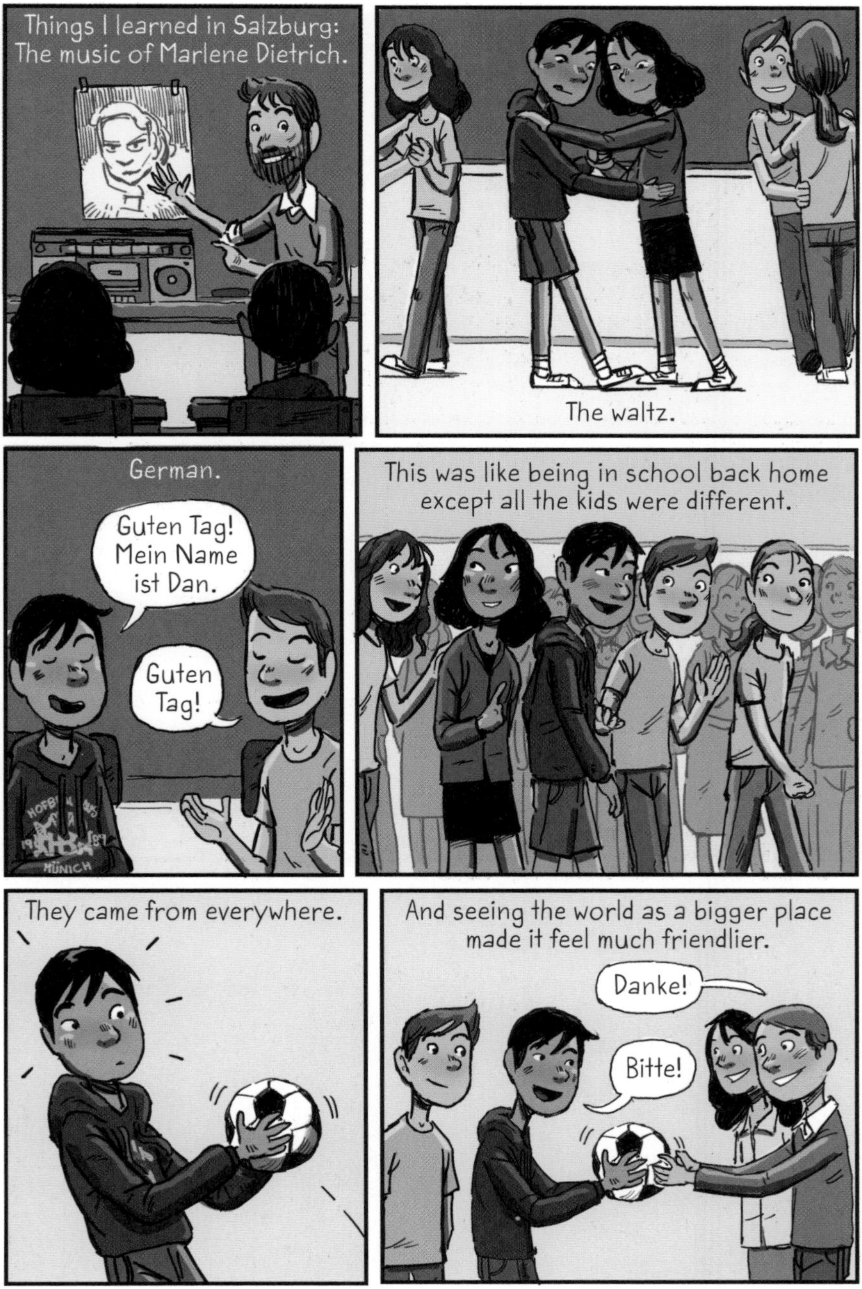
Things I learned in Salzburg: The music of Marlene Dietrich.
The waltz.
German.
Guten Tag! Mein Name ist Dan.
Guten Tag!
This was like being in school back home except all the kids were different.
They came from everywhere.
And seeing the world as a bigger place made it feel much friendlier.
Danke!
Bitte!

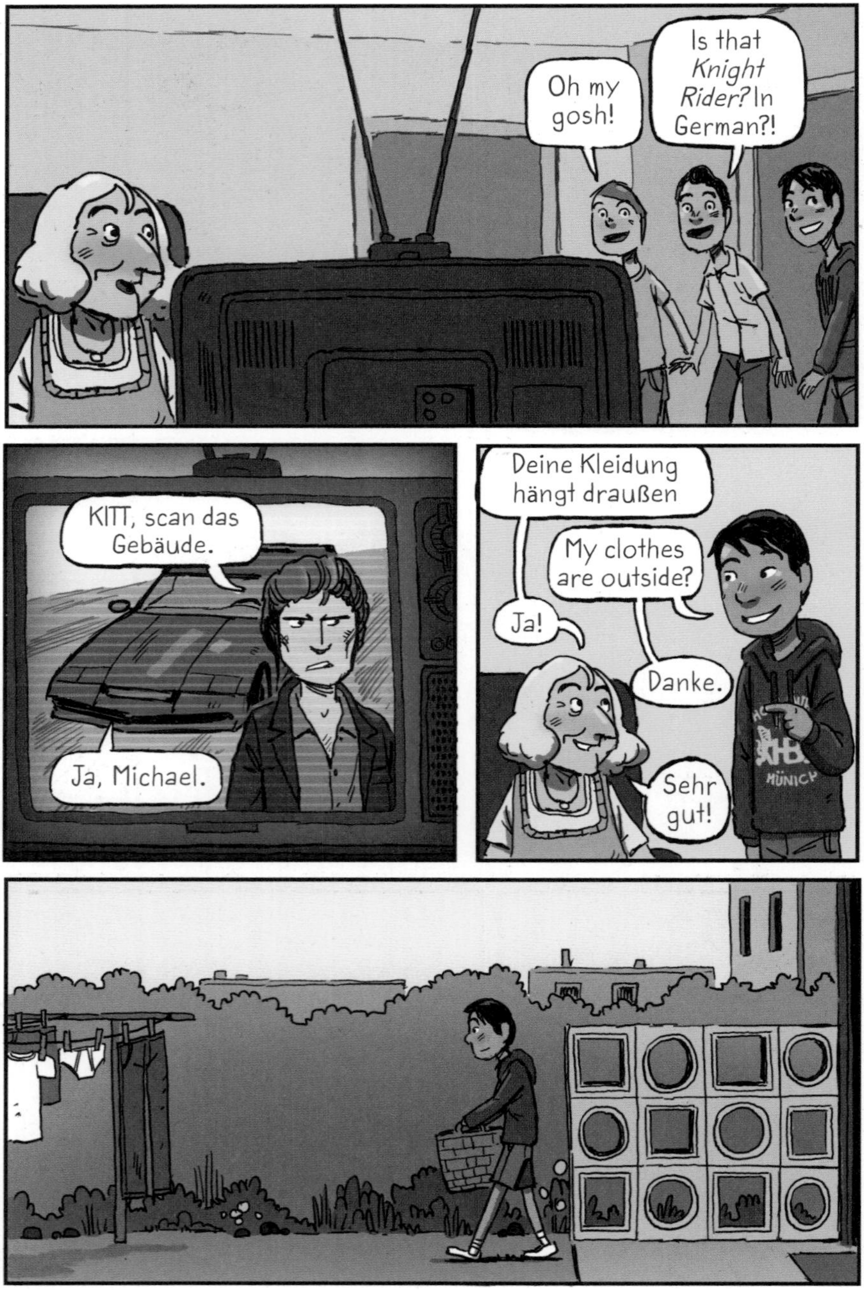
Oh my gosh!
Is that *Knight Rider?* In German?!
KITT, scan das Gebäude.
Ja, Michael.
Deine Kleidung hängt draußen
My clothes are outside?
Ja!
Danke.
Sehr gut!
MÜNICH

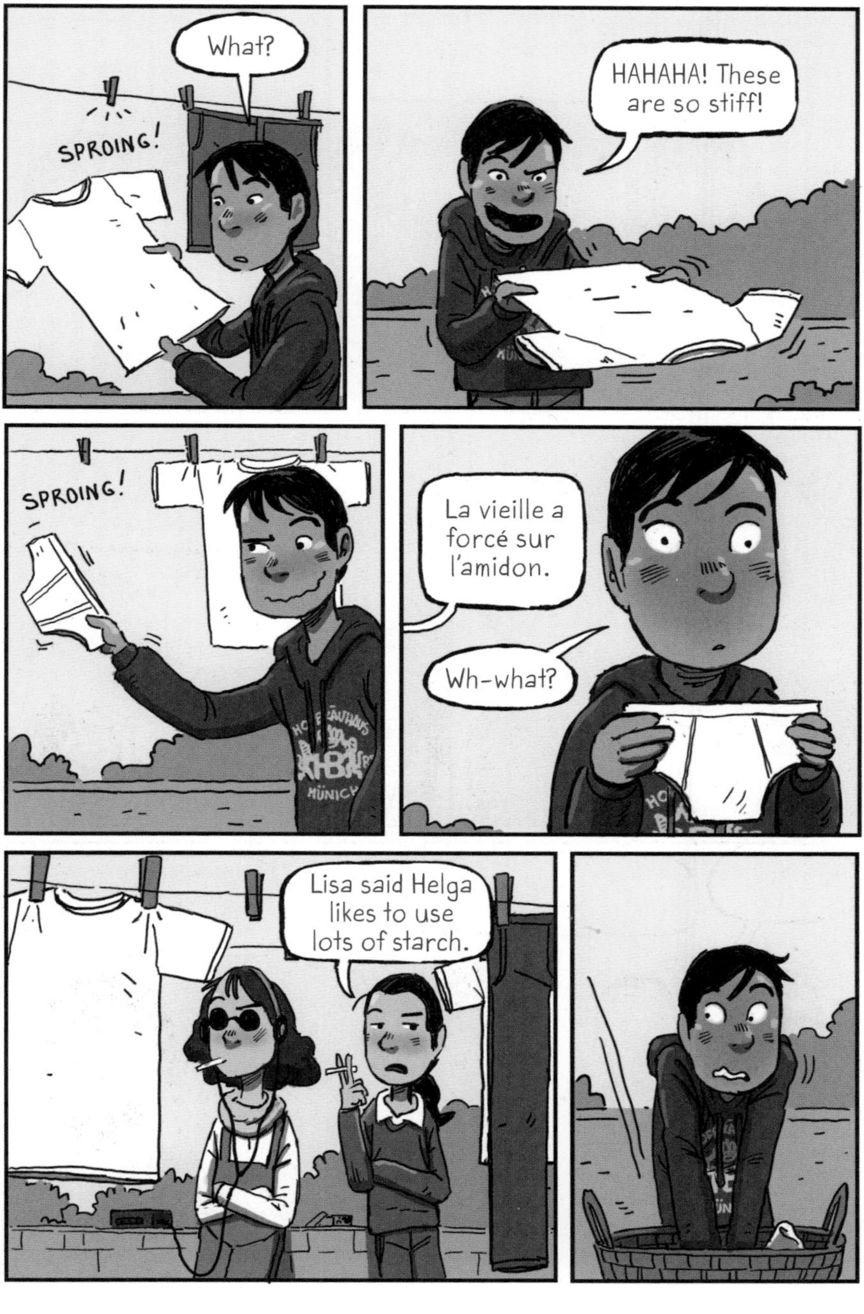
What?
SPROING!
HAHAHA! These are so stiff!
SPROING!
La vieille a forcé sur l'amidon.
Wh-what?
Lisa said Helga likes to use lots of starch.

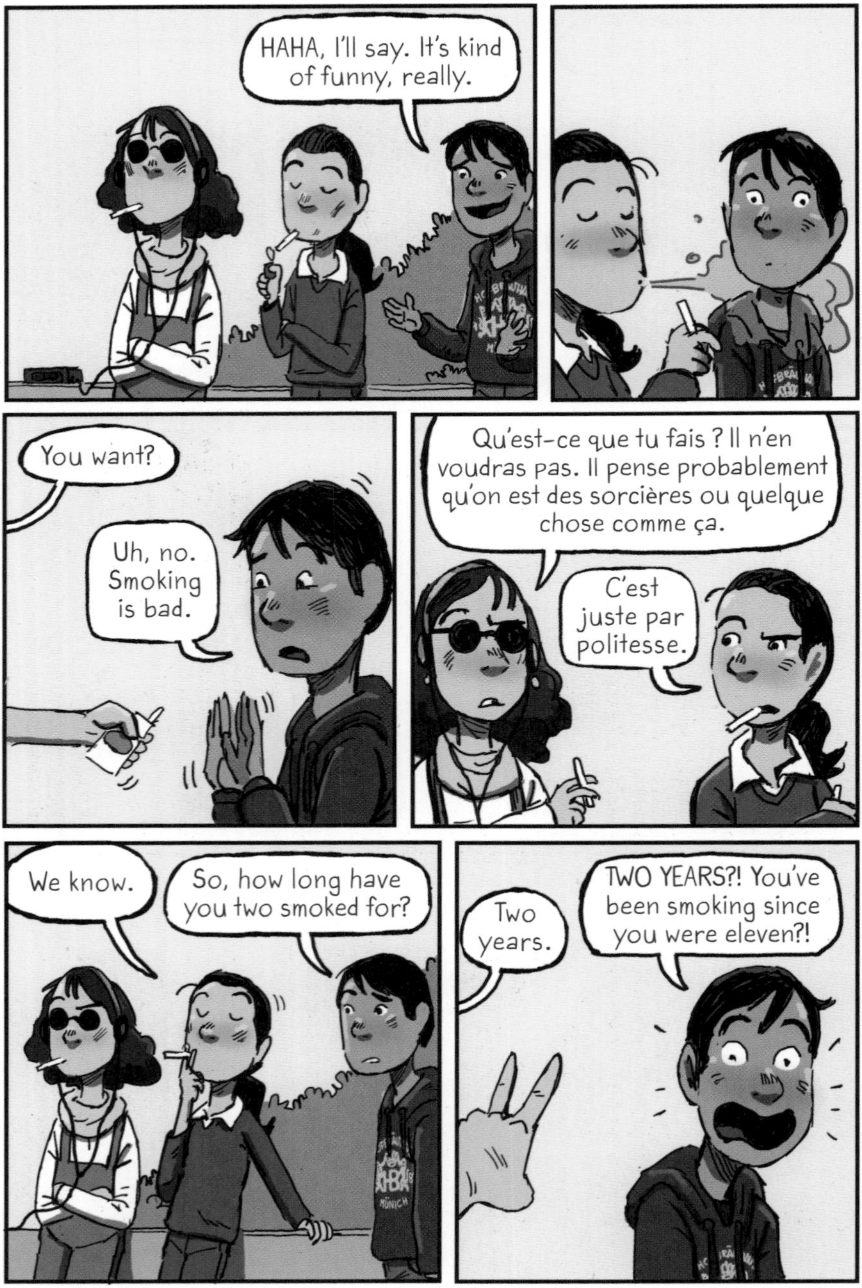
HAHA, I'll say. It's kind of funny, really.
You want?
Uh, no. Smoking is bad.
Qu'est-ce que tu fais ? Il n'en voudras pas. Il pense probablement qu'on est des sorcières ou quelque chose comme ça.
C'est juste par politesse.
We know.
So, how long have you two smoked for?
Two years.
TWO YEARS?! You've been smoking since you were eleven?!

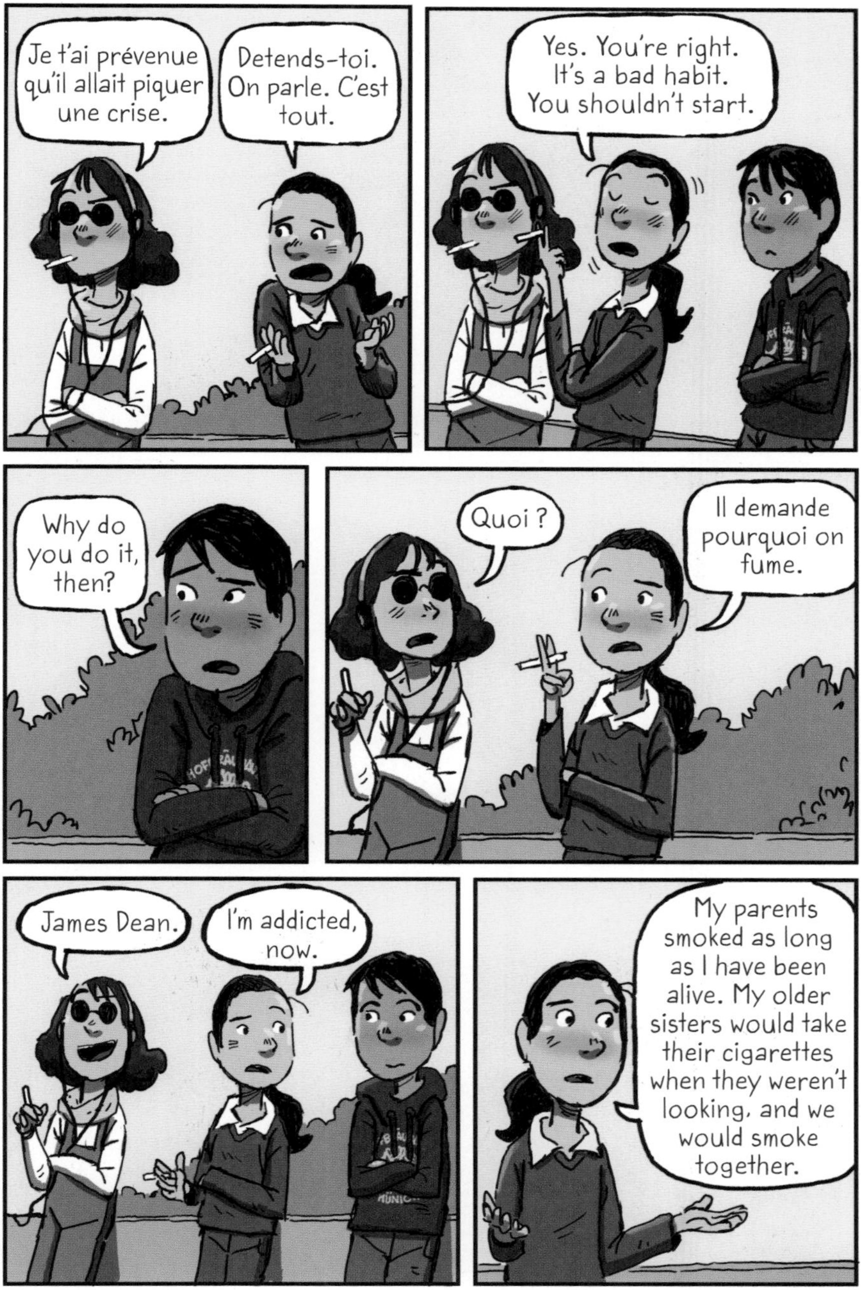
Je t'ai prévenue qu'il allait piquer une crise.
Detends-toi. On parle. C'est tout.
Yes. You're right. It's a bad habit. You shouldn't start.
Why do you do it, then?
Quoi ?
Il demande pourquoi on fume.
James Dean.
I'm addicted, now.
My parents smoked as long as I have been alive. My older sisters would take their cigarettes when they weren't looking, and we would smoke together.

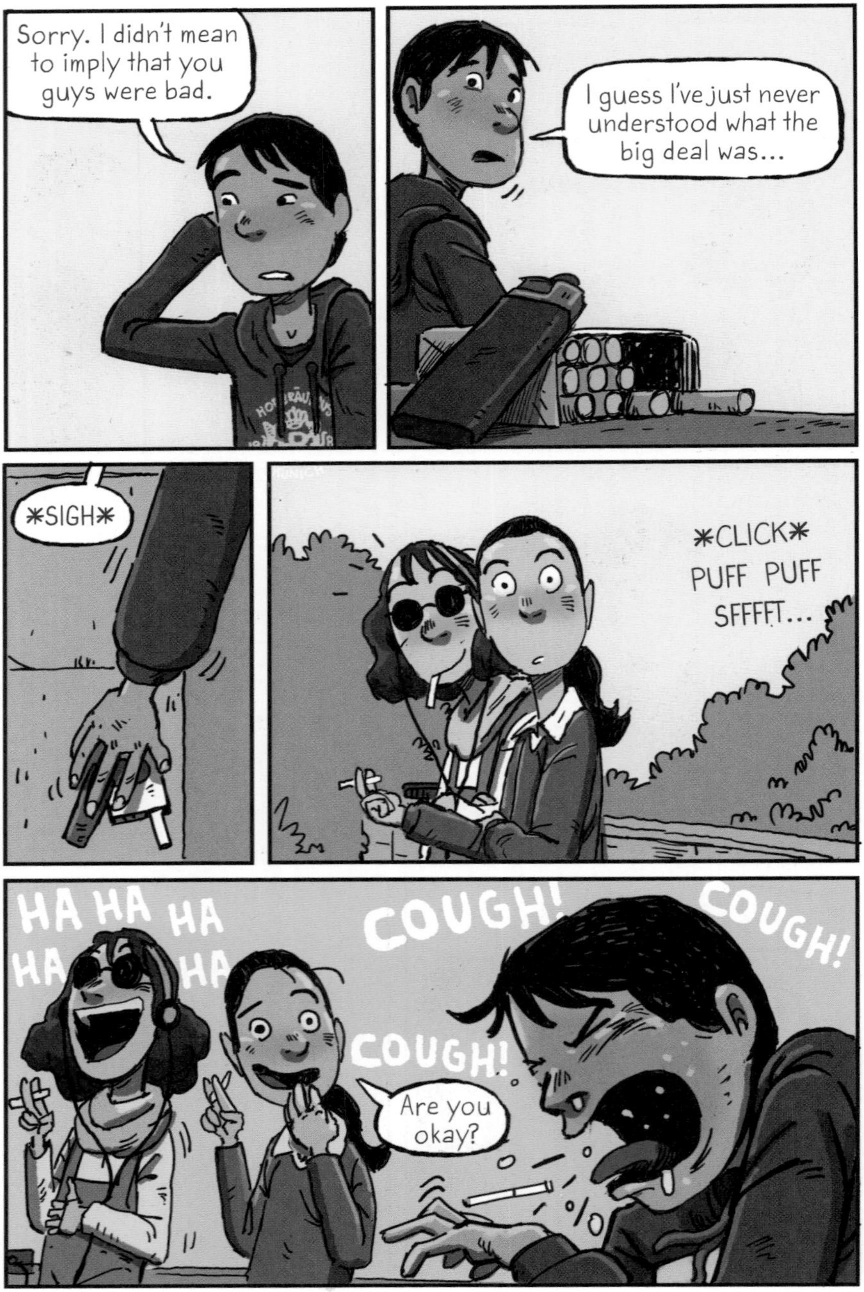
Sorry. I didn't mean to imply that you guys were bad.
I guess I've just never understood what the big deal was...
SIGH
CLICK
PUFF PUFF
SFFFFT...
HA HA HA
HA HA
COUGH!
COUGH!
COUGH!
Are you okay?

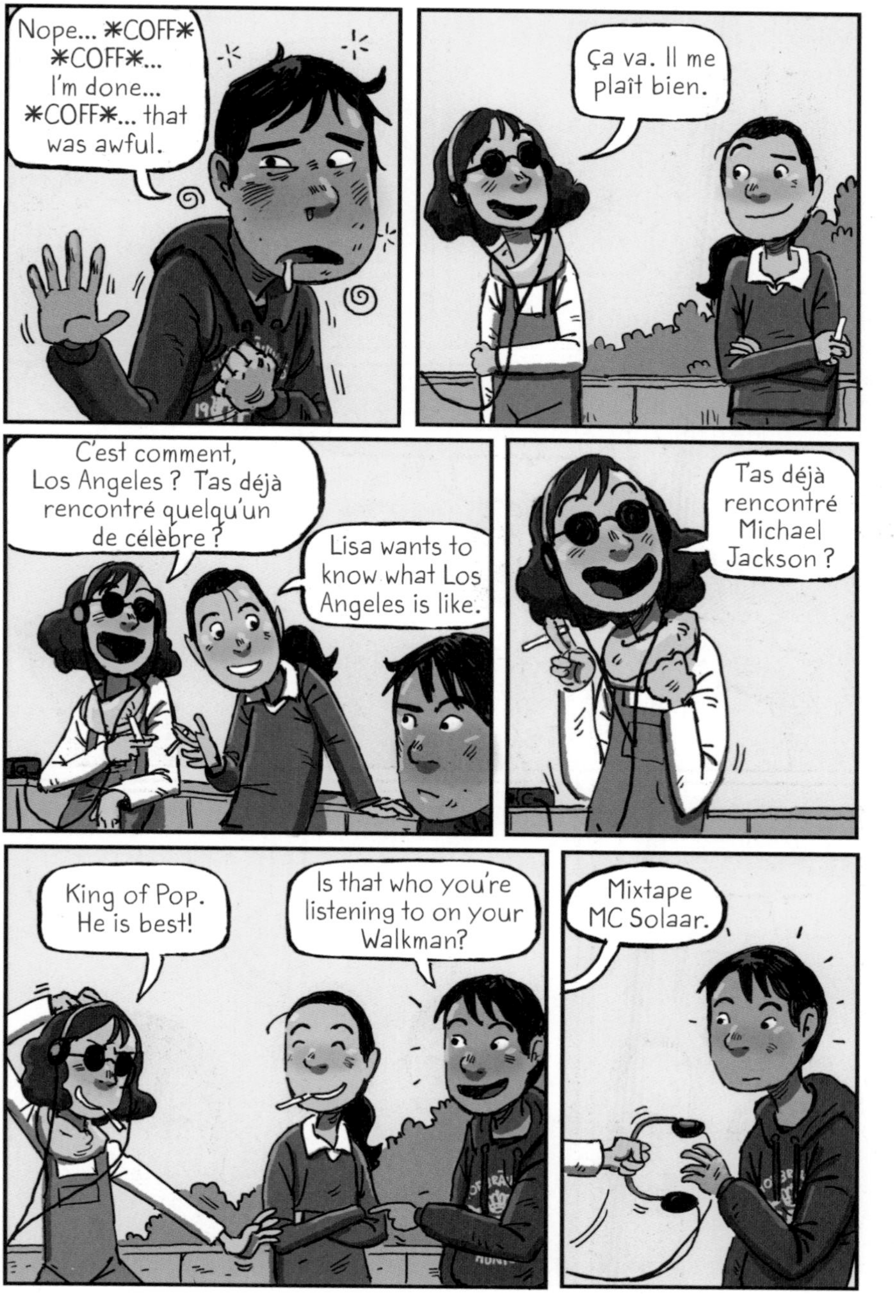
Nope... ✱COFF✱
✱COFF✱...
I'm done...
✱COFF✱... that
was awful.
Ça va. Il me
plaît bien.
C'est comment,
Los Angeles ? T'as déjà
rencontré quelqu'un
de célèbre ?
Lisa wants to
know what Los
Angeles is like.
T'as déjà
rencontré
Michael
Jackson ?
King of Pop.
He is best!
Is that who you're
listening to on your
Walkman?
Mixtape
MC Solaar.

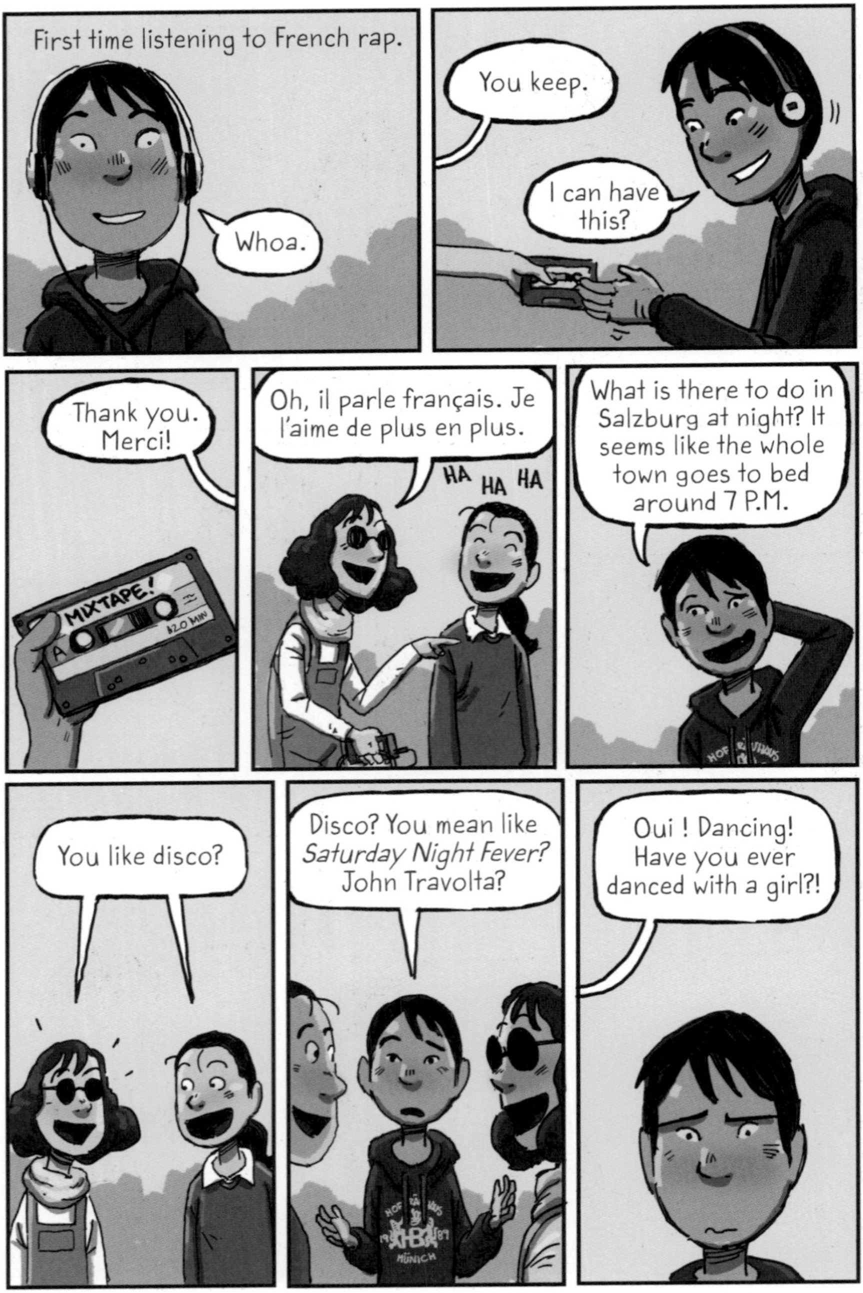
First time listening to French rap.
Whoa.
You keep.
I can have this?
Thank you. Merci!
MIXTAPE!
120 MIN
Oh, il parle français. Je l'aime de plus en plus.
HA HA HA
What is there to do in Salzburg at night? It seems like the whole town goes to bed around 7 P.M.
You like disco?
Disco? You mean like *Saturday Night Fever?* John Travolta?
MÜNICH
Oui ! Dancing! Have you ever danced with a girl?!

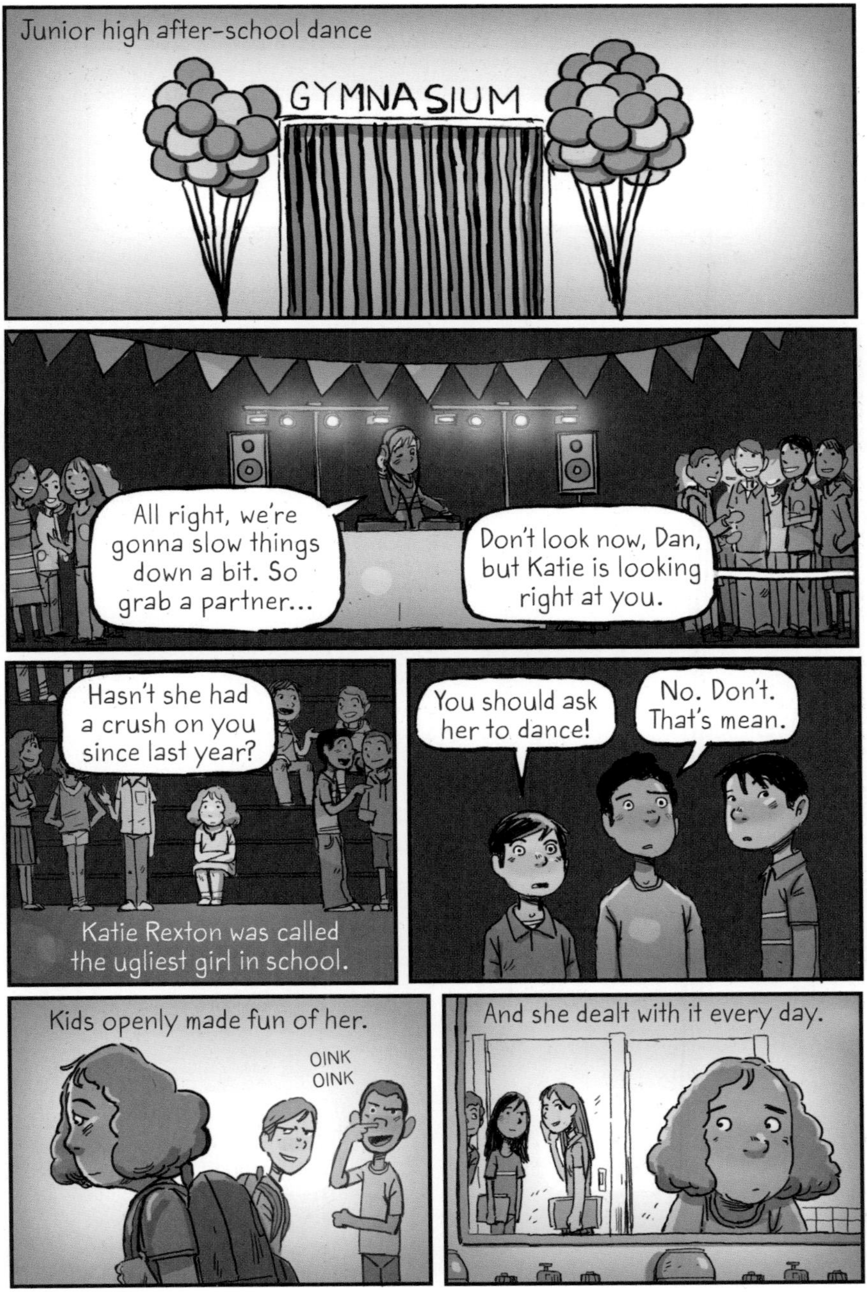
Junior high after-school dance
GYMNASIUM
All right, we're gonna slow things down a bit. So grab a partner...
Don't look now, Dan, but Katie is looking right at you.
Hasn't she had a crush on you since last year?
Katie Rexton was called the ugliest girl in school.
You should ask her to dance!
No. Don't. That's mean.
Kids openly made fun of her.
OINK OINK
And she dealt with it every day.

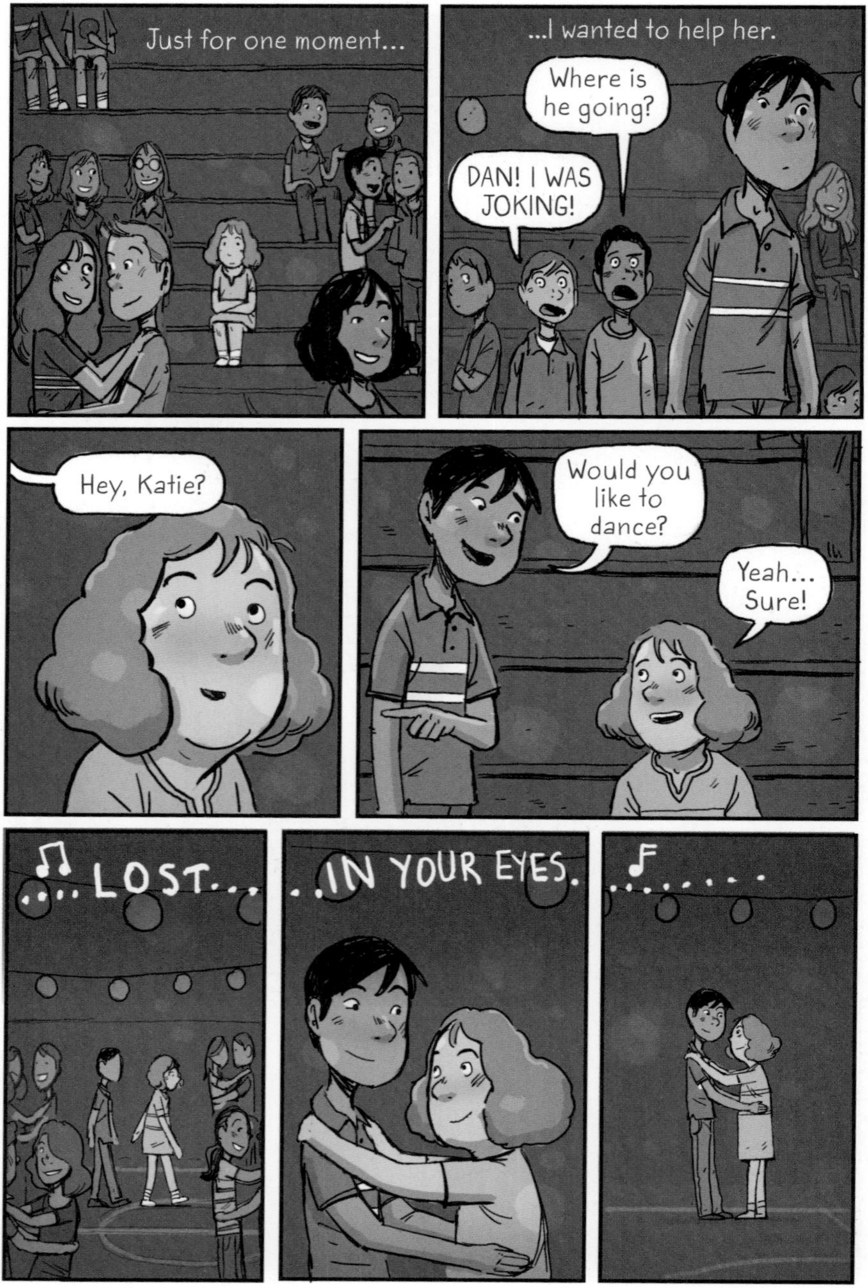
Just for one moment...
...I wanted to help her.
Where is he going?
DAN! I WAS JOKING!
Hey, Katie?
Would you like to dance?
Yeah... Sure!
...LOST...
...IN YOUR EYES.

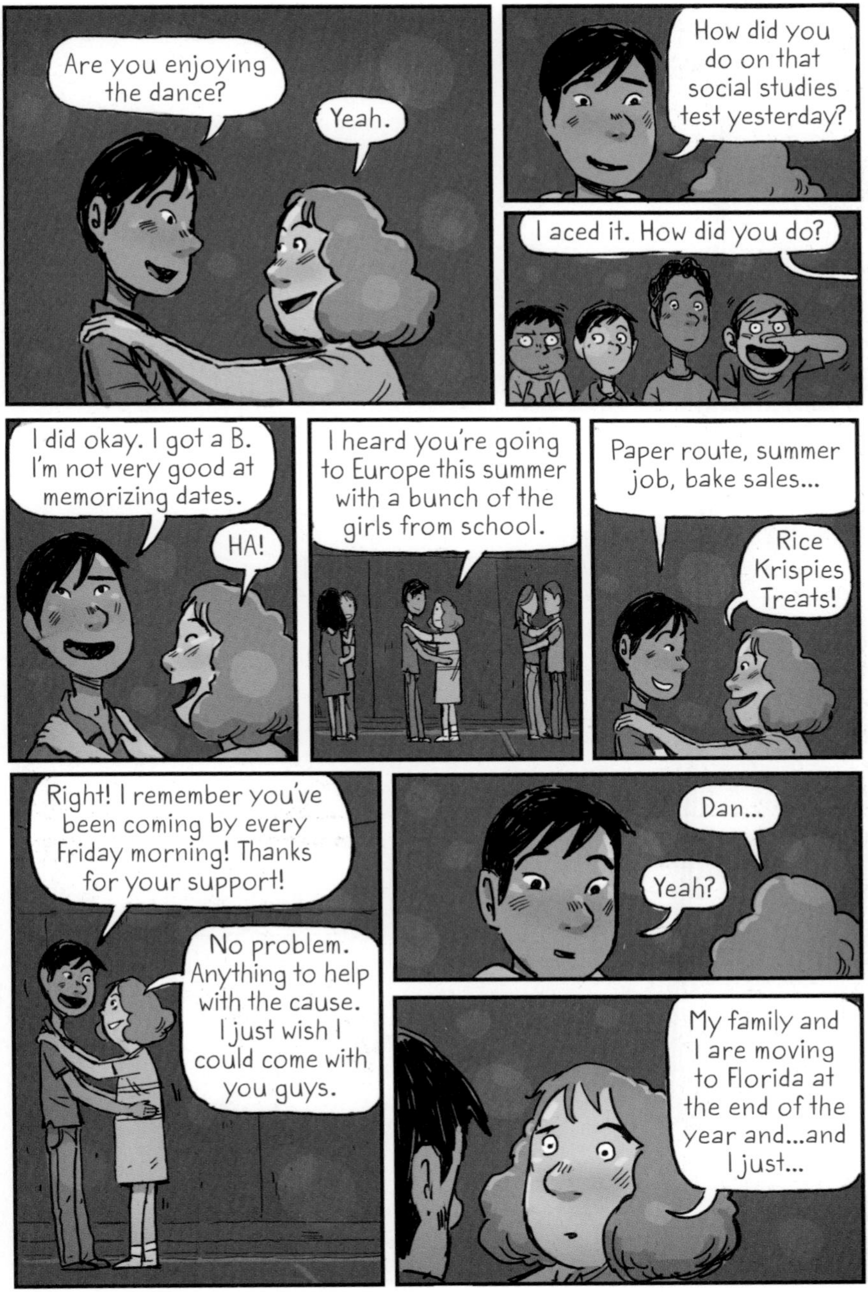
Are you enjoying the dance?
Yeah.
How did you do on that social studies test yesterday?
I aced it. How did you do?
I did okay. I got a B. I'm not very good at memorizing dates.
HA!
I heard you're going to Europe this summer with a bunch of the girls from school.
Paper route, summer job, bake sales...
Rice Krispies Treats!
Right! I remember you've been coming by every Friday morning! Thanks for your support!
No problem. Anything to help with the cause. I just wish I could come with you guys.
Dan...
Yeah?
My family and I are moving to Florida at the end of the year and...and I just...

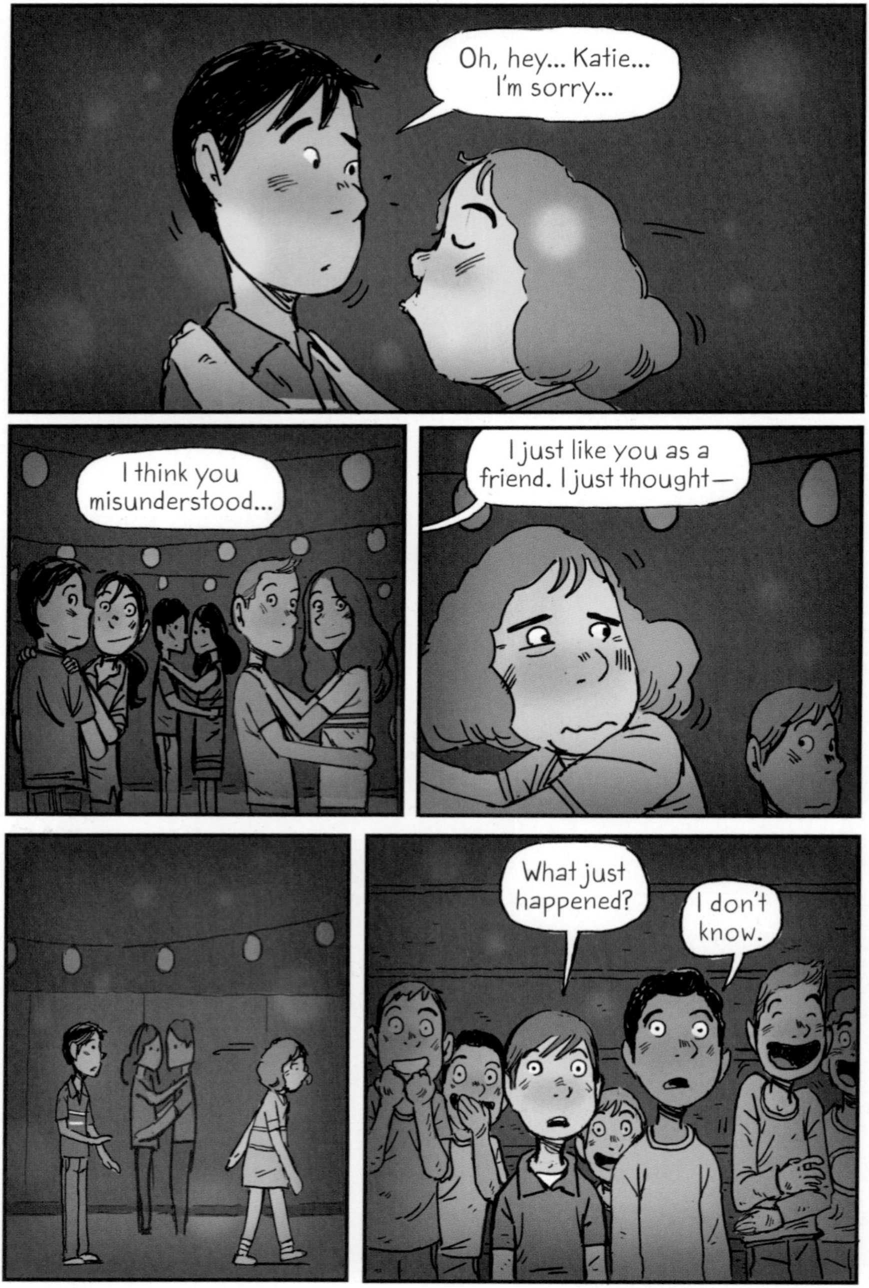
Oh, hey... Katie...
I'm sorry...
I think you misunderstood...
I just like you as a friend. I just thought—
What just happened?
I don't know.

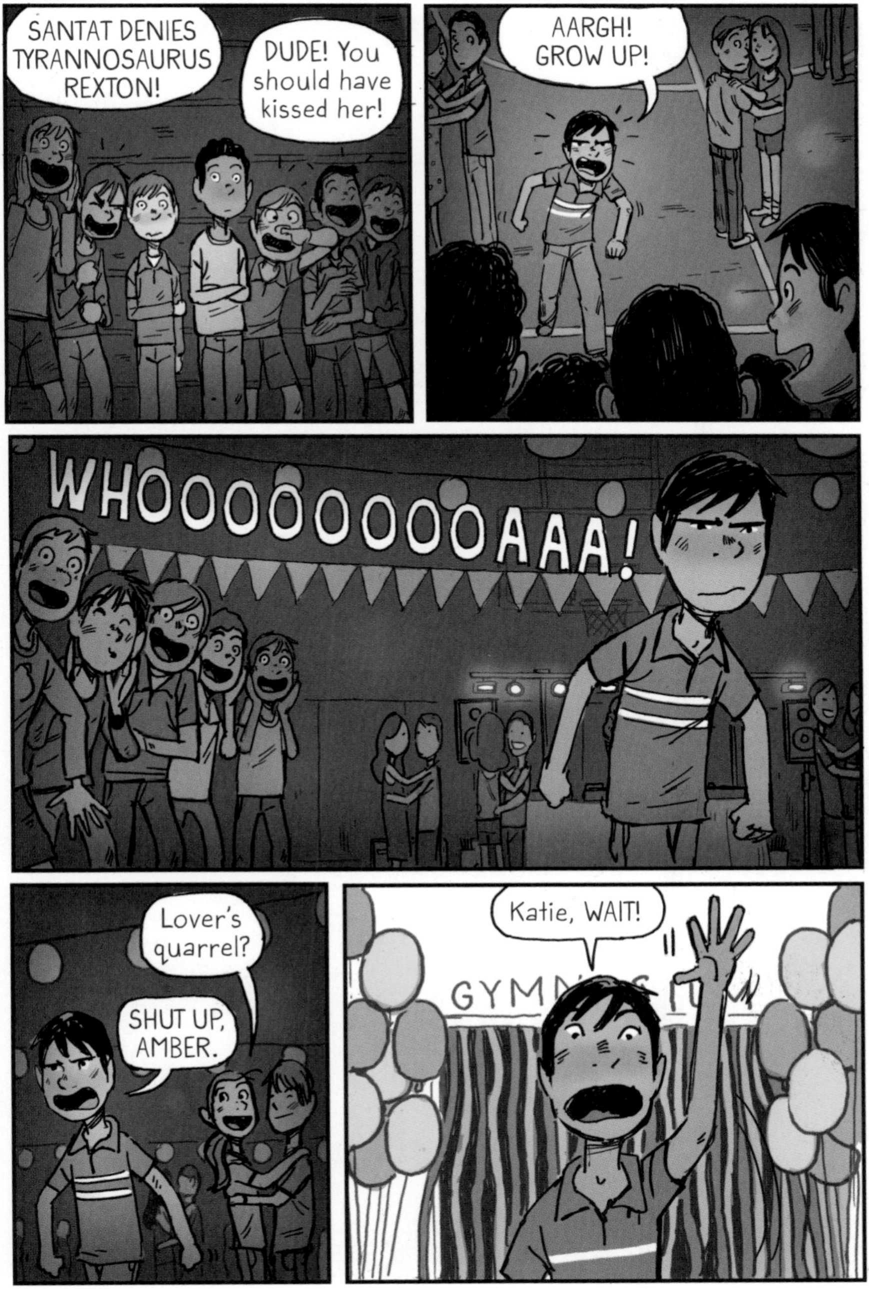
SANTAT DENIES TYRANNOSAURUS REXTON!
DUDE! You should have kissed her!
AARGH! GROW UP!
WHOOOOOOOOOAAA!
Lover's quarrel?
SHUT UP, AMBER.
Katie, WAIT!
GYMN

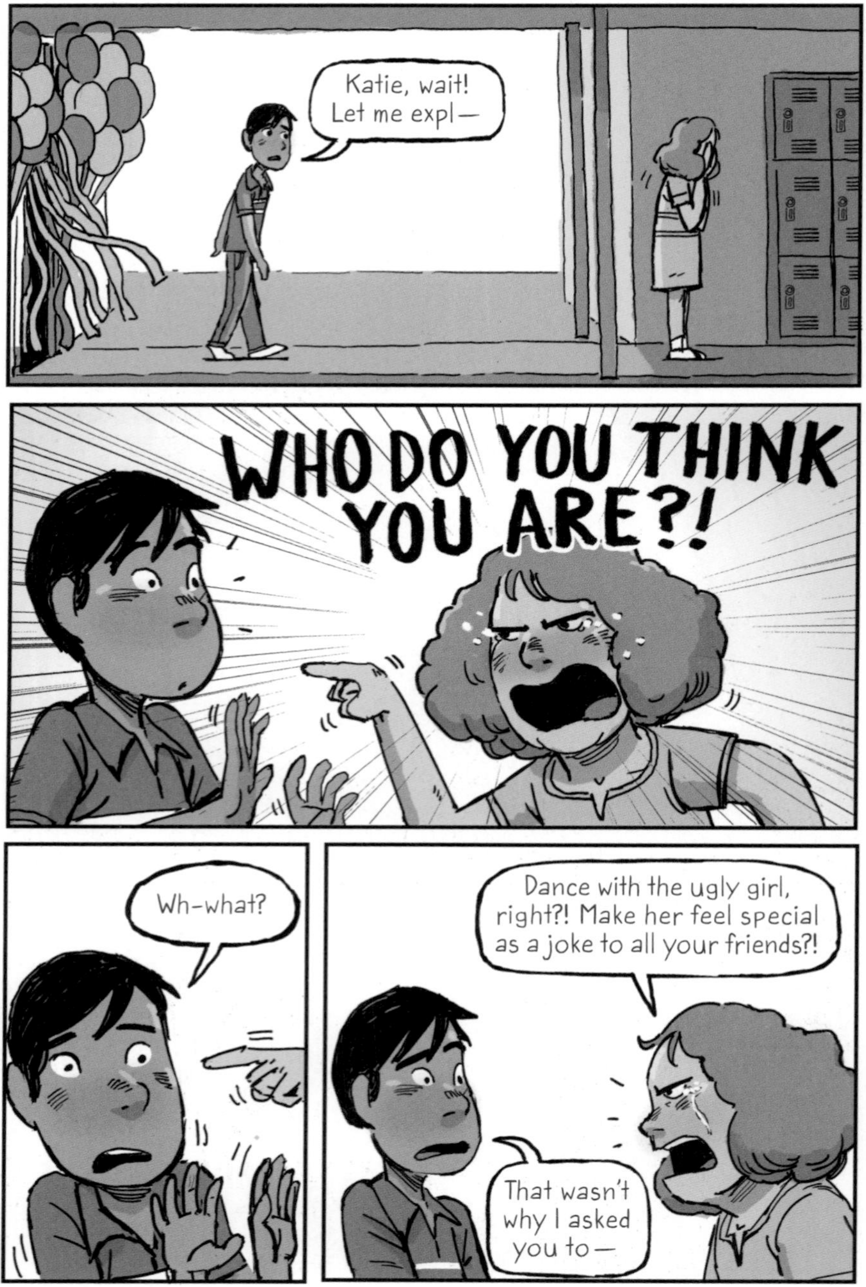
Katie, wait! Let me expl—
WHO DO YOU THINK YOU ARE?!
Wh-what?
Dance with the ugly girl, right?! Make her feel special as a joke to all your friends?!
That wasn't why I asked you to—

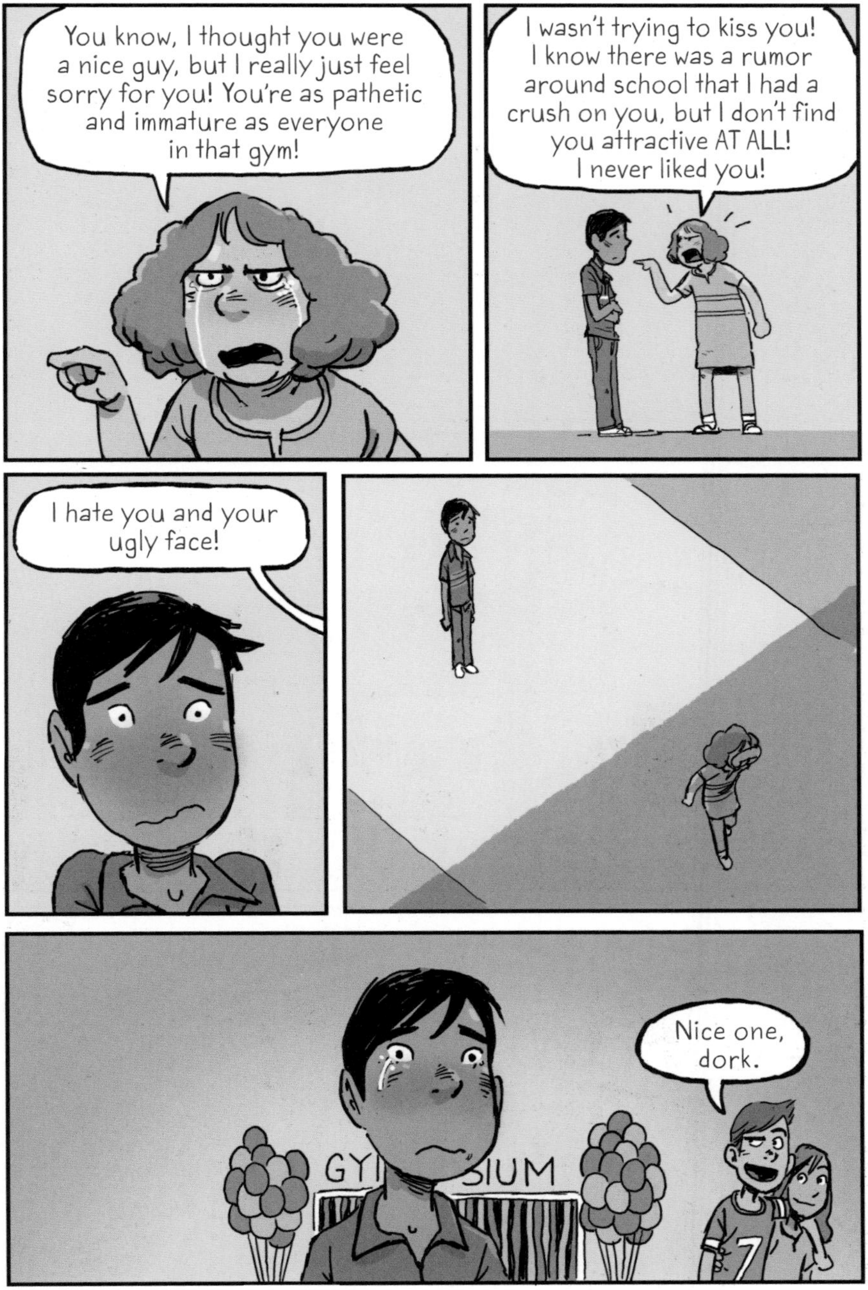
You know, I thought you were a nice guy, but I really just feel sorry for you! You're as pathetic and immature as everyone in that gym!
I wasn't trying to kiss you! I know there was a rumor around school that I had a crush on you, but I don't find you attractive AT ALL! I never liked you!
I hate you and your ugly face!
GY SIUM
Nice one, dork.

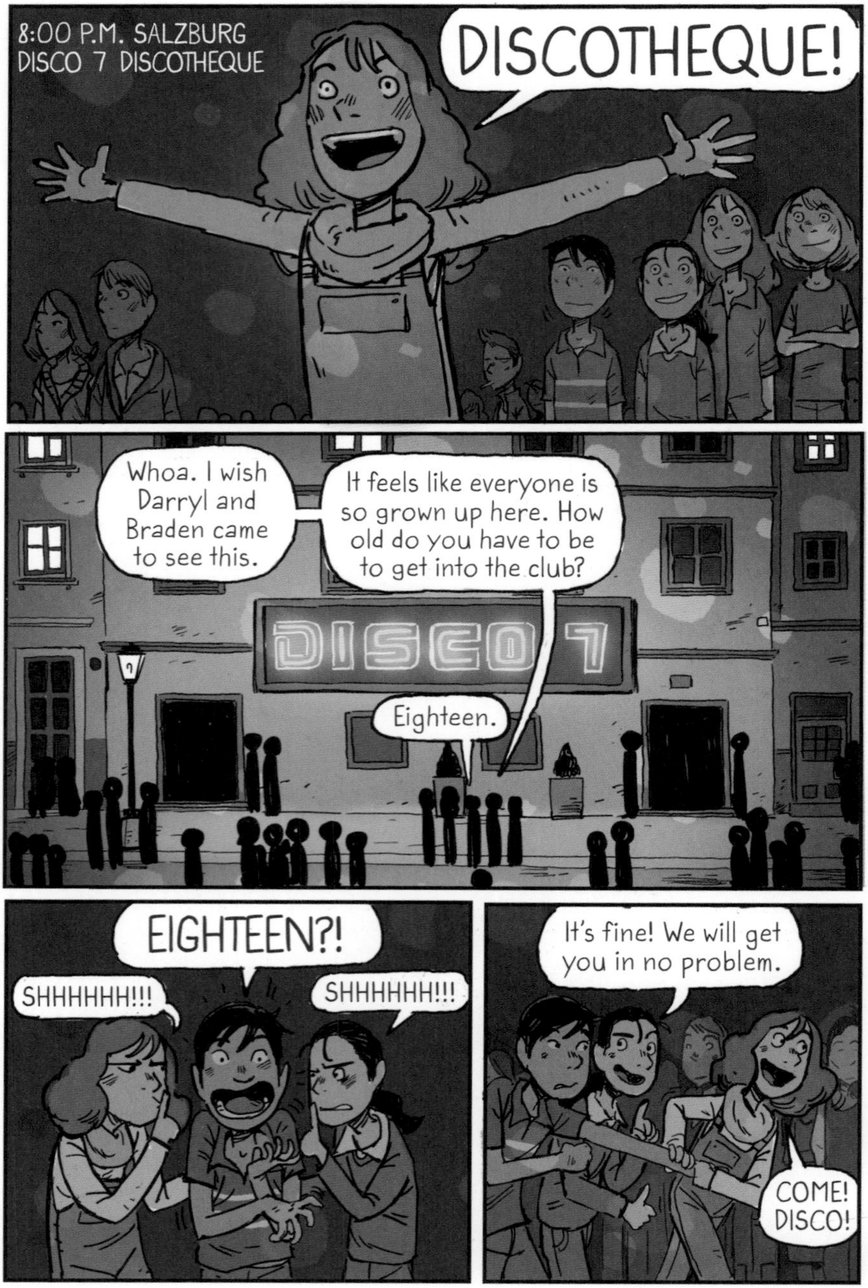
8:00 P.M. SALZBURG
DISCO 7 DISCOTHEQUE
DISCOTHEQUE!
Whoa. I wish Darryl and Braden came to see this.
It feels like everyone is so grown up here. How old do you have to be to get into the club?
DISCO 7
Eighteen.
EIGHTEEN?!
SHHHHHH!!!
SHHHHHH!!!
It's fine! We will get you in no problem.
COME! DISCO!

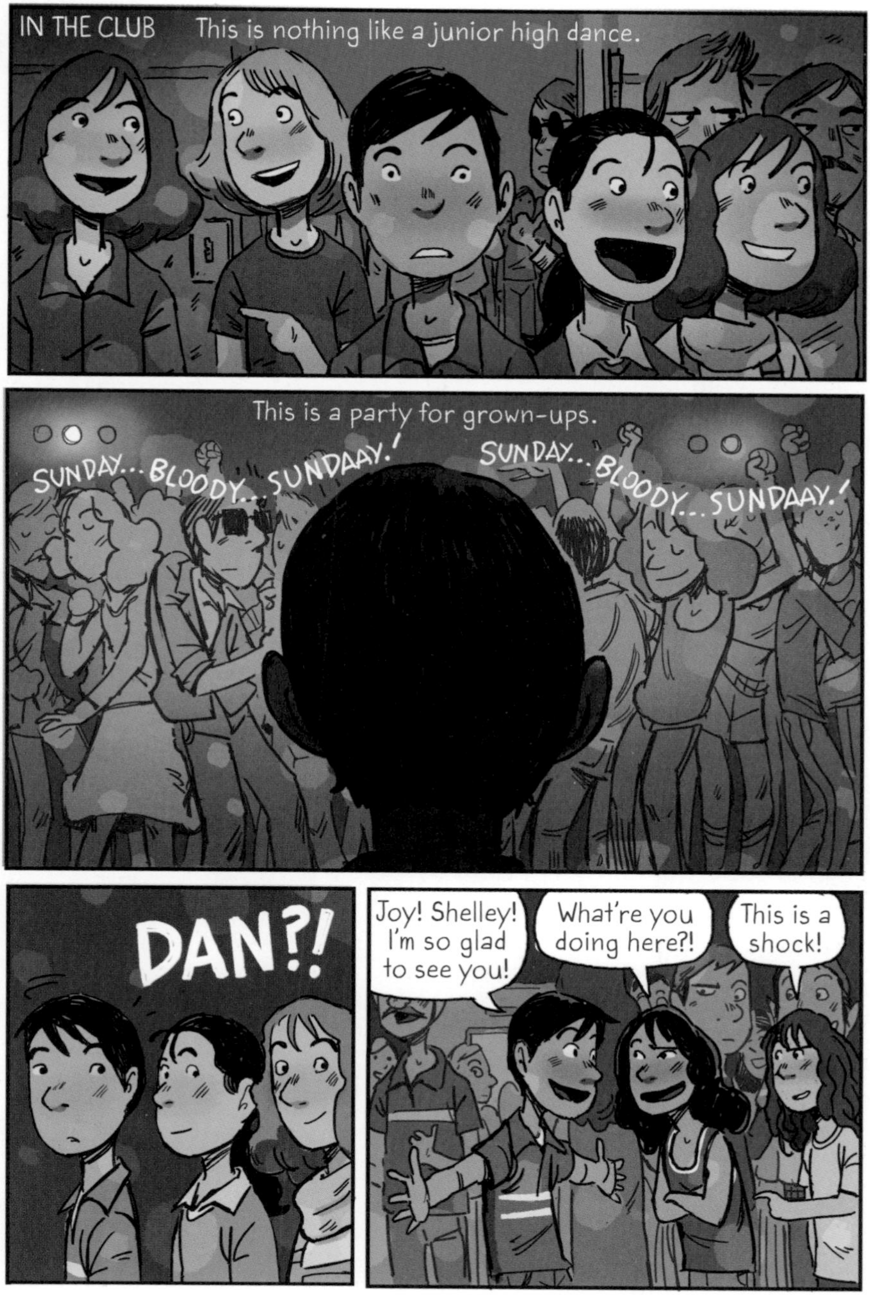

IN THE CLUB
This is nothing like a junior high dance.
This is a party for grown-ups.
SUNDAY... BLOODY... SUNDAAY.!
SUNDAY... BLOODY... SUNDAAY.!
DAN?!
Joy! Shelley! I'm so glad to see you!
What're you doing here?!
This is a shock!

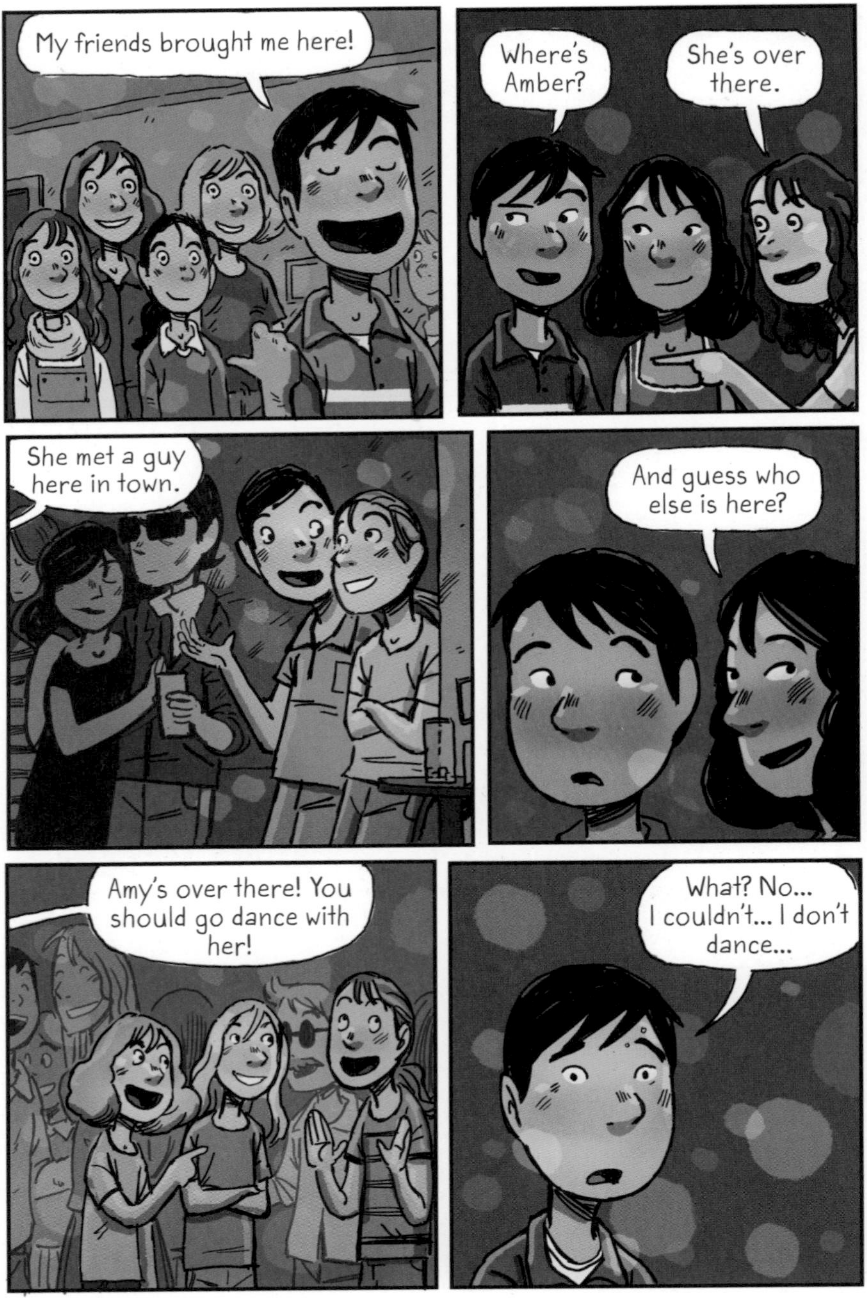
My friends brought me here!
Where's Amber?
She's over there.
She met a guy here in town.
And guess who else is here?
Amy's over there! You should go dance with her!
What? No... I couldn't... I don't dance...

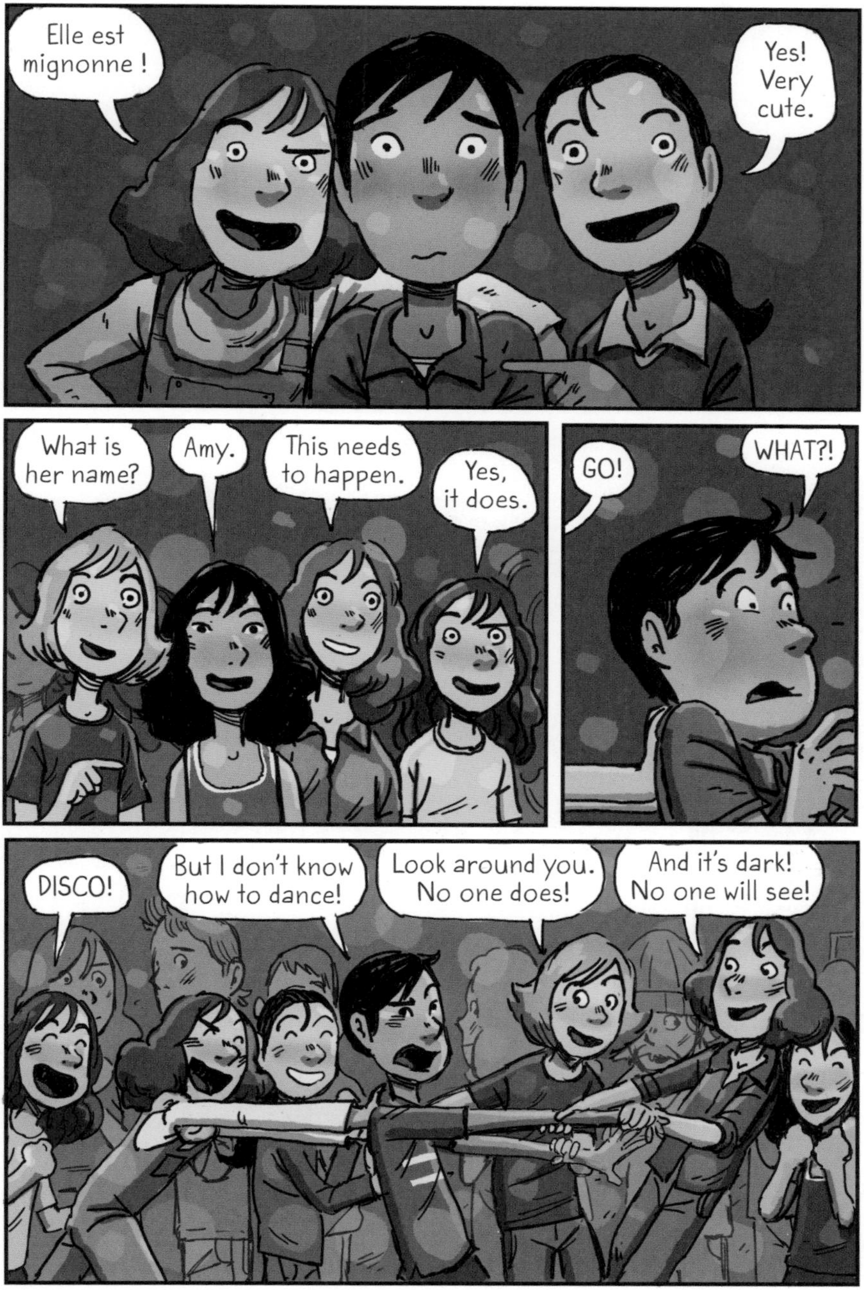
Elle est mignonne !
Yes! Very cute.
What is her name?
Amy.
This needs to happen.
Yes, it does.
GO!
WHAT?!
DISCO!
But I don't know how to dance!
Look around you. No one does!
And it's dark! No one will see!

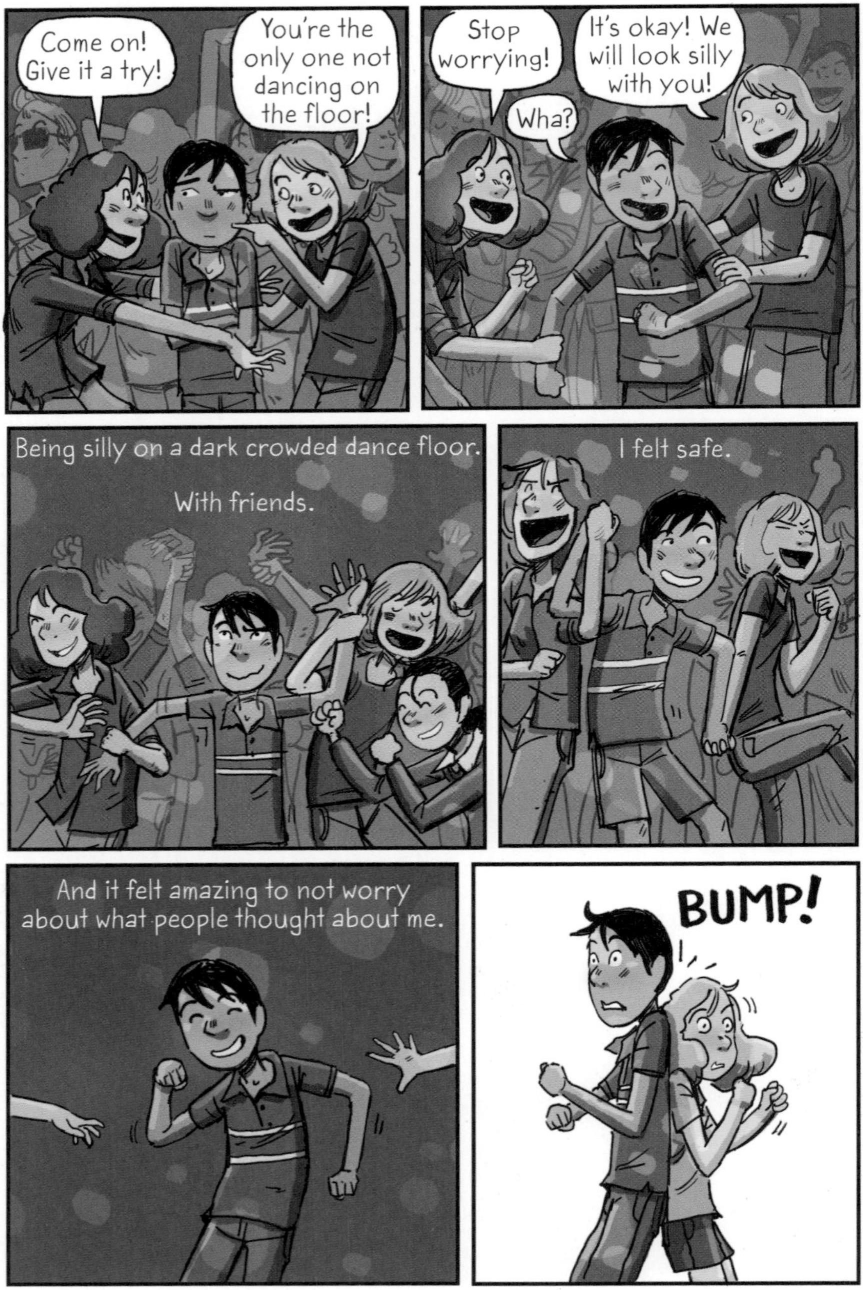
Come on! Give it a try!
You're the only one not dancing on the floor!
Stop worrying!
Wha?
It's okay! We will look silly with you!
Being silly on a dark crowded dance floor.
With friends.
I felt safe.
And it felt amazing to not worry about what people thought about me.
BUMP!

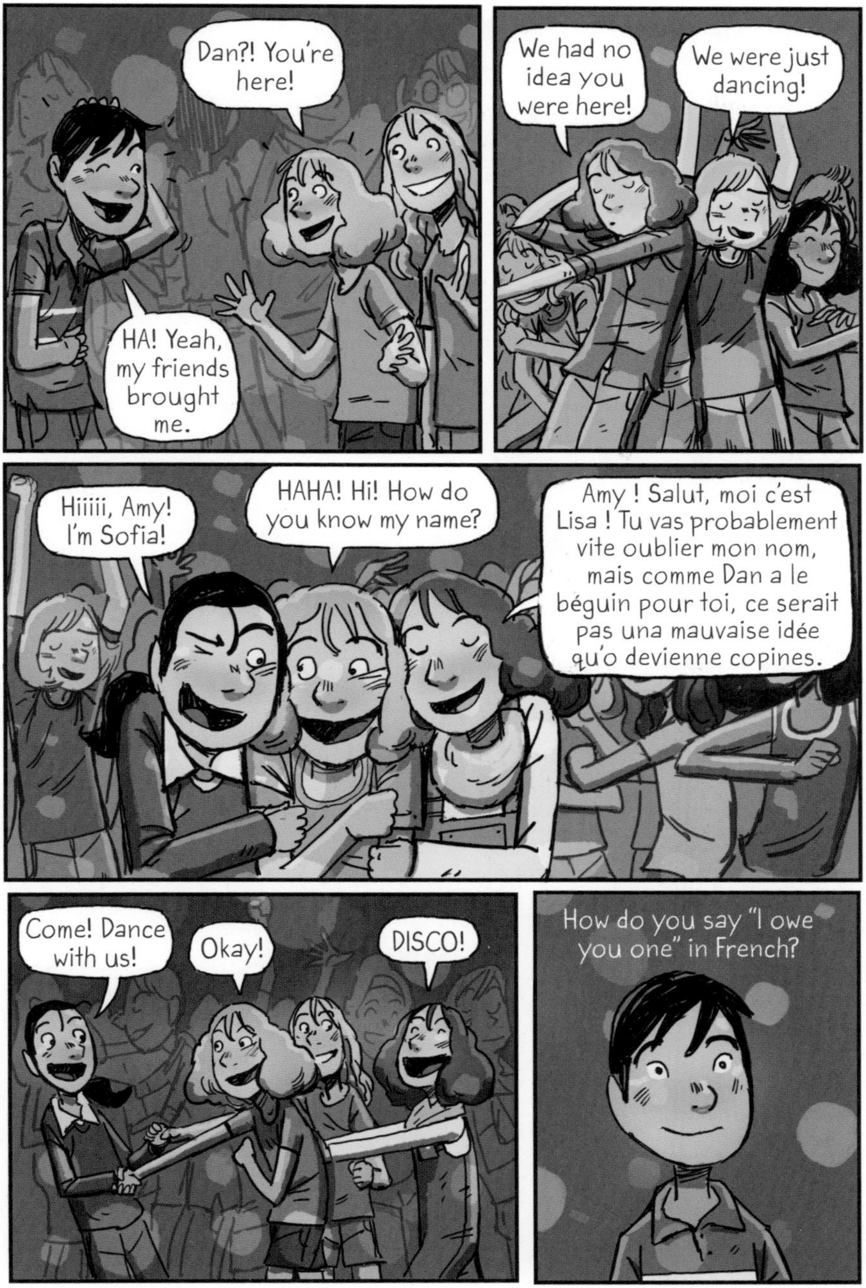
Dan?! You're here!
HA! Yeah, my friends brought me.
We had no idea you were here!
We were just dancing!
Hiiiii, Amy! I'm Sofia!
HAHA! Hi! How do you know my name?
Amy ! Salut, moi c'est Lisa ! Tu vas probablement vite oublier mon nom, mais comme Dan a le béguin pour toi, ce serait pas una mauvaise idée qu'o devienne copines.
Come! Dance with us!
Okay!
DISCO!
How do you say "I owe you one" in French?

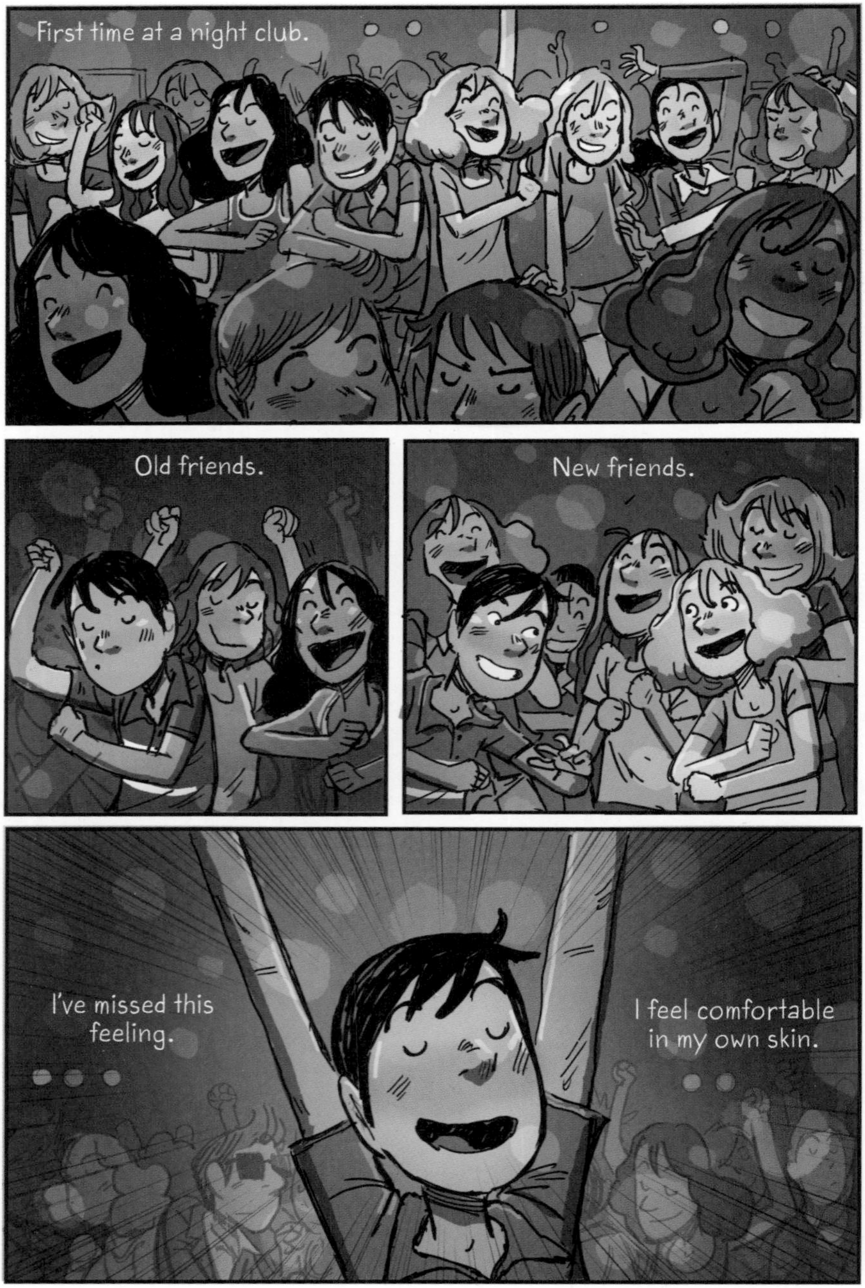
First time at a night club.
Old friends.
New friends.
I've missed this feeling.
I feel comfortable in my own skin.

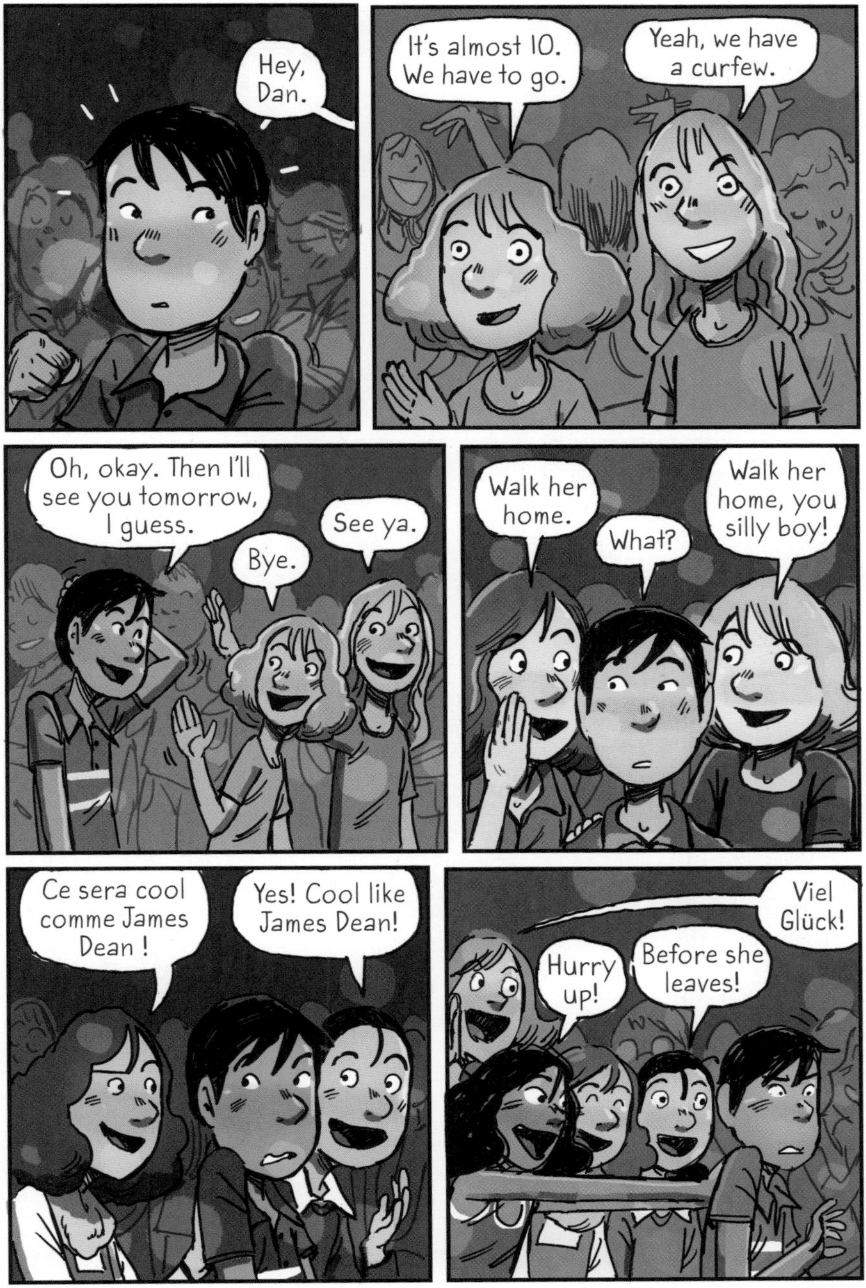
Hey, Dan.
It's almost 10. We have to go.
Yeah, we have a curfew.
Oh, okay. Then I'll see you tomorrow, I guess.
Bye.
See ya.
Walk her home.
What?
Walk her home, you silly boy!
Ce sera cool comme James Dean !
Yes! Cool like James Dean!
Viel Glück!
Hurry up!
Before she leaves!

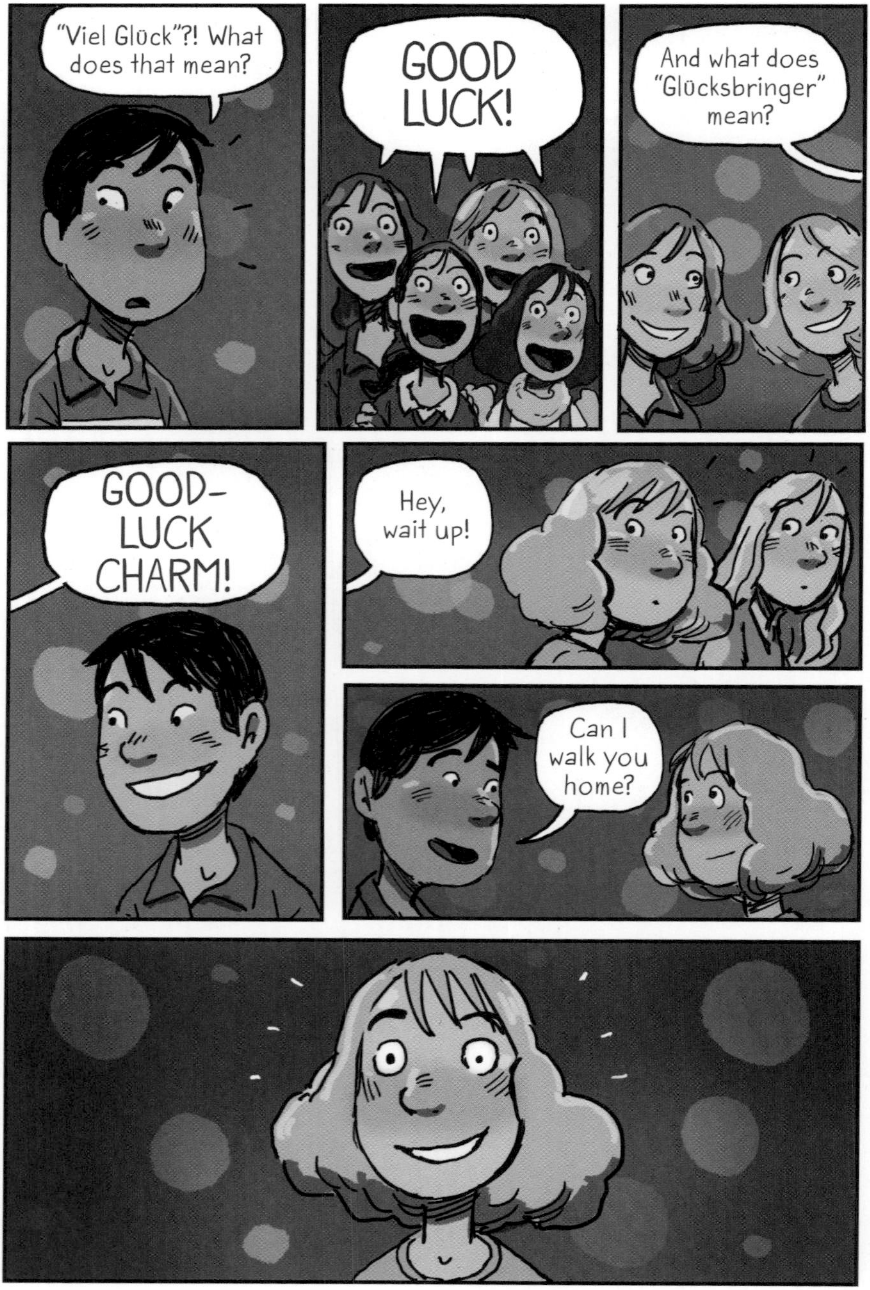
"Viel Glück"?! What does that mean?
GOOD LUCK!
And what does "Glücksbringer" mean?
GOOD-LUCK CHARM!
Hey, wait up!
Can I walk you home?

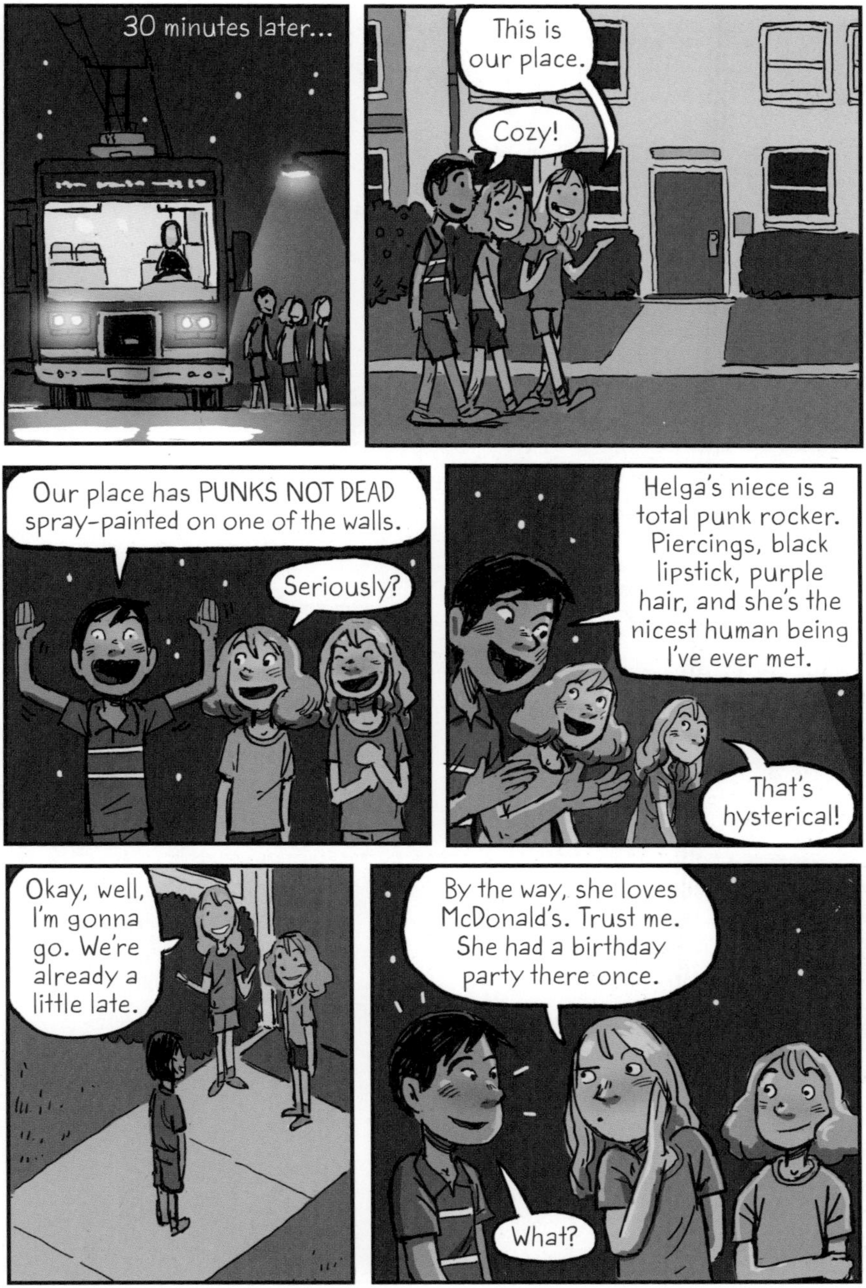
30 minutes later...
This is our place.
Cozy!
Our place has PUNKS NOT DEAD spray-painted on one of the walls.
Seriously?
Helga's niece is a total punk rocker. Piercings, black lipstick, purple hair, and she's the nicest human being I've ever met.
That's hysterical!
Okay, well, I'm gonna go. We're already a little late.
By the way, she loves McDonald's. Trust me. She had a birthday party there once.
What?

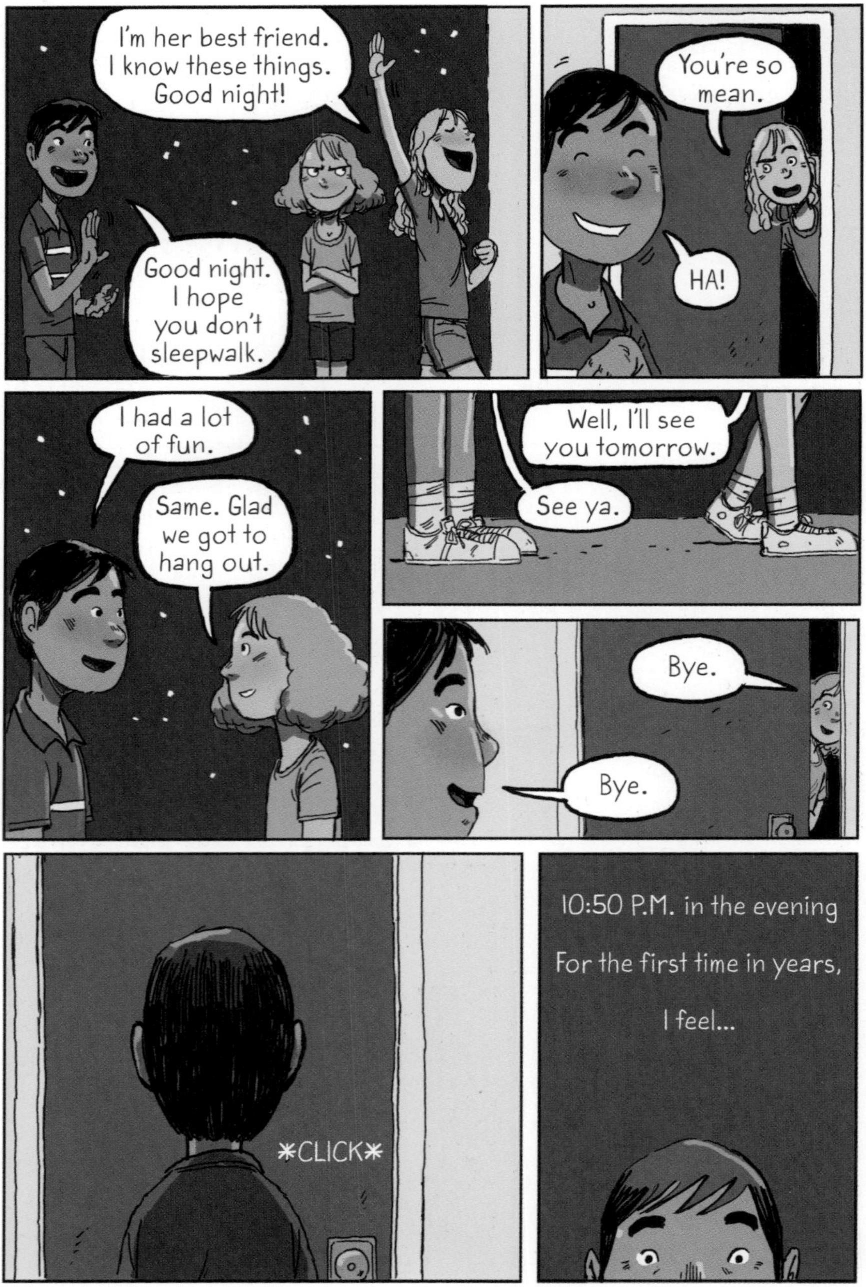
I'm her best friend.
I know these things.
Good night!
Good night.
I hope
you don't
sleepwalk.
You're so
mean.
HA!
I had a lot
of fun.
Same. Glad
we got to
hang out.
Well, I'll see
you tomorrow.
See ya.
Bye.
Bye.
CLICK
10:50 P.M. in the evening
For the first time in years,
I feel...

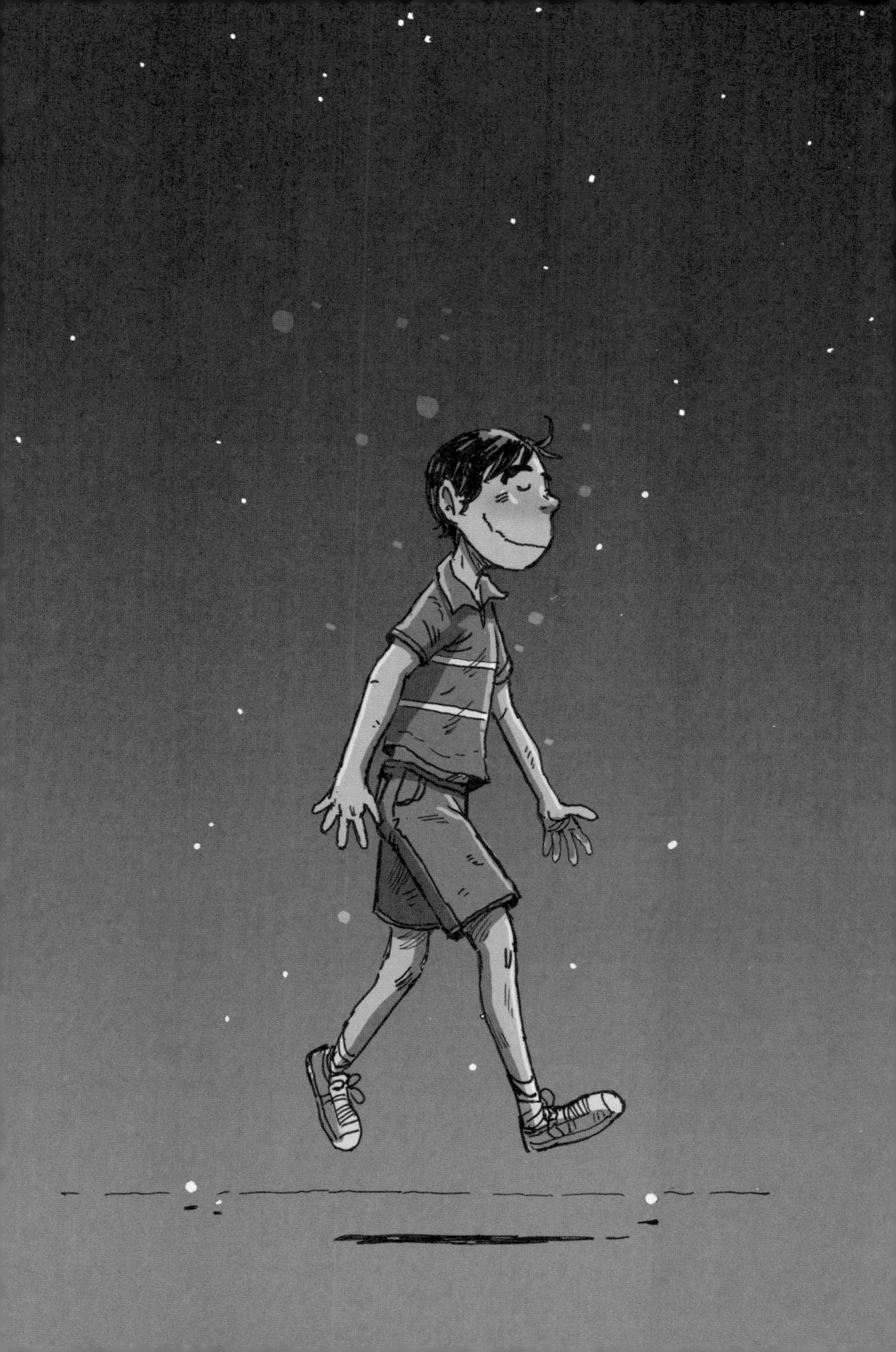

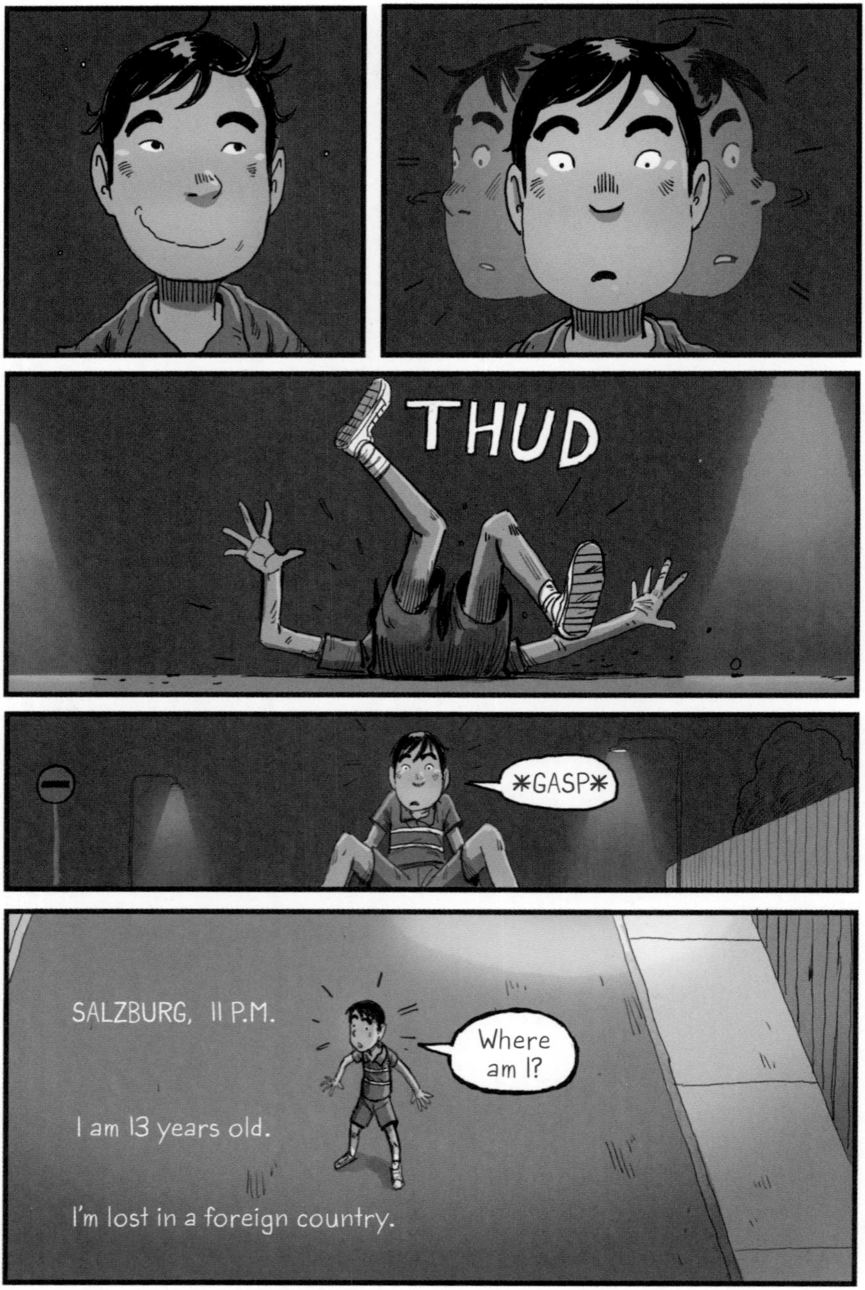
THUD
GASP
SALZBURG, 11 P.M.
Where am I?
I am 13 years old.
I'm lost in a foreign country.

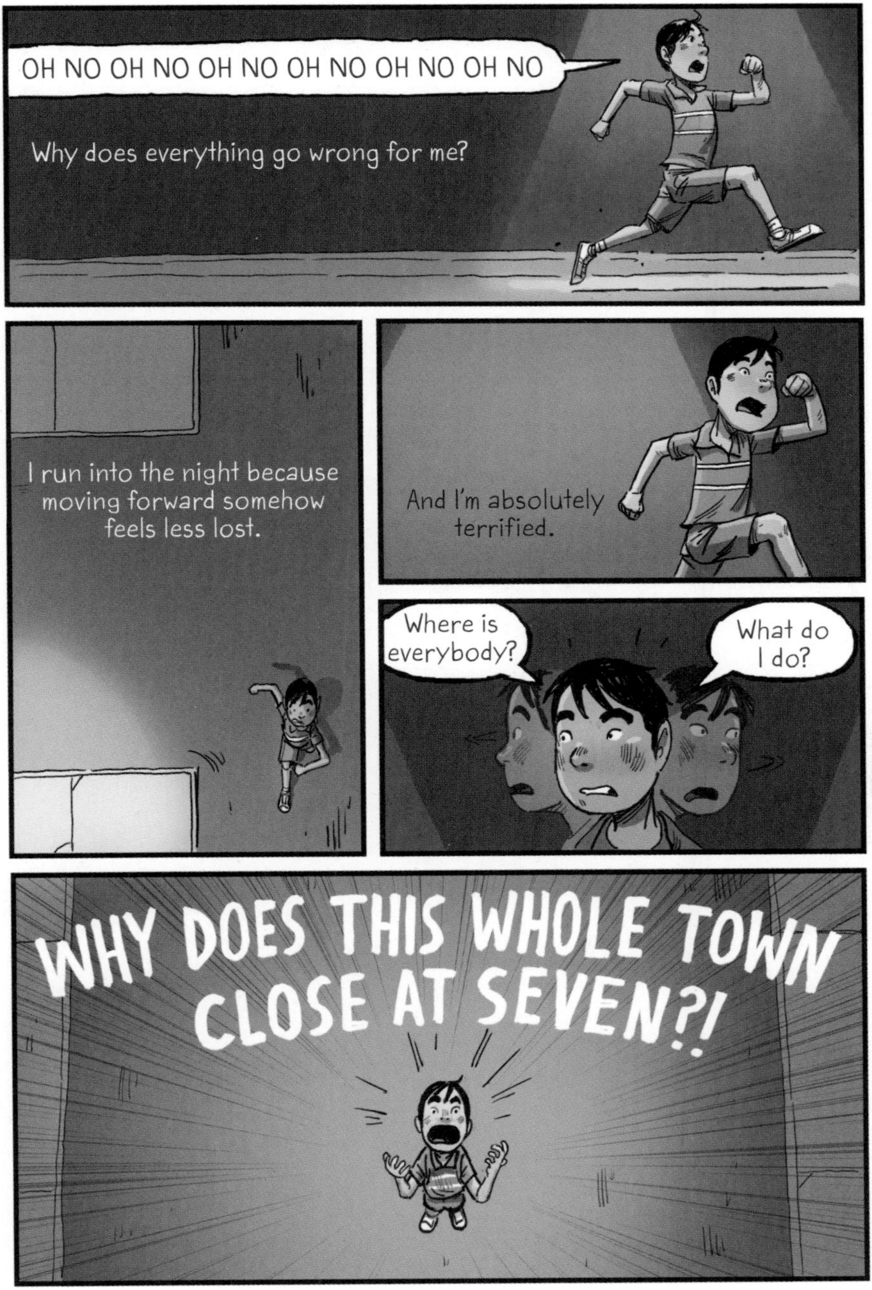
OH NO OH NO OH NO OH NO OH NO OH NO
Why does everything go wrong for me?
I run into the night because moving forward somehow feels less lost.
And I'm absolutely terrified.
Where is everybody?
What do I do?
WHY DOES THIS WHOLE TOWN CLOSE AT SEVEN?!

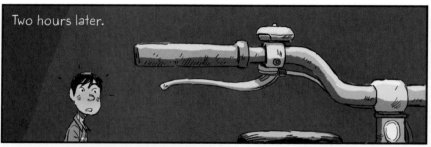
Two hours later.

None of these bikes have any locks on them...

In America, this entire bike rack would be pillaged and nothing would be left.

Should I take one? I'm lost in a foreign country. People would understand, right?

I shouldn't steal.

But I have no idea where I am.

What if I get mugged or worse?

Killed!?

Just this once.

I'm sorry to the owner of this bicycl—

HEY!

Oh no.

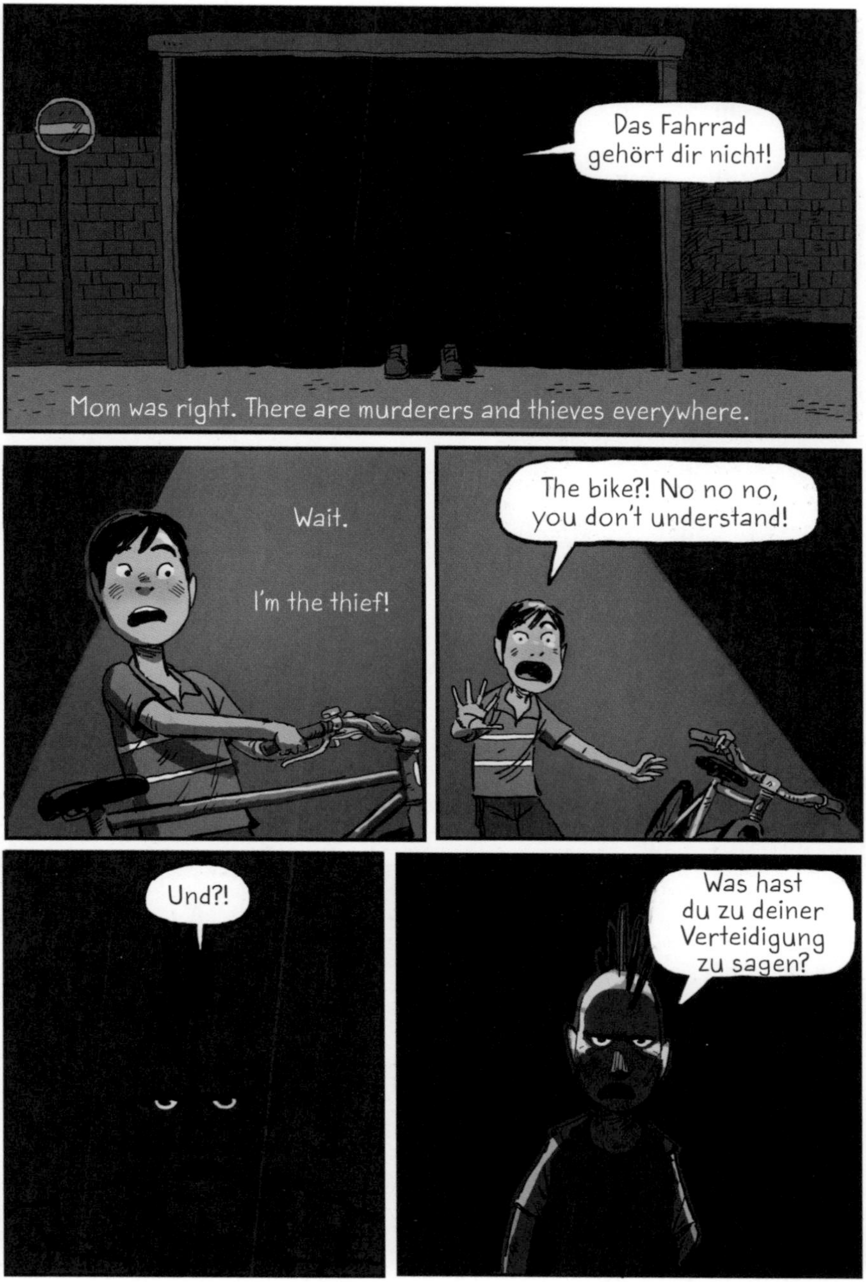
Das Fahrrad gehört dir nicht!
Mom was right. There are murderers and thieves everywhere.
Wait.
I'm the thief!
The bike?! No no no, you don't understand!
Und?!
Was hast du zu deiner Verteidigung zu sagen?

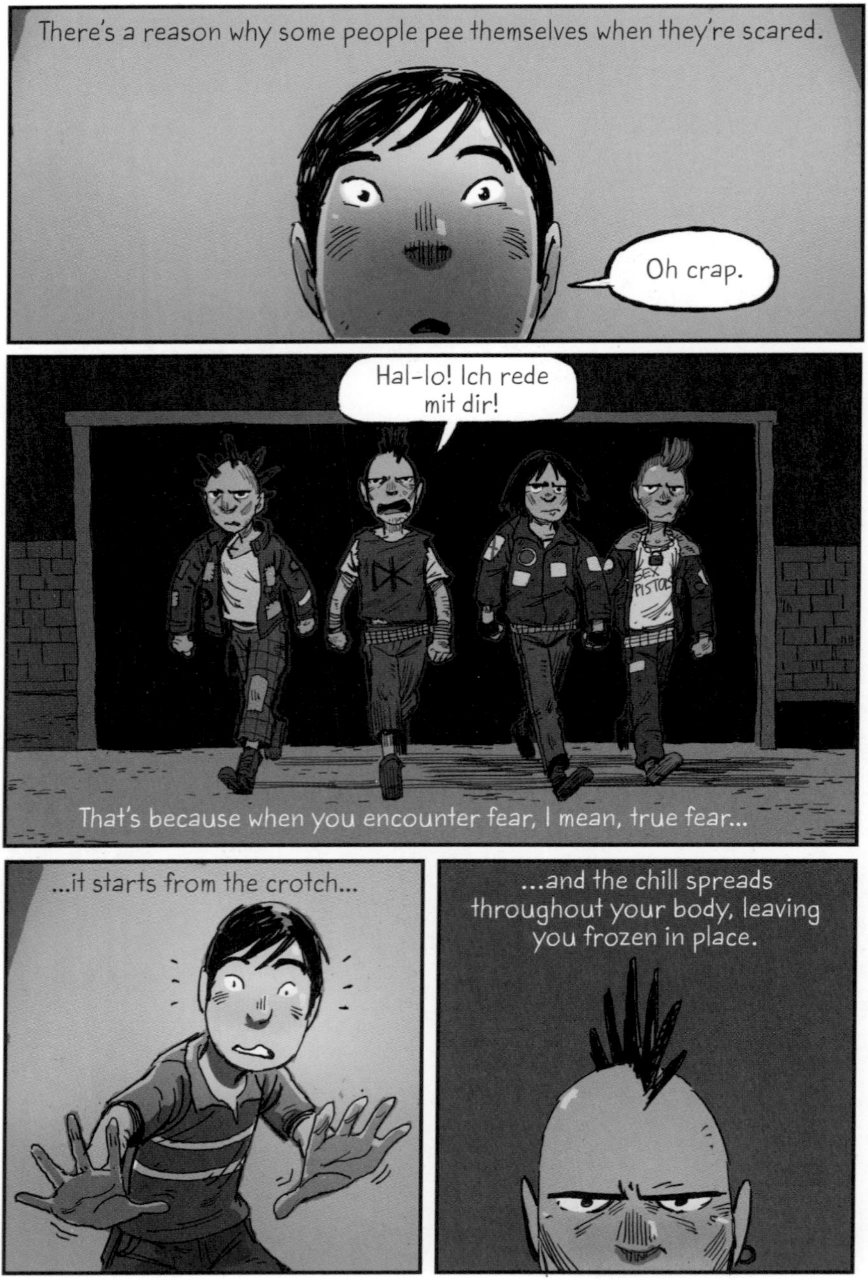
There's a reason why some people pee themselves when they're scared.
Oh crap.
Hal-lo! Ich rede mit dir!
That's because when you encounter fear, I mean, true fear...
...it starts from the crotch...
...and the chill spreads throughout your body, leaving you frozen in place.

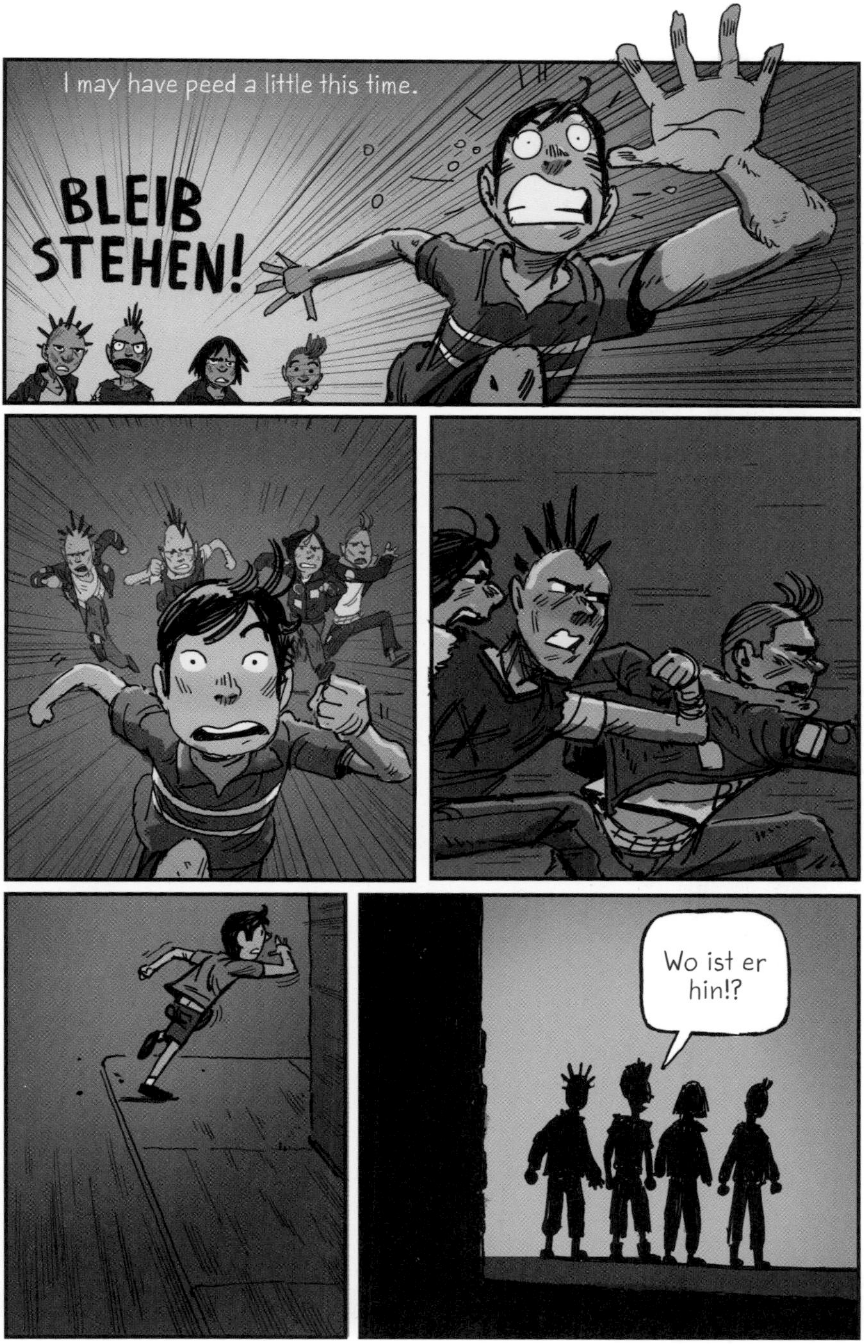
I may have peed a little this time.
BLEIB STEHEN!
Wo ist er hin!?

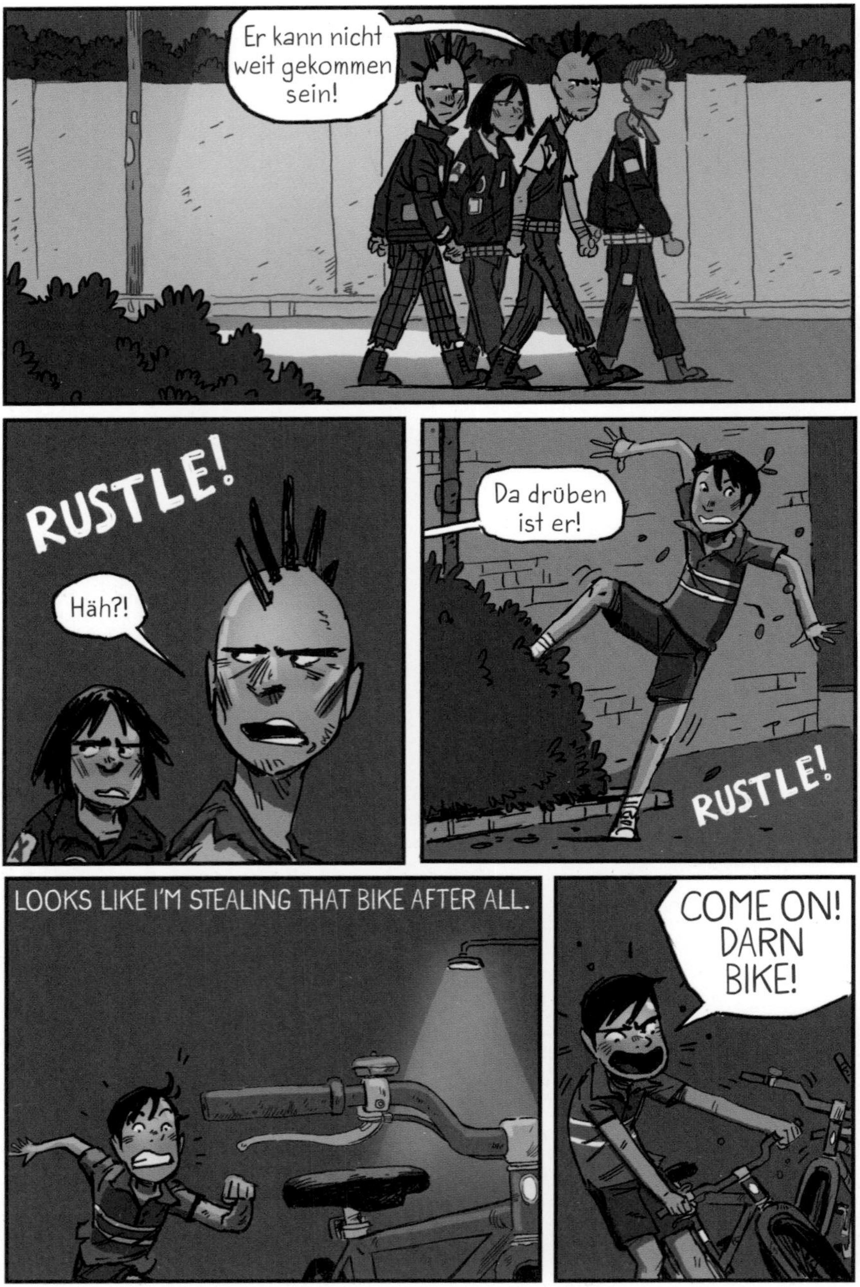
Er kann nicht weit gekommen sein!
RUSTLE!
Häh?!
Da drüben ist er!
RUSTLE!
LOOKS LIKE I'M STEALING THAT BIKE AFTER ALL.
COME ON! DARN BIKE!

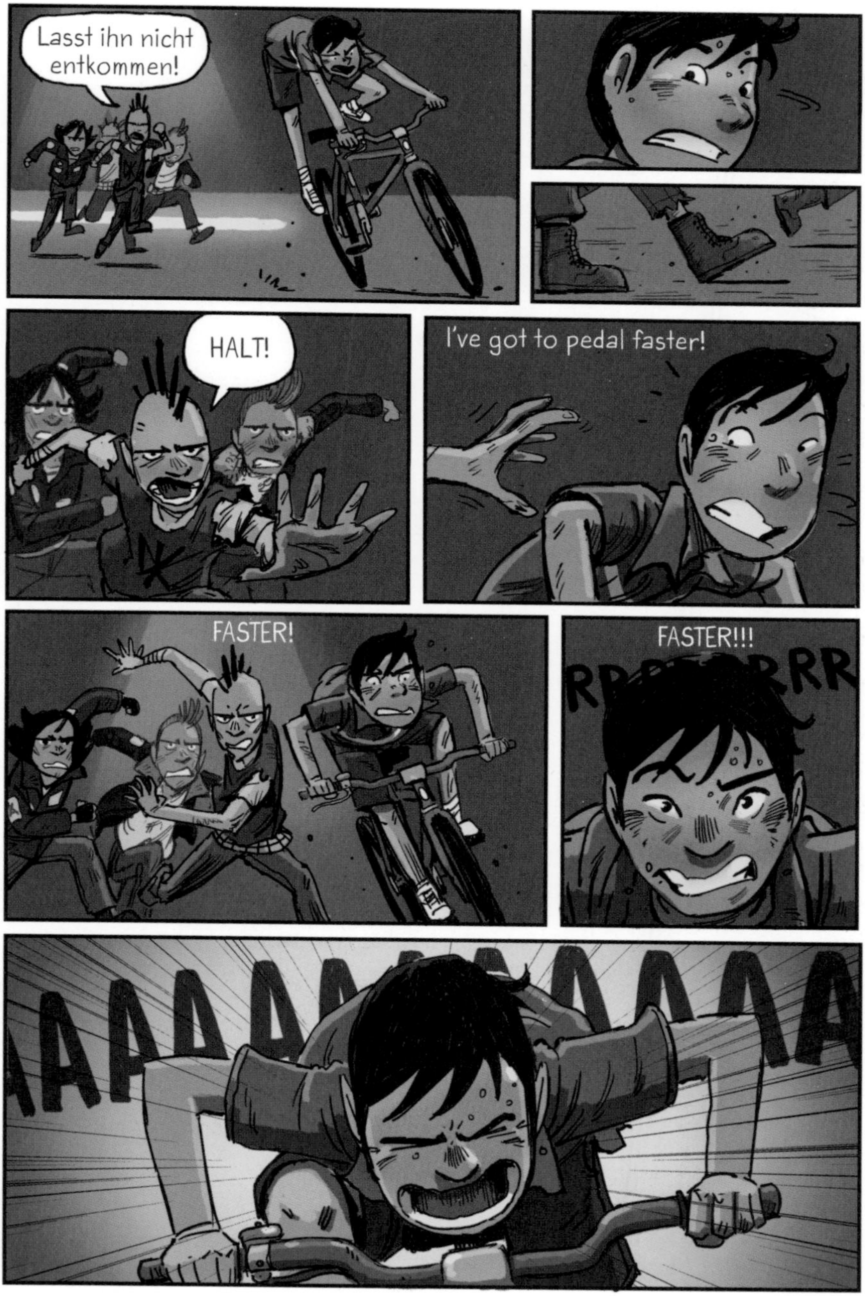
Lasst ihn nicht entkommen!
HALT!
I've got to pedal faster!
FASTER!
FASTER!!!
RRRRRRR
AAAAAAAAAAAA

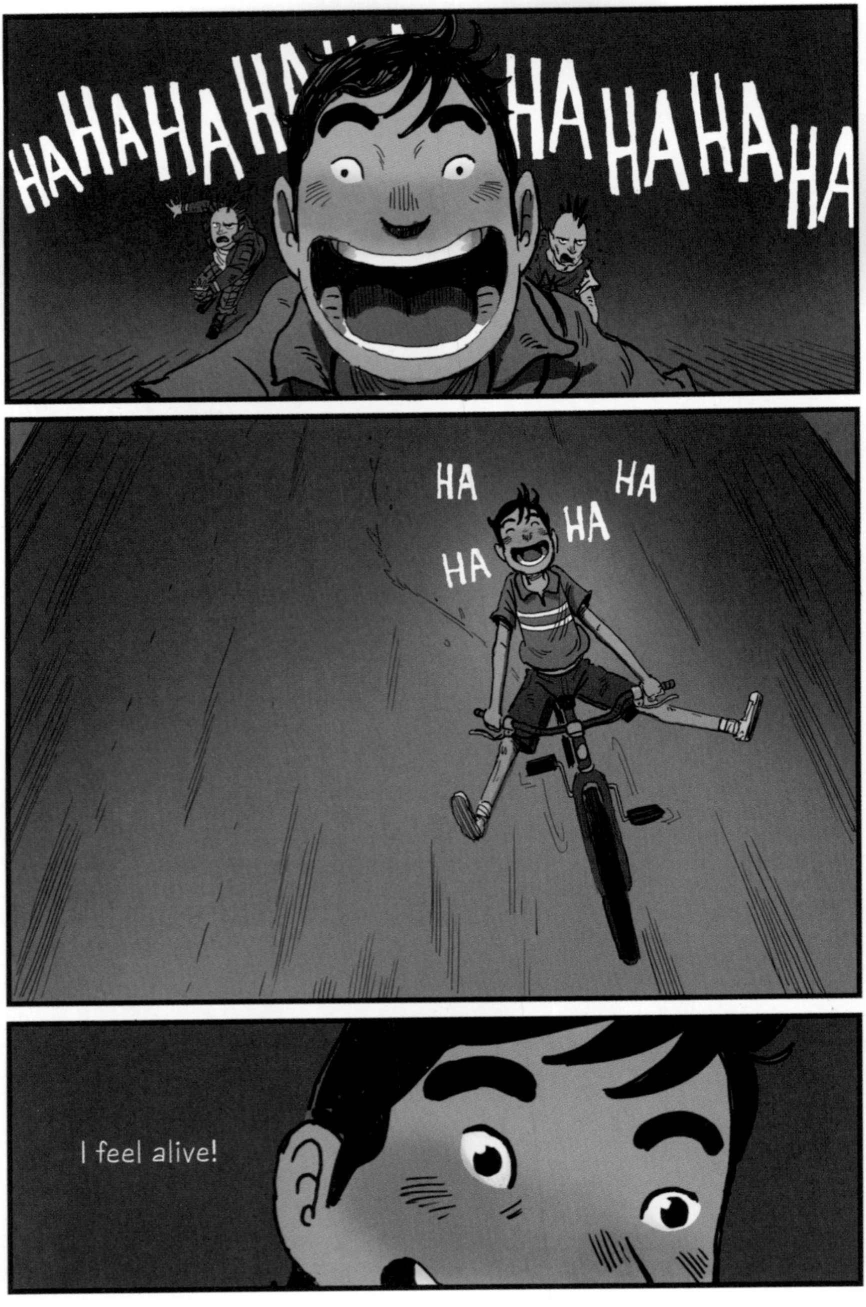
HAHAHAHAHA HAHAHAHAHA
HA
HA
HA
HA
I feel alive!

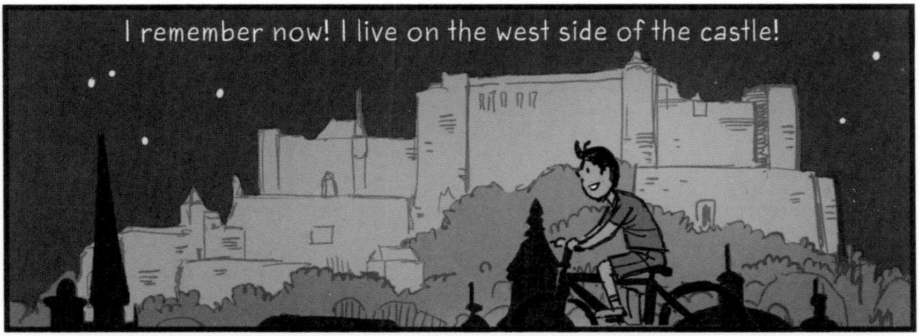
I remember now! I live on the west side of the castle!

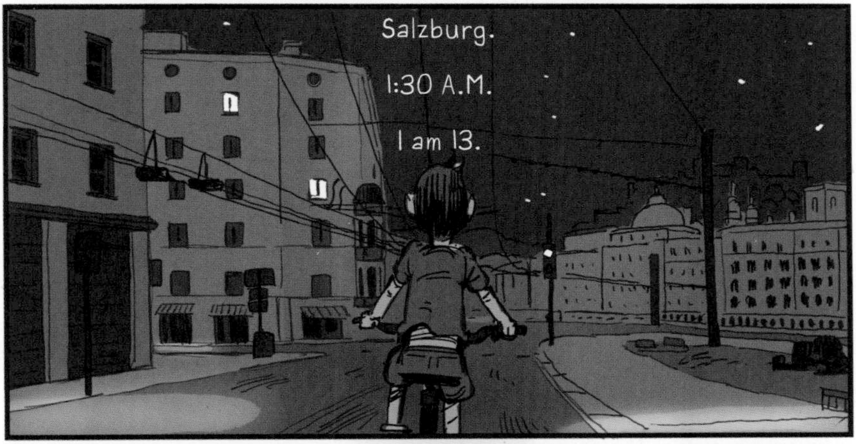
Salzburg.
1:30 A.M.
I am 13.

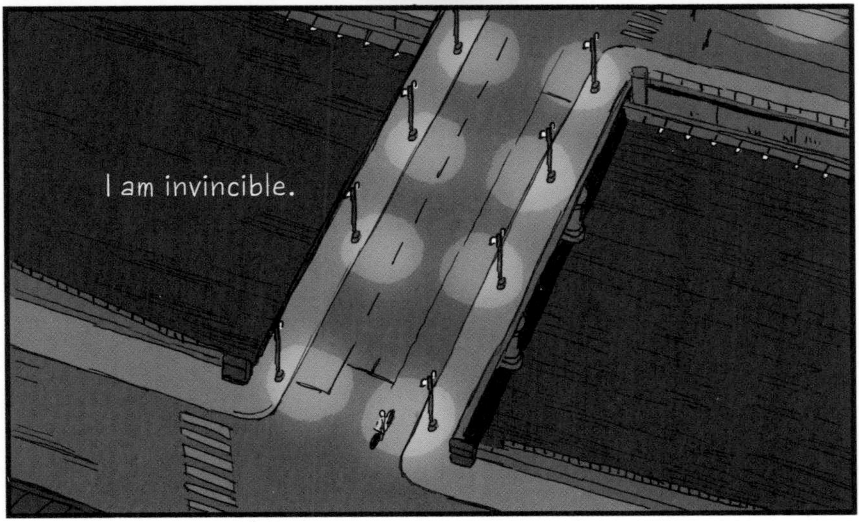
I am invincible.

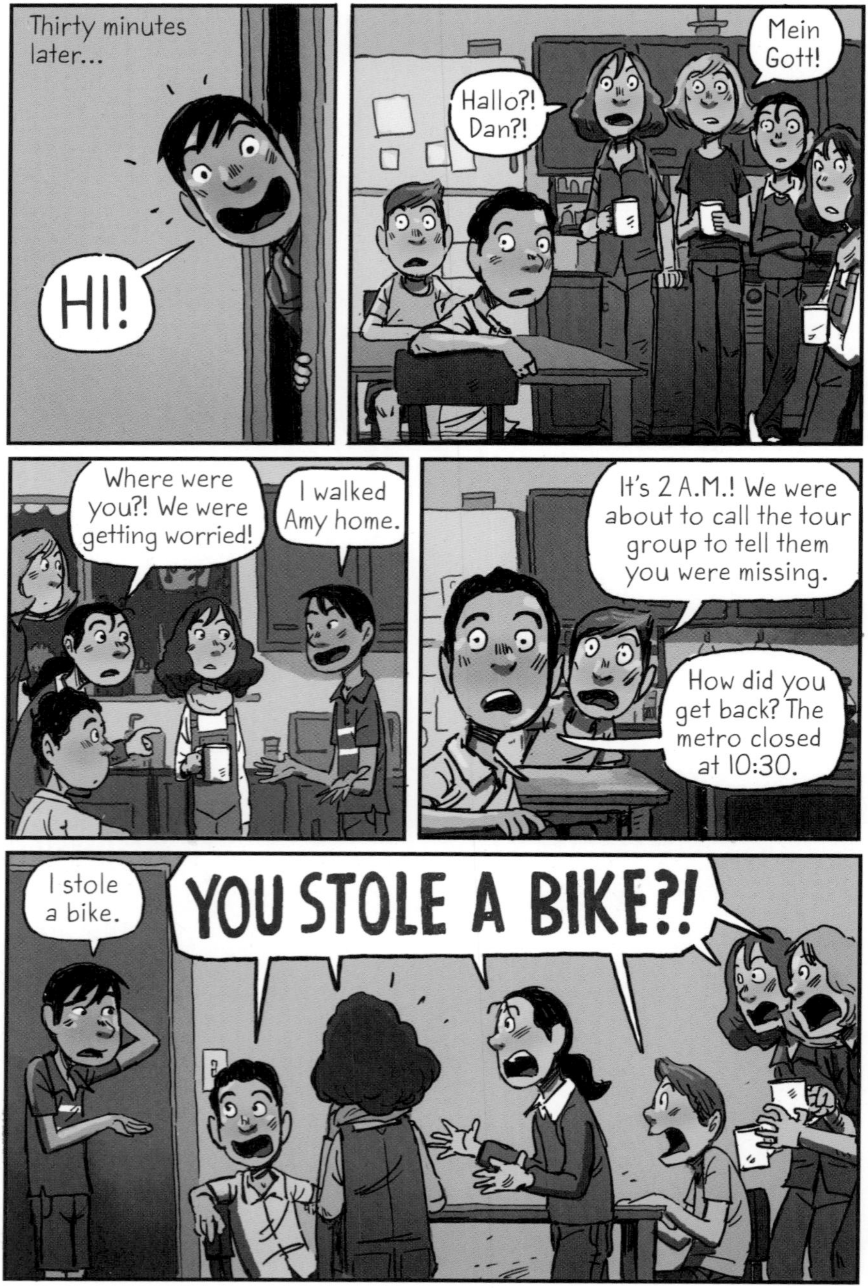
Thirty minutes later...
HI!
Hallo?! Dan?!
Mein Gott!
Where were you?! We were getting worried!
I walked Amy home.
It's 2 A.M.! We were about to call the tour group to tell them you were missing.
How did you get back? The metro closed at 10:30.
I stole a bike.
YOU STOLE A BIKE?!

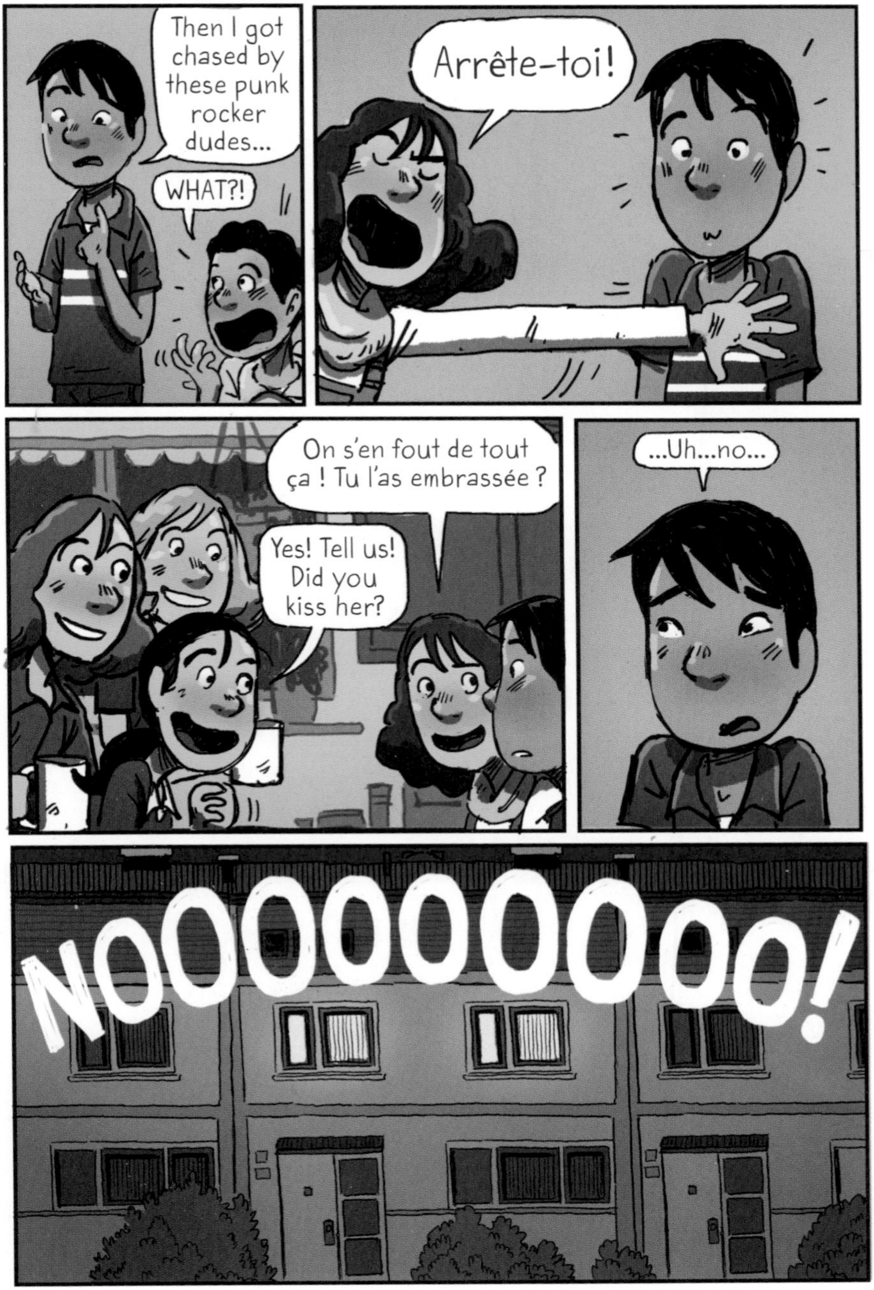

Then I got chased by these punk rocker dudes...
WHAT?!
Arrête-toi!
On s'en fout de tout ça ! Tu l'as embrassée ?
Yes! Tell us! Did you kiss her?
...Uh...no...
NOOOOOOOOO!

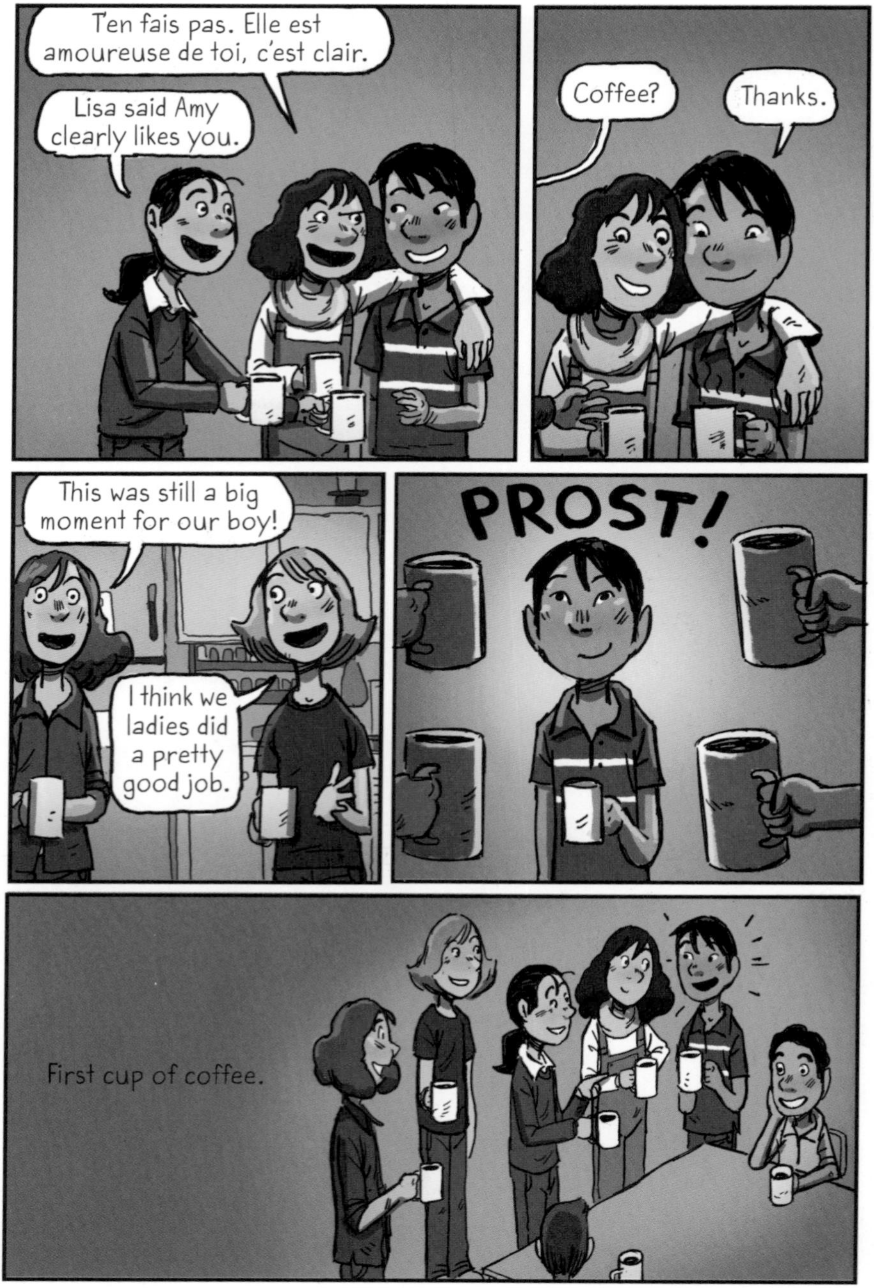
T'en fais pas. Elle est amoureuse de toi, c'est clair.
Lisa said Amy clearly likes you.
Coffee?
Thanks.
This was still a big moment for our boy!
I think we ladies did a pretty good job.
PROST!
First cup of coffee.

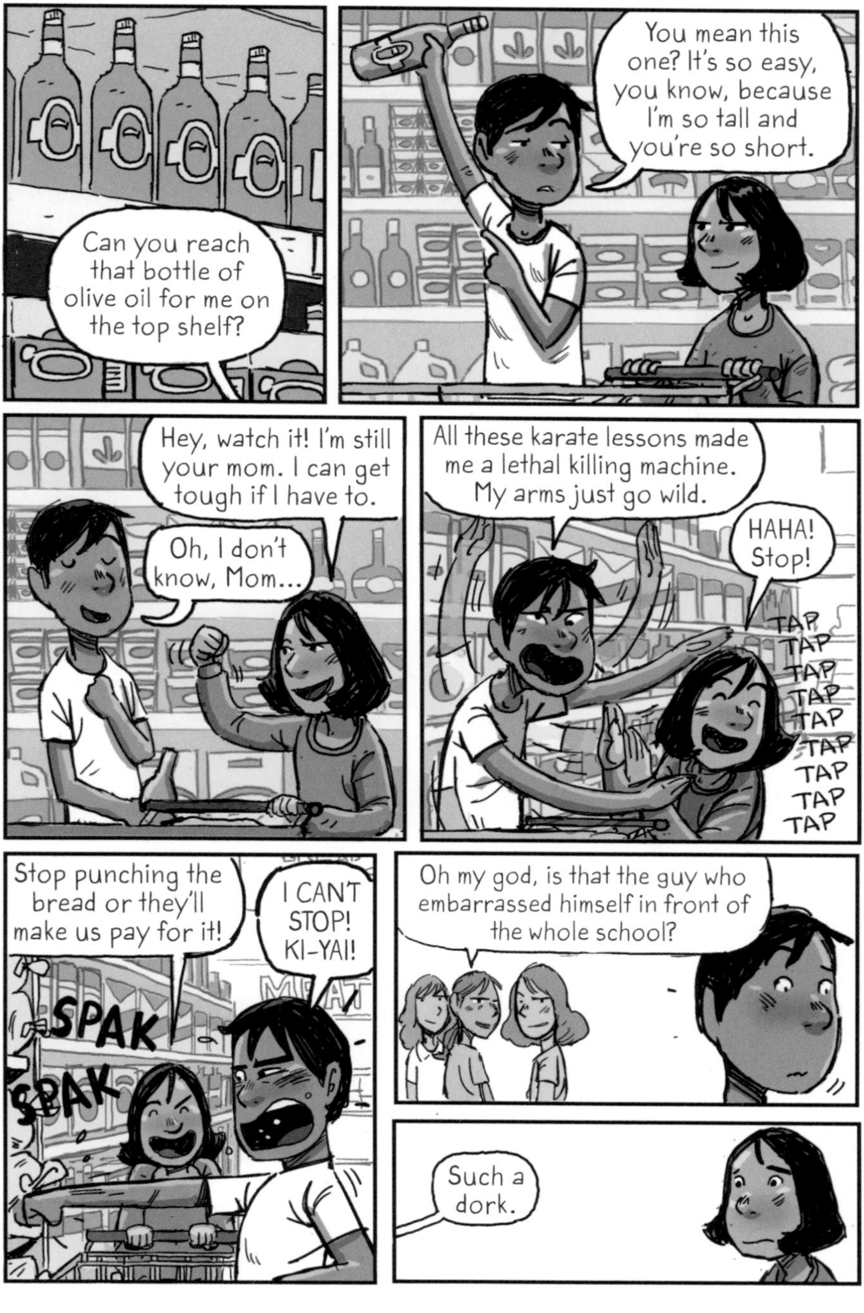

Can you reach that bottle of olive oil for me on the top shelf?
You mean this one? It's so easy, you know, because I'm so tall and you're so short.
Hey, watch it! I'm still your mom. I can get tough if I have to.
Oh, I don't know, Mom...
All these karate lessons made me a lethal killing machine. My arms just go wild.
HAHA! Stop!
TAP TAP TAP TAP TAP TAP TAP TAP TAP
Stop punching the bread or they'll make us pay for it!
I CAN'T STOP! KI-YAI!
SPAK
SPAK
Oh my god, is that the guy who embarrassed himself in front of the whole school?
Such a dork.

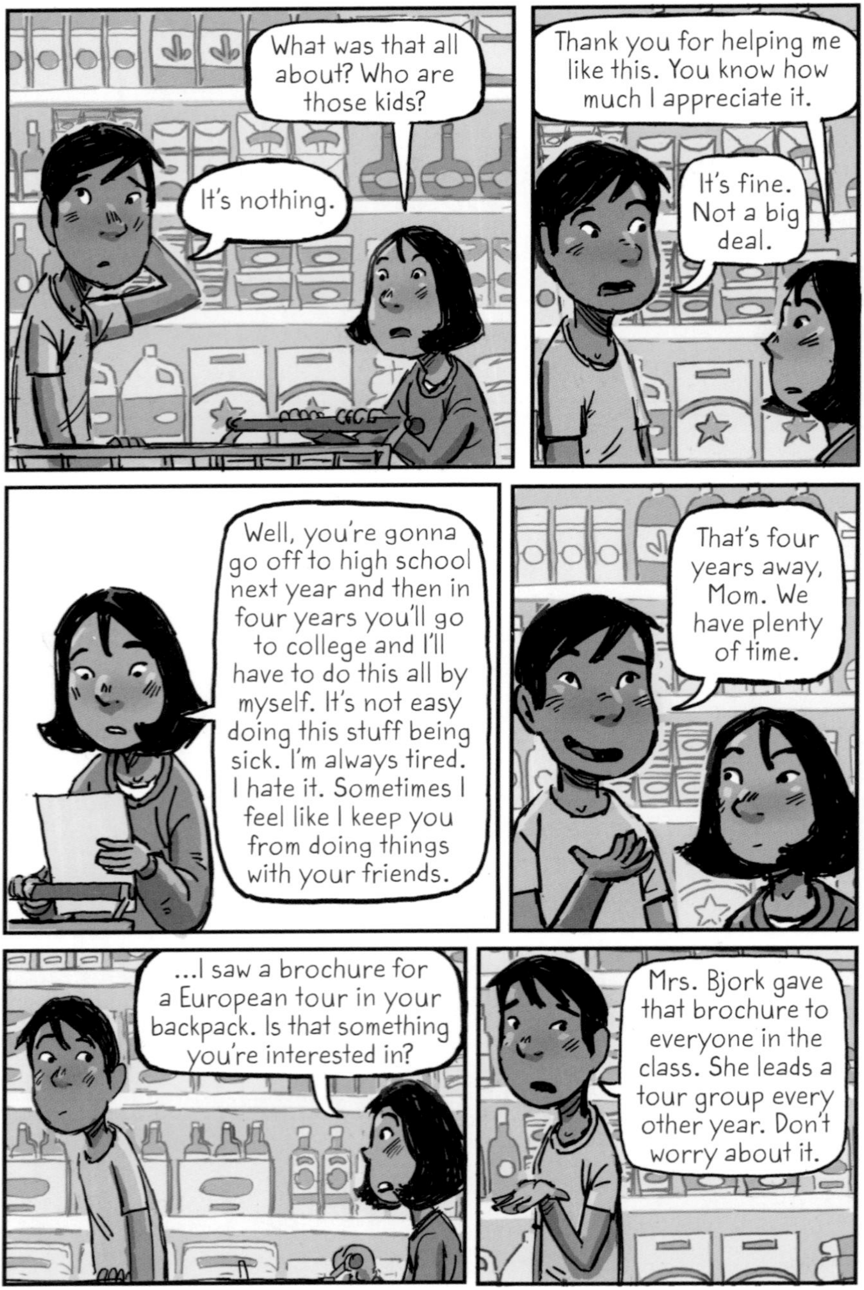
What was that all about? Who are those kids?
It's nothing.
Thank you for helping me like this. You know how much I appreciate it.
It's fine. Not a big deal.
Well, you're gonna go off to high school next year and then in four years you'll go to college and I'll have to do this all by myself. It's not easy doing this stuff being sick. I'm always tired. I hate it. Sometimes I feel like I keep you from doing things with your friends.
That's four years away, Mom. We have plenty of time.
...I saw a brochure for a European tour in your backpack. Is that something you're interested in?
Mrs. Bjork gave that brochure to everyone in the class. She leads a tour group every other year. Don't worry about it.

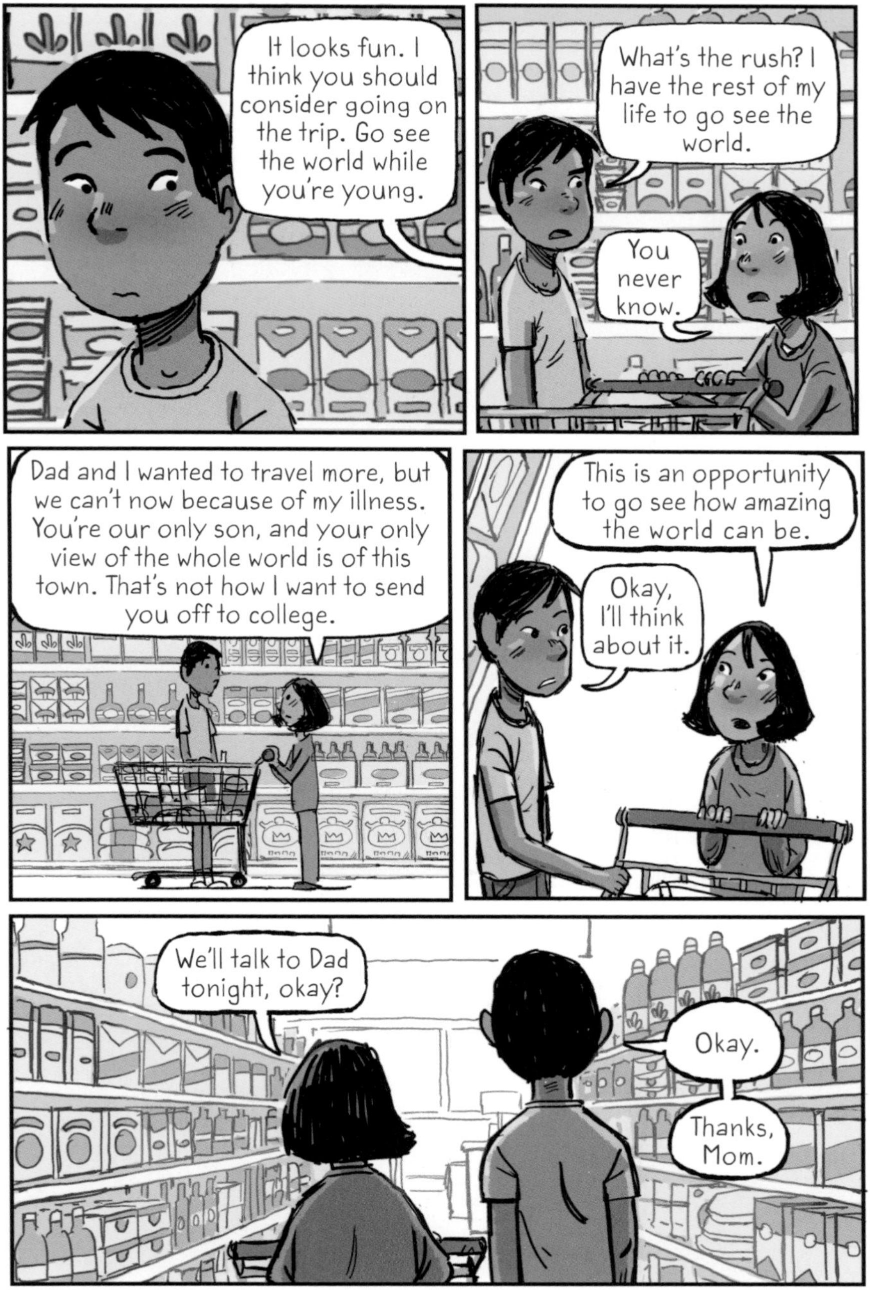
It looks fun. I think you should consider going on the trip. Go see the world while you're young.
What's the rush? I have the rest of my life to go see the world.
You never know.
Dad and I wanted to travel more, but we can't now because of my illness. You're our only son, and your only view of the whole world is of this town. That's not how I want to send you off to college.
This is an opportunity to go see how amazing the world can be.
Okay, I'll think about it.
We'll talk to Dad tonight, okay?
Okay.
Thanks, Mom.

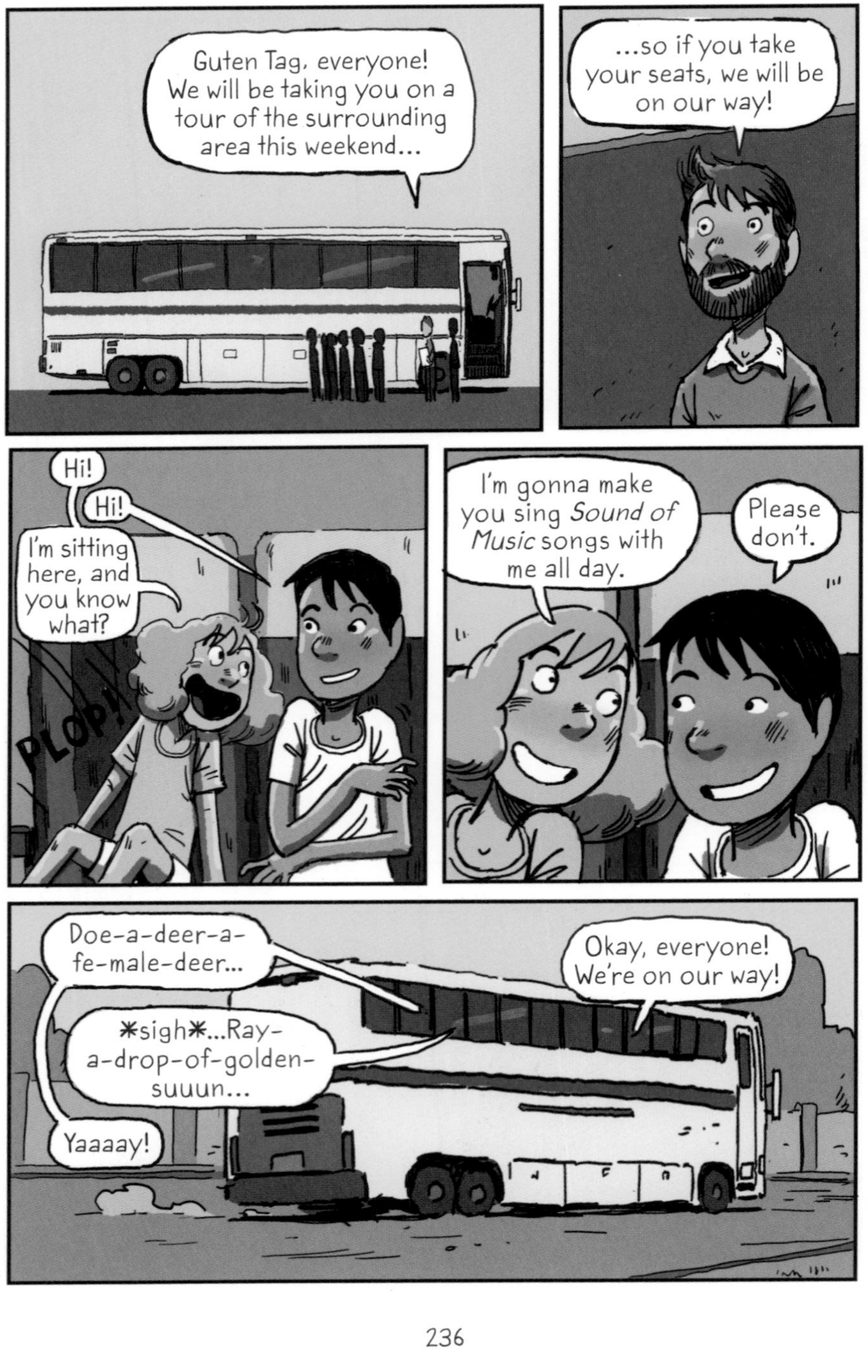
Guten Tag, everyone! We will be taking you on a tour of the surrounding area this weekend...
...so if you take your seats, we will be on our way!
Hi!
Hi!
I'm sitting here, and you know what?
PLOP!
I'm gonna make you sing *Sound of Music* songs with me all day.
Please don't.
Doe-a-deer-a-fe-male-deer...
sigh...Ray-a-drop-of-golden-suuun...
Yaaaay!
Okay, everyone! We're on our way!

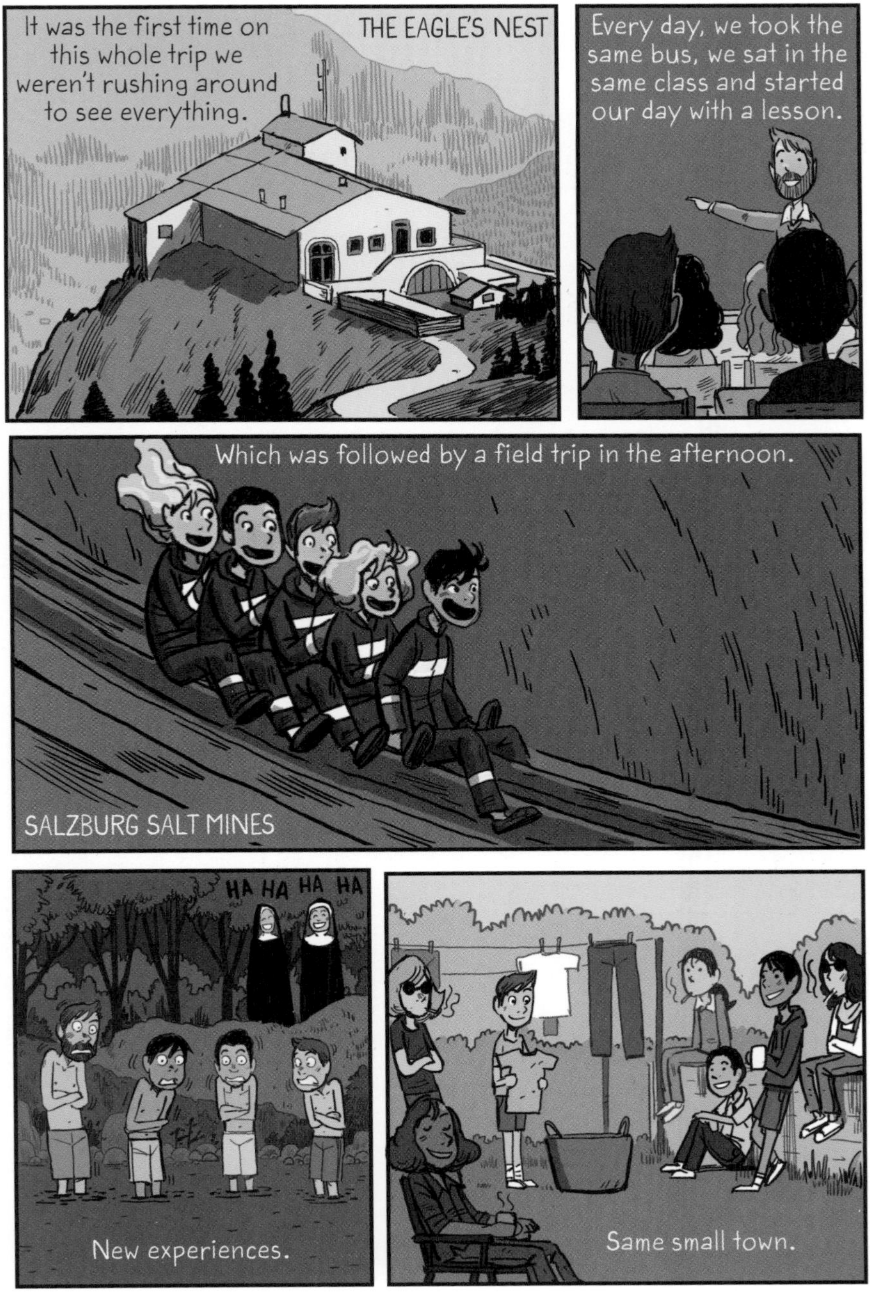
It was the first time on this whole trip we weren't rushing around to see everything.
THE EAGLE'S NEST
Every day, we took the same bus, we sat in the same class and started our day with a lesson.
Which was followed by a field trip in the afternoon.
SALZBURG SALT MINES
HA HA HA HA
New experiences.
Same small town.

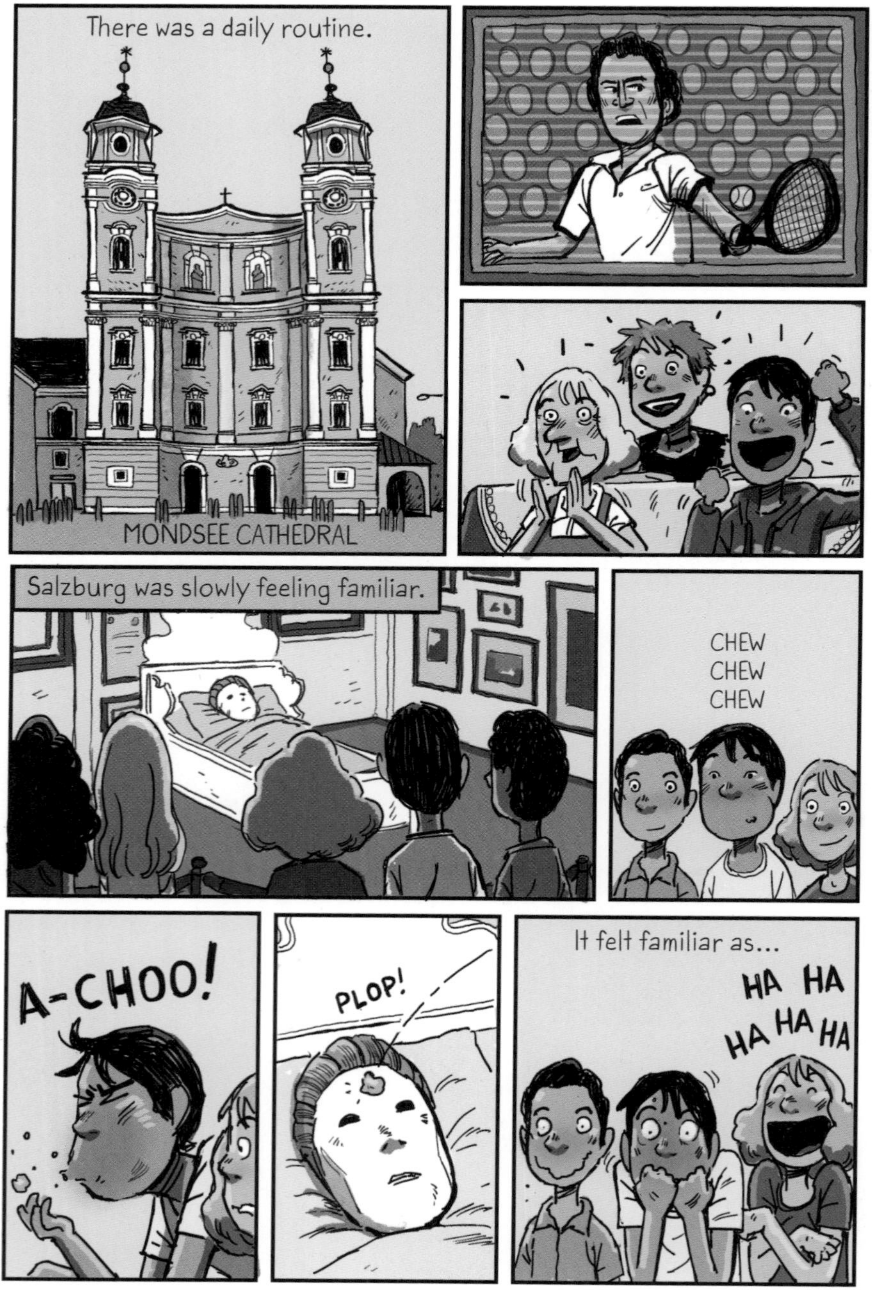
There was a daily routine.
MONDSEE CATHEDRAL
Salzburg was slowly feeling familiar.
CHEW
CHEW
CHEW
A-CHOO!
PLOP!
It felt familiar as...
HA HA
HA HA HA

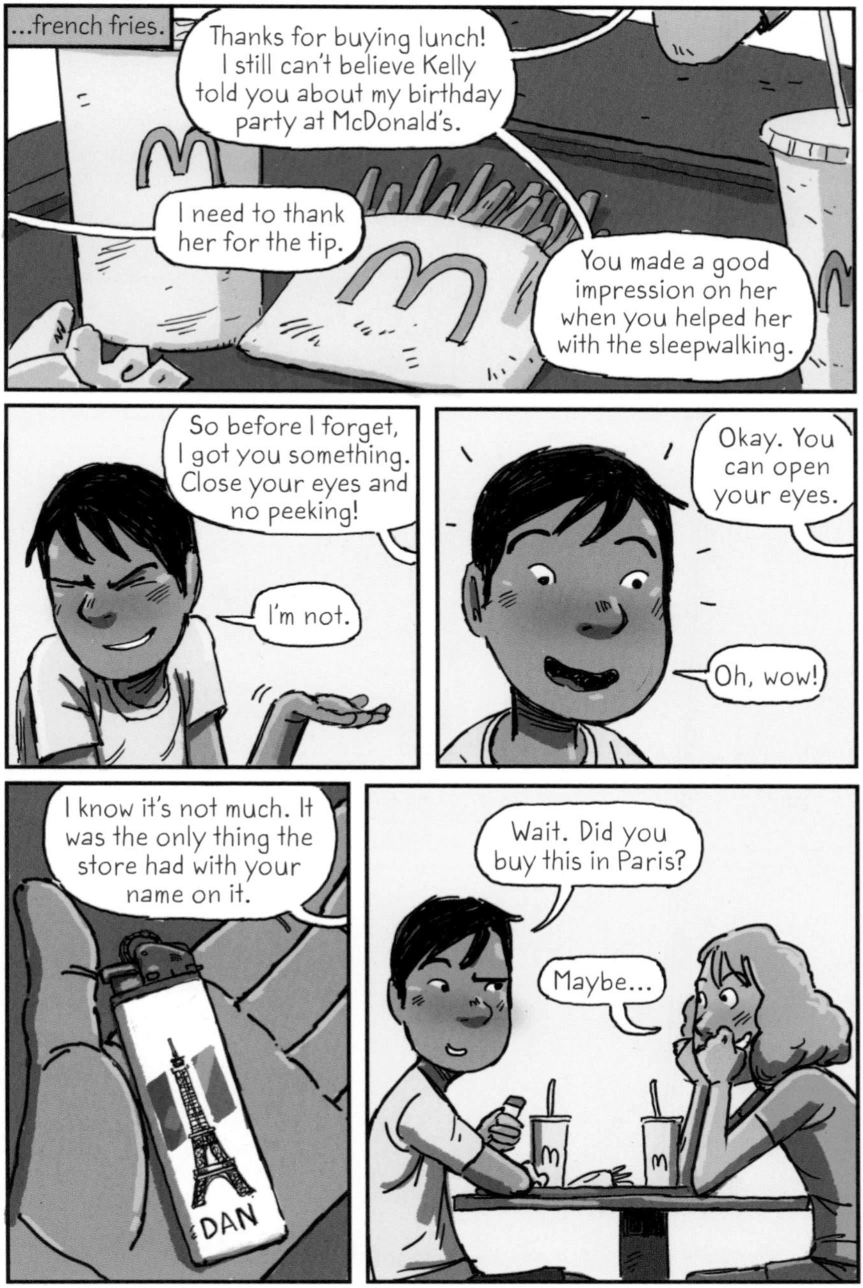

...french fries.
Thanks for buying lunch! I still can't believe Kelly told you about my birthday party at McDonald's.
I need to thank her for the tip.
You made a good impression on her when you helped her with the sleepwalking.
So before I forget, I got you something. Close your eyes and no peeking!
I'm not.
Okay. You can open your eyes.
Oh, wow!
I know it's not much. It was the only thing the store had with your name on it.
DAN
Wait. Did you buy this in Paris?
Maybe...

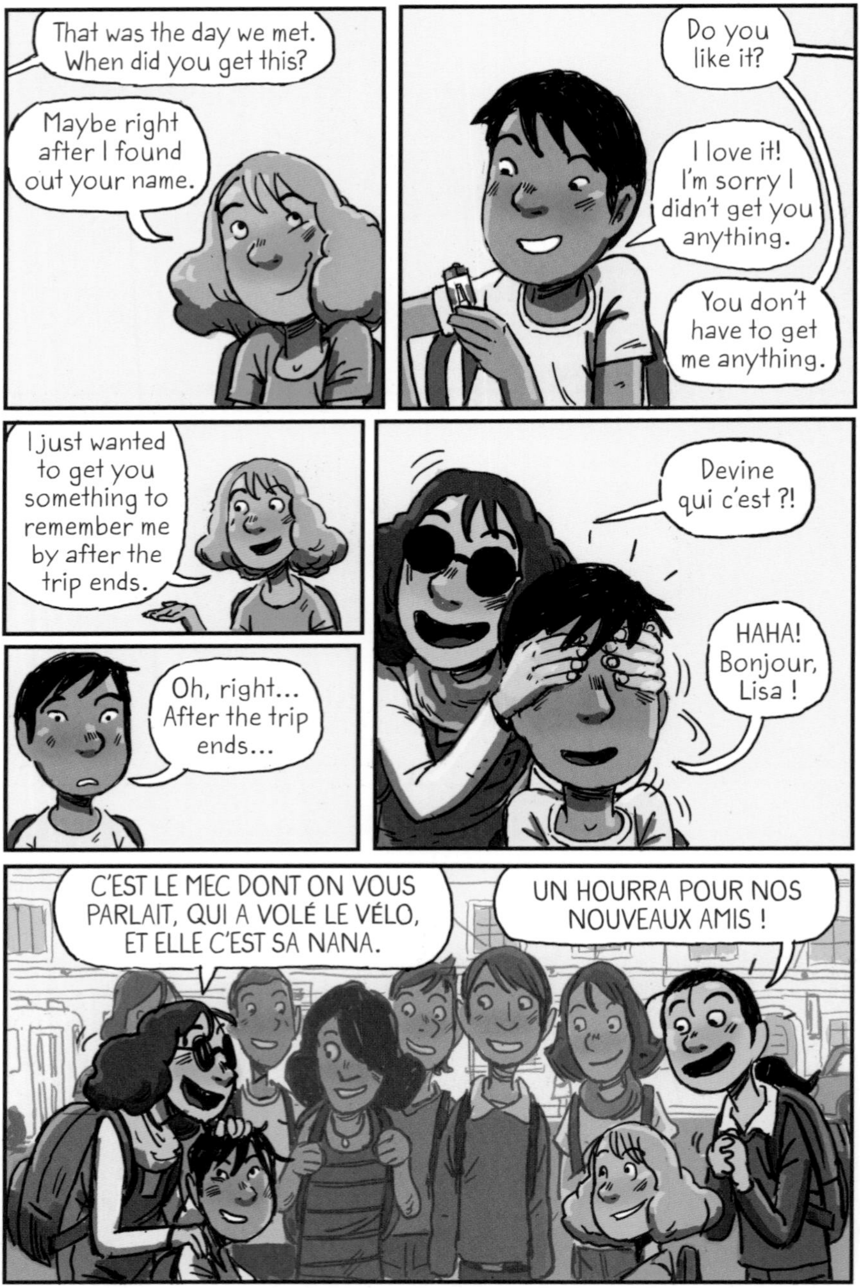
That was the day we met. When did you get this?
Maybe right after I found out your name.
Do you like it?
I love it! I'm sorry I didn't get you anything.
You don't have to get me anything.
I just wanted to get you something to remember me by after the trip ends.
Oh, right... After the trip ends...
Devine qui c'est ?!
HAHA! Bonjour, Lisa !
C'EST LE MEC DONT ON VOUS PARLAIT, QUI A VOLÉ LE VÉLO, ET ELLE C'EST SA NANA.
UN HOURRA POUR NOS NOUVEAUX AMIS !

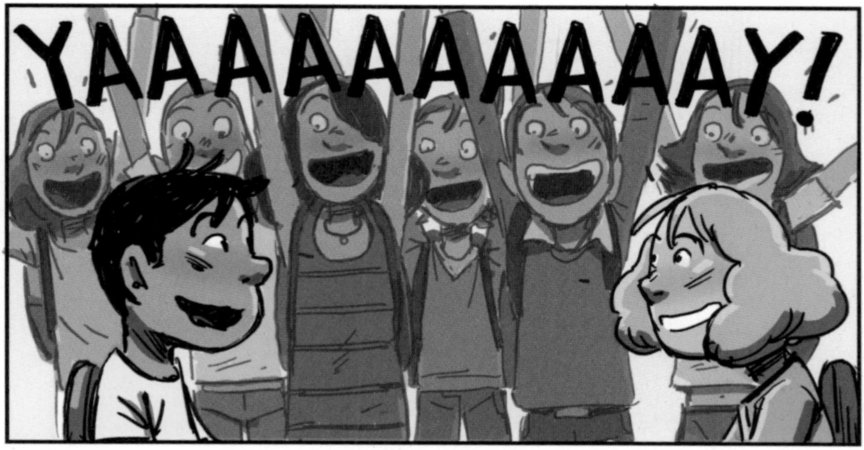

YAAAAAAAAAAY!

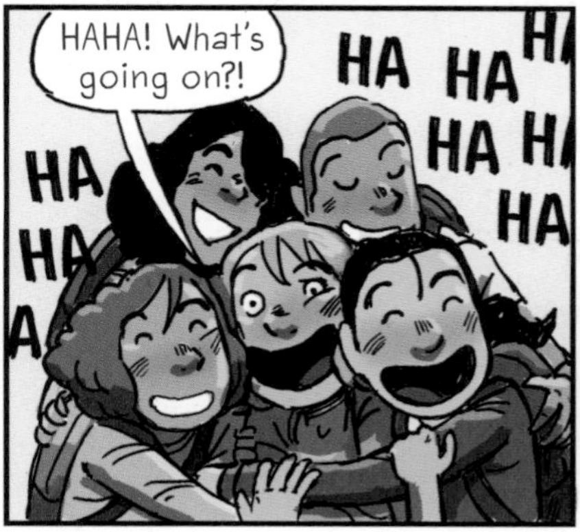

HAHA! What's going on?!
HA HA
HA
HA
HA
HA
HA

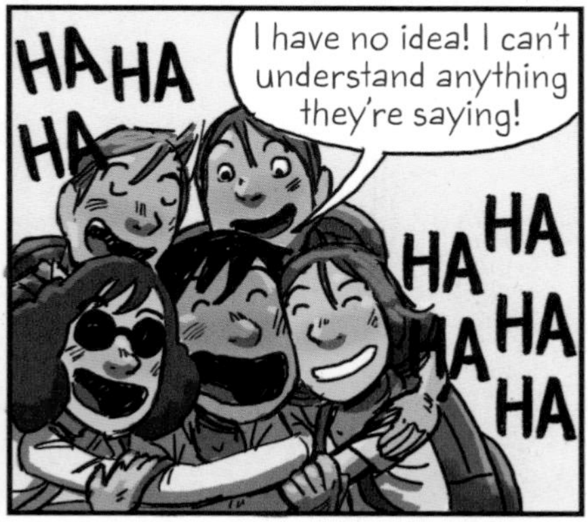

HAHA
I have no idea! I can't understand anything they're saying!
HA
HA
HA
HA
HA

*The French don't usually hug as a greeting, so I don't know why this happened.

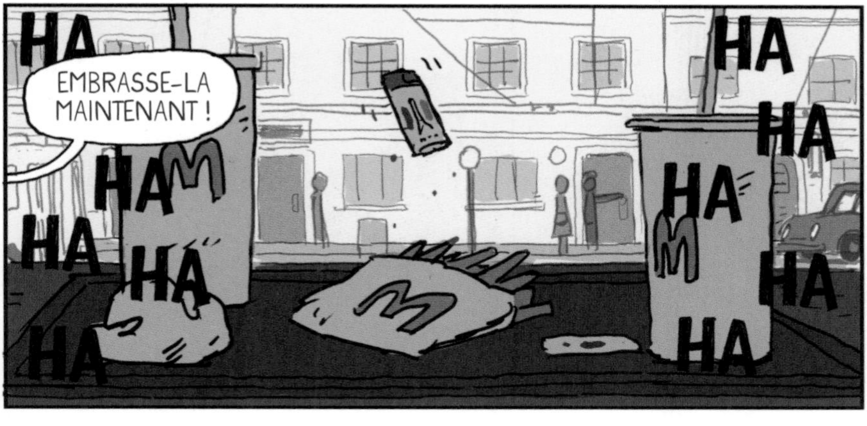

HA
EMBRASSE-LA MAINTENANT !
HA
HA
HA
HA
HA
HA
HA
HA
HA

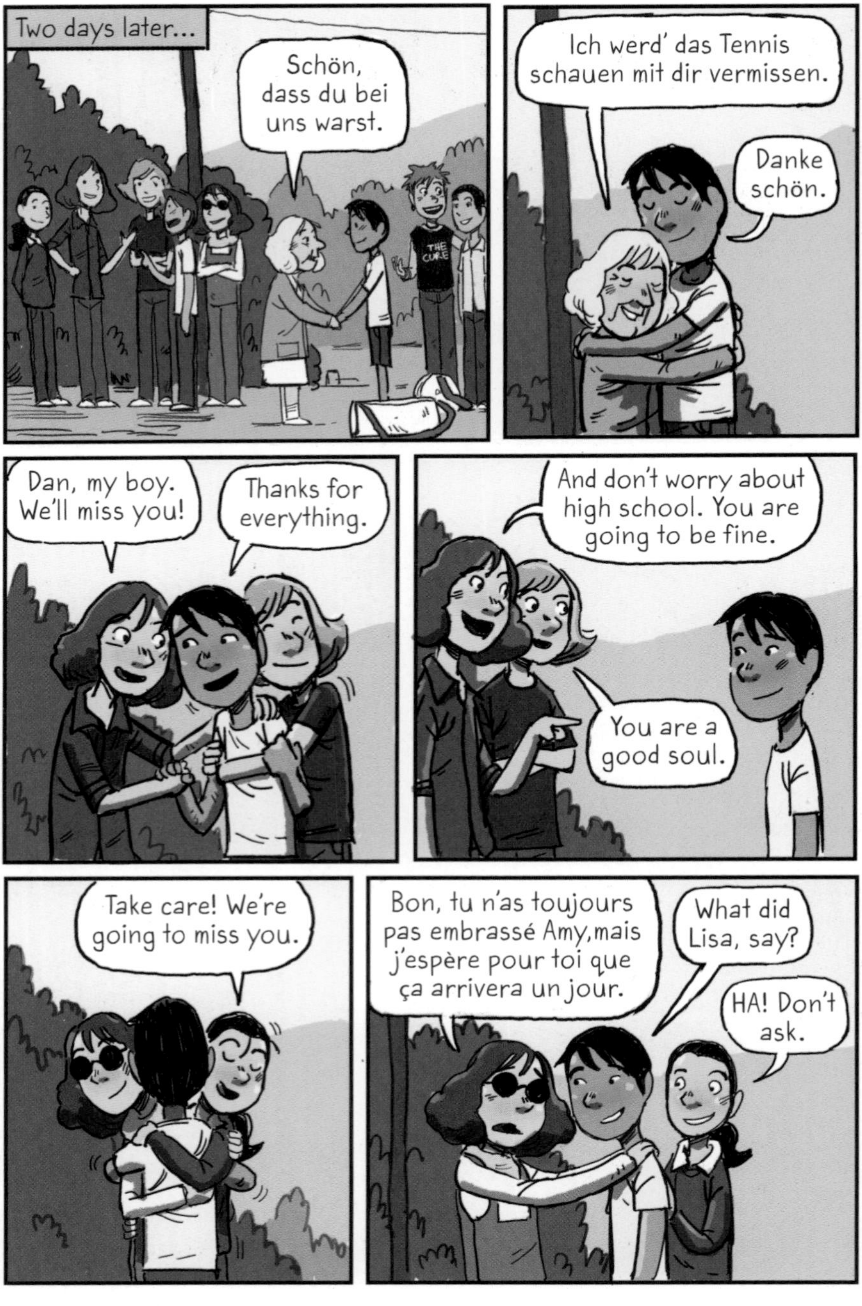
Two days later...
Schön, dass du bei uns warst.
Ich werd' das Tennis schauen mit dir vermissen.
Danke schön.
Dan, my boy. We'll miss you!
Thanks for everything.
And don't worry about high school. You are going to be fine.
You are a good soul.
Take care! We're going to miss you.
Bon, tu n'as toujours pas embrassé Amy,mais j'espère pour toi que ça arrivera un jour.
What did Lisa, say?
HA! Don't ask.

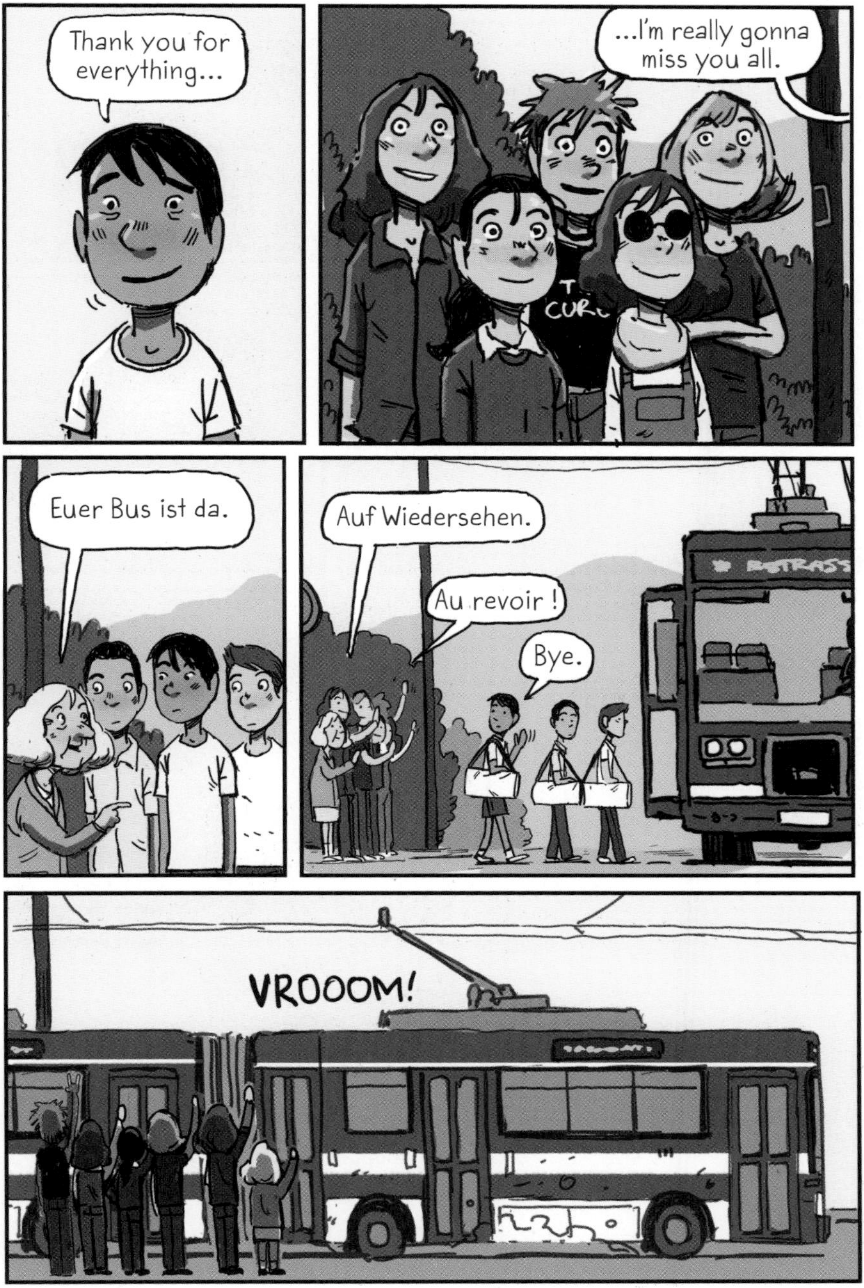
Thank you for everything...
...I'm really gonna miss you all.
Euer Bus ist da.
Auf Wiedersehen.
Au revoir !
Bye.
VROOOM!

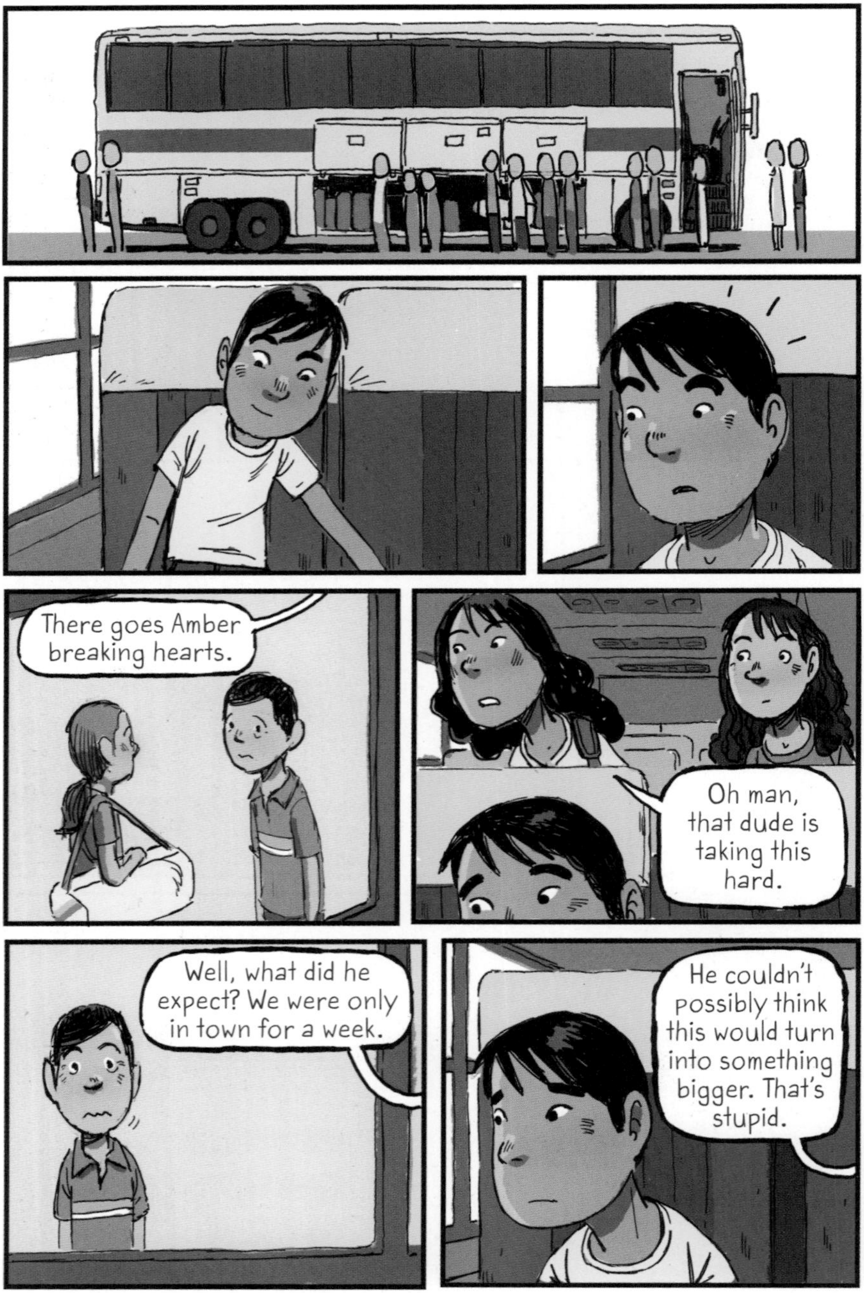
There goes Amber breaking hearts.
Oh man, that dude is taking this hard.
Well, what did he expect? We were only in town for a week.
He couldn't possibly think this would turn into something bigger. That's stupid.

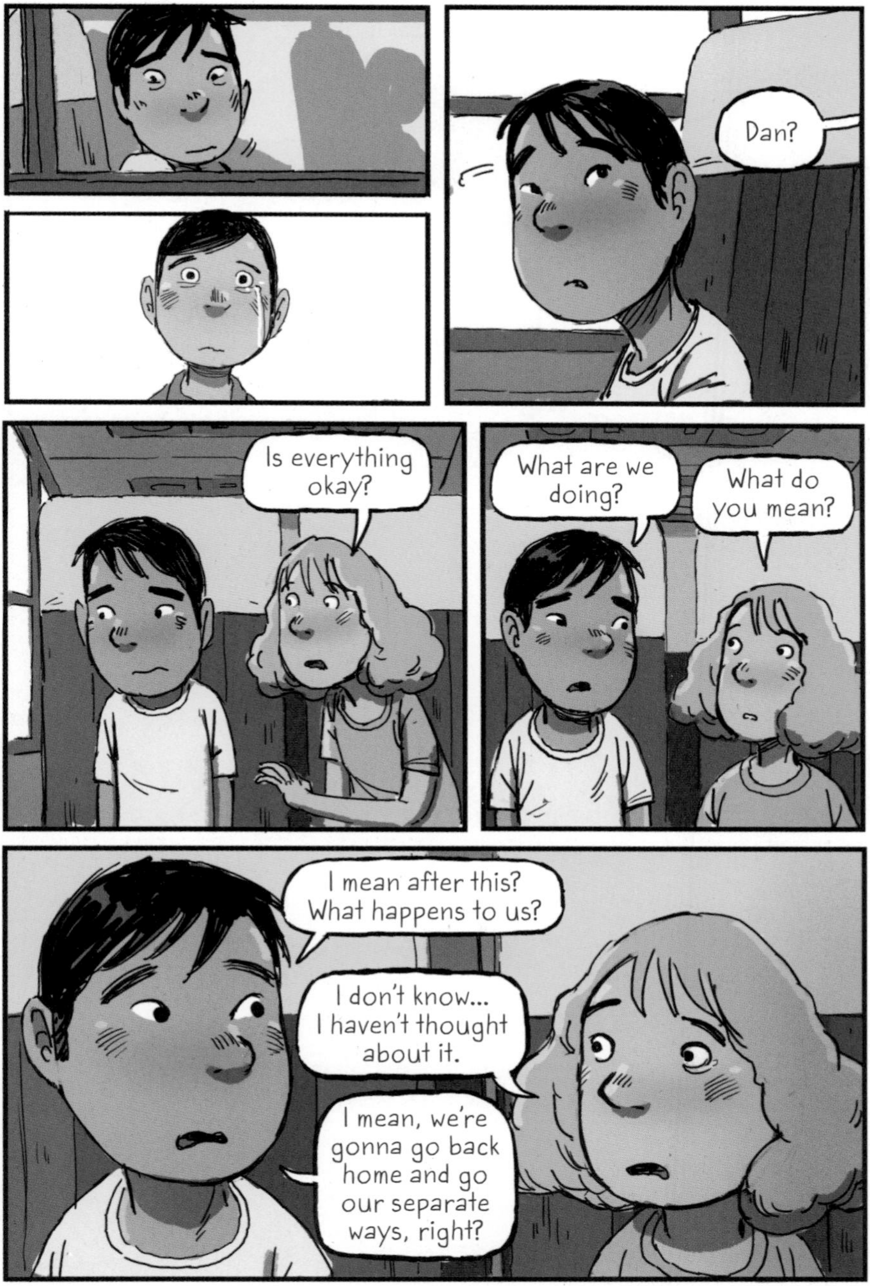
Dan?
Is everything okay?
What are we doing?
What do you mean?
I mean after this? What happens to us?
I don't know... I haven't thought about it.
I mean, we're gonna go back home and go our separate ways, right?

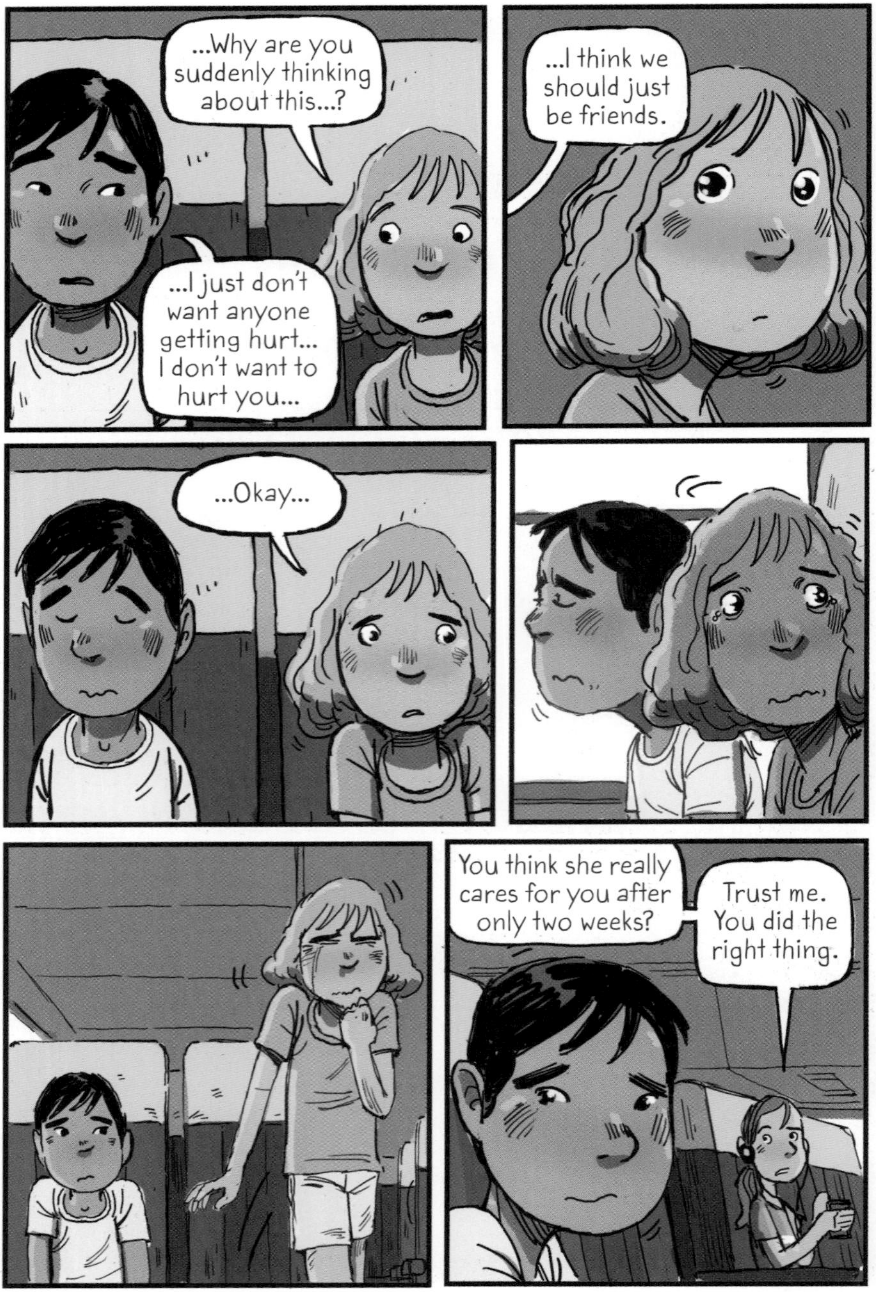
...Why are you suddenly thinking about this...?
...I just don't want anyone getting hurt... I don't want to hurt you...
...I think we should just be friends.
...Okay...
You think she really cares for you after only two weeks?
Trust me. You did the right thing.

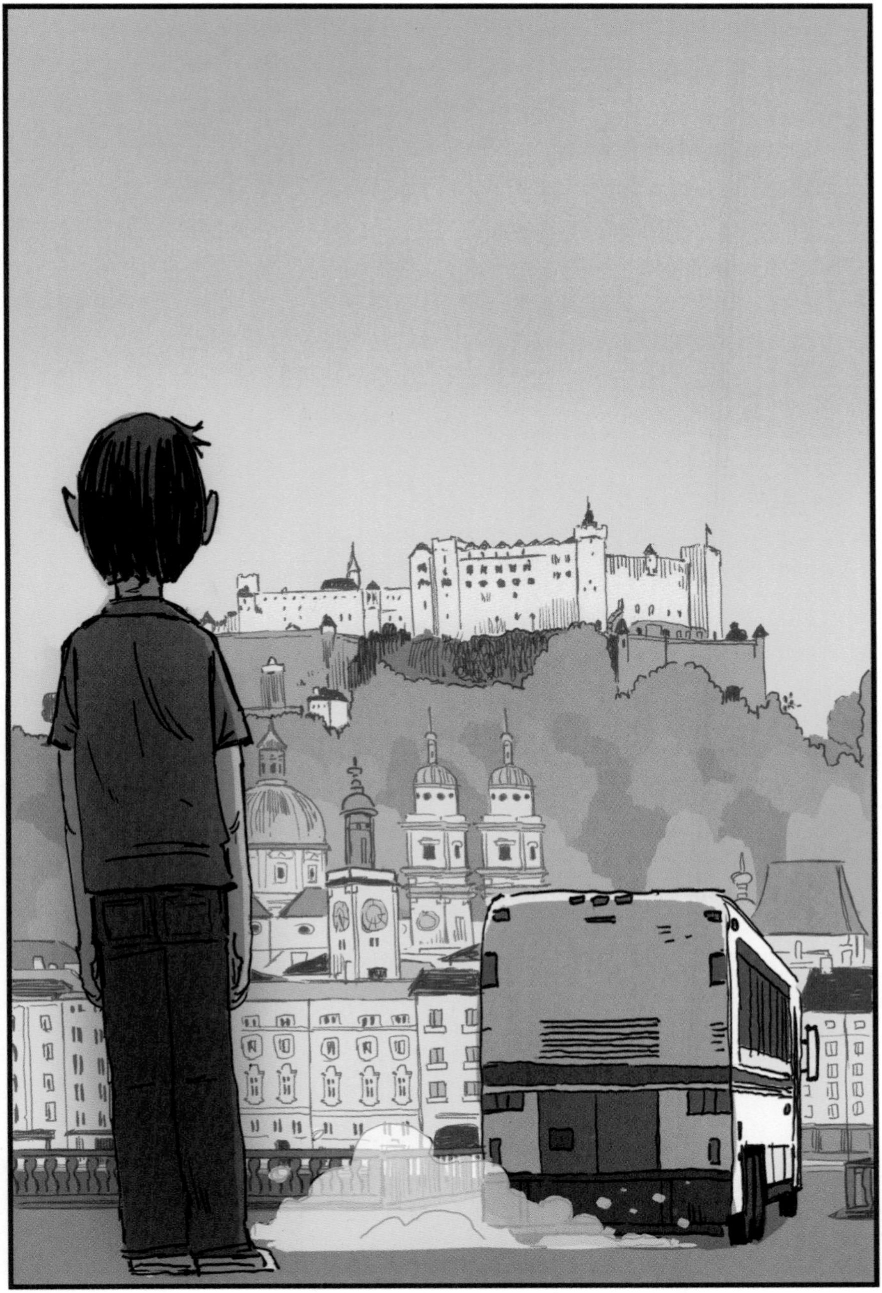

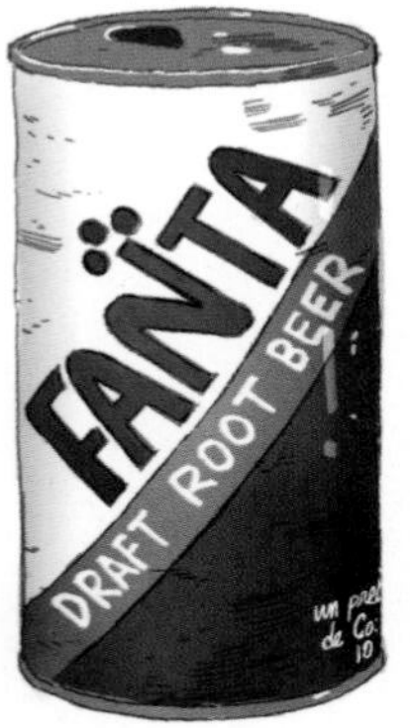
FANTA
DRAFT ROOT BEER

VIENNA

(4 DAYS LEFT IN THE TRIP)

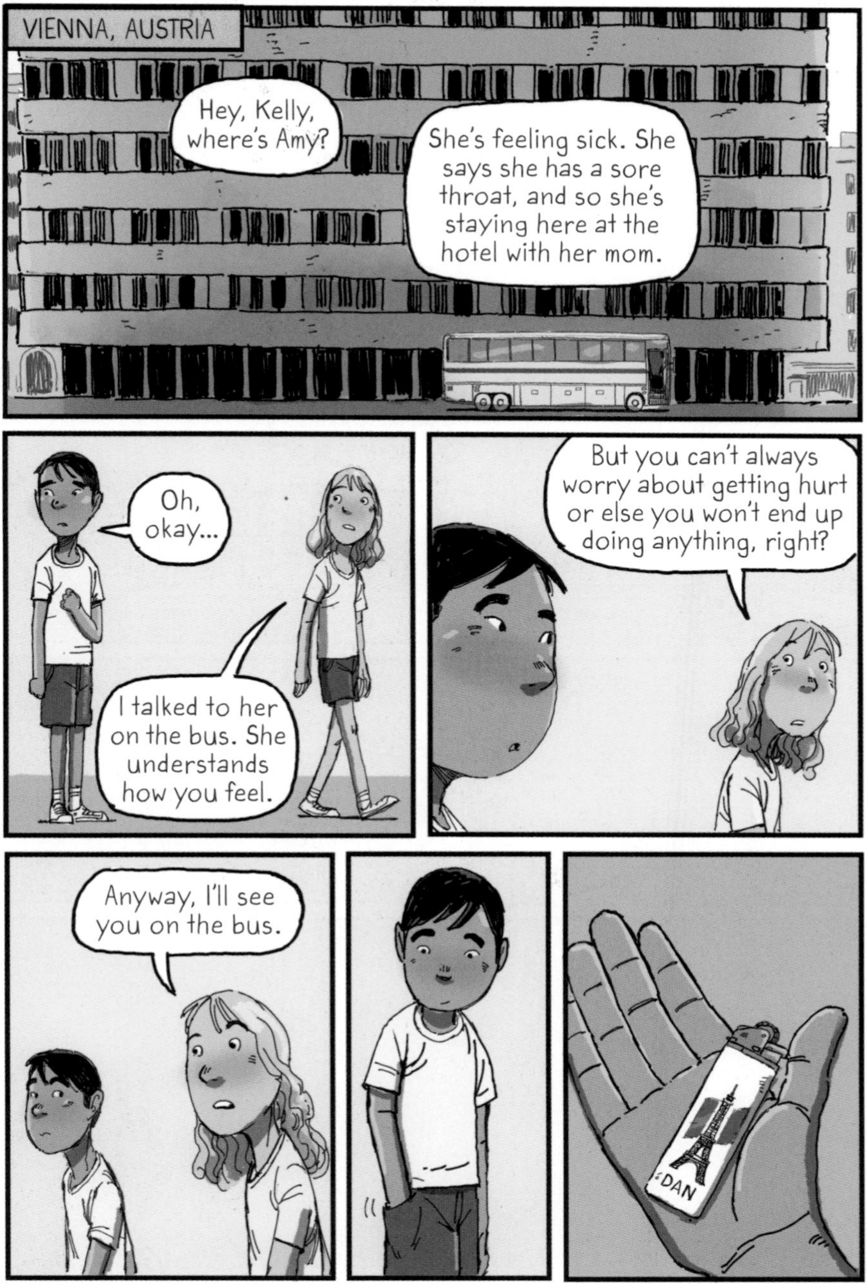
VIENNA, AUSTRIA
Hey, Kelly, where's Amy?
She's feeling sick. She says she has a sore throat, and so she's staying here at the hotel with her mom.
Oh, okay...
I talked to her on the bus. She understands how you feel.
But you can't always worry about getting hurt or else you won't end up doing anything, right?
Anyway, I'll see you on the bus.
DAN

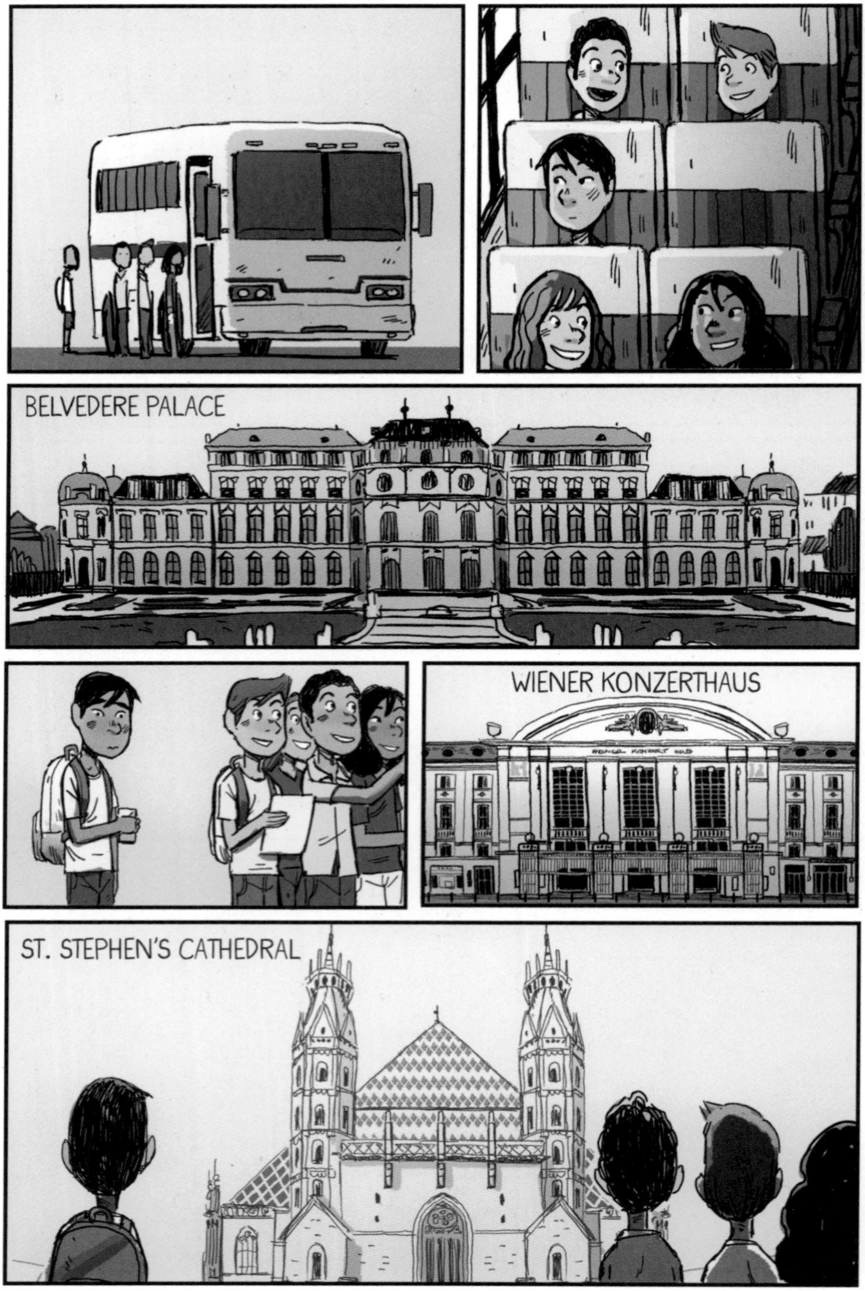
BELVEDERE PALACE
WIENER KONZERTHAUS
ST. STEPHEN'S CATHEDRAL

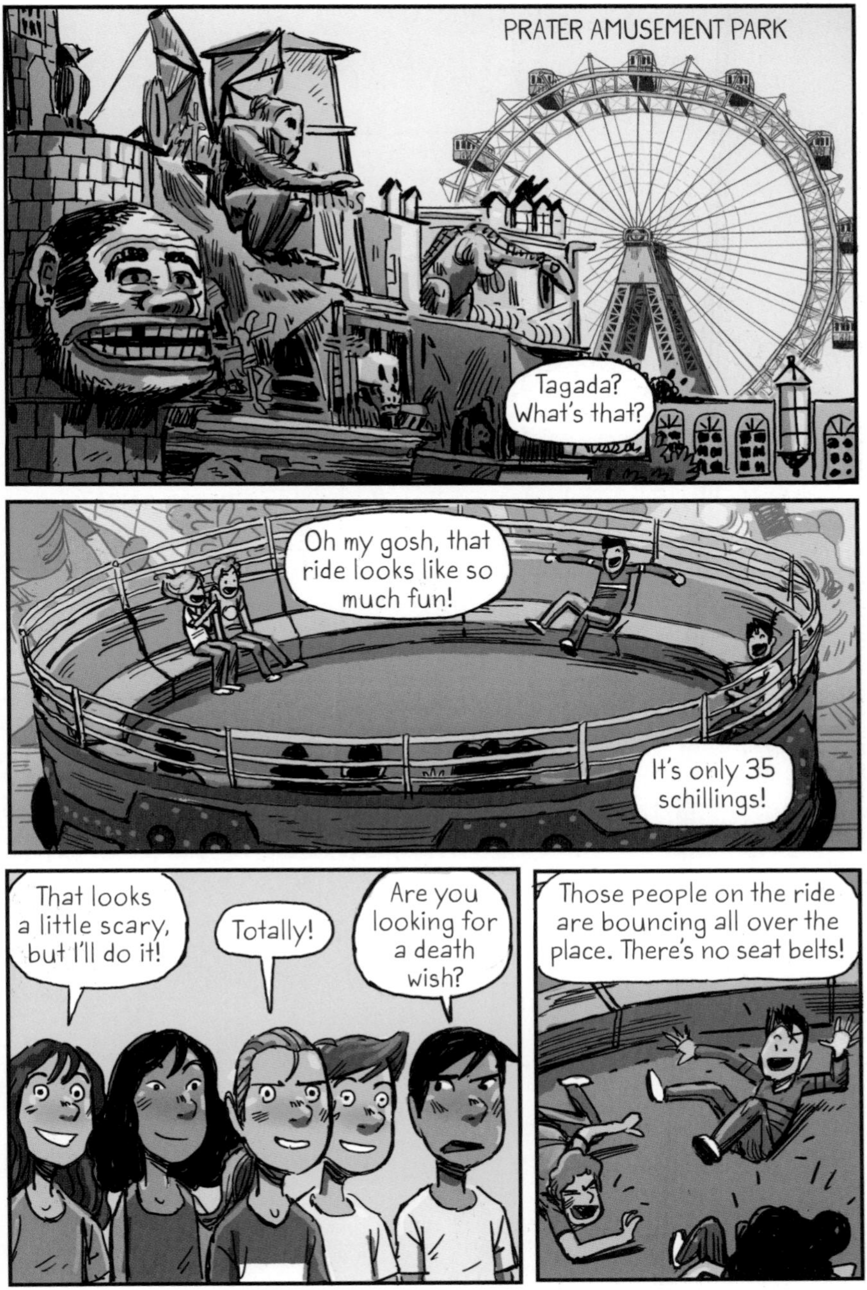
PRATER AMUSEMENT PARK
Tagada? What's that?
Oh my gosh, that ride looks like so much fun!
It's only 35 schillings!
That looks a little scary, but I'll do it!
Totally!
Are you looking for a death wish?
Those people on the ride are bouncing all over the place. There's no seat belts!

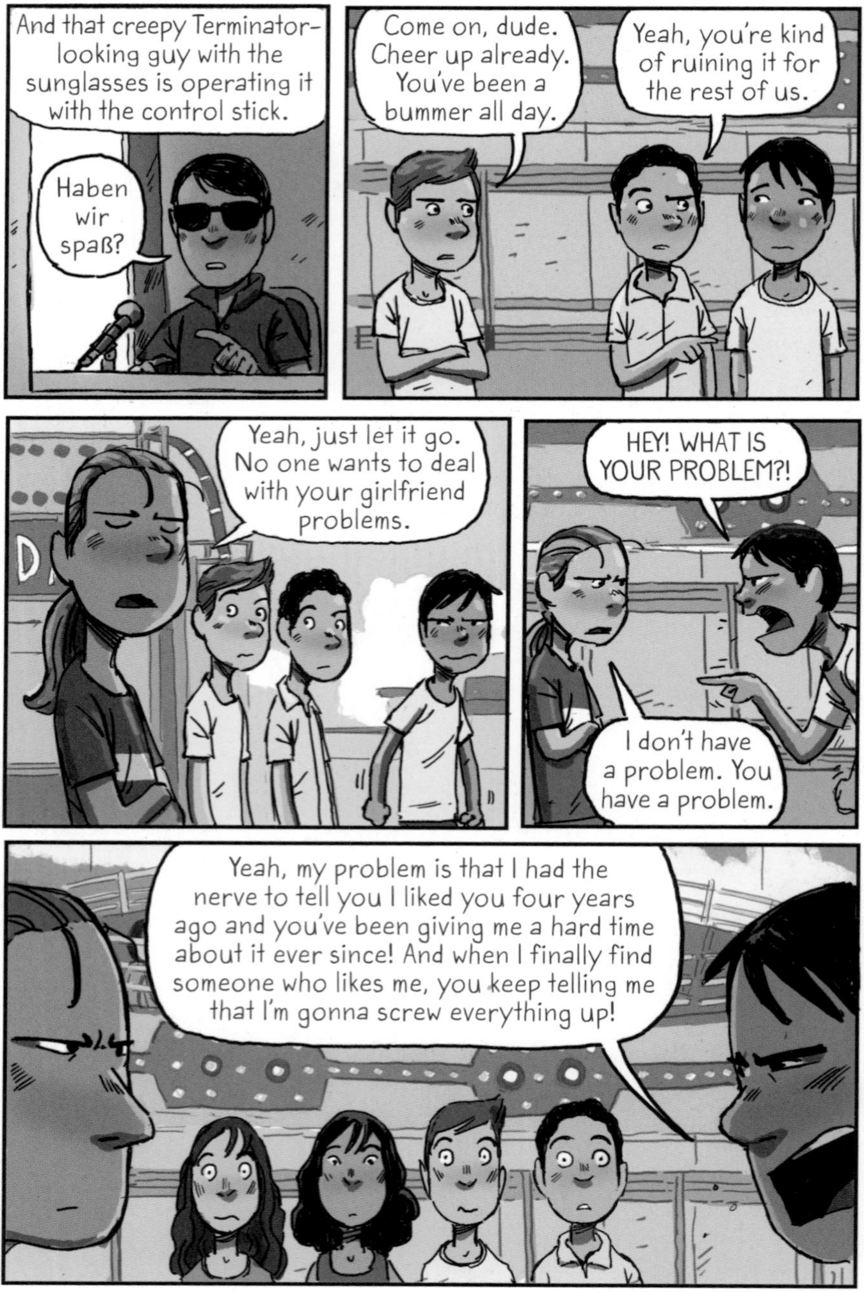

And that creepy Terminator-looking guy with the sunglasses is operating it with the control stick.
Haben wir spaß?
Come on, dude. Cheer up already. You've been a bummer all day.
Yeah, you're kind of ruining it for the rest of us.
Yeah, just let it go. No one wants to deal with your girlfriend problems.
HEY! WHAT IS YOUR PROBLEM?!
I don't have a problem. You have a problem.
Yeah, my problem is that I had the nerve to tell you I liked you four years ago and you've been giving me a hard time about it ever since! And when I finally find someone who likes me, you keep telling me that I'm gonna screw everything up!

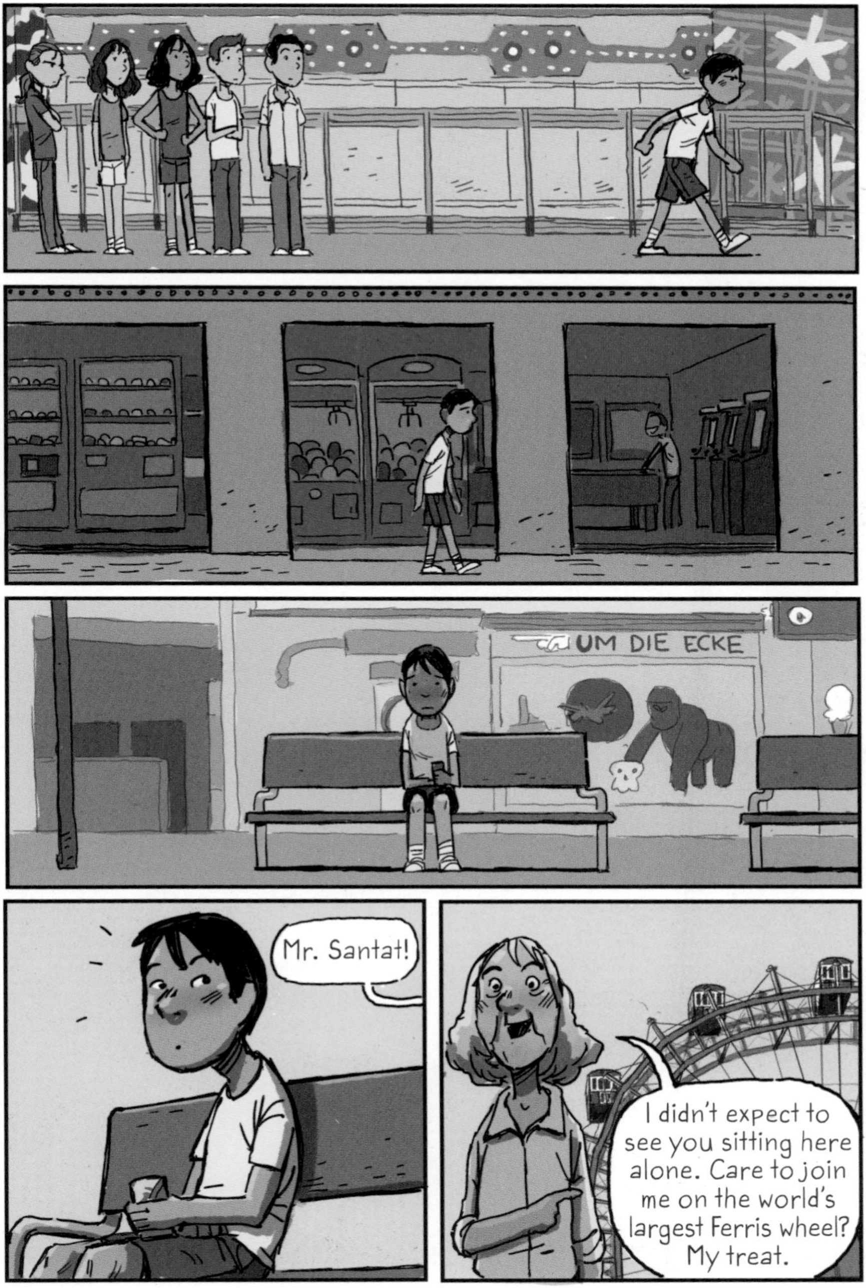
UM DIE ECKE
Mr. Santat!
I didn't expect to see you sitting here alone. Care to join me on the world's largest Ferris wheel? My treat.

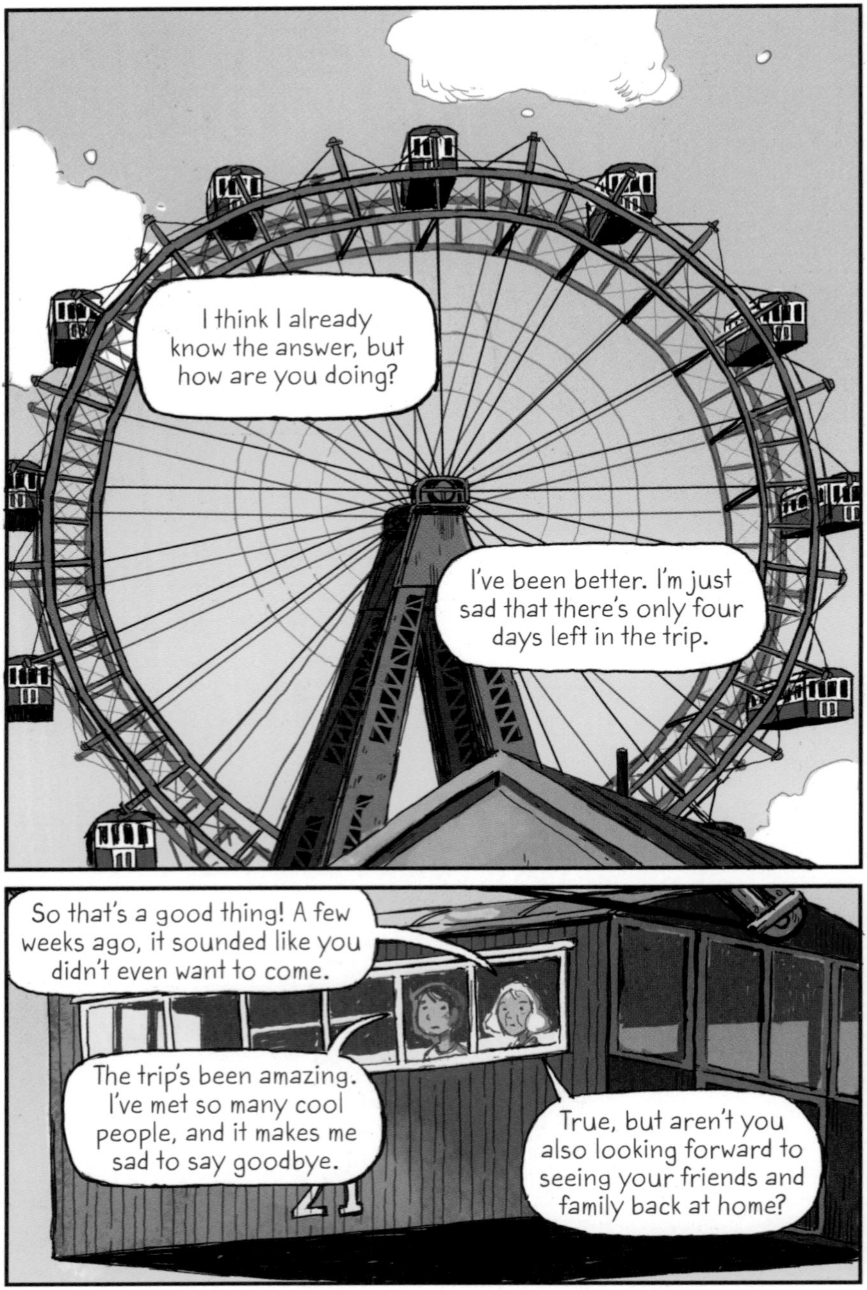
I think I already know the answer, but how are you doing?
I've been better. I'm just sad that there's only four days left in the trip.
So that's a good thing! A few weeks ago, it sounded like you didn't even want to come.
The trip's been amazing. I've met so many cool people, and it makes me sad to say goodbye.
True, but aren't you also looking forward to seeing your friends and family back at home?
21

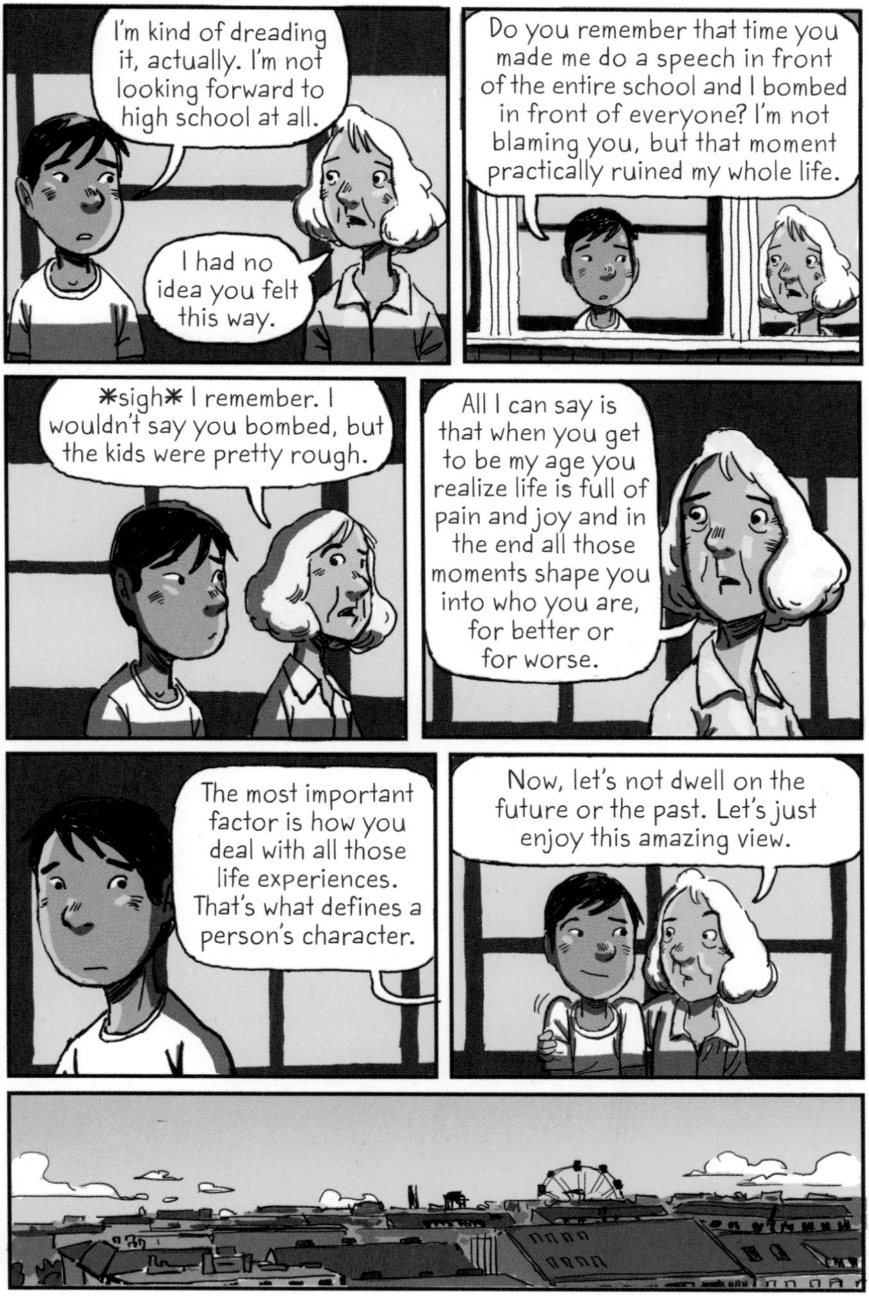
I'm kind of dreading it, actually. I'm not looking forward to high school at all.
I had no idea you felt this way.
Do you remember that time you made me do a speech in front of the entire school and I bombed in front of everyone? I'm not blaming you, but that moment practically ruined my whole life.
sigh I remember. I wouldn't say you bombed, but the kids were pretty rough.
All I can say is that when you get to be my age you realize life is full of pain and joy and in the end all those moments shape you into who you are, for better or for worse.
The most important factor is how you deal with all those life experiences. That's what defines a person's character.
Now, let's not dwell on the future or the past. Let's just enjoy this amazing view.

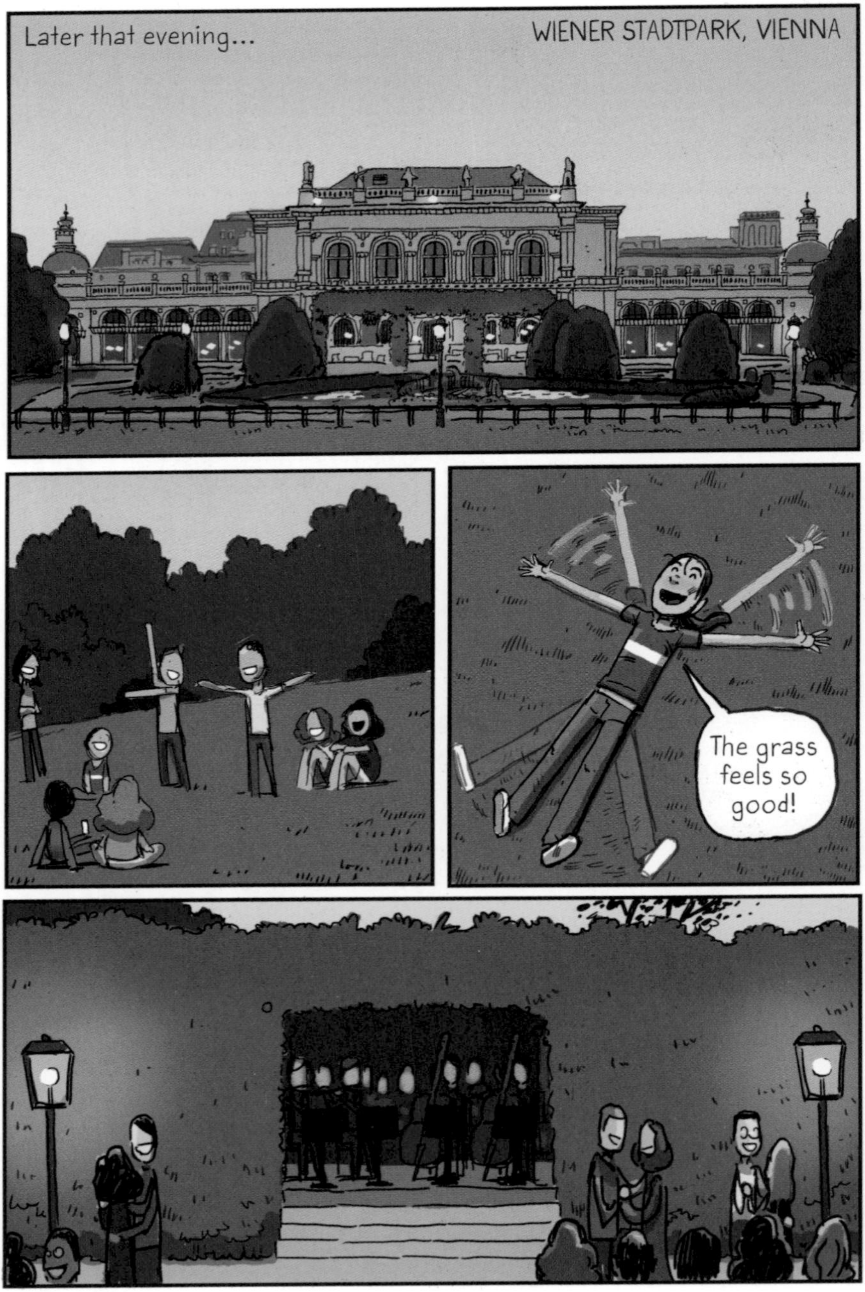
Later that evening...
WIENER STADTPARK, VIENNA
The grass feels so good!

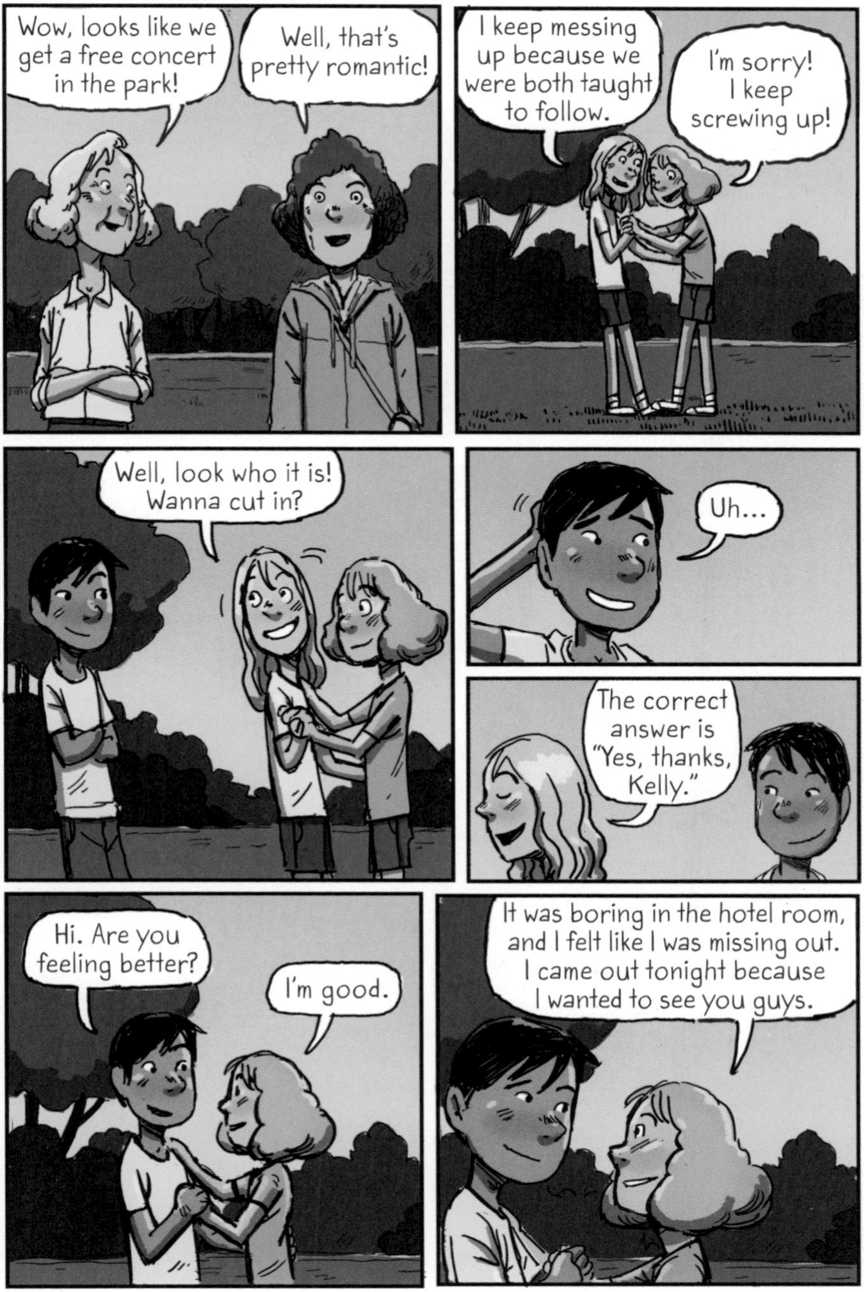
Wow, looks like we get a free concert in the park!
Well, that's pretty romantic!
I keep messing up because we were both taught to follow.
I'm sorry! I keep screwing up!
Well, look who it is! Wanna cut in?
Uh...
The correct answer is "Yes, thanks, Kelly."
Hi. Are you feeling better?
I'm good.
It was boring in the hotel room, and I felt like I was missing out. I came out tonight because I wanted to see you guys.

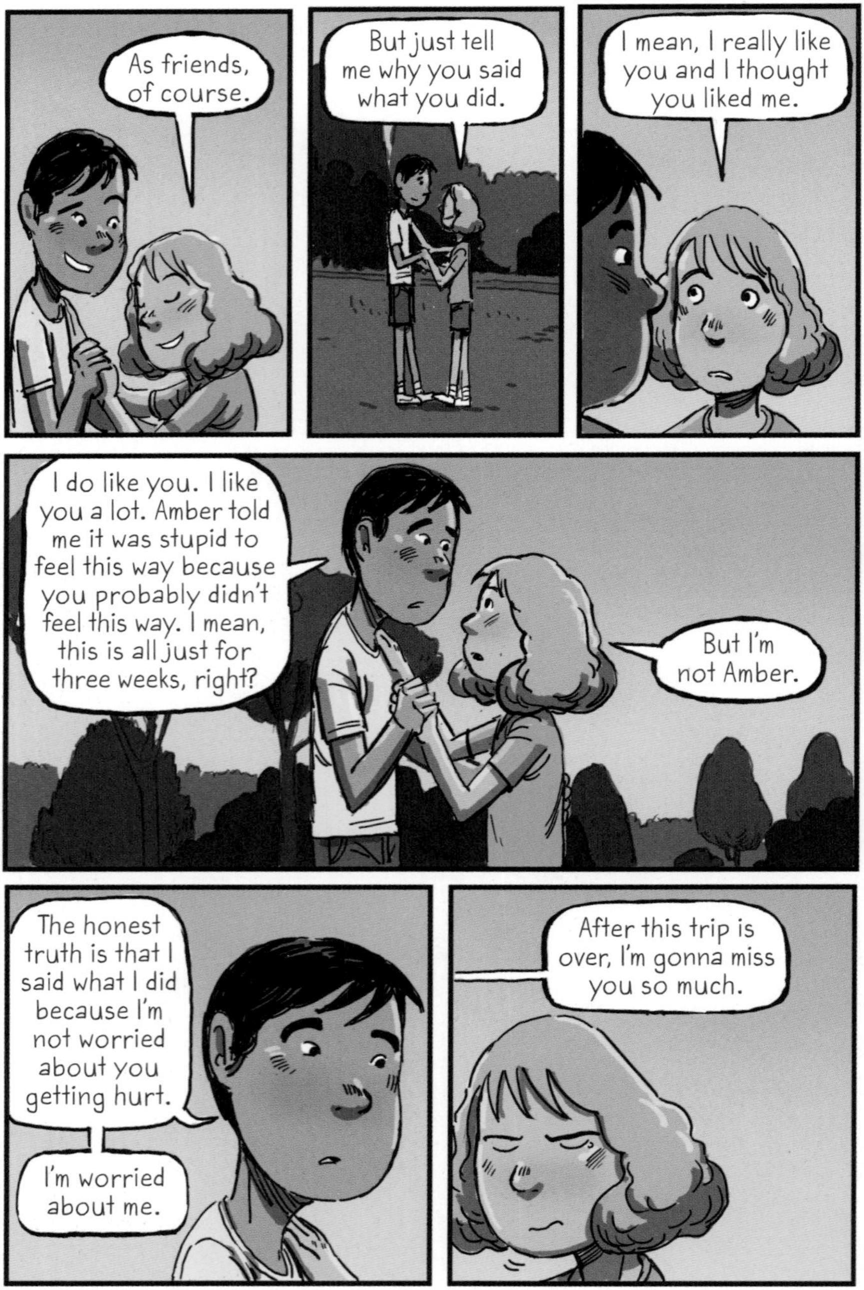
As friends, of course.
But just tell me why you said what you did.
I mean, I really like you and I thought you liked me.
I do like you. I like you a lot. Amber told me it was stupid to feel this way because you probably didn't feel this way. I mean, this is all just for three weeks, right?
But I'm not Amber.
The honest truth is that I said what I did because I'm not worried about you getting hurt.
I'm worried about me.
After this trip is over, I'm gonna miss you so much.

Amy...

Leave me alone.

sigh

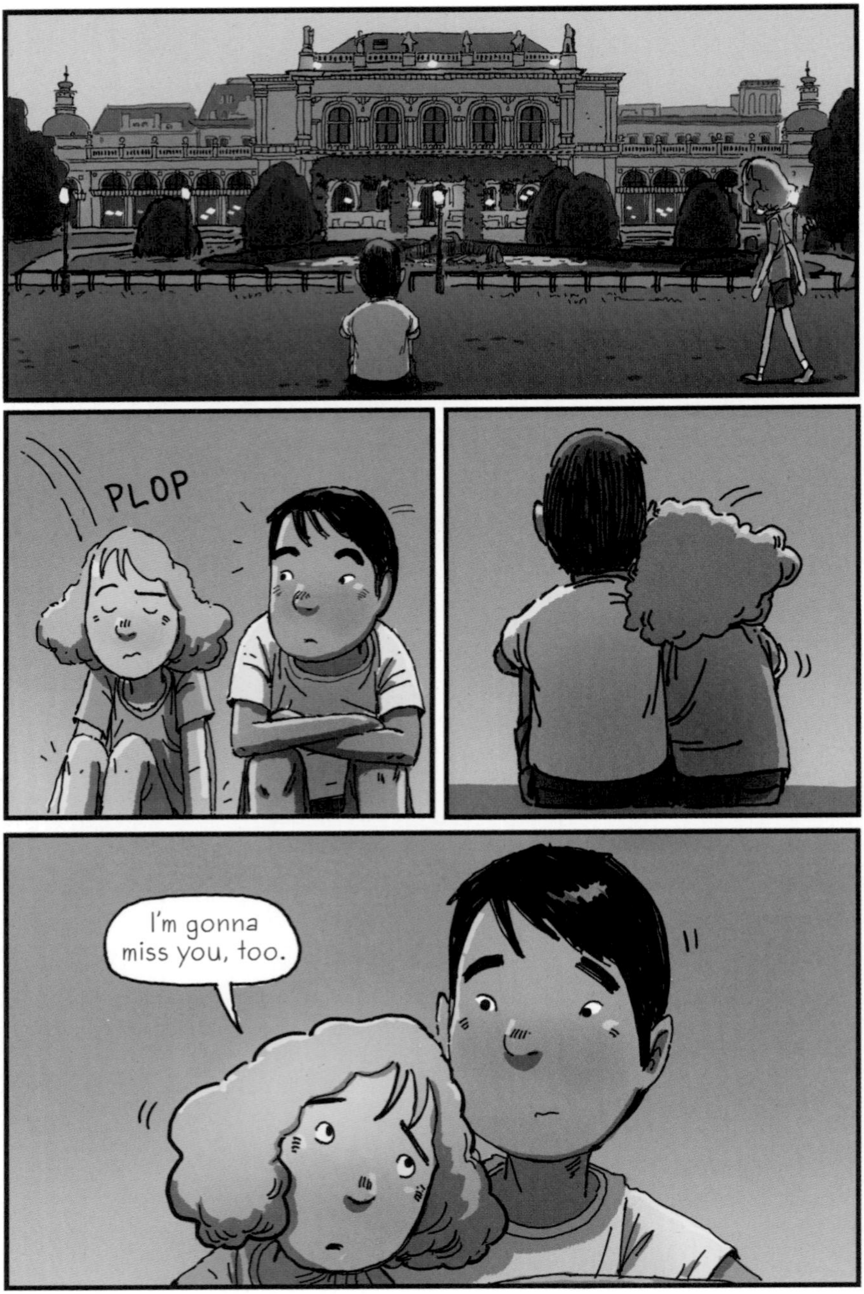
PLOP
I'm gonna miss you, too.

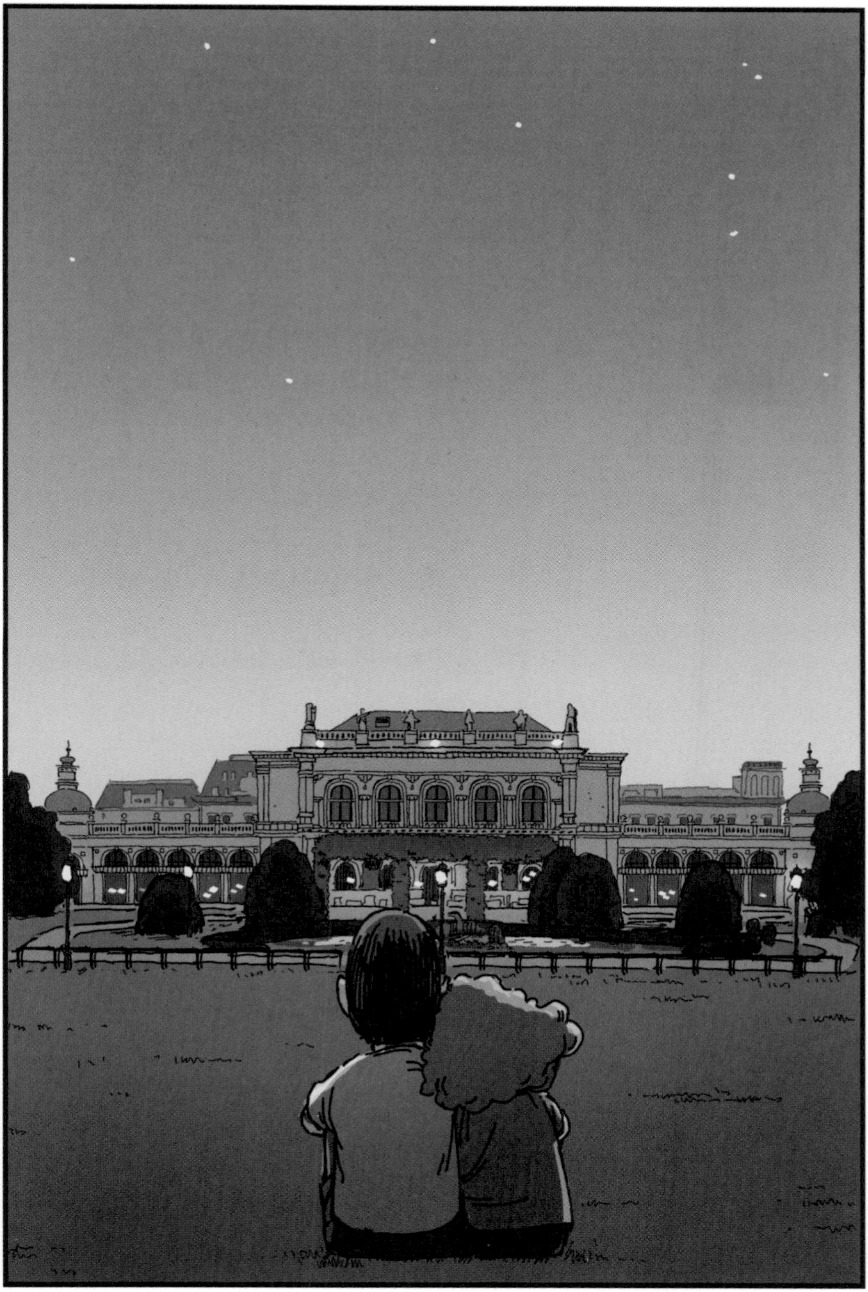

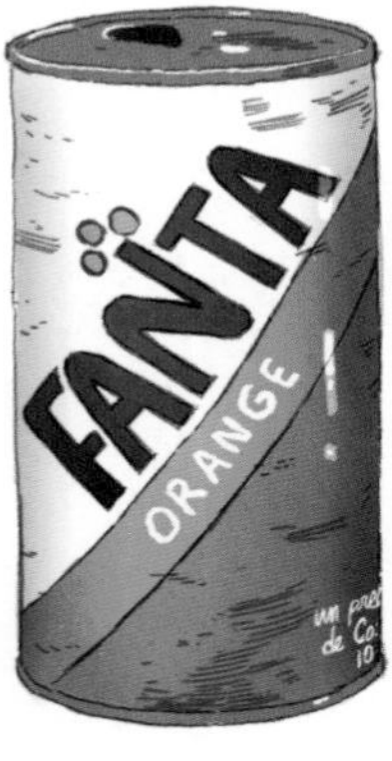
FANTA
ORANGE

LONDON

(2 DAYS LEFT IN THE TRIP)

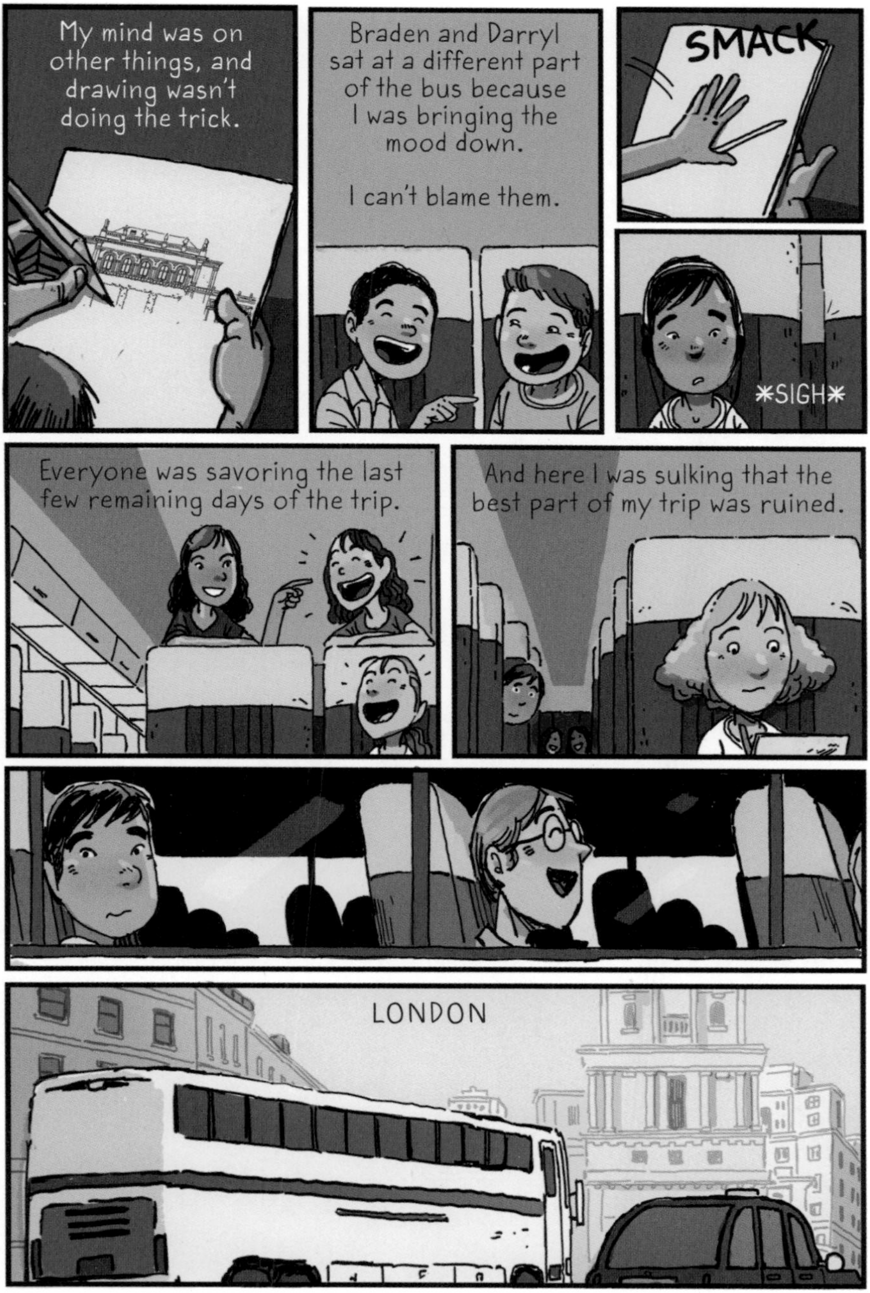
My mind was on other things, and drawing wasn't doing the trick.
Braden and Darryl sat at a different part of the bus because I was bringing the mood down.
I can't blame them.
SMACK
SIGH
Everyone was savoring the last few remaining days of the trip.
And here I was sulking that the best part of my trip was ruined.
LONDON

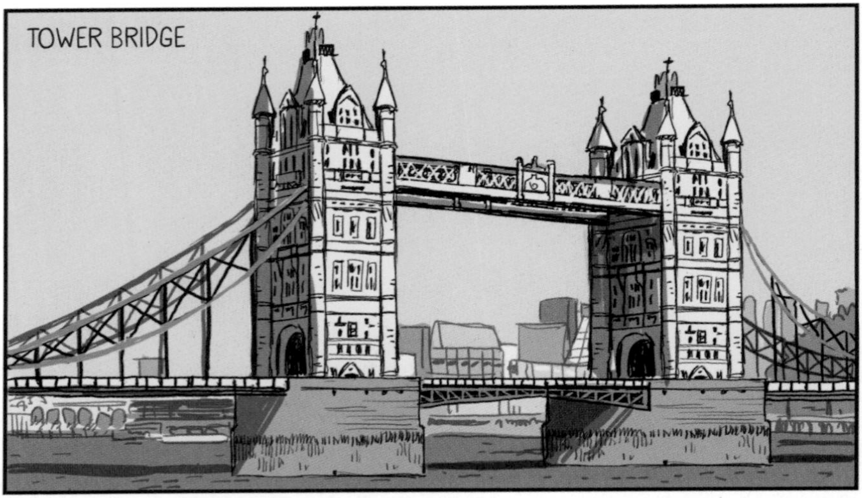
TOWER BRIDGE

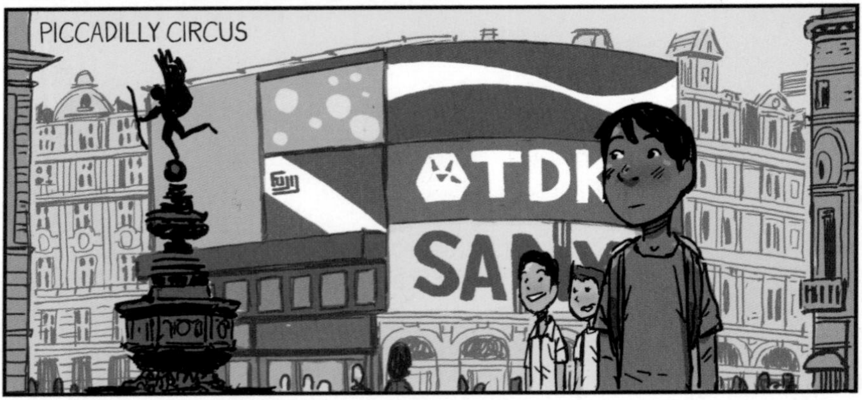
PICCADILLY CIRCUS
TDK
SANY

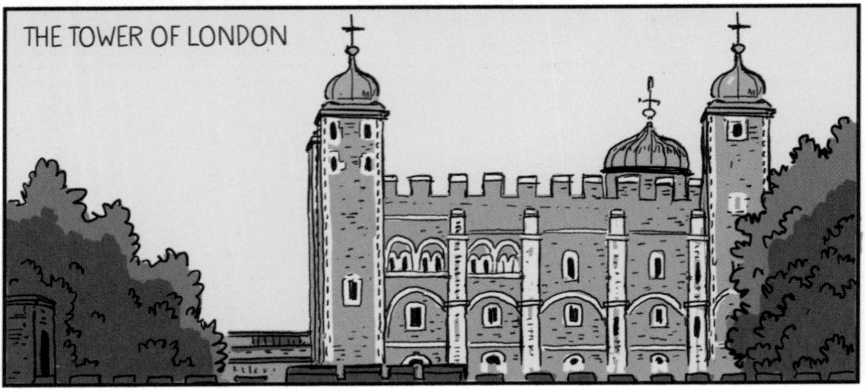
THE TOWER OF LONDON

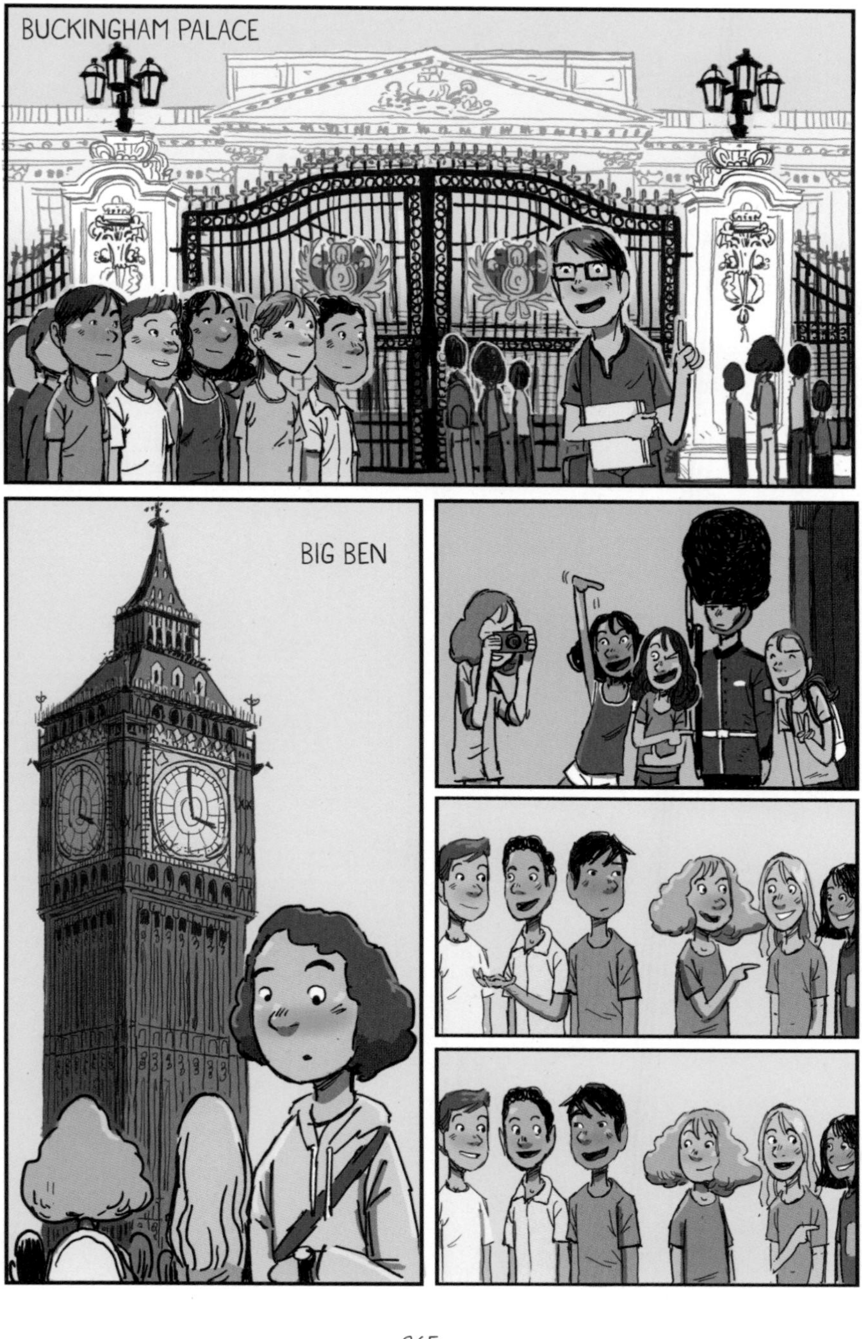
BUCKINGHAM PALACE
BIG BEN

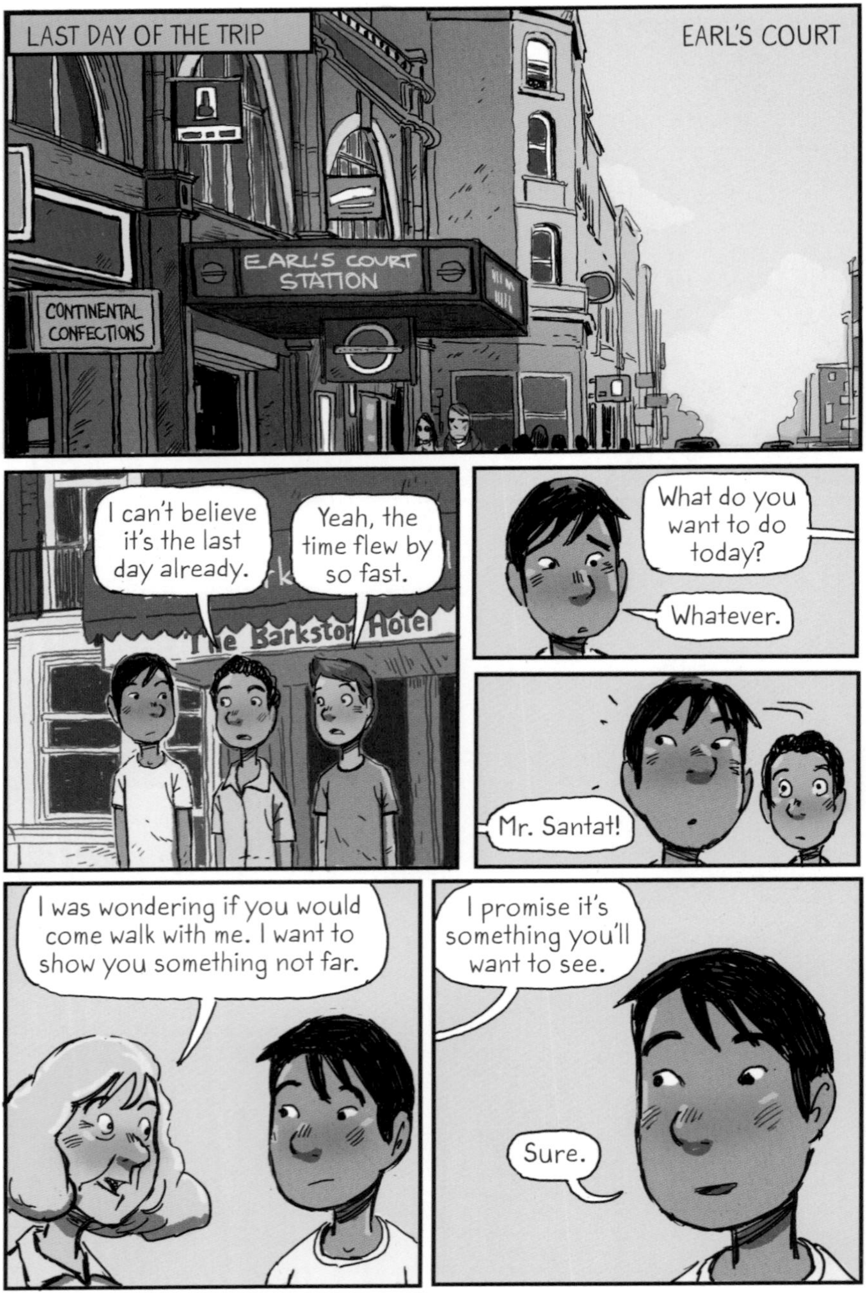
LAST DAY OF THE TRIP
EARL'S COURT
EARL'S COURT STATION
CONTINENTAL CONFECTIONS
The Barkston Hotel
I can't believe it's the last day already.
Yeah, the time flew by so fast.
What do you want to do today?
Whatever.
Mr. Santat!
I was wondering if you would come walk with me. I want to show you something not far.
I promise it's something you'll want to see.
Sure.

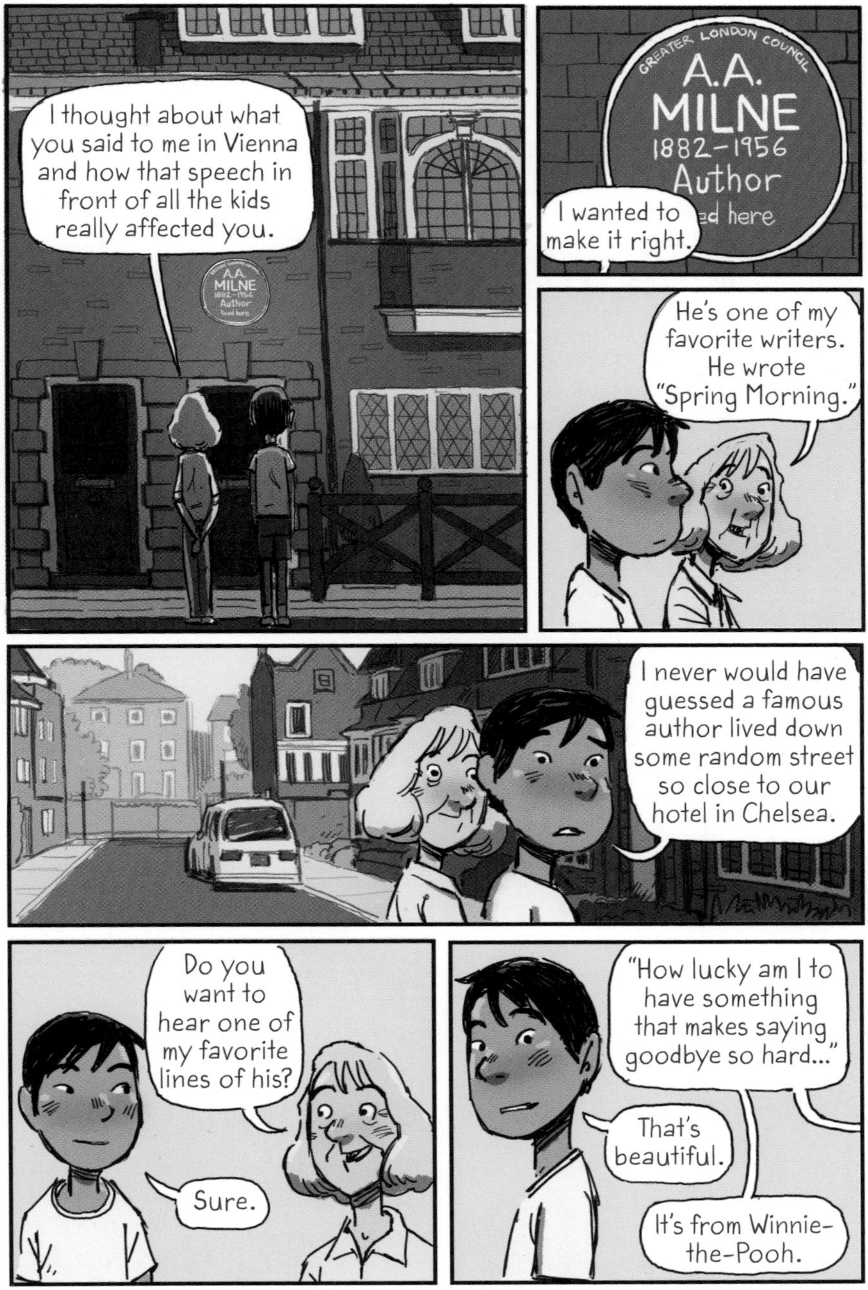
I thought about what you said to me in Vienna and how that speech in front of all the kids really affected you.
GREATER LONDON COUNCIL
A.A. MILNE
1882–1956
Author
I wanted to make it right.
He's one of my favorite writers. He wrote "Spring Morning."
I never would have guessed a famous author lived down some random street so close to our hotel in Chelsea.
Do you want to hear one of my favorite lines of his?
Sure.
"How lucky am I to have something that makes saying goodbye so hard..."
That's beautiful.
It's from Winnie-the-Pooh.

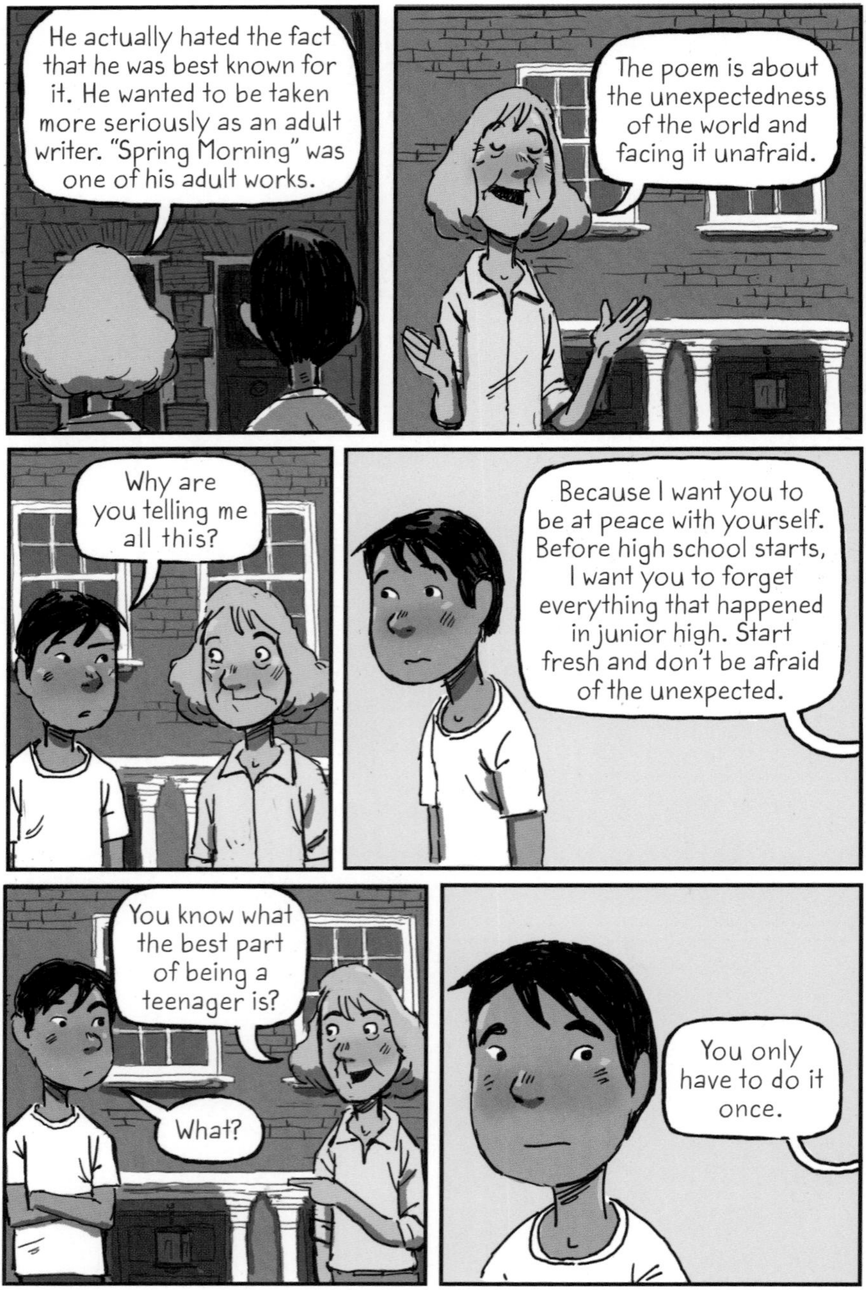
He actually hated the fact that he was best known for it. He wanted to be taken more seriously as an adult writer. "Spring Morning" was one of his adult works.
The poem is about the unexpectedness of the world and facing it unafraid.
Why are you telling me all this?
Because I want you to be at peace with yourself. Before high school starts, I want you to forget everything that happened in junior high. Start fresh and don't be afraid of the unexpected.
You know what the best part of being a teenager is?
What?
You only have to do it once.

Now here we are at a spot in Hyde Park known as the Speakers' Corner.

Later that morning...

This is where the term "standing on your soapbox" originated. This is a place where anyone can speak their minds freely.

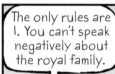

The only rules are
1. You can't speak negatively about the royal family.

2. You must be at least six inches off the grounds of the Queen's property.

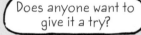

Does anyone want to give it a try?

No one has anything to say? Then let's continue on!

269

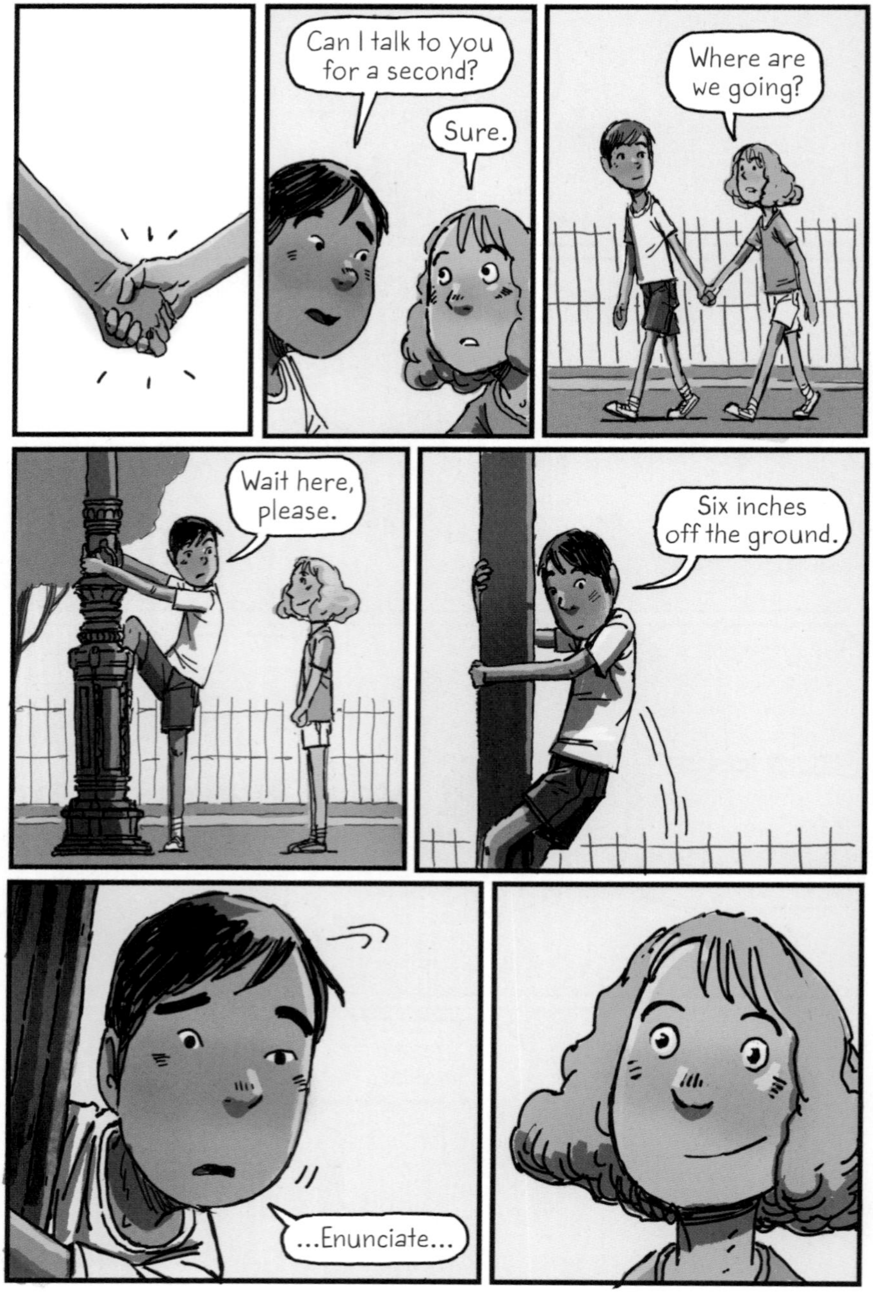
Can I talk to you for a second?
Sure.
Where are we going?
Wait here, please.
Six inches off the ground.
...Enunciate...

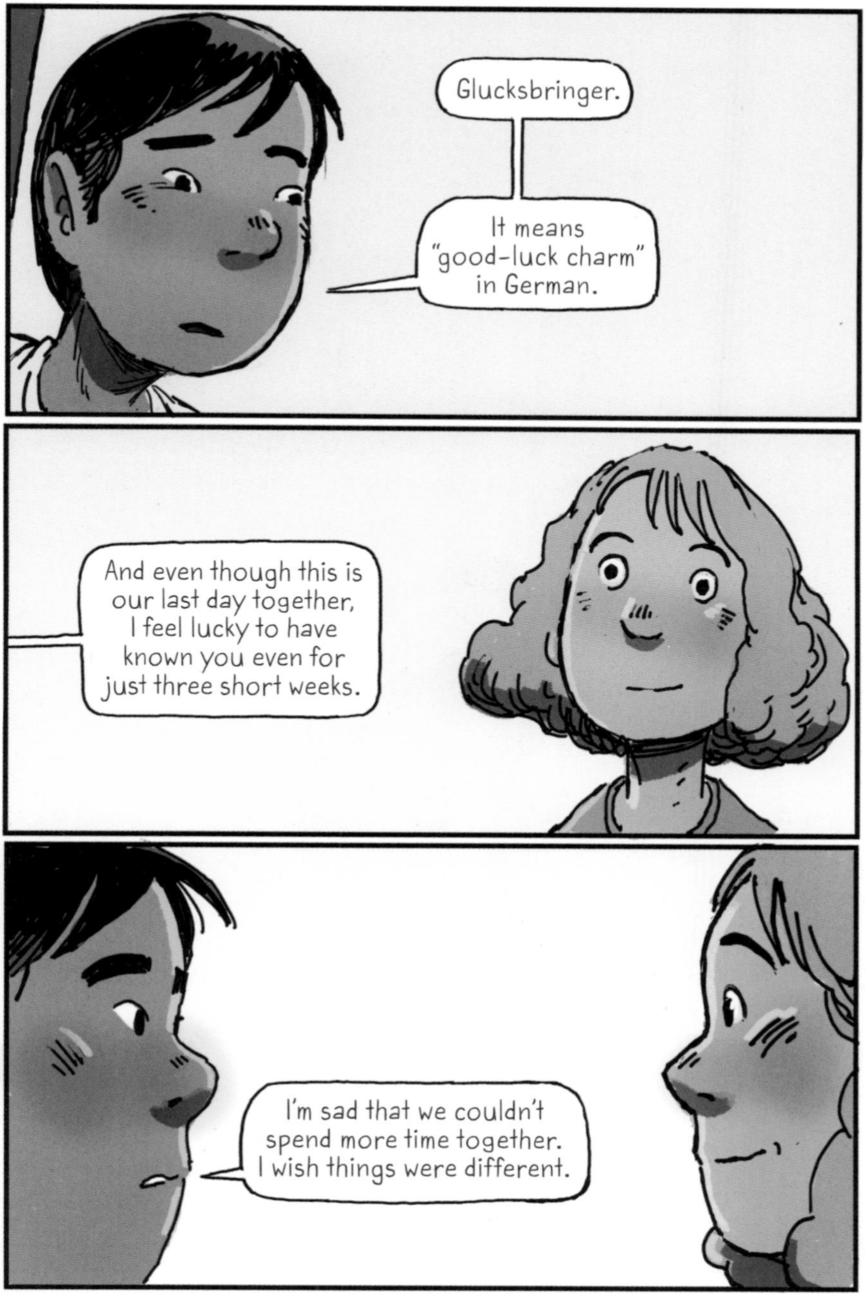
Glucksbringer.
It means "good-luck charm" in German.
And even though this is our last day together, I feel lucky to have known you even for just three short weeks.
I'm sad that we couldn't spend more time together. I wish things were different.

...How lucky am I to have something
that makes saying goodbye so hard...

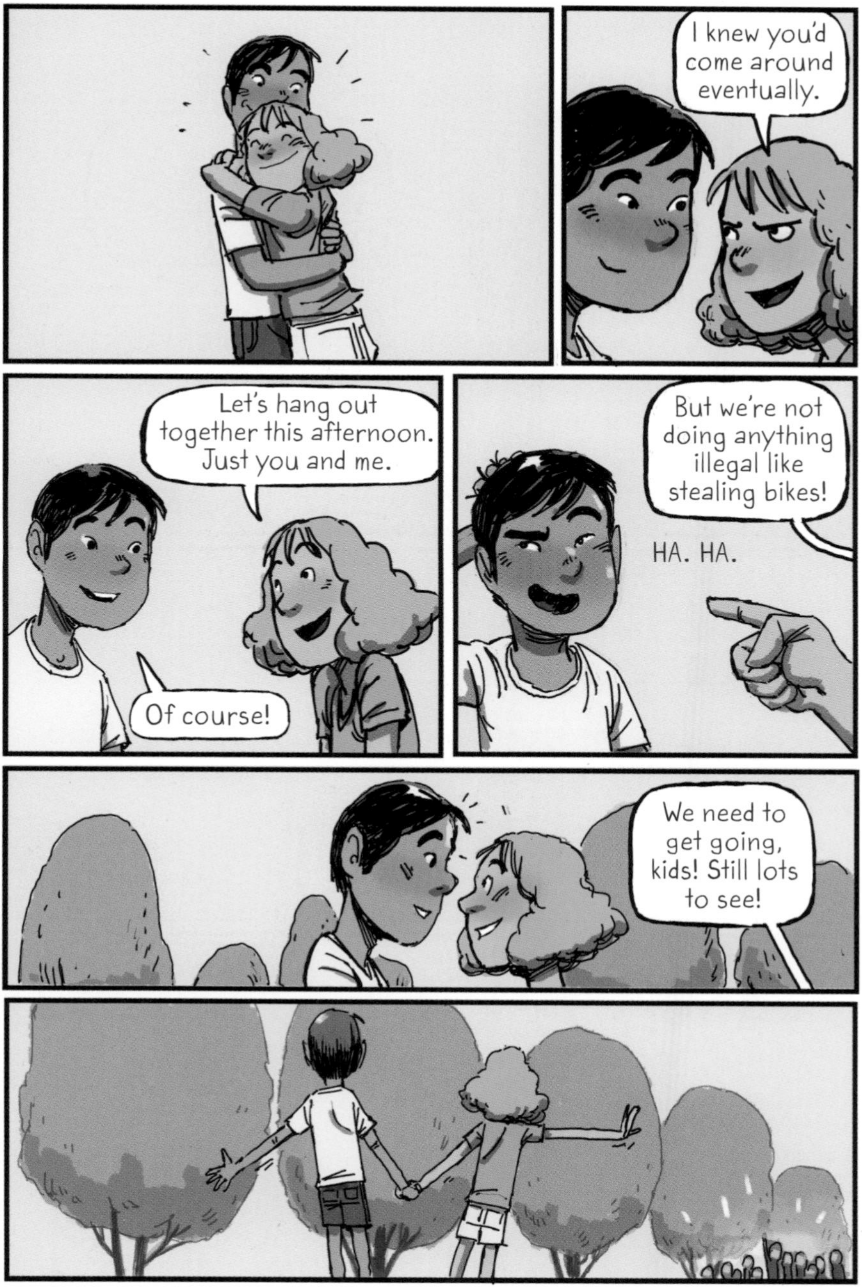
I knew you'd come around eventually.
Let's hang out together this afternoon. Just you and me.
Of course!
But we're not doing anything illegal like stealing bikes!
HA. HA.
We need to get going, kids! Still lots to see!

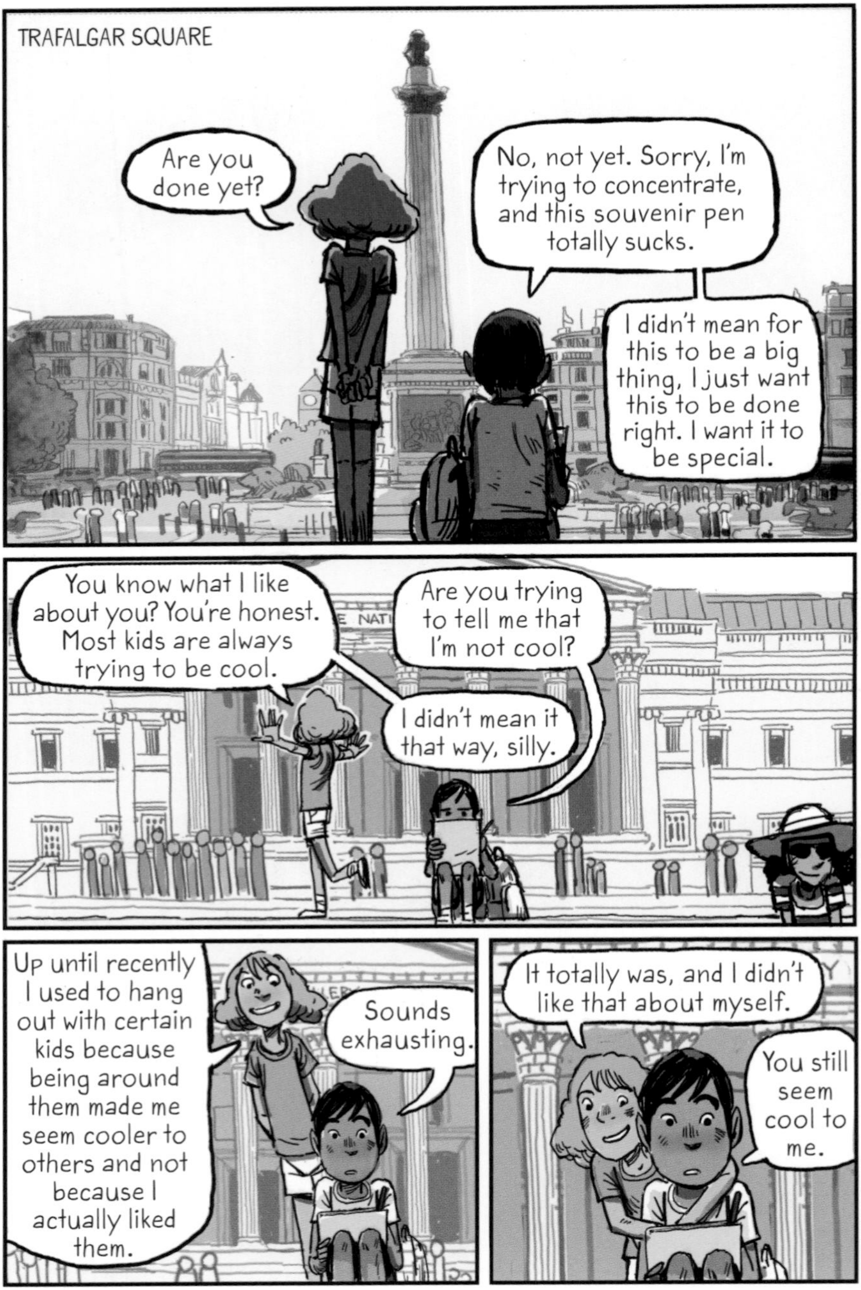
TRAFALGAR SQUARE
Are you done yet?
No, not yet. Sorry, I'm trying to concentrate, and this souvenir pen totally sucks.
I didn't mean for this to be a big thing, I just want this to be done right. I want it to be special.
You know what I like about you? You're honest. Most kids are always trying to be cool.
Are you trying to tell me that I'm not cool?
I didn't mean it that way, silly.
Up until recently I used to hang out with certain kids because being around them made me seem cooler to others and not because I actually liked them.
Sounds exhausting.
It totally was, and I didn't like that about myself.
You still seem cool to me.

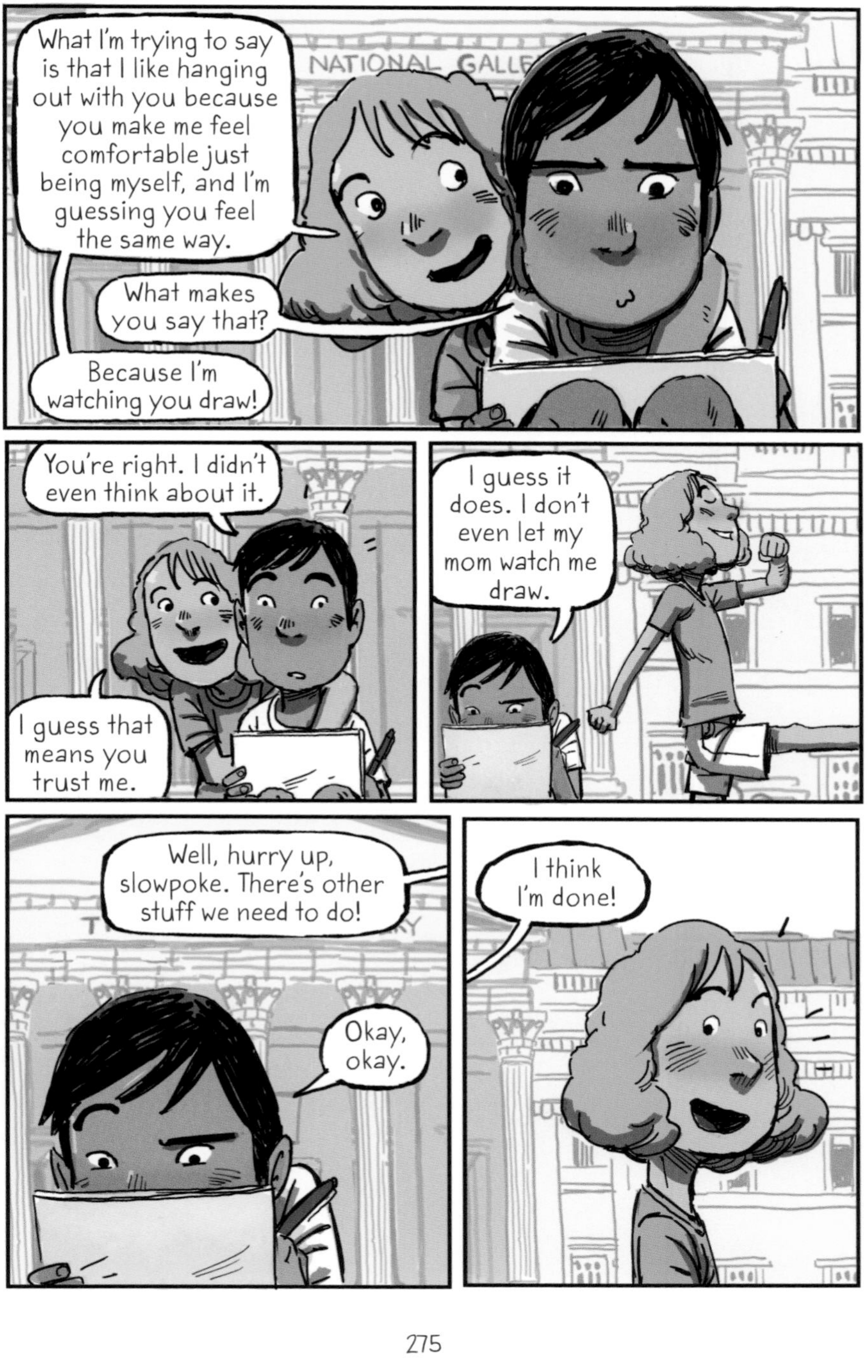
NATIONAL GALLE
What I'm trying to say is that I like hanging out with you because you make me feel comfortable just being myself, and I'm guessing you feel the same way.
What makes you say that?
Because I'm watching you draw!
You're right. I didn't even think about it.
I guess that means you trust me.
I guess it does. I don't even let my mom watch me draw.
Well, hurry up, slowpoke. There's other stuff we need to do!
Okay, okay.
I think I'm done!

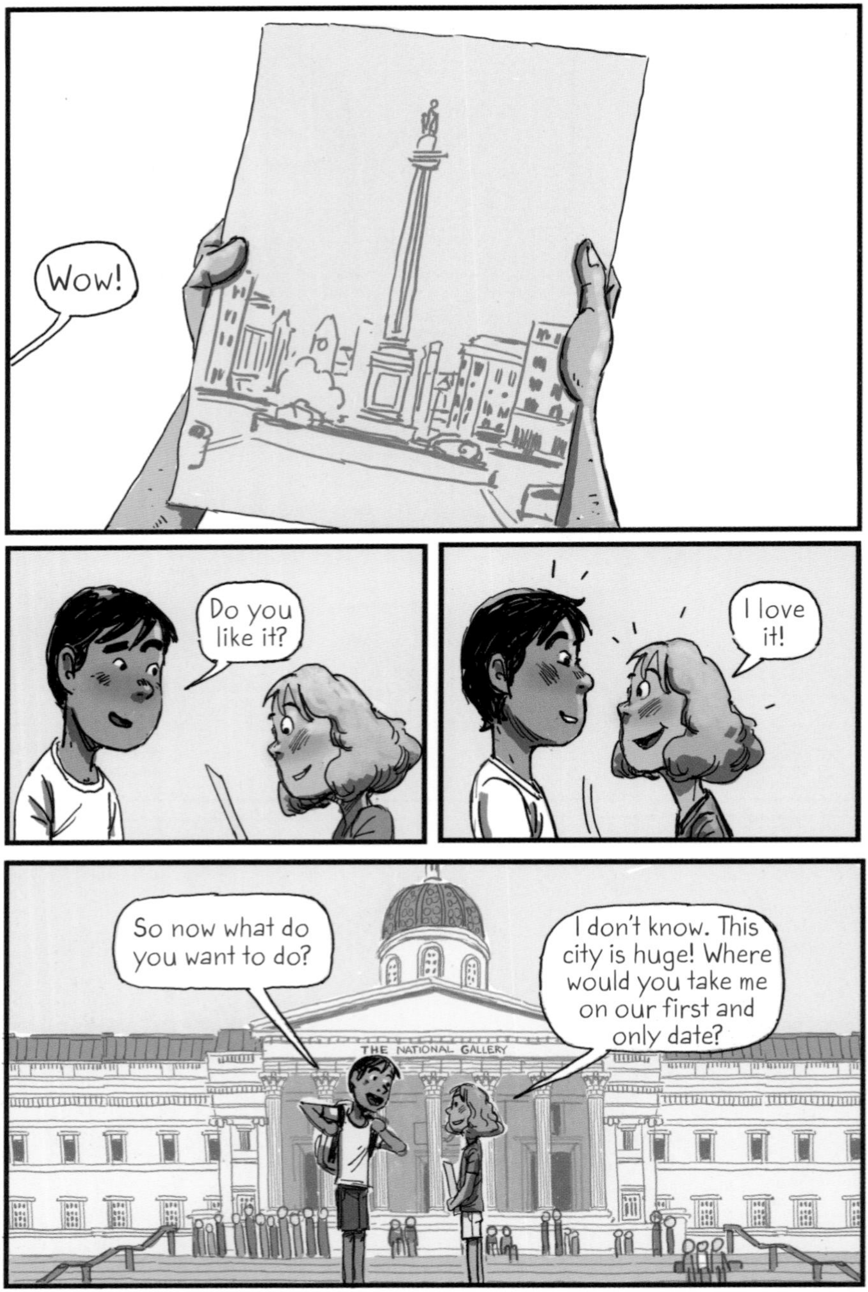
Wow!
Do you like it?
I love it!
So now what do you want to do?
THE NATIONAL GALLERY
I don't know. This city is huge! Where would you take me on our first and only date?

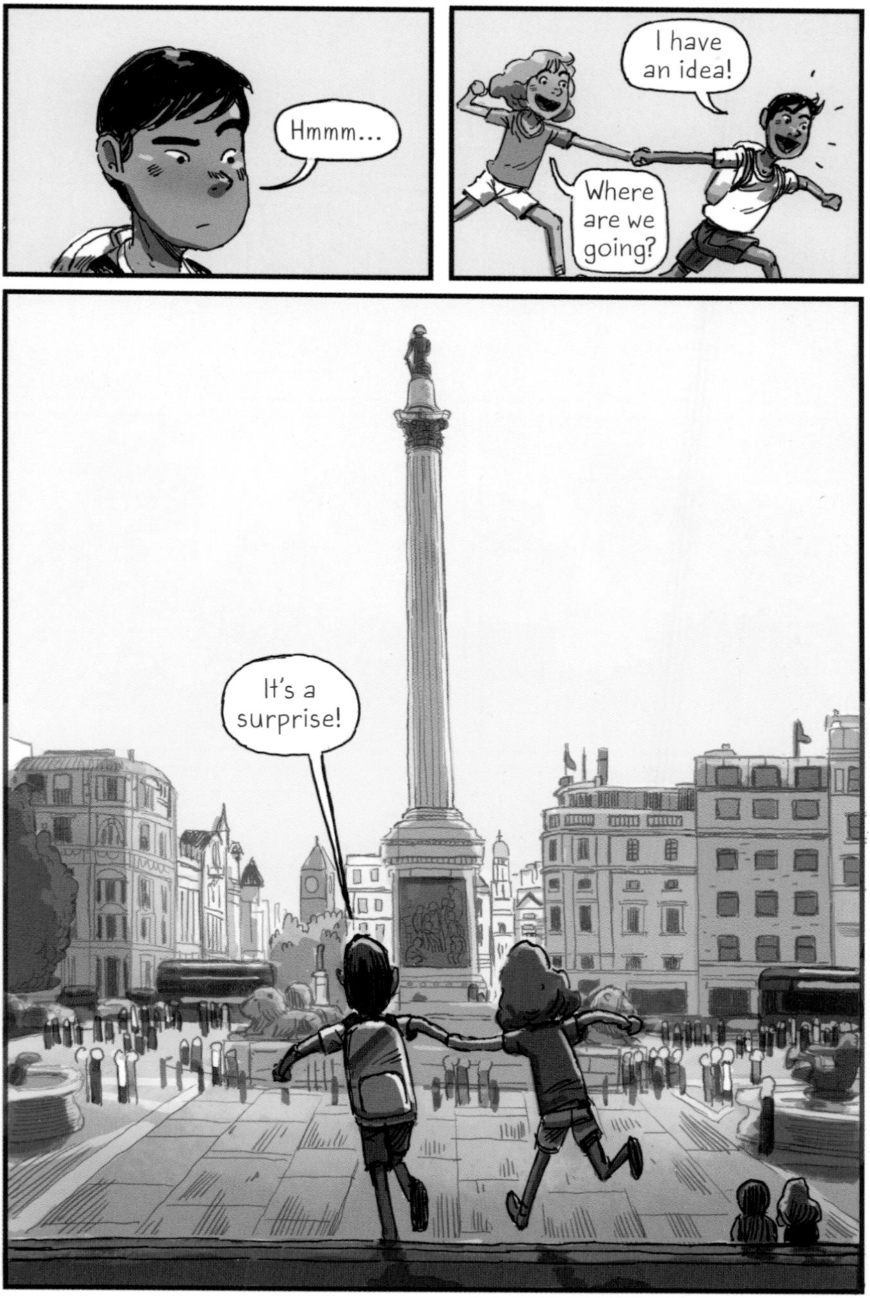
Hmmm...
I have an idea!
Where are we going?
It's a surprise!

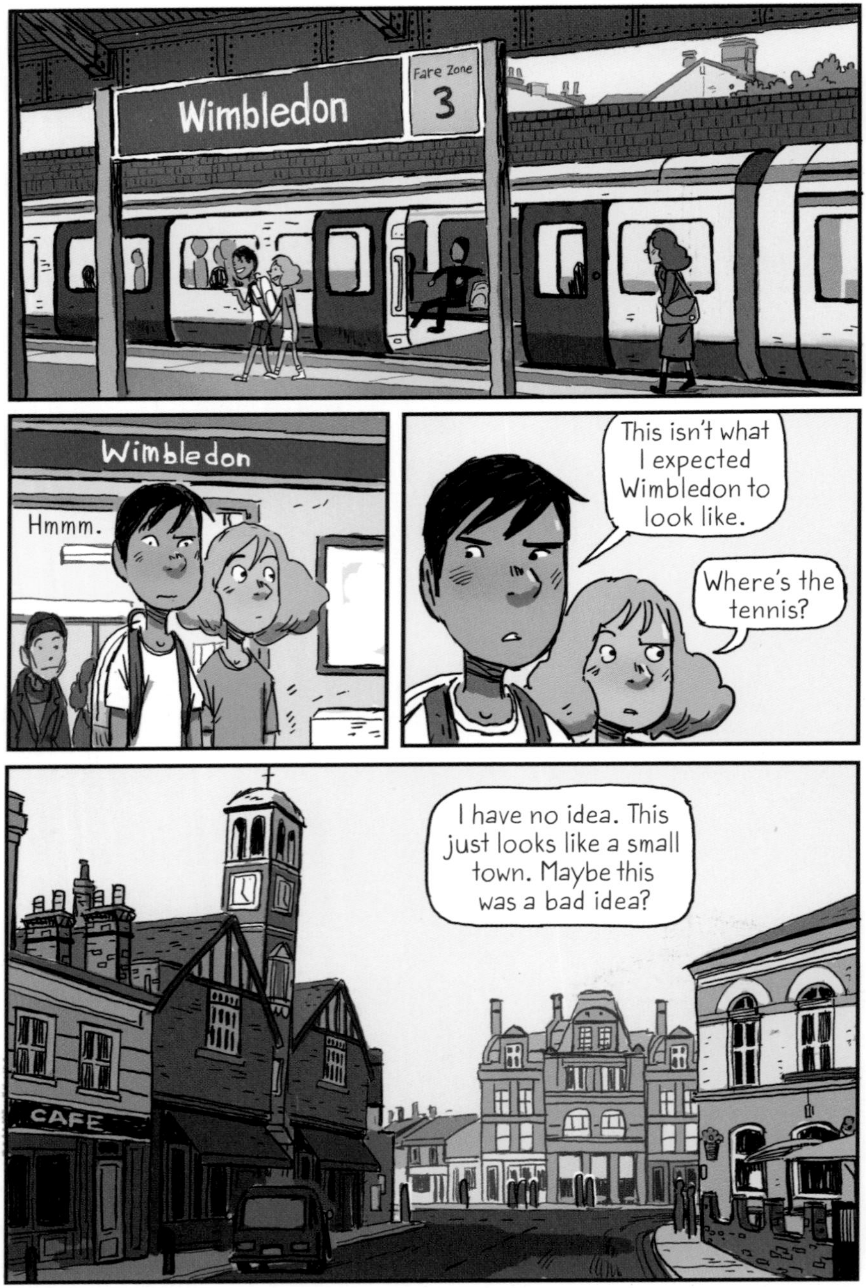
Wimbledon
Fare Zone 3
Wimbledon
Hmmm.
This isn't what I expected Wimbledon to look like.
Where's the tennis?
I have no idea. This just looks like a small town. Maybe this was a bad idea?
CAFE

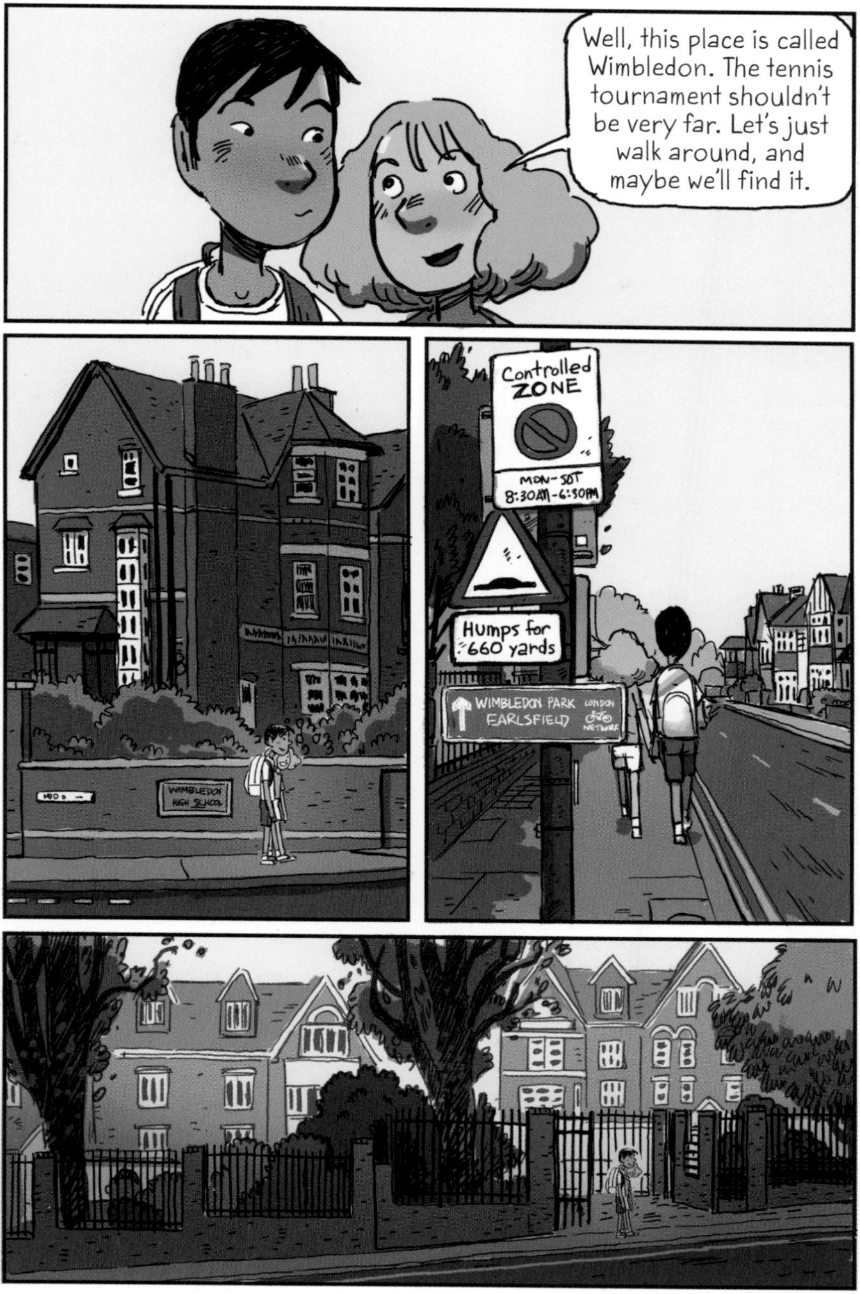
Well, this place is called Wimbledon. The tennis tournament shouldn't be very far. Let's just walk around, and maybe we'll find it.
WIMBLEDON HIGH SCHOOL
Controlled ZONE
Humps for 660 yards
WIMBLEDON PARK
EARLSFIELD

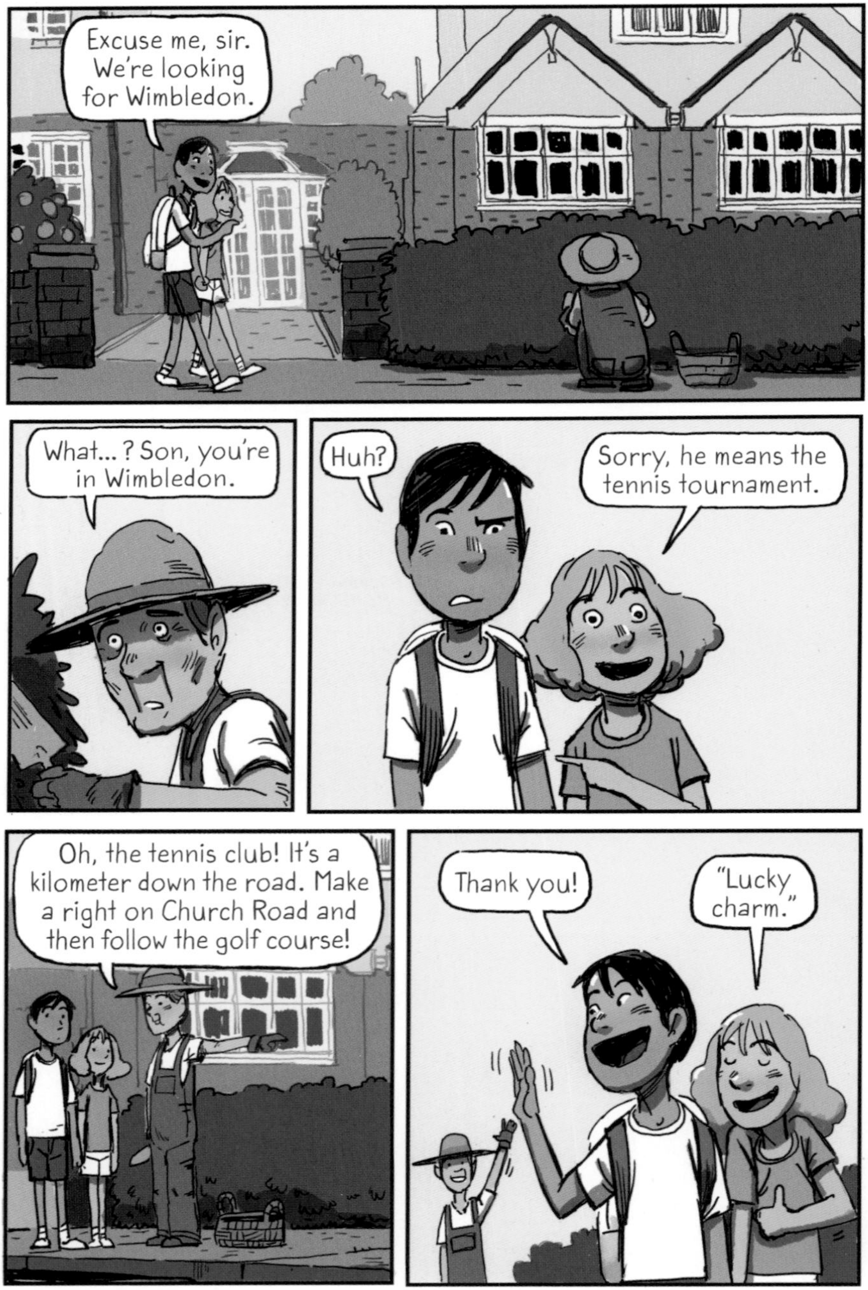
Excuse me, sir. We're looking for Wimbledon.
What... ? Son, you're in Wimbledon.
Huh?
Sorry, he means the tennis tournament.
Oh, the tennis club! It's a kilometer down the road. Make a right on Church Road and then follow the golf course!
Thank you!
"Lucky charm."

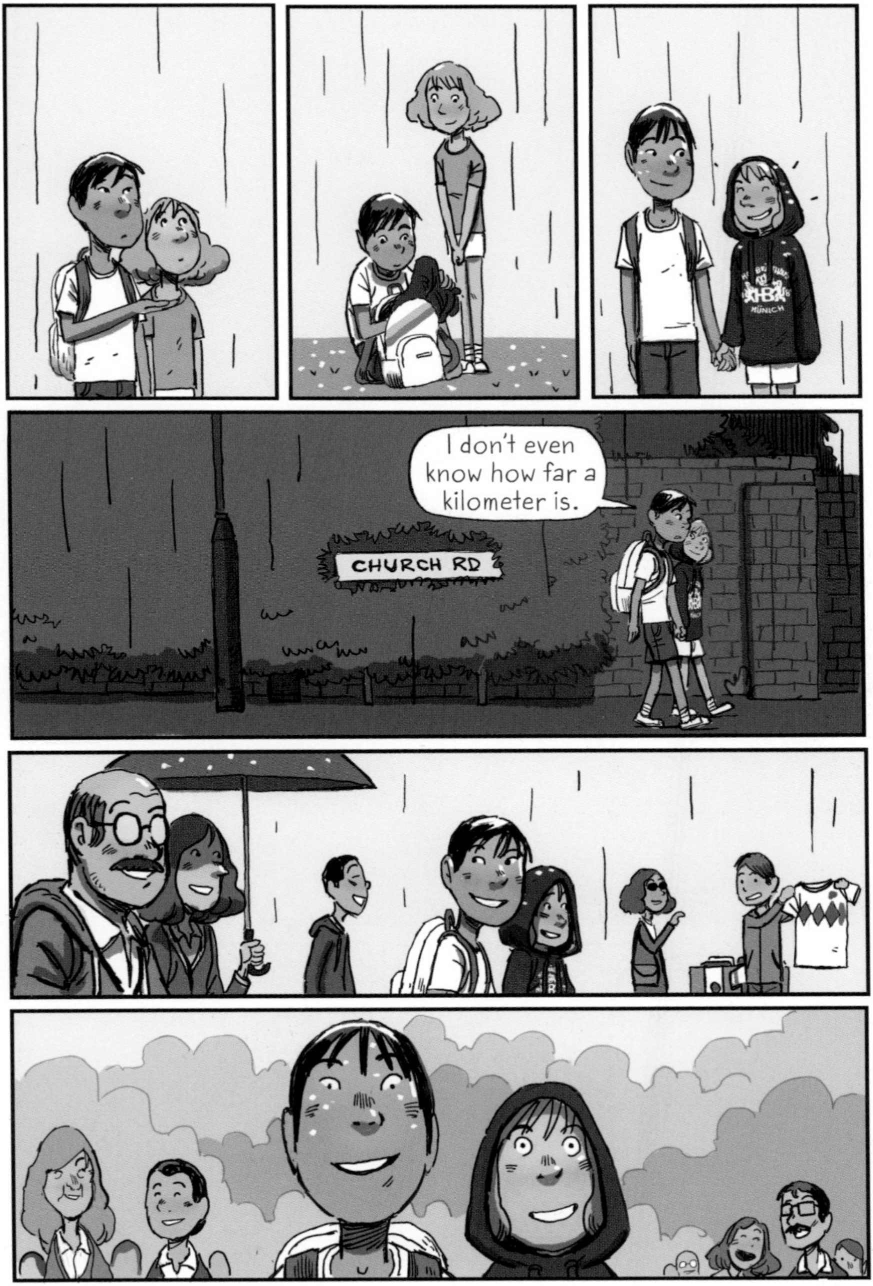
I don't even know how far a kilometer is.
CHURCH RD

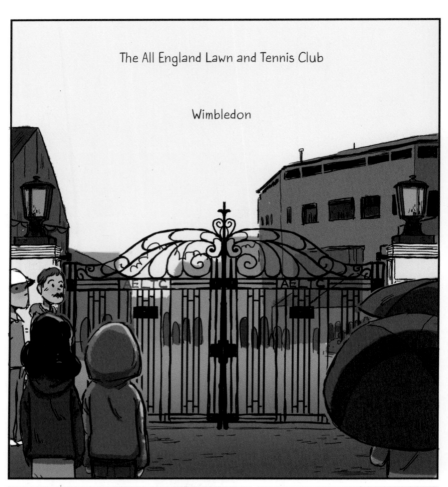

The All England Lawn and Tennis Club

Wimbledon

All right, folks, we'll be letting people onto the grounds in about 15 minutes! Please have your three pounds ready for the attendant!

WE CAN GO IN!

THE LAWN TENNIS CHAMPIONSHIPS WIMBLEDON 1989
ORDER OF PLAY   FRIDAY 7th JULY

| CENTRE COURT |
| No.1 COURT |
| No.2 COURT |
| No.3 COURT |
| No.4 COURT |
| No.5 COURT |
| No.6 COURT |
| No.7 COURT |
| No.8 COURT |
| No.9 COURT |
| No.10 COURT |
| No.11 COURT |
| No.12 COURT |
| No.13 COURT |
| No.14 COURT |

Since there's a rain delay, I wonder if we can see Centre Court?

Well, we made it this far. It's worth a shot.

Just keep walking.

211

GASP

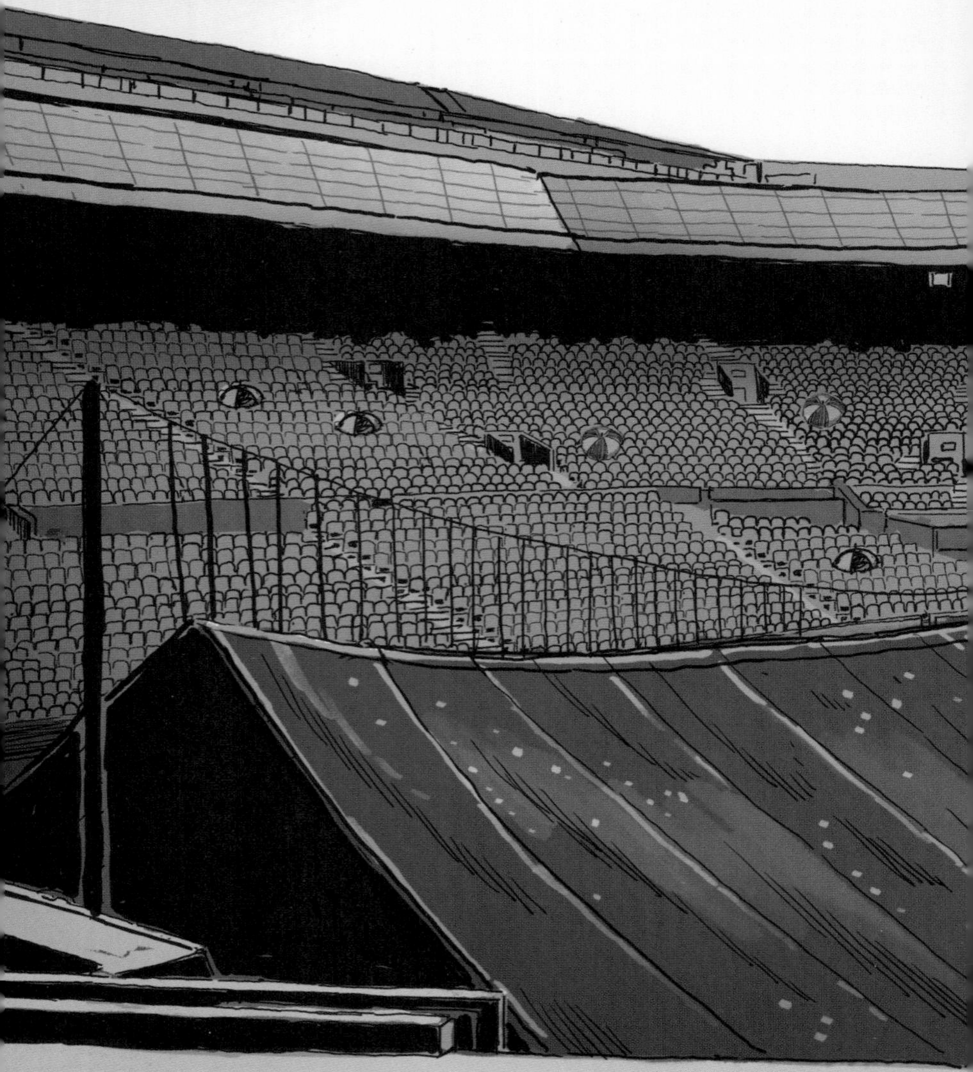

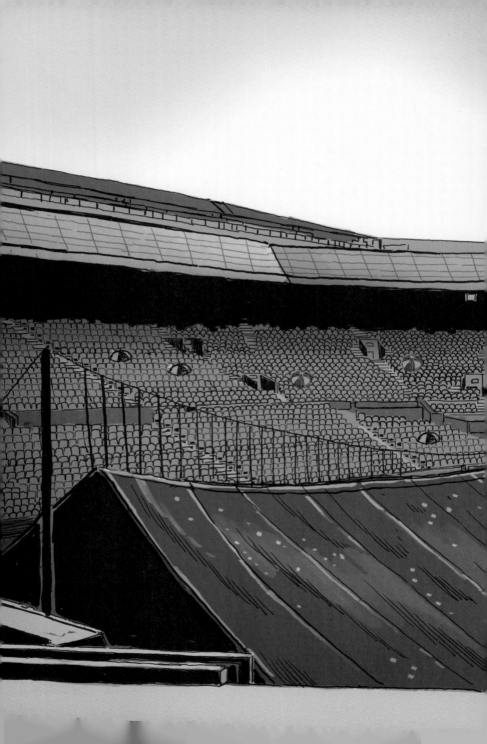

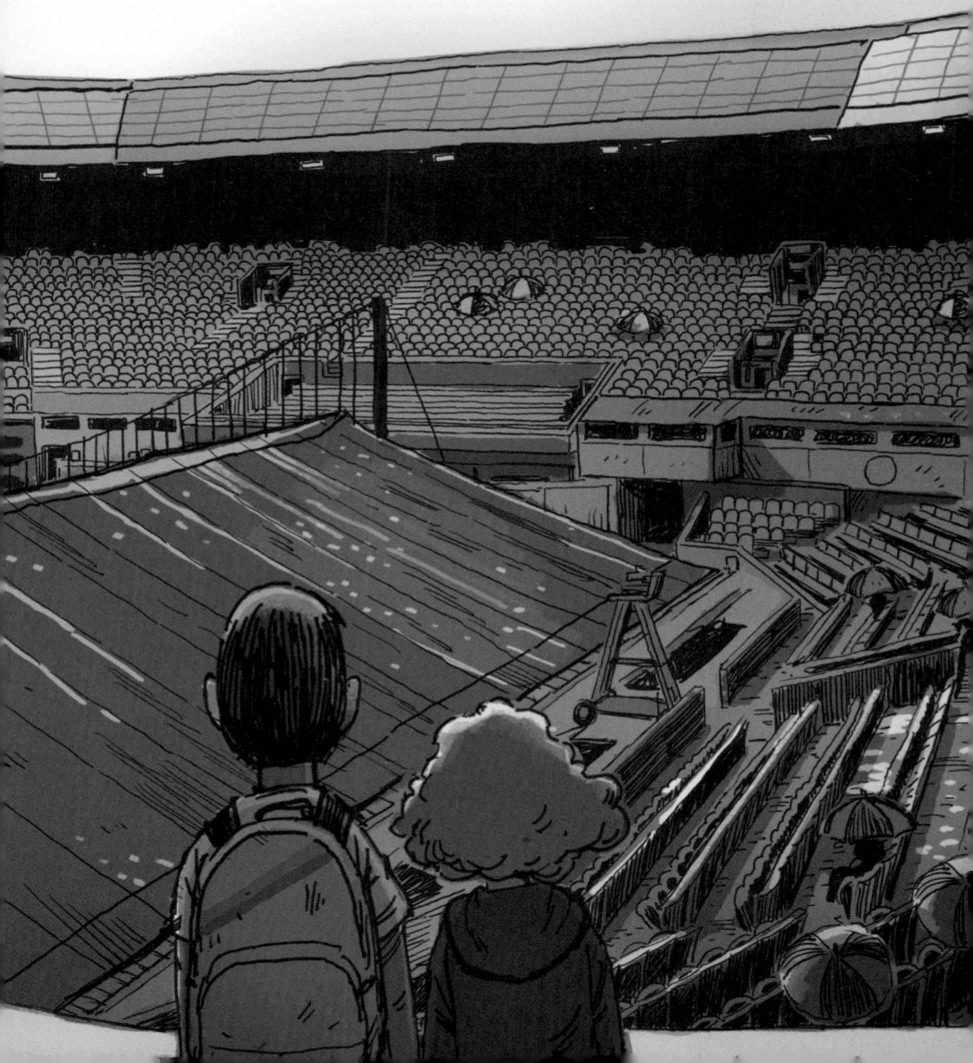

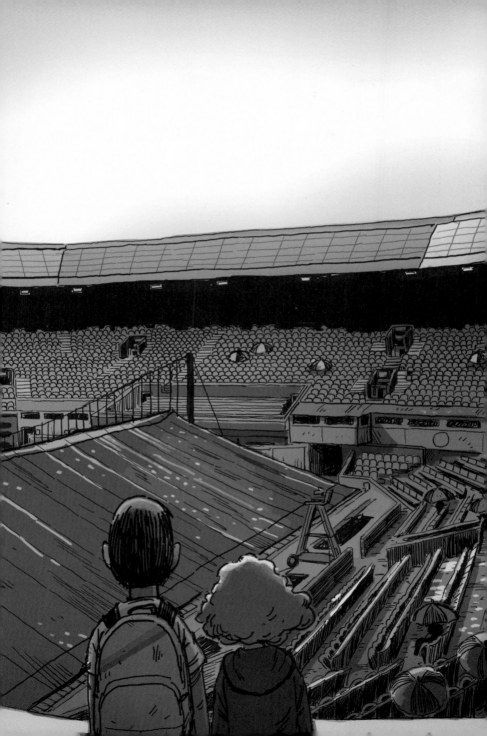

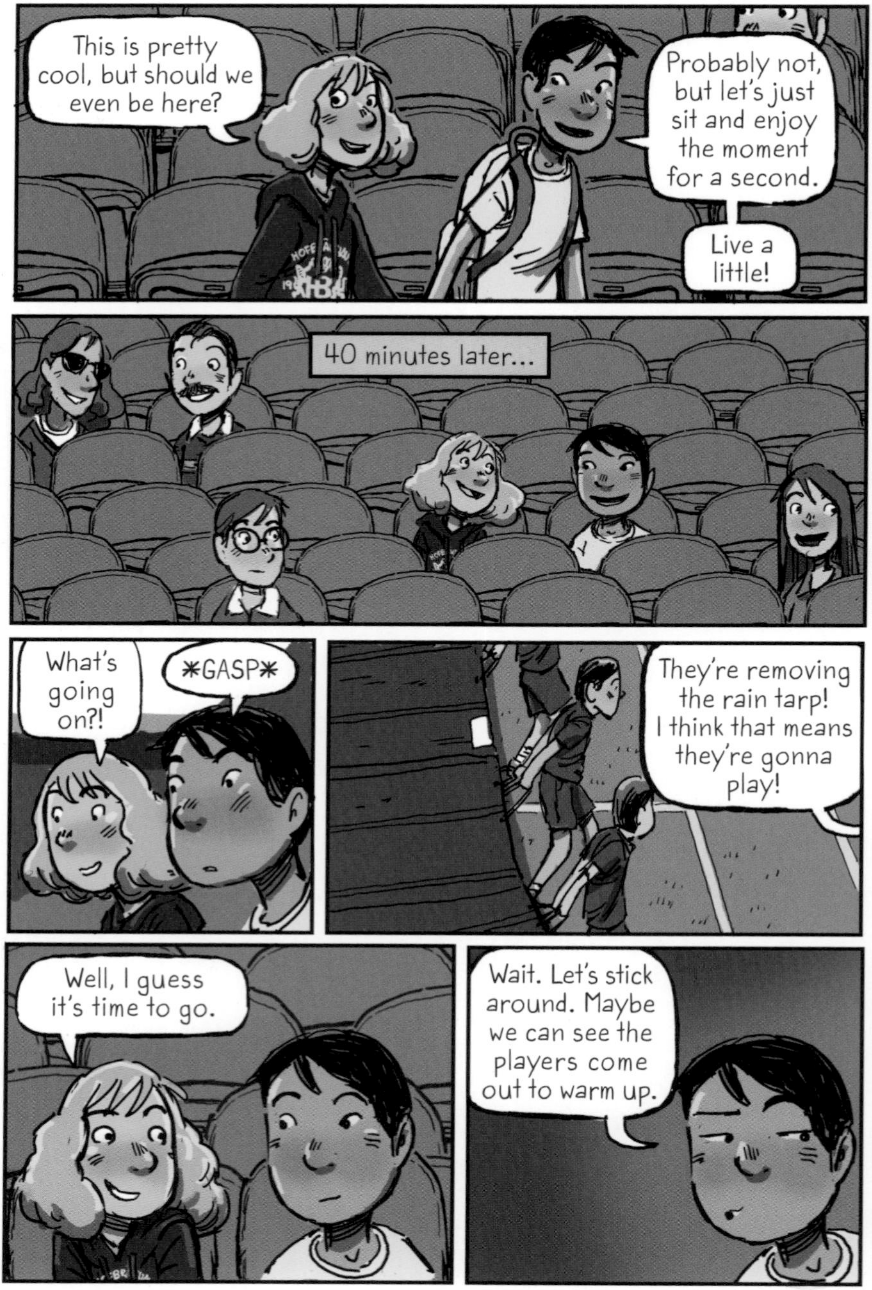
This is pretty cool, but should we even be here?
Probably not, but let's just sit and enjoy the moment for a second.
Live a little!
40 minutes later...
What's going on?!
GASP
They're removing the rain tarp! I think that means they're gonna play!
Well, I guess it's time to go.
Wait. Let's stick around. Maybe we can see the players come out to warm up.

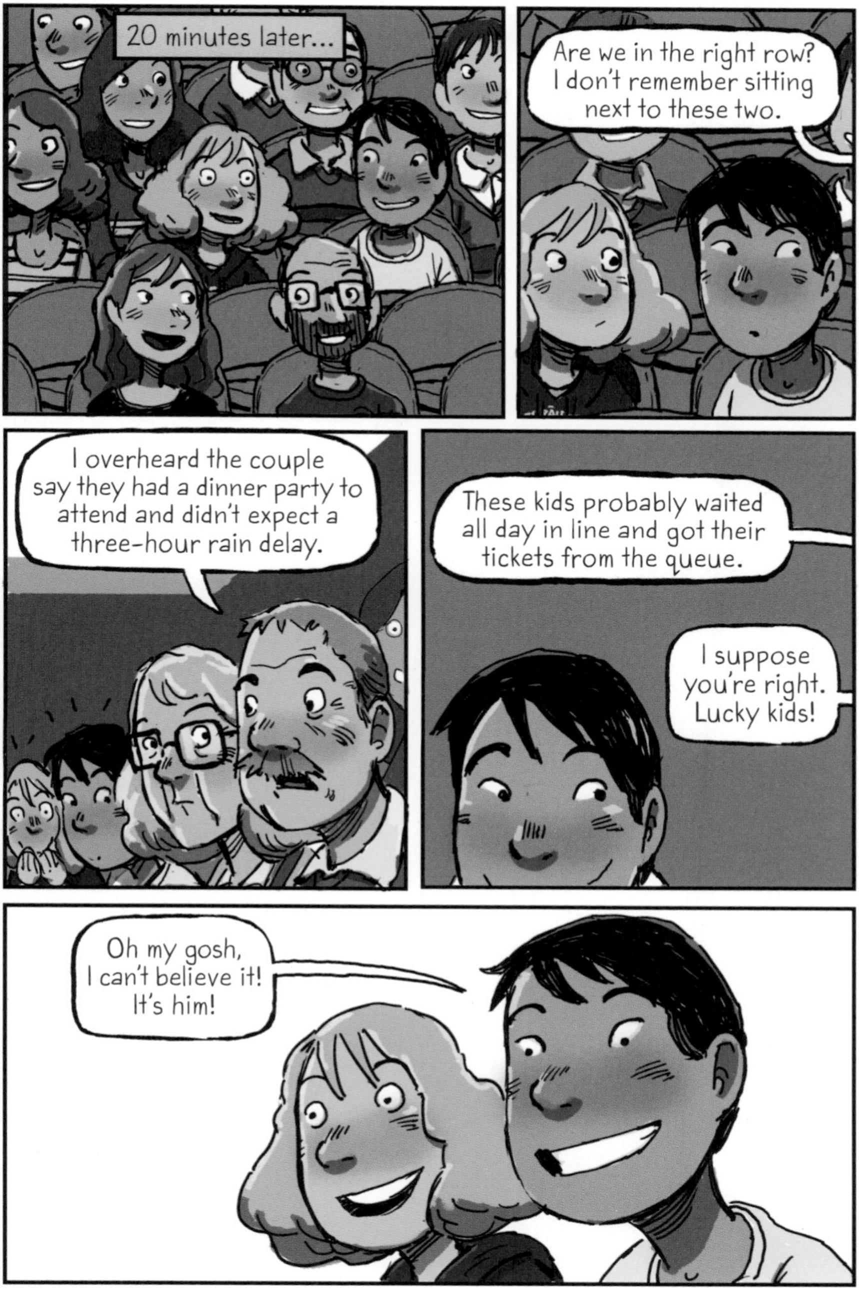
20 minutes later...
Are we in the right row? I don't remember sitting next to these two.
I overheard the couple say they had a dinner party to attend and didn't expect a three-hour rain delay.
These kids probably waited all day in line and got their tickets from the queue.
I suppose you're right. Lucky kids!
Oh my gosh, I can't believe it! It's him!

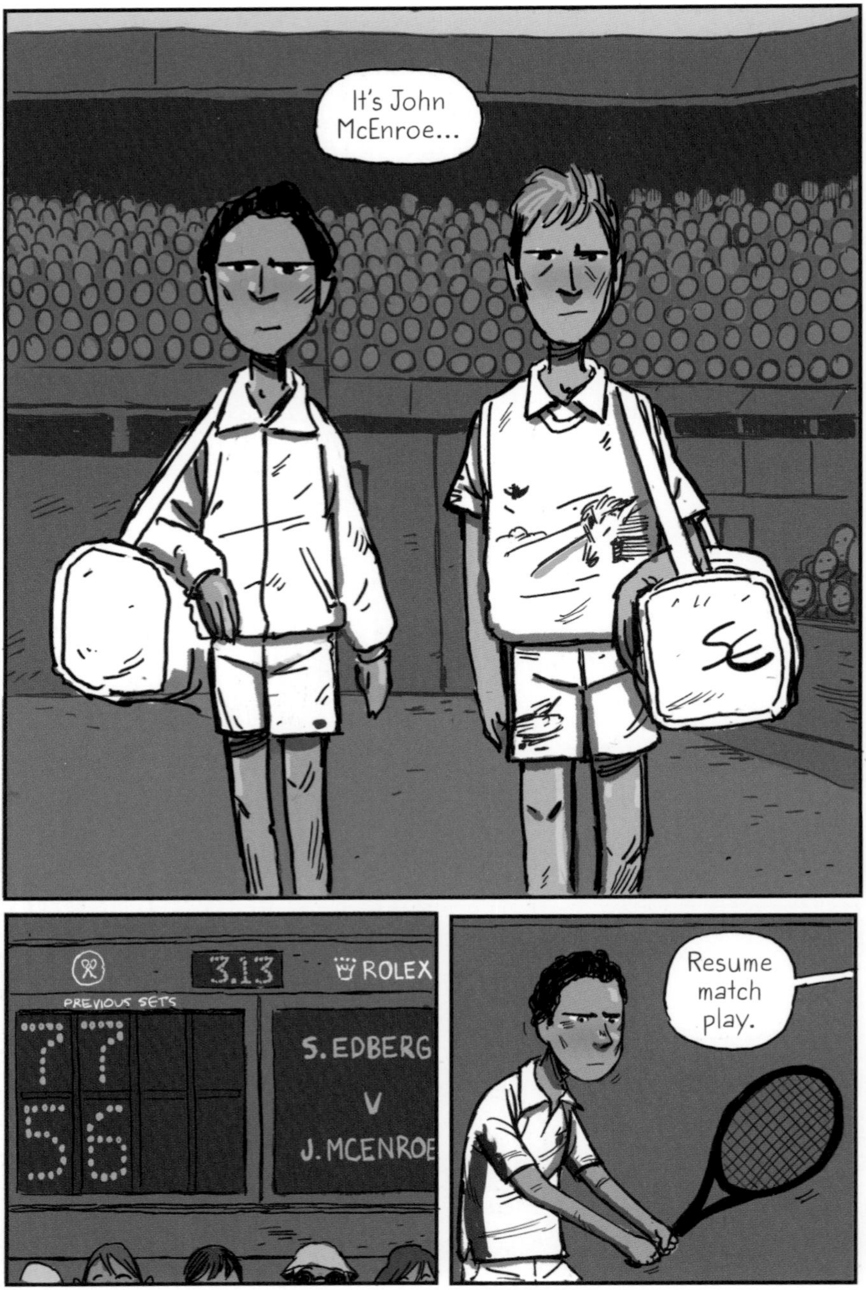
It's John McEnroe...
3.13
ROLEX
PREVIOUS SETS
7 7
5 6
S. EDBERG
V
J. MCENROE
Resume match play.

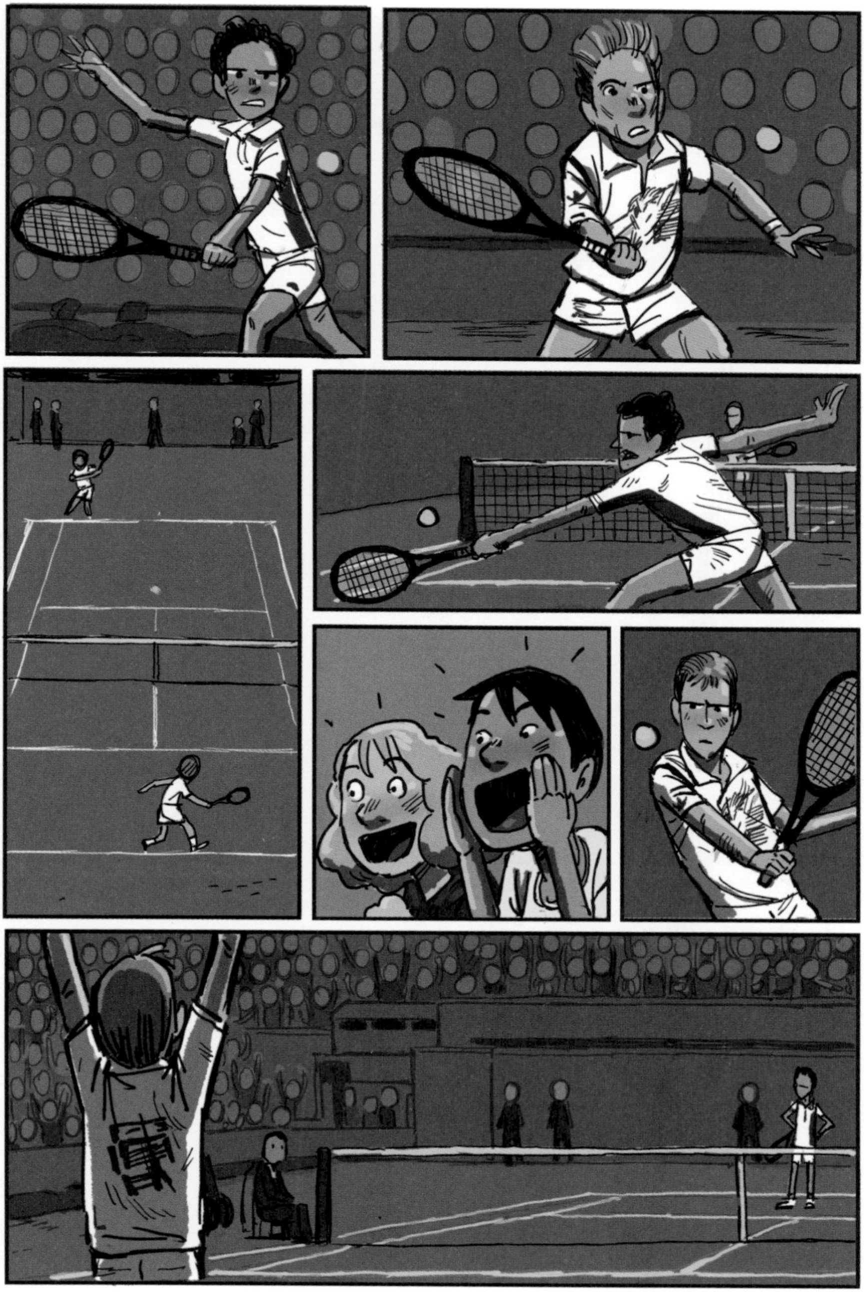

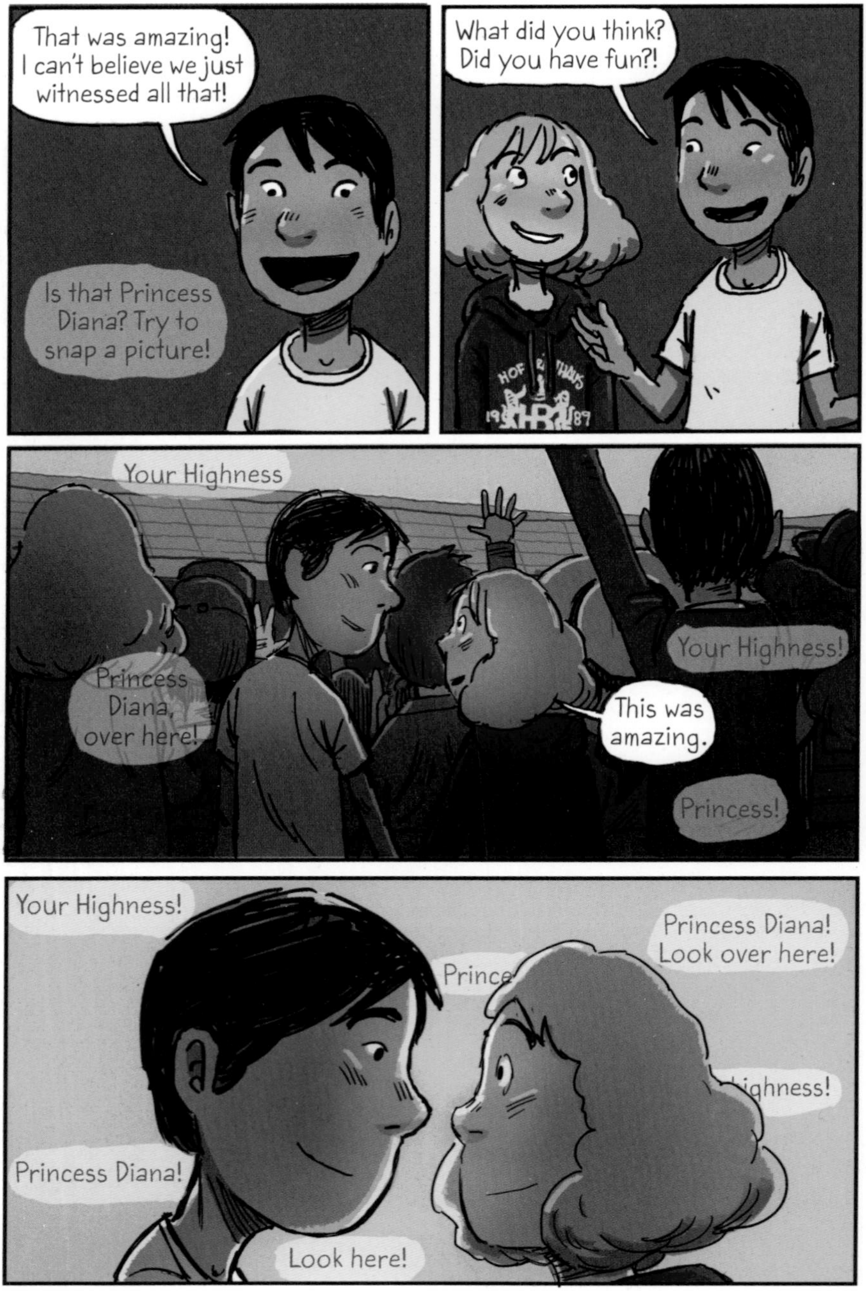
That was amazing! I can't believe we just witnessed all that!
Is that Princess Diana? Try to snap a picture!
What did you think? Did you have fun?!
HOF 19 HB 87
Your Highness
Princess Diana, over here!
Your Highness!
This was amazing.
Princess!
Your Highness!
Princess Diana! Look over here!
Prince
ighness!
Princess Diana!
Look here!

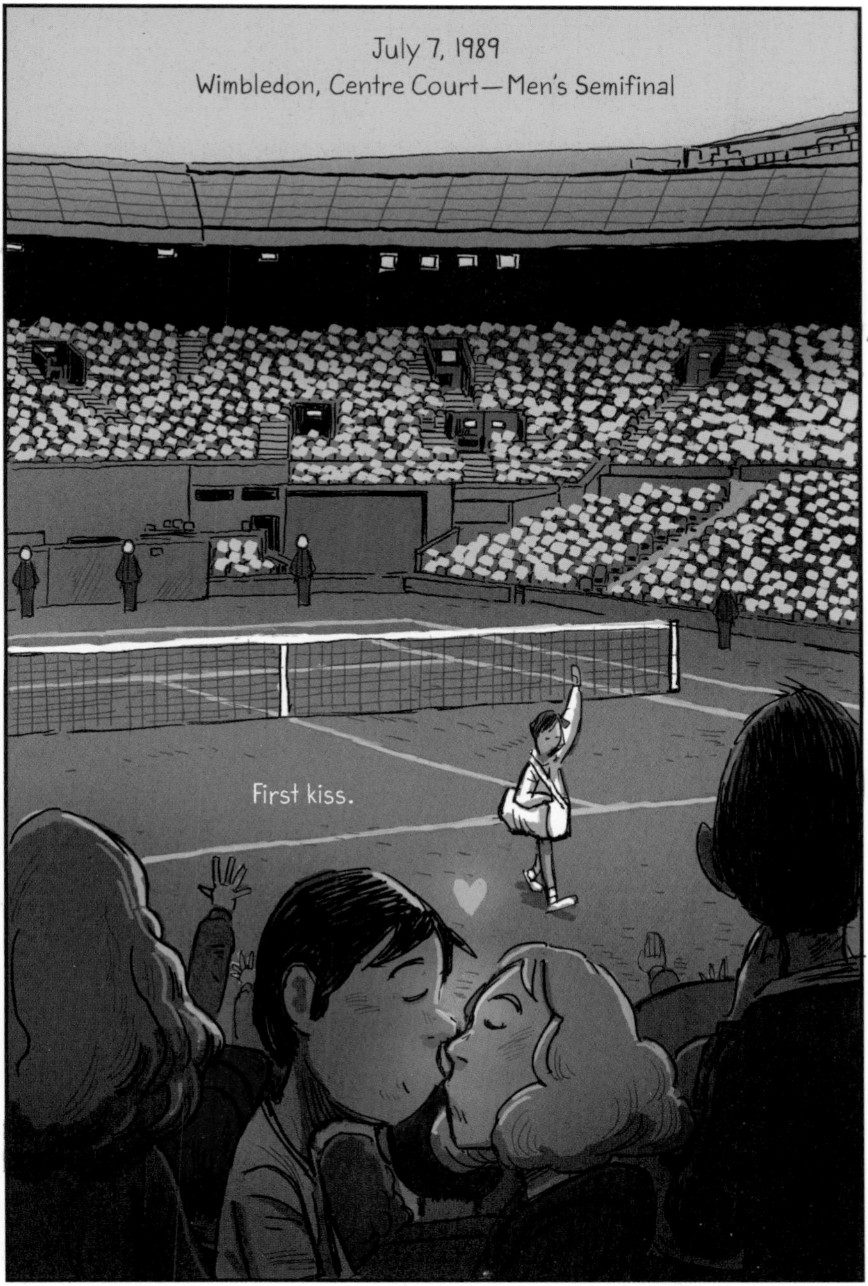
July 7, 1989
Wimbledon, Centre Court—Men's Semifinal
First kiss.

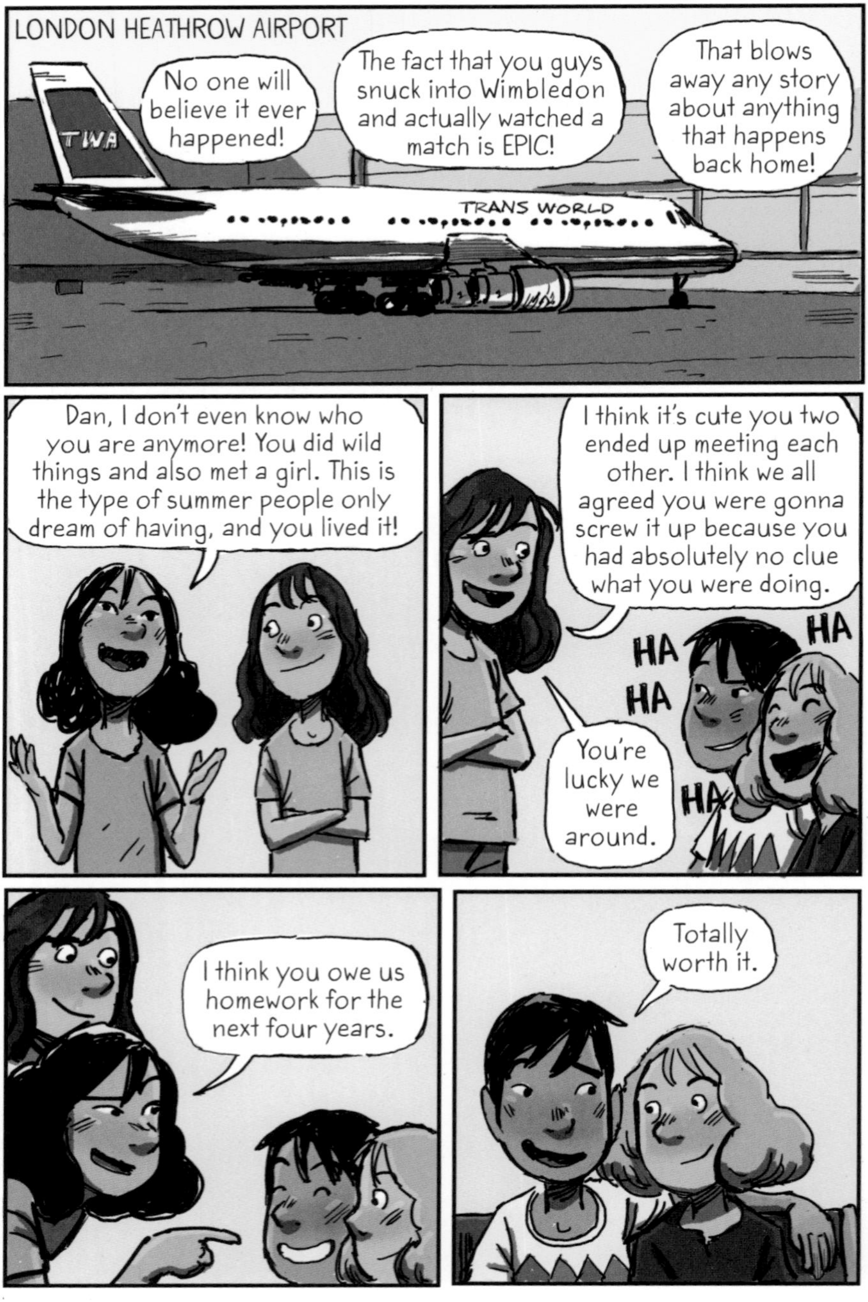
LONDON HEATHROW AIRPORT
No one will believe it ever happened!
The fact that you guys snuck into Wimbledon and actually watched a match is EPIC!
That blows away any story about anything that happens back home!
TWA
TRANS WORLD
Dan, I don't even know who you are anymore! You did wild things and also met a girl. This is the type of summer people only dream of having, and you lived it!
I think it's cute you two ended up meeting each other. I think we all agreed you were gonna screw it up because you had absolutely no clue what you were doing.
HA HA HA HA
You're lucky we were around.
I think you owe us homework for the next four years.
Totally worth it.

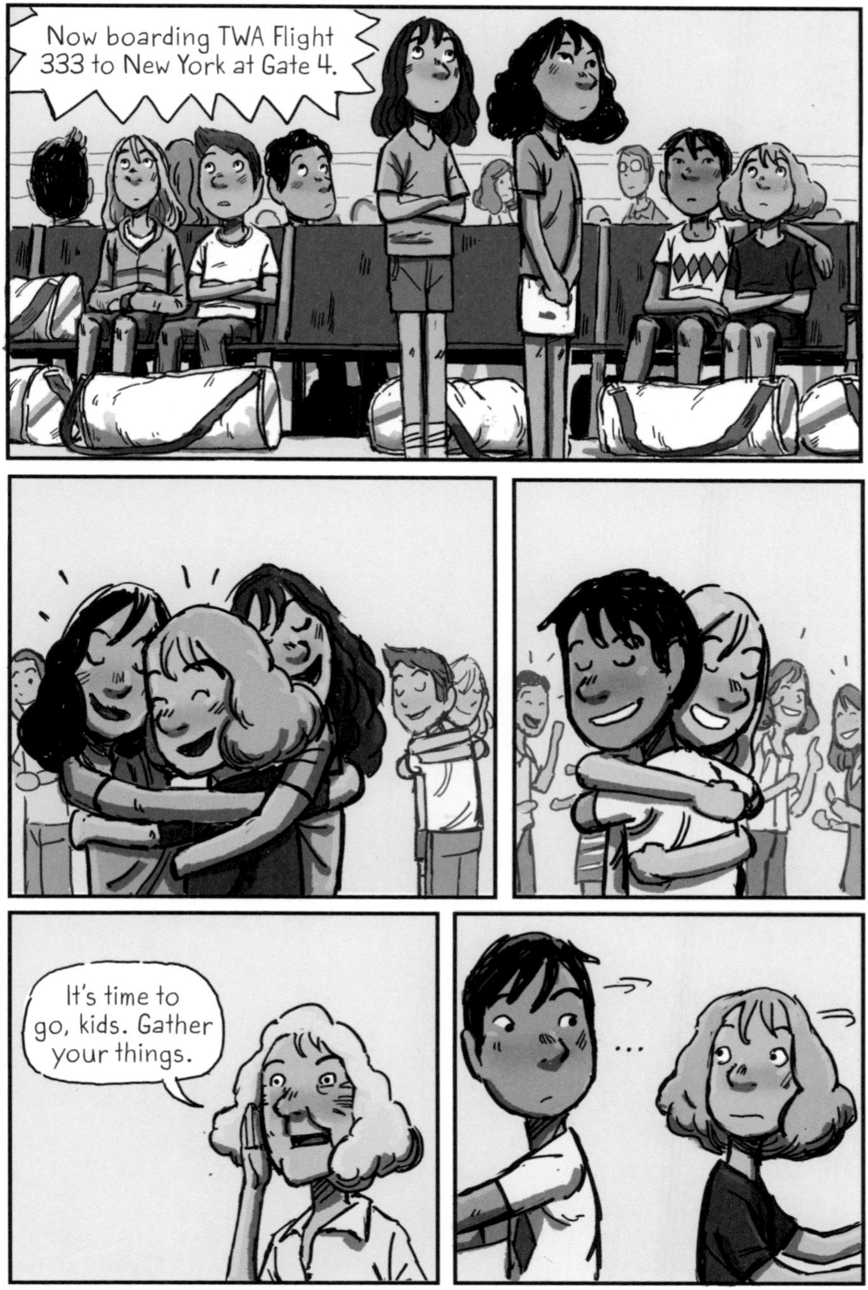
Now boarding TWA Flight 333 to New York at Gate 4.
It's time to go, kids. Gather your things.
...

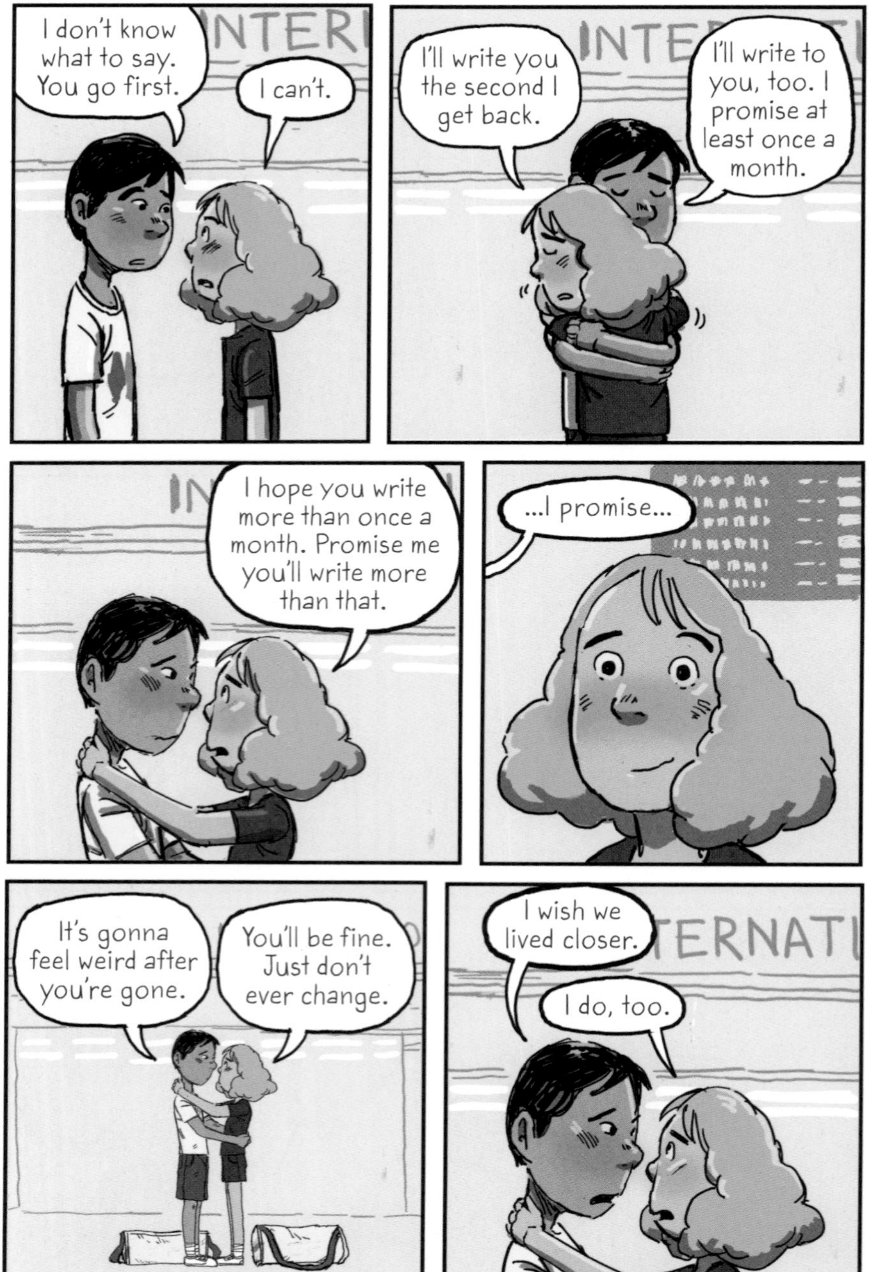
I don't know what to say. You go first.
I can't.
I'll write you the second I get back.
I'll write to you, too. I promise at least once a month.
I hope you write more than once a month. Promise me you'll write more than that.
...I promise...
It's gonna feel weird after you're gone.
You'll be fine. Just don't ever change.
I wish we lived closer.
I do, too.

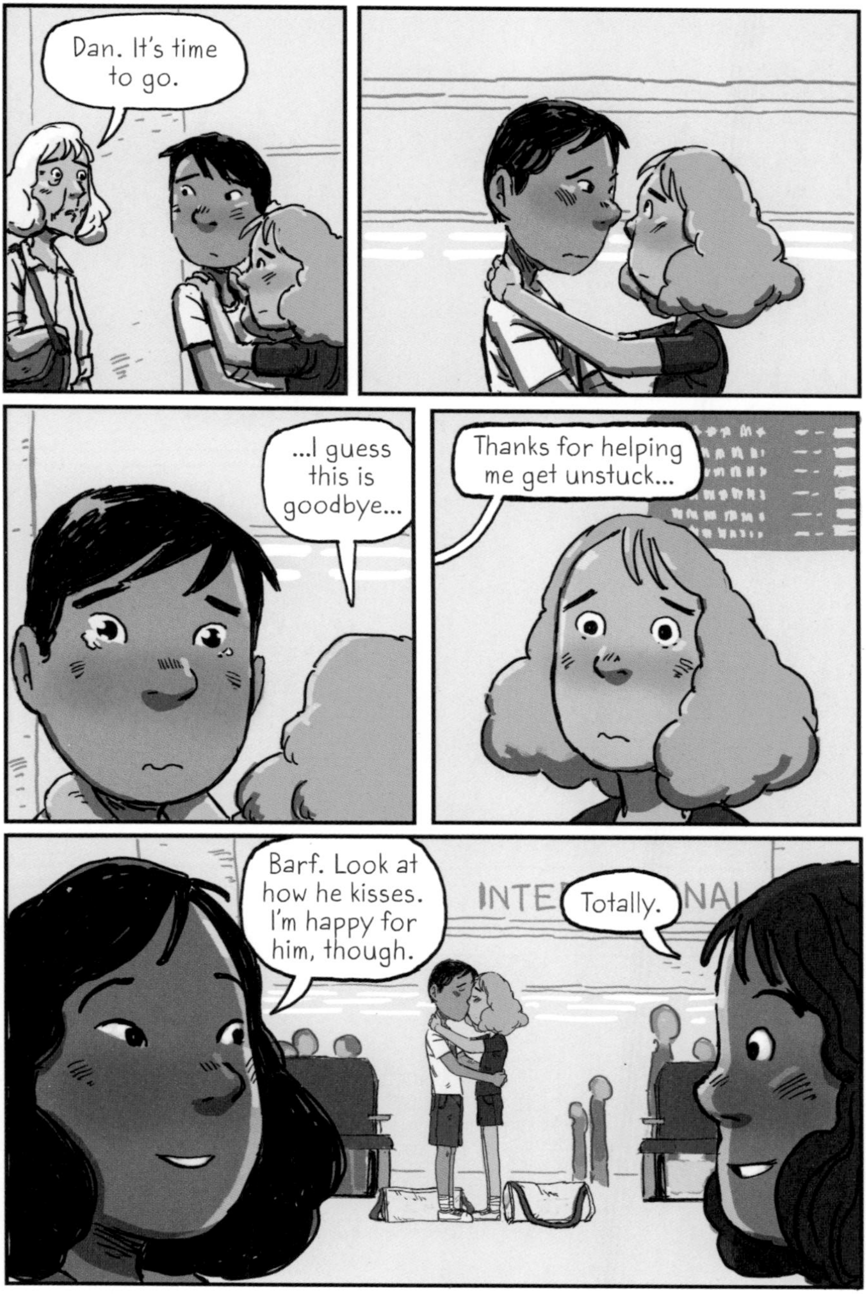

Dan. It's time to go.
...I guess this is goodbye...
Thanks for helping me get unstuck...
Barf. Look at how he kisses. I'm happy for him, though.
INTER NAL
Totally.

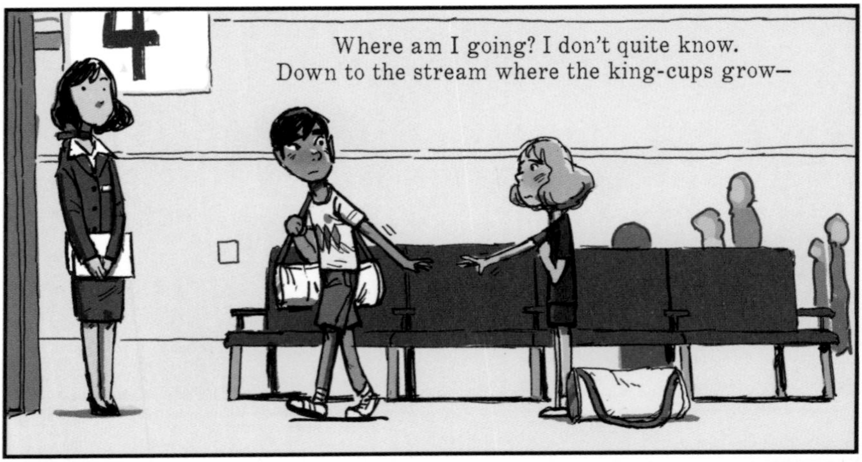
4
Where am I going? I don't quite know.
Down to the stream where the king-cups grow–

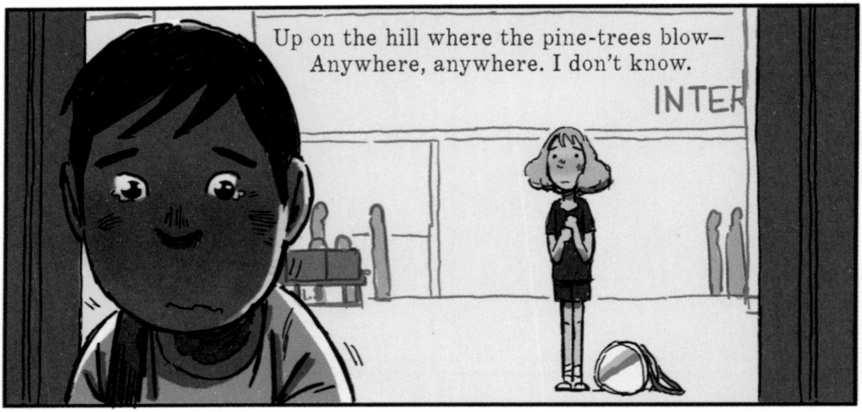
Up on the hill where the pine-trees blow–
Anywhere, anywhere. I don't know.
INTER

Where am I going? The clouds sail by,
Little ones, baby ones, over the sky.

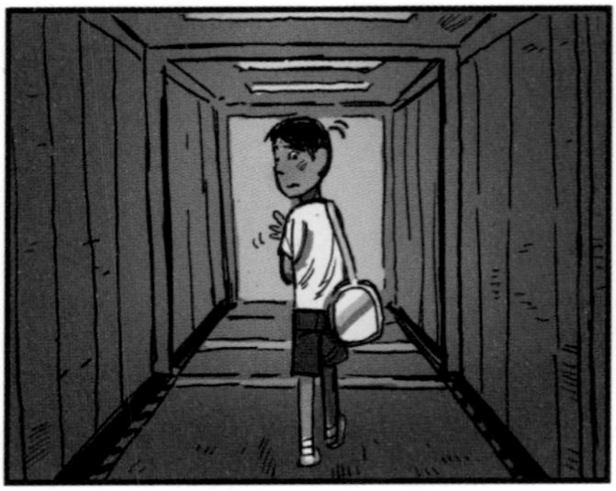

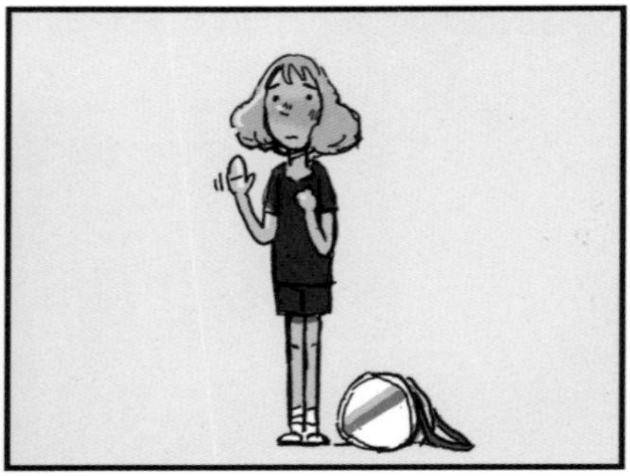

Where am I going? The shadows pass,
Little ones, baby ones, over the grass.

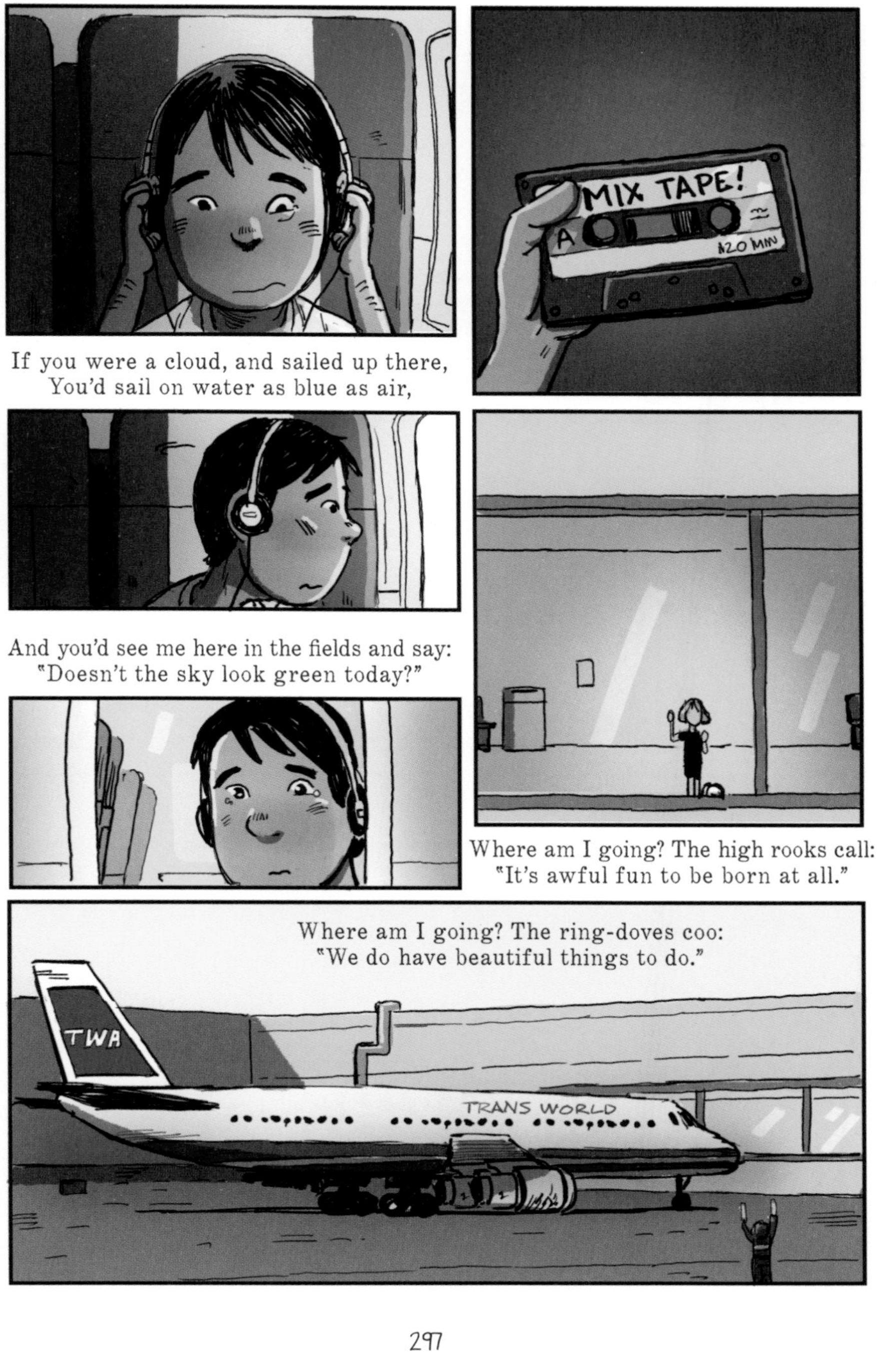
If you were a cloud, and sailed up there,
You'd sail on water as blue as air,
MIX TAPE!
A
120 MIN
And you'd see me here in the fields and say:
"Doesn't the sky look green today?"
Where am I going? The high rooks call:
"It's awful fun to be born at all."
Where am I going? The ring-doves coo:
"We do have beautiful things to do."
TWA
TRANS WORLD

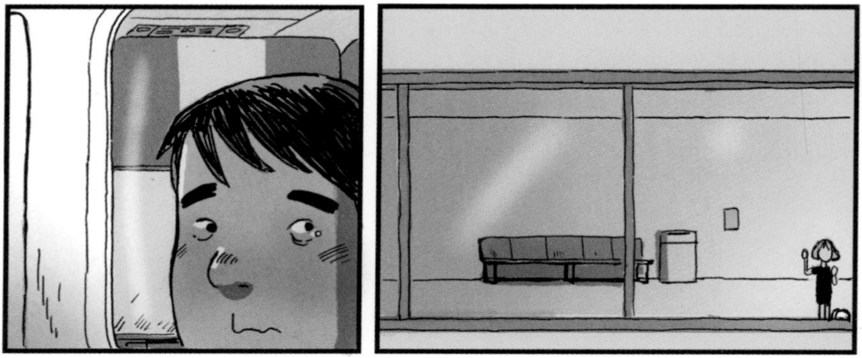

If you were a bird, and lived on high,
You'd lean on the wind when the wind came by,

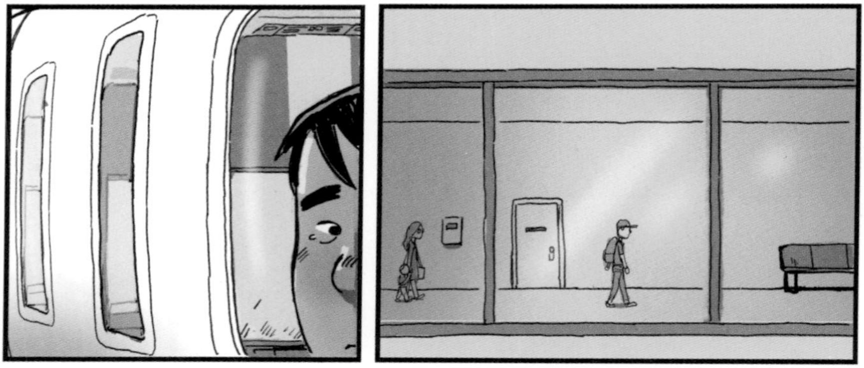

You'd say to the wind when it took you away:
"That's where I wanted to go today!"

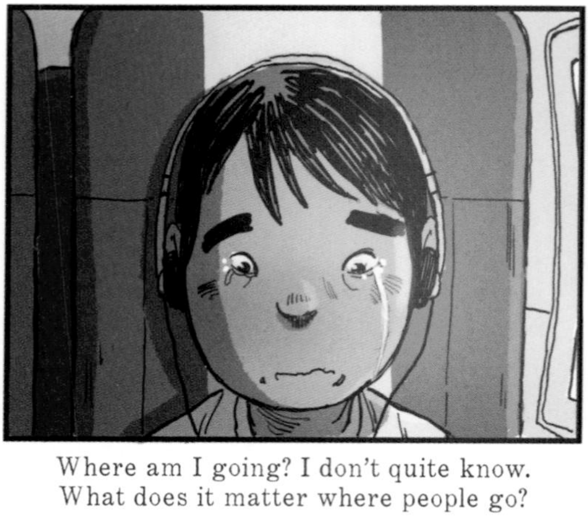

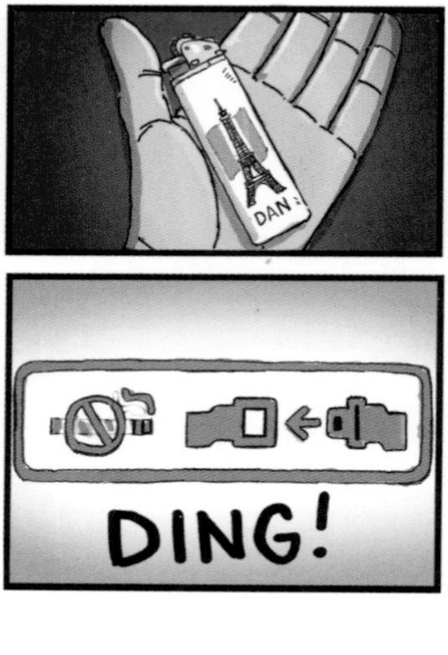
DAN
DING!

Where am I going? I don't quite know.
What does it matter where people go?

Down to the wood where the blue-bells grow—

Anywhere, anywhere. I don't know.

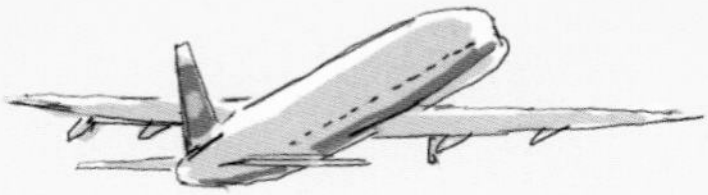

First broken heart.

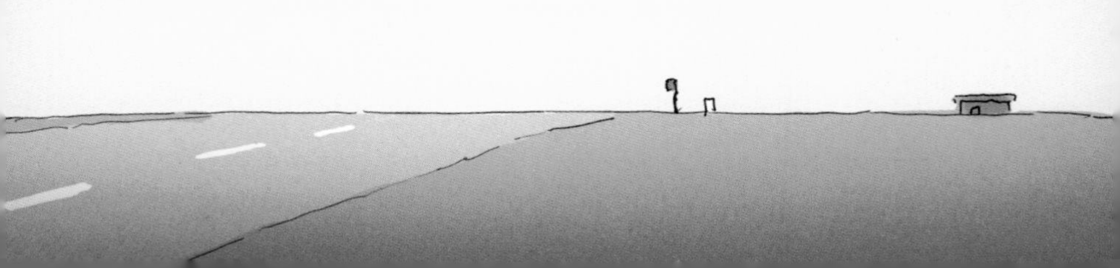

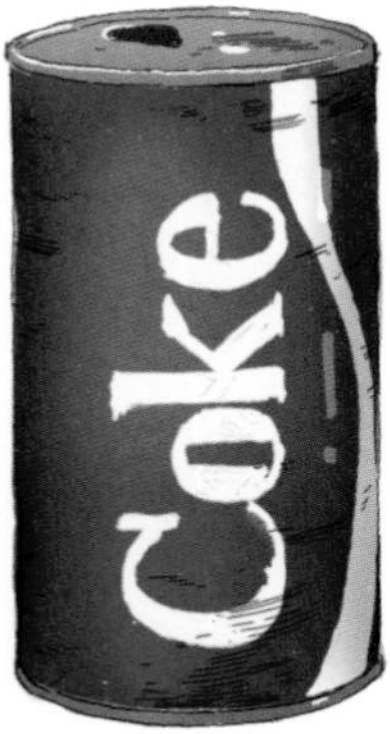
Coke

HOME

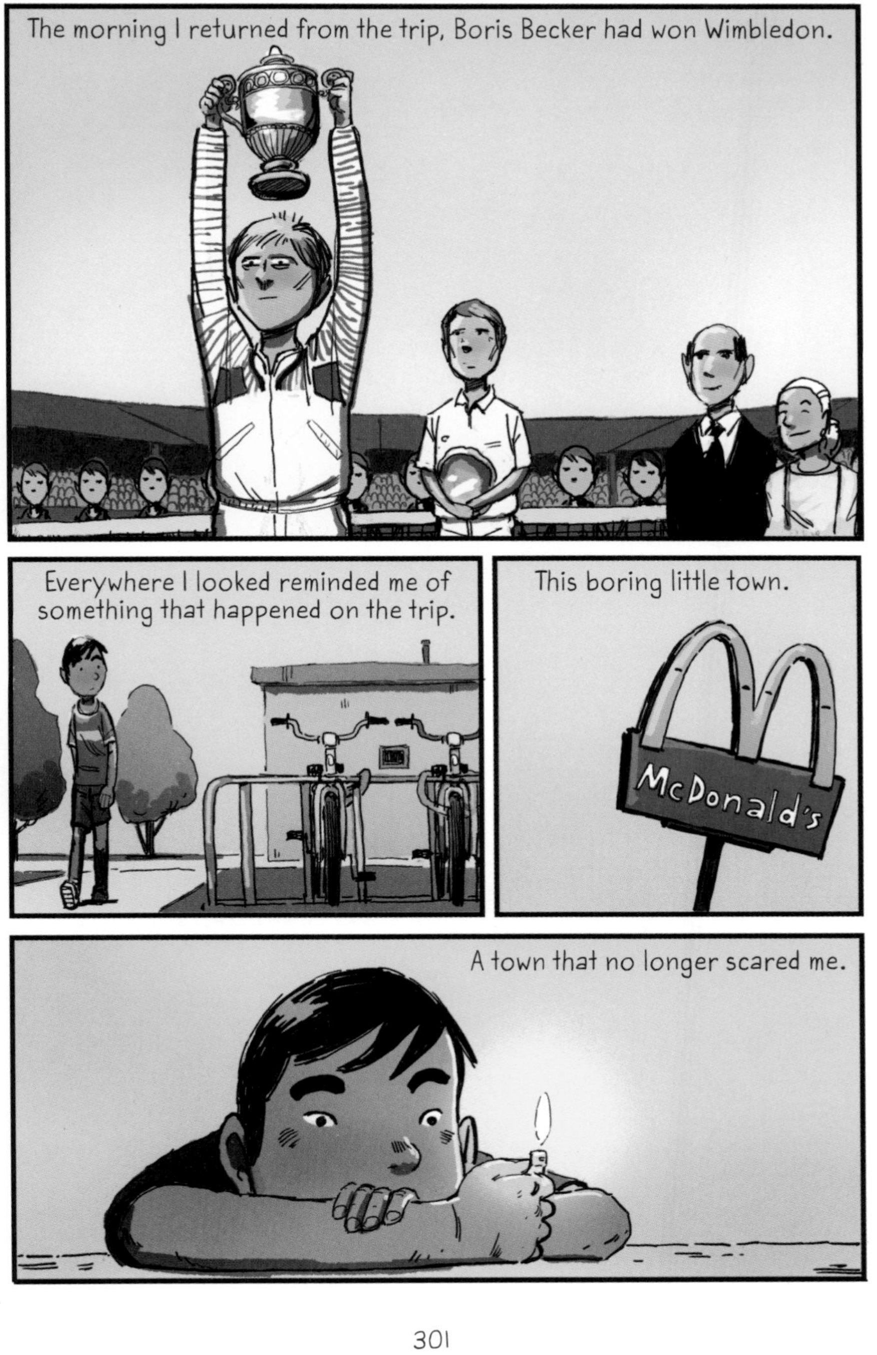
The morning I returned from the trip, Boris Becker had won Wimbledon.
Everywhere I looked reminded me of something that happened on the trip.
This boring little town.
McDonald's
A town that no longer scared me.

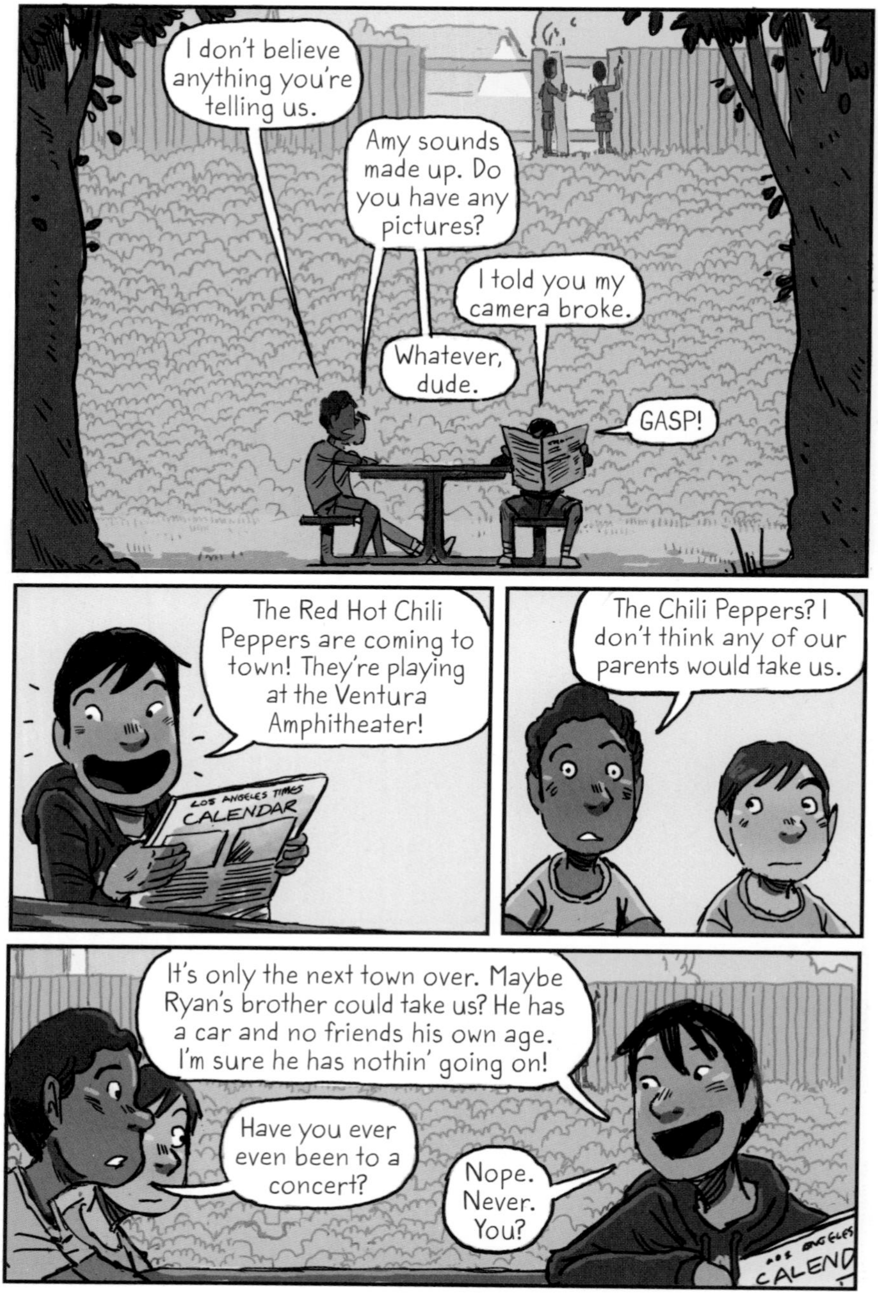
I don't believe anything you're telling us.
Amy sounds made up. Do you have any pictures?
I told you my camera broke.
Whatever, dude.
GASP!
The Red Hot Chili Peppers are coming to town! They're playing at the Ventura Amphitheater!
LOS ANGELES TIMES
CALENDAR
The Chili Peppers? I don't think any of our parents would take us.
It's only the next town over. Maybe Ryan's brother could take us? He has a car and no friends his own age. I'm sure he has nothin' going on!
Have you ever even been to a concert?
Nope. Never. You?
CALEND

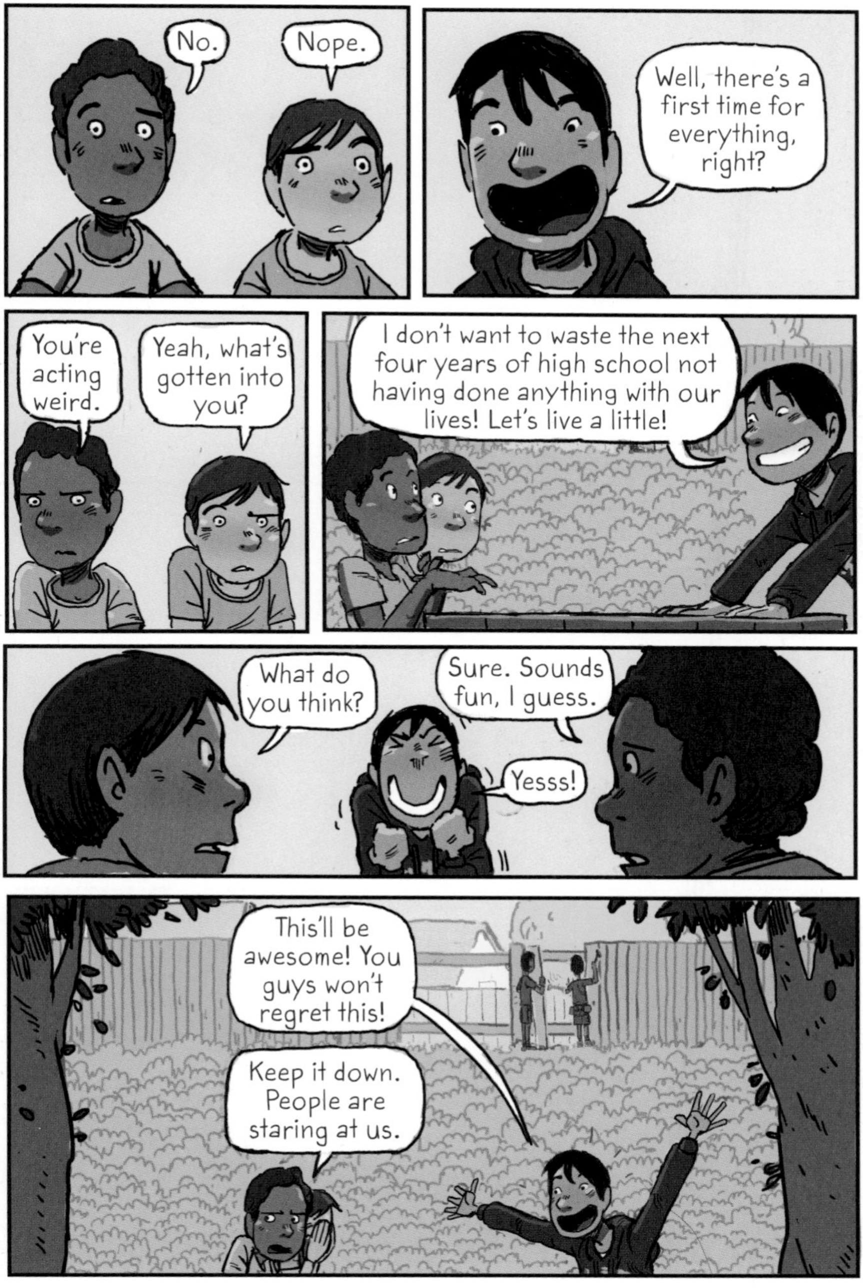
No.
Nope.
Well, there's a first time for everything, right?
You're acting weird.
Yeah, what's gotten into you?
I don't want to waste the next four years of high school not having done anything with our lives! Let's live a little!
What do you think?
Sure. Sounds fun, I guess.
Yesss!
This'll be awesome! You guys won't regret this!
Keep it down. People are staring at us.

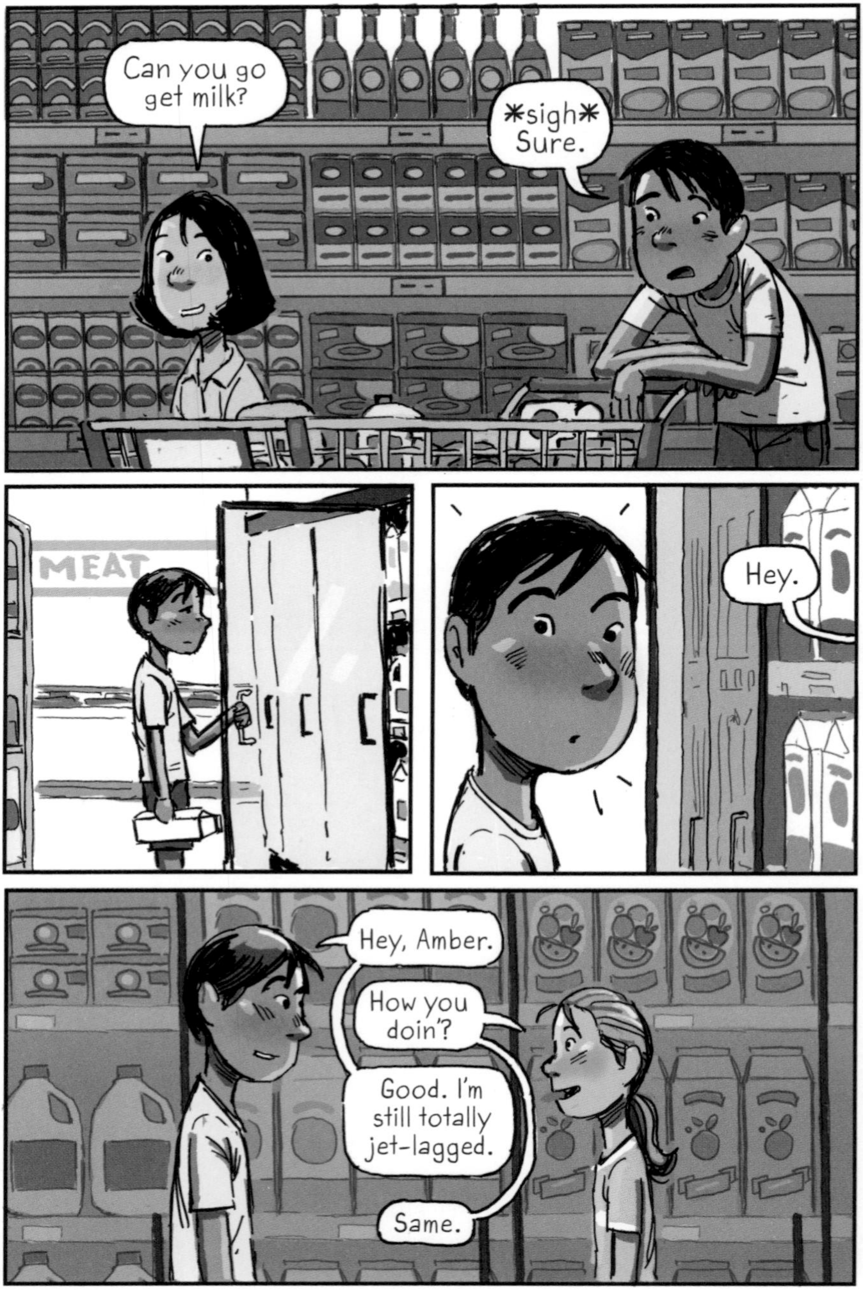
Can you go get milk?
sigh Sure.
MEAT
Hey.
Hey, Amber.
How you doin'?
Good. I'm still totally jet-lagged.
Same.

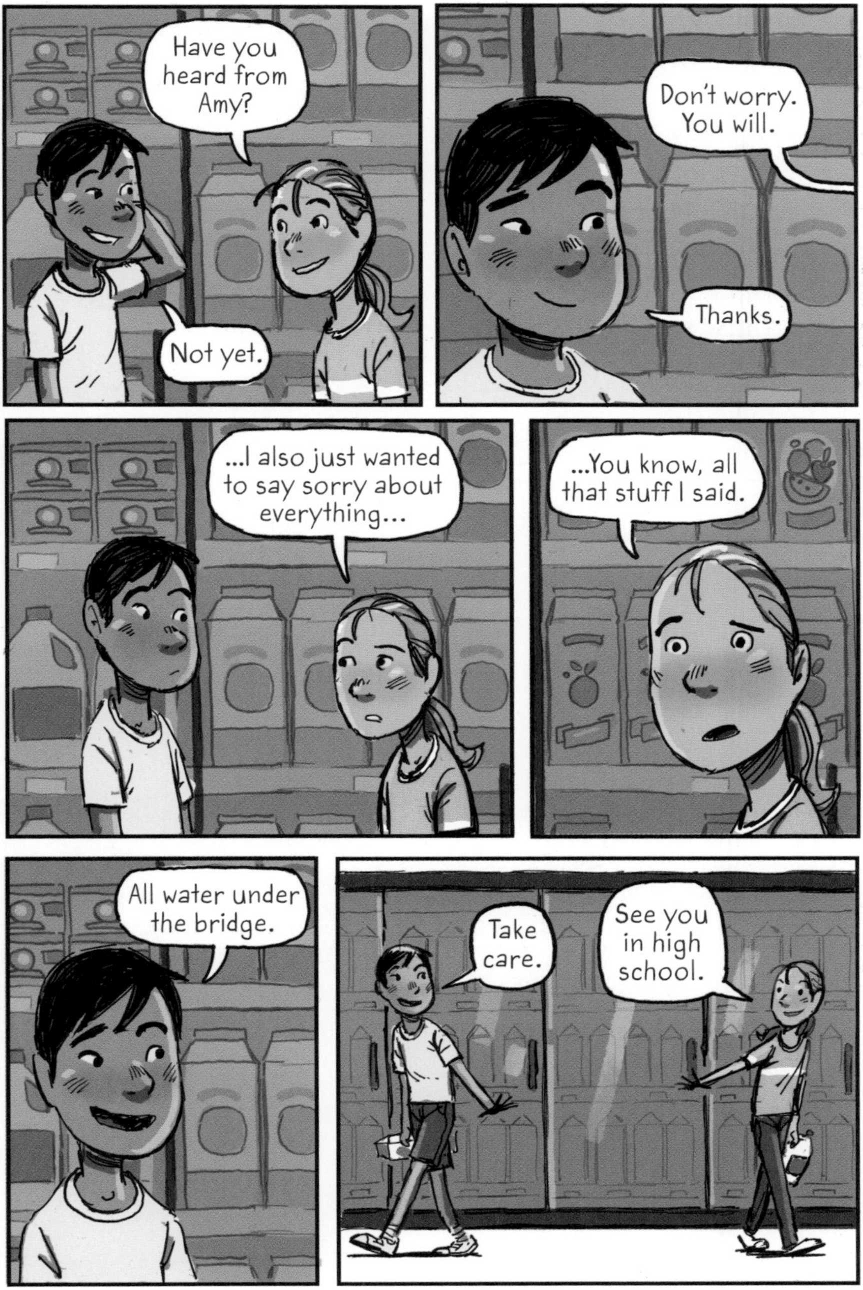
Have you heard from Amy?
Not yet.
Don't worry. You will.
Thanks.
...I also just wanted to say sorry about everything...
...You know, all that stuff I said.
All water under the bridge.
Take care.
See you in high school.

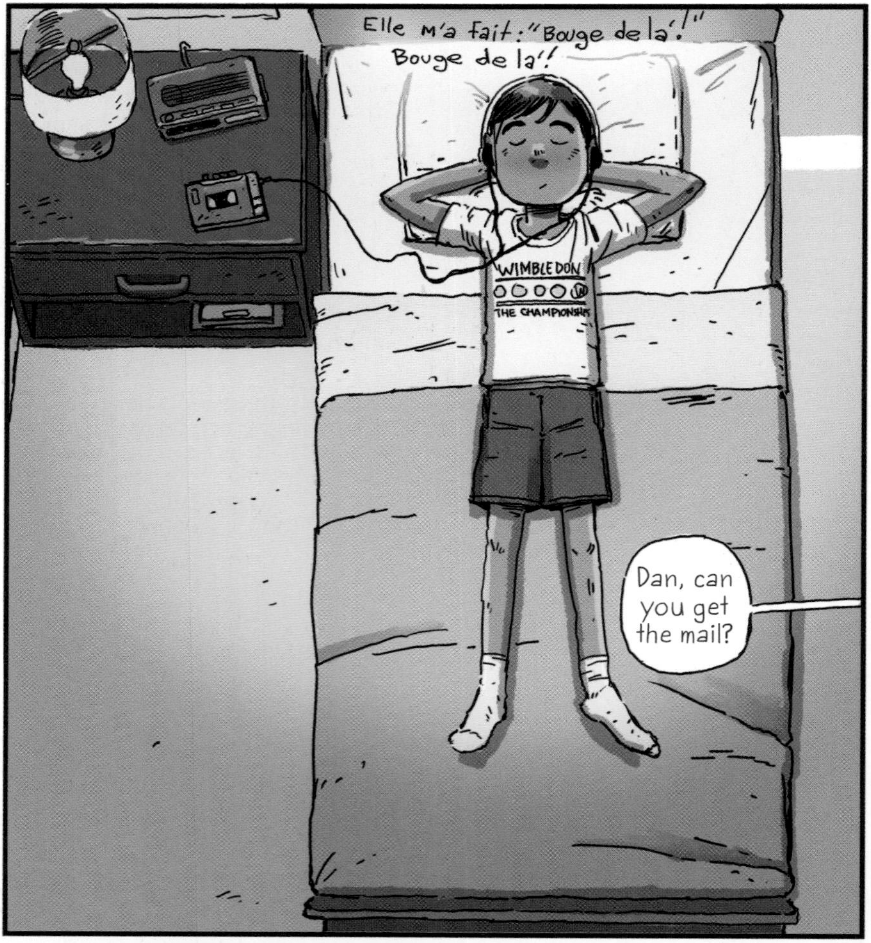
Elle m'a fait: "Bouge de là!"
Bouge de là!
WIMBLEDON
THE CHAMPIONSHIPS
Dan, can you get the mail?

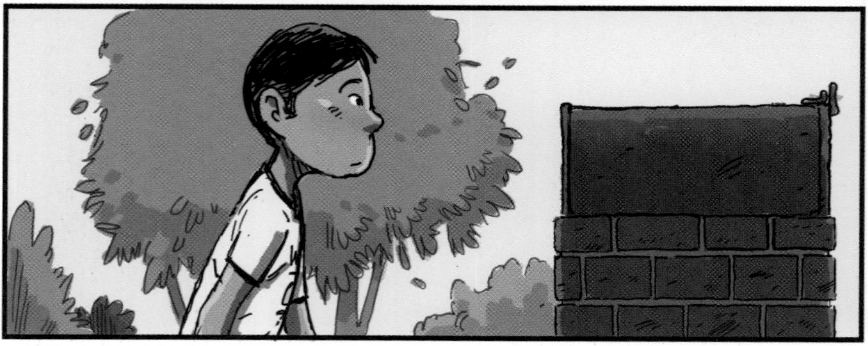

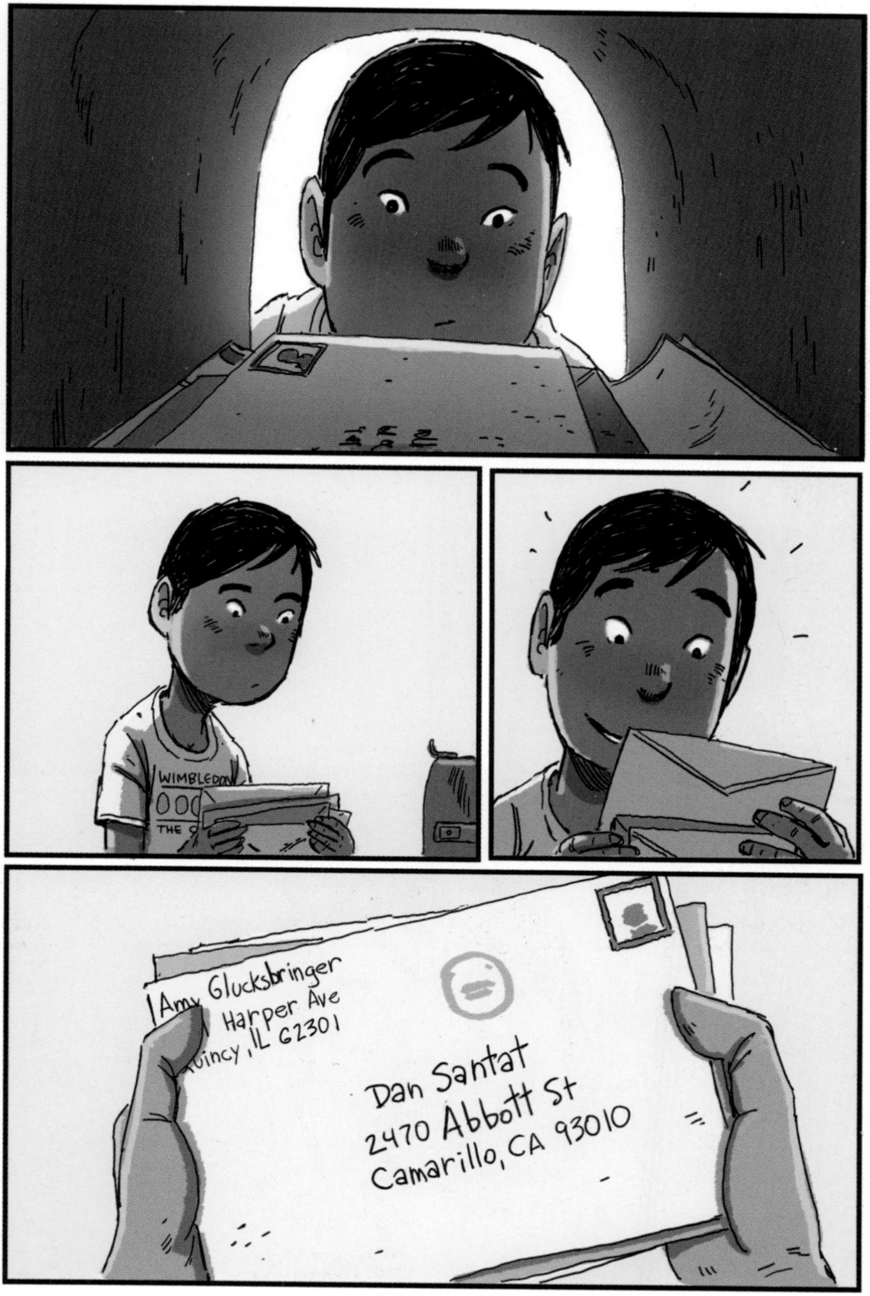
Amy Glucksbringer
Harper Ave
IL 62301
Dan Santat
2470 Abbott St
Camarillo, CA 93010

First letter.

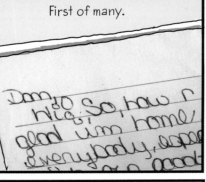

First of many.

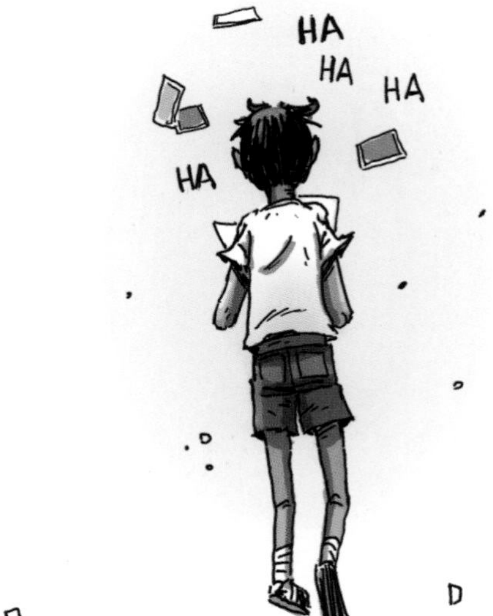
HA
HA
HA
HA

AUTHOR'S NOTE

1989 was quite a year to remember in Europe. The Louvre reopened, the Eiffel Tower was celebrating its 100th Anniversary, and the Berlin Wall would fall later that year. For me, 1989 was the year I learned to like myself, and this trip was one of the happiest and most memorable events from my childhood.

It was also a much different time. There was a larger middle class, flights were more affordable, and the internet wasn't around to give us a peek at the world outside of our tiny little towns and help us connect with people. Generation X was a generation of kids who ventured outdoors oftentimes with little to no adult supervision. It was normal back then. There were no cell phones, or Uber, or GPS maps, just a vast world to explore and endless amounts of time.

When I talk about this trip with the folks who went with me, we all are shocked by what we were allowed to get away with at that age, and we agree that we would never let any of our own kids do those same things. Even though these events really happened to me, I do not think kids should drink alcohol, smoke cigarettes, or steal bicycles. I included those scenes in the book because I understand how curious kids can be at that age. We should all be open to new experiences in our lives, but we can also learn from our mistakes.

When we got back, Joy, Shelley, Amber, and I continued to high school, and things were much better for me. Despite that awful experience of reciting the poem in front of the entire middle school, it was quickly forgotten by most kids after a few years. We slowly matured, and I settled in with a good group of friends with similar interests. High school, much like the world, was big enough to carve out my own niche. Amy and I continued to write letters to each other for six more years, but fell out of touch midway through college. Luckily, we reconnected in 2007 through social media (along with other kids from the trip), and we are all still friends to this day.

Middle school was a tough period in my life. It took time and life experiences like this trip for me to get to know myself, eventually feel more comfortable in my own skin, and not let other people determine how I feel about myself.

We all have only one life to live, so why not live it to its fullest? I encourage you all to try something new, whether it be grand or small. Try a new food, learn a new skill, do something that scares you. It's okay to be embarrassed. Be patient with yourself. Go at your own pace, but most importantly, go find adventure.

It may be good.

It may be bad.

But in the end, you'll know yourself better, and at the very least you'll have a story to tell.

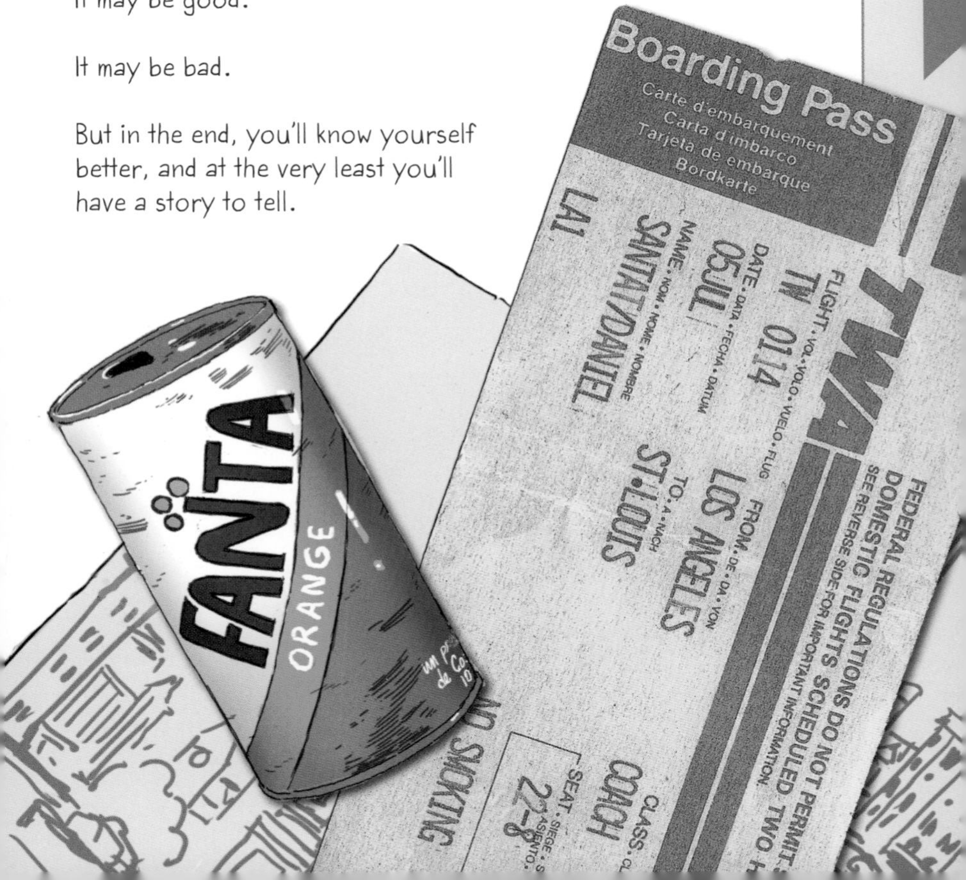
Boarding Pass
Carte d'embarquement
Carta d'imbarco
Tarjeta de embarque
Bordkarte
TWA
FLIGHT • VOL • VOLO • VUELO • FLUG
TW 0114
DATE • DATA • FECHA • DATUM
05JUL
NAME • NOM • NOME • NOMBRE
SANTAT/DANIEL
LAI
FROM • DE • DA • VON
LOS ANGELES
TO • A • NACH
ST. LOUIS
FEDERAL REGULATIONS DO NOT PERMIT
DOMESTIC FLIGHTS SCHEDULED TWO
SEE REVERSE SIDE FOR IMPORTANT INFORMATION.
CLASS
COACH
SEAT • SIEGE • ASIENTO
NO SMOKING
FANTA
ORANGE

RECREATING OLD MEMORIES

While pretty much everything in this trip actually happened, some events and names were modified. For instance, I really did sneak into Wimbledon and watch the 1989 Men's Semifinal, but it happened on the second day of the trip rather than the last (and it was with Darryl).

But all the feelings I had about everyone were 100% true. As time passes, memories slowly become fragments, and you try to piece together the remaining portions that you have. What doesn't change or fade are the emotions I felt. Three decades later, as I made this book, those feelings feel as fresh as if I went on that trip yesterday. Thirteen-year-old Dan is still well inside me.

During my research, I interviewed some of my friends from the trip. A few remembered events differently, some had completely forgotten certain events even happened at all, while others added a new, interesting perspective to certain stories with unexpected details. The most helpful piece of research was from Amy, who was kind enough to send me lots of photos and transcribe all her journal entries from the whole trip—complete with dates, places we visited, and hotels we stayed at. And yes, we both kept all our letters. There were other amazing stories and other fantastic people I met on the trip, but unfortunately, there are only so many pages in a book.

Day 1 of the trip!

Viennese Giant Ferris Wheel

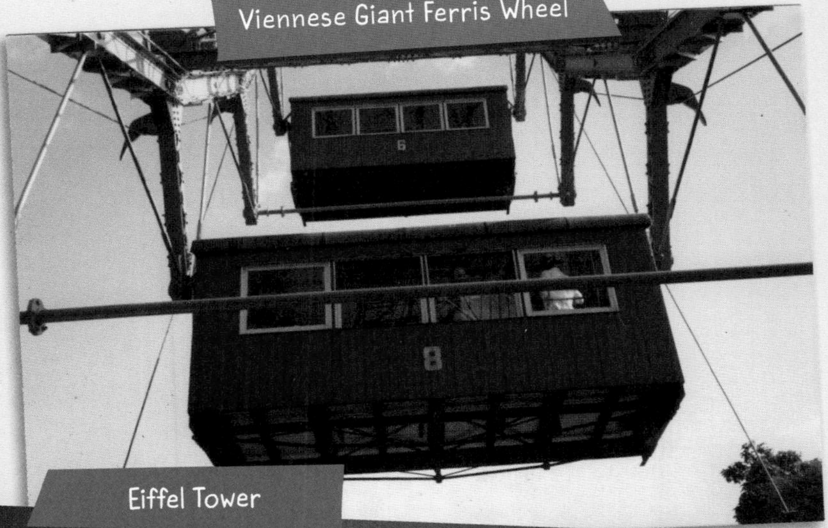

6
8

Eiffel Tower

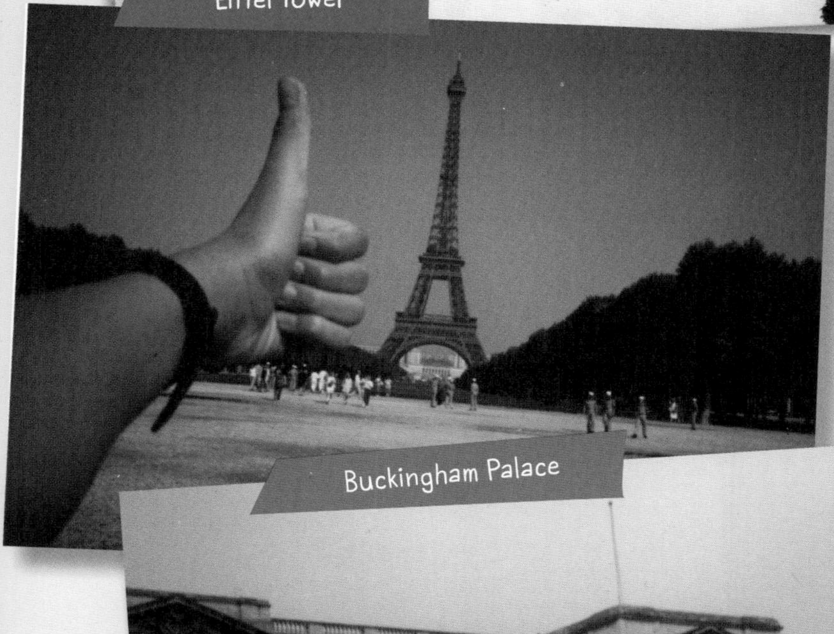

Buckingham Palace

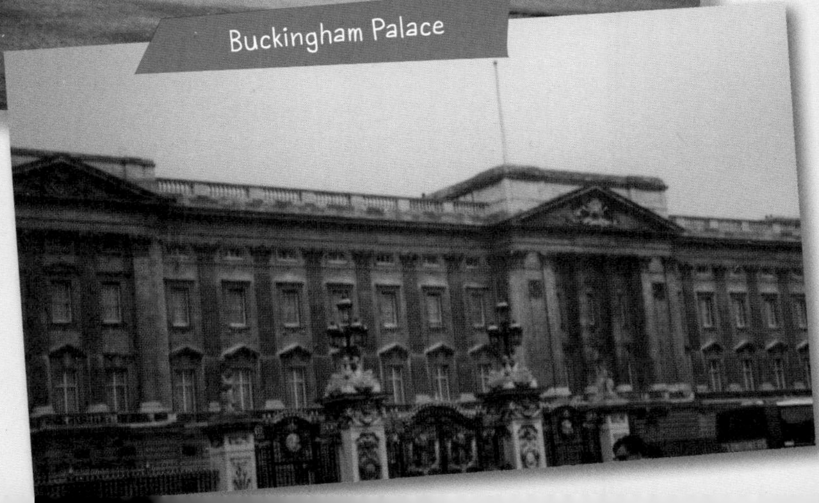

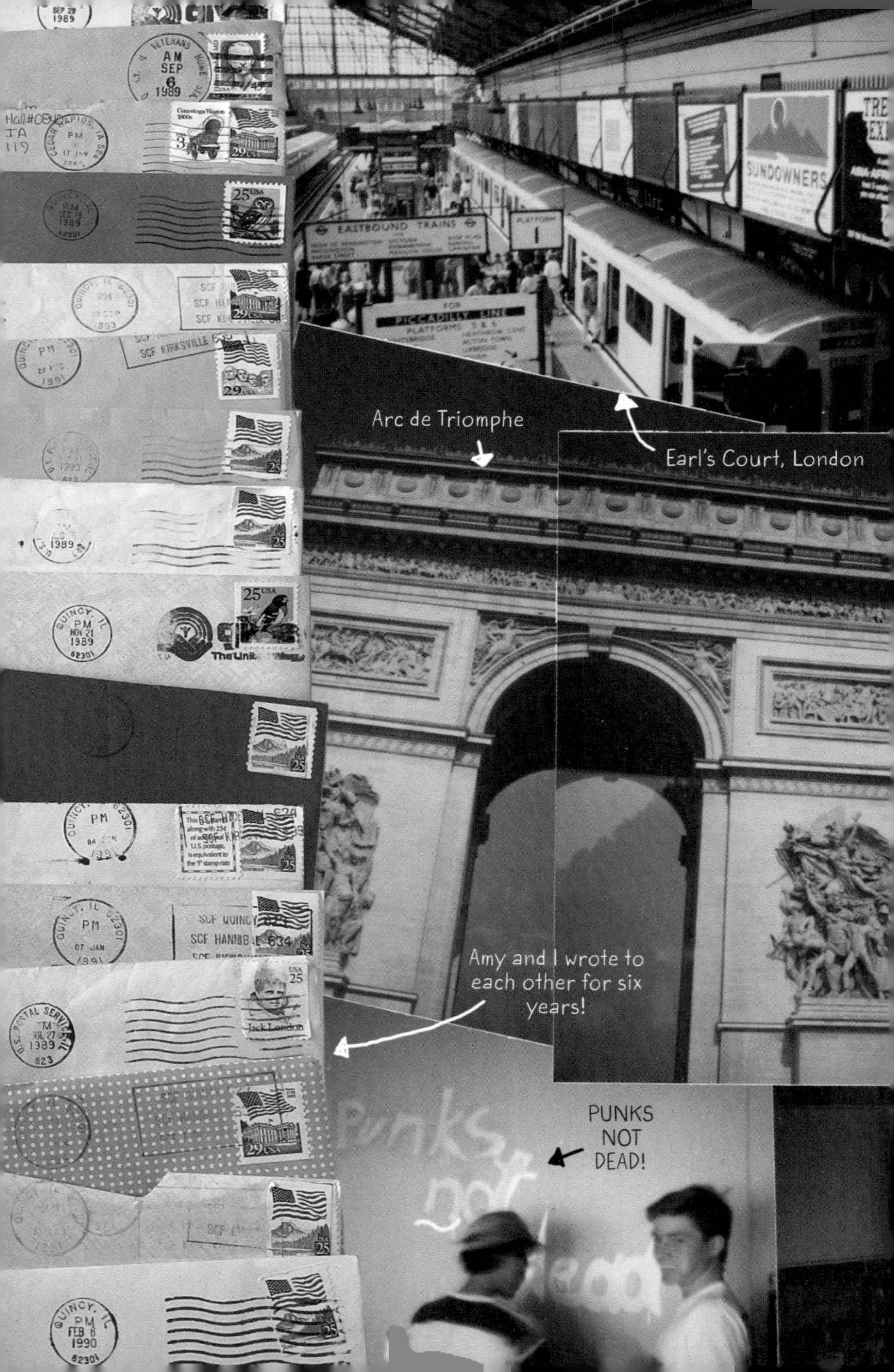

Arc de Triomphe
Earl's Court, London
EASTBOUND TRAINS
PLATFORM 1
FOR PICCADILLY LINE PLATFORMS 5 & 6
SUNDOWNERS
Amy and I wrote to each other for six years!
PUNKS NOT DEAD!

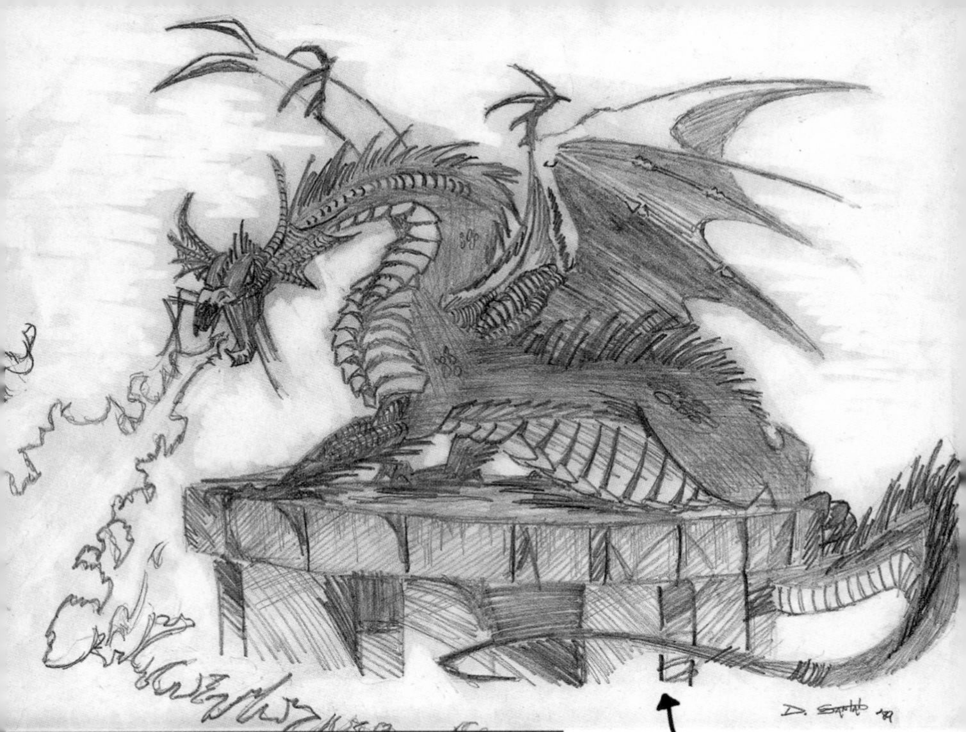

The dragon drawing I made for Joy. I had forgotten I drew this, and she reminded me while I was making this book.

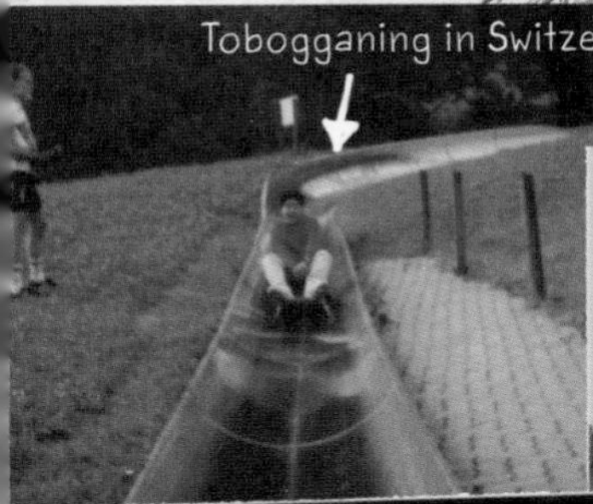

Tobogganing in Switzerland

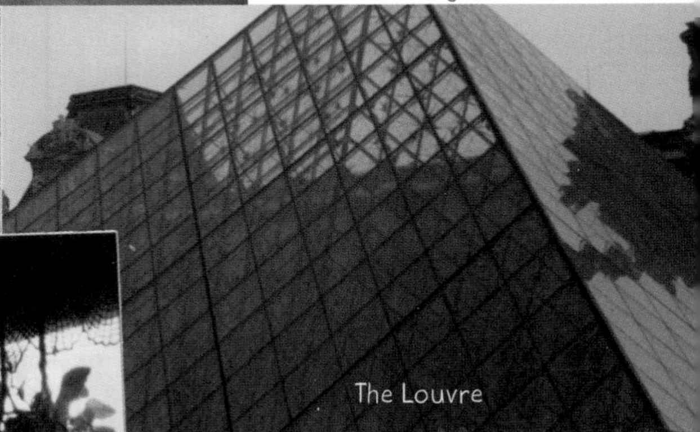

The Louvre

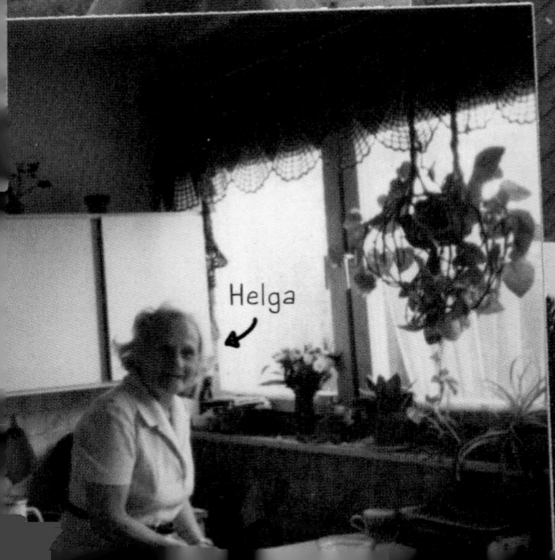

Helga

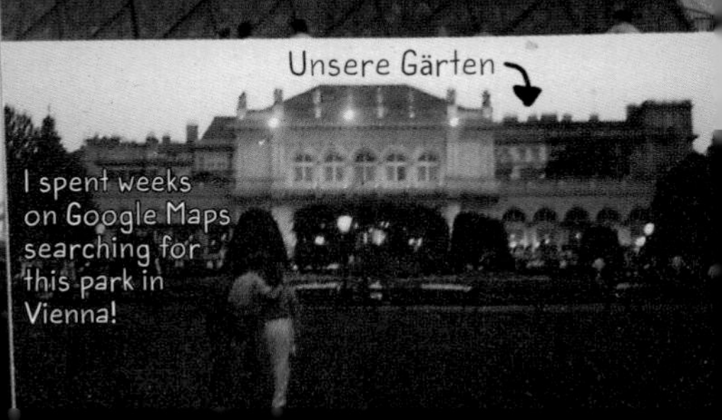

Unsere Gärten

I spent weeks on Google Maps searching for this park in Vienna!

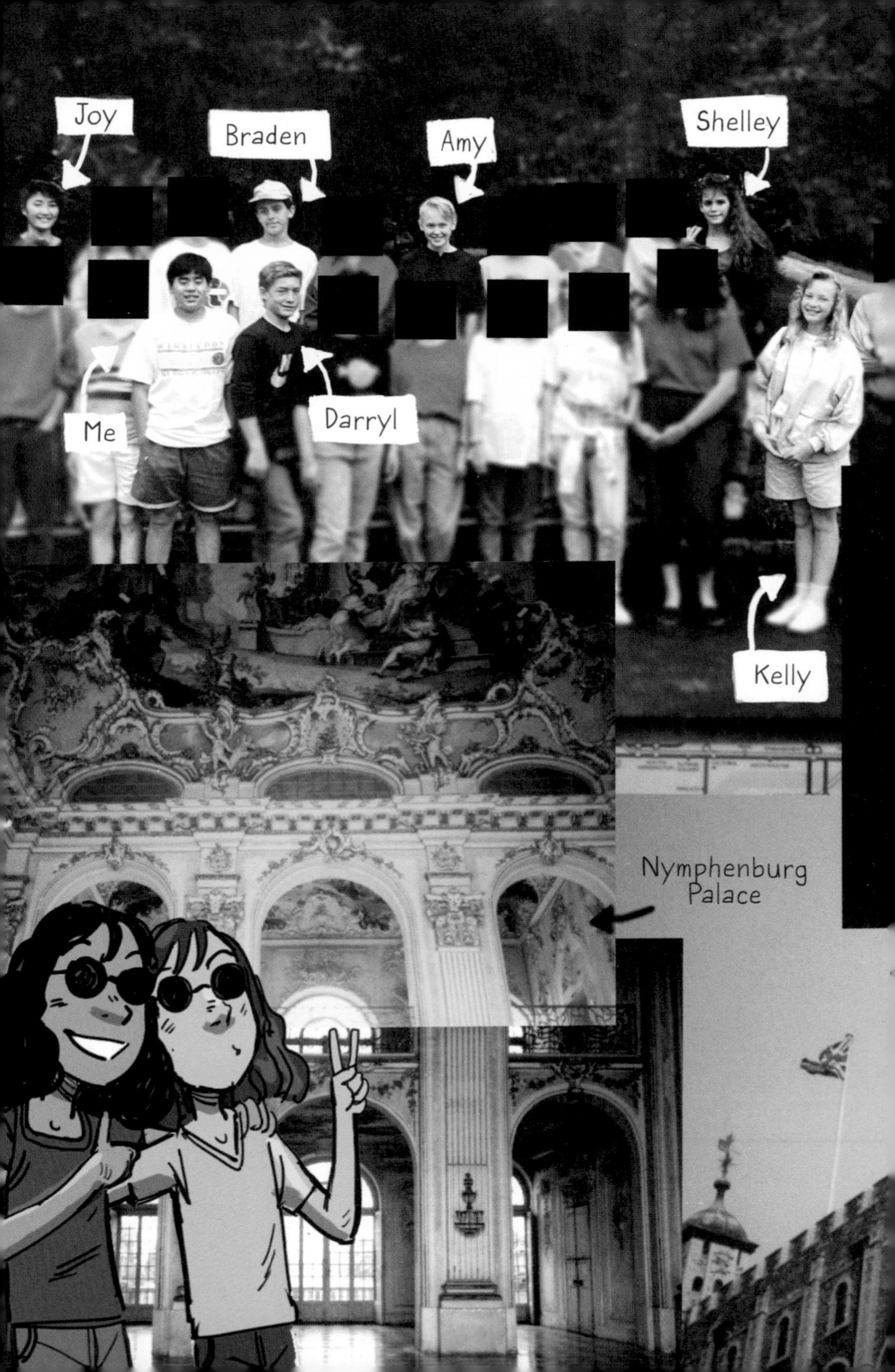
Joy
Braden
Amy
Shelley
Me
Darryl
Kelly
Nymphenburg Palace

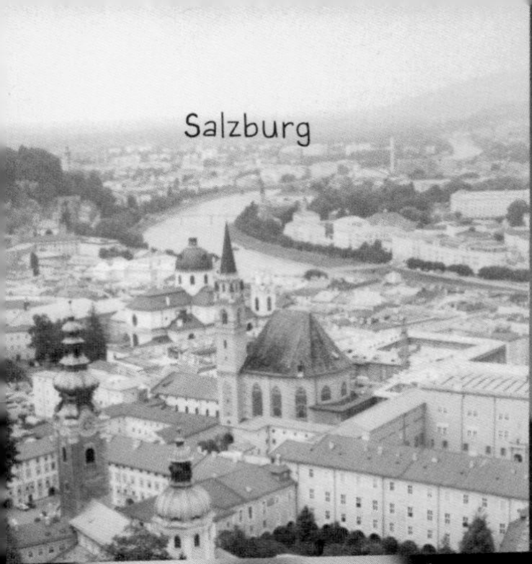

Salzburg

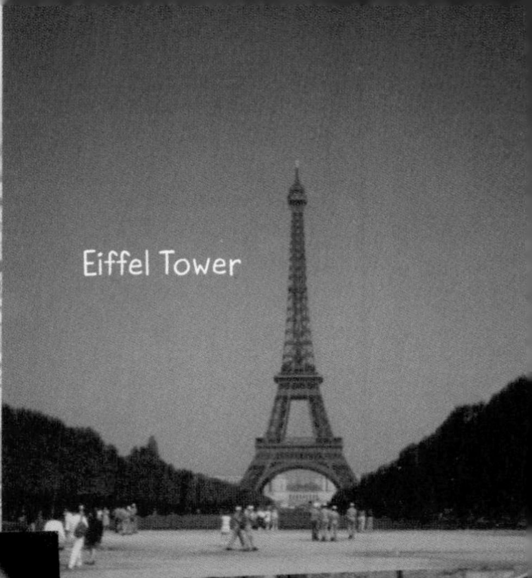

Eiffel Tower

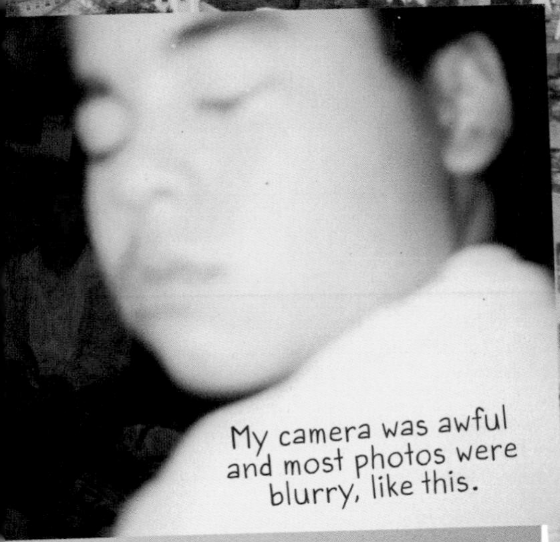

My camera was awful and most photos were blurry, like this.

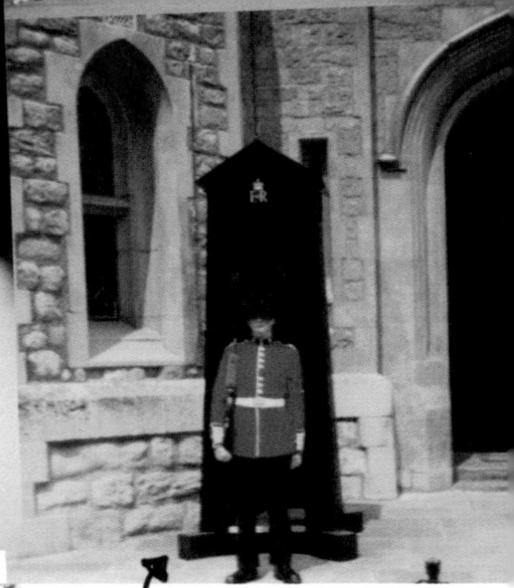

British Guard

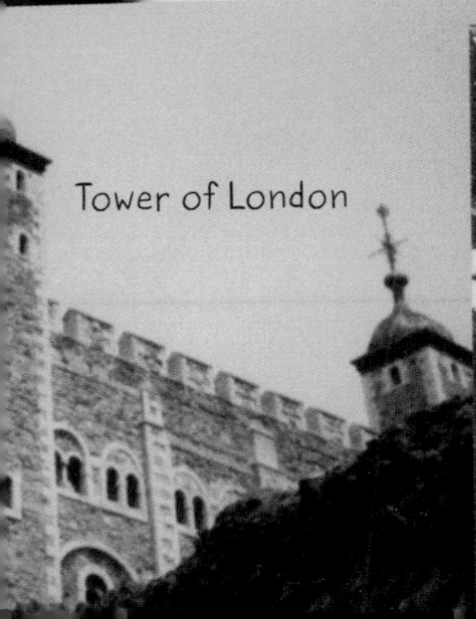

Tower of London

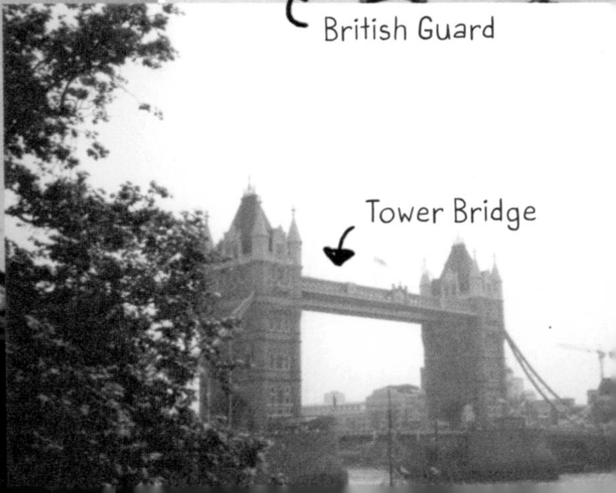

Tower Bridge

ACKNOWLEDGMENTS

Just like the busload of friends I had on that trip who helped me regain my confidence in life, there are many folks to thank for helping me find the path to finishing this memoir. My editor, Connie Hsu, and I have been friends and colleagues for many years. She has always brought out the best in my work, and, in this case, she has also been my personal therapist as I navigated and dissected old childhood feelings.

My agent, Jodi Reamer, guided me through many difficult years as I tried to write a graphic memoir. This one started out as a completely different story. It's never easy to analyze your awkward and personal moments to share them with the world. Jodi told me not to panic and assured me that the story would reveal itself when the time was right.

Abe Erskine was my fabulous colorist on this project, and they did a masterful job on setting the mood for each scene. I look forward to seeing their future endeavors as they pursue their own graphic stories.

I'd like to give a shout-out to the whole crew at Macmillan for helping me make this book the best it could be. Special thanks to Kirk Benshoff, Sunny Lee, Nicolás Ore-Giron, Alexa Blanco, Helen Seachrist, Jen Healey, Morgan Kane, Mary Van Akin, Calista Brill, Mark Siegel, Jen Edwards, Allison Verost, and Jen Besser.

Thanks to Kelly Murphy and Antoine Revoy for providing the French translations while Andrea Offerman went above and beyond in providing German translations specific to their regions. They are as equally talented artists and storytellers as they are friends.

I'd like to thank my trusty group of expert authors: Raina Telgemeier, Shannon Hale, LeUyen Pham, Vera Brosgol, Laurel Snyder, Renée Kurilla, Lisa Yee, and Cecil Castellucci. They read my story and offered their guidance to help me maintain the integrity of the women's voices for this book.

I'd like to thank my kids, Alek and Kyle, for asking me the question about when I first fell in love, which planted the seed for this story, and my wife, Leah, for her love and support during this process.

Finally, generous thanks to all the people from 1989 who helped me live a little: Mrs. Bjork, Joi, Richelle, Gail, Dawn, Meghan, Krystle, Matt, Darren, Brandon, Kellee, Allison, Zoe, and last but certainly not least, the real Amy.

—DAN

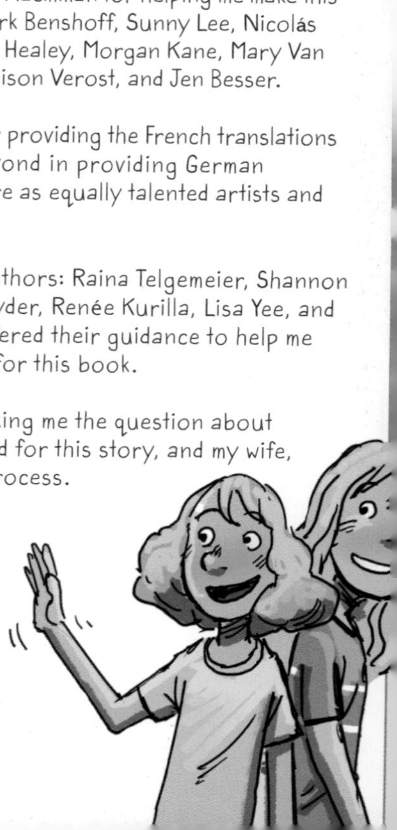

Wimbledon,
Centre Court, 1989

(I didn't take pictures during the match for fear of getting caught!)

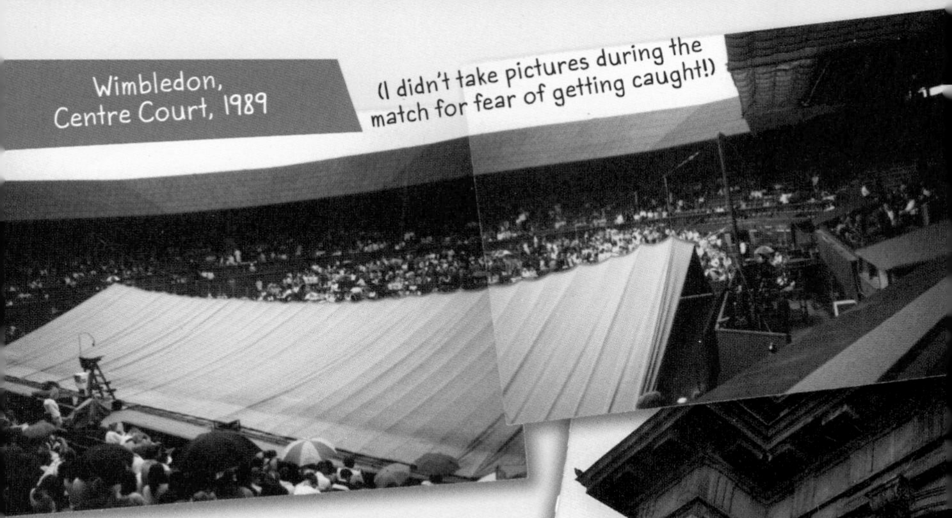

Last day of the trip

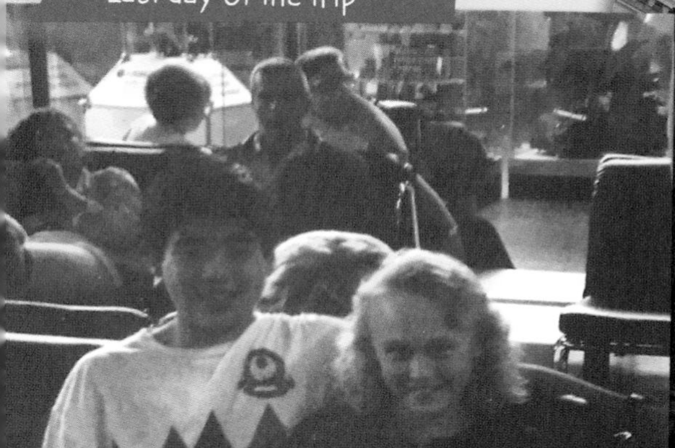

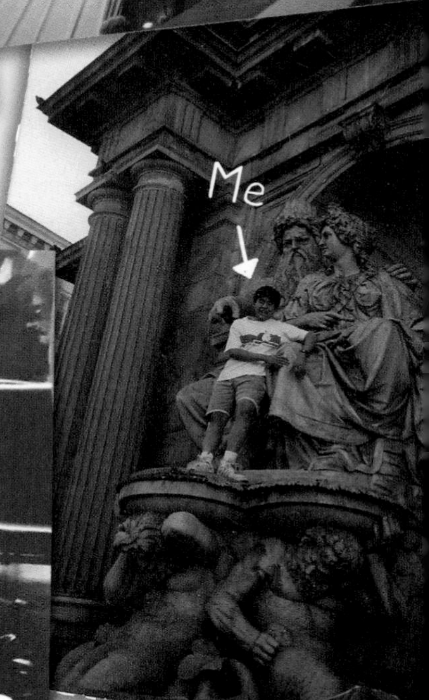
Me

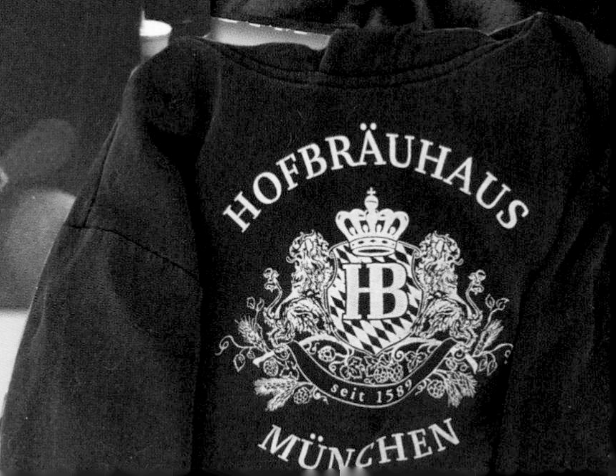
HOFBRÄUHAUS
HB
seit 1589
MÜNCHEN

Still have the hoodie
and it still fits!

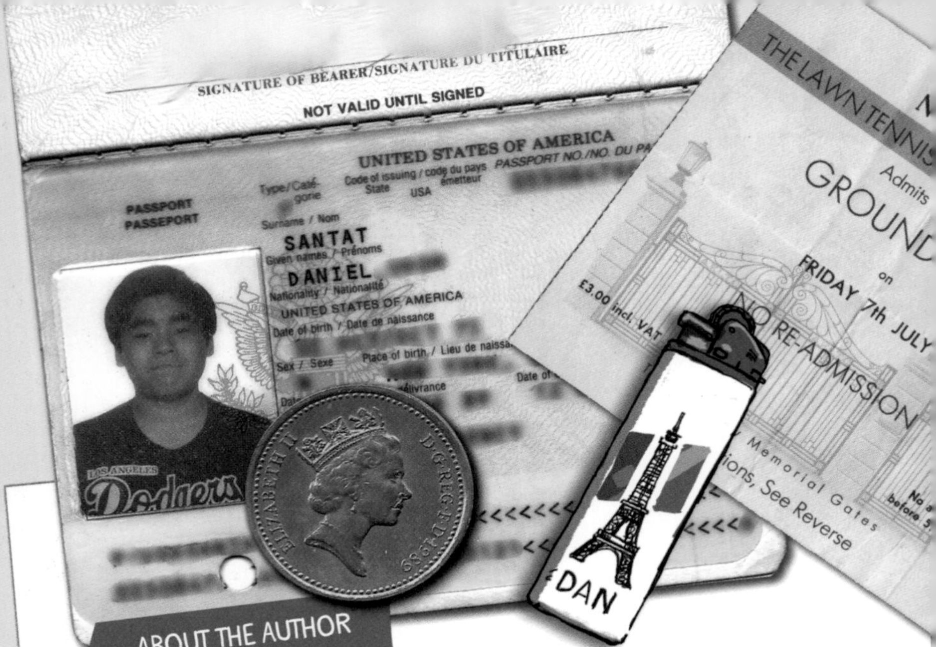
SIGNATURE OF BEARER/SIGNATURE DU TITULAIRE
NOT VALID UNTIL SIGNED
UNITED STATES OF AMERICA
PASSPORT
PASSEPORT
Type/Caté-gorie
Code of issuing / code du pays émetteur
State
USA
PASSPORT NO./NO. DU PA
Surname / Nom
SANTAT
Given names / Prénoms
DANIEL
Nationality / Nationalité
UNITED STATES OF AMERICA
Date of birth / Date de naissance
Sex / Sexe
Place of birth / Lieu de naissa
LOS ANGELES
Dodgers
ELIZABETH II D·G·REG·F·D 1989
THE LAWN TENNIS
Admits
GROUND
on
FRIDAY 7th JULY
£3.00 incl. VAT
NO RE-ADMISSION
Memorial Gates
ions, See Reverse
DAN

ABOUT THE AUTHOR

DAN SANTAT is a graduate of the Art Center College of Design and has published over one hundred books for children. His most notable titles include *The Adventures of Beekle: The Unimaginary Friend*, which won the Randolph Caldecott Medal in 2015, the #1 *New York Times*–bestselling road trip/time travel adventure *Are We There Yet?*, and the *New York Times*–bestselling book *After the Fall (How Humpty Dumpty Got Back Up Again)*, which was named on many best book of the year lists, including for NPR and the New York Public Library. His artwork is also featured in numerous picture books, chapter books, and middle grade novels, including Dav Pilkey's Ricky Ricotta series.

Dan lives in Southern California with his wife, two kids, and many, many pets.

WWW.DANSANTATBOOKS.COM

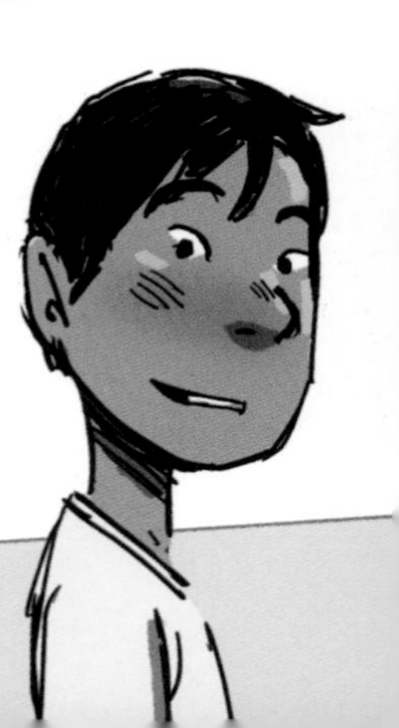